DEMOCRACY
AND
DEMOCRATIZATION

DILEMMAS IN WORLD POLITICS

Series Editor

George A. Lopez, University of Notre Dame

Dilemmas in World Politics offers teachers and students of international relations a series of quality books on critical issues, trends, and regions in international politics. Each text examines a "real world" dilemma and is structured to cover the historical, theoretical, practical, and projected dimensions of its subject.

EDITORIAL BOARD

FORTHCOMING TITLES

Steve Chan
**East Asian Dynamism: Growth, Order, and
Security in the Pacific Region, second edition**

□ □ □

Jack Donnelly
International Human Rights

□ □ □

Barry B. Hughes
International Futures

□ □ □

V. Spike Peterson and Anne Sisson Runyan
Global Gender Issues

□ □ □

Sarah Tisch and Michael Wallace
**Dilemmas of Development Assistance:
The What, Why, and Who of Foreign Aid**

□ □ □

Ted Robert Gurr and Barbara Harff
Ethnic Conflict in World Politics

□ □ □

Frederic S. Pearson
The Spread of Arms in the International System

DEMOCRACY AND DEMOCRATIZATION

■ ■ ■

Processes and Prospects in a Changing World

Georg Sørensen

UNIVERSITY OF AARHUS

Westview Press

BOULDER □ SAN FRANCISCO □ OXFORD

Dilemmas in World Politics Series

Copyright © 1993 by Westview Press, Inc.

Published in 1993 in the United States of America by Westview Press, Inc., 5500 Central Avenue, Boulder, Colorado 80301-2877, and in the United Kingdom by Westview Press, 36 Lonsdale Road, Summertown, Oxford OX2 7EW

Library of Congress Cataloging-in-Publication Data
Sørensen, Georg, 1948–
   Democracy and democratization : processes and prospects in a changing world / Georg Sørensen.
      p.   cm. — (Dilemmas in world politics)
   Includes bibliographical references and index.
   ISBN 0-8133-1526-3. — ISBN 0-8133-1527-1 (pbk.)
   1. Democracy.   2. World politics—1989–   I. Title.   II. Series.
JC423.S69   1993
321.8—dc20   92-28614
                                                                                      CIP

Printed and bound in the United States of America

The paper used in this publication meets the requirements
of the American National Standard for Permanence of Paper
for Printed Library Materials Z39.48-1984.

10   9   8   7   6   5   4   3   2

For Lisbet and Mathilde

□ □ □

Contents

□ □ □

Tables and Figures

□ □ □

Acknowledgments

I am grateful to friends and colleagues for their help and encouragement. Series editor George Lopez started this project by inviting me to submit a book proposal on democracy and democratization. Comments from Frances Hagopian and several members of the Dilemmas editorial board helped improve the proposal. Jennifer Knerr and Rachel Quenk from Westview were always ready with advice and support as the project moved along. Jørgen Elklit, Hans-Henrik Holm, Hans-Jørgen Nielsen, Ole Nørgaard, and Palle Svensson read the manuscript, or parts of it, and provided extensive comments that definitely improved the final product. Comments from Westview's two anonymous reviewers of the manuscript were also very useful. Jonna Kjær aided in preparing the final version of the manuscript. Special thanks to Beverly LeSuer, whose expert editorial input significantly improved the readability of the book. Libby Barstow guided it through the final production stage. Any shortcomings that remain are my responsibility. Finally, I am grateful, once again, for the constant support and encouragement of my wife, Lisbet.

Georg Sørensen

Acronyms

ASEE	authoritarian state elite enrichment regime
CCP	Chinese Communist party
CSCE	Conference on Security and Cooperation in Europe
DDR	Deutsche Demokratische Republik
GDP	gross domestic product
GNP	gross national product
HDI	Human Development index
IMF	International Monetary Fund
NATO	North Atlantic Treaty Organization
NGO	nongovernmental organization
NIC	newly industrializing country
OECD	Organization for Economic Cooperation and Development
PPP	purchasing power parities
TNC	transnational corporation
UN	United Nations
UNDP	United Nations Development Programme

□ □ □

Introduction

A statement often repeated nowadays, both in scholarly circles and in the mass media, is that democracy has made great progress in the world in recent years. The reasons for the statement are simple: In a brief period of time, a large number of countries have commenced a process of democratization. In Eastern Europe, the totalitarian systems are being replaced by democracies; in Africa, the one-party systems headed by strongmen, personally in charge of the state, are challenged by opposition forces exploiting newly gained political liberties; in Latin America, the military dictatorships began crumbling several years ago; in many Asian countries, authoritarian systems are moving—or being forced to move—in a democratic direction.

The swift progress of democracy in many countries has raised hopes for a better world; the expectations are that democracy will not only promote political liberties and other human rights but will also lead to rapid economic development and increased welfare as well as to international relations characterized by peaceful cooperation and mutual understanding. In this book, we will examine the prospects for these great expectations. A necessary first step is to clarify the concept of democracy. This is done in Chapter 1, which introduces different views of democracy, discusses ways of measuring democracy, and identifies the countries that presently qualify as democratic. Next, we need to know whether democracy is advancing in a sustainable fashion. This issue is the theme of Chapter 2. A model is introduced that demonstrates that the process of **democratization**—that is, the movement from authoritarian to democratic forms of rule—is a lengthy one involving different phases. The major part of the chapter is devoted to the formulation of four propositions, each of which spells out an important characteristic of democracy's degree of progress and sustainability. Following this groundwork, we are ready to ask about the domestic and international consequences of democracy. Chapter 3 concentrates on possible domestic consequences for economic development, welfare, and human rights. Chapter 4 turns to the international consequences of democracy: Will it pave the way for a more peaceful and cooperative world? Finally, Chapter 5 considers the future of democracy and democratization against the background of an optimistic and a pessimistic scenario.

In one sense it is true, then, that democracy has made great progress in the world in recent years. We shall see, however, that the way in which democratization has occurred calls into question whether democratic advancement will continue and whether potential positive effects of democracy will be forthcoming. This is the central dilemma surrounding the current transitions toward democracy. Chapters 2, 3, and 4 further investigate particular aspects of this dilemma. Chapter 2 emphasizes that the processes of democratization in recent years are frail openings with democracy still restricted in many ways and with no guarantees of further democratic progress. Chapter 3 argues that economic development and welfare improvement will not necessarily be forthcoming from these fragile democracies. Indeed, there may be a trade-off between democratic stability and welfare progress. Chapter 4 asserts that a more peaceful world as a result of the current democratizations—although a theoretical possibility—is by no means assured. In short, current democratic advancement is taking place in a way that may well jeopardize continued democratic progress.

The book concludes with a chapter on the future of democracy, followed by discussion questions for each chapter and a list of recommended readings for students interested in further study of democracy and democratization.

ONE

□ □ □

What Is Democracy?

D emocracy is a form of government in which the people rule. The concrete way in which this form of goverment should be organized and
the question of which conditions and preconditions it requires have been
intensely debated for several centuries. Indeed, the early contributions to
this discussion go back to ancient Greece. It is my contention that in order
to understand democracy and its present position in the world, one must
have an awareness of the most important debates about the meaning of
democracy; a notion of the core features of democracy relevant for today's
world; and an understanding of how economic, social, and cultural conditions affect the quality of democracy. Thus, each of these elements is addressed in this chapter. The aim is merely to introduce the important issues; references will be given to sources with in-depth treatments.

The term democracy comes from the combination of two Greek words:
demos (people) and *kratos* (rule). The definition "rule by the people" may
sound innocently straightforward, but it immediately raises a number of
complex issues. The most important ones were aptly summarized in a recent report:

□ who are to be considered 'the people'?
□ what kind of participation is envisaged for them?
□ what conditions are assumed to be conducive to participation? Can the
disincentives and incentives, or costs and benefits, of participation be
equal?
□ how broadly or narrowly is the scope of rule to be construed? Or, what is
the appropriate field of democratic activity?
□ if 'rule' is to cover 'the political', what is meant by this? Does it cover (a)
law and order? (b) relations between states? (c) the economy? (d) the domestic or private sphere?

☐ must the rules of 'the people' be obeyed? What is the place of obligation and dissent?

☐ what mechanisms are created for those who are avowedly and actively 'non-participants'?

☐ under what circumstances, if any, are democracies entitled to resort to coercion against some of their own people or against those outside the sphere of legitimate rule?[1]

It readily appears that a discussion of democracy must involve not only the *theory* about possible ways of organizing rule by the people but also the *philosophy* about what ought to be (that is, the best ways of constructing government) and an understanding of *practical experiences* with the ways in which government has been organized in different societies at different times.

Such considerations are often interwoven in a highly complex manner. At the same time, the most significant contributions to the deliberations about democracy have one important element in common: They have been set against the context of contemporary society as those who have made these contributions perceive it. The debate about democracy therefore has an inbuilt dynamic: It develops and grows to incorporate new aspects and dimensions when the societal context—or the analyst's perception of it—changes.

Thus, Plato's critique of democracy in Athens was set against what he saw as the decline of the city, its defeat in the war with Sparta, and the decay of morality and leadership. In Athens, democracy meant the rule by the poor majority. People could do pretty much as they liked; there was no respect for authority in the family, in schools, or elsewhere. Eventually, Plato reasoned, laws would not be respected but would be seen as attacks on the freedom of the people. This situation would lead to **anarchy** (the absence of political authority) and chaos, paving the way for tyranny (rule by a single dictator). Plato's solution was to recommend rule by the wise, trained, and educated—that is, the philosophers.[2]

Aristotle voiced similar criticisms of democracy, which he also saw as a form of government devoted only to the good of the poor. Developing a position taken by Plato in his later writings, Aristotle argued for some room for popular influence, for example in the making of laws. Such considerations pointed toward a combination of monarchy and democracy, a "mixed state"[3] where a separation of powers ensured a balance of forces between the main groups in society.

With the decline of Athens, the debate about democracy was put on hold for a very long time. In the feudal system of the Middle Ages, power was not vested in elected bodies; it was based on rank that could be attained only through inheritance or by force. "No popular movement, however enraged, would think that its aims could be achieved by getting the vote. And in the nations and independent city-states of the later Middle Ages also, power was not to be sought in that way."[4]

A new body of thought on democracy, based on modern society, did not emerge until the nineteenth century, although its beginnings can be traced to the Renaissance and Niccolo Machiavelli (1469–1527). During this span of time from the Renaissance to the nineteenth century, ideas about democracy took shape in the context of the development of modern, industrial-capitalist society. A large number of highly diverse contributions to the debate about democracy were made during this period, but it is not possible or necessary to give an exhaustive account of them here. The intention in what follows is more modest: to reach a conception of the core features of democracy in the modern sense and to point out main areas where the content and conditions of this conception are still debated.

LIBERAL DEMOCRACY AND ITS CRITICS

Liberalism developed in opposition to the medieval, hierarchical institutions, the despotic monarchies whose claim to all-powerful rule rested on the assertion that they enjoyed divine support. Liberalism attacked the old system on two fronts. First, the liberalists fought for a rollback of state power and the creation of a sphere of **civil society** where social relations, including private business, nonstate institutions, family, and personal life, could evolve without state interference. "Gradually, liberalism became associated with the doctrine that individuals should be free to pursue their own preferences in religious, economic and political affairs—in fact everything that affected daily life."[5] An important element in this regard was the support of a market economy based on the respect for private property.

The second element of early liberalism was the claim that state power was based not on natural or supernatural rights but on the will of the sovereign people. Ultimately, this claim would lead to demands for democracy—that is, for the creation of mechanisms of representation that assured that those who held state power enjoyed popular support. Yet the creation of such mechanisms was not a primary concern of early liberalism. The tradition that became liberal democracy was liberal first (aimed at restricting state power over civil society) and democratic later (aimed at creating structures that would secure a popular mandate for holders of state power). Even when the focus was on democracy, the liberals had various reservations. They feared that democracy would impede the establishment of a liberal society.[6] In a sense the development of liberal democratic thinking evolved around the settling of the complex relationship between these two elements.

The unfolding of thinking on liberal democracy has been instructively summarized by C. B. Macpherson in three different models that he called (1) protective democracy, (2) developmental democracy, and (3) equilibrium democracy.[7] Instead of presenting these models in detail, I will include elements from them in a discussion of more recent debates and critiques with the aim of identifying some of the important issues that have been raised in the different stages of thinking about democracy.

The earliest model of liberal democracy, derived around 1820, builds on contributions from Jeremy Bentham and James Mill. Macpherson called it protective democracy because of the model's preoccupation with the protection of citizens from government and its attempts to ensure that governors would pursue policies in accordance with the interests of citizens as a whole. The way to such protection was seen as universal franchise. The vote gave political power; "one person, one vote" provided self-protection because the rulers could be removed.

In practice, however, Bentham and Mill were willing to accept severe restrictions in the right to vote; women and large sections of the working classes did not enjoy this privilege.[8] Their cause was more liberal than democratic: The aim was to restrict the sphere of politics, especially that of governmental activity and institutions. Civil society should be left to itself, meaning that such issues as "the organization of the economy or violence against women in marriage (rape) are thought of as non-political, an outcome of 'free' private contracts in civil society, not a public issue or a matter for the state".[9]

This concern with negative freedom, that is, freedom of the citizens from pervasive political authority, was echoed some 150 years later in the reflections of the so-called New Right or neo-liberalists. Their preoccupation was with the rollback of a state that keeps expanding its regulatory and redistributive activities in the name of general welfare and social justice.

The leading figure of the New Right, Friedrich von Hayek, makes a sharp distinction between liberalism and democracy. He calls the former a doctrine about what the law ought to be and the latter a doctrine about the manner of determining what will be the law[10]. For Hayek democracy is of only secondary importance. The highest political end is liberty, which can be achieved only if there are strict limits on the activities of governments. Government intervention in civil society must aim at protecting life, liberty, and estate, which basically means creating the best possible framework for the operation of the free market. There can be no room, for example, for redistributive measures because they would jeopardize the free choice of individuals in the free market.[11]

In this view democracy is desirable as a mechanism for securing that the majority will decide what the law should be. It is vital, however, that democratic majorities respect the limitations on government activity. If they do not, democracy will be in conflict with liberty, and if that is the case, Hayek is "not a democrat."[12]

In summary, it is possible to point to both very early and very recent contributions in the liberal democratic tradition whose primary concern is with the restriction of political authority over citizens. Liberty is individual freedom in the realm of civil society. Democracy can be a means of achieving this end but is not the end itself. If there is a democratic core in this way of thinking, it is the principle of the political equality of citizens. In what follows it will appear that this principle can lead in a quite different direction from the one taken by the proponents of protective democracy and can result in a much more central and positive role for democracy.

*   *   *

John Stuart Mill (1806–1873), the son of James Mill, was more enthusiastic about democracy than his father was. The younger Mill saw democracy as an important element in free human development. Participation in political life could lead toward the "highest and harmonious expansion of individual capacities."[13] At the same time, J. S. Mill shared one of the basic assumptions of the protective democrats: The maximum freedom of citizens required a limitation on the scope of the state's activity. His vision was one of representative government in combination with a free-market economy.

Thus, in important ways J. S. Mill followed familiar liberal views concerning the restriction of the scope of government and governmental activity. With regard to enfranchisements, it can even be said that he took a step backward. His father had argued for universal franchise, at least in principle; but J. S. Mill recommended a system of **plural voting** (one in which some members of the electorate have more votes than others) in order to give the "wiser and more talented" more votes than "the ignorant and less able."[14] It is in two other respects that the younger Mill was more democratic than his father. First, in the moral dimension, he saw participation in the political process as a way to liberty and self-development. The importance of participation has been stressed by other thinkers both before and after Mill, as we shall see in a moment. Second, J. S. Mill directly confronted a number of inequalities in mid-nineteenth-century English society that he considered obstacles to the democratic process. He severely criticized the subjection of women and pointed to the need for complete equality between the sexes as a precondition for human development and democracy. He was highly critical of the extreme inequalities of income, wealth, and power, which hindered the human development of the lower classes. Mill's ideas of participation and equality create a tension in his work because they are hard to reconcile with his positions concerning a restricted government committed to laissez-faire (which can be interpreted as doing nothing about the inequalities) and a plural voting system in favor of the well-educated (which is hardly a radical commitment to equality).[15]

Several other thinkers have shared Mill's preoccupation with participation as an important element of democracy and his concern that socioeconomic inequality is a main barrier to democracy and political equality. An early contribution in this respect was made by Jean-Jacques Rousseau (1712–1778) almost a hundred years before J. S. Mill. Rousseau's point of departure was a small, preindustrial community. He criticized the notion of representation, saying that citizens should be directly involved in the making of their laws; otherwise, there is no freedom. "The English people believes itself to be free, it is gravely mistaken; it is free only during the election of Members of Parliament; as soon as the members are elected, the people are enslaved; it is nothing."[16] In other words, real freedom calls for participation in the form of direct democracy.

Rousseau's ideas about the role of participation in democracy have often been rejected because they are seen as irrelevant for modern, large-scale society. But in more recent contributions, C. B. Macpherson and Carol Pateman have argued that Rousseau's ideas are indeed compatible with modern society and that representative government can be combined with elements of direct participation and indeed ought to be if democracy is to be more than merely formal.[17] According to Macpherson and Pateman, structures of participation in local society and in the workplace will vastly improve the quality of representative democracy. A participatory society would make the common man "better able to assess the performance of representatives at the national level, better equipped to take decisions of national scope when the opportunity arose to do so, and better able to weigh up the impact of decisions taken by national representatives on his own life."[18]

Like J. S. Mill, Rousseau felt that socioeconomic inequality would prevent citizens from equal political rights. In other words, with vast socioeconomic inequalities there could be no political democracy. In his critical analysis of capitalism, Karl Marx (1818–1883) related the existence of inequality with the class division produced by capitalist society itself. In Marx's view, in a capitalist society a free market and a state based on politically equal citizens are simply formalities that hide the reality of rule by the capitalist class. The only way to achieve real political and economic equality and a full democratization of state and society is to abolish the capitalist system and replace it with socialism and ultimately communism.[19] Thus, Marx agreed with Hayek that there is a sharp distinction between liberalism and democracy, but he drew the opposite conclusion: In order to achieve liberty and democracy, it is necessary to reject liberal capitalism.

In the debate about the relationship between capitalism and democracy, the liberalist tradition maintains that only a capitalist system can provide the necessary basis for liberty and democracy. The Marxist tradition finds that capitalism must be replaced by socialism as the necessary basis for democracy. The liberal view has prevailed insofar as the noncapitalist countries that have declared adherence to the Marxist tradition have been unable to construct political systems that can claim to be more democratic than the liberal democracies based on capitalism.

Yet the debate does not end there. Far from all of the capitalist systems in the world are also democratic. And it should be stressed that one does not have to be a Marxist in order to see the obstacles to democracy stemming from economic inequality. In a recent contribution, Robert Dahl stated that modern corporate capitalism tends to "produce inequalities in social and economic resources so great as to bring about severe violations of political equality and hence of the democratic process."[20] Dahl went on to suggest a system of cooperative control over the economy. This view of the need to extend democratic decision-making beyond government, to economic and social life as well, is also expressed in other recent contributions.[21]

Thus, the current debate about capitalism and democracy is not greatly concerned about the abolition of capitalism; the debate is between such thinkers as Hayek, on the one side, who wanted to protect life, liberty, and estate by rolling back government intervention in civil society, and a liberal cum social democratic group, on the other side, that argues for the necessity of a more reformed capitalism with less inequality and more democracy, not only in strictly political affairs but also in social and economic life.[22]

THE MEANING OF DEMOCRACY

It is clear from this brief overview of important debates concerning democracy that the questions asked at the beginning of this chapter about the meaning of rule by the people involve so many complex elements that they are far from easily answered. Indeed, a full answer to the question of what democracy means today requires a theory of contemporary society supported by substantial normative considerations about the type of people's rule that is desirable, which cannot be pursued here. Instead, I will illustrate the scope of this debate by outlining two conceptions of democracy with contemporary relevance: one rather narrow, the other very comprehensive. From each side, they help delimit the territory within which the debate about democracy has taken place.

The narrow concept was formulated by Joseph Schumpeter. For him democracy was simply a political method, a mechanism for choosing political leadership. The citizens are given a choice among rival political leaders who compete for their votes. Between elections, decisions are made by the politicians. At the next election, citizens can replace their elected officials. This ability to choose between leaders at election time is democracy. In Schumpeter's words, "The democratic method is that institutional arrangement for arriving at political decisions in which individuals acquire the power to decide by means of a competitive struggle for the people's vote."[23]

At the opposite end of the spectrum we have the very comprehensive notion of democracy suggested by David Held. Held combined insights of the liberal and the Marxist traditions in order to arrive at a meaning of democracy that supports a basic principle of autonomy:

> Individuals should be free and equal in the determination of the conditions of their own lives; that is, they should enjoy equal rights (and, accordingly, equal obligations) in the specification of the framework which generates and limits the opportunities available to them, so long as they do not deploy this framework to negate the rights of others.[24]

The enactment of this principle, which Held called **democratic autonomy,** requires both a high degree of accountability of the state and a democratic reordering of civil society. It foresees substantial direct participation in local community institutions as well as self-management of cooperatively owned enterprises. It calls for a bill of rights that goes beyond the right to cast a vote to include equal opportunity for participation and for discovering individual preferences as well as citizens' final control of the political agenda. Also included are social and economic rights to ensure adequate resources for democratic autonomy. "Without tough social and economic rights, rights with respect to the state could not be fully enjoyed; and without state rights new forms of inequality of power, wealth and status could systematically disrupt the implementation of social and economic liberties."[25]

In the area between the narrow notion of political democracy suggested by Schumpeter and the extremely comprehensive understanding presented by Held lies the debate about what democracy is and what it ought to be. Looking at democracy this way helps us understand that it is a dynamic entity that has been given many different definitions; its meaning remains subject to debate.

This approach can also help us see the possibility of emphasizing different aspects of democracy in framing one's own understanding of the concept. It is not surprising, for example, that conditions in many developing countries have led to an emphasis on the need to meet basic economic rights and equal opportunities for participation, as stressed in Held's comprehensive notion of democracy. Extreme material poverty makes democracy difficult:

> Where the members of a community suffer from chronic malnutrition and frequent illness, participation in common affairs that is both broad and deep is difficult to maintain. Where the lot of the masses is often that of acute hunger, or where disease runs rampant, the expectation of any genuine democracy among such masses is naive.[26]

It is against such a background that Julius Nyerere, the former president of Tanzania, said that the struggle for freedom in Africa is basically a struggle for freedom from hunger, disease, and poverty.

In the industrialized countries, where extreme poverty is not the main problem, there can be other impediments to democracy—for example, the lack of economic, social, and, consequently, political equality stressed by Dahl. At the same time, many of us would agree that the Western industrialized countries are, in a basic respect, democracies, particularly according to the narrow concept of political democracy provided by Schumpeter.

One general conclusion that can be drawn from this discussion of the meaning of democracy is that there can be no talk of the "**end of history**"[27] even if the authoritarian, noncapitalist regimes of the East have collapsed. (The end of history is a phrase coined by Francis Fukuyama to describe the end point of humankind's ideological evolution and the universalization of Western liberal democracy as the final form of human government.) There is still plenty of room for the development of different variations or models of democracy.

*   *   *

In another respect this view of the meaning of democracy is less helpful. It does not give us much guidance in determining whether specific countries are democratic. For that purpose we need a precise concept that provides a clear identification of what democracy essentially is. It is necessary, in other words, to cut through the debates in order to find a tool with which we can identify democracy by its core features, as a form of government in which the people rule. Most helpful would be a narrow concept that focuses on democracy as a specific type of political system. In the very broad concept, democracy is not only a political but also a specific social and economic system. In other words, if we were to use the broad concept we would be able to find very few, if indeed any, empirical cases of democracy. Furthermore, when democracy is seen in a narrow sense as a political system, it is easier to ask questions about the relationships between this political system, on the one hand, and the economic and social dimensions, on the other. It must be emphasized that although the narrow concept of democracy provides the most adequate starting point for the analysis intended here, it is not a normative choice of the "best kind" of democracy.

A contribution by Robert A. Dahl is helpful in defining democracy as a political system. Dahl emphasized the responsiveness of the government to the preferences of its citizens, considered as political equals, as a key characteristic of democracy. Such responsiveness requires that citizens must have opportunities to (1) formulate their preferences, (2) signify their preferences to their fellow citizens and the government by individual and collective action, and (3) have their preferences weighed equally in the conduct of the government. These three opportunities, in turn, are dependent on the following institutional guarantees:

1. Freedom to form and join organizations
2. Freedom of expression
3. Right to vote
4. Eligibility for public office
5. Right of political leaders to compete for support
   5a. Right of political leaders to compete for votes
6. Alternative sources of information
7. Free and fair elections
8. Institutions for making government policies depend on votes and other expressions of preference[28]

When these conditions are met, we have a political democracy. It is sometimes referred to as a liberal democracy because of its focus on the form of government. Dahl noted that there is no country in which these conditions are perfectly satisfied; he therefore prefers the term **polyarchy** for concrete systems and reserves the democracy label for the nonexistent, ideal type. In this book the term democracy or political democracy will be used for the systems Dahl would call polyarchies.

In principle, the eight conditions outlined by Dahl make up our definition of political democracy. Yet for practical purposes it will be helpful to come up with an even more condensed definition that summarizes the basic elements of political democracy. The eight conditions cover three main dimensions of political democracy, namely *competition, participation,* and *civil and political liberties.*[29] Against this background, political democracy can be viewed as a system of government that meets the following conditions:

□ Meaningful and extensive *competition* among individuals and organized groups (especially political parties) for all effective positions of government power, at regular intervals and excluding the use of force

□ A highly inclusive level of *political participation* in the selection of leaders and policies, at least through regular and fair elections, such that no major (adult) social group is excluded

□ A level of *civil and political liberties*—freedom of expression, freedom of the press, freedom to form and join organizations—sufficient to ensure the integrity of political competition and participation[30]

This is the definition of political democracy that is to be employed in the present volume.

Our first task in attempting to determine whether a specific country is a democracy is to look for the presence of the elements of competition, participation, and liberties in that country, not just on the formal level but in real practice. (There are many examples of political leaders who pay lip service to democratic ideals without meeting them in practice.) This task is complicated by the fact that many countries meet the conditions specified by the three dimensions in varying degrees.

Thus, it is necessary to decide on some minimum value that should be met with regard to each dimension for a country to qualify as democratic. For those that do not qualify, further differentiation is necessary because they vary substantially in their degrees of nondemocracy. For example, Mexico may not have been fully democratic in the postwar period, but it has been much more democratic than Chile has been under the Pinochet dictatorship. Differentiating degrees of nondemocracy is another substantial task; in the area between full democracy and nondemocracy (or authoritarian rule), there is room for highly different types of semi-democracies and semi-authoritarian systems.[31]

Unfortunately, there is no agreement among scholars about which of the dimensions are most important in determining whether there is democracy or about what precise minimum value should be applied for each of the dimensions. Moreover, just trying to analyze the particular conditions specified by the three dimensions can often be difficult (e.g., was an election rigged; do opposition parties get fair possibilities for competing?).

We shall return to attempts to measure political democracy in a moment. It is helpful first to look briefly at processes of democratization based on the concept of democracy we have just outlined and to indicate the relationship between political democracy as competition, participation, and liberties and the very broad concept of democracy formulated by Held.

When democracy is defined in terms of competition, participation, and liberties, it is clear that the process of democratization, the change of a political system from nondemocratic toward more democratic, can take place in different ways. Dahl identified two principal routes toward democracy: one with a focus on competition, the other with a focus on participation.[32] Increased participation (or **inclusiveness**) means that the proportion of citizens who enjoy political rights and liberties increases. Nondemocratic regimes may exclude a large majority of the population from participation. In democratic regimes the entire adult population enjoys the full range of rights and liberties.

Competition (or **liberalization**) concerns the extent to which rights and liberties are available to at least some members of the political system. Increasing liberalization means increasing the possibility for political opposition and competition for government power. Figure 1.1 illustrates possible paths from nondemocratic rule toward democracy, each involving a different degree of participation and competition.

Four countries are mentioned in the figure. Denmark is an example of a democracy in which the entire adult population enjoys the full range of rights and liberties. In the former USSR, elections were regularly held and all adults had the right to vote, but opposition to the ruling Communist party was not possible. In other words, there was a high degree of participation but there was no political competition and there were no real liberties, such as freedom of expression, the right to form organizations, and access to alternative sources of information. Therefore, the USSR was not a democracy. The present process of democratization in the former USSR is first and foremost a process of liberalization, of increased political competition backed by real rights and liberties. In South Africa, the situation is different. For many years, a white minority has enjoyed the political rights and liberties necessary for political competition, whereas the black majority has been excluded from participation. In this case, the process of democratization is primarily one of increasing participation through the inclusion of the black population. Finally, the dictatorship in Chile under Augusto Pinochet has offered neither competition nor participation to any parts of the population. Since 1988, Chile has undergone a process of democratization that has increased both liberalization and participation, but it has not yet made the full transition to democracy. The processes of democratization will be subject to further scrutiny in Chapter 2, where additional concrete examples of different paths toward democracy will be given.

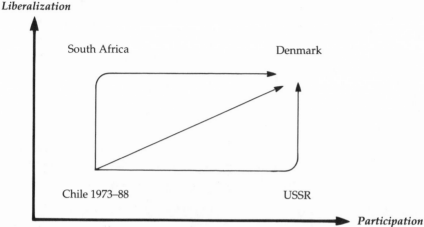

FIGURE 1.1   Dimensions of democratization

Source: Modified from Robert A. Dahl, *Polyarchy: Participation and Opposition* (New Haven: Yale University Press, 1971), p. 7, and Paille Svensson, "The Liberalization of Eastern Europe," *Journal of Behavioral and Social Sciences* 34 (1991): 56.

How does the comprehensive notion of democracy outlined by Held fit into this picture? Held's concept of democracy can be seen as an expansion of political democracy in two respects: further liberalization and more participation. In other words, having reached political democracy, further democratization is still possible according to the broad concept of democracy set forth by Held. On one dimension, this means additional liberalization: Formal political rights and liberties may be worth little if citizens are not secured equal rights in a more substantial manner. For example, without a welfare state that prevents extreme material poverty and steep socioeconomic inequalities, it is not possible for the poor sections of the population to fully enjoy their political rights. Only with poverty eradicated can formally equal rights be translated into substantially equal rights.

It is also possible to extend the other dimension, participation. According to our definition of political democracy, participation concerns government and public institutions. In Held's notion of democracy, participation is extended to social institutions and the economy (note his suggestions about the self-management of enterprises and participation in local community institutions). The movement from political democracy toward Held's notion of democratic autonomy is summarized in Figure 1.2.

The figure demonstrates how the combination of extended liberalization and participation defines the movement from political democracy to-

	WELFARE DEMOCRACY	DEMOCRATIC AUTONOMY
Substantive benefits and entitlements	WELFARE DEMOCRACY	DEMOCRATIC AUTONOMY
Formal rights and liberties	POLITICAL DEMOCRACY	SOCIAL DEMOCRACY

LIBERALIZATION ▲

Public institutions and governmental processes   Social institutions and economic processes

PARTICIPATION ▶

FIGURE 1.2   The movement from political democracy toward democratic autonomy

Source: Modified from Guillermo O'Donnell and Philippe C. Schmitter, *Transitions from Authoritarian Rule: Tentative Conclusions About Uncertain Democracies* (Baltimore: Johns Hopkins University Press, 1986), p. 13.

ward democratic autonomy. It must be stressed that focus in this volume is *not* on the processes going beyond political democracy. The focus is on the processes of democratization depicted in Figure 1.1—that is, the movement from authoritarian rule toward political democracy. Therefore, the terms democracy and political democracy will be used interchangeably.

We now have (1) a definition of political democracy as participation, competition, and civil and political liberties; (2) a notion of paths of democratization; and (3) a sense of the relationship between political democracy and the much broader concept of democratic autonomy. The following section looks at attempts to measure democracy, using our definition of political democracy as the starting point.

ATTEMPTS TO MEASURE DEMOCRACY

With the difficulties it involves, it is no surprise that the measurement of democracy has become its own branch of political science surrounded by an ongoing debate about best ways of devising and combining indicators. Because of the large number of difficulties in this domain, one should treat attempts at estimating the quantity of democracy with caution. The indexes and overviews are helpful as starting points, but a closer inspection of countries must follow.

The most recent attempt to measure the degree of democracy in a large number of countries using Dahl's concept of democracy as a starting point was undertaken by Tatu Vanhanen.[33] Unfortunately, his study, which covers the years 1980 to 1988, does not provide data about the most recent transitions toward democracy. Therefore, I shall rely on another well-known attempt at measuring democracy, namely the Freedom House index.[34]

The index employs one dimension for competition and participation (called political rights) and one dimension for civil liberties. For each dimension a seven-point scale is used, so that the highest ranking countries (that is, those with the highest degree of democracy) are one-ones (1-1's) and the lowest are seven-sevens (7-7's). In other words, the index attempts to reflect the space of semi-democracy or semi-authoritarianism between outright authoritarian (7-7) and fully democratic (1-1) regimes (see Fig. 1.3).

Countries with an average rating between 1 and 2.5 are considered free; those with an average between 3 and 5.5 are partly free; and those with ratings from 5.5 to 7 are considered not free. Although the Freedom House distinction between rights and liberties differs from the breakdown of components in the definition of democracy we are employing, both basically cover the same dimensions. Therefore, the Freedom House index can function as an approximate measurement of political democracy as defined in this book.

The 1991 Freedom House survey of independent countries with more than one million inhabitants identified forty-four countries as free. The list, shown in Table 1.1, is ordered according to combined average ratings. When countries with fewer than one million inhabitants were included (bringing the total number of states in the world to 165), the Freedom House survey for 1990–1991 classified sixty-five countries as free, fifty as partly free, and another fifty as not free.[35]

Two caveats are worth stressing in relation to the Freedom House survey and other indexes. First, they provide only rough approximations of the possible presence and status of democracy in a country. They are incapable of revealing many of the features of political systems. For example, the features that made one scholar characterize Japan as soft authoritarian do not come clearly forward in any of these indexes. Chalmers Johnson presented the following argument:

> Since 1947, despite its adoption of a formally democratic constitution and the subsequent development of a genuinely open political culture, Japan seems to have retained many **"soft authoritarian"** features in its governmental institutions: an extremely strong and comparatively unsupervised state administration, single-party rule for more than three decades, and a set of economic priorities that seems unattainable under true political pluralism during such a long period.[36]

Classification of Countries	Political rights Rating 1–7	Civil liberties Rating 1–7
	Combined average ranking	
Free	1–2.5	
Partly Free	3–5.5	
Not free	5.5–7	

FIGURE 1.3 The Freedom House index for measuring democracy. Note that countries with a 5.5 average are classified as either partly free or not free depending on which raw scores the overall ranking summarizes.

Source: Based on R. Bruce McColm, "The Comparative Survey of Freedom: 1991," Freedom Review 22, no. 1 (1991): 14.

TABLE 1.1   The Freedom House Index Classification of Free Countries (with greater than one million inhabitants), 1991

Average rating: 1
Australia	Finland	Norway
Austria	Ireland	Spain
Belgium	Italy	Sweden
Canada	Japan	Switzerland
Costa Rica	Netherlands	United States
Denmark	New Zealand	

Average rating: 1.5
Botswana	Greece	Uruguay
France	Portugal	
Germany	United Kingdom	

Average rating: 2
Argentina	The Gambia	Mauritius
Chile	Hungary	Poland
Czechoslovakia	Israel	Venezuela
Ecuador	Jamaica	

Average rating: 2.5
Bolivia	Honduras	Namibia
Brazil	India	Papua New Guinea
Dominican Republic	Korea, South	Thailand

Source: Data from R. Bruce McColm, "The Comparative Survey of Freedom: 1991," Freedom Review 22, no. 1 (1991): 23.

Indeed, Japan may be superficially characterized as a parliamentary democracy, but its political system is profoundly different from the Western system, with power in Japan vested in institutions to which there are no clear parallels in the West.[37] Other commentators have been even harsher in their criticism of what they see as the lack of real democracy in Japan, but the political rights and political liberties dimensions employed by Freedom House do not reveal such problems.[38]

Thus, actual cases of democracy are often highly dissimilar in important dimensions. We may include such systems as those of the United States, Botswana, Denmark, Costa Rica, Japan, and Jamaica under the general term democracies, but the specific structures of their political systems, their political culture, and their socioeconomic environments are substantially different. One scholar has suggested making the following distinctions between various types of democratic regimes: presidential versus parliamentary; majoritarian versus representational; two-party versus multiparty; distribution of power among parties; extremist multiparty; and consociational. He defined a **consociational democracy** as one that has mechanisms serving to promote compromise and consensus among groups in society.[39]

Therefore, detailed analysis of specific cases is necessary in order to ascertain in a more profound manner their democratic qualities. It is only at the level of the individual case that one can study the interplay between formal freedoms, political processes, and the larger context of socioeconomic and other conditions that affect the quality of democracy. Furthermore, if we agree with Held that democracy is made much more difficult by extreme material poverty, then it also becomes relevant to look at socioeconomic conditions as co-determinants of the quality of democracy, even if these conditions are not included in the definition of democracy as a political system. The Human Development index compiled by the United Nations Development Programme (UNDP) provides systematic, comparative information on these conditions.[40]

In countries like India, where more than half of the adult population is illiterate and close to one-half of the population lives below the poverty line, a vigorous democracy is more difficult to achieve than in countries with better socioeconomic conditions. This observation is also relevant for many African countries, where the situation is similar or even worse, and for such countries as Bangladesh, Pakistan, Haiti, Bolivia, and Nepal.

Some scholars draw the dramatic conclusion that it is impossible to have democracy in any meaningful sense in materially very poor societies.[41] That might be going too far. Socioeconomic conditions do affect the *quality* of political democracy but they do not prevent the development of a democratic system.

At the same time, it is necessary to be aware that socioeconomic inequalities can impede real political equality in industrialized countries as well. Some data on socioeconomic conditions in industrialized countries can also be found in the UNDP report.[42]

The second caveat that should be stressed with regard to the indexes that estimate degrees of democracy concerns the "new" democracies, which will be analyzed in further detail in the next chapter. These democracies are in the early stages of what might be a long process of transition from authoritarian toward democratic rule. In other words, the ratings these new democracies receive in the indexes are really only snapshots of regimes that are "on the move"—that is, in a process of transition from one form of regime toward another.

TIME HORIZONS
AND LEVELS OF ANALYSIS

It is useful to introduce two additional elements in this general presentation of the meaning and prevalence of democracy. The first is the historical dimension. One must remember that in historical terms, democracy as it has been defined here is a very recent phenomenon. Only four countries—Australia, Finland, New Zealand, and Norway—had extended suffrage to women before World War I. And even if we look for "male democracies" in existence then, we would not find many cases; the constitutional monarchies in nineteenth-century Europe cannot be considered fully democratic because their cabinets were not responsible to elected Parliaments in a clear-cut manner.[43]

Thus, the semi-democracies of nineteenth-century Europe became fully democratic only in the twentieth century, and several of them, including Italy, Germany, Austria, and Spain, suffered setbacks to nondemocratic rule in the 1920s and 1930s. Consequently, it is only for the period after World War II that one can talk about extended, stable democratic rule in the industrialized countries of Western Europe and North America.

In the developing countries of Asia, Africa, and Latin America, there have been only a handful of enduring democracies, among them Costa Rica, India, Venezuela (from 1958), and Jamaica (from 1962). In recent years, transitions toward more democratic rule have taken place in a large number of developing countries and countries of Eastern Europe. The question must be asked whether this phenomenon is a prelude to an era of many more stable democracies than we have seen so far or is merely a fragile flourish that can easily suffer setbacks to nondemocracy. This issue will be addressed in Chapter 2.

The other dimension that must be introduced here concerns levels of analysis. Until now, our discussion about what democracy is and where it can be found has focused on the state: Does this or that country have democracy or not? But this level of analysis is clearly insufficient. There is an international or global level "above" the states and a local level "below" them that must also be taken into account.

How does the *international system* affect prospects for democracy in individual countries? To answer this question, one must analyze the dominant trends in the international system and the different ways in which they affect specific countries. It is probably universally agreed that during the postwar period there has been an enormous increase in all types of exchange between countries, including trade, investment, communication, and travel. In other words, there is a higher degree of **interdependence** (situations characterized by mutual dependence between countries or among actors in different countries) than ever before.[44]

Against this background, ideas about democracy and human rights have been increasingly diffused. Russian Nobel laureate Andrei Sakharov called the United Nations declaration of human rights the common glue that binds all ideologies together, and state leaders have felt a growing need to appeal to democratic ideas in order to legitimize their rule. There is no doubt that the Helsinki factor—the pressure from the West for more respect for basic human rights in Eastern Europe and the Soviet Union—has played an important part in the democratic openings there, as we shall see in Chapter 2. Yet leading Western countries such as the United States, France, and Great Britain have not provided consistent support for the promotion of democracy in all parts of the world. They have, on several occasions, supported nondemocratic leaders in Asia, Africa, and Latin America for reasons of national interest.

At the same time, individual countries are to an increasing degree being subjected to international forces over which they have little control. It is true, as Dahl pointed out, that this has always been the case: "Not just conflict but also trade, commerce, and finance have always spilled over state boundaries. Democratic states, therefore, have never been able to act autonomously, in disregard of the actions of outside forces over which they had little or no control."[45] But recent tendencies are more than just replays of this theme. In developing countries, for example, dependence on international structures has increased in the wake of the debt crisis, which has expanded the power over single countries of such international organizations as the International Monetary Fund (IMF) and the World Bank. The frustration of these countries to this increased dependency came out clearly in a speech by Julius Nyerere of Tanzania in 1979: "When did the IMF become an International Ministry of Finance? When did nations agree to surrender their power of decision making?"[46] The IMF response to questions such as these would probably be that the fund acts only on the basis of agreements entered by countries on a voluntary basis.

No clear conclusion emerges from these brief remarks on the effects of the international system on democracy in single countries. I shall return to the issue in the coming chapters. What we may note for now is that actors in the international system can either promote or try to prevent democracy in single countries. Moreover, the dynamics of dependence and interdependence in the international system directly affect the scope of democratic decision-making at the national level. In general, one must expect large and socioeconomically strong countries to be much less susceptible to international pressures and challenges than is the case with smaller, socioeconomically weak countries.

Let me turn to the *local level* of analysis. Until now we have assumed that democracy at the level of national government in a country means that democracy also prevails at the local level. Yet this need not always be the case. Examples from India and China illustrate this point.

India is one of the most stable democracies in the developing world. It adopted a democratic constitution in 1950, and for only eighteen months, in 1975-1977, during the so-called emergency declared by Indira Gandhi, was there nondemocratic rule. However, democracy at the national or macro level of the political system has not meant that democracy was brought to all localities. The Congress party attained its dominant position in India's vast countryside by making alliances that enforced the traditional patterns of domination. Congress dealt with the electorate through "existing patron-brokers who, as landowners and caste-leaders, had no desire to jeopardize their positions by transforming local social structures. In adapting to local conditions, the party thus increasingly became tied to age-old patterns of status and leadership."[47] Against this background, it is not surprising that democratic India has set in motion programs that, although claiming to promote welfare and participation at the local level, have in fact had the opposite effect: making the poor majority even worse off and strengthening the traditional structures of dominance and subordination.[48]

In China, political democracy like that found in India was never seriously on the agenda. The Chinese Communist party (CCP) is a Bolshevik party; it did not propose to fight for the interests of all Chinese but only for the interests of workers and poor peasants against internal and external class enemies. Further, the democracy it sought for workers and poor peasants was the democracy of leadership from above combined with some degree of participation from below, and it gave special status to the small faction of the population (less than 1 percent in 1949) who were members of the party.[49]

But it can be claimed that the Communists, within this overall structure of authoritarian socialist rule, also promoted at least some elements of democracy at the local level. They did so through what was called the mass line, which took at least five different forms.[50] First, grass-roots and county-level leaders were given a high degree of latitude in ensuring that higher-level instructions were in accordance with local needs, conditions, and opinions. Second, cadres were sent to the villages to work and live alongside the peasants, under similar circumstances, in order to share their experiences and learn from rural life. Third, secret ballot elections were held regularly at village, township, county, and regional levels, providing a democratic and representative character to local government. "The only restriction was the 'three-thirds' principle, according to which one-third of offices were to be filled by CCP members, one-third by non-CCP leftists, and one-third by liberals."[51] Fourth, popular political expression in the form of the "big character poster" (*dazibao*, or wall poster) was encouraged. And, finally, the armed forces were to take part in civilian affairs under rules that required their subordination to civil authority.

The difference between China and India at the local level is quite clear: The authoritarian Chinese government has pushed structural reforms and systems of local participation that have done more for democratic change at the micro level than the so-called reforms attempted by democratic India. I am not suggesting that this contradiction between democracy (or nondemocracy) at the national level and nondemocratic tendencies (or the opposite) at the local level can be widely generalized. The core of the matter is that a national framework of democracy does not guarantee real democracy at the local level and an authoritarian national framework does not completely block democratic elements at the local level.

Yet one can expect such contradictions to become less pronounced in the long run. It can indeed be argued that India's democracy has grown stronger at the local level since independence and that overall authoritarianism is increasingly the order of the day in China. In other words, in the long run, democracy at the national level and democracy at the local level tend to reinforce each other, but in the short-to-medium run there may be discrepancies between the two. It is important to be aware of these discrepancies in overall assessments of democracy.

CONCLUSION

Democracy means rule by the people. A more precise definition is difficult to formulate because democracy is a dynamic entity that has acquired many different meanings over the course of time. Much of this dynamic comes from changes in society and from the different interpretations by analysts of the consequences of these changes for democracy. With the very different levels and ways of development of societies in today's world, it is not surprising that the meaning of democracy continues to be the subject of debate.

Yet for analytical purposes we need to develop a concept that provides a clear identification of what democracy essentially is. The core of political democracy has three dimensions: competition, participation, and civil and political liberties. When we study the status of democracy in a specific country, the first step is to look for these three elements. In this context it is helpful to consult one of the indexes on democracy—for example, the Freedom House index. In order to make a comprehensive assessment of democracy, one must carefully scrutinize the individual country as well because democratic systems vary greatly in their institutional patterns and along other dimensions. Socioeconomic conditions also affect the quality of democracy. Finally, it is necessary to be aware of the international setting above and the local conditions below the level of national government.

It can be argued that this procedure is too comprehensive and requires analysis of "everything." It is true that one will often have to stop short of completing all of these stages. Even in the present volume the discussion is limited to the transition from authoritarian rule to political democracy and to the consequences of democracy. Yet it is important to be aware of the full agenda if one wishes to evaluate specific cases of democracy in a more comprehensive manner.

TWO

□ □ □

Processes of Democratization

What conditions are conducive to the formation of a political democracy? The first two sections of this chapter introduce the debate
about the effects of general economic, social, and other conditions on the
rise of democracy. Some conditions favor democracy more than others,
but it will be argued that for a full understanding one must study the interplay between these conditions, on the one hand, and the choices made
by political actors, on the other.

And why have such a large number of countries begun the transition
toward democracy in recent years? A model of the process of democratization will be introduced that demonstrates that the movement from authoritarian to democratic rule is a complex, long-term process involving
different phases; the current transitions are only in the beginning of this
process. The bulk of this chapter is devoted to the formulation of four
propositions, each of which spells out an important characteristic of the
current transitions. The propositions serve to substantiate the dilemma
identified in the introduction: Democracy has made progress in terms of
democratic openings, but it has progressed in a way that does not bode
well for further democratic consolidation. The result may just as easily be
a democratic deadlock in which frail and unconsolidated democracies fail
to meet the hopes and promises invested in them by the majorities of the
populations.

THE SEARCH FOR
DEMOCRACY'S PRECONDITIONS

What pattern of economic, social, cultural, and other conditions is most
favorable to the rise of democracy? It was noted in Chapter 1 that the

spread of democracy is a relatively recent phenomenon. The implication seems to be that it takes the conditions brought about by modern, industrial society to produce democracy. This idea was behind the famous thesis by Seymour M. Lipset: "The more well-to-do a nation, the greater the chances that it will sustain democracy."[1]

Modernization and wealth will always be accompanied by a number of factors conducive to democracy: higher rates of literacy and education, urbanization, the development of mass media. Moreover, wealth will also provide the resources needed to mitigate the tensions produced by political conflict.[2] A large number of empirical analyses inspired by the Lipset hypothesis tended to support it. Thus, in 1971 Robert Dahl considered it "pretty much beyond dispute" that the higher the socioeconomic level of a country, the more likely that it would be a democracy.[3]

But this expectation far from always holds true. Argentina has had many years of authoritarian rule despite a relatively high level of per capita income; the same can be said of Taiwan and South Korea. In the latter cases, rapid economic development has even been accompanied by a fairly equal distribution of income. In his analysis of the major South American cases, Guillermo O'Donnell developed an argument that turned the Lipset thesis on its head: Authoritarianism, not democracy, seemed to him to be the more likely concomitant of the highest levels of modernization. O'Donnell's reasoning went as follows: The process of industrial modernization that was taking place in several Latin American countries in the 1960s and early 1970s had very little to offer the large majority of the populations. Therefore, in order to pursue this model in the face of popular resistance, the ruling elite needs an authoritarian system.[4]

A second set of preconditions (the first set being associated with modernization and wealth) often brought forward in the attempt to determine the factors that favor democracy concerns **political culture**—that is, the system of values and beliefs that defines the context and meaning of political action. If political culture is tied in with the larger system of culture in a society, is it possible to identify cultural values and beliefs that are especially conducive to democracy?

One of the frequent answers to this question is that Protestantism supports democracy whereas Catholicism in many cases, especially in Latin America, works against it. In more general terms, some cultures emphasize hierarchy, authority, and intolerance more than others. It seems reasonable to expect that they are less conducive to democracy. Islam and Confucianism are like Catholicism in this regard.

Yet it is difficult to demonstrate a systematic relationship between specific cultural patterns and the prevalence of democracy.[5] Moreover, cultural systems are subject to dynamic change. It may be that Catholicism did, at one point in history, work against democracy in Latin America, but the Catholic church also played an active role in the opposition toward authoritarian rule in the 1980s.[6]

A third set of preconditions favoring democracy is associated with the social structure of society, that is, the specific classes and groups making up the society. Is it possible to identify certain groups and classes that consistently favor democracy (for example, the middle classes, industrial bourgeoisie, workers) and others that consistently work against it (for example, traditional landowners)?

In his historical account of the roots of democracy and dictatorship, Barrington Moore concluded that "a vigorous and independent class of town dwellers has been an indispensable element in the growth of parliamentary democracy. No bourgeois, no democracy."[7] Conversely, landowners tend to support democracy only under special circumstances, such as when small-scale farming is dominant and there is a relatively equal distribution of land. Against Barrington Moore's thesis it must be said that the bourgeoisie does not consistently work for democracy. It has in fact been argued that the opposite is closer to the truth. According to Goran Therborn, democracy has "always and everywhere" been brought about in a popular struggle against the leading sections of the bourgeoisie.[8]

The final set of possible preconditions to be mentioned here is made up of **external factors,** the economic, political, ideological, and other elements that constitute the international context for the processes that take place in single countries. It was argued in Chapter 1 that no straightforward conclusion is possible regarding the effect of external factors on democracy. The developing countries of the Third World are those most susceptible to external influence, especially by the leading Western countries. It is customary among modernization theorists to consider this influence beneficial for the promotion of democracy.[9] Dependency theorists have drawn the opposite conclusion: The inequalities and distortions of the economies and societies of the Third World, brought about by their dependent position in the world economic system, make democracy very difficult.[10]

Four sets of possible preconditions for democracy have now been identified. It is possible to continue the list, of course. Dahl named seventeen variables, classified into seven categories, that are conducive to democracy.[11] Larry Diamond, Juan Linz, and Seymour Lipset employed a similar procedure in the introduction to their study of democracy in developing countries.[12] Yet for every factor seen as conducive to democracy, counterexamples can be put forward. Moreover, in many countries, different preconditions may exist that point in different directions: For example, cultural factors may be conducive to democracy while economic factors may not be.

The situation is somewhat frustrating. It is possible to point out a number of preconditions that can reasonably be expected to favor or obstruct the possibilities for democracy. But in every case it is also possible to give counterexamples, where the expectations have not held true.

Thus, a fixed model or law about democracy cannot be formulated. We cannot say that if x, y, or n preconditions are present, there will be democracy. In one sense, it is fortunate that a law of this kind is infeasible. For it would leave little or no room for the choices taken by political actors. Such choices make a difference. Juan Linz has noted that in some situations "even the presence of an individual with unique qualities and characteristics—a Charles de Gaulle, for instance—can be decisive and cannot be predicted by any model.[13]

In some cases, as we shall see, democracy can emerge even when none, or very few, of the preconditions listed as conducive to democracy are present. Economic, social, cultural, and other structural conditions may well act as constraints decreasing the likelihood for democracy to occur, but they do not themselves make the policy choice about whether there will be a democratic system.

However, recognizing the importance of choices taken by political actors does not mean that the search for preconditions is completely useless. Actors cannot make any kind of choice in a given situation. They are constrained by the structures—the preconditions—that are the result of the country's development in previous periods. Therefore, one must look at the interplay between economic, social, cultural, and other preconditions created in earlier periods and the decisions taken by current political actors.

The preconditions set the stage; they form the scene on which the actors play.[14] The preconditions cannot foretell whether the actors will produce democracy or not, but they can provide some information about what kind of outcome we can expect from the players. Although very poor countries with adverse social, economic, and other preconditions may well move toward democracy (as can be seen currently in some African countries), we can expect that outcome to be much more rare than in countries with more favorable preconditions. We must also expect the democracies emerging under such adverse conditions to be highly unstable, frail, and vulnerable.

In the final analysis, there is no way around a more detailed study of the interplay of actors and structures in concrete settings. Before we move in that direction, however, it is useful to discuss in more general terms the choices made by political actors.

WHEN DO POLITICAL ACTORS
CHOOSE DEMOCRACY?

Democracy does not fall from heaven. It is brought about by individuals and groups, by social actors, who fight for it. Adam Przeworski has made a penetrating analysis of the choices taken by the important actors in moving their countries toward democracy.[15] His starting point was the contention that democracy basically introduces a degree of uncertainty in the political process. In a democracy, no single group can be sure that its interests will ultimately prevail. Even the most powerful group, be it local or foreign business, armed forces, bureaucracy, or other privileged elements, must be ready to face the possibility that it can lose out in conflicts with other groups, which means that its interests may not be looked after. In other words, in democracies actors may choose policy reforms that attack the power and privilege of dominant groups.

Given this situation, it is not difficult to see why the nonprivileged, who were barred from political influence during authoritarian rule, struggle for a democratic polity that will give them access to political influence. But why should members of the dominant forces, who held together in the power bloc behind nondemocratic, authoritarian rule, suddenly opt for a democratic solution that may entail a threat to their interests?

They may try to avoid the democratic option, of course. That is, they may strive to keep the authoritarian system. Insofar as there is regime change, it is merely from one type of authoritarian regime to another. Alternatively, democracy may prevail, even against the wishes of the dominant forces, because the authoritarian regime suffers defeat in a foreign or a civil war or simply disintegrates due to internal division.[16]

However, transitions to democracy are only very rarely based on the complete defeat of the elites who stood behind the previous authoritarian rule. In the vast majority of cases the transition to democracy is based on negotiations with the forces backing the authoritarian regime. The question then becomes: Why should the forces behind authoritarian rule enter such negotiations?

There can be several reasons. Democratic openings are often preceded by a split in the coalition of forces behind authoritarian rule, a split between hard-liners and soft-liners.[17] The latter may seek more democratic forms of rule—perhaps in order to get the upper hand in a conflict with hard-liners—in the face of internal and external pressures and perhaps also due to normative commitments to democracy.

More pragmatic reasons for such a move have to do with problems for which democracy can provide a solution. For example, democracy can help restore the legitimacy of the existing social order and it can provide an open and regularized system of decision-making that can result in a better environment for conducting business. According to one scholar, "Another benefit not to be minimized is the international recognition that accompanies democratization. This can yield dividends in the form of inflows of foreign aid and loans."[18]

The point is that the elites' support of democracy is often based on self-interest; therefore, it is both fragile and conditional.[19] During the negotiations accompanying transitions toward democracy, the elites will try to stack the cards in order to make sure that the democratic institutions that are set up do not threaten their basic interests. This can be done in several ways. Adam Przeworski gave as an example the Brazilian elections held in 1982, where "the authoritarian government used every possible legal instrument to secure *a priori* advantage for the pro-government party and to secure to itself the eventual majority in the presidential electoral college."[20] These were some of the measures taken in Brazil: First, the authoritarian rulers allowed the formation of additional parties, with the aim of splitting the opposition; second, they created obstacles that made it difficult for those parties that were popular before the authoritarian rulers took over in 1964 to register; third, they made it more difficult for illiterates to cast their ballots, as they were expected to vote against the government.

Przeworski drew the somber conclusion that democratization is possible only "if there exist institutions that provide a reasonable expectation that interests of major political forces would not be affected highly adversely under democratic competition, given the resources these forces can muster."[21] In other words, elite groups will support democracy only insofar as they feel certain that their interests will be looked after under more democratic conditions. Thus, the democratic institutions that are set up as a result of negotiations with elite groups may be restricted in various ways, as, for example, is the case in Brazil. Moreover, the elite groups may require that the policies of the new, democratically based governments contain inbuilt social and economic conservatism. In summary, when transitions toward democracy are the result of negotiations with the forces behind the previous, authoritarian regime, it is likely that the new democracy will be restricted in various respects, as will be its room for maneuvering in terms of social and economic reform measures.

I shall argue later that the majority of transitions toward democracy in recent years have indeed been of this negotiated variety. Although it is clearly necessary to examine specific cases in order to study the variations in the actual compromises behind the transitions, one cannot help being somewhat pessimistic regarding the further development of democracy as well as regarding the prospects for substantial reform that would benefit the less privileged.

WHY THE RECENT SURGE
TOWARD DEMOCRACY?

The previous sections have discussed the general conditions for democracy and the need to study the interplay between those conditions and the choices made by political actors. In this section, these elements are put to use in an attempt to answer the question: Why has there been a recent surge toward democracy in so many countries?

It is useful to present some information about the spread of democracy. More than thirty countries made transitions toward democracy between 1974 and 1990. The result has been a near doubling of the number of democratic regimes. The transitions began in southern Europe (Greece, Spain, and Portugal). The next wave was in Latin America (Argentina, Uruguay, Peru, Ecuador, Bolivia, Brazil, and Paraguay) and in Central America (Honduras, El Salvador, Nicaragua, Guatemala, and Mexico). Then came the transitions in Eastern Europe (Poland, Czechoslovakia, Hungary, Romania, Bulgaria, and the former German Democratic Republic). The most recent wave has been in Africa and in the former Soviet Union. Finally, transitions toward democracy have taken place in Asia over the entire period since the early 1970s (in Papua New Guinea, Thailand, Pakistan, Bangladesh, the Philippines, South Korea, Taiwan, Mongolia, and Nepal).

The changes are impressive, and they do indeed give evidence of democratic progress in a large number of countries in a relatively short span of time. But some caveats should be taken into account. First, in some countries—for example, Thailand—there have already been setbacks toward authoritarian rule. Second, the transitions recorded here do not give the full picture; those countries that underwent changes toward more or less democracy without changing category are not represented.[22] Third, a number of the countries mentioned are not yet full democracies; they are in the early phases of a transition toward democracy, as I shall argue in further detail later. Finally, it is useful to put the democratic progress of 1974–1991 in a larger historical context. Much depends on the way in which the time periods are defined. The progress since 1974 must be seen against the background of a large number of democratic breakdowns in earlier periods, especially between the mid-1960s and the early 1970s.

In 1984, Samuel Huntington wrote that "it would be difficult to argue that the world was more or less democratic in 1984 than it had been in 1954."[23] Seen from this perspective, the democratic progress between 1974 and 1984 merely regained the distance lost by the setbacks of earlier periods. Most of the "new" democracies in Latin America, Eastern Europe, and Asia that have appeared since 1984 are thus in the category of *re*democratizations, that is, returns to more democratic conditions after periods of nondemocratic rule.

Even if this is the case, the moves toward democracy in recent years are significant and must be explained. No single factor can account for these events. There are complex patterns of internal and external elements, of various conditions that interplay with different groups of actors. Moreover, the movements toward democracy in different parts of the world during the last fifteen years must be explained in different ways. Ideally, the movements should be untangled country by country, but space does not allow this. Therefore, we will look at events in major regions as well as events in some specific countries. Finally, although the question "Why has there been a recent surge toward democracy?" really covers two analytically separate issues—the breakdown of authoritarian systems and the move toward democracy instead of toward another authoritarian system—a sharp distinction between these two elements will not be made in the discussion that follows. However, I shall have more to say about the reasons behind moves toward democracy later in this chapter.

The first cluster of transitions took place in the mid-1970s in southern Europe, specifically in Greece, Portugal, and Spain. In all three cases, splits within the authoritarian regimes led to their downfall. At the same time, these countries experienced distinct phases of authoritarian breakdown followed by the erection of democracy.

In Spain, Francisco Franco had made arrangements for the continuation of authoritarian rule well before his death. Admiral Carrero Blanco was to take responsibility for the government and Juan Carlos, a monarch educated under Franco's supervision, was to become head of state. But the scheme was interrupted by the assassination of Carrero Blanco; with him out of the picture, Juan Carlos was left with a high degree of freedom to maneuver when he took over as head of state after Franco died in 1975. In retrospect, it is easy to see internal and external elements conducive to change in democratic direction. Internally, a process of rapid economic growth had strengthened new social groups of workers, members of the middle classes, and students with a quest for political change. It was also becoming clear that membership in the European Community, which Spain badly wanted (as did Greece and Portugal), would require political changes. But in 1975, political democracy was only one of the options open to the main actors, and it took what one observer has called "exceptionally skilled leaders in the regime and the opposition" to negotiate the transition and further consolidate a democratic regime.[24]

In Portugal, dictator Antonio Salazar drained the country of resources by holding onto a Portuguese empire in Africa for much too long. Increasing guerrilla activity in the colonies meant that close to one-half of the national budget went to defense. Middle-ranking officers fed up with the situation staged a coup in 1974, which led to an incredibly intense period of political experimentation and debate by literally hundreds of new political groups that sprang up after the long period of authoritarian rule. The end result of political democracy appeared only in 1976.

In Greece, the transition went faster. The military colonels' junta ordered a general mobilization of troops in response to the Turkish invasion of Cyprus on July 20, 1974, but it quickly became apparent that the junta did not even enjoy the full support of its own ranks. When the Joint Chiefs of Staff decided the next day to seek a political solution to the crisis, the return of civilian rule was made possible.

The second important cluster of transitions toward democracy took place in Latin America during, roughly speaking, the first half of the 1980s. As in southern Europe, the Latin American countries felt some pressure for democracy from various organizations in Western Europe and the United States. But internal dynamics had an even greater influence. One important set of reasons concerns problems brought about by the models of economic development that were pursued under authoritarian rule. In many cases, a ruling elite coalition led by the military had used authoritarian rule to promote a strategy of economic development for the benefit of a strict minority. Production was focused on durable consumer goods for the upper middle classes (cars, consumer electronics, and so forth), and no attention was paid to the basic needs of the poor majority. By the early 1980s, these models ran into serious problems. According to one observer, the Latin American countries were "unified by crisis, foreign debt, economic stagnation . . . inflation, rising unemployment and growing social inequalities."[25] The economic crisis did not have purely domestic roots, however. The second round of sharply increasing oil prices hit most Latin American countries hard. One way to cover the increases in expenditure was to borrow more money abroad. When the real interest rate on such loans increased dramatically, as occurred during the 1980s, the economic crisis was seriously aggravated.

In some countries, with Brazil as the most important example, the authoritarian regimes could draw on records of very high rates of economic growth despite the fact that the distribution of the benefits was extremely uneven. However, when the economic crisis set in, the regimes underwent a process of **delegitimation**—that is, they could no longer point to a basis for their right to govern. In other countries (for example, Argentina and Bolivia), authoritarian rulers could not even point to achievements in terms of economic growth; characterized by corruption and incompetence, their regimes were in even more vulnerable positions.

The problems led to divisions within the authoritarian regimes—that is, the split between hard-liners and soft-liners mentioned earlier. These divisions in turn weakened the authoritarian regimes' grip on society and allowed for a process of liberalization with better possibilities for public debate, oppositional activity, and criticism of the political system. As a result, demands for democracy were reinforced and the legitimacy of authoritarian rule was further decreased. At the same time, the quest for political democracy began to receive a higher priority than ever before in many social groups in Latin America. In the days of harsh authoritarianism, there was a tendency for the polarization of forces as well as of outlooks; fascism and socialism were seen by many as the only feasible alternatives for the region. There was no possibility of a middle path. But with liberalization, the notion of political democracy gained new strength; it is supported by bishops and priests, by journalists and professors, and by labor and other social movements.[26]

In several Latin American countries, the process of democratization proceeded slowly, beginning with the regimes' liberalization. In Argentina, however, economic failures inspired the authoritarian military rulers to embark on the Falkland Islands/Islas Malvinas adventure, and the regime collapsed as a result of defeat in the war. Yet neither Argentina nor the countries that experienced a more gradual transition have moved very far on the road toward political democracy.

If we take one step further ahead in time, we come to the next region in which dramatic changes toward democracy have taken place: Eastern Europe. The early beginnings were in Poland, where Solidarity was founded in 1980 in an attempt by the workers to improve their economic conditions. At first, the demands were for autonomous unions, not political reform. But it quickly became clear that union autonomy could not be achieved without changes in the political system. Yet even though there were splits within the ruling party, it appeared impossible to reach agreement on a model for political reform in Poland. It was not until 1989 that the **totalitarian** regimes (authoritarian regimes in which the state attempts to control every aspect of the citizens' lives) began to fall in Eastern Europe. There had been popular uprisings on several previous occasions—in East Germany in 1952, in Hungary in 1956, and in Czechoslovakia in 1968—but they did not result in political reform. What was different in 1989? One experienced observer pointed to three basic factors, which he labeled "Gorbachev," "Helsinki," and "Tocqueville."[27]

The election of Mikhail Gorbachev signaled new Soviet policies toward Eastern Europe. Before Gorbachev came to power, the Brezhnev doctrine, which supported Soviet intervention in Eastern Europe against "unacceptable" regime changes, was in effect. Under Gorbachev, it was changed to the so-called Sinatra doctrine: "You do it your way." Gorbachev's influence can be seen more directly in the following: It was a telephone call from Gorbachev in August 1989 that urged the Polish

Communists to permit the formation of a government led by a member of Solidarity (Tadeusz Mazowiecki); and when he was a guest of honor in East Germany at the country's fortieth anniversary in October 1989, Gorbachev told Erich Honecker that "the problems of DDR [Deutsche Demokratische Republik] must be solved in Berlin, not in Moscow."[28]

Yet even in the absence of Soviet assistance, the ruling elites of Eastern Europe could have sent their own troops against the popular demonstrations. Why did they hesitate? The Helsinki factor points to the Western attempt to promote respect for human rights in Eastern Europe through the Helsinki accords, which in turn opened for some countries the possibility of Western economic assistance. The Helsinki factor worked together with the Tocqueville factor. The latter points to the old ruling elite's loss of belief in its own right to rule, in its own legitimacy:

> A few kids went into the streets and threw a few words. The police beat them. The kids said: You have no right to beat us! And the rulers, the high and mighty, replied, in effect: Yes, we have no right to beat you. We have no right to preserve our rule by force. The end no longer justifies the means!
>
> In fact, the ruling elites, and their armed servants, distinguished themselves by their comprehensive unreadiness to stand up in any way for the things in which they had so long claimed to believe, and their almost indecent haste to embrace democratic capitalism.[29]

The popular demonstrations themselves still have to be better explained, however. The mounting economic crisis in Eastern Europe meant that the centrally planned economic system was increasingly unable to deliver dynamic performance and satisfy even the most basic needs of the population. It was a similar situation that brought Gorbachev to power in the Soviet Union. The intention on the side of the rulers was to reform and dynamize the system through more intensive cooperation with the West.

But the opening of the system posed a threat to the ruling elite: Without the important condition of isolation, the integrated power structure of the totalitarian system became much more difficult to sustain. In other words, the authoritarian political system and the centrally planned economy based on state ownership are pillars in a mutually supportive system of power, production, and distribution. Tinkering with the system at one point, such as by decentralizing economic control in order to make the enterprises cooperate with foreign firms, creates repercussions in the entire system.[30] The situation puts the ruling elites in a serious dilemma: Their attempts at reforming the system create tensions that threaten their power positions. Yet radical initiatives were necessary to prevent the socioeconomic crisis from running out of control.

The elites proved incapable of devising solutions to this dilemma. Instead, they created a moral dilemma as well. The regimes' propaganda machineries were employed to convince everyone that all was going well and that great progress was being achieved, but the message had to sound increasingly hollow to an educated population well aware of the true state of affairs. Ultimately, the gulf between truth and propaganda, between what people could say and what they thought, became intolerable. The demand for truth became as important as the demand for bread, and writers and intellectuals became the driving force in the struggle against the old regimes. The demand for improved material conditions was critical, but no less critical was the demand for freedom of the mind.[31]

Let us proceed to Africa, where the most recent transitions toward democracy have taken place. When the Berlin Wall fell in 1989, thirty-eight out of forty-five states in Africa south of the Sahara were governed by civilian or military one-party systems in various shades of authoritarianism. No more than eighteen months later, more than half of them had either held competitive multiparty elections or made commitments to do so.[32]

It is clear that the rapid changes in Eastern Europe were an important catalyst in Africa. On the one hand, those changes signaled that the cold war division, which had helped uphold nondemocratic regimes in both the Western and the Eastern camps in Africa, was coming to an end. On the other hand, they provided inspiration for the popular movements that were already mobilizing in Africa.

Thus, developments in Eastern Europe stimulated upheavals that were already under way for internal reasons, including severe economic crises, stagnation and increasing foreign debt, corruption, and economic and political mismanagement. There have also been structural changes that have increased the prospects for democratic demands: A higher degree of urbanization and of education has resulted in a population that is less bound by tradition and long-standing political leaders and that has less patience for authoritarianism.[33]

With these developments, traditional ideas about specific forms of African governance have lost currency. There were two main elements in traditional thinking: decision-making by consensus and the concept of one-party democracy. Decision-making by consensus grew out of the famous notion of the palaver tree, where people met to discuss issues for as long as was necessary, that is, until a consensus was reached. In this way, a majority could not impose its will on a minority because all individuals participated in the process. Ideally, the consensus reached by everyone would ensure that all individual differences were taken into account. The one-party system is the logical organizational framework for this kind of decision-making. In addition, the one-party system should, ideally, help to avoid the wasting of energy on fruitless political competition in an environment in which there are much more urgent tasks of economic and social development. Yet the real functioning of consensus and one-party rule has been far from the ideals. Decision-making by consensus is not applicable to large and complex societies with many different interest groups; and one-party rule has, in many cases, become a thin veil over authoritarian, corrupt rule by dictators who seek to favor themselves and their own tribes or ethnic groups.[34] The African system of personal rule will be further described later in this chapter.

In many cases, such as in Côte d'Ivoire and Gabon, incumbent leaders have seen the writing on the wall and have tried to ride with the waves of democratic change instead of being swept aside by them. They have, for example, given in to opposition demands for free elections (though it is true that they have done so at a time when opposition forces are poorly organized and unready to compete with powerful leaders with economic resources and mass media control).

One additional external factor is important in this regard: the role of the donor countries and agencies that provide the economic aid that is vital for most African states. The pressure from major donors for changes in a democratic direction as a condition for further economic assistance has been increasing in recent years. It is a piece of advice that few African countries can afford to ignore. Of particular importance is the French position, at least for Francophone Africa, which is heavily dependent on aid from France. (The **Francophone countries** are the states in Africa that had been under French colonial rule and retain special ties with France.) In June 1990, the president of France told leaders from Francophone Africa that "the sooner you organize free elections, the better it will be for the youth of your countries who need to express themselves."[35]

Finally, there has been a domino effect in Africa: Once changes begin to occur in some countries, there is an increased likelihood that other countries will move in the same direction. A similar effect can be seen in other regions, for example in Latin America, where first Peru and then Ecuador, Argentina, Bolivia, Uruguay, and Brazil moved toward democracy within a decade. In Eastern Europe, democratization caught on even faster in a whole cluster of countries. At the same time, it is clear that the domino effect is tied to changes in international conditions that affect several countries simultaneously (for example, the change of donors' attitudes toward Africa and the new Soviet policies toward Eastern Europe). It must be borne in mind, however, that these external changes have a maximum effect only when they are combined with an internal setting receptive to democracy.

It is more difficult to summarize events in Asia, where the transitions have not been clustered in a specific period but have been spread over the last two decades. Furthermore, there have also been moves away from democracy in Asia, toward authoritarianism, which makes the picture even more confusing. And countries in Asia have substantially different levels of development and therefore have different economic, social, and political structures. Even so, democracy has moved forward in recent years in the poorest and least developed of countries (Nepal), in the most well-to-do states (South Korea and Taiwan), and in countries in between (Thailand and the Philippines). There is hardly a common denominator. Three rather different cases, namely the Philippines, Nepal, and Taiwan, may demonstrate the scope of the Asian transitions in terms of both socioeconomic background and actual political processes.

The Philippines had some experience with unstable democracy before Ferdinand Marcos introduced martial law in 1972 in a society on the move toward industrialization. Yet his ploy was not totally unpopular. Martial law provided a measure of order and stability; violence by various oppositional groups decreased, agrarian reform measures and a streamlining of the administrative apparatus paved the way for a period of rapid economic growth. By 1980, however, the steam had gone out of the early measures. Rising import prices, not least for oil, a shrinking market for Philippine exports, and increasing foreign debt set the stage for an economic crisis. At the same time, Marcos and his first lady, Imelda, together with a small group of cronies, became the subject of increasing criticism because of their monopolistic control of the most important industries. The IMF was not willing to help mitigate the debt problem as long as Marcos refused to de-monopolize the economy, an act that would mean turning against his own cronies. In the countryside, the activities of Communist guerrillas increased dramatically. Yet Marcos probably could have weathered the storm had it not been for the killing of opposition leader Benigno Aquino by his own security forces. The murder caused opposition forces to rally and produced a movement for reform within the army that was sponsored by Defense Minister Juan Ponce Enrile. The murder also led to strong criticism from the United States. Marcos attempted to fence off critics by offering to compete with an opposition candidate in a free election. Corazon Aquino won the contest, albeit not with a clear mandate. At this point, Marcos tried to invalidate the election but was unable to do so, lacking internal support from the military and external support from the United States.[36]

In Nepal, the basis for democratization was radically different from the situation in the Philippines. Nepal is a small, poor country whose economy is dominated by agriculture and some tourism. It is, economically and otherwise, highly dependent on its giant neighbor, India. In early 1990, the form of regime in Nepal was absolute monarchy, as it had been for more than two hundred years. But in that year the king and his government came under pressure from three sides. First, the country had been involved in a yearlong deadlock on a trade and transit treaty with

India, and the lack of a solution was beginning to create shortages of essential goods in the economy. Second, international aid donors were increasing their pressure for improvements in the human rights situation in the country. Finally, the groups in opposition to the government were inspired by the events in Eastern Europe to increase their drive for political changes, and for the first time opposition forces from the Left and the Right worked together.

The king and the government stood firm at first, instructing the police to clamp down on demonstrators and banning opposition newspapers. But as the confrontation increased, the king started leaning toward a compromise, and he eventually called upon a moderate opposition leader to form a new government. In the subsequent phase, the king and the cabinet struggled for control over the process of drafting a new constitution, which was intended to lead to a constitutional monarchy. Eventually, the king assured for himself the role of political arbiter and was empowered, for example, to declare an emergency without cabinet approval.[37]

In Taiwan, democratization has been influenced by economic success rather than failure. For many years, the state has pushed and guided economic development. Contrary to the Philippine case, politics in Taiwan has been relatively untouched by corruption and malpractice. Having lost badly to the Communists in the civil war on the mainland, Nationalist leaders were determined to clean up their act and promote rapid economic development on the island. Fifty years of Japanese colonial rule over Taiwan had left a strong infrastructure, a productive agriculture, and a population with a comparatively high level of education. Furthermore, the United States was very willing to assist Taiwan economically and otherwise as a consequence of the cold war confrontation with communism. The authoritarian regime produced a startling success in terms of economic development. But politically, it was being undermined by the very same process: Rapid economic development produces stronger social forces outside the state apparatus, including private business, the industrial labor force, and the middle classes. These developments tend to put new demands on the state. One of the important demands in recent years has been for a more democratic society. Yet the first general election, in late 1990, appears to have rewarded the government's achievements—the Nationalist party won a comfortable victory at the polls.

The cases described here underline the fact that there is nothing automatic about transitions away from authoritarianism. Such transitions involve a long sequence of events in which different types of actors stand in the center of the political stage, and the final outcome is not decided before hand. When transitions are looked at in retrospect, as we have done here, explanations for why changes occurred tend to revolve around a search for the obvious: Knowing that an authoritarian regime fell, we can try to stack all the odds that seemed to work against it and in favor of democracy. It is sobering to recall that not many years ago scholars were busily occupied with similar sequences of events going in the exact opposite direction—from more or less genuine democracies toward authoritarian rule. The exercise then was similar to the present one: Knowing that democracy broke down, one could try to stack all the odds that seemed to work against it and in favor of authoritarianism.

One way to avoid this fatalistic overtone is to demonstrate the fragility of many of the democratic openings that have taken place and to stress how they might just as easily fall back toward authoritarianism as continue toward more authentic democracy. The early transitions in southern Europe appear to be the most consolidated, whereas the recent democratic openings in Africa are the most fragile, having moved only a short distance away from authoritarianism. The mere passage of time, however, is no guarantee for a continued process of democratization. Several problems facing the current democratic openings are discussed in a subsequent section of this chapter. But first it will be helpful to introduce a model that contains a precise picture of the different phases involved in the transition from authoritarian to democratic rule.

PROCESSES OF TRANSITION
AND CONSOLIDATION

The transition from nondemocracy to democratic rule is a complex process involving several phases. In the typical contemporary case, the beginning of the process is marked by crisis within and the eventual breakdown of the nondemocratic regime. If the transition to democracy begins with the realization of the authoritarian rulers that they must leave office, then this phase ends with the installation, based on free elections, of a new government.

But the process does not end there. The new regime will often be a restricted democracy, more democratic than the previous one but not yet fully democratic. Several phases of "democratic deepening" may be necessary before this latter stage is reached. And then the regime still has to be consolidated, which is said to occur when democracy is seen by all major political actors as "the only game in town." There is often considerable overlap between these phases.

It is important to realize that the phases outlined here are not necessarily negotiated in a smooth, linear manner. There may be crises and setbacks. And the result of regime change need not necessarily be democracy. The typical pattern for many developing countries has indeed been one of seesawing between authoritarianism and frail democracy.

Moreover, the full process toward consolidated democracy may take a long time, often several decades. In the case of Great Britain, the full process took more than two hundred years.

A more concrete impression of the phases and problems involved in the transition toward democracy can be attained with the use of a simple model that describes some of the main elements in the transition process (see Fig. 2.1). It is a slightly modified version of a model created by Dankwart Rustow.[38]

The model has one background condition, national unity, which must be in place before it is possible to conceive of a transition toward democracy. According to Rustow, national unity simply indicates that "the vast majority of citizens in a democracy-to-be . . . have no doubt or mental reservations as to which political community they belong to."[39] There may well be ethnic or other cleavages between groups in the population; it is only when such divisions lead to basic questioning of national unity that the problem must be resolved before a transition to democracy becomes feasible. National unity was an issue in India and Pakistan and is an issue today in Yugoslavia and in the former Soviet Union. Democratization demands a settling of the national question: Who are the nations that are going to democratize?

The issue will emerge elsewhere, as well. For example, in China any process of democratization will have to settle the issue of Tibet's claim for autonomy. Empires held together by force must confront the national unity question as a precondition for a process of democratization; rulers and policies cannot change in a democratic manner if the boundaries do not endure. As one observer stated, "The people cannot decide until somebody decides who are the people."[40]

The principle also seems to apply to situations in which established democracies have to confront crises concerning national unity: If these matters are not resolved in a democratic manner (for example, through minority guarantees or local autonomy for the group in question), the result will be the breakdown of democracy combined with repression of the minority group or civil war, as in the case of Sri Lanka. Again, a return to democracy presupposes that the question of national unity is resolved.

With national unity as the single background condition, the first phase in the transition toward democracy is the *preparatory phase*. It contains first and foremost what Rustow called a prolonged and inconclusive political struggle. Some individuals, groups, and classes challenge the nondemocratic rulers. Democracy may not be their main aim; it can be a means to another end or a byproduct of a struggle for other ends, such as a more equal society, a better distribution of wealth, the extension of rights and freedoms, and so forth. The composition of the groups behind the challenge to the rulers varies from country to country and also over time

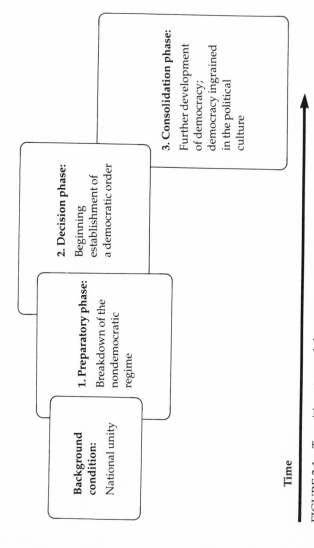

Background condition: National unity

1. Preparatory phase: Breakdown of the nondemocratic regime

2. Decision phase: Beginning establishment of a democratic order

3. Consolidation phase: Further development of democracy; democracy ingrained in the political culture

Time

FIGURE 2.1   Transitions toward democracy: A model

Source: Based on Dankwart Rustow, "Transitions to Democracy," *Comparative Politics* 2, no. 3 (1970).

periods. As Rustow stated, "No two existing democracies have gone through a struggle between the very same forces over the same issues and with the same institutional outcome."[41]

The phases often overlap. In India, for example, the preparatory phase of the struggle for democracy began long before national unity and independence had been achieved. The same coalition of forces in the National Congress movement that struggled for national independence struggled for a democratic political system.

Other scholars have analyzed the preparatory phase. Alfred Stepan outlined ten different paths from nondemocratic toward democratic rule.[42] They are differentiated according to the nature of the previous authoritarian regime, the constellation of political and social forces in the various societies, and the different international contexts in which the transitions take place. The contemporary transitions toward democracy include cases of democratization initiated from within the authoritarian regimes (for example, in Latin America) as well as cases mainly triggered by external forces (for example, in Eastern Europe).

In Chapter 1, two basic dimensions of the process of democratization were identified, namely liberalization (or competition) and inclusiveness (or participation). According to the comparative study of transitions in Latin America and southern Europe by O'Donnell and Schmitter, the typical beginning of the transition to democracy is a period of liberalization. In this period, the incumbent authoritarian rulers extend a measure of civil and political rights to individuals and groups. Space for oppositional political activity (for public competition) is thereby created, albeit within a framework still controlled by the authoritarian regime. This phase began in Brazil, for example, with the suspension of press censorship in 1974. It was overlapped by a later phase of increased participation, which culminated in the election of a civilian president in 1985.[43]

A similar phase of liberalization occurred in several of the East European countries. It began with single-party pluralism, where the population was allowed to choose among different candidates of the same (Communist) party. But this development was not enough to convey legitimacy on the old rulers. In a following phase, increased opposition led to the introduction of different versions of multiparty systems in Poland, Hungary, and the Soviet Union by the late 1980s.[44]

Now let us return to our description of Rustow's model. The second phase is the *decision phase*, in which there is "a deliberate decision on the part of political leaders to . . . institutionalize some crucial aspect of democratic procedure."[45] Again, it is clear that there can be overlap with the previous (preparatory) phase. The decision may be split into several subphases. England provides a prime example of this type of incremental democratization: The compromise of 1688 started the process, and it was completed only in 1928 when suffrage was extended to women. Even when the time period is much shorter, as in Brazil, the decision phase may involve several steps. Indeed, I shall argue in a moment that many countries presently in transition toward democracy are stuck in the early phase of the decision step, having made some moves toward democracy but having far from completed the transition.

If the time period is very short, opposition forces have few opportunities to organize themselves into proper actors on the political arena. In Romania, for example, where there was no preceding process of liberalization and where a quick outburst of popular uprising toppled the old regime, a provisional government was formed "whose plans are uncertain and might not lead to a democracy."[46]

Thus, the pace of transition influences the outcome. So does the institutional legacy of authoritarian rule. To what extent is it possible to build on political parties, interest associations, local governments, and social movements from the period of authoritarian rule? In some cases, such as Portugal and Chile, such institutions were destroyed to the extent that the government following the democratic transition had to start almost from scratch in building new institutions. In other cases, such as Brazil and Peru, structures from previous phases of democratic rule have survived and can be put to use in the transition.[47] In Eastern Europe the new regimes have hardly anything to build on, with the exception of the organizations created in some countries during the liberalization phase. Africa's problems in this regard stem from the fact that in nearly all countries experiences with democracy have been sporadic, and democratic organizations have not been effectively institutionalized.

Probably the most important factor influencing the outcome of the decision phase is the makeup of the leading coalition behind the transition. The crucial distinction is between transitions dominated by the elites who were also behind the old, authoritarian regimes, and transitions in which mass actors have gained the upper hand. The former can be called "transitions from above." As Terry Lynn Karl stated, "Here traditional rulers remain in control, even if pressured from below, and successfully use strategies of either compromise or force—or some mix of the two—to retain at least part of their power."[48] Karl stressed in her analysis of Latin American cases that transitions from above are the most frequently encountered type of transition. Insofar as there have been transitions from below, they have been unable to lead to stable democracy:

> To date, however, *no* stable political democracy has resulted from regime transitions in which mass actors have gained control, even momentarily, over traditional ruling classes. Efforts at reform from below . . . have met

with subversive opposition from unsuppressed traditional elites, as the cases of Argentina (1946–51), Guatemala (1946–54) and Chile (1970–73) demonstrate.[49]

Of the recent transitions in Latin America, Karl classified those in Uruguay, Brazil, Chile, and Ecuador as transitions from above. Borderline cases are Peru and Argentina. Three further cases were also transitions from above (Mexico, Guatemala, and El Salvador), but they are in an earlier phase of moving from nondemocratic rule. In Latin America, there have been no examples of transitions from below in the last two decades that have resulted in democracy.

In a recent contribution, Karl and Schmitter argued that several of the transitions in southern and Eastern Europe can also be seen as transitions from above, although they stressed that classification is often difficult because of the complex historical patterns in single cases.[50] Examples of transitions from above in Europe include Spain, Turkey, Hungary, Bulgaria, and the Soviet Union. In the latter case, the classification is due to the controlled process of perestroika led by Mikhail Gorbachev; after the unsuccessful August 1991 coup by the old Communist elites, their influence on the transition was substantially reduced.

A transition from above may lead to a restricted democracy that is less capable than a nonrestricted democracy of making reform policies that go against vested elite interests. I shall return to this issue in a moment. The final phase of the transition to democracy must be briefly introduced first. It is the *consolidation phase*. What is consolidation? There is no agreement about the proper definition. The most demanding version states that consolidation is not reached until all the democratic institutions have been formed and the new democracy has proved itself capable of transferring power to an opposition party; it has, so to speak, proved capable of confronting the most difficult challenges. But this kind of understanding may lead to the assertion that almost no democratic regime can ever be seen as fully consolidated. Therefore, I follow the more modest definition suggested by Juan Linz, who states that a **consolidated democracy**

> is one in which none of the major political actors, parties, or organized interests, forces, or institutions consider that there is any alternative to democratic processes to gain power, and that no political institution or group has a claim to veto the action of democratically elected decision makers. This does not mean that there are no minorities ready to challenge and question the legitimacy of the democratic process by nondemocratic means. It means, however, that the major actors do not turn to them and they remain politically isolated. To put it simply, democracy must be seen as the "only game in town."[51]

Seen as a process, consolidation clearly overlaps with the decision phase. The gradual progression of decisions leading from more restricted democracy toward more real democracy can be seen as elements leading toward increased consolidation. The democratic deepening process in the decision phase is an early phase of consolidation. As long as there are major powerful groups and institutions, such as the armed forces in Latin America or the old elites (the **nomenklatura**) in Eastern Europe, that may try to circumvent or veto democratically made decisions, democracy is not fully consolidated.[52]

It can be argued that consolidation is not a purely political process but is one that also demands social and economic change. Without changes made to correct the vast inequalities in many societies, there may be decreased political support for democratically elected leaders and a "spiral of delegitimation" of the democratic regime.[53]

The final phase of consolidation is the process whereby democratic institutions and practices become ingrained in the political culture. Not only political leaders but the vast majority of political actors and of the population come to see democratic practices as part of the right and natural order of things.[54] With a few possible exceptions, this stage has not been reached in any of the transitions that have taken place in the last two decades.

*　　*　　*

From the background condition of national unity, the process of transition from nondemocratic rule to democracy has been described as occurring in three phases, which will most often overlap in the real world. They are the preparatory phase, characterized by a political struggle leading to the breakdown of the nondemocratic regime; the decision phase, where clear-cut elements of a democratic order are established; and the consolidation phase, where the new democracy is further developed and, eventually, democratic practices become an established part of the political culture.

It is important to stress once again that there is nothing inevitable about these phases. There is no historical law that defines this transition process as the natural order of things. As already mentioned, the natural order in many developing countries seems to be an uneasy seesaw between authoritarianism and frail democracy. Consequently, it cannot be expected that all the countries of the world will sooner or later pass through all of these stages and end up as consolidated democracies. After all, only a minority of the countries in the world can be considered democratic today. Moreover, I shall argue later that most of the newcomers in this fortunate category are plagued by serious problems.

FOUR PROPOSITIONS
ABOUT THE CURRENT TRANSITIONS
TOWARD DEMOCRACY

Each transition toward democracy has its own unique characteristics. In order to know the specific conditions of each case (its distinctive constellation of forces and institutional setup) and in order to determine in what way and how far the transition toward democracy has advanced, analyses of individual countries are necessary. But a large number of case studies cannot be undertaken here. Instead, I have chosen to advance four propositions about characteristic features of the transitions in the recent surge toward democracy. Each proposition contains what I believe is an important characteristic of the large majority of these transitions. Within the context of each proposition, I will refer to concrete examples; but it is important to stress that the features described are relevant for most of the transitions currently taking place. There are only a few exceptions, which will be pointed out in due course.

My suggestion is that the large majority of the current transitions can be described as being restricted, frail and unconsolidated, and plagued by acute social and economic problems. In terms of the model outlined earlier in this chapter, these transitions are thus still in the early phases of change; the countries are seeing the breakdown of their nondemocratic regimes and the early establishment of a democratic order. In some cases (for example, Yugoslavia and the former Soviet Union) the question of national unity is not even finally decided.

Against this rather pessimistic analysis only one encouraging element is put forward, namely that the process of popular mobilization and organization in the struggle for democracy has reached levels not seen before. This high level of mobilization and organization will make it more difficult for the new regimes to revert to more authoritarian forms of rule.

Restricted Democracies

Restricted democracies are political systems with some democratic elements but also with limits on competition, participation, and liberties. Frequently, they are characterized by the presence of elite groups whose members reserve the right to interfere in the democratic process in order to protect their interests. In the case of democratic transitions from above, such interference can be part of the actual basis of the whole movement toward democracy. In others words, the elite groups (the military, traditional economic elites, and leading politicians) may make the transition toward democracy dependent on the acceptance of a set of agreements, or **political pacts,** that define vital areas of interest for the elites. An example from Brazil may illustrate this point.[55]

An authoritarian regime led by the military came to power in Brazil in 1964. Some ten years later, a process of liberalization began, and it culminated in the formation of the New Republic with the election of a civilian president in 1985. The return of the civilian regime was orchestrated by the military in alliance with other elite groups. A series of political pacts engineered the return to civilian rule. In several important respects, these pacts serve to restrict democracy. First, the military had retained its influence in the New Republic, not only over its own affairs but also over domestic affairs. The constitutional clauses that have served as the basis for military intervention in domestic affairs remain in place. Even more important, six out of twenty-two cabinet members are uniformed officers.[56]

In addition, the New Republic has reinforced the Brazilian tradition of clientelism. Frances Hagopian stated that "guaranteed access to state resources was the price traditional elites extracted for supporting democratization."[57] The democratic opposition to authoritarian rule led by Tancredo Neves secured access to power only by promising state spoils to the traditional elites who had supported authoritarian rule. The elites were given political posts, the right to appoint federal and local state jobs, money for specific projects, and so forth. According to Hagopian, federal and state cabinets are directly based on clientelism. Therefore, these organs do not have the implementation of conceived policies as their main aim. They are geared more toward "diverting their resources to the areas of greatest political return for the ministers and secretaries that head them."[58] Political parties are also affected. They orient their activities toward this system of sharing the spoils and thereby distort the nature of political representation.

In the Brazilian case, the military is the leading force in the pact-making process. But the military is not always the dominant elite force. The negotiations between elite factions that paved the way for democracy in Uruguay in 1984 illustrate more of a compromise between dominant groups. With less influence of the military, the new democracy may have more room to maneuver; the military is less able to fully preserve its privileges and to prevent civilian control.[59]

A case that falls somewhere between Brazil and Uruguay with regard to the influence of elites on the political system is the recent transition toward democracy in Chile. The early process of liberalization was firmly controlled by the authoritarian regime under Pinochet. But the dictator lost the important plebiscite in 1988, which was supposed to secure him a new term in office. His loss paved the way for increased influence of the opposition on the transition. However, Pinochet has been able to restrict the new democracy in vital areas and preserve a high degree of influence for nondemocratic organs, among them the National Security Council and the armed forces.[60]

Overall, these variations in the influence of elite factions are a matter of degree. In all of the cases the new democracy is restricted by elite agreements about basic rules of the game. If this situation has a positive side, seen from a democratic viewpoint, it is that such agreements may be conducive to an orderly and continuous transition toward democracy.[61] The negative side, of course, is that the pacts severely restrict the democracy that comes out of the transition process. Moreover, they create a framework in which political actors may be unable to push socioeconomic reforms that would benefit the poor. This point is stressed in Terry Lynn Karl's analysis of Latin America:

> Even as these democracies guarantee a greater respect for law and human dignity when compared to their authoritarian predecessors, they may be unable to carry out substantive reforms that address the lot of their poorest citizens. If this scenario should occur . . . the democratic transitions of the 1980s that survive could prove to be the "frozen" democracies of the 1990s.[62]

Karl's remarks are less concerned with restrictions on the political system that come out of pact-making processes than with the dangers of the lack of economic change that may result from the restricted democracies. I shall return to the issue of economic consequences of democracy in the next chapter. Here it is important to stress that the lack of economic change may have serious political repercussions; namely, it may be the catalyst for a spiral of delegitimation. Ironically, then, the pact-making between elites that makes the orderly and continuous transition possible also sets the stage for a later phase of potential instability and deadlock.

Even in the absence of explicit agreements between elite factions, there can be strong forces affecting the progress of the new democratic institutions. Such forces can restrict democracy through direct intervention in the democratic process, which, clearly, can create a highly unstable political climate. The most important example of such forces in the Latin American context is of course the military, but there is frequently an interplay with civilian groups appealing to the military for intervention.

The most pressing matter affecting the military in the transition from authoritarian rule is often the issue of settling responsibility for the past. Bringing military officers to justice would seem to be a crucial task for new democratic rulers. But the military in Latin America is strong enough to avoid such moves, even in the absence of pact agreements. The situation in Argentina provides an instructive example. The military suffered a dramatic loss of legitimacy and prestige after Argentina's defeat in the war with England in 1982. The new democratic government under Raúl Alfonsin moved swiftly to penalize the armed forces and purge them of undesirable elements. For the first time in Argentina since 1930, authoritarian military rulers had to answer for their actions before a court of law. However, the summoning of active officers by the courts was more than the military could accept, and rebellions broke out in 1987. Alfonsin had to retreat from all decisions regarding punishment of the military; the only officers imprisoned were those who were behind the first juntas.[63]

Argentina is not the most extreme example. In Central American countries the military has ruled out any discussion concerning accountability for the past. In these countries, and also in Peru and Colombia where domestic violence abounds, the military is the only nationwide state authority.[64] Elected civilian governments face the imminent danger of military coups, which may be provoked for a variety of reasons, including severe economic crisis, mass movements of urban and rural poor that elude control by traditional elites, disagreement among political factions, and perceived threats to the interests of the military itself.[65]

Robert Dahl noted in his 1971 study that democracy (polyarchy) is "of course impossible unless the military is sufficiently depoliticized to permit civilian rule."[66] It is clear that this condition is far from being met in most Latin American countries today. The militaries have entered pact agreements that restrict democracy or directly intervene in the democratic process in order to safeguard what they see as vital interests, not least the preservation of their own autonomy and power.

This description of restricted democracies has focused on the transitions in Latin America. The situation with regard to new democracies in others parts·of the world is not identical. But in all restricted democracies, as in the Latin American cases, there are strong forces outside the full control of the new democratic institutions, forces that in various ways restrict democratic rule.

Frail, Unconsolidated Democracies

Restricted democracies are also unconsolidated democracies, according to the definition of the elements of democracy set forth in Chapter 1. Therefore, the Latin American transitions are also examples of frail and unconsolidated democracies. This section focuses on the aspect of consolidation whereby democratic institutions and practices become ingrained in the political culture. The discussion is centered around the African transitions.

Nowhere does the consolidation of democracy face larger obstacles than in sub-Saharan Africa, where the foundation on which democracy must be built, in terms of the existing institutions of state and their positions in society, is very weak. The African state has failed both economically and politically: In general, Africans are as poor today as they were thirty years ago.[67] At the same time, the large majority of African states have so far failed to institutionalize any form of effective rule, be it authoritarianism or democracy. What is the problem?[68]

One plausible answer to this question, provided by Richard Sandbrook and also by other scholars, points to the lack of legitimacy that characterized postcolonial African states.[69] At independence, there were no strong social forces in society that were capable of disciplining political leaders. And the latter had no moral basis or legitimizing ideology from which they could demand compliance of citizens and bureaucrats. Precolonial, traditional legitimacy was no longer a relevant foundation. The type of government that filled this vacuum was a form of **neo-patrimonialism.** (Neo-patrimonialism must be understood against the background of patrimonialism, which is the name used by Max Weber to describe any type of government that originated from a royal household and that has a ruler who treats matters of state as his or her personal affair. Present-day systems of this type, such as the system of personal rule in Africa, are examples of neo-patrimonialism.)

Personal rule is based on personal loyalty, especially toward the leading figure of the regime, the strongman. All the important positions in the state, whether bureaucratic, political, military, or police, are filled with the loyal followers of the strongman, his relatives, friends, kinsmen, and tribesmen. Their loyalty to the strongman is reinforced by their sharing of the spoils of office.[70]

The strongman commands a web of informal networks, or **patron-client relationships,** within which two main forms of spoils are distributed. Both emanate from the strongman and his followers' control of the state. They are access to the state's resources in the form of jobs, contracts, favorable loans, opportunities for illegal gain, and so forth, and access to resources not directly controlled by the state but subject to state regulation, such as import permits and business licenses.

The final element in personal rule, in addition to the strongman and clientelism, is an armed force personally loyal to the regime. Because of the state's lack of legitimacy and the fact that many people are excluded from the rewards resulting from clientelism, rulers must resort to coercion or the threat of it for survival. Thus, in determining the degree of democracy in African states, one should focus less on the differences between civilian and military regimes and more on the direct and indirect political influence of the armed forces.[71]

It is against this background that different varieties of frail democracy and authoritarianism have developed in most African states. The study of regime change in Africa has aptly been characterized as "the study of the collapse of the 'tutelary' democratic regimes introduced during decolonization and the emergence of various types of authoritarian regimes."[72] The grafting of more democratic procedures, such as multiparty systems and open presidential elections, is now in the cards or has already been effectuated in many African states. But it is clear that the consolidation of democracy will be possible only if more profound changes in the structure of personal rule take place.

For this reason several scholars have stressed the need for the establishment of order, stability, and civility in the African political systems.[73] Otherwise, democracy runs the risk of deteriorating to a caricature, the direct opposite of what it claims to be in theory. According to one analysis, democracy has deteriorated in this way in Ghana and Nigeria. In the latter case, corruption among politicians has swelled due to the country's income from the export of oil. "In a political climate in which the democratic control of government was regarded by politicians of all parties as a license to plunder the state, the 1983 elections deteriorated into an extended round of electoral fraud and violence. . . . Instead of controlling the government, democracy has been a method of stealing from the people."[74]

It remains a question whether the democratic openings that are sweeping across Africa can activate the profound changes that are needed in order to consolidate democracy. What must be stressed here is the frail, unconsolidated nature of the African democratic openings. It is clear that the system of personal rule presents a very difficult background for the consolidation of democracy. One scholar, who used the term *sultanistic regimes* for these systems, stressed that the downfall or weakening of the leading strongman leaves "a vacuum in society that makes the establishment and consolidation of democratic politics extremely difficult."[75]

It is not hard to find evidence in support of this view from the current African scene. With the introduction of multiparty systems, swarms of political parties have been formed. They are most often separated along ethnic lines and led by individuals with no clear ideological visions but with ambitions of becoming strongmen in their own right, controlling their own political networks. Thus, 1,800 candidates of twenty-six political parties ran for election in Benin, a country of four million inhabitants. Fourteen candidates were on the ballot for the presidential election. Ninety-six parties have requested registration in Zaire. There is a real danger, then, that the democratic openings will result primarily in tugs-of-war along ethnic lines in the competition for the vacant seats of the strongmen.

That possibility holds, of course, only if the strongmen's seats are really vacant. In several cases, incumbent leaders have preempted the new winds of democracy and have succeeded in staying in power by engineering transitions from above. A recent situation in Côte d'Ivoire provides an example. Felix Houphouet-Boigny, who has been president for several decades, took the opposition by surprise in 1990 by quickly giving in to its demands for open presidential and legislative elections. In a country in which there had not been opposition activity for thirty years, twenty-six political groups were summoned by the president and told about the forthcoming elections. Opposition requests for a delay in order to gain time for getting organized were rejected—the argument was that the demand for instant elections came from the opposition itself. As a result, the election could be controlled by the president's own party, which also has a large measure of control over the media. Both the president and his party scored comfortable victories at the elections. Against this background, one may speculate whether the current pressure from Western donors for multiparty systems and political democracy in Africa can have counterproductive effects. The Western countries themselves are examples of the fact that democracy cannot be installed overnight; it is a long-term process of gradual change. When quick fixes of imposing multiparty systems, for example, are substituted for the long haul of patiently paving the way for a democratic polity, the result may be that a thin layer of democratic coating is superimposed upon a system of personal rule without changes in the basic features of the old structure.[76]

Robert A. Dahl listed five conditions that he feels are most favorable for the development of stable polyarchy—that is, stable democratic rule. They are

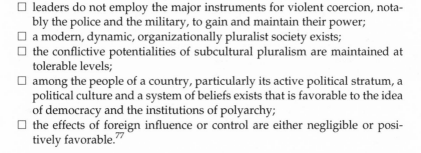

- □ leaders do not employ the major instruments for violent coercion, notably the police and the military, to gain and maintain their power;
- □ a modern, dynamic, organizationally pluralist society exists;
- □ the conflictive potentialities of subcultural pluralism are maintained at tolerable levels;
- □ among the people of a country, particularly its active political stratum, a political culture and a system of beliefs exists that is favorable to the idea of democracy and the institutions of polyarchy;
- □ the effects of foreign influence or control are either negligible or positively favorable.[77]

With the last point being a possible exception, none of these conditions are met in the African countries today. Neither are they altogether present in the large majority of countries in Asia and Latin America or even in Eastern Europe. Against this background, there is not much hope that the recent democratic openings will progress into consolidated democracies. But it is important to note that these conditions, although the most favorable ones for the development of a consolidated democracy, are not prerequisites for its development. A relatively stable democracy is not impossible in the absence of some, or even most, of these conditions; in Africa this fact is demonstrated by the case of Botswana, which has had a democratic political system for more than two decades.[78] At the same time, the popular mobilization and organization that can be seen in the current democratic openings present some hope for the future. I shall return to this idea in a moment. One final problematic characteristic of the new democracies must be introduced first.

Democracies Plagued by Acute Social and Economic Problems

The vast majority of the current transitions toward democracy face severe economic and social problems. These problems must be expected, considering the fact that economic crisis is most often an important factor behind the ousting of the earlier, authoritarian rulers. The authoritarian governments leave office, but they also leave an inheritance of acute economic problems for the new democratic administrations to tackle.

The 1980s has been called the lost decade in Latin America because in many countries the average real income per capita returned to the level of the late 1970s. The decisive factor in the Latin American crisis is the spiraling foreign debt. By 1987, the debt burden had reached 46 percent of the region's gross national product (GNP) and more than four times the value of its exports. In addition to the debt, the countries have been faced with the problems of trying to curb inflation while trying to avoid stagnation and rising unemployment.

The economic and social crisis is even more severe in Africa. In many countries the problem is one of mere survival in the face of famine and drought. They have increasingly relied on aid from donors, both international organizations and single countries in the North. In this context it is important to note that no additional aid seems to be forthcoming as a result of the democratic openings. Current public opinion in the North seems to be that starvation and death are more acceptable in Africa than elsewhere or are unavoidable there. In other words, the conditions that are being imposed concerning democratization do not promise more aid if they are met; they promise less aid if they are not met.

Although social and economic crisis is a factor in most of the current transitions toward democracy, the focus in this section is on Eastern Europe. The political transitions there take on a special significance because they must transpire in the context of a profound change in the economic structure. This change, in turn, will deeply affect the entire social profile of society and thus the whole basis for democratic regimes. Moreover, there is no available blueprint or model for the economic transition from a centrally planned economy to some form of capitalism.

The planned economies have been locked in an evil circle of stagnation, lack of innovation, and low productivity. The days are long gone when people believed in the official *Polish Encyclopedia* definition of economic crisis, according to which "crisis is a phenomenon solely connected with the capitalist economies and does not occur in other socioeconomic systems."[79] Earlier attempts at injecting change into the planned economies left the groundwork of the system basically unchanged. The current metamorphosis, in contrast, aims at transforming the basic pillars of the system. Three fundamental economic changes must take place so that the economies are transformed (1) from being closed to being integrated in the world market; (2) from being centrally planned to being market guided; and (3) from being collectively and state owned to being based on private ownership.

With regard to the first necessary transformation, gradual openings toward the world market began in some countries, such as Hungary, long before the political events of 1989. What is in the cards now is a much faster and more comprehensive process of world market integration than seen earlier. Judged on the basis of previous experiences, the transition is going to be difficult. Demand for all kinds of imports in Eastern Europe far exceeds the countries' capacity for exporting. Several export articles, moreover, such as textiles and foodstuffs, must compete with traditional industries of southern European members of the European Community, which makes market access difficult. The result of high import needs combined with low export capacity is rapidly increasing foreign debt, as has already been demonstrated in Poland and Hungary. In those countries, debt amounts in relation to exports had already reached Latin American levels by the mid-1980s. Thus, even though this period is one of rapidly rising expectations in the Eastern European populations, those countries must curb imports because they are unable to pay for them. In this context, one of the serious criticisms against the IMF stabilization programs (for example, in Poland) is that they are more directed toward maintaining a country's external economic balance than toward securing a smooth overall transformation of the economy.

The second basic transformation is from centrally planned control to economies based on the market forces. The problem here is that the mere retreat of central planning does not in itself leave the economy with a smoothly functioning free market. A market economy functions only if it is backed by the necessary institutional and legal frameworks. Needed, for example, are an independent banking system that can provide credit for enterprises at levels determined strictly by commercial criteria; an unemployment support system, without which the dismissal of workers and the shutdown of unproductive enterprises on a large scale is unfeasible; and a legal back-up system that can lay the ground rules for free competition among firms. These systems cannot be created overnight; and in the transition period between one system and the other, which may take several years or even more than a decade, there is ample room for profiteering, speculation, and black market activity.

Another aspect of the transition toward a market-based economy has to do with the attitudes of the population. The introduction of the market system will be accompanied by rapidly increasing inequalities, widespread unemployment, and sharply rising prices; yet the wages of many employees will remain relatively fixed. As one scholar has put it, it is simply not possible to meet the economic challenges and simultaneously "provide the population with administrative guarantees of a life without losses and conflicts."[80] All of this goes squarely against the deeply ingrained egalitarian social values held by substantial parts of the populations.[81] Consequently, the issue arises about the extent to which the populations are ready to support such changes. In the long run, when the benefits of change will be more readily apparent, there may be no problem. But in the short and medium run, the economic changes constitute a "valley of tears" for which enthusiastic support by the large, negatively affected groups, may not be forthcoming.[82] Therefore, one cannot assume that there will be a straightforward, mutually reinforcing relationship between democratization in the political sphere and changes toward a market economy in the economic sphere in Eastern Europe; it is quite possible that large groups may use their newly gained political influence to resist rapid economic change.[83] Such resistance may in turn undermine the socioeconomic basis for a consolidated democratic order because such an order cannot be built without profound economic changes.

The final element in the economic transformation of Eastern Europe, the move from collective, state-owned enterprise to a system based on private ownership, is plagued by major practical difficulties because few, if any, private citizens are capable of or interested in buying the large industrial enterprises. Thus, there has been discussion in several countries about issuing peoples' shares or giving away the enterprises to the employees. But there is another, more precarious aspect of this transformation. When privatization of state enterprises is combined with the elimination of the central planning machinery, the very power basis of the old elite is undermined. To what extent will the old party-state apparatus resist such changes by sabotaging reform programs, and what will the consequences be for the fledgling democracies?

There are no straightforward answers. The power of the old elites in Eastern Europe, the *nomenklatura,* has been compared to the power of the military in Latin America. In these terms, the Latin American democracies worry about "the *Gorrilla* question," and the new democracies in Eastern Europe worry about "the *nomenklatura* question."[84] The countries find themselves in a precarious balance: When the old elites retain a high degree of influence on the transition process, the result is the restricted democracies identified in the Latin American context. If they are cut off from influence, they may utilize whatever remains of their power positions to destabilize the new, fragile democracies.

In this sense, the current situation in Eastern Europe is at an impasse: A potential, virtuous circle in which economic reform is reinforced by a process of democratic consolidation stands against a potential, vicious circle of democratic decay reinforced by economic crisis. The outcome is far from certain; most probably it will vary across countries. It is clear, however, that a smooth passage for the Eastern European countries toward consolidated democracies and sound economies capable of meeting the demands for higher standards of living cannot be taken for granted. For some countries in Eastern Europe, the future may just as easily be a Latin American version of reality. One scholar has succinctly outlined this perspective:

> Forget for a moment the geographical location and put Poland in the place of Argentina, Hungary in the place of Uruguay. You will see states weak as organizations, political parties and other associations that are ineffectual in representing and mobilizing, economies that are monopolistic, over-protected and over-regulated, agricultures that cannot feed their own people, public bureaucracies that are overgrown, welfare services that are fragmentary and rudimentary. And would you not conclude that such conditions breed governments vulnerable to pressure from large firms, populist movements of doubtful commitment to democratic institutions, armed forces that sit menacingly at the sidelines, church hierarchies torn between authoritarianism and social justice, nationalist sentiments vulnerable to xenophobia?[85]

But the countries of Eastern Europe are not doomed to failure; neither are those of Latin America, Africa, or Asia. One of the most encouraging elements in the recent democratic openings is the process of popular mobilization and organization that has taken place in the context of the fight for democracy. This theme is explored in the following section.

Popular Mobilization and Organization in the Struggle for Democracy

The three propositions presented so far paint a rather gloomy picture of the current processes of transition toward democracy. But there is also a more promising aspect, which is the focus here. It concerns popular mobilization and organization. The discussion earlier in this chapter of transitions from above may have conveyed the impression that regime change is often imposed by competing elites on a docile population that is inarticulate in political matters. Such a picture is false. Even in the cases where elites dominate the process of transition, there is a large measure of popular activity. So-called ordinary men and women, workers, students, peasants, and office clerks are taking risks in distributing propaganda against authoritarian regimes, are organizing illegal groups, and in some cases are even directly assaulting the seats of power.[86]

In some cases the different movements come together in a popular upsurge, where diverse groups from all corners of society join together to form a greater whole, identifying itself as "the people" and demanding democracy and the removal of the old rulers.[87] But the point to be stressed here is that the process of popular mobilization and organization is more than this brief, intense outburst that dies away quickly. It begins during authoritarian rule and continues in a new setting after the first elections have taken place. In that sense, the popular mobilization behind a transition toward democracy includes two different elements: the new social movements that emerged as various types of self-help organizations during authoritarian rule and the overall resurrection of civil society that takes place during the transition itself.

The term "new social movements" encompasses a wide range of rural and urban associations. In the Latin American context, self-help projects concerning housing, community health care, popular education, consumer and producer cooperatives, and the defense of rural land rights have emerged, as have activities of "protest and conflict, lobbying and pressuring government agencies and politicians."[88] In Africa, a similar array of groups, together with ethnic and kinship associations and regional or home-town groupings, has emerged.[89] The new social movements have often appeared because of the difficulties created by authoritarian rule; the self-help organizations are a strategy of survival. Some of the organizations in Africa are working outside the formal economy in an attempt to cater for basic needs locally or in cooperation with nearby communities.[90]

During the transition phase these new social movements are joined by human rights groups, amnesty committees, and other civil associations; in some countries in Latin America, the justice and peace commissions of the Catholic church have played an important role. Their critique of the authoritarian regime's abuses combined with their demands for democracy help to secure basic political, legal, and social rights. Finally, during the transition process the organizations of civil society that were suppressed during authoritarian rule often reappear on the political stage, including trade union associations, professional groups (lawyers, engineers, social workers, journalists, and so forth), and university associations.

The emergence of a stronger civil society in the context of the struggle for democracy has a wider perspective. These diverse associations constitute the plural society that is an important precondition for a thriving democracy because they create power centers outside the state. Moreover, their internal organizations create forums for the education of citizens in democratic decision-making. In this sense, the associations can act as "seedbeds of democracy."[91]

Thus, the transition toward democracy creates a more open environment in which the associations of civil society have much better possibilities for functioning. But the changes in society cause questions to be raised about the relationship between the movements and the emerging political parties. In many cases, the new social movements were organized in direct opposition to the state apparatus and orthodox party politics. Yet the best way to support the nascent democracy seems to be by becoming active in the political parties.

In Brazil, for example, this issue has divided many of the grass-roots movements. But there is evidence that a large number of activists have gone into party politics since the early 1980s. Some observers have argued that this trend signifies a substantial strengthening of the Brazilian party system because it helps move the parties away from their earlier role as clientelistic machines centered on the advancement of individual leaders. In other words, an institutionalization of the party system is taking place, which provides a stronger basis for democracy in Brazil: "The influx of movement activists into the party system . . . brought an ideological coherence and structuring to the system that is entirely novel in Brazilian politics."[92]

The pattern of popular mobilization and organization in the Eastern European transitions has been radically different from that in Latin America. In Eastern Europe the associations of a civil society were nearly nonexistent before the transitions began (the church is the only major exception); all aspects of people's lives, from cradle to grave, took place in the context of organizations that were linked with the party-state apparatus. Therefore, the democratic demands did not come from a medley of different associations; such associations simply did not exist. The decisive dividing line was between "them," the party-state elite, and "us," the people. The democratic demands came from the people, and the organizational structures corresponded to this all-encompassing showdown; the popular organizations simply included all of the people—Civic Forum in Czechoslovakia, Neues Forum in East Germany, Solidarity in Poland. But the demands of the people, in turn, were for the very right to organize in a civil society, to form associations outside the control and interference of the party-state. This process has now begun, with the socioeconomic changes previously discussed, and it is clearly a long-term undertaking; one scholar has ventured that it is going to take at least one generation.[93]

The flurry of popular activity briefly described here does not apply in equal measure to all the current transitions toward democracy. In many cases in Africa and elsewhere, the democratic openings have been a distinctly urban affair, and popular activity has been sporadic. Yet the over-all picture is quite clear: The transitions toward democracy are accompa-nied by decisive upsurges in popular mobilization and organization. A strengthening of civil society is taking place, which improves the condi-tions for democracy and simultaneously makes the reversal to authoritar-ian rule more difficult.

At the same time, however, the transition toward democracy creates a new political environment with new challenges to the popular move-ments. The rallying point of a common enemy—the authoritarian government—is no longer there. The challenge has shifted from cooperating in a common goal of removing old rulers to working toward institutionalizing a democratic competition between the interests and vi-sions of various groups in the population. The demands put on the skills and commitments of leading actors to meet this challenge are different from those required during the transition itself. The actors must, accord-ing to one observer of Latin America, "demonstrate the ability to differen-tiate political forces rather than to draw them all into a grand coalition, the capacity to define and channel competing political projects rather than seek to keep potentially divisive reforms off the agenda, and the willing-ness to tackle incremental reforms . . . rather than defer them to some later date."[94] In other words, the popular mobilization and organization in it-self improves the prospects for democracy; but the way this popular power is utilized is a decisive element in the difficult process that will de-termine whether democracy will be consolidated.

CONCLUSION

In this chapter we have studied processes of democratization, first in a general sense and then with a focus on the current transitions toward de-mocracy. It was stressed that it is impossible to draw up a general law to the effect that democracy will always emerge provided certain precondi-tions are present. It is more productive to conceive of an interplay be-tween social, cultural, economic, and other conditions, on the one hand, and decisions taken by political actors, on the other.

No single factor can account for the contemporary surge toward de-mocracy. Each case involves a complex pattern of internal and external el-ements; in each, various conditions interplay with different groups of ac-tors. Furthermore, the movements toward democracy in different parts of the world during the last fifteen years must be explained in different ways. Within the scope of this book it is not possible to unravel the pro-cesses country by country. Therefore, we looked at events in major re-gions of the world and reviewed a few specific country examples in detail. One must always keep in mind the danger caused by hindsight:

Explaining past events can easily become a search for the obvious because we already know what happened.

In more general terms, the process of transition to democracy can be described with a simple model. The background condition of the model is national unity, and the overlapping phases of the transitions are (1) the preparatory phase, characterized by a political struggle leading to the breakdown of the nondemocratic regime; (2) the decision phase, where clear-cut elements of a democratic order are established; and (3) the consolidation phase, where the new democracy is further developed, and, eventually, democratic practices become an established part of the political culture.

The phases do not represent a predetermined path that all countries will or must follow. There is no historical law that says that regimes must move from authoritarian to democratic; a more accurate description of the typical pattern in the developing world is an uneasy fluctuation between authoritarianism and frail democracy.

It was argued that the large majority of the current transitions are in the early phases of moving toward democracy. More specifically, they can be described as restricted democracies that are frail and unconsolidated and plagued by acute social and economic problems. The only characteristic of the transitions that paints a more optimistic picture is that the process of popular mobilization and organization in the struggles for democracy has reached higher levels than seen before, thereby making reversals to authoritarianism more difficult.

When an overall assessment is made, one must be skeptical about the prospects for many of the new democracies. The large measure of elite influence in the early stages of the move away from authoritarianism can lead to a later phase of instability and stalemate during which it can prove impossible to further develop and strengthen democracy. Furthermore, the optimal conditions for the consolidation of democracy are not present in the large majority of the new democracies. Finally, the economic and social crisis that exists in these countries makes a smooth passage toward consolidated democracy even more difficult.

It may well be that determined groups of actors will be able to consolidate democracy in some countries, despite the generally adverse conditions. The transition in Spain is an example, but Spain also had the external incentive of a European Community demanding democratization as a membership condition. Portugal and Greece have also advanced toward relatively stable and consolidated democracies.

In the developing world, only a few countries present reasonably favorable conditions for democratic consolidation. South Korea and Taiwan, for example, have reached high levels of economic development, and early agrarian reforms and a labor-intensive model of industrial development have kept socioeconomic inequality at a comparatively low level. At the same time, the successful economic development has helped bring forward strong social forces outside the state apparatus, including private business and the industrial labor force. This process has created new demands on the state, and important among them has been the demand for a more democratic society. In both countries, long periods of authoritarianism are now being succeeded by more democratic forms of rule. With the ending of the cold war, the Western excuse for supporting authoritarian regimes because they are in the front line of the confrontation with the Soviet bloc is no longer valid. Given this new combination of internal and external conditions, there seem to be good prospects for the further development of democracy in these countries.

But these cases are exceptions rather than the rule. The general picture is much more gloomy; in most cases, the odds seem to weigh heavily against the further development and consolidation of the frail democratic openings that have taken place in recent years. These openings inspired a wealth of analyses on transitions toward democracy. Unfortunately, there is imminent risk that the next set of analyses will deal with democratic decay rather than democratic consolidation.

THREE

□ □ □

Domestic Consequences of Democracy: Growth and Welfare?

I s democracy really worth the trouble? Does it pave the way for improvements in spheres of life other than those narrowly connected
with political freedoms? For the populations of the countries currently
undergoing transitions toward more democratic rule, this issue is pain-
fully crucial. This chapter looks at consequences of democracy with regard to economic development, which we will define as growth and welfare. The relationship between democracy and human rights is also
addressed. Whereas democracy was treated as a dependent variable in
Chapter 2, where we were looking for conditions favorable to the rise of
democracy, democracy is treated as an independent variable in this chapter, where we are looking at its effects on economic development. In this
chapter, we will consider the question of whether democracy, once it is attained, will be able to fulfill expectations of improved performance in
terms of economic growth and welfare. The scholars who have addressed
this issue are not all optimists; some even see a trade-off between political
democracy on the one hand and economic development on the other. The
main standpoints in the theoretical debate are outlined, and a survey of
the empirical studies addressing the question is provided.[1] It will reject
the notion of a general trade-off between democracy and economic development, but I will also demonstrate why economic development and welfare improvement will not necessarily be forthcoming from the new democracies.

THE DEBATE ON DEMOCRACY
AND DEVELOPMENT

Many scholars see an incompatibility between democracy and economic growth for both economic and political reasons. The economic reasons relate to the fact that growth requires an economic surplus available for investment. Such a surplus can be either invested or consumed. Hence, the only way to increase the investable surplus is to reduce consumption. The argument is that a democratic regime will not be able to pursue policies of curbing consumption (holding down real wages) because the consumers are also voters, and they will punish the politicians next time they get the chance at the ballot box. Therefore, in a democratic system, political leaders have to cater to the short-term demands of the population. In the words of an Indian economist: "Under a system in which lawmakers . . . seek the approval of the electorate, the politician cannot afford . . . to follow any policies which will not produce tangible benefits for the electorate by the time the next election comes around."[2]

Accordingly, there is an incompatibility in the short and medium run between economic growth (investment) and welfare (consumption): You cannot have your cake and eat it too. Those who have economic reservations about democracy focus on the tendency for democratic leaders to be persuaded by the electorate to promote too much welfare and, consequently, too little growth. Their actions jeopardize the whole basis for welfare promotion in the long run.

Those with political reservations about democracy take as their starting point the fact that economic development is best promoted when there is a high degree of political stability and order.[3] Democracy is counterproductive in this regard because it opens the already weak institutions of the developing countries to all kinds of pressures from different groups in society. Instability and disorder are the result, especially in countries in which there is a massive potential for conflict stemming from numerous religious, ethnic, regional, and class divisions. In other words, the policies for change that have the objective of long-run national development can best be promoted by governments insulated from the crisscrossing political pressures of a democratic polity. In that sense, authoritarianism is best suited for the promotion of change.[4]

Another argument that scholars have made to show that authoritarian rule is better suited than democracy to promote economic development is based on the fact that the odds are increasingly being stacked against the successful promotion of development and thus the demands for comprehensive state action in order to promote development have increased dramatically over time. There is more competition from the world market and a higher internal urgency for development than was the case when the industrialized Western countries went through the early phases of development. Indeed, the processes of development then and now are qualitatively different. And in this century there has been no case of successful economic development without comprehensive political action involving massive state intervention in the economy. Such concerted state action is difficult, if not impossible, under democratic conditions.[5]

The current tasks of nation-building are indeed formidable. "It is almost inconceivable how the process can be managed without recourse to dictatorship," exclaimed one scholar,[6] and his words succinctly summarize the position of those seeing an incompatibility between democracy and economic development. At the same time, it must be stressed that the trade-off is seen as a temporary one. Political order and governmental authority are needed in order to get through the early, difficult stages of economic development. Only at a later stage do participation and distribution become relevant. The position was summarized neatly by Gabriel Almond and G. Bingham Powell: "State building and economy building are logically prior to political participation and material distribution, since power sharing and welfare sharing are dependent on there being power and welfare to share."[7]

Critics of the viewpoint that there is a trade-off between democracy and economic growth challenge all of the arguments that have been set forth. They counter the economic argument about democracy hurting growth as follows. Although it is true that specific amount of economic surplus can be either invested or consumed but not both, the conclusion that there is thus sharp contradiction between growth and welfare is not as straightforward as it seems. For example, public expenditure in such areas as health and education constitutes investment in human capital, which simultaneously improves welfare for large groups in the population. Indeed, many economists advocate a strategy of development that emphasizes basic human needs because in that area it is possible to have growth and welfare simultaneously.[8] If we can have simultaneous growth and welfare, the argument in favor of authoritarianism because of democracy's tendency to promote too much welfare weakens severely. Indeed, the choice may be not between growth and welfare but between two different kinds of investment policy—one that supports welfare and one that does not. And it can be argued that a democratic government is more likely to promote the former policy and an authoritarian government the latter.[9]

Next, the critics turn the argument that democracy cannot secure order and stability on its head by pointing out that authoritarianism can mean arbitrary rule and undue interference in citizens' affairs. Only a democracy can provide the predictable environment in which economic development can prosper. Moreover, political and economic pluralism reinforce each other. Without basic civil and political liberties, citizens will not feel secure to consistently pursue economic goals.[10] In that sense, there is a mutually reinforcing relationship between democracy and economic development.

Finally, there is the argument concerning the need for comprehensive and concerted state action in order to promote economic development. Although strong state action may be needed, it cannot be taken for granted that a strong state capable of taking a leading role in economic development efforts is also necessarily a nondemocratic state. In other words, a strong state and an authoritarian state are not synonymous. A strong state has an efficient and noncorrupt bureaucracy, a political elite willing and able to give priority to economic development, and well-designed policies for pursuing development goals. A strong state in this sense is not necessarily authoritarian.[11] The argument concerning democracy's effects on economic development are summarized in Figure 3.1.

In sum, the view of the critics is not so much that democracy is invariably better suited for promoting economic development than is authoritarian rule (for there may be cases in which authoritarian rule has helped produce a faster rate of growth during certain periods). The view is that the arguments presented by those advocating a trade-off between democracy and development are simply not strong enough to support a general claim of the superiority of authoritarianism for economic development. In other words, democracy and development cannot be seen as generally incompatible even if there are some cases of fast growth under authoritarian conditions. Some countries with harsh authoritarian rule have not shown the economic development benefits identified by the trade-off advocates.

So is there a trade-off between democracy and development? A fairly large number of analyses have been conducted in an attempt to answer this question, yet the answer remains inconclusive.[12] Perhaps the most comprehensive study is a survey by Robert Marsh of the performance of ninety-eight countries between 1955 and 1970. He concluded that "political competition/democracy does have a significant effect on later rates of economic development; its influence is to *retard* the development rate, rather than to facilitate it. In short, among the poor nations, an authoritarian political system increases the rate of economic development, while a democratic political system does appear to be a luxury which hinders development."[13] A similar conclusion was reached by Yousseff Cohen following his study of economic growth in a number of Latin American countries.[14]

Dirk Berg-Schlosser, in his analysis of African regimes, stated that authoritarian systems have a "strong positive effect on the overall rate of GNP growth,"[15] but he also emphasized that democratic (polyarchic) re-

	Democracy impedes economic development	Democracy can promote economic development
Economic reasons	Democracy is unable to reduce consumption in favor of investment. Thus, economic growth suffers.	Democratic investment in basic human needs is good for economic growth.
Political reasons	Democracy increases the pressure on weak institutions. Concerted state action is more difficult. The state is weak.	Democracy provides a stable political environment and the basis for economic pluralism. Democracy means legitimacy: A strong state is often also a democratic state.

FIGURE 3.1   Democracy: Does it promote or impede economic development?

gimes have done better than should be expected: "Thus polyarchic systems fare quite well both in terms of GNP growth and the improvement of the basic quality of life. They also have the best record concerning normative standards (protection of civil liberties and freedom from political repression)."[16] Dwight King reached a similar conclusion in his study of six Asian countries: "If performance is evaluated in terms of material equality and welfare rather than growth, and is examined diachronically over the past decade and within differentiated population groups (rural, landless, and near landless), democratic-type regimes (Malaysia, Sri Lanka) have performed better than bureaucratic-authoritarian ones (Indonesia, Philippines, Thailand)."[17]

G. William Dick examined the growth record of seventy-two countries between 1959 and 1968. He categorized the countries according to their form of government: authoritarian, semi-competitive, or competitive. He readily admitted that the data are not unambiguous, but he maintained that the "results certainly do not support, and tend to refute, the view that authoritarian countries are universally capable of achieving faster economic growth in the early stages of development than countries having competitive political systems."[18]

Thus, as mentioned earlier, no clear answer to the trade-off question emerges from these studies, and it seems that there is little help to be had from the review of additional analyses, as a recent survey has demonstrated.[19] The question inevitably arises of whether it is really a meaningful exercise to seek a definite answer through these largely quantitative analyses of large numbers of cases covering limited periods of time. Dick's contribution provides a good example of the problems involved. First, it does not seem reasonable to base such an analysis on a period covering less than a decade. The economic performance of developing countries varies substantially over time, and nine years is not a representative period. Second, whereas a small number of cases would not be representative, a large number of cases invariably presents problems with regime classification. The best growth performers in Dick's analysis are the so-called semi-competitive countries. According to the definition he used and data from 1970, Algeria, Ethiopia, South Africa, and Nicaragua under Anastasio Somoza are classified not as authoritarian but as semi-competitive. But one can easily argue that such regimes should be considered authoritarian, and then the whole basis for Dick's conclusion would disappear.

The other contributions are plagued by similar problems. Thus, what we learn from these analyses is that there are a large number of countries that are not clearly identifiable as democratic or authoritarian and that countries move very fast between the categories, being semi-democratic yesterday, authoritarian today, and semi-democratic tomorrow. Each time they make a stop in one of the categories, they lend their economic performance data, often covering only a few years, to a different argument in these investigations.

If all the overwhelming methodological problems could be solved, would it then be possible to come up with a universally relevant answer to the trade-off question? I contend that it is impossible to arrive at a law-like statement concerning the effects of regime form on economic development. How can we say "When this is the form of regime, democratic or authoritarian, we can expect such and such in terms of economic development" when very dissimilar entities are covered by the label democratic and by the label authoritarian? I am not saying that the form of regime is irrelevant for economic development. But when theorizing on the relationship, we need to be less ambitious, in the middle range. Instead of attempting to make universal statements about the relationship between regime form and economic development, we should look for systematic relationships between development outcomes and *different types* of democratic and authoritarian systems, and we should study outcomes in comparable pairs of democratic and authoritarian cases.

Both of these pathways are tried out in the sections that follow. We will look first at a pair of comparable cases, one authoritarian and one democratic, and then at different types of authoritarian and democratic systems.[20]

INDIA VERSUS CHINA

India and China are very large, populous, and predominantly agrarian countries. They both had a rather low level of social and economic development in 1950, following India's independence in 1947 and the Chinese revolution in 1949. Today, India is one of the most stable political democracies in the developing world, whereas China is under authoritarian socialist rule. It may be that India's democracy is less than perfect and that some democratic elements have been present in China (see Chapter 1), but the overall difference is clear. Thus we have a democratic and an authoritarian country that have had stable regime forms for more than three decades and that have a number of basic traits in common, including similar levels of development in 1950. They are good candidates for comparing development outcomes of democratic and authoritarian regimes.

Economic development as defined here includes two elements, growth and welfare. Let us first look at the economic growth of China and India, shown in Table 3.1.We must bear in mind that growth statistics are seldom fully reliable, and there is also a problem with comparability. Note that the levels of GNP were roughly equal in China and India in 1989— $330 and $340, respectively. If the 1965–1989 growth rates are also reliable, we must conclude that India's per capita income in 1965 should have been nearly twice that of China, which is contrary to all available evidence.[21] Real GDP (gross domestic product) in terms of purchasing power parities (PPP) dollars is a more valid figure than per capita GNP, and when this value is used, the difference in growth rates becomes more trustworthy.

These data problems cannot be fully settled here. Although the exact magnitudes of the growth rates are in question, I see no reason to doubt that the overall growth rate in China has been substantially higher than in India. On one important dimension the difference is not dramatic— namely, agricultural growth between 1950 and 1980. Before discussing this point further, let me make a few more general remarks on the growth figures.

The data in Table 3.1 seem to fully confirm the trade-off argument insofar as authoritarian China has achieved much higher growth rates than has democratic India. Those who believe that there is a trade-off between democracy and economic growth would probably contend that the authoritarian Chinese regime has consistently held down consumption and given first priority to investment. Morever, the regime has been able to avoid disorder and instability while consistently pursuing a strategy of rapid change.

There is some truth to those contentions: Except during the 1980s, the Communist leadership has invariably put investment before consumption. During the twenty years from 1956 through 1976, high rates of investment were made possible only by curbing consumption to a level that, in the rural areas, was not very much above subsistence.[22] But there is more to the story. Elements other than the mere curbing of consump-

TABLE 3.1   Economic Growth in China and India

Indicators	China	India
GNP per capita, 1989 (dollars)	330	340
Real GDP per capita, 1989 (PPP$)[a]	2,656	910
Annual growth rate, GDP per capita (%)		
1965–1980	6.9	3.6
1980–1989	9.7	5.3
Industrial growth (% per annum)		
1950–1980[b]	12.1	5.5
1980–1989	12.6	6.9
Agricultural growth (% per annum)		
1950–1980[c]	3.1	2.3
1980–1989	6.3	2.9

[a]PPP (purchasing power parities): An attempt to measure real GDP in terms of domestic purchasing powers of currencies, thereby avoiding the distortions of official exchange rates.
[b]Figures for China are for 1953–1982; those for India are for 1956–1979.
[c]Figures for China are for 1952–1977.

Sources: United Nations Development Programme, *Human Development Report 1992* (New York: Oxford University Press, 1992); World Bank, *World Development Report 1991* (New York: Oxford University Press, 1991); Pranab Bardhan, *The Political Economy of Development in India* (Delhi: Oxford University Press, 1984); Jürgen Domes, *The Government and Politics of the PRC: A Time of Transition* (Boulder: Westview, 1985).

tion contributed to the high growth rates. Most important was that the regime initiated far-reaching reforms in industry and agriculture that made economic surpluses available for investment. The surpluses had previously accrued to private landowners and capitalists. At the same time the reforms increased productivity, especially in agriculture. Several analysts have pointed out that the lack of such basic reforms is responsible for a large, unrealized growth potential in Indian agriculture.[23] It is a main thesis in Barrington Moore's contribution that big landowners and moneylenders in India appropriate a large part of the agrarian surplus and spend it unproductively.[24] A number of scholars have echoed that opinion in more recent analyses, and it is a fact that the taxation of agricultural income in India has been extremely low, yielding only 1 percent of total tax proceeds in 1980–1981.[25] The strategy of the Green Revolution adopted in some areas of India in the mid-1960s aimed at increasing production through the use of modern inputs, such as chemical fertilizers, pesticides, irrigation, and new crop varieties. The strategy has increased output where implemented, but it has not radically improved the overall growth rate in agriculture or paved the way for a substantially higher contribution from agriculture toward industrial growth.

Yet there are some less attractive elements in the Chinese growth record that must also be discussed. The power of the authoritarian regime to organize rapid economic growth also involves the power to commit horrible mistakes and even persevere in such mistakes, as occurred during the so-called Great Leap Forward, initiated in 1958, which was supposed to boost production to the extent that China could be among the highly industrialized countries in ten years time. The Leap was a failure in industry and a disaster in agriculture; the production of food grain dropped in 1959 to the level of 1953. Only in 1978 did the per capita output of food grain reach the level of 1956.[26] In industry, output increased dramatically at first, but it then dropped at a similar speed in 1961–1962. Behind the rise in output was a complete lack of consideration for quality and for the cost of resources; behind the decline was an increasing organizational chaos and a misallocation of resources. In what can be seen only as an extreme arrogance of power, Mao Zedong, for reasons of personal pride, held onto the strategy of the Great Leap for some time even after it had proven catastrophically wrong.[27]

The Stalinist growth strategy that was employed in China must also be questioned from a more general perspective. It gave top priority to heavy industry while holding agriculture in an iron grip, allowing very few possibilities of increasing both investment and consumption in agriculture.[28] It is certainly this strategy that explains the substantial difference between Chinese industrial and agricultural rates of growth before 1980. It also helps explain why agricultural growth in China before 1980 was only slightly higher than in India (if, indeed, it was at all higher, given the uncertainty of the data).

The Stalinist strategy was changed after Mao's death. His successor, Deng Xiaoping, has pushed for reforms in industry and agriculture aimed at decentralization and a more prominent role for market forces. Such reforms are behind the much improved rates of growth in agriculture since 1980, but it has proven difficult to implement similar reforms in industry. China is currently in a phase of transition. Few people are interested in reverting to the old system of a highly centralized economic and political structure (with the exception, perhaps, of the groups in the state apparatus whose power hinges on that system), yet it has proven difficult to move toward a more decentralized, market-based system because the institutional preconditions are not present. These preconditions include a set of rules for conducting competition and for defining what is legal and illegal. Indeed, there is a lot of "official speculation" at the moment because these rules are not clear.[29] Also, there is no independent banking system for providing credit on commercial terms. And, perhaps most important, since the Tiananmen demonstrations in 1989 the leadership has been uncertain about how far it wishes to move down the road of reform. In short, the transformation toward another system is far from smooth and easy.

We have discussed economic growth in China and India. Let us now turn to the other aspect of economic development, welfare. There is no single best indicator for the level of welfare, but the United Nations Development Programme (UNDP) has in recent years published the *Human Development Report,* which ranks countries according to some of the best indicators. Drawing primarily on these data, Table 3.2 outlines the welfare achievements in China and India.

Even when we allow for some uncertainty in the data, there is no doubt about the general tendency: China has achieved a substantially higher level of welfare according to these indicators than has India. China's rating in the composite Human Development index is twice that of India's. Note that the figures in the table are averages for the population as a whole. The situation for the poor is much worse. The percentage of the population living in **absolute poverty,** that is, at a minimum level of subsistence or below, is as high as 40 in India, and this percentage has basically remained unchanged since that country's independence. With a population increase from 360 million to more than 800 million between 1950 and 1988, there has been, of course, a dramatic increase in the number of very poor people. The corresponding percentage of the population living in absolute poverty in China is between 12 and 15.[30]

These data go squarely against the expectation that democratic regimes will give in to the electorate's demands for tangible benefits and will thus give priority to immediate welfare demands rather than to the long-term goals of investment and growth. The pertinent question is, of course, the following: Why has democratic India not done more for welfare?

Improved welfare for the masses has always received high priority in the development goals of Indian governments. But it is a long way from political rhetoric to actual welfare progress. First, good wishes must be translated into concrete political initiatives, and even in this early process we see a reduction in the rhetorical "welfare impulse." Second, to the extent that political measures are actually taken, there is a lack of implementation, especially in the rural sector. Welfare measures are perceived as a threat to the elite, who then fight to keep them from being carried out. Programs concerning the redistribution of land, tenancy regulations, minimum wage regulations, and the protection of the rural poor have all been subject to such resistance.[31] And when implementation does take place, there are often leakages in the delivery pipeline. Funds often end up in the hands of corrupt officials or middlemen; benefits are diverted at the end of the pipeline in favor of nontargeted, upper-income recipients.[32]

These are some of the mechanisms behind the lack of welfare progress in India. Their existence can be explained by looking at the structure of socioeconomic and political power that forms the basis of democracy in that country. Since independence, the Congress party has been dominated by

TABLE 3.2   Welfare in China and India

Indicators	China	India
Life expectancy at birth, 1990 (years)	70.1	59.1
Adult literacy rate, 1985 (%)	68.2	44.1
Mean years of schooling, 1980	4.8	2.2
Under-age-five mortality rate (per thousand)	47 ·	154
Human Development index rank[a]	0.614	0.308

[a]The Human Development Index (HDI) is composed of three indicators: life expectancy, education, and income. For each indicator, a worldwide maximum (1) and minimum (0) are identified, and each country is then ranked according to its position. The combined average of the three positions is the HDI; the closer it is to 1, the better the ranking. See United Nations Development Programme, *Human Development Report 1991* (New York: Oxford University Press, 1991), pp. 88–91.

Source: Figures from United Nations Development Programme, *Human Development Report 1991* (New York: Oxford University Press, 1991), p. 120. The under-age-five mortality rate is based on UNICEF data, quoted from Jean Drèze and Amartya Sen, *Hunger and Public Action* (Oxford: Clarendon Press, 1989), p. 204.

three groups: the urban professionals, the bourgeoisie in industry and trade, and the rural landowning elite. It is, roughly speaking, the interests of these groups that have been looked after in the development policies of administrations led by the Congress party.[33]

Therefore, if we ask who have been the primary beneficiaries of the development policies conducted by the Indian state since independence, three groups emerge. First, there is the Indian bourgeoisie (or industrial capitalist class). With their control of a powerful nucleus of monopolistic undertakings, the bourgeoisie has enjoyed a protected domestic market and has benefited from a large public sector supplying the industrial infrastructure and other basic inputs at low prices; public financial institutions have provided a cheap source of finance, and the level of taxation has never constituted a serious burden.

Second, there are the rich farmers. They have benefited from price support for farm products and from a wide range of subsidized inputs (fertilizer, power, and water, for example). Moreover, the threat of land reform has been held in check, and there has been no significant taxation of agricultural income and wealth.

The third group is the bureaucracy, that is, the professionals and white-collar workers in the public sector. The benefits to this group have come from the substantial expansion of the public sector, partly by direct intervention in the economy in the form of public enterprises and partly through indirect controls; the bureaucracy has the power to grant licenses, subsidies, and other favors sought by the private sector.

In sum, Indian governments have presided over this coalition constituting roughly the top 20 percent of the population. It is a dominant coalition, and its position is reinforced because the government policies further, in the long run, the interests of its members.[34] The development policies of the state have never significantly been outside of the orbit of what is acceptable to the dominant coalition. The mass of poor people is too unorganized, divided, and politically weak to radically change this state of affairs.

Why, then, is there a much better welfare situation in China, in spite of an authoritarian government pushing economic growth? On the one hand, the reforms in agriculture not only promoted growth, but also welfare. According to one estimate, the poorest fifth of the rural households increased its share of the overall income from 6 to 11 percent as a consequence of the agrarian reform.[35] On the other hand, a number of measures were taken that were aimed directly at welfare improvement. Three areas stand out in this respect, namely health, education, and public distribution systems. The average health situation in the country was substantially improved by the system of public health care erected in the 1950s and expanded to cover the rural areas during the 1960s. In addition to preventive care, the usual domain of public health care, this system also includes curative health care.[36] With regard to education, 93 percent of the relevant age-groups attended primary school in 1983, and even if more than one-third of the pupils from the rural areas drop out, the level of education has been considerably improved. Finally, the social security system in China includes the distribution of food through public channels that have extensive coverage.[37]

Yet there are also welfare elements in India's favor. Democratic India has avoided policy excesses, such as China's Great Leap Forward, that can lead to catastrophic situations. There has been no severe famine in India since independence; warning signals of such disasters are quickly relayed through a relatively free press, and the democratic government is prompted to take swift countermeasures. The situation is different in China. There was, for example, no free press to expose the failures of the Great Leap Forward and the severe famine that followed in its wake. The famine is estimated to have killed between 16.5 and 29.5 million people. At the same time, the more open political system in India has not provided protection against endemic undernutrition. Jean Drèze and Amartya Sen stated that "every eight years or so more people die in India because of its higher regular death rate than died in China in the gigantic famine of 1958–61. India seems to manage to fill its cupboard with more skeletons every eight years than China put there in its years of shame."[38]

In summary, the overall results in the growth and welfare aspects of economic development put authoritarian China ahead of democratic India. Radical reforms in China paved the way for economic development, which has provided a decent level of living for the large majority. The reforms could not have been implemented without a strong leadership bent on pushing such policies, perhaps even to the point of using coercion against opponents. But these radical reforms have also involved conflicts and mistaken policies that have led to human suffering and loss of life. Moreover, the other side of the strong, determined leadership is that it has promoted a system in which there is a blatant lack of basic civil and political rights.

In India the democratic government has, by and large, protected the basic civil and political rights of the people. Policy excesses have been avoided, as have human catastrophes such as large-scale famines. But democracy has also maintained a highly unequal social structure headed by a dominant elite whose members resist far-reaching change that would benefit the poor. The lack of progress on the welfare dimension in India has led to human suffering and loss of life, not through spectacular disasters like in China but through the quiet, continuous suffering of the 40 percent of the population who are in absolute poverty.

TYPES OF AUTHORITARIAN SYSTEMS

Comparison of the cases of India and China helped shed a more nuanced light on the theoretical debate over economic development outcomes of democratic and authoritarian regimes. Yet the debate obviously cannot be settled on the basis of one pair of cases. The comparison says nothing about the relationship between India/China and other examples of authoritarian and democratic regimes. Even if the India/China contrast does not give very high marks to Indian democracy, it is necessary to know more about different types of authoritarian and democratic systems and how India and China fit into this larger picture before further conclusions can be drawn. I shall argue in the sections that follow that China is indeed not very typical of the large group of authoritarian systems. China belongs, together with a few other countries, to a rather exclusive group of authoritarian developmentalist regimes that have been capable of promoting both economic growth and welfare. When we look at development outcomes, the large number of authoritarian systems belong to two less attractive groups: Either they push growth but not welfare or, even worse, they push neither. Regimes in this latter group do not have economic development as their main aim: Their ultimate goal is the enrichment of the elite, which controls the state. These three main types of authoritarian systems are outlined in Figure 3.2 and are further described in the sections that follow.

Authoritarian Developmentalist Regimes

The distinctive feature of an **authoritarian developmentalist regime** is its capability of promoting both growth and welfare. The government is

Regime type	Aspects of economic development		Country example
	Growth	Welfare	
Authoritarian developmentalist regime	+	+	Taiwan; China
Authoritarian growth regime	+	–	Brazil under military rule
Authoritarian state elite enrich-ment regime	–	–	Zaire under Mobutu

FIGURE 3.2   Types of authoritarian systems and their consequences for economic development

reform oriented and enjoys a high degree of autonomy from vested elite interests. It controls a state apparatus with the bureaucratic, organizational capacity for promoting development and is run by a state elite that is ideologically committed toward boosting economic development in terms of growth as well as welfare. China is an example of a socialist authoritarian developmentalist regime. There is also a capitalist variety, with Taiwan being an example. Even if they are often seen as opposites, Taiwan and China have several traits in common in addition to their authoritarian political systems. Taiwan, like China, pushed economic development through radical agrarian reform and the transfer of economic surplus from agriculture to industry. As in China, there has been a high degree of state involvement in the economy.

But the countries also have a number of dissimilar characteristics, some of which account for the fact that Taiwan has in several respects been more successful than its socialist counterpart.[39] First, the starting point experiences of the countries when they began to pursue economic development (around 1949) were different: China was engaged in a vicious civil war during the first half of the twentieth century; in the same period, orderly Japanese rule in Taiwan provided a basis for advances in economic development. Second, centralized planning like that in China has not been employed in Taiwan; the regime there has never attempted to monopolize economic power. The path taken by Taiwan more closely resembles the Japanese model, with a combination of market forces and private property and with heavy state guidance of the market, than the Chinese model. Taiwan seems to have struck a sound balance between the stagnation problems of "too much state" and the ultraliberalism of uncontrolled market forces that do not automatically serve the goals of economic development. Third, Taiwan has experienced a smooth process of growth and productivity increases in both agriculture, with its system of family farms, and industry, with its emphasis on light, labor-intensive manufacturing supported by public enterprises. In this process of economic reform, Taiwan has not experienced the severe setbacks due to policy failures that characterize China. The entire process has been supported by significant economic aid from the United States. China, conversely, imitated a Stalinist model of industrial growth, which overemphasized heavy industry and left very little room for growth in light industry and agriculture. It followed this policy until the late 1970s. In addition, China was internationally isolated for a long period, and its ties with the Soviet Union during the 1950s did not yield much economic assistance compared to what Taiwan received from the United States.

Yet what must be stressed here is the basic similarity of China and Taiwan as members of the category of authoritarian developmentalist regimes. There are only a few other candidates for this type of authoritarian regime. The most obvious ones are the two Koreas.[40] South Korea has many traits in common with Taiwan, whereas North Korea has a socialist regime that has taken centralization of political and economic control even further than has China. There are also a few borderline cases that share some of the features of authoritarian developmentalist regimes; examples are Singapore on the capitalist side and Cuba on the socialist side.

Authoritarian Growth Regimes

The second major type of authoritarian regime is the **authoritarian growth regime,** an elite-dominated government that promotes economic growth but not welfare. Brazil during military rule, from 1964 until the present period of redemocratization, is a good example of this form of rule. As an authoritarian growth regime, Brazil exhibited the following characteristics: It pursued economic growth objectives with the aim of building a strong national economy (which, in turn, could provide the basis for a strong military power), and it respected the long-term interests (but not necessarily the immediate interests) of the dominant social forces while it looked to the workers and peasants of the poor majority for the economic surplus needed to get growth under way.

The Brazilian regime was thus an explicitly elite-oriented model of development. It rested on an alliance between local private capital, state enterprises, and transnational corporations. The elite orientation of the model applies to the supply side of development (for the emphasis was on consumer durables) as well as to the demand side (for industrialization was capital intensive, with most benefits going to a small layer of skilled and white-collar employees and workers). The poor majority did not really benefit from the growth process; many had urgent needs in the areas of basic health, housing, education, and gainful employment.[41] Redistributive reform measures, including agrarian reform, could have helped push the welfare dimension of economic development, but what the regime undertook, especially in its early years, was exactly the opposite kind of redistribution. After having cut off popular organizations from political influence, the regime dramatically reduced real wages and took other measures that led to a substantial income concentration favoring the richest 20 percent of the population.[42]

The military regimes that imposed authoritarian rule in Uruguay, Chile, and Argentina in the early and mid-1970s attempted to implement models of economic growth with similar features. However, they were less successful than the Brazilian regime with regard to economic growth. In contrast to Brazil, these countries opened their economies to external shocks through the pursuit of ultraliberal economic policies, which, before corrective measures were taken, led to deindustrialization—that is, toward a dismantling of the existing industrial base.[43] Even so, these cases have a basic feature in common: The authoritarian regimes attempted to one-sidedly pursue economic growth in an alliance with elite interests.

Authoritarian State Elite Enrichment Regimes

The final major type of authoritarian rule, the **authoritarian state elite enrichment** (ASEE) regime, promotes neither growth nor welfare; its main aim is rather the enrichment of the elite, which controls the state. It is often based on autocratic rule by a supreme leader. Although the leader's actions may not make sense when judged by the standards of formal development goals set up by the regime, they are perfectly understandable through the lenses of patronage and clientelistic politics. It is clear that several African regimes, with their systems of personal rule as described in Chapter 2, are candidates for this category of authoritarianism. One observer has described the system as one of clan politics: "The clan is a political faction, operating within the institutions of the state and the governing party; it exists above all to promote the interests of its members . . . and its first unifying principle is the prospect of the material rewards of political success: loot is the clan's totem."[44]

The surplus that comes into the hands of the leadership through its control of the state is distributed among the clan or a coalition of clans, which in turn provide political support for the leader. It is not, of course, an equal pattern of distribution; the lion's share of the benefits accrues to the supreme leader and a small elite around him. There is no clear distinction between politicians and civil servants; the latter are actively involved in efforts to gain personal advantage from their public posts.

Thus, despite official claims to the contrary, the ruling elite takes no real interest in economic development, be it in terms of growth or welfare. The main aim of the regime is self-enrichment. Attainment of this goal requires an act of balancing against potential opponents (who are paid off or held down by force) and, as mentioned, also requires the distribution of spoils. Both may have side effects in terms of promoting either welfare or growth, but, again, this outcome is not the main aim.

Zaire under Mobutu may be the clearest example of an ASEE regime.[45] The inner circle of the Mobutu clan consists of a few hundred people, Mobutu's "fraternity." The lucrative positions in the state, diplomatic corps, party, army, secret police, and the Presidency are reserved for clan members.[46] They directly claim some 20 percent of the national budget, and their income is complemented through smuggling (diamonds and gold) and private sales of copper. Mobutu himself has a personal share in all foreign undertakings operating in Zaire, and his family controls 60 percent of the domestic trade net. He has accumulated enormous wealth and is recognized to be one of the three richest people in the world.

Hence, the defining characteristic of the ASEE regime is simply that the elite who control the state are preoccupied with enriching themselves. Other examples from Africa that fit this description are the Central African Republic under Jean Bedel Bokassa and Uganda under Idi Amin. Examples of authoritarian regimes outside Africa that are also candidates for the ASEE category are Haiti under François and Jean-Claude Duvalier (Papa and Baby Doc), Nicaragua under Somoza, and Paraguay under Alfredo Stroessner.

*   *   *

What can be learned from this typology of authoritarian regimes? First, it is not possible to generalize across authoritarian systems in terms of their capacities for promoting economic development. Different authoritarian regimes vary greatly in this respect. In this chapter, we described three main categories of authoritarian systems: the authoritarian developmentalist regimes, capable of promoting both growth and welfare; the authoritarian growth regimes, which give priority to economic growth; and the ASEE regimes, which promote neither growth nor welfare. Second, authoritarianism does not automatically generate economic growth, order, and stability, as those advocating a trade-off between democracy and economic development contend. The authoritarian growth regime is perhaps the type closest to the mainstream view of authoritarian regimes held by those advocating the trade-off. Under this system, economic growth is promoted at the expense of the welfare of the majority of the population. Although proponents of this system seem to think that a long phase of growth can provide a good basis for improving welfare at a later stage, the case of authoritarian Brazil appears to demonstrate the opposite. In that country, a number of impediments prevented the expected trickle-down effect from making itself felt on a scale at which it could significantly contribute to welfare improvement.[47] One important reason was the specific elite orientation of the growth process.

Finally, the typology sets the trade-off debate in a new light by emphasizing the diversity of authoritarian regimes. If we examine the ASEE regime in Zaire, we find that authoritarianism is definitely worse for economic development than its rumor; if we study the authoritarian developmentalist regime in Taiwan, we find that authoritarianism is much better for economic development than its rumor.

Against this background, and with the knowledge that authoritarian developmentalist systems of the Taiwan type are few and far between, it is easy to reject the argument that there is a trade-off between democracy and economic development on the ground that most authoritarian systems do not fare any better than democracies in the area of development. And then there is no reason to sacrifice the rights and liberties associated with democracy. Before we draw final conclusions, however, let us take a closer look at different types of democracies.

TYPES OF DEMOCRATIC SYSTEMS

It is more difficult to create a typology of democratic systems than one of authoritarian systems simply because there are very few relatively stable democracies in the developing world. If we do not count very small countries with populations of less than one million, only Costa Rica (with a population of three million) has been a stable democracy for as long as India. Venezuela and Colombia come close to a similar stability. Yet there is a common denominator between these stable cases and the majority of the current transitions discussed in Chapter 2 that is significant for their economic development outlooks. They are all **elite-dominated democracies** (systems in which traditional rulers remain in control, even if pressured from below, and successfully use strategies of either compromise or force—or some mix of the two—to retain at least part of their power).

Elite-Dominated Democracies

Indian democracy, in the vein of the current transitions toward democracy, was achieved by an elite-dominated coalition with three main groups: the urban professionals, who founded the Congress movement in 1885; the Indian business community in trade and industry; and the rural landowning elite. The masses of poor peasants supported the elite coalition's struggle for independence and democracy; they rallied behind

Gandhi as the great leading figure who would be instrumental in welding this alliance between elite groups and the poor masses. Yet the support of the poor peasants did not really upset the rural elite. Gandhi's vision of the future of the Indian villages included no threat to their position, and it was the rural elite, not the landless peasants, who controlled the Congress organization at the local level.[48]

We have already seen that the continued elite dominance in the Indian democracy shaped and set the limits of what could be achieved in terms of economic development. The process of economic development has mainly served the interests of the elite groups in the dominant coalition. The respect for elite interests has impeded the capacity of Indian democracy to mobilize resources for economic growth and welfare improvement through basic agrarian and other reforms.

In Chapter 2, the majority of the current transitions toward democracy were characterized as transitions from above—that is, elite-dominated transitions. We saw the fears expressed there that the regimes may become **frozen democracies,** which is Terry Lynn Karl's term for restricted elite-dominated democracies that are unwilling to transgress the narrow limitations imposed on them by the elite factions who engineered the transitions to democracy in the first place. They are unwilling to carry out substantive reforms that address the lot of the poor citizens. Against the background of the Indian experience with some forty years of elite-dominated democracy, such fears are well founded; there has been economic development in India both in terms of growth and welfare, but as a whole the process has offered much too little to the mass of poor people.

But it is important to emphasize another point raised in Chapter 2: Democracy introduces a degree of uncertainty in the political process. It opens channels for popular pressure on the rulers. Even elite-dominated democracies may be pushed in the direction of more effective reform measures, as can be seen in the following case study of Costa Rica.

In Costa Rica, democracy was based on political pacts between elite factions. The three main groups in the dominant coalition in Costa Rica are the elites in export agriculture and in industry (including foreign investors) and the members of the state bureaucracy.[49] They shared the benefits of a development model that is based on export agriculture and promotes industrialization and a strong role for the state in certain areas. Thus, export agriculture has received constant government support, the level of taxation has been quite modest, and the agrarian reform measures have been no threat. Although industrialists have had to accept that agriculture could not be restructured according to the specific needs of industrialization, industry has received ample support in terms of external protection, low tariffs for inputs, tax exemptions, and comprehensive infrastructural support from the public sector. The bureaucracy has grown stronger through the rapid expansion of a great variety of institutions in the public sector, which has provided a solid basis from which further benefits could be negotiated from the state.

In this sense, Costa Rican democracy may be seen as "a masked hegemony of competing elites who have explicitly agreed to respect one another's interests."[50] Policies are based on a balance between different elites respecting one another's basic interests. Thus, welfare programs have been kept within limits acceptable to the dominant interests. Radical social programs of structural change have been avoided, as have economic policies that could pose a serious threat to any elite faction. As a result, welfare improvements in Costa Rica rest on the shaky basis of an agrarian export economy saddled with a heavy (and increasing) foreign debt.

Yet, within these limitations, the dominant coalitions in Costa Rica have supported governments that have promoted substantial welfare programs. As shown in Table 3.3, the overall achievements of the country are fairly impressive with respect to welfare, whereas the economic growth achievements have been more ordinary, especially during the crisis period in the 1980s. It should be noted that the average figures given in Table 3.3 conceal the existence of a fairly large group of people at the bottom of the ladder that has made much less progress. Although there are very few at the level of actual starvation, one estimate from 1977 put the share of the population living at the subsistence level at 17 percent.[51] Most of these people belong to the rural landless or the urban populations from the city slums. The economic crisis of the 1980s has meant a setback for the majority of the population. As early as 1982, real wages were back at the level of 1970 and cutbacks in state expenditure had hit several social programs.

Still, the elite-dominated democracy of Costa Rica has fared relatively well in terms of welfare. Several elements go into explaining this achievement. First, the nature of elite rule in Costa Rica during the nineteenth and early twentieth centuries was different from that in most other countries in Latin America. Costa Rica did not have a system with Indians and slaves under the control of a rural elite; there was an independent peasantry, and the rural working class was free from feudal ties binding them to rural patrons. Second, the dominant stratum of coffee barons supported liberal values of religious freedom, freedom of the press, and the promotion of public education. A law for free, compulsory education was passed in 1884, and the educational level of the population combined with open public debate paved the way for the formation of a variety of groups and associations that fed demands into the political system.[52] Third, the democracy established after 1948 has a reputation for fair and honest elections in a political system geared toward negotiation and compromise. In

TABLE 3.3 Welfare and Growth in Costa Rica

Life expectancy at birth, 1990 (years)	74.9
Adult literacy rate, 1985 (%)	91.8
Mean years of schooling, 1980	5.6
Human Development index rank[a]	0.876
Real GDP per capita, 1988 (PPP$)[b]	4,320
Annual growth rate, GNP per capita (in percent)	
1965–1980	3.3
1980–1988	0.2

[a]The Human Development Index (HDI) is composed of three indicators: life expectancy, education, and income. For each indicator, a worldwide maximum (1) and minimum (0) are identified, and each country is then ranked according to its position. The combined average of the three positions is the HDI; the closer it is to 1, the better the ranking. See United Nations Development Programme, *Human Development Report 1991* (New York: Oxford University Press, 1991), pp. 88–91.

[b]PPP (purchasing power parities): An attempt to measure real GDP in terms of domestic purchasing powers of currencies, thereby avoiding the distortions of official exchange rates.

Source: Figures from United Nations Development Programme, *Human Development Report 1991* (New York: Oxford University Press, 1991), pp. 119, 164.

dramatic contrast to its Central American neighbors, Costa Rica disbanded its army in 1949.

The case of Costa Rica demonstrates that elite-dominated democracies need not fare as poorly as, for example, India has fared in welfare terms. They are capable of transforming toward a higher degree of responsiveness to mass demands. But the political background of Costa Rica contains some rather unique features, which are hard to find in other elite-dominated democracies, that allowed it to move in this direction. The egalitarian values of the dominant coalition led to a social and political environment that was conducive to the organization of popular forces at an early stage. These elements provided the basis for welfare policies and for the formation of "a system of stable liberal democracy without parallel in Latin America."[53]

As shown by this case study, elite-dominated democracies can address welfare issues. Unfortunately, there are few elite-dominated democracies that have conditions similar to those that were instrumental for bringing this result about in Costa Rica.

Mass-Dominated Democracies

Mass-dominated democracies are systems in which mass actors have gained the upper hand over traditional ruling classes. They push for reforms from below, attacking the power and privilege of the elites. A prominent example of this system of rule is the Unidad Popular (Popular Unity) government under Salvador Allende in Chile between 1970 and 1973. The government was elected on a program promising massive improvement for low-income and poor groups in terms of wage and salary increases and better social and housing conditions. It also promoted measures for making the economy more effective; policies would be geared to faster growth and increased popular control. It implemented policies for the redistribution of land through agrarian reform and for the nationalization of the mineral sector, something that it also foresaw for the largest enterprises in the private sector.[54]

Although successful in its first year in power, the Unidad Popular faced rapidly growing resistance from landowners, industrialists, and the middle sectors. A process of radicalization took place in which an increasingly united opposition faced a government that was divided internally over whether it should radically confront or moderately accommodate its political adversaries. It was this situation that in 1973 culminated in the military coup led by Augusto Pinochet. This example underlines the fragility of mass-dominated democracies; they easily lead toward hostile confrontation, which may then result in a return to authoritarian rule.

The fate of the Unidad Popular and other mass-dominated democracies in Latin America has led to rather pessimistic conclusions regarding the future possibilities for such systems in the region, as we saw in Chapter 2. Set in a broader perspective, the picture may be a bit brighter. It should be possible for mass-dominated democracies to proceed more cautiously along the road of reform than did Unidad Popular, for example, and thereby avoid the kind of all-encompassing showdown that took place in Chile. A government that has been successful in this way is the Left Front rule in West Bengal, India, which came to power in 1977.[55] At the same time, democracies have transformative capacities. The development of most West European democracies since the nineteenth century can be seen as a process beginning with elite-dominated systems and then gradually transforming toward more mass-dominated systems. The latter, in turn, are responsible for the welfare states built since the 1930s. The process of gradual transformation paved the way for elite acceptance of social reforms and equity policies.

*   *   *

From the examples given we can see that the economic development prospects of democratic systems, especially concerning the likelihood of improvements for the underprivileged, depend on the nature of the ruling coalitions behind the democracies. Highly restricted, elite-dominated democracies may be virtually "frozen" in that their room for maneuver in addressing welfare issues and also in promoting resources for economic growth is set within the very narrow limits of continued support for the status quo. If, as was argued earlier, most of the current transitions toward democracy are from above (that is, elite-dominated), the pessimistic projection that many of the current transitions will develop into frozen democracies remains rather convincing.

Mass-dominated democracies are not frozen in this way. They contain the potential for substantial reform going against vested elite interests. But such reform may lead to confrontation with elite forces and to the subsequent undermining of democracy itself.

Yet there is a space between these extremes where relatively stable democracy and economic progress can go hand in hand. The elite-dominated systems are not necessarily locked in their frozen positions forever. They have transformative capacities that may lead to a higher responsiveness to popular demands. The Scandinavian welfare states are examples of countries that have undertaken this transformation.

DEMOCRACY AND ECONOMIC
DEVELOPMENT IN PERSPECTIVE

Drawing on the typologies of authoritarian and democratic systems presented in this chapter and the comparative considerations discussed, we can now derive some general conclusions regarding the possible trade-off between democracy, on the one hand, and economic development, on the other. First, there is not a one-to-one relationship between the form of regime (democratic or authoritarian) and development outcomes for the simple reason that different types of democratic and authoritarian regimes have different development capacities. If we compare the elite-dominated type of democracy with the authoritarian developmentalist regime, as was done in the India/China comparison, it is possible to argue that there is a trade-off between democracy and development because the authoritarian developmentalist regime performs better in development than the elite-dominated democracy does. This conclusion, however, is not strong enough to support the notion of a *general* trade-off between democracy and development; other types of authoritarian systems perform worse in economic development than the authoritarian developmentalist ones, and the democratic regimes might come out on top in comparisons with those systems.

Second, with regard to the relatively few authoritarian developmentalist systems that perform well in economic development, we need to demonstrate in precise terms how and to what extent the suspension of civil and political rights can be justified in order to promote economic development. For example, although it may well be that socialist authoritarianism in China provided the regime with a freedom of maneuver that paved the way for the radical redistribution of land to the benefit of the rural masses, the development benefits hardly justify a blanket trade-off between development and all types of civil and political rights. As one scholar has noted, such violations as "torture, disappearances, and arbitrary executions can almost always be eliminated with no costs to development; rights to nationality and to equality before the law would also seem to have very low development costs; due process is likely to be a bit more costly, but the burden seems bearable. . . . In other words, tradeoffs of civil and political rights must be selective, flexible, and rather specific if they are to be justified at all."[56] Therefore, even in those cases where the trade-off seems justified, it is necessary to examine which rights really require suspension in order to promote development.

We have stated that the theory of a general trade-off between democracy and development must be rejected. Yet rejection of that statement does not mean that democracy and economic development automatically go hand in hand, mutually reinforcing each other. Behind the rejected trade-off are other, equally serious dilemmas. First, there seem to be a fairly large number of both authoritarian *and* democratic systems that, for different reasons, do not perform well in terms of economic development. The ASEE regimes and the elite-oriented authoritarian growth regimes, together with the elite-dominated frozen democracies, seem to hold out few promises for a process of economic development that will benefit the large masses of poor people.

Second, with regard to the main types of democracies, there seems to be a trade-off between stability, on the one hand, and the capacity for promoting rapid economic development, on the other. The elite-dominated democracies by far hold the best prospects for stability, as the Latin American experiences illustrate; at the same time, elite dominance can often mean support for the status quo and little development progress. Mass-dominated democracies promise more rapid economic advance through reforms attacking vested elite interests, but instability and reversion to authoritarianism may be the result. It was argued earlier that there is a space between these extremes where democracy and economic development can go hand in hand. Democracies have transformative capacities, as the case of Costa Rica demonstrates; but not many of the present transitions toward democracy hold the promise of being able to strike the necessary balance between democratic stability and economic development.

DEMOCRACY AND HUMAN RIGHTS

Development is concerned not only with progress in material terms (food, housing, health service, education, and so forth); it also involves a nonmaterial aspect that has to do with human freedom, identity, and security.[57] The latter can be gathered under the umbrella of human rights, especially civil and political human rights.[58] They include such elements as the prohibition of torture, the right to a fair trial and to equal protection under the law, freedom from arbitrary arrest, freedom of movement and residence, and freedom of thought, conscience, and religion.

What is the relationship between democracy and human rights? Does democracy promote human rights? On first impression, the answers seem to be straightforward. The definition of political democracy given in Chapter 1 involved civil and political rights: freedom of expression, freedom of the press, freedom of association, and the right of political participation. If civil and political rights are part of the definition of democracy itself, then democracies, one would think, must promote those rights. Democracies may not always promote, for example, economic development, but at least they provide for basic civil and political rights.

One scholar has tried to sort out the relationship between political democracy as measured by Freedom House and the pattern of human rights violations based on information from the U.S. State Department. As shown in Table 3.4, the democratic ("free") systems respect rights to a much higher degree than the authoritarian ("not free") systems.

However, further scrutiny reveals problems at two points. First, the relationship between democracy and the promotion of human rights is not perfect. Many democracies promote the basic political freedoms associated with democracy while they violate other human rights. Such violations are monitored by Amnesty International. In recent years even the long-standing and consolidated democracy of Denmark has been mentioned in Amnesty's report on human rights violations (the case in question had to do with the state's violation of the right to humane treatment under detention for some visitors from developing countries). Therefore, if rights are defined in a very broad sense, even the most democratic countries might not fully provide all of them. This point is supported by data in the Human Freedom index constructed by United Nations Development Programme.[59] The index lists forty rights and freedoms, including social and economic equality for ethnic minorities, freedom for independent newspapers and book publishing, and freedom from capital punishment. It then ranks countries according to the extent to which they respect these forty different rights. None of the eighty-eight countries listed in 1985 observed all of the freedoms. Sweden and Denmark topped the list, with thirty-eight out of forty freedoms guaranteed to their people. They were followed by the Netherlands with thirty-seven, and Finland, New Zealand, and Austria with thirty-six. Some democracies had rather low scores, such as India (fourteen), Colombia (fourteen), Israel (nineteen), Spain (twenty-six), and Italy (twenty-nine). At the bottom of the list were Iraq (zero!), Libya (one), and China (two). Yet, although this information may cast some democracies in an unfavorable light, it does not

TABLE 3.4 Democracy and Human Rights, 1990: Percentage of States Committing Selected Violations

Human Rights Violations	Not Free	Free
Summary executions	11	2
Disappearances	56	20
Massacres	24	3
Arbitrary arrest	88	31
No fair or decent trial	86	23
Torture	84	25

Source: Based on Berto Jongman, "Why Some States Kill and Torture While Others Do Not," *PIOOM Newsletter and Progress Report* 3, no. 1 (1991): 9.

seem to break the general rule that democracies show higher respect for human rights than do authoritarian systems, even if this respect may not be complete.

But there is a second problem with the contention that democracy and human rights are two sides of the same coin. It has to do with the incompleteness of many of the transitions toward democracy. Many regimes are still restricted democracies in which there is also insufficient respect for civil and political rights.

In addition, some transitions provoke turbulence and instability, which can also have negative effects for human rights. In this context one scholar has emphasized that not only authoritarian rule but also the breakdown of authority involves major human rights violations.[60] The breakdown of authority means the weakening of the authority of a government (democratic or authoritarian) to the point that it is on the verge of losing power or to the point that it must employ harsh means to hold on to power.[61] Thus, a high violation of human rights can be seen in crisis-ridden transitions toward democracy, where weak civilian goverments are struggling to stay in authority. In other words, the political freedoms (competition, participation) may indicate fairly democratic conditions, but the breakdown of authority leads to a high degree of human rights violation. Many countries fall into this category, including Colombia, El Salvador, Paraguay, Peru, Bulgaria, Nicaragua, Panama, the Philippines, Turkey, and Sri Lanka.

In summary, democracies as a rule give higher respect to human rights in general than authoritarian regimes do. When countries are viewed against a very comprehensive list of human rights, it appears that many democracies violate some of them. Furthermore, transitions toward democracy may lead to breakdowns of authority, which can result in even higher human rights violations than would be the case under stable authoritarian conditions. Thus, stable and consolidated democracy correlates with a high respect for human rights in general, but the move toward democracy and the early phases of democratic opening that characterize the majority of the current transitions can produce situations with a high degree of human rights violation.

CONCLUSION

This chapter opened by asking whether democracy is really worth the trouble and by asking if it paves the way for improvements in spheres of life other than those narrowly connected with political freedoms. A number of reasons were given for an affirmative answer to both questions. Not only is democracy a value in itself, but it helps promote other civil and political rights. Furthermore, although democracies may not invariably perform better than authoritarian systems in terms of economic development, the notion of a general trade-off between democracy and development was rejected. Most of the authoritarian systems are oppressive, and they are also poor performers in terms of economic development.

At the same time, transitions toward democracy do not guarantee a promised land of rapid economic development and a vastly improved human rights situation. The elite-dominated frozen democracies seem to hold out few promises for a process of economic development that would benefit the large groups of poor people. The transitions themselves can lead to situations of instability and the breakdown of authority that involve higher human rights violation than before. The promise of democracy is not that of automatic improvement in areas of life that are not narrowly connected with political freedoms; it is the creation of a window of opportunity, a political framework where groups struggling for development and human rights have better possibilities than before for organizing and expressing their demands. Democracy offers the opportunities; it does not offer guarantees of success.

FOUR

□ □ □

International Consequences of Democracy: Peace and Cooperation?

Will the spread of democracy mean the end of war? Can we look forward to a more peaceful world focused on cooperation toward mutual gain instead of conflict and violence? This chapter examines the consequences for international relations of the spread of democracy. Democracy is again treated as the independent variable; the aim is to discover its effects on relations between states and on the nature of the international system.

The scholarly debate contains widely diverging views. One school of thought expects profoundly positive consequences from the spread of democracy; another completely rejects the importance of democracy for international relations. We shall see that these seemingly contrasting views are not entirely incompatible, but first the main arguments in the theoretical debate must be presented.

THE DEBATE ON DEMOCRACY AND PEACE

The argument that democracy is an important force for peace has as its most forceful advocate the German philosopher Immanuel Kant. In his essay "Perpetual Peace," which was published in 1795, Kant developed his argument in several stages.[1] First, he pointed to a natural tendency for states to organize in the form of liberal republics because that system of rule bestows legitimacy on the political leaders and promotes popular support for the state, making it well suited to face foreign threats. In other words, states not organized as liberal republics will tend to be unsuccessful.

A "liberal republic" corresponds roughly to what is called a political democracy in this book. Thus, the establishment of democracies in the world is a natural tendency according to Kant, although there may be many setbacks. Once established, democracies will lead to peaceful relations because democratic governments are controlled by the citizens and therefore will not enter into violent conflict that may subject the citizens to bloodshed and war. In Kant's words,

> If the consent of the citizens is required in order to decide that war should be declared . . . nothing is more natural than that they would be very cautious in commencing such a poor game, decreeing for themselves all the calamities of war. Among the latter would be: having to fight, having to pay the costs of war from their own resources, having painfully to repair the devastation war leaves behind, and, to fill up the measure of evils, load themselves with heavy national debt that would embitter peace itself and that can never be liquidated on account of constant wars in the future.[2]

One of the great social scientists of the twentieth century, Joseph Schumpeter, has also supported the notion of peaceful democracies. His reasoning is similar to Kant's. Schumpeter has argued that imperialist expansion and war benefit only a minority of profiteers, arms producers, and members of the military establishment. Therefore, "no democracy would pursue a minority interest and tolerate the high costs of imperialism."[3]

There is some empirical support for these views. A study by R. J. Rummel looked at libertarian states (meaning those emphasizing political and economic freedom) and contrasted the involvement of these "free" states in conflict at or above the level of economic sanctions with that of "nonfree" and "partly free" states. The conclusion was that of the violence during the period 1976 to 1980, only 24 percent of the free states were involved, compared with 26 percent of the partly free and 61 percent of the nonfree states. In other words, the more libertarian a state, the less it is involved in foreign violence. Rummel further claimed that a number of previous studies support this conclusion.[4]

However, several recent studies have rejected the idea that democracies are more peaceful than other regimes. Melvin Small and J. David Singer studied wars between 1816 and 1965 and found no significant differences between democracies and other regimes in terms of frequency of war involvement. This conclusion was supported by Steve Chan in his study of wars between 1816 and 1980; it was also supported by Erich Weede's study of war involvement between 1960 and 1980. It should be noted that Rummel's study lends itself to criticism because it covers only the period 1976 to 1980. The studies based on longer periods of observation deserve more credibility. In addition, Rummel's way of surveying the literature can be criticized.[5] Indeed, there is overwhelming consensus among scholars that democracies have gone to war as often as have other types of regimes.

But the debate does not end there because the empirical studies have come up with a finding that revives the optimists' hopes for democracy as a road to peace. Although democracies are as war-prone as other types of regimes, democracies do not fight one another: *"Even though liberal states have become involved in numerous wars with nonliberal states, constitutionally secure liberal states have yet to engage in war with each other."*[6] The empirical investigations provide substantial support for this claim. The observation was first emphasized by Dean Babst in 1964, and it has been confirmed in numerous studies since then.[7] Indeed, one scholar has called the assertion that democracies do not fight each other "one of the strongest nontrivial or nontautological statements that can be made about international relations."[8]

This finding, then, is the basis of the present optimism among many scholars and policymakers. Their reasoning goes as follows: The number of democracies in the world has increased rapidly in recent years and democracies do not fight one another; therefore, we can look forward to a much more peaceful world with international relations characterized by cooperation instead of conflict. If their assertion is true, it seems that profound revision is also needed of the dominant theoretical paradigm in international relations, namely **realism.** (Realism, in this context, is a theoretical perspective on international relations that purports to analyze the world as it really is, not as it ought to be. According to this perspective, conflict in the real world is imminent due to forces inherent in human nature and due to the way the world's populations have chosen to organize in the form of independent, sovereign states that respect no authority outside or above themselves.) With realism, the major characteristic of the international system is the lack of authority above the sovereign nation-states, which is what makes the system an unsafe anarchy where states constantly have to fear violent conflict with other states. If we are to believe that democracies do not fight one another, then a substantial modification of the notion of anarchy leading to violent conflict is called for.

Before we move on with these issues, however, it is helpful to return to Kant. Kant was well aware that democracy would lead not to the total abolishment of war, but only to peace between democracies. His point of departure was outlined earlier: There are constitutional mechanisms in democracies that restrain them from going to war because of the burdens war imposes on the population. Yet these restraints are effective only in relations with other democracies. Why only there? Kant gave two reasons—one moral, the other economic. The moral reason has to do with the common values of legitimate rights held by democracies and with the mutual respect and understanding between democracies. These bonds lead to what Kant called a **pacific union,** which is not a signed treaty but a zone of peace based on the common moral foundation of the democracies (see Fig. 4.1). Peaceful ways of solving domestic conflicts are seen as morally superior to violent behavior, and this view is transferred to international relations between democracies. The beginning of cooperation starts a virtuous circle of increasing cooperation: "As culture grows and men gradually move towards greater agreement over their principles, [these agreed-upon principles] lead to mutual understanding and peace."[9] The transparency of democracies is important for the whole process. Freedom of expression and free communication help establish mutual understanding internationally and help assure that political representatives act in accordance with citizens' views domestically.

The economic reason is based on the benefits from international trade and investment. In the pacific union it is possible to focus on what Kant called "the spirit of commerce," the possibility for mutual gain for those involved in international economic cooperation. The development of economic interdependence which occurs when notions of autarky (self-sufficiency) are set aside and the pursuit of mutual economic gain is given priority, further strengthens the pacific union.

In sum, there are three elements behind Kant's claim that democracy leads to peace. The first is the mere existence of democracies, with their culture of peaceful conflict resolution. Second, the democracies hold common moral values, and the bonds they forge because of these values lead to the formation of a pacific union. Finally, the pacific union is strengthened through economic cooperation and interdependence. All three elements are necessary in order to make the connection between democracy and peace. But it is important to bear in mind that democracies continue to go to war with nondemocratic regimes, with whom they have no common moral foundation. Between the democracies themselves, peace is predicated upon the existence of a pacific union with ties of economic interdependence. These elements do not come about automatically; they are formed in a process in which the early results of cooperation lead to further cooperative efforts. There can be reversals, a backsliding toward the use of violence, warned Kant, but ultimately the pacific union will expand and provide perpetual peace among all democratic nations. As Kant has also argued for the victory of democracy as the superior form of state, it follows that in the end peace will prevail among all nations.

Such is the positive vision formulated by Kant. In order to evaluate its prospects in relation to the current processes of democratization, it is nec-

1. **Democratic norms of** **peaceful resolution of conflict**
2. **Peaceful relations among** **democratic states** **based on a common moral foundation**
3. **Economic cooperation among democracies;** **ties of interdependence**

FIGURE 4.1   Elements of Kant's pacific union among democracies

essary to further examine each of the elements of Kant's vision in a contemporary context. We will look first at the domestic scene and then at international relations.

THE DOMESTIC SCENE: FOREIGN POLICY IN DEMOCRACIES

Democracies show restraint in their relations with other democracies but not with nondemocratic regimes. Why the possible belligerence toward the latter? Although relations between the states within the pacific union are characterized by cooperation, outside the pacific union the power struggle between states for security, resources, and prestige continues; there, the realist picture of an international system characterized by anarchy applies. Democracies have reasons to be skeptical in their relations with governments that cannot claim to represent their peoples. As one observer has written, "Because nonliberal governments are in a state of aggression with their own people, their foreign relations become for liberal governments deeply suspect. In short, fellow liberals benefit from a presumption of amity; nonliberals suffer from a presumption of enmity."[10] War as the outcome of conflict is always a possibility under these circumstances.

Further, democratic regimes can go to war for crusade reasons—that is, in order to promote democratic values in new areas. In this sense, "The very constitutional restraint, shared commercial interests, and international respect for individual rights that promote peace among liberal societies can exacerbate conflicts in relations between liberal and non-liberal societies."[11] This view helps explain the liberal democratic vigilance toward nondemocratic areas, especially the self-imposed "white man's burden" of bringing civilized government and order to the colonies. Obviously, this view is very ethnocentric: Western civilization is seen as vastly superior to the "barbarian" ways of the indigenous peoples of the colonies; thus, it is only reasonable that the colonies are being subjected to Western leadership, if necessary by force. Later, the liberation movements of the colonies turned the argument against their Western masters: Self-government, so ran their claim, is a legitimate right according to democratic principles. This counterargument led many colonial masters to lose faith in their right to rule and provided an important impetus to the process of decolonization.[12]

Finally, it can be argued that democracy introduces an element of irrationality to foreign policy-making. Instead of using prudence in international relations, democracies may succumb to whims of public opinion or moods of possible belligerence or appeasement that may result in confused, unwise policies. Walter Lippmann argued that public opinion has forced governments "to be too late with too little, or too long with too much, too pacifist in peace and too bellicose in war, too neutralist or appeasing in negotiation or too transient."[13]

This irrationality in foreign policy-making introduces a dilemma in the way democracies conduct foreign affairs: The democratic framework of government is a cornerstone of the pacific union, but at the same time democracy can lead to imprudent, adventurous policies toward nondemocratic regimes. Removing this irrationality from policy-making would seem to require an executive more unrestrained from the representative legislature than current executives are, but change in that direction would, in turn, threaten the basis for the pacific union. In other words, "completely resolving liberal dilemmas may not be possible without threatening liberal success."[14]

It is against the background of this dilemma that a long-standing debate is taking place about the proper amount of public influence on foreign policy in democracies. There are two main positions. On one side, there are those who agree with John Locke's argument that foreign policy should be left to the experts. He was supported in this view by Alexis de Tocqueville, who feared that foreign policy subjected to a democratic process would lead to poor results. A democracy, said Tocqueville in 1835, is "unable to regulate the details of an important undertaking, to persevere in a design, and to work out its execution in the presence of serious obstacles. It cannot combine its measures with secrecy, and will not await their consequences with patience."[15]

On the other side are supporters of the argument that a genuine democratic process in foreign policy will help secure peace. It was set forth by a British member of Parliament, Arthur Ponsonby, in 1915, following the outbreak of World War I, which Ponsonby considered a demonstration of the failure of the elite model of decision-making:

> When a small number of statesmen, conducting the intercourse of nations in secrecy, have to confess their inability to preserve good relations, it is not an extravagant proposal to suggest that their isolated action should be supplemented and reinforced by the intelligent and well-informed assistance of the peoples themselves.[16]

These views about how much public democratic influence there ought to be in foreign policy are normative ones. What is the actual situation in the real world? There is no straightforward answer. Later in this section some empirical studies of the issue will be described, but first the argument concerning a possible incompatibility between democracy and the conduct of foreign policy will be analyzed. One author listed three points in support of the argument that democracy and foreign policy are incompatible.[17] The first concerns the conditions involved in bargaining with outsiders. Democratic openness and the internal disunity associated with democracy can lead to poor results in a process of bargaining. Furthermore, it seems wise to leave such negotiations in the hands of professionals, who are the experts in bargaining. There is also the need for secrecy, which is difficult to meet if foreign affairs are subjected to normal democratic debates and procedures.

The second point concerns the stakes involved in foreign policy. Foreign policy concerns the security of the nation, its survival. Therefore, citizens cannot afford, so runs the argument, to put such issues to open and free debates. It is critically important that they unite behind their leaders; opposition under such circumstances is not only disloyal, it may imperil the safety of the nation.

Finally, there is the issue of remoteness. Foreign affairs are far removed from the bread-and-butter issues that dominate domestic politics, with their clear implications for individual citizens. It is not that foreign policy is unimportant. It is simply that it is much more difficult for ordinary citizens to see the consequences that specific foreign policy options will have on their lives than it is for them to anticipate the outcome of domestic policies. It follows from this argument that foreign affairs should play an unobtrusive role in the political deliberations of the voters. The majority of voters feel that such matters can be left to the experts.[18]

An argument made against these three points is that they fail to differentiate between the various issue areas of foreign affairs. A common distinction is between the high politics of national security and the low politics of other foreign policy areas, such as those concerned with trade, finance, investment, the environment, and a host of other issues. It is clear that the points concerning the incompatibility between democracy and foreign policy pertain to the area of high politics rather than to the area of low politics.[19] But even in the area of national security, it can be said that from a democratic viewpoint it is simply unacceptable to leave issues isolated from the normal mechanisms of democracy. This normative debate will not be pursued further here. In what follows, I shall focus on some empirical investigations concerning the actual degree of democratic influence on the high-politics area of foreign affairs.

One problem facing such investigations is the difficulty in determining what is actually meant in operational terms by more democracy and less democracy in foreign affairs. In most cases, focus is on the role of public opinion. To what extent does public opinion influence the high-politics area of foreign policy? A recent study by Thomas Risse-Kappen compared the role of public opinion in the various responses of four countries—the United States, France, Germany, and Japan—to changes in Soviet foreign policy from Leonid Brezhnev (late 1970s) to Mikhail Gorbachev (late 1980s).[20] His conclusion was that mass public opinion does matter in each country; policymakers in liberal democracies do not decide against an overwhelming public consensus. However, the author went on to say that "there are discernible limits to the impact of the general public on foreign and security policies. Rarely does general public opinion directly affect policy decisions or the implementation of specific policies."[21] He argued that the major impact of the public is indirect, through its influence on elite groups. The elites have the final say, but elite groups whose opinions are in line with public preferences are likely to prevail. Finally, Risse-Kappen contended that variations in domestic structures in the four countries can explain the differences in policy outcomes that were sometimes seen even when there were similar public attitudes and similar influences from the international environment. Domestic structures encompass three elements: the degree of centralization of political institutions, the degree of state dominance over policy networks, and the degree of polarization between groups in society.

Other studies confirm the view that public opinion does matter in foreign affairs, albeit not in a direct manner but through the influence on elite groups. In the words of Bruce Russett and Harvey Starr, public opinion affects policy primarily

by setting broad limits of constraint and identifying a range of policies within which decision makers must choose if they are not to face retaliation in competitive elections. These constraints are clearly quite broad, though they are likely to be felt more intensely the closer a particular decision time is to a national election. Of course, this still begs the question about how strongly mass opinion is itself merely shaped or controlled by elites who command public attention and the mass media.[22]

What light do these studies shed on the debate concerning the domestic aspect of democracy and peace? We started with the straightforward assertion by Kant that democracies will be peaceful because citizens will see to it that governments stay out of bloodshed and war. It seems that the link between the views of citizens and the outcomes in terms of foreign policy decisions is much more indirect, blurred, and complex than indicated by Kant. The restraint shown by democracies in their relations with other democracies is not directly attributable to the influence of peace-loving citizens on the decisionmakers.

Thus, it appears necessary to look for other factors that can help explain peace between democracies. One possibility that is consistent with Kant's general framework is that democracy promotes norms and expectations among citizens as well as among policymakers that support the peaceful resolution of conflicts with other democracies. Here, the decisive element is not the constraining influence of citizens on elites; it is the democratic political culture, which holds that "states have the right to be free from foreign intervention. Since morally autonomous citizens hold rights to liberty, the states that democratically represent them have the right to exercise political independence. Mutual respect for these rights then becomes the touchstone of international liberal theory."[23] This democratic political culture rules out ideological motives for democracies to act in expansionist ways against one another and makes it extremely difficult for democratic elites to legitimate wars against other democracies.[24]

Furthermore, democracy helps remove some of the important reasons for expansionism and the quest for domination that characterized regimes before the advent of democracy. External belligerence could flow from the desire of nondemocratic rulers to bolster their domestic positions; it could also stem from the rulers' quests for recognition, not only from their own subordinates but from other states as well.[25] In democracies, the recognition of leaders rests on a qualitatively different foundation. Democratic regimes may still go to war against states that they regard as illegitimate, but the democratic political culture makes it very difficult for them to wage war on regimes that are based on a democratic legitimacy.

The core of the matter is that democratic norms of peaceful conflict resolution and democratic norms recognizing other peoples' right to self-determination introduce an element of restraint or caution in the way in which democracies conduct international relations. These domestic elements of the democratic political culture help explain the peaceful relations between democracies. In a moment we will discuss the international dimension, but first it is useful to consider this domestic element in relation to the current processes of democratization.

*   *   *

We have made the argument that the peaceful behavior of democracies is predicated upon the existence of a democratic culture with well-defined norms concerning the peaceful resolution of conflict and the right of others to self-determination. If we wish to examine the prospects for a more peaceful world, a relevant question is therefore whether such a peaceful democratic culture can be found in the large number of democracies that are currently emerging.

In Chapter 2 it was demonstrated that the transition from a nondemocratic to a democratic form of regime is a long and complex process involving several overlapping phases. Three such phases were identified: the preparatory phase, characterized by a political struggle leading to the breakdown of the nondemocratic regime; the decision phase, where clear-cut elements of a democratic order are established; and, finally, the consolidation phase, where the new democracy is further developed and where democratic practices eventually become an established part of the political culture.

It appears from this description that the emergence of a democratic culture is a long-term process that occurs as part of the consolidation phase. During this phase, democracy begins to be seen as "the only game in town" and both political actors and the population come to view democratic practices as the right and natural order of things. It was argued in Chapter 2 that the new democracies cannot be seen as consolidated; on the contrary, they were described as restricted, frail, and unconsolidated.

It follows that the norms of a democratic culture for the peaceful resolution of conflict have not yet become characteristics of the new democracies. A closer look at some of the recent transitions confirms this view. In Latin America, the military continues to be a dominant player in several countries. In some of them, domestic conflict has resulted in a breakdown of authority accompanied by a high level of domestic violence. In others, the rule of law has not yet been applied to the military, which continues to circumvent the democratic process. In Africa, the corrupt practices of personal rule remain strong in spite of the democratic openings. In Eastern Europe, a civil society is only beginning to emerge, and the rule of law is challenged by the *nomenklatura,* who have retained a good deal of power. In short, a democratic culture is beginning to emerge in the new democracies, but it is highly disputable whether this culture has grown strong enough to constitute the domestic basis for peaceful relations between democracies.

It is difficult to come up with a very definite conclusion in this area because we do not know the precise extent to which a democratic culture has to be developed in order to provide the necessary basis for peaceful relations. Michael Doyle has indicated that a democratic culture (which he called "the pacifying effects of liberalism") has to be deeply ingrained before it can form the basis for peaceful relations. Bruce Russett has emphasized that "it is not clear what threshold of democratic norms and practices must be crossed to achieve peace."[26]

With the continuing high levels of domestic violence in several Latin American and African countries, there are good reasons to be pessimistic. Perhaps the best one can say is that a substantial number of countries are moving in the right direction for the moment—that is, they are moving in the direction of a stronger democratic culture. But it will certainly take some time before democratic culture is deeply ingrained, and there are no guarantees against setbacks or reversals.

These considerations concern only the domestic basis for the pacific union envisaged by Kant. The possible zone of peace between democracies also contains an international dimension, which is the theme of the following section.

INTERNATIONAL RELATIONS: COOPERATION BETWEEN DEMOCRACIES

The international dimension of Kant's vision of peace between democracies is dependent on two related elements, one moral, the other economic. I shall treat them separately in the sections that follow.

Moral Aspects of Cooperation Among Democracies

According to Kant, the moral element that helps form the framework for peaceful relations between democratic states is based on the common principles of cooperation, mutual respect, and understanding. Such principles were indeed emerging in Europe in the early nineteenth century. It was a period during which the major European powers were expanding their territories in an attempt to achieve worldwide dominance, but it was also a time during which they worked out rules of behavior among themselves that can be seen as an important step toward the common standards envisaged by Kant.

The mutual understanding between the European powers rested on two basic principles: the recognition of the absolute sovereignty of states and the treatment of states as juridically equal.[27] On this basis, four principles came to form the framework for relations between the European states. The first was the balance of power, which has been called a systematic practice of anti-hegemonialism. The basic idea was that any state could be prevented from growing too powerful relative to the others through the shifting of alliances away from it, thereby hindering its rise to dominance. The second was the codification of a set of practices of interaction among states in order to form a body of international law. The third was the use of congresses for the purpose of settling the affairs of the European states; at the congresses, the states passed treaties to conclude wars and made additional agreements on general rules. The most important congresses were in Westphalia in 1648, in Utrecht in 1713, and in Vienna in 1815. The fourth was diplomatic dialogue. The application of the first three principles—balance of power, international law, and congresses—took place through diplomatic dialogue. Taken together the four principles formed the basis of a consensus among the European states. As one observer stated, "In the eighteenth century Europe came to be regarded as a single diplomatic commonwealth made up of a number of independent states 'resembling each other in their manners, religion and degree of social improvement,' or in other words operating within the framework of a common culture."[28]

It is important to emphasize that the European states did not form the full-fledged pacific union envisaged by Kant. The participating states were by no means full democracies, and the agreed-upon standards of behavior did not entirely rule out war between them. But Kant saw the pacific union as a long-term project, and many scholars view the standards of cooperation and common culture among the European states as an important first step. In recent scholarship, these relations between the European states have been looked upon as the foundation for an **international society.** Hedley Bull and Adam Watson defined an international society as

> a group of states (or more generally, a group of independent political communities) which not merely form a system, in the sense that the behavior of each is a necessary factor in the calculations of the others, but also have established by dialogue and consent common rules and institutions for the conduct of their relations, and recognize their common interest in maintaining these arrangements.[29]

If the relations between European states in the eighteenth and nineteenth centuries form the beginning of an international society, what is the present status of the international society? There is no uniform agreement about the common understanding that currently exists between the states in the world. A recent analysis by Barry Buzan argues that the present international society is in fairly good shape by historical standards. A main reason for its status is the fact that the sovereign territorial state is nearly universally accepted as the fundamental unit of political legitimacy: "The fundamental organizing principle of sovereign states treating each other as juridical equals reigns almost unchallenged as the basic political norm of the system."[30] On this basis, diplomacy and international law continue to provide a framework for cooperative behavior.

Kant regarded free communication as an important means of establishing a common international understanding, but he could hardly have foreseen the extent to which television and other mass media have, in the words of one observer, "brought the entire world to the instant attention of any listener."[31] The possibilities for instantly relaying information about events that occur anywhere in the world have dramatically improved the conditions for mutual insight and understanding among peoples and leaders alike. Some scholars speculate that a new global culture is emerging on the basis of these and related developments.[32] It is much easier to agree with their forecasts now than only a few years ago. The collapse of the totalitarian regimes and planned economies in Eastern Europe seems to have paved the way for a much stronger adherence to the norms of liberal capitalism—that is, to the combination of political democracy and a market economy. As was stressed in Chapter 1, systems based on these principles are not alike; they can take many different forms. But there appears to be a much higher consensus now regarding the adoption of the core features of liberal capitalism and the rejection of the two radical alternatives: fascism, on the one hand, and totalitarian communism, on the other.[33]

How do these developments relate to the prospects for peaceful relations among democracies that are bound by a common understanding? Following Kant's logic, we would expect that the general trends described here would be especially strong in the relationships between democracies with a common moral foundation. Consequently, we should expect norms to have developed between the democracies (especially the consolidated ones) that secure their devotion to the peaceful resolution of conflict.

This seems to be the case when we look at the relations among the well-established democracies in the industrialized West (including Japan). Western Europe, North America, Japan, Australia, and New Zealand have developed into a security community, which means that they constitute a group of states that do not prepare for, expect, or fear the use of military force in their relations with one another.[34] Several other factors have been important in the development of this security community, including economic cooperation and interdependence (on which I shall have more to say in a moment) and the cooperation between the Western powers in the alliance against the Eastern bloc. Yet, according to Kant's reasoning, the decisive element in the development of a security community between the partners in the Western alliance would not be the negative characteristic of a common enemy, but the positive shared foundation of democracy and cooperation. This view helps explain why violent hostilities could break out between the NATO partners Turkey and Greece in a period during which they were both governed by military dictatorships.[35]

However, the peaceful relations between the Western industrialized democracies have not been extended in equal measure to the democracies in the developing world. Relations between the United States and some democracies in Latin America provide an illustration. On a rhetorical level, the U.S. posture has been in perfect harmony with Kant's view of democracies seeking to promote democratic values in relations with other countries ever since Woodrow Wilson set forth the rules for his administration's relationship with Latin America:

> We hold, as I am sure all thoughtful leaders of republican government everywhere hold, that just government rests always upon the consent of the governed, and that there can be no freedom without order based upon law and upon the public conscience and approval. We shall look to make these principles the basis of mutual intercourse, respect and helpfulness between our sister republics and ourselves.[36]

In more recent times as well, the promotion of democratic values has been formulated as a guiding principle for U.S. policies. Yet both now and in the past, other elements of perceived national interest have competed with the goal of promoting democracy. Since 1945, an important issue has been the struggle against communism and Soviet influence in Latin America; another concern has been the protection of U.S. economic interests in the region. Both of these issues have been allowed to override concerns for the promotion of democracy on several occasions. A situation that occurred in the Dominican Republic in the early 1960s provides an instructive example. At that time a democratically elected leadership under Juán Bosch set out to promote economic development through nationalist economic policies that went against some American economic interests in the country. When Bosch faced the prospect of a military coup, Washington decided to opt for the authoritarian military dictatorship. John F. Kennedy formulated the alternatives as follows: "There are three possibilities, in descending order of preference, a decent democratic regime, a continuation of the Trujillo regime [a military dictatorship], or a Castro regime. We ought to aim at the first, but we can't really renounce the second until we are sure we can avoid the third."[37] Thus, fearing that the democratic Bosch regime would develop into a Castro regime, the United States found it safest to back a military dictatorship. This action aided the struggle against communism and protected U.S. economic interests, but it hardly promoted democracy or economic welfare policies in the Dominican Republic.

A situation in Chile provides another example. In 1970, Chile already had a record as one of the most stable and long-lasting democracies in Latin America. The elections in 1970 brought Salvador Allende, a candidate backed by a left-wing Popular Unity coalition, to power. His economic policies aimed at redistributive reforms went against vested elite interests, including U.S. economic interests in Chile. Washington had attempted to prevent Allende's election through the support of rival candidates; after his election the United States became actively involved in supporting the opposition in the political parties, the Chilean military, and elsewhere.[38] The confrontation culminated in the military coup led by Augusto Pinochet in 1973, which paved the way for more than fifteen years of harsh military dictatorship in Chile.

It is not that the United States went to war with Allende's Chile; in that sense, Kant has not been disproved. Yet, as the events in Central America in the 1980s show, covert involvement with economic, military, and expert support for opposition forces can develop to a point where the distinction between such activities and open war becomes fairly academic.[39]

In any case, these and other examples are hardly evidence of Kant's expectation about democracies developing peaceful relations based on a common understanding and a shared moral foundation. Why do we see these hostile developments in relations between democracies? The reason for the hostilities in the examples given in this section are straightforward: The United States turns against some democracies because it fears that they will hurt U.S. economic interests or they will develop into communist regimes, which threaten U.S. security, or they will do both. Thus, not every kind of democracy is smoothly integrated in the pacific union envisaged by Kant; and it appears that those that are met with enmity instead of amity are the mass-dominated democracies, defined in Chapter 2 as regimes in which mass actors have gained the upper hand and push for reforms from below, attacking the power and privilege of the elites.

This situation creates two related dilemmas, one concerning the prospects for economic development and welfare improvement and the other the prospects for the peace between democracies. If international support (that is, support from the dominant countries in the developed world) is forthcoming only to the elite-dominated democracies, the possibilities for welfare improvement for the poor as a result of the democratic transitions may be very limited, as was argued in some detail in Chapter 3. And the resulting lack of welfare progress may threaten the prospects for the pacific union. As one scholar has argued, "Increasing worldwide adherence to democratic political norms and practices cannot alone bear all the weight of sustaining peace. Greater prosperity and economic justice, especially in the third world, must also bear a major part."[40] In short, the problem is that the necessary welfare progress may not be forthcoming when support is given only to the elite-dominated democracies, and the lack of welfare progress that results threatens not only economic improvement but also the possibilities for a pacific union.

How will relations between the dominant democracies in the North and the democracies in the South develop after the end of the cold war? It is too early to give a firm answer. On the one hand, there is basis for optimism: Because Soviet communism is no longer a threat, the dominant liberal democracies led by the United States ought to be able to accept the mass-dominated democracies in the South with more ease than before. The latter can no longer be seen as prospective allies of a world communist movement because such a movement no longer exists. On the other hand, the record to date supports a more pessimistic view. The dominant liberal democracies, as well as the international organizations they lead, such as the International Monetary Fund and the World Bank, have made their provision of aid dependent on the new democracies' promotion of strictly liberal principles, such as privatizations, public sector cutbacks, free market policies, and the protection of private property.[41] In addition, U.S. policies toward Central America, for example, have not changed significantly since the end of the cold war.

What about the new democracies in Eastern Europe? Even though the preferences of the leading Western democracies are for clearly liberal democratic systems in Eastern Europe, the scenario of Western support for an "East European Trujillo" is not likely. The countries in Eastern Europe share a common past with Western Europe and are in the process of reviving old relationships and building new ones. Two of the East European countries, Hungary and Czechoslovakia, have joined the Council of Europe, whose very foundation is the recognition of common moral values of personal freedom, political independence, democracy, and the rule of law. Through the context of the Conference on Security and Cooperation in Europe (CSCE), all the East European countries including the Soviet Union have expressed their commitment to basic democratic values and the peaceful resolution of conflict. If the process of democratization proceeds successfully, there is reason to believe that most of the East European countries can become full members of the security community that has developed in Western Europe. Leading politicians in both Hungary and Czechoslovakia have already expressed the wish that their countries become full members of the North Atlantic Treaty Organization (NATO). In the words of Czech foreign minister Jiří Dienstbier: "The only thing wrong with NATO is that we don't belong to it." The future may well see the North Atlantic Treaty Organization transformed into a Democratic Europe Treaty Organization.[42]

In this section we have discussed Kant's vision of peaceful cooperation between democracies based on their common moral foundation. It was argued that such cooperation has indeed developed among the consolidated democracies of the North. In regard to relations with democracies in the Third World, the picture is less clear. Mass-dominated democracies there are seen as a threat to U.S. economic and security interests. They are met with enmity rather than amity. Even if the result has not been open war, this enmity poses a clear threat to the prospects for a pacific union among democracies. The East European countries, however, appear to have good prospects for joining a larger European security community.

Economic Cooperation Between Democracies

The final element upon which Kant's pacific union among democracies rests is economic cooperation. When countries focus on the spirit of commerce, they develop mutually beneficial ties of trade and investment as well as other economic relations. These ties, in turn, strengthen the bonds of peace among them.

The flow of goods and money, as well as of people, messages, and other forms of intercourse between countries, has indeed increased by leaps and bounds since the time of Kant's writing. As early as in 1975, one scholar argued that "recent decades reveal a general tendency for many forms of human interconnectedness across national boundaries to be doubling every ten years."[43] World trade went from $77 billion in 1953 to $2,694 billion in 1988, and trade has increased much faster than has economic growth. International financial flows have grown even faster than trade; for example, the London Eurodollar market, which borrows and lends dollars outside of the United States, turns over $300 billion each working day, which comes to $75 trillion a year.[44]

According to Kant's reasoning, economic exchange should be especially well developed among democracies. This premise also appears to hold true when we look at the Western industrialized democracies, but it is clear that other factors, such as the size of the national economy, the level of economic development, and the nature of economic policies, may play an even larger role than the presence of democracy in determining levels of economic intercourse.[45] Thus, a country with a large national economy, like the United States or India, has a relatively smaller share of its total economic activity crossing its borders than countries with small economies, like Costa Rica and Denmark. Countries with high levels of economic development, like Japan and Sweden, have much greater external trade than countries with low levels of development, such as Nepal and Bangladesh. Finally, countries with development policies aimed at the international market, for example, Taiwan and the Netherlands, have greater levels of external activity than countries with more inward strategies, such as China and North Korea.

In any case, there is a high degree of mutual economic dependence, or economic interdependence, among the Western industrialized democracies in Europe, North America, Japan, Australia, and New Zealand. These countries not only meet the third of Kant's conditions for a pacific union, economic cooperation, but also the other two discussed earlier, namely a developed democratic culture with norms of peaceful conflict resolution and a common moral understanding cultivated on this basis. They constitute a **security community,** which can be described as a contemporary version of Kant's pacific union. Karl Deutsch defined a security community as follows:

> A *security community* is a group of people which has become 'integrated'. By *integration* we mean the attainment, within a territory, of a *'sense of community'* and of institutions and practices strong enough and widespread enough to assure . . . dependable expectations of 'peaceful change' among its population. By sense of community we mean a belief . . . that common social problems must and can be resolved by processes of 'peaceful change'.[46]

In other words, although there may be problems within security communities that require change, and there may also be economic and other areas of conflict between the members, the groups within the security communities are determined to promote change and solve conflicts through peaceful means, without using threats of force.

It is more difficult to gauge the prospects for economic cooperation in Eastern Europe. On the one hand, as argued in Chapter 2, there is reason to be pessimistic concerning the possibilities for rapid economic transformation and world market integration of Eastern Europe. On the other hand, economic aid from the West to facilitate the economic changes appears to be forthcoming, and leading decisionmakers in the European Community foresee the admission of at least some East European countries to that organization by the end of the 1990s. The countries that are going to be admitted first are also those with the highest level of economic development: Czechoslovakia and Hungary. Their membership will help them develop ties of economic cooperation, which will strengthen their position in a European security community. In contrast, the less developed East European countries with looser ties to the Community will have more of a dependent "South status" in the realm of economic relations.

Let me now focus on North-South relations. There have not been many stable democracies in the South, and even the relatively few countries that are stable democracies have not experienced mutually rewarding economic relationships with the democracies in the North. North-South relations are characterized by unilateral dependence of the South on the North, not by mutually beneficial interdependence. Heeding the liberal advice of integrating in the international division of labor has produced mixed results in the South. The countries' dependence on exports of raw materials and agricultural products combined with the dominant presence of transnational corporations from the North in their domestic markets has not convinced the South about the mutually beneficial effects of economic exchange. In fact, some of the most successful countries of the South—including South Korea and Taiwan, the two most successful newly industrializing countries (NICs)—have used rather unliberal strategies of protection from the world market and have promoted a high degree of state intervention in the economy in order to get their economic development processes under way.[47]

For many years, radical theorists of development advised countries in the South to opt out of the international division of labor and look instead to economic self-reliance combined with cooperation among the poor countries themselves.[48] Today, most theorists advise the countries to find an optimal combination of integration in the world market and self-reliance. Unfortunately, they make these recommendations at a time when the problem of foreign debt is more serious than ever for many countries and the export market for typical southern products, such as raw materials and agricultural products, is stagnant or shrinking.[49]

Furthermore, the countries of the South are not equal members of the Bretton Woods system, the organizational system created at the end of World War II to coordinate economic cooperation and development; and the two most important organizations from the South's point of view, the IMF and the World Bank, are dominated by the leading democracies of the North. As one scholar has said, "Although power is unequally distributed in the West, all members have access to both formal and informal management systems. In North-South relations, in contrast, there is no well-developed system with access for all. The South has been regularly excluded from the formal and informal processes of system management. North-South relations are controlled by the North as a subsidiary of the Western system."[50]

There seems no reason to expect substantial improvement in the position of the South in the international economic system as a consequence of the end of the cold war. If anything, there is reason to suspect change for the worse. With the end of ideological confrontation between East and West, the leading powers will be less interested in economically supporting friends in the developing world; the major Western donors will tend to focus on aid toward economic reconstruction in the East instead of in the South. To make matters worse, several of the South's export products will be met by increasing competition from the East in areas where the international market is stagnant.

Scholars often emphasize the need to differentiate between the various groups of countries in the South; and it is true that there are dramatic differences between the poorest countries in Africa at one extreme and the NICs in Southeast Asia at the other extreme. But none of these groups appears to be able to look forward to economic improvements in coming years. The NICs are being met with rising protectionism in their main market, the United States; they also have to face such internal problems as environmental degradation and demands for welfare improvement.[51] The poorest countries in Africa face a crisis of mere survival; many of them have been subjected to economic administration by the IMF and the World Bank, but the problems these countries face are so severe that the policies prescribed by the international institutions offer little hope for improvement in the short or medium run. Indeed, the World Bank itself admitted in a recent report that "the outlook for Africa is potentially devastating."[52]

Focus in this section has been on Kant's third basic pillar of a pacific union, mutually beneficial economic cooperation between democracies. Such economic cooperation has indeed developed between the stable, industrialized democracies in the West—that is, Western Europe, North America, Japan, Australia, and New Zealand. For the South, however, economic relations are characterized by dependence rather than interdependence. Integration in the world market has been a mixed blessing for the countries there; even with the end of the cold war, there is no prospect for an improved economic position for the South in the global system. Therefore, democracies in the South have not developed the mutually beneficial ties of economic cooperation with the leading democracies in the North that in Kant's view constitute the third necessary element of a pacific union. Prospects for Eastern Europe are better, especially for the countries that will join the European Community.

PEACE AS A RESULT OF DEMOCRACY?

In the past, democracies have not gone to war against one another, and the number of democracies in the world has increased rapidly in recent years. So will the spread of democracy bring a bright future with peace among nations? The theoretical foundation for expecting peace to flow from democracy is set forth by Immanuel Kant. His pacific union of democracies rests on three pillars: first, the mere existence of democracies with their culture of peaceful conflict resolution; second, the moral bonds that are forged between the democracies on the basis of their common moral foundations; and third, the democracies' economic cooperation toward mutual advantage.

This chapter has analyzed each of these conditions in the light of recent processes of democratization. With regard to the first, it is evident that a democratic culture with norms of peaceful conflict resolution has not yet developed in the new democracies. Democratic norms must be ingrained before the domestic basis of the pacific union will be secure, and such development of the political culture will take some time. There may be setbacks toward nondemocratic forms of rule.

The second condition is existence of common moral bonds between democracies. Such relations have indeed developed among the consolidated democracies of the West. Furthermore, there is reason to believe that the security community made up of the Western stable democracies can be extended to include the new democracies in Eastern Europe, provided there are no severe setbacks in their further democratization. The democracies in the South may or may not be included; in the past, the United States has turned against the mass-dominated democracies in the South in order to protect its perceived economic or security interests. If such policies continue, the pacific union is in double jeopardy: Mass-dominated democracies are left out and elite-dominated democracies in the South may well fail to produce the welfare progress that is necessary for a sustained peace.

The final condition is the existence of ties of mutually beneficial economic cooperation between democracies. Such economic interdependence is highly developed among the consolidated democracies in the West. At least some of the new democracies in Eastern Europe are set to be integrated into these economic networks through their anticipated membership in the European Community. For the democracies in the South, however, continued one-sided economic dependence rather than interdependence is the order of the day, even after the end of the cold war.

In short, the emergence of a global pacific union embracing all the new and old democracies cannot be taken for granted. The pacific union with its zone of peace is a long-term project. For the project to be successful, the three basic conditions laid down by Kant must be met by all of the democracies. Presently, a pacific union is a reality among the industrialized democracies in the West, and it may expand to include several of the new democracies in the East. Yet most of the democracies in the South fail to meet at least two of Kant's conditions. And instead of exhibiting further progress, they may backslide toward authoritarian rule.

What are the consequences of the existence and expansion of a pacific union for the dominant theoretical paradigm in international relations—

realism? The next section of this chapter addresses the realist critique of Kantian visions.

PEACEFUL DEMOCRACIES AND REALIST THOUGHT

Kant's vision of a peaceful world of democracies belongs to a school of thought labeled **idealism.** The basic notion of idealist thinking is the view that conflict and violence can be overcome if the world is organized according to certain principles. Harmony is possible if man gives priority to the "right" ideas; with regard to Kant, the right idea would be that of democracy. This notion is rejected by *realist* thought, which claims to analyze the world as it really is, not as it ought to be. In the real world, conflict is imminent due to forces inherent in human nature and due to the fact that the world's populations have chosen to organize in the form of independent, sovereign states that respect no authority outside or above themselves. Early realist thought stressed the quest for power and dominance stemming from human nature as the basic reason for conflict; more recent contributions, often termed neorealist, emphasize the structure of the state system as the reason. The sovereign states respect no higher authority than themselves; there is no world government. In that sense, *anarchy* is the basic feature of the state system. With anarchy conflict is imminent. States cannot really trust one another, and one state's attempt to increase its safety by increasing its weaponry is unavoidably a threat to the security of other states. In short, as long as there are sovereign nation-states, there will be a state-system characterized by anarchy. As long as there is anarchy, there is a threat of violent conflict. In such a system, perpetual peace as envisaged by Kant is impossible.

It is not surprising, therefore, that according to many neorealists, "the theory of peace-loving democracies is unsound."[53] It is the aim in this section to discuss John Mearsheimer's neorealist critique of Kant's visions of democracy and peace. It will be argued that the distance between an analysis based on Kant, on the one hand, and neorealist thought, on the other, is much smaller than implied by Mearsheimer. On the basis of a more nuanced concept of anarchy than the one employed by Mearsheimer, we will see that the results described in the discussion of democracy and peace are perfectly compatible with neorealist analysis.

Mearsheimer started by attacking the logic of Kant's theory linking democracy and peace.[54] The first point, as has been discussed, concerns the assertion that democracies are more peaceful than authoritarian systems because the people in the former are more hesitant to go to war. Mearsheimer noted that democracies are as likely to fight wars as are other systems and that the public may be no less war-prone than authoritarian leaders are. His arguments do not contradict Kant; the general war-proneness of democracies has already been noted, as has been the fact that the restraint shown by democracies in their relations with other democracies is not directly attributable to the influence of peace-loving citizens on the decisionmakers. The suggestion offered here was that a democratic culture of peaceful resolution of conflict introduces an element of restraint in the ways in which democracies conduct international relations. This element alone is not enough to explain the existence of a pacific union among democracies, but it is one of the three basic pillars of the pacific union.

The next point made by Mearsheimer criticizes the notion of a common moral foundation between democracies—that is, the second pillar of a pacific union. He claimed that moral bonds compete with other factors that are drawing toward conflict instead of peace, such as nationalism and religious fundamentalism. However, Kant did not deny the existence of these countervailing elements. His claim was, quite simply, that in relations between democracies with ingrained democratic cultures the competing factors will, most likely, *not* override the common moral foundation. Mearsheimer did not provide examples to support his argument, probably because there are none.

We have now reached the central point in Mearsheimer's attack on the logic of the theory. His argument is worth quoting in full:

> The possibility always exists that a democracy will revert to an authoritarian state. This threat of backsliding means that one democratic state can never be sure that another democratic state will not change its stripes and turn on it sometime in the future. Liberal democracies must therefore worry about relative power among themselves, which is tantamount to saying that each has an incentive to consider aggression against the other to forestall future trouble. Lamentably, it is not possible for even liberal democracies to transcend anarchy.[55]

Kant was well aware of the possibility of reversals toward authoritarian rule. That countries may backslide in that way does not invalidate the notion of a pacific union. The decisive point in Mearsheimer's argument is his inference that because there can be setbacks, anarchy remains the basic feature of the system regardless of the form of regime of the state. Anarchy prevails with all its dreadful but unavoidable consequences of imminent conflict and risk of war. Thus, the basic disagreement between idealists and neorealists concerns whether anarchy will prevail and whether it can be modified or even abolished in a pacific union of democracies.

Is it possible for liberal democracies to transcend anarchy? To answer this question, we need to take a closer look at the concept of anarchy. We know that anarchy is a rather abstract and imprecise characteristic of relations between sovereign states. If we categorize the states of the world in different subsystems, it is possible to give a more precise description of the relations between states in each subsystem. Such subsystems have been termed **security complexes,** that is, "groups of states whose primary security concerns link together."[56] Europe, the Gulf, and South Asia are examples. It then becomes possible to analyze the patterns and degrees of amity and enmity exhibited by the states within a specific group in more precise terms. It seems that the vast majority of neorealist analyses recognize the point that different security complexes can exhibit different degrees of anarchy.[57]

Can we further identify these different degrees of anarchy? A Danish scholar has suggested the following distinctions: At one extreme is what might be called raw anarchy; security is built on alliances and a balance of power achieved by deterrence. At the other extreme is the security community as defined by Deutsch; member countries are determined to solve conflicts by peaceful means, without fighting each other physically. In between are two middle stations, an immature and a mature security regime.[58] In the former, conflicts between states dominate, but amity is also possible. In the latter, states exhibit greater cooperation than they would if they were following only their short-term self-interests.[59] Such a continuum is shown in the accompanying illustration. Power politics dominates relations at the raw anarchy extreme; peaceful cooperation toward mutual gain dominates relations at the security community extreme.

Raw anarchy	Immature security regime	Mature security regime	Security community

The version of anarchy that Deutsch called a security community is exactly the pacific union envisaged by Kant. It is thus perfectly possible, even on the basis of neorealist reasoning, to conceive of a pacific union—a security community between consolidated democracies. Note that the general concept of anarchy still applies to the states in a security community: They are sovereign states that do not recognize an authority above or outside themselves. At the same time, it is clear that ties of cooperation and interdependence dominate relations between states in a security community. Mainstream neorealist analyses of deterrence and balance of power are thus more applicable to states in raw anarchy relationships than to states in communities in which cooperation dominates.

Mearsheimer would object that such security communities may not endure; there can be backslides toward more raw forms of anarchy. He is right; Kant also feared such developments. But security communities can also develop toward even further integration, as is currently happening, according to many observers, in the European Community. The Community has taken over political functions that were earlier the prerogative of the single member states; if the process of integration continues along the present path, the result will be a united Europe, a new state, a new unitary international actor. Anarchy between the old member states would be ruled out for good because they would have accepted a new, central authority above the old nation-states. Contrary to Mearsheimer's argument, it thus appears that it *is* possible for liberal democratic states to transcend anarchy. It must be emphasized, however, that the process of integration in the Community has not yet reached this point.

This takes us to the second path of criticism brought forward by Mearsheimer. He claimed that history provides no clear test of the theory that democracies do not fight each other. He raised the objection that several democracies have come close to fighting one another—for example, the United States and Allende's Chile. If Wilhelmine Germany is classified as a democracy, or a quasi-democracy, then World War I becomes a war among democracies. But these examples stem from the misunderstanding that the pacific union springs into existence between countries as soon as they meet a minimum definition of democracy. It does not. The pacific union is built upon a domestic foundation of democratic culture as well as two international pillars. All three must be in place for the pacific union to be effective, which is not the case in these examples.

Mearsheimer's other complaints concern the lack of a proper test of the theory of peaceful democracies. He pointed to the fact that democracies have been few in number over the past two centuries, and thus there have not been many situations in which two democracies have been in a position to fight each other. When there actually have been such situations, Mearsheimer's claim is that "there are other persuasive explanations for why war did not occur. . . . These competing explanations must be ruled out before the peace loving democracies theory can be accepted."[60]

If a proper test of the theory must meet Mearsheimer's requirement that all other competing explanations be ruled out, then there will never be a proper test of the theory. In international relations, as well as in other branches of social science, there is no possibility for laboratory experiments. One cannot in a clinical fashion isolate one single factor, such as democracy, from all other possibly relevant factors in the relationships between countries. The same constraints also pertain to Mearsheimer's theory of peaceful relations between states, which comes out of mainstream neorealism. He claimed that periods of peace between democracies (as well as between all other types of regimes) are due to patterns of alliances in the anarchic state system; in short, two or more states hold together because they face larger threats from other states in the system. Again, it is not possible to completely isolate this element of alliance patterns from all other possibly relevant factors. Theories in social science cannot be subjected to this kind of testing. It should be added that Mearsheimer would have a hard time explaining the hostilities in the 1970s between NATO countries Greece and Turkey with his theory of peace, which focuses solely on alliance and threat patterns.

Although laboratory tests of these theories are not possible, recent historical developments may provide a fairly strong test of Kant versus Mearsheimer. The case is the security community in Western Europe. According to Mearsheimer, the absence of war among Western democracies since 1945 is explained by the Soviet threat; with this threat gone, the Western partners no longer have an external enemy to hold them together. Mearsheimer's theory would predict that relations among them will tend to deteriorate toward raw anarchy, maybe even war. According to Kant, the pacific union among the Western democracies rests on the three pillars of a democratic culture, a common moral foundation, and economic interdependence. Those pillars are not affected by the presence or absence of a Soviet threat. Thus, Kant's theory would predict that the security community will remain intact and perhaps even expand due to the process of democratization in Eastern Europe.

Mearsheimer's arguments are set forth in his article in the journal *International Security*, cited earlier in this section. Several other scholars have recently argued in the vein of Kant that the security community will remain in place.[61] As I have already indicated, I find the arguments for a continued security community much more convincing than Mearsheimer's raw anarchy scenario. Indeed, the current process of further integration in the European Community is a movement toward even stronger cooperation. If the process continues in this direction, it could lead, possibly, to anarchy being transcended.

CONCLUSION

Kant's theory of a possible pacific union between democracies is basically sound. But it is a mistake to think that a pacific union automatically extends to include countries that are in the early stages of a long and tenuous process of democratization or countries that have not developed moral bonds and economic interdependence. The current processes of democratization increase the possibilities for a larger pacific union, but by no means do they guarantee its realization. In particular, the prospects are poor for the inclusion of the new democracies in the South in the pacific union.

Finally, it is possible to accept Kant's vision without rejecting the basic insights of neorealism. The distance between Kant's idealism and neorealism is often overdrawn, as in Mearsheimer's analysis. A pacific union is the type of anarchy called a security community. It is only when theorists place a one-sided emphasis on raw anarchy and see patterns of alliance and threat between anonymous states as the only factors leading to peace and war that there seems to be an insurmountable gulf between neorealist and Kantian thinking.

FIVE

□ □ □

The Future of Democracy and Democratization

The preceding chapters have focused on the large number of transitions toward democracy in recent years and have examined the possible effects of these transitions on economic development and international relations. This chapter explores the future of democracy and democratization. Will the processes of democratization continue in force with many more countries becoming democratic and with the new democracies moving toward greater democratic consolidation, or will there be reversals toward authoritarianism? It will quickly become apparent that forecasting is difficult; the ability to explain past events does not, unfortunately, necessarily mean that one can make accurate predictions about the future. What individual actors and social movements will do is to some extent unpredictable. But with the knowledge we have about the general framework that sets the stage for the actors, we can outline some possibilities in the form of scenarios. Although we cannot know if these forecasts will prove true, they can help inform our thinking about the future.

In a recent, much debated essay, Francis Fukuyama predicted the end of history. With the collapse of communism, he argues, there is no longer a viable alternative to the Western type of liberal democracy that is based on a market economy. We are looking at, said Fukuyama, "the end of history as such: that is, the end point of mankind's ideological evolution and the universalization of Western liberal democracy as the final form of human government.[1] According to this reasoning, the liberal democracy model is more than merely dominant; it is the only one left to choose. The alternatives have proven unviable. The transitions toward democracy discussed in this book constitute the early stage of a process that will lead to the victory of democracy on a world scale.

Fukuyama's essay has attracted substantial critique. Samuel Huntington, a scholar who rejects Fukuyama's vision, is much more skeptical about the future of democracy:

> History has proved both optimists and pessimists wrong about democracy. Future events will probably do the same. Formidable obstacles to the expansion of democracy exist in many societies. The third wave, the "global democratic revolutions" of the late twentieth century, will not last forever. It may be followed by a new surge of authoritarianism sustained enough to constitute a third reverse wave. That, however, would not preclude a fourth wave of democratization developing some time in the twenty-first century.[2]

Another line of argument against the "end of history" thesis is centered on the fact that democracy is not a fixed entity. Not only does it come in different organizational forms (parliamentary vs. presidential; majoritarian vs. representational; two-party vs. multiparty; and so forth), but there are also qualitative differences between the various concepts of democracy that have been put forth. Consider, for example, the two concepts outlined in Chapter 1: the narrow one by Joseph Schumpeter, where democracy is a method for choosing political leadership, and the comprehensive notion by David Held, where democracy is defined as a system in which individuals are free and equal in the determination of the conditions of their own lives. With Held's notion of democracy, the electorate has a greater influence on the state than Schumpeter allows. In addition, the people directly participate in local community institutions and manage cooperatively owned enterprises. This latter element highlights the fact that the two definitions also carry dissimilar implications for the political control of the economic sphere: from the rule of market forces based on private property, on the one hand, to a very high degree of political influence and control over the economy, on the other.

These models may be extremes, but they illustrate the significant diversity that continues to exist within the boundaries of democracy. In short, the necessity to navigate among these varieties of democracy is hardly compatible with the notion of end of history.[3]

This debate relates to the dilemmas of democracy and democratization discussed in this book. Democracy has made great progress throughout the world in recent years; but the characteristics of the new democracies call into question whether democratic advancement will continue and whether positive effects from democracy will be forthcoming. Chapter 2 stressed that the recent transitions from authoritarianism have resulted in frail, restricted democracies that are unconsolidated and plagued by severe social and economic problems. Chapter 3 emphasized that economic development and a general improvement of human rights are not necessarily forthcoming from these fragile democracies. Finally, Chapter 4 stressed that a more peaceful world will not necessarily be secured as a result of the present processes of democratization and that the inclusion of all of the new democracies in a pacific union is a long-term project with no guarantee of success.

It appears that future developments will take place on a playing field demarcated by two extremes. At one end is a very optimistic scenario in which democratic progress continues on all counts; more countries become democratic and the movement toward consolidated democracies takes place in the systems in which the democratic transition is already under way. At the other end is a pessimistic scenario in which a process of democratic decay sets in that may engulf not only the new democracies in the South and the East but also the consolidated democracies in the West. It is helpful to outline the two scenarios in more detail before proceeding to discuss what is likely to happen.

THE OPTIMISTIC SCENARIO:
A SPRINGTIME OF DEMOCRACY

According to this scenario, the trend of democratization will continue in an increasing number of countries and will be accompanied by a democratization of the international system. One scholar has talked about the need, in a world of rapidly increasing interdependence, for **horizontal accountability,** which he defines as the representative mechanisms that "enable citizens to influence the decisions that are made in neighboring societies and that directly affect them."[4] In such a world, citizens of nation-states are profoundly affected by decisions made outside their borders, whether they concern political, economic, or environmental issues.

In the optimistic scenario, further democratization on national and local levels will lead to democratization on the level of the international system. The United Nations (UN) may be the point of departure. In earlier times, it was hardly possible to see the UN as an expression of a global popular, democratic will. It was an assembly of governments, many of which were authoritarian and unrepresentative. With further democratization at the national level, it will become possible to change the nature of the UN toward a genuine democratic world assembly. According to one scholar,

> Possibly, too, the United Nations can be weaned gradually away from the state system and begin to serve the cause of humanity as a whole, not naively, but rather fulfilling a mandate from a war-weary world to protect the planet from the adverse effects of antagonistic sovereign national wills and

gradually incubating the growth and strengthening of world community structures and sentiments.[5]

Such developments can already be seen in some regional contexts, notably the European Community. Democratic organs above the states, on the Community level, are in the process of being strengthened in the context of further cooperation and integration.

Tendencies for democratization on the international level, according to this scenario, will go hand in hand with democratic deepening at the national level. In the consolidated democracies of the industrialized West, the peace dividend from the end of the cold war will be employed toward strengthening the welfare state and alleviating economic inequality. These developments will be combined with more democratic elements of participation and citizen's control in the local community and in enterprises, in accordance with the model of democratic autonomy outlined by David Held.[6]

In the East, democratization reinforced by advances in economic reform will dominate. The reintegration of the former planned economies into a network of European economic and political cooperation will significantly help the process. Hungary and Czechoslovakia will become members of the European Community before the end of the 1990s; other countries will negotiate association agreements as a first step toward full membership. The more successful countries will set an example for the others. Thus, the "new" countries from the dissolved Soviet empire will emulate the democratic and economic reforms of their forerunners and will seek close collaboration with the European Community.

In the South, the time of the dictators will have finally ended. The great powers will no longer support nondemocratic regimes for national security reasons. Both the internal and the external pressures toward democratization will substantially increase. The rise of democracy will be supported by a process of demilitarization, which will reduce the influence of the armed forces in the developing societies. The regimes of long-standing dictators, such as Mobutu in Zaire and Daniel Arap Moi in Kenya, will finally begin to succumb to democratic forces. With the cold war over, a number of perennial conflicts in the developing world can finally be solved: in South Africa, Angola, Ethiopia, and Campuchea, for example. Perhaps even a peace settlement in the Middle East is conceivable. And it is not mere conflict resolution that will take place in these areas; the countries will be involved in the early steps toward democratization. With the existence of more democratic and responsive political systems, the road will be open to a process of economic development and increasing standards of living, which in turn will reinforce the process of democratization.

THE PESSIMISTIC SCENARIO:
DEMOCRATIC DECAY

If democracy suffers setbacks in many countries there will be implications on the international level. Organizations such as the UN will become much less representative and undemocratic forces will become more powerful. In fact, the wheels are turning in this direction now. Large transnational corporations (TNCs) are becoming stronger; in the 1980s, the six hundred largest TNCs accounted for close to one-fourth of the entire global production of goods. Today, the so-called free market trade between countries is not free at all; much of it is **intrafirm trade**—that is, trade across borders but between different units of the same corporation. In the early 1980s, close to one-third of the total exports from the United States, Japan, and the United Kingdom was in the form of intrafirm trade.[7]

Other organizations that are far from representative of the peoples of the world are also becoming more powerful in the international system. The **Group of Seven** (G7) is a case in point. This small group of the most economically (and militarily) powerful capitalist nations, made up of the United States, Japan, Germany, Great Britain, France, Italy, and Canada, calls the tune of the world economy with far-reaching implications for the majority of the world's peoples. It was to the G7, not to the economically powerless UN, that Mikhail Gorbachev turned for assistance for economic reform. For the poor countries of the South, the World Bank and the IMF are the more important organizations; but even if the scope of membership in these organizations is broader than in the G7, they are not democratic. They are controlled by a relatively small group of rich nations.

In short, it can be argued that the dominant organizations on the level of the international system are basically nondemocratic. It can also be argued that their ascent on the international level may well be accompanied by democratic decay on the national level. Consider the consolidated democracies in the West, the heartland of victorious liberal democracy. Are we not forced to admit that there is no longer a vigorous political life in these countries? Instead, there is an increasing lack of interest in politics and a public debate characterized by diffidence and bereft of really significant issues. This argument was recently made in a number of French contributions to the debate on democracy.[8] The authors put some of the blame for democratic decay on a lack of political parties that are really different in important respects; only parties that are really different can raise debates about truly significant issues and sharpen our awareness of competing visions of the future. There is also a growing tendency for rising economic and social inequalities, which lead to political inequality. It is not that Western democracies will become authoritarian; more likely the substance of democracy will simply dry up, and democracy in the West will become an increasingly empty shell of formal political practices.

In the East and South, democratic decay will be of a more tangible kind. The East will likely see a vicious circle of democratic decay reinforced by economic crisis. Aid from the West is far from sufficient to help secure a smooth passage toward a market economy. As the economic crisis grows, ethnic conflict will become more intense. A recent U.S. Times-Mirror poll on European attitudes confirms the gloomy prospect for intensified ethnic conflict. The poll found that in every Eastern European country sampled, at least 40 percent of the respondents felt hostile to the main national minority.[9] Against a background of economic breakdown and ethnic confrontation, democratic consolidation cannot proceed. Old elites are called in by the disillusioned population to run proto-fascist governments that are turned against ethnic minorities.

The countries of the South will likely slide back and forth between restricted democracy and outright authoritarianism. Because the frozen, elite-dominated democracies are incapable of meeting popular expectations of economic improvement and further political reform, there will be an erosion of support for democratic institutions. The increasing social unrest will confirm the apprehension among elites that further democratization may indeed threaten their established dominance. At the same time, the decreasing support for democratic institutions will reduce the perceived costs of authoritarian solutions. Consequently, the military will again intervene in many countries, as it has already done in Sudan, Nigeria, Haiti, and Thailand. The large majority of developing countries will again come under authoritarian rule.

WEIGHING THE ALTERNATIVES

When discussing possible future developments, we can probably be certain of only one thing: that reality will never come out as one-sided as depicted in the scenarios we painted, where the bleak future of across-the-board democratic decay stands against the hopeful vision of a total democratic victory. Reality will be something in between, a mixture of the two extremes. The hard part is predicting precisely what kind of mixture and what kind of flavor (optimistic or pessimistic) will dominate. To make such predictions would require a more concrete analysis of regions (South, East, and West) and specific countries within regions. In other words, we would need to take steps down the ladder of abstraction from the very general trends outlined in the scenarios toward more detailed analyses of specific areas. A complete analysis of this kind is not possible in the present context. Instead, let us look at the prospects for additional countries entering a process of transition toward democracy and the prospects for democratic consolidation in the South in the light of international trends, on the one hand, and activities at the local level, on the other.

According to recent contributions by Robert Dahl and Samuel Huntington, we should not expect many more countries to become part of the present wave of democratization. Dahl emphasized that the conditions favoring democracy (polyarchy) are not strong in the presently nondemocratic countries; thus, we can infer that we should not expect a further spread of democracy.[10] Dahl also pointed out that in the consolidated democracies, countries that have been democratic for twenty years or more, the breakdown of democracy is extremely rare. Therefore, he concluded that

> neither the optimistic nor the pessimistic scenario is likely to prove correct. Short of a major catastrophe such as a deep and prolonged economic collapse or a nuclear war, polyarchy will continue in the large core of countries where democratic institutions have existed for a generation or more. At the margins of this core of stable democracies, transformations of both kinds are likely to occur.[11]

In other words, some countries may begin transitions toward democracy and others may backslide to authoritarianism; but the overall number of democracies will remain basically unchanged. Dahl made this conclusion before the recent changes in Eastern Europe, which bear witness to the fact that unforeseen events may occur. He did not predict the large number of transitions to democracy that were to occur in Eastern Europe. But the decisive push there was the lifting of Soviet dominance, and it is hard to think of other areas of the world in which actions by a major power could result in a similar drive toward democracy. Thus, Dahl's prediction may well apply to the global situation.

Huntington reached a conclusion that is similar to Dahl's. He noted that the large majority of the countries that democratized between 1974 and 1990 had some previous experience of democracy. The present ninety or more nondemocratic countries have always been nondemocratic. The fact that these countries have always been nondemocratic does not render democratization impossible, but it does make it more difficult.[12] Furthermore, many of the nondemocratic countries exhibit cultures, such as Islam or Confucianism, that are inimical to democracy. Like the situation just mentioned, such cultural traits do not render democratization impossible but make it more difficult. Finally, economic development and the eradication of poverty have been central features behind many of the earlier processes of democratization; but the prospects for rapid economic development in the poorest countries today are not good. Consequently, the lack of economic progress will inhibit a process of democratization. Huntington summarized as follows: "In China, the obstacles to democratization are political, economic, and cultural; in Africa they are overwhelmingly economic; and in the rapidly developing countries of East Asia and in many Islamic countries, they are primarily cultural."[13]

If we combine these rather gloomy conclusions concerning the prospects for the further spread of democracy with the results of the analyses in this book, which also presented a somber view of the prospects for further democratic consolidation in many of the new democracies, we could not help but reach a pessimistic conclusion. Yet it is worth extending our analysis, which has mainly focused on democracy at the national, governmental level, to a look at the main trends at the international level ("above" the nation-state) and the local, grass-roots level ("below" the nation-state). From these focal points, we will explore the chances for further democratization in the South, the area most in need of more democracy. We will also demonstrate how trends at the international and the local levels influence possibilities for democratization at the national level.

International Trends and Democratization in the South

In this discussion we will distinguish between international ideological, economic, and political trends. *Ideological* tendencies will be discussed first. In this area, it is important to note the rising popularity of political democracy. "Never in recorded history," wrote Robert Dahl in 1989, "have state leaders appealed so widely to democratic ideas to legitimate their rule," and the trend in this direction has grown even stronger since then.[14] Theorists who were earlier critical of democracy's potential now see it as the way forward; for example, a well-known Latin American scholar recently proclaimed that "democracy is the only path which Latin American countries can follow to modernity."[15] This statement is all the more remarkable when one notes that a widespread mistrust of political democracy had been prevalent in earlier periods among the popular forces in Latin America, which are now the central forces in the struggle for democracy. In Africa, the one-party system is no longer being supported as the ideal framework for consensual decisionmaking and for the promotion of economic and social development. Finally, in Eastern Europe, people no longer buy into the official position that political leadership by what was understood to be the party of the masses, the Communist party, is infinitely more democratic than liberal democracy on the basis of a capitalist society. On this point, the vast variety of new political movements in Eastern Europe are in agreement. As one observer noted,

In politics they are all saying: There is no "socialist democracy," there is only democracy. And by democracy they mean multi-party, parliamentary democracy as practiced in contemporary Western, Northern, and Southern Europe. They are all saying: There is no "socialist legality," there is only legality. And by that they mean the rule of law, guaranteed by the constitutionally anchored independence of the judiciary.[16]

There appears to be only one major ideological opponent to the dominant idea of political democracy, and that is Islam. But even if Islam is strong in several countries in Asia and Africa, the current Islamic revival must be set against the quest for modernization that is also at work in the heartlands of Islam. In Saudi Arabia, the process of modernization has given democratic ideas a much stronger foothold.[17] At the same time, the case of Algeria demonstrates the paradoxical situation that democratic openings can bring forward Islamic forces at the elections, which were suppressed during earlier periods of authoritarian rule. Algeria will be an interesting case study of the extent to which democratic progress is at all compatible with a political scene distinguished by strong elements of Islamic forces.

We have seen that the idea of democracy is very strong at the global ideological level. Let us now examine the *economic* prospects for the South from a global perspective. Can we foresee a period of economic progress that will help sustain democratization? It has already been noted that growth prospects for the countries of the South are not good. A closer look at international economic trends confirms the gloomy picture.

First, there is a long-term trend of deteriorating terms of trade for the South's main export commodities, primary products. The trend has been at work since the early twentieth century, and it has turned increasingly against the South since the beginning of the 1970s. The World Bank index of real prices of thirty-three nonfuel primary commodities fell from 130 in the boom year of 1974 to 70 in 1988 (1979–1981 = 100), a decline of 46 percent. Real petroleum prices fell from index 120 to 40 in 1988.[18]

Second, the overall demand for the South's main export products is gradually declining. World trade in agricultural raw materials (cotton, sisal, jute, wool, and so forth) has declined in absolute terms since 1960; the growth rate for trade in manufactured products is more than twice as high as the rate for world trade in agricultural products. In short, due to better utilization and substitution by synthetic products, the industrialized countries have less need for the agricultural raw materials of the Third World.

Furthermore, the role of the South as a reservoir of cheap labor is rapidly declining in importance, as is its role as a market for industrial products from the North. The cost of labor plays a less important role in economic decisions today than in the past; hence, the difference between labor costs in the North and South no longer acts as a strong incentive for attracting foreign investment to the South. At the same time, the large majority of countries in the South have stagnant markets with low purchase power and thus are of little interest to Northern investors. Kari Levitt summarized as follows: "The brutal truth is that the industrialised world has decreasing need for the countries of the periphery, either as sources of raw material, or as markets, or as cheap labor."[19]

Finally, there is the debt problem. Developing country debt increased from $753 billion in 1982 to $1,159 billion in 1988. Interest and loan repayments are a constantly increasing burden. As a matter of fact, net financial transfers are now going from the poor to the rich, from South to North. Net annual transfers were $36 million in 1985; by 1988 annual net transfers had stabilized at more than $50 billion annually.[20]

In short, it is clear that the economic outlook for the developing world is gloomy; the industrialized countries have less need for the South at a time when the South's dependence on the North is greater than ever. From the viewpoint of international economic trends, there is no prospect for a process of vigorous economic development that can help sustain democratization in the South.

What about the *political* aspect of North-South relations? Until recently North-South politics was to a large extent determined by the cold war. The Soviet Union had its group of client states in the South, as did the United States. In the cold war period, between 1946 and 1988, the top ten recipients of U.S. aid were all countries that were important to the West from the viewpoint of the confrontation with the Soviet Union; that is, aid depended less on needs in terms of poverty and more on geostrategic position in the East-West struggle. For this reason, substantial aid was given to such countries as South Korea and Taiwan.

With the end of the cold war, less aid may be forthcoming because the cold war argument for it is gone. At the same time, it may be in the North's best interest to provide aid to the South to help it solve some new problems that are arising there. For example, efficient solutions to environmental problems in the South will require economic aid from the North. The provision of such aid is a matter of self-interest for the North: Pollution problems do not respect borders. Another area of concern is migration: Without substantial economic improvement in the South, a sharply increasing number of people will try to emigrate to the rich countries, legally or otherwise. One possible measure by which the North can avoid the unpleasant prospect of being seen as a fortress of the rich that shuts off access to upwards of 80 percent of world's population is continued or even increased aid. In this context, there is a tendency for regionalization. Each of the major centers in the North—the United States, Japan, and Western Europe—concentrates relations on "its" region in the South: Latin America for the United States, Southeast Asia for Japan, and Africa for Europe.

Furthermore, the end of the cold war has had the good effect of reducing the tendency to protect corrupt and inefficient rulers in the South just because they were "good friends" of the West. In addition, the respect for human rights and the demand for political reform are receiving higher priority as preconditions for economic aid. The code word for such preconditions is **political conditionality;** as noted in Chapter 2, it has already helped bring forward a process of democratization in Africa. It is clear that political conditionality will receive higher priority in coming years. For example, the donor countries in the European Community recently decided that "good government," that is, the respect for human rights, efforts at democratization, and the struggle against corruption and mismanagement, is going to be a condition for receiving economic aid. Countries that fail to meet these demands will risk losing their aid. Such policies are also supported by Japan and the United States, and it is expected that they will be adopted by the broader group of Western donors in the Organization for Economic Cooperation and Development (OECD) Development Assistance Committee. If adopted, these policies will come into effect in 1992. Although it is possible that countries may, at times, use political conditionality as a smokescreen covering vested donor interests, it is a step forward compared with earlier policies of silently accepting dictators and tyrants.

This section looked at international trends pertaining to possibilities for democratization in the South. Ideologically, democracy is stronger than ever; politically, the end of the cold war has meant more serious attempts by the North to promote democracy in the South; economically, there is no reason to expect improvement that may help foster processes of democratization. The international trends thus draw in opposite directions. To get a better understanding of whether democratization will proceed, we therefore must look at the interplay between these international trends and the internal preconditions that prevail in specific countries. The internal preconditions for meeting the external challenges vary greatly from country to country in the South in terms of their levels of economic and social development and cultural-ideological outlooks. We shall not go into specific cases here but will instead focus on democracy at the local level. It is the interplay of the international level (discussed in this chapter), the national level (which has been in main focus in this book), and the local level that determines whether democratization will move forward. What are the dynamics at the local level?

The Local Level: Democracy's Roots

It was indicated in Chapter 1 that there can be a discrepancy between the degree of democracy at the national and local levels. Chapter 2 briefly described the popular mobilization that is a part of the early process of democratization. It is clear from the discussion in that chapter that a viable process of democratic development must be firmly rooted at the local level. Otherwise, democracy will be more of a formal structure for resolving conflicts between different, primarily urban elites than a system of benefit to the whole population. At the same time, there is no simple, straightforward relationship between micro-level participation and macro-level democracy. If popular participation is strictly confined to the micro level, it can take place in the framework of an authoritarian, even oppressive central government. What is needed at the micro level, therefore, is participation that is linked to broader arenas; such participation would involve "organized efforts to increase control over resources and regulative institutions in given social situations . . . on the part of groups and movements hitherto excluded from such control."[21]

There has been an increasing debate in recent years about possible ways in which popular participation and peoples' control over their own lives can be strengthened. The most comprehensive contribution is by Guy Gran.[22] His strategy contains three elements. First, it is necessary to raise the consciousness of people who are not members of the economic and political elites so that they achieve an understanding of the social reality in which they live and their possibilities for actively changing it. Gran was inspired by Brazilian educator Paolo Freire, who called this process **conscientization.** The second element is organization of the poor, although not in the hierarchical, bureaucratized sense; the structure of organization must be horizontal, with a high degree of member influence, and it must be open to everybody. The main task is to activate and educate the members to the role of actively involved citizens. The final element concerns the structure of local society. Gran saw it as vitally important that citizens are secured equal access to influence decisions concerning their own lives. He proposed organizing local society into relatively small units, each responsible for several aspects of its members' conditions. Such a structure provides a possibility for putting the problems that must be solved in order of priority; that is, people decide locally about the utilization of scarce resources. It is clear that the units must be highly decentralized if they are to secure a real influence for locally organized groups.

Gran's vision is part of an increasingly strong trend toward greater political, cultural, social, and economic empowerment of the poor and underprivileged. Many nongovernmental organizations (NGOs) involved in aid have popular empowerment as their main goal. Ideally, the NGO volunteers can function as the educators who can help spark the first element of Gran's strategy, the raising of consciousness.

There are also many examples of grass-roots initiatives, which come from the poor themselves, that have the aim of improving the position of this segment of the population. In a recent study of such initiatives in Sri Lanka and Brazil, Denis Goulet made the following assessment:

> Participation began largely as a defense mechanism against the destruction wrought by elite problem solvers in the name of progress or development. From there it has evolved into a preferred form of "do-it-yourself" problem solving in small-scale operations. Now, however, many parties to participation seek entry into larger, more macro, arenas of decision making. Alternative development strategies centering on goals of equity, job creation, the multiplication of autonomous capacities, and respect for cultural diversity—all these require significant participation in macro arenas. Without it, development strategies will be simultaneously undemocratic and ineffectual. Without the developmental participation of non-elites, even political democracy will largely be a sham.[23]

In other words, change at the local level toward increased participation and empowerment of the poor is an important element in a process of democratization. Seen from the micro perspective, the initiatives fostering such change are just as important as the changes themselves, or even more so, for a process of empowerment of the poor and underprivileged. Take, for example, a water project that installs taps to provide water to a village. The organization of village women to control and maintain the water supply is a piece of social change that may have more immediate and tangible consequences for democratization in that village than the announcement of an election at the national level. In Sri Lanka, the Buddhist Sarvodaya movement has successfully initiated projects in several thousand villages based on its vision of meeting people's basic needs (education, health care, farming, community services) in a context of bottom-up participation and popular control.[24] In Latin America, progressive elements of the Catholic church have promoted a large number of communal self-management projects both in the cities and in the countryside.[25]

Yet it must be stressed that the micro level of popular participation and empowerment is closely interrelated with the level of national government: Without democratization at the national level, the scope of local initiatives is strictly limited; without democratic change at the local level, the national democratic framework is primarily a formal shell. Enduring, qualitative changes in the national political structure require durable, qualitative changes in the structure of the economy and in civil society.[26]

Thus, change at the local level is an important factor for the overall success of a process of democratization. It is difficult to assess the extent to which change at the local level will be made in the current transitions toward democracy. As indicated earlier, one can point to a large number of concrete examples of local activities toward empowerment; but it is also clear that in many cases the early phases of democratization have been concentrated on a rather narrow range of elite activity.

*   *   *

No definite conclusion emerges from these brief considerations on international and local dynamics with regard to the future of democracy and democratization. On both levels one can point to positive and negative elements from the viewpoint of democratic progress. It can be argued that discussion of the international level "above" and the micro level "below" the level of national government increases the complexity of the democratization issue rather than reducing it. Yet, it is important to be aware of the different levels and the interplay between them. All of these elements must be studied in a full investigation of the prospects for democratization in specific regions and countries.

CONCLUSION

The discussion about the meaning of democracy in Chapter 1 formed the basis for our assessment of the processes of democratization under way in many countries and for our examination of the possible domestic and international consequences of democracy. A basic dilemma was identified at the beginning: The democratic openings we have seen are a mere beginning; by no means do they ensure further democratization or additional benefits in the form of economic development, peace, and cooperation. Each of the main chapters in this book has focused on a particular aspect of this dilemma: the processes of democratization in Chapter 2, the consequences for economic development and human rights in Chapter 3, and the consequences for peace among nations in Chapter 4. In Chapter 5, the future of democracy and democratization was evaluated against the framework of an optimistic and a pessimistic scenario. If our final assessment leans toward the pessimistic scenario, we may do well to remember a fundamental lesson learned in recent years: The future is not predetermined; expected patterns of development can be fundamentally changed by the actions of individuals and groups on both the local and the national level. It is the sum of these actions that determine whether democracy will prevail. Perhaps to a higher extent than ever before, the responsibility for future developments rests heavily with the actors in the democracies of the industrialized countries—that is, with us. Not only are we responsible for the way in which democracy fares in our own countries; we also control the basic framework of the international system, the economic, political, and ideological dimensions of which influence the possibilities of democratization in the South and the East. Our willingness to contribute to the solution of economic and other problems in these regions is of major importance for their future prospects for democratization. Furthermore, if the dilemmas of the current processes of democratization carry any weight, we are forced to be more concerned not only with democracy in general but also with the specific kinds of democracy that are emerging in the present world. Support for elite-dominated, restricted democracies will not be enough. Without a more solid, popular basis, today's fragile democracies may well be tomorrow's authoritarian dictatorships.

□ □ □

Discussion Questions

CHAPTER ONE

1. Give a broad and a narrow definition of democracy. What are the arguments in favor of each?

2. According to Julius Nyerere, the former president of Tanzania, the struggle for freedom in the Third World is primarily a struggle for freedom from hunger, disease, and poverty, and not so much a struggle for political rights and liberties. Is that true?

3. In 1968, a progressive military junta took power in Peru and did away with the democratic political system. The military government went on to launch much more far-reaching measures against poverty and poor living conditions for the mass of people than had been seen under the previous, democratic government, which was dominated by an elite. Which regime is more democratic: the one that upholds a democratic political system that serves mainly an elite or the one that does away with the democratic political system in order to promote the struggle for freedom from hunger, disease, and poverty?

4. Discuss the assertion that only a capitalist system can provide the necessary basis for democracy. Which elements in capitalism can promote democracy and which can impede it?

CHAPTER TWO

1. Some conditions favor the rise of democracy more than others. What are the most favorable economic, social, and cultural conditions for democracy? Why is it that democracy may emerge in places where the conditions for it are adverse?

2. Are there common factors that help explain the recent surge toward democracy in many countries, or must democratization in different parts of the world be explained in different ways?

3. Outline the phases in the transition toward democracy according to the model described in this chapter and apply the model to your own country. Is your country a consolidated democracy? How much time has passed since the move toward democracy began in your country? What light does the experience of your own country shed on the process of transition to democracy in other countries?

4. What arguments can you make for and against the assertion that democracy has made great progress in the world during the past decade?

CHAPTER THREE

1. What arguments have been made in support of the view that there is a trade-off between political democracy and economic development? What arguments have been made against this view? Is it possible to settle this debate on the basis of empirical analyses?

2. This chapter identifies three types of authoritarian systems: authoritarian developmentalist regimes, authoritarian growth regimes, and authoritarian state elite enrichment regimes. Which of these types is the most common today? How do elite-dominated and mass-dominated democracies differ?

3. Sometimes the early process of democratization brings neither welfare improvement nor a better human rights situation. Is this an argument against democracy?

CHAPTER FOUR

1. What are the arguments in favor of the contention that the spread of democracy will lead to the creation of a peaceful world? Democracies have not gone to war with one another in the past, but they have been few in number and have not had many opportunities to fight one another. Is this knowledge about the past a reliable guide to the actions of democracies in a future world where, possibly, a large number of democracies can come into conflict?

2. Do you think that a more peaceful world will result from the current processes of democratization? Why or why not?

3. Evaluate current developments in the European Community in light of the debate between a Kantian view and Mearsheimerian neorealism. Which of these views, if any, is correct?

CHAPTER FIVE

1. What arguments can you give in support of the optimistic and the pessimistic scenarios that were described as a basis for discussion of the future of democracy and democratization? Is the trend in your own country toward more or less democracy? In what way?

2. What would a really democratic world order look like? Would it not be dominated by the poor majority of the world's population from China, India, and elsewhere in the South? And would the major policy aim of such an order not be the redistribution of wealth from North to South?

□ □ □

Notes

CHAPTER ONE

1. David Held, *Models of Democracy* (Cambridge: Polity Press, 1987), p. 2.

2. Ibid., pp. 28–33. See also Arne Naess et al., *Democracy, Ideology, and Objectivity* (Oslo: Oslo University Press, 1956), p. 78n.

3. Held, *Models of Democracy*, p. 32.

4. C. B. Macpherson, *The Life and Times of Liberal Democracy* (Oxford: Oxford University Press, 1977), p. 13.

5. Held, *Models of Democracy*, p. 41n.

6. See Goran Therborn, "The Rule of Capital and the Rise of Democracy," *New Left Review* 103 (1977): 3.

7. Macpherson, *The Life and Times*; see also Held, *Models of Democracy*.

8. See Macpherson, *The Life and Times*, pp. 35–39.

9. Held, *Models of Democracy*, p. 69.

10. F. A. Hayek, *The Constitution of Liberty* (London: Routledge and Kegan Paul, 1960), p. 103.

11. See Held, *Models of Democracy*, pp. 248–252.

12. Quoted from ibid., p. 248.

13. See ibid., p. 86.

14. See ibid., p. 94.

15. See Macpherson, *The Life and Times*, pp. 60–64, and Held, *Models of Democracy*, pp. 100–104.

16. Quoted from Held, *Models of Democracy*, p. 75.

17. Macpherson, *The Life and Times*; Carol Pateman, *Participation and Democratic Theory* (Cambridge: Cambridge University Press, 1970); Carol Pateman, *The Problem of Political Obligation: A Critique of Liberal Theory* (Cambridge: Polity Press, 1985).

18. Pateman, *Participation and Democratic Theory*, p. 110.

19. See the discussion of Marx in Held, *Models of Democracy*, pp. 105–143.

20. Robert A. Dahl, *A Preface to Economic Democracy* (Cambridge: Polity Press, 1985), p. 60.

21. See, for example, Carol C. Gould, *Rethinking Democracy* (New York: Cambridge University Press, 1988).

22. For a summary of the current debate, see Charles F. Andrain, "Capitalism and Democracy Revisited," *Western Political Quarterly* 37, no. 4 (1984): 652–664.

23. Joseph Schumpeter, *Capitalism, Socialism and Democracy* (1942; reprint, London: Allen and Unwin, 1976), p. 260.

24. Held, *Models of Democracy*, p. 271.

25. Ibid., p. 285.

26. Carl Cohen, *Democracy* (New York: Free Press, 1971), p. 109n; see also Gavin Kitching, *Rethinking Socialism: A Theory for a Better Practice* (London: Methuen, 1983), p. 49.

27. Francis Fukuyama, "The End of History?" *The National Interest*, no. 16 (1989): 3–18.

28. Robert A. Dahl, *Polyarchy: Participation and Opposition* (New Haven: Yale University Press, 1971), p. 3.

29. Hans-Jørgen Nielsen grouped these eight conditions in a similar way in *Den Chilenske Transitionsproces* (The Chilean process of transition) (Aarhus: University of Aarhus, Institute of Political Science, 1991), p. 5.

30. Larry Diamond, Juan J. Linz, and Seymour Martin Lipset (eds.), *Democracy in Developing Countries*. Vol. 2: *Africa* (Boulder: Lynne Rienner, 1988), p. xvi.

31. For such attempts at differentiation in African and Latin American countries, respectively, see Richard Sklar, "Democracy in Africa," *African Studies Review* 26, no. 3/4 (1983): 11–25, and Karen L. Remmer, "Exclusionary Democracy," *Studies in Comparative International Development* 20, no. 4 (1985–1986): 64–86.

32. Dahl, *Polyarchy*, p. 4.

33. Tatu Vanhanen, *The Process of Democratization: A Comparative Study of 147 States, 1980–88* (New York: Taylor and Francis, 1990).

34. R. Bruce McColm, "The Comparative Survey of Freedom: 1991," *Freedom Review* 22, no. 1 (1991): 5–24. For a general survey of attempts to measure democracy, see *Studies in Comparative International Development* 25, no. 1 (1990).

35. McColm, "The Comparative Survey of Freedom," p. 6.

36. Chalmers Johnson, "Political Institutions and Economic Performance: The Government-Business Relationship in Japan, South Korea, and Taiwan," in Frederic C. Deyo (ed.), *The Political Economy of the New Asian Industrialism* (Ithaca: Cornell University Press, 1987), p. 137. Emphasis added.

37. See, for example, Karl van Wolferen, *The Enigma of Japanese Power* (New York: Knopf, 1989).

38. See John Woronoff, *Politics the Japanese Way* (London: Macmillan, 1988); Roy Thomas, *Japan: The Blighted Blossom* (Vancouver: New Star, 1989).

39. Mark Gasiorowski, "The Political Regimes Project," *Studies in Comparative International Development* 25, no. 1 (1990): 112n.

40. United Nations Development Programme (UNDP), *Human Development Report 1991* (New York: Oxford University Press, 1991).

41. See Kitching, *Rethinking Socialism*, p. 48.

42. UNDP, *Human Development Report 1991*.

43. See Therborn, "The Rule of Capital."

44. See Robert O. Keohane and Joseph S. Nye, Jr., *Power and Interdependence: World Politics in Transition* (Boston: Little, Brown, 1977).

45. Robert A. Dahl, *Democracy and Its Critics* (New Haven: Yale University Press, 1989), p. 319.

46. Quoted from John Loxley, "The Devaluation Debate in Tanzania," in Bonnie K. Campbell and John Loxley (eds.), *Structural Adjustment in Africa* (London: Macmillan, 1989), p. 15.

47. J. R. Scott, *Comparative Political Corruption* (Englewood Cliffs, N.J.: Prentice-Hall, 1972), p. 137.

48. For an example of such a program, see O. M. Prakash and P. N. Rastogi, "Development of the Rural Poor: The Missing Factor," *IFDA Dossier* 51 (1986); see also Georg Sørensen, *Democracy, Dictatorship and Development: Economic Development in Selected Regimes of the Third World* (London: Macmillan, 1991), ch. 2.

49. See Mark Blecher, *China: Politics, Economics and Society* (London: Frances Pinter, 1986), p. 104.

50. Ibid., p. 25n.

51. Ibid., p. 26.

CHAPTER TWO

1. Seymour Martin Lipset, "Some Social Requisites of Democracy: Economic Development and Political Legitimacy," *American Political Science Review* 53 (1959): 75.

2. Samuel P. Huntington, "Will More Countries Become Democratic?" *Political Science Quarterly* 99, no. 2 (1984): 199.

3. Robert A. Dahl, *Polyarchy: Participation and Opposition* (New Haven: Yale University Press, 1971), p. 65.

4. Guillermo O'Donnell, *Modernization and Bureaucratic-Authoritarianism: Studies in South American Politics* (Berkeley: University of California, Institute of International Studies, 1973).

5. See Huntington, "Will More Countries Become Democratic?" p. 209.

6. See Terry Lynn Karl, "Dilemmas of Democratization in Latin America," *Comparative Politics* 23, no. 1 (1990): 4.

7. Barrington Moore, Jr., *Social Origins of Dictatorship and Democracy: Lord and Peasant in the Making of the Modern World* (Boston: Beacon Press, 1966), p. 418.

8. Goran Therborn, "The Rule of Capital and the Rise of Democracy," in David Held et al. (eds.), *States and Societies* (Oxford: Martin Robertson, 1983), p. 271.

9. See Huntington, "Will More Countries Become Democratic?" p. 206.

10. See, for example, Fernando Henrique Cardoso, "Dependent Capitalist Development in Latin America," *New Left Review* 80 (1973): 83–95.

11. Dahl, *Polyarchy*, pp. 202–208.

12. Larry Diamond, Juan J. Linz, and Seymour Martin Lipset (eds.), *Democracy in Developing Countries*. Vol. 2: *Africa* (Boulder: Lynne Rienner, 1988), pp. ix–xxix.

13. In Juan J. Linz and Alfred Stepan (eds.), *The Breakdown of Democratic Regimes: Crisis, Breakdown and Reequilibration* (Baltimore: Johns Hopkins University Press, 1978), p. 5. See also Dankwart A. Rustow, "Transitions to Democracy," *Comparative Politics* 2, no. 3 (1970): 337–365.

14. For a similar view, see Karl, "Dilemmas of Democratization."

15. Adam Przeworski, "Democracy as a Contingent Outcome of Conflicts," in Jon Elster and Rune Slagstad (eds.), *Constitutionalism and Democracy* (Cambridge: Cambridge University Press, 1988), pp. 59–81.

16. Ibid., p. 71.

17. See Guillermo O'Donnell and Philippe C. Schmitter, *Transitions from Authoritarian Rule: Tentative Conclusions About Uncertain Democracies* (Baltimore: Johns Hopkins University Press, 1986), p. 19.

18. Richard Sandbrook, "Liberal Democracy in Africa: A Socialist-Revisionist Perspective," *Canadian Journal of African Studies* 22, no. 2 (1988): 253.

19. See ibid., p. 254.

20. Przeworski, "Democracy as a Contingent Outcome," p. 69.

21. Ibid., p. 79.

22. For example, the categories used by Freedom House are free, partly free, and not free. Between 1990 and 1991, twenty-one countries experienced gains in freedom without changing category, and sixteen countries showed declines in freedom without changing category. See R. Bruce McColm, "The Comparative Survey of Freedom: 1991," *Freedom Review* 22, no. 1 (1991): 9.

23. Huntington, "Will More Countries Become Democratic?" p. 197.

24. Donald Share, "Transitions to Democracy and Transition Through Transaction," *Comparative Political Studies* 19, no. 4 (1987): 545. See also three articles on which my remarks draw: Kenneth Medhurst, "Spain's Evolutionary Pathway from Dictatorship to Democracy," *West European Politics* 7, no. 2 (1984): 30–50; P. Nikiforos Diamandouros, "Transition to, and Consolidation of, Democratic Politics in Greece, 1974–83: A Tentative Assessment," *West European Politics* 7, no. 2 (1984): 50–72; Thomas C. Bruneau, "Continuity and Change in Portuguese Politics: Ten Years After the Revolution of 25 April 1974," *West European Politics* 7, no. 2 (1984): 72–83.

25. Francisco C. Weffort, quoted from Hélgio Trindade, "Presidential Elections and Political Transition in Latin America," *International Social Science Journal* 128 (1991): 301–314.

26. See Fernando Henrique Cardoso, "Democracy in Latin America," *Politics and Society* 15, no. 1 (1986–1987): 32.

27. Timothy Garton Ash, "Eastern Europe: The Year of Truth," *The New York Review of Books*, February 15, 1990, pp. 17–22.

28. Quoted from Ole Nørgaard, "De post-stalinistiske samfund og demokratiet" (The post-Stalinist societies and democracy), *Politica* 23, no. 3 (1991): 246.

29. Ash, "Eastern Europe," p. 19.

30. See Nørgaard, "De post-stalinistiske samfund," pp. 241–259.

31. See Adam Przeworski, "The 'East' Becomes the 'South'? The 'Autumn of the People' and the Future of Eastern Europe," *PS Political Science and Politics* 24, no. 1 (1991): 21.

32. See Samuel Decalo, "The Process, Prospects and Constraints of Democratization in Africa" (Paper delivered at the XVth World Congress of the International Political Science Association, Buenos Aires, July 21–25, 1991), p. 2.

33. Ibid., p. 8.

34. See Jacques-Mariel Nzouankeu, "The African Attitude to Democracy," *International Social Science Journal* 128 (1991): 374.

35. Quoted from Decalo, "Democratization in Africa," p. 11.

36. See Karl D. Jackson, "The Philippines: The Search for a Suitable Democratic Solution, 1946–86," in Larry Diamond, Juan J. Linz, and Seymour Martin Lipset (eds.), *Democracy in Developing Countries*. Vol. 3: *Asia* (Boulder: Lynne Rienner, 1989), pp. 231–267.

37. See Niranjan Koirala, "Nepal in 1990: End of an Era," *Asian Survey* 31, no. 2 (1991): 134–140.

38. Rustow, "Transitions to Democracy."

39. Ibid., p. 350.

40. W. Ivor Jennings, quoted from ibid., p. 351.

41. Ibid., p. 354.

42. Alfred Stepan, "Paths Toward Redemocratization: Theoretical and Comparative Considerations," in Guillermo O'Donnell, Philippe C. Schmitter, and Laurence Whitehead (eds.), *Transitions from Authoritarian Rule: Comparative Perspectives* (Baltimore: Johns Hopkins University Press, 1988), pp. 64–85.

43. O'Donnell and Schmitter, *Transitions from Authoritarian Rule.*

44. See Nørgaard, "De post-stalinistiske samfund," p. 14.

45. Rustow, "Transitions to Democracy," p. 355.

46. Juan J. Linz, "Transitions to Democracy," *The Washington Quarterly* 13, no. 3 (1990): 156.

47. O'Donnell and Schmitter, *Transitions from Authoritarian Rule*, pp. 21–23.

48. Karl, "Dilemmas of Democratization," p. 9.

49. Ibid., p. 8.

50. Terry Lynn Karl and Philippe C. Schmitter, "Modes of Transition in Latin America, Southern and Eastern Europe," *International Social Science Journal* 128 (1991): 269–284.

51. Linz, "Transitions to Democracy," p. 158.

52. Ibid.

53. Jose Nun, "Democracy and Modernization, Thirty Years After" (Paper delivered at the XVth World Congress of the International Political Science Association, Buenos Aires, July 21–25, 1991), p. 23.

54. For a case study, see Thomas R. Rochon and Michael J. Mitchell, "Cultural Components of the Consolidation of Democracy in Brazil" (Paper delivered at the annual meeting of the American Political Science Association, Washington, D.C., August 28–31, 1991).

55. Some of what follows draws on Georg Sørensen, "Democracy and the Developmental State" (Institute of Political Science, University of Aarhus, 1991, Mimeographed).

56. See Frances Hagopian, "'Democracy by Undemocratic Means?' Elites, Political Pacts, and Regime Transition in Brazil," *Comparative Political Studies* 23, no. 2 (1990): 154–157.

57. Ibid., p. 157.

58. Ibid., p. 159.

59. See Karl, "Dilemmas of Democratization," p. 14.

60. For a case study of the Chilean transition, see Hans-Jørgen Nielsen, *Den Chilenske Transitionsproces* (The Chilean process of transition) (Aarhus: University of Aarhus, Institute of Political Science, 1991).

61. This argument is made by O'Donnell and Schmitter, *Transitions from Authoritarian Rule*, p. 66.

62. Karl, "Dilemmas of Democratization," p. 13.

63. See Juan Rial, "Transitions in Latin America on the Threshold of the 1990s," *International Social Science Journal* 128 (1991): 299; Carlos H. Waisman, "Argentina: Autarkic Industrialization and Illegitimacy," in Larry Diamond, Juan J. Linz, and Seymour Martin Lipset (eds.), *Democracy in Developing Countries*. Vol. 4: *Latin America* (Boulder: Lynne Rienner, 1989), p. 102.

64. Rial, "Transitions in Latin America," p. 290.

65. Karl, "Dilemmas of Democratization," p. 12.

66. Dahl, *Polyarchy*, p. 50.

67. World Bank, *Sub-Saharan Africa: From Crisis to Sustainable Growth. A Long-Term Perspective Study* (Washington, D.C.: World Bank, 1989), p. 1.

68. Some of what follows draws on Sørensen, "Democracy and the Developmental State."

69. Richard Sandbrook, *The Politics of Africa's Economic Stagnation* (Cambridge: Cambridge University Press, 1985); Richard Sandbrook, "The State and Economic Stagnation in Tropical Africa," *World Development* 14, no. 3 (1986): 319–332; Goran Hyden, *No Shortcuts to Progress: African Development Management in Perspective* (London: Heinemann, 1983); Robert Jackson and Carl G. Rosberg, *Personal Rule in Black Africa: Prince, Autocrat, Prophet, Tyrant* (Berkeley: University of California Press, 1982).

70. Sandbrook, "The State and Economic Stagnation," p. 324.

71. Ibid.

72. Ruth Berins Collier, *Regimes in Tropical Africa: Changing Forms of Supremacy 1945–75* (Berkeley: University of California Press, 1975), p. 22.

73. See, for example, Robert Jackson and Carl G. Rosberg, "Democracy in Tropical Africa: Democracy Versus Autocracy in African Politics," *Journal of International Affairs* 38, no. 2 (1985): 305.

74. Ibid., p. 301.

75. Linz, "Transitions to Democracy," p. 146.

76. See the article by Ole Therkildsen, "Democracy Is Forced down Africa's Throat," in the Danish newspaper *Information*, January 3, 1992, p. 2. At the same time, it must be admitted that there are no simple or straightforward answers to the question about the best ways to promote democracy. The final chapter in this book has some remarks on the strategy of promoting democracy from the grass-roots level.

77. Robert A. Dahl, *Democracy and Its Critics* (New Haven: Yale University Press, 1989), p. 314.

78. For a case study of Botswana, see John D. Holm, "Botswana: A Paternalistic Democracy," in Diamond, Linz, and Lipset (eds.), *Democracy in Developing Countries*, Vol. 2, pp. 179–217.

79. Quoted from Timothy Garton Ash, *The Polish Revolution* (London: Hodder & Stoughton, 1985), p. 1.

80. Janos Kis, "Turning Point in Hungary," *Dissent* (Spring 1989): 238.

81. See Ole Nørgaard, "Reflections on the Revolutions in Eastern Europe" (Institute of Political Science, University of Aarhus, 1990, Mimeographed).

82. "A valley of tears" is an expression used by Ralf Dahrendorf in a lecture on Eastern Europe in Oslo, 1990.

83. Nørgaard, "De post-stalinistiske samfund," and Paul G. Lewis, "Democratization in Eastern Europe," *Coexistence* 27 (1990): 245–267.

84. Karl and Schmitter, "Modes of Transition," p. 272.

85. Przeworski, "The 'East' Becomes the 'South'?" p. 23n.

86. See Linz, "Transitions to Democracy," p. 152.

87. O'Donnell and Schmitter, *Transitions from Authoritarian Rule*, p. 54.

88. David Lehmann, *Democracy and Development in Latin America* (Cambridge: Polity Press, 1990), p. 150.

89. Naomi Chazan, "The New Politics of Participation in Tropical Africa," *Comparative Politics* 14, no. 2 (1982): 172.

90. Sandbrook, *The Politics of Africa's Economic Stagnation*, p. 148.

91. Sandbrook, "Liberal Democracy in Africa," p. 262.

92. Rochon and Mitchell, "Cultural Components," p. 17.

93. Ralf Dahrendorf, lecture on Eastern Europe, Oslo, 1990.

94. Karl, "Dilemmas of Democratization," p. 17.

CHAPTER THREE

1. For a recent overview of the debate, see Larry Sirowy and Alex Inkeles, "The Effects of Democracy on Economic Growth and Inequality: A Review," *Studies in Comparative International Development* 25, no. 1 (1990): 126–157. Some of what follows draws on Georg Sørensen, *Democracy, Dictatorship and Development: Economic Development in Selected Regimes of the Third World* (London: Macmillan, 1991).

2. B. K. Nehru, "Western Democracy and the Third World," *Third World Quarterly* 1, no. 2 (1979): p. 57n. See also V. Rao, "Democracy and Economic Development," *Studies in Comparative International Development* 19, no. 4 (1984–1985): 67–82.

3. Samuel P. Huntington, *Political Order in Changing Societies* (New Haven: Yale University Press, 1968).

4. David E. Apter, *The Politics of Modernization* (Chicago: University of Chicago Press, 1965).

5. See Dieter Senghaas, *The European Experience: A Historical Critique of Development Theory* (Leamington Spa/Dover: Berg Publishers, 1985), and Dieter Senghaas, "China 1979," in J. Habermas (ed.), *Stichworte zur "Geistigen Situation der Zeit,"* Vol. 1 (Frankfurt Main: Suhrkamp, 1979), p. 435.

6. J. A. Hall, *Powers and Liberties: The Causes and Consequences of the Rise of the West* (Harmondsworth: Penguin, 1986), p. 222.

7. Gabriel Almond and G. Bingham Powell, *Comparative Politics: A Developmental Approach* (Boston: Little, Brown, 1978), p. 363. See also Samuel P. Huntington, "The Goals of Development," in Myron Weiner and Samuel P. Huntington (eds.), *Understanding Political Development* (Boston: Little, Brown, 1987), p. 19, and Irene Gendzier, *Managing Political Change: Social Scientists and the Third World* (Boulder: Westview, 1985), ch. 6.

8. See Hollis Chenery et al., *Redistribution with Growth* (London: Oxford University Press, 1974), and Paul Streeten et al., *First Things First: Meeting Basic Human Needs in Developing Countries* (New York: Oxford University Press, 1981).

9. See Grace Goodell and John P. Powelson, "The Democratic Prerequisites of Development," in Raymond Gastil (ed.), *Freedom in the World: Political Rights and Civil Liberties* (New York: Freedom House, 1982), pp. 167–176, and Atul Kohli, "Democracy and Development," in John Lewis and Valeriana Kallab (eds.), *Development Strategies Reconsidered* (New Brunswick, N.J.: Transaction Books, 1986), pp. 153–182.

10. Richard Claude, "The Classical Model of Human Rights Development," in Richard Claude (ed.), *Comparative Human Rights* (Baltimore: Johns Hopkins University Press, 1976), pp. 6–50.

11. See Georg Sørensen, "Democracy and the Developmental State" (Institute of Political Science, University of Aarhus, 1991. Mimeographed).

12. See the overview in Sirowy and Inkeles, "The Effects of Democracy on Economic Growth."

13. Robert M. Marsh, "Does Democracy Hinder Economic Development in the Latecomer Developing Nations?" *Comparative Social Research* 2 (1979): 244.

14. Yousseff Cohen, "The Impact of Bureaucratic-Authoritarian Rule on Economic Growth," *Comparative Political Studies* 18, no. 1 (1985): 123–136.

15. Dirk Berg-Schlosser, "African Political Systems: Typology and Performance," *Comparative Political Studies* 17, no. 1 (1984): 143.

16. Ibid., p. 121.

17. Dwight Y. King, "Regime Type and Performance: Authoritarian Rule, Semi-Capitalist Development and Rural Inequality in Asia," *Comparative Political Studies* 13, no. 4 (1981): 477.

18. G. William Dick, "Authoritarian Versus Nonauthoritarian Approaches to Economic Development," *Journal of Political Economy* 82, no. 4 (1974): 823.

19. Sirowy and Inkeles, "The Effects of Democracy on Economic Growth."

20. Some of these considerations draw on Sørensen, *Democracy, Dictatorship and Development.*

21. See Jean Drèze and Amartya Sen, *Hunger and Public Action* (Oxford: Clarendon Press, 1989), p. 206n.

22. See C. Ka and M. Selden, "Original Accumulation, Equity and Late Industrialization: The Cases of Socialist China and Capitalist Taiwan," *World Development* 14, no. 10/11 (1986): 1300n.

23. See, for example, Francine Frankel, "Is Authoritarianism the Solution to India's Economic Development Problems?" in Atul Kohli (ed.), *The State and Development in the Third World* (Princeton: Princeton University Press, 1986), pp. 154–161.

24. Barrington Moore, Jr., *Social Origins of Dictatorship and Democracy: Lord and Peasant in the Making of the Modern World* (Boston: Beacon Press, 1966), p. 355.

25. Pranab Bardhan, *The Political Economy of Development in India* (Delhi: Oxford University Press, 1984), p. 56. See also Rajni Kothari, *Politics in India* (Delhi: Orient Longman, 1982), p. 352n, and K. Subbarao, "State Policies and Regional Disparity in Indian Agriculture," *Development and Change* 16, no. 4 (1985): 543.

26. A. Piazza, *Food Consumption and Nutritional Status in the PRC* (Boulder: Westview, 1986), p. 36.

27. Carl Riskin, *China's Political Economy: The Quest for Development Since 1949* (Oxford: Oxford University Press, 1987), p. 276.

28. See Ka and Selden, "Original Accumulation," p. 1301.

29. Clemens Stubbe Østergaard and Christina Petersen, "Official Profiteering and the Tiananmen Square Demonstrations in China" (Paper delivered at the Second Liverpool Conference on Fraud, Corruption and Business Crime, Liverpool, April 17–19, 1991).

30. See Sørensen, *Democracy, Dictatorship and Development.*

31. G. Etienne, *India's Changing Rural Scene 1963–79* (New Delhi: Oxford University Press, 1982), pp. 152–158; J. Breman, "I Am the Government Labour Officer . . . State Protection for Rural Proletariat of South Gujarat," *Economic and Political Weekly* 20, no. 4 (June 15, 1985): 1043–1056.

32. Bardhan, *The Political Economy of Development in India*, p. 4.

33. The following analysis draws heavily on Bardhan, *The Political Economy of Development in India.*

34. See A. Rudra, "Political Economy of Indian Non-Development," *Economic and Political Weekly* 20, no. 21 (May 25, 1985), p. 916.

35. Riskin, *China's Political Economy*, p. 235.

36. See Piazza, *Food Consumption and Nutritional Status*, p. 176.

37. Drèze and Sen, *Hunger and Public Action*, p. 209.

38. Ibid., p. 215.

39. See, for example, Thomas B. Gold, *State and Society in the Taiwan Miracle* (New York: M. E. Sharpe, 1986).

40. Jon Halliday, "The North Korean Enigma," in Gordon White et al. (eds.), *Revolutionary Socialist Development in the Third World* (Brighton: Wheatsheaf, 1983), pp. 114–155; Clive Hamilton, *Capitalist Industrialization in Korea* (Boulder: Westview, 1986).

41. Peter T. Knight, "Brazilian Socio-Economic Development: Issues for the Eighties," *World Development* 9, no. 11–12 (1981).

42. Sylvia Ann Hewlett, *The Cruel Dilemmas of Development: Twentieth Century Brazil* (New York: Basic Books, 1980).

43. See C. Ominami, "Déindustrialisation et restructuration industrielle en Argentine, au Brésil et au Chili," *Problemas D'Amerique Latine* 89 (1988): 55–79.

44. D. Cruise O'Brien, quoted from Goran Hyden, *No Shortcuts to Progress: African Development Management in Perspective* (London: Heineman, 1983), p. 37.

45. David Gould, "The Administration of Underdevelopment," in Guy Gran (ed.), *Zaire: The Political Economy of Underdevelopment* (New York: Praeger, 1979), pp. 87–107; Salua Nour, "Zaire," in Dieter Nohlen and Franz Nuscheler (eds.), *Handbuch der Dritten Welt*, vol. 4 (Hamburg: Hoffmann und Campe), pp. 468–522.

46. Nour, "Zaire," p. 512.

47. See Hewlett, *The Cruel Dilemmas of Development*, and Knight, "Brazilian Socio-Economic Development."

48. See Sørensen, *Democracy, Dictatorship and Development*, ch. 2.

49. See Charles D. Ameringer, *Democracy in Costa Rica* (New York: Praeger, 1982); John A. Peeler, *Latin American Democracies: Colombia, Costa Rica, Venezuela* (Chapel Hill: University of North Carolina Press, 1985).

50. Peeler, *Latin American Democracies*, p. 129.

51. See C. Hall, *Costa Rica: A Geographical Interpretation in Historical Perspective* (Boulder: Westview, 1985), p. 270.

52. Ameringer, *Democracy in Costa Rica*, p. 19.

53. J. A. Booth, "Costa Rica," in Larry Diamond, Juan J. Linz, and Seymour Martin Lipset (eds.), *Democracy in Developing Countries. Vol. 4: Latin America* (Boulder: Lynne Rienner, 1989), p. 417.

54. The remarks on Chile are based on Jakob J. Simonsen and Georg Sørensen, *Chile 1970–73: Et eksempel på Østeuropæisk udviklingsstrategi?* (Aarhus: University of Aarhus, Institute of Political Science, 1976).

55. See Atul Kohli, *The State and Poverty in India: The Politics of Reform* (Cambridge: Harvard University Press, 1987).

56. Jack Donnelly, "Human Rights and Development: Complementary or Competing Concerns?" *World Politics* 36, no. 2 (1984): 281n.

57. See, for example, Johan Galtung, "Why the Concern with Ways of Life?" in Council for International Development Studies, *The Western Development Model and Life Style* (Oslo: University of Oslo, 1980).

58. See Jack Donnelly, *Human Rights and World Politics* (Boulder: Westview, 1993).

59. United Nations Development Programme (UNDP), *Human Development Report 1991* (New York: Oxford University Press, 1991), p. 20.

60. See Richard Falk, *Human Rights and State Sovereignty* (New York: Holmes and Meier, 1981), pp. 63–124.

61. See Stephen Marks, "Promoting Human Rights," in Michael T. Klare and Daniel C. Thomas, *World Security: Trends and Challenges at Century's End* (New York: St. Martin's Press, 1991), p. 303.

CHAPTER FOUR

1. An English version of Kant's "Perpetual Peace" can be found in Hans Reiss (ed.), *Kant's Political Writings* (Cambridge: Cambridge University Press, 1970). My summary of Kant's ideas relies heavily on three articles by Michael W. Doyle: "Kant, Liberal Legacies and Foreign Affairs," *Philosophy and Public Affairs* 12, no. 3 (1983): 205–235; "Kant, Liberal Legacies and Foreign Affairs, Part 2," *Philosophy and Public Affairs* 12, no. 4 (1983): 323–354; and "Liberalism and World Politics," *American Political Science Review* 80, no. 4 (1986): 1151–1169.

2. Quoted from Reiss, *Kant's Political Writings*, p. 100.

3. Quoted from Doyle, "Liberalism and World Politics," p. 1153.

4. See Rudolph J. Rummel, "Libertarianism and International Violence," *Journal of Conflict Resolution* 27, no. 1 (1983): 27–71.

5. See Melvin Small and J. David Singer, "The War-Proneness of Democratic Regimes," *The Jerusalem Journal of International Relations* 1, no. 4 (1976): 50–69; Steve Chan, "Mirror, Mirror on the Wall . . . Are the Freer Countries More Pacific?" *Journal of Conflict Resolution* 28, no. 4 (1984): 617–648; Erich Weede, "Democracy and War Involvement," *Journal of Conflict Resolution* 28, no. 4 (1984): 649–664. Yet it should be added that studies such as Chan's (cited in note 5), which are based on very long periods of observation, face other difficulties because, as was demonstrated in Chapter 1, the concrete content of the entity called "democracy" changes over time.

6. Doyle, "Kant, Liberal Legacies and Foreign Affairs," p. 213.

7. Dean Babst, "Elective Governments—A Force for Peace," *The Wisconsin Sociologist* 3, no. 1 (1964): 9–14; see also Small and Singer, "The War-Proneness of Democratic Regimes"; Chan, "Mirror, Mirror"; Bruce Russett, "Democracy and Peace," in B. Russett, H. Starr, and R. J. Stoll, *Choices in World Politics: Sovereignty and Interdependence* (New York: Freeman and Company, 1989), pp. 245–261; and James Lee Ray, "The Future of International War" (Paper delivered at the Annual Meeting of the American Political Science Association, Washington, D.C., August 29 to September 1, 1991).

8. Russett, "Democracy and Peace," p. 245.

9. Reiss, *Kant's Political Writings*, p. 114.

10. Doyle, "Liberalism and World Politics," p. 1161.

11. Doyle, "Kant, Liberal Legacies and Foreign Affairs, Part 2," p. 324n. This quotation was italicized in the original.

12. See Russett, "Democracy and Peace," p. 250.

13. Walter Lippmann, *Essays in the Public Philosophy* (Boston: Little, Brown, 1955), p. 20.

14. Doyle, "Kant, Liberal Legacies and Foreign Affairs, Part 2," p. 344.

15. Quoted from Kjell Goldmann, "'Democracy Is Incompatible with International Politics': Reconsideration of a Hypothesis," in K. Goldmann, S. Berglund, and G. Sjöstedt, *Democracy and Foreign Policy* (Aldershot: Gower, 1986), p. 2.

16. Ibid. There are several modern versions of Ponsonby's argument. See, for example, Jørgen Christensen, *Demokratiet og sikkerhedspolitikken*, Vols. I and II (Democracy and security policy) (Aarhus: University of Aarhus, Institute of Political Science, 1990).

17. See Goldmann, "'Democracy Is Incompatible with International Politics,'" pp. 5–8.

18. Ibid., p. 7n.

19. Further distinctions have been made that focus the argument concerning incompatibility primarily on diplomatic security policy. They are outlined in ibid., pp. 27–31.

20. Thomas Risse-Kappen, "Public Opinion, Domestic Structure, and Foreign Policy in Liberal Democracies," *World Politics* 43, no. 4 (1991): 479–513.

21. Ibid., p. 510.

22. Bruce Russett and Harvey Starr, *World Politics: The Menu for Choice* (New York: W. H. Freeman, 1985), p. 250. See also Hans-Henrik Holm, "The Democratic Victory: What Will Happen to Foreign Policy?" in Wojtech Kostecki (ed.), *Eastern*

Europe in Transition: A Chance or Threat to Peace? Proceedings of a seminar (Warsaw: Polish Institute of International Affairs, 1991), pp. 44–63; and Kurt Taylor Gaubatz, "Election Cycles and War," *Journal of Conflict Resolution* 35, no. 2 (1991): 212–245.

23. Doyle, "Kant, Liberal Legacies and Foreign Affairs," p. 213.

24. See Stephen Van Evera, "Primed for Peace: Europe After the Cold War," *International Security* 15, no. 3 (1990/1991): 26n.

25. Ibid., p. 25.

26. Doyle, "Kant, Liberal Legacies and Foreign Affairs," p. 213; Russett, "Democracy and Peace," p. 260.

27. Adam Watson, "European International Society and Its Expansion," in Hedley Bull and Adam Watson (eds.), *The Expansion of International Society* (Oxford: Clarendon Press, 1988), p. 23.

28. Ibid., p. 24n.

29. Ibid., p. 1.

30. Barry Buzan, *People, States and Fear: An Agenda for International Security Studies in the Post–Cold War Era* (Hemel Hempstead: Harvester Wheatsheaf, 1991), p. 169.

31. Daniel Bell, *The Coming of Post-Industrial Society: A Venture in Social Forecasting* (New York: Basic Books, 1973), p. 317.

32. See, for example, James N. Rosenau, *Turbulence in World Politics: A Theory of Change and Continuity* (Princeton: Princeton University Press, 1990), pp. 416–443.

33. See Barry Buzan, "New Patterns of Global Security in the Twenty-First Century," *International Affairs* 67, no. 3 (1991): 431–451.

34. See Karl Deutsch and S. A. Burrell, *Political Community and the North Atlantic Area* (Princeton: Princeton University Press, 1957). See also Buzan, "New Patterns of Global Security," p. 436.

35. See Volker Rittberger, "Zur Friedensfähigkeit von Demokratien," *Aus Politik und Zeitgeschichte*, no. 44 (1987): 3–12.

36. Speech printed in the *New York Times*, March 12, 1913, p. 1, quoted from Cole Blasier, "The United States and Democracy in Latin America," in James M. Malloy and Mitchell A. Seligson (eds.), *Authoritarians and Democrats: Regime Transition in Latin America* (Pittsburgh: University of Pittsburgh Press, 1987), pp. 219–233.

37. Quoted from Doyle, "Kant, Liberal Legacies and Foreign Affairs, Part 2," p. 335.

38. See, for example, James Petras and Morris Morley, *How Allende Fell* (Nottingham: Spokesman, 1974).

39. On U.S. involvement in Central America, see Thomas Carothers, *In the Name of Democracy: U.S. Policy Toward Latin America in the Reagan Years* (Los Angeles: University of California Press, 1991).

40. Russett, "Democracy and Peace," p. 256.

41. See Aldo C. Vacs, "Ambiguous Crusade, Uncertain Commitment: International Factors and the Transition to Democracy in the 1980s" (Paper delivered at the XVth World Congress of the International Political Science Association, Buenos Aires, July 21–25, 1991). See also Richard Sandbrook, "Taming the African Leviathan," *World Policy Journal* 7, no. 4 (1990): 673–701.

42. See Timothy Garton Ash, "Ten Thoughts on the New Europe," *The New York Review of Books*, June 14, 1990; the Dienstbier quotation is from page 22 of this article.

43. Alex Inkeles, "The Emerging Social Structure of the World," *World Politics* 27, no. 4 (1975): 479.

44. See Barry B. Hughes, *Continuity and Change in World Politics* (Englewood Cliffs, N.J.: Prentice-Hall, 1991), p. 328n. For the view that the growth of trade and investment should not be exaggerated relative to the levels in the early twentieth century, see Janice E. Thompson and Stephen D. Krasner, "Global Transactions and the Consolidation of Sovereignty," in E-O. Czempiel and J. Rosenau (eds.), *Global Changes and Theoretical Challenges* (Lexington, Mass.: Lexington Books, 1989), pp. 195–220.

45. See Stephen D. Krasner, "State Power and the Structure of International Trade," *World Politics* 28, no. 3 (1976): 317–348.

46. Deutsch and Burrell, *Political Community*, p. 5.

47. See, for example, Frederic C. Deyo (ed.), *The Political Economy of the New Asian Industrialism* (Ithaca: Cornell University Press, 1987).

48. See, for example, J. Galtung, P. O'Brien, and R. Preiswerk (eds.), *Self-Reliance: A Strategy for Development* (London: Bogle-L'Overture, 1980).

49. For the changes in strategy, see Georg Sørensen, "Strategies and Structures of Development: The New 'Consensus' and the Limits to Its Promises," *European Journal of Development Research* 3, no. 2 (1991): 121–146. For a discussion of the shrinking market opportunities and other problems for the South, see John Ravenhill, "The North-South Balance of Power," *International Affairs* 66, no. 4 (1990): 731–748.

50. Joan Edelman Spero, *The Politics of International Economic Relations* (London: George Allen & Unwin, 1985), p. 169n.

51. See Walden Bello and Stephanie Rosenfeld, "Dragons in Distress: The Crisis of the NICs," *World Policy Journal* 7, no. 3 (1990): 431–469.

52. See Sandbrook, "Taming the African Leviathan," and John Ravenhill, "Reversing Africa's Economic Decline: No Easy Answers," *World Policy Journal* 7, no. 4 (1990): 703–732. For discussion of the debt crisis in Latin America, see David Felix, "Latin America's Debt Crisis," *World Policy Journal* 7, no. 4 (1990): 733–771. The quote is from World Bank, *Sub-Saharan Africa: From Crisis to Sustainable Growth* (Washington, D.C.: World Bank, 1989), p. 185.

53. John J. Mearsheimer, "Back to the Future: Instability in Europe After the Cold War," *International Security* 15, no. 1 (1990): 49.

54. Ibid., pp. 49–51.

55. Ibid., p. 50.

56. Buzan, *People, States and Fears*, p. 190.

57. The argument is set forth at length on a neorealist basis in ibid., pp. 186–229.

58. Ole Wæver, "Conflicts of Vision: Visions of Conflict," in Ole Wæver et al. (eds.), *European Polyphony: Perspectives Beyond East-West Confrontation* (London: Macmillan, 1989), pp. 283–327.

59. Robert Jervis, "Security Regimes," *International Organization* 36, no. 2 (1982): 357.

60. Mearsheimer, "Back to the Future," p. 50.

61. Two significant contributions supporting Kantian arguments are Van Evera, "Primed for Peace," and Richard H. Ullman, *Securing Europe* (Princeton: Princeton University Press, 1991). See also the debate on Mearsheimer's contribution in *International Security* 15, no. 2 (1990): 191–200, and *International Security* 15, no. 3 (1990/1991): 216–222.

CHAPTER FIVE

1. Francis Fukuyama, "The End of History?" *The National Interest*, no. 16 (1989): 4.

2. Samuel P. Huntington, "Democracy's Third Wave," *Journal of Democracy* 2, no. 2 (1991): 33. See also Samuel P. Huntington, "No Exit: The Errors of Endism," *The National Interest*, no. 17 (1989): 3–11.

3. For an example of how the debate continues and the many unanswered questions, see "Roundtable Discussion: Politics, Economics, and Welfare," in Ian Shapiro and Grant Reeher (eds.), *Power, Inequality, and Democratic Politics: Essays in Honor of Robert A. Dahl* (Boulder: Westview, 1988), pp. 153–167.

4. Robert C. Johansen, "A Policy Framework for World Security," in Michael T. Klare and Daniel C. Thomas, *World Security: Trends and Challenges at Century's End* (New York: St. Martin's Press, 1991), p. 412.

5. Richard Falk, *Human Rights and State Sovereignty* (New York: Holmes & Meier, 1981), p. 103.

6. David Held, *Models of Democracy* (Cambridge: Polity Press, 1987), pp. 267–301.

7. UN Centre on Transnational Corporations, *Transnational Corporations in World Development* (New York: United Nations, 1988), p. 92.

8. Pascal Bruckner, *La mélancolie démocratique* (Paris: Editions du Seuil, 1990); Oliver Mongin, *La peur du vide* (Paris: Editions du Seuil, 1990).

9. See Neal Ascherson, "Old Wounds Exposed by Post-Communist Thaw," *The Independent*, October 6, 1991.

10. Robert A. Dahl, *Democracy and Its Critics* (New Haven: Yale University Press, 1989), p. 314. The conditions outlined by Dahl were set forth in Chapter 2 of this volume.

11. Ibid., p. 315.

12. Huntington, "Democracy's Third Wave," p. 21.

13. Ibid., p. 33.

14. Dahl's quote appears in *Democracy and Its Critics*, p. 313.

15. Francisco C. Weffort, "A America errada," *Lua Nova* 21 (1990): 39.

16. Timothy Garton Ash, "Eastern Europe: The Year of Truth," *The New York Review of Books*, February 15, 1990, p. 21.

17. See, for example, Rebekka Sylvest, *Værdier og udvikling i Saudi-Arabien* (Values and development in Saudi Arabia) (Aarhus: University of Aarhus, Institute of Political Science, 1991). For the role of Islam as a carrier of anti-Western sentiment, see Barry Buzan, "New Patterns of Global Security in the Twenty-First Century," *International Affairs* 67, no. 3 (1991): 441n.

18. See Kari Levitt, "Debt, Adjustment and Development: Looking to the 1990s," *Economic and Political Weekly,* July 21, 1990, p. 1586. It should be stressed that using 1974 as the base year maximizes the deterioration in terms of trade for the South. If other base years or different time spans are used, the deterioration is less dramatic.

19. Ibid., p. 1587.

20. Ibid., p. 1589.

21. The quotation is by Marshall Wolfe and is included in Denis Goulet, "Participation in Development: New Avenues," *World Development* 17, no. 2 (1989): 165.

22. Guy Gran, *Development by People: Citizen Construction of a Just World* (New York: Praeger, 1983).

23. Goulet, "Participation in Development," p. 175n. For additional examples of participation and organization from below, see, for example, Robert Chambers, *Rural Development: Putting the Last First* (London: Longman, 1983); Andreas Fuglesang and Dale Chandler, *Participation as Process—What We Can Learn from Grameen Bank, Bangladesh* (Oslo: Norad, n.d.).

24. See Goulet, "Participation in Development."

25. See David Lehmann, *Democracy and Development in Latin America: Economics, Politics and Religion in the Postwar Period* (Cambridge: Polity Press, 1989).

26. Because durable, qualitative changes at the local level are a prerequisite for durable, qualitative changes at the national level, the cutbacks in aid to nondemocratic regimes (as a result of political conditionality policies) do not include a termination of projects aimed at empowerment of the poor—for example, the NGO projects mentioned earlier.

□ □ □

Suggested Readings

Andrain, Charles F. "Capitalism and Democracy Revisited." *Western Political Quarterly* 37, no. 4 (1984): 652–664.

Ash, Timothy Garton. "Eastern Europe: The Year of Truth." *The New York Review of Books,* February 15, 1990, 17–22.

Babst, Dean. "A Force for Peace." *Industrial Research* 14 (April 1972): 55–58.

Bardhan, Pranab. *The Political Economy of Development in India.* Delhi: Oxford University Press, 1984.

Berg-Schlosser, Dirk. "African Political Systems: Typology and Performance." *Comparative Political Studies* 17, no. 1 (1984): 121–151.

Bull, Hedley, and Adam Watson (eds.). *The Expansion of International Society.* Oxford: Clarendon Press, 1988.

Buzan, Barry. "New Patterns of Global Security in the Twenty-First Century." *International Affairs* 67, no. 3 (1991): 431–451.

_____ . *People, States and Fear: An Agenda for International Security Studies in the Post–Cold War Era.* Hemel Hempstead: Harvester Wheatsheaf, 1991.

Carothers, Thomas. *In the Name of Democracy: U.S. Policy Toward Latin America in the Reagan Years.* Los Angeles: University of California Press, 1991.

Chan, Steve. "Mirror, Mirror on the Wall ... Are the Freer Countries More Pacific?" *Journal of Conflict Resolution* 28, no. 4 (1984): 617–648.

Cohen, Yousseff. "The Impact of Bureaucratic-Authoritarian Rule on Economic Growth." *Comparative Political Studies* 18, no. 1 (1985): 123–136.

Dahl, Robert A. *Polyarchy: Participation and Opposition.* New Haven: Yale University Press, 1971.

_____ . *A Preface to Economic Democracy.* Cambridge: Polity Press, 1985.

_____ . *Democracy and Its Critics.* New Haven: Yale University Press, 1989.

Diamond, Larry, Juan J. Linz, and Seymour Martin Lipset (eds.). *Democracy in Developing Countries.* Vol. 1: *Persistence, Failure, and Renewal.* Vol. 2: *Africa.* Vol. 3: *Asia.* Vol. 4: *Latin America.* Boulder: Lynne Rienner, 1988, 1989.

Dick, William G. "Authoritarian Versus Nonauthoritarian Approaches to Economic Development." *Journal of Political Economy* 82, no. 4 (1974): 817–827.

Donnelly, Jack. "Human Rights and Development: Complementary or Competing Concerns?" *World Politics* 36, no. 2 (1984): 255–284.

_____ . *Human Rights and World Politics.* Boulder: Westview, 1993.

Doyle, Michael W. "Kant, Liberal Legacies and Foreign Affairs." *Philosophy and Public Affairs* 12, no. 3 (1983): 205–235.

———— . "Kant, Liberal Legacies and Foreign Affairs, Part 2." *Philosophy and Public Affairs* 12, no. 4 (1983): 323–354.

———— . "Liberalism and World Politics." *American Political Science Review* 80, no. 4 (1986): 1151–1169.

Falk, Richard. *Human Rights and State Sovereignty.* New York: Holmes and Meier, 1981.

Frankel, Francine. "Is Authoritarianism the Solution to India's Economic Development Problems?" In Atul Kohli (ed.), *The State and Development in the Third World.* Princeton: Princeton University Press, 1986, pp. 154–161.

Fukuyama, Francis. "The End of History?" *The National Interest,* no. 16 (1989): 3–18.

Galtung, Johan. "Why the Concern with Ways of Life?" In Council for International Development Studies, *The Western Development Model and Life Style.* Oslo: University of Oslo, 1980, pp. 46–71.

Gaubatz, Kurt Taylor. "Election Cycles and War." *Journal of Conflict Resolution* 35, no. 2 (1991): 212–245.

Goldmann, Kjell. "'Democracy Is Incompatible with International Politics': Reconsideration of a Hypothesis." In K. Goldmann, S. Berglund, and G. Sjöstedt, *Democracy and Foreign Policy.* Aldershot: Gower, 1986, pp. 1–44.

Goodell, Grace, and John P. Powelson. "The Democratic Prerequisites of Development." In Raymond Gastil (ed.), *Freedom in the World: Political Rights and Civil Liberties.* New York: Freedom House, 1982, pp. 167–176.

Goulet, Denis. "Participation in Development: New Avenues." *World Development* 17, no. 2 (1989): 165–178.

Gran, Guy. *Development by People: Citizen Construction of a Just World.* New York: Praeger, 1983.

Hagopian, Frances. "'Democracy by Undemocratic Means?' Elites, Political Pacts, and Regime Transition in Brazil." *Comparative Political Studies* 23, no. 2 (1990): 147–170.

Held, David. *Models of Democracy.* Cambridge: Polity Press, 1987.

Holm, Hans-Henrik. "The Democratic Victory: What Will Happen to Foreign Policy?" In Wojtech Kostecki (ed.), *Eastern Europe in Transition: A Chance or Threat to Peace?* Proceedings of a seminar (Warsaw: Polish Institute of International Affairs, 1991), pp. 44–63.

Huntington, Samuel P. "Will More Countries Become Democratic?" *Political Science Quarterly* 99, no. 2 (1984): 193–218.

———— . "No Exit: The Errors of Endism." *The National Interest,* no. 17 (1989): 3–11.

———— . "Democracy's Third Wave." *Journal of Democracy* 2, no. 2 (1991): 12–34.

Hyden, Goran. *No Shortcuts to Progress: African Development Management in Perspective.* London: Heinemann, 1983.

Jackson, Robert, and Carl G. Rosberg. *Personal Rule in Black Africa: Prince, Autocrat, Prophet, Tyrant.* Berkeley: University of California Press, 1982.

Johansen, Robert C. "A Policy Framework for World Security." In Michael T. Klare and Daniel C. Thomas (eds.), *World Security: Trends and Challenges at Century's End.* New York: St. Martin's Press, 1991, pp. 401–425.

Karl, Terry Lynn. "Dilemmas of Democratization in Latin America." *Comparative Politics* 23, no. 1 (1990): 1–21.

King, Dwight Y. "Regime Type and Performance: Authoritarian Rule, Semi-Capitalist Development and Rural Inequality in Asia." *Comparative Political Studies* 13, no. 4 (1981): 477–504.

Kohli, Atul. "Democracy and Development." In John Lewis and Valeriana Kallab (eds.), *Development Strategies Reconsidered*. New Brunswick, N.J.: Transaction Books, 1986, pp. 153–182.

_____. *The State and Poverty in India: The Politics of Reform*. Cambridge, Mass.: Harvard University Press, 1987.

Lehmann, David. *Democracy and Development in Latin America*. Cambridge: Polity Press, 1990.

Lewis, Paul G. "Democratization in Eastern Europe." *Coexistence* 27 (1990): 245–267.

Linz, Juan J. "Transitions to Democracy." *The Washington Quarterly* 13, no. 3 (1990): 143–164.

Lipset, Seymour M. "Some Social Requisites of Democracy: Economic Development and Political Legitimacy." *American Political Science Review* 53, no. 1 (1959): 69–106.

McColm, R. Bruce. "The Comparative Survey of Freedom: 1991." *Freedom Review* 22, no. 1 (1991): 5–24.

Macpherson, C. B. *The Life and Times of Liberal Democracy*. Oxford: Oxford University Press, 1977.

Marsh, Rodney M. "Does Democracy Hinder Economic Development in the Latecomer Developing Nations?" *Comparative Social Research* 2 (1979): 215–248.

Mearsheimer, John J. "Back to the Future: Instability in Europe After the Cold War." *International Security* 15, no. 1 (1990): 5–56.

Nehru, B. K. "Western Democracy and the Third World," *Third World Quarterly* 1, no. 2 (1979): 53–70.

O'Donnell, Guillermo, and Philippe C. Schmitter. *Transitions from Authoritarian Rule: Tentative Conclusions About Uncertain Democracies*. Baltimore: Johns Hopkins University Press, 1986.

O'Donnell, Guillermo, Philippe C. Schmitter, and Laurence Whitehead (eds.). *Transitions from Authoritarian Rule: Comparative Perspectives*. Baltimore: Johns Hopkins University Press, 1988.

Pateman, Carol. *Participation and Democratic Theory*. Cambridge: Cambridge University Press, 1970.

Rao, V. "Democracy and Economic Development." *Studies in Comparative International Development* 19, no. 4 (1984/1985): 67–82.

Reiss, Hans (ed.). *Kant's Political Writings*. Cambridge: Cambridge University Press, 1970.

Risse-Kappen, Thomas. "Public Opinion, Domestic Structure, and Foreign Policy in Liberal Democracies." *World Politics* 43, no. 4 (1991): 479–513.

Rosenau, James N. *Turbulence in World Politics: A Theory of Change and Continuity*. Princeton: Princeton University Press, 1990.

Rummel, Rudolph J. "Libertarianism and International Violence." *Journal of Conflict Resolution* 27, no. 1 (1983): 27–71.

Rustow, Dankwart A. "Transitions to Democracy." *Comparative Politics* 2, no. 3 (1970): 337–365.

Sandbrook, Richard. "The State and Economic Stagnation in Tropical Africa." *World Development* 14, no. 3 (1986): 319–332.

——— . "Liberal Democracy in Africa: A Socialist-Revisionist Perspective." *Canadian Journal of African Studies* 22, no. 2 (1988): 240–267.

Senghaas, Dieter. *The European Experience: A Historical Critique of Development Theory.* Leamington Spa/Dover: Berg Publishers, 1985.

Sirowy, Larry, and Alex Inkeles. "The Effects of Democracy on Economic Growth and Inequality: A Review." *Studies in Comparative International Development* 25, no. 1 (1990): 126–157.

Small, Melvin, and J. David Singer. "The War-Proneness of Democratic Regimes." *The Jerusalem Journal of International Relations* 1, no. 4 (1976): 50–69.

Sørensen, Georg. "Democracy and the Developmental State." Institute of Political Science, University of Aarhus, 1991. Mimeo.

——— . *Democracy, Dictatorship and Development: Economic Development in Selected Regimes of the Third World.* London: Macmillan, 1991.

——— . "Strategies and Structures of Development: The New 'Consensus' and the Limits to Its Promises." *European Journal of Development Research* 3, no. 2 (1991): 121–146.

Studies in Comparative International Development 25, no. 1 (1990).

Therborn, Goran. "The Rule of Capital and the Rise of Democracy." *New Left Review* 103 (1977): 3–41.

Ullmann, Richard H. *Securing Europe.* Princeton: Princeton University Press, 1991.

United Nations Development Programme (UNDP). *Human Development Report 1991.* New York: Oxford University Press, 1991.

Van Evera, Stephen. "Primed for Peace: Europe After the Cold War." *International Security* 15, no. 3 (1990/1991): 7–57.

Weede, Erich. "Democracy and War Involvement." *Journal of Conflict Resolution* 28, no. 4 (1984): 649–664.

Weiner, Myron, and Samuel P. Huntington (eds.). *Understanding Political Development.* Boston: Little, Brown, 1987.

□ □ □

Glossary

Absolute poverty indicates the minimum level of subsistence in a specific country. The basic human needs are not met at this level of subsistence. Disease, malnutrition, and illiteracy are common.

Anarchy is the absence of political authority. The international system is anarchic because of the absence of a central political authority above the sovereign states.

An **authoritarian developmentalist regime** is a reform-oriented system that enjoys a high degree of autonomy from vested elite interests. The regime controls a state apparatus with the bureaucratic capacity for promoting development and is run by a state elite ideologically committed to boosting economic development in terms of growth and welfare.

An **authoritarian growth regime** is an elite-dominated system focused on building a strong national economy. The long-term interests of the dominant social forces are respected, whereas the workers and peasants of the poor majority are looked to for providing the economic surplus needed to get growth under way.

The **authoritarian state elite enrichment regime** has as its main aim the enrichment of the elite who control the state. Neither economic growth nor welfare is an important goal. This type of regime is often based on autocratic rule by a supreme leader. The government of Zaire, led by Mobutu, is an example.

Civil society is the realm of social relations not regulated by the state. It includes all nonstate institutions, such as interest groups, associations, civil rights groups, and youth movements. In a totalitarian system, the state attempts to absorb civil society; in such a system, all types of organizations are under state control.

Conscientization is a term introduced by Paolo Freire to describe the process whereby people achieve an understanding of the social reality in which they live and their possibilities for actively changing it.

A **consociational democracy** is a type of democratic system that is characterized by mechanisms serving to promote compromise and consensus among the groups in society. Such mechanisms include federalist systems, special legislative practices, and state agencies that facilitate intergroup compromise.

A **consolidated democracy,** according to Juan Linz, is one in which none of the major political actors consider that there is any alternative to democratic processes to gain power, and no political institution or group has a claim to veto the action of

157

democratically elected decisionmakers. In short, democracy is seen as the "only game in town."

Delegitimation must be understood against the background of legitimacy, which indicates a government's right to govern based on such criteria as popular acceptance, the constitutional process, or economic or other achievements. Delegitimation sets in when the government can no longer point to a basis for its right to govern.

Democratic autonomy is the very broad concept of democracy set forth by David Held. It includes direct participation in local community institutions, active control of elected politicians through the party system, and social as well as economic rights to ensure adequate resources for citizens' political activity. It also foresees self-management of cooperatively owned enterprises.

Democratization refers to the process of change toward more democratic forms of rule. The first phase involves the breakdown of the nondemocratic regime. In the second phase, the elements of a democratic order are established. During the third phase, consolidation, the new democracy is further developed; eventually, democratic practices become an established part of the political culture.

Elite-dominated democracies are systems in which traditional rulers remain in control, even if pressured from below, and successfully use strategies of either compromise or force—or some mix of the two—to retain at least part of their power.

The **"end of history"** is a phrase coined by Francis Fukuyama to describe the end point of humankind's ideological evolution and the universalization of Western liberal democracy as the final form of human government.

External factors are the economic, political, ideological, and other elements that constitute the international context for the processes that take place in single countries. They often have a profound influence on those processes.

Francophone Africa is the name used to describe the countries in Africa that had been under French colonial rule and that retain special ties with France. The countries making up Francophone Africa are Mauritania, Senegal, Mali, Côte d'Ivoire, the Central African Republic, Burkina Faso, Congo, Gabon, and Cameroun.

Frozen democracies is Terry Lynn Karl's label for restricted, elite-dominated democracies that are unwilling to carry out substantive reforms that address the lot of the poor.

The **Group of Seven (or G7)** includes the seven most economically and militarily powerful capitalist nations: the United States, Japan, Germany, Great Britain, France, Italy, and Canada. The group meets periodically to discuss global issues.

Horizontal accountability is defined by Robert Johansen as the ability of citizens to influence the decisions that are made in neighboring societies and that directly affect them. It is achieved through democratic international institutions that guarantee rights for global minorities as well as majorities.

Idealism, in the context of this book, is the view that conflict and violence can be overcome if the world is organized according to certain ideas or principles. Harmony is possible if priority is given to the "right" ideas.

The degree of **inclusiveness** (or participation) describes the number of citizens in a society who enjoy political rights and liberties. Nondemocratic regimes may exclude the large majority of the population from participation. In democratic regimes the entire adult population enjoys the full range of rights and liberties.

Interdependence is a word used to describe situations characterized by mutual dependence between countries or among actors in different countries.

An **international society,** according to Hedley Bull and Adam Watson, is a group of states that have established by dialogue and consent common rules and institutions for the conduct of their relations, and they recognize their common interest in maintaining these arrangements.

Intrafirm trade refers to trade across national borders but between different units of the same corporation.

Liberalization is the process of increasing the possibilities for political opposition and for competition for government power. Often the first steps involve improving the possibilities for open public debate, allowing criticism of the authoritarian regime, and allowing open oppositional activity.

Mass-dominated democracies are systems in which mass actors have gained the upper hand over traditional ruling classes.

Neo-patrimonialism must be understood against the background of patrimonialism, which is the name used by Max Weber to describe any type of government that originated from a royal household and that has a ruler who treats matters of state as his or her personal affair. Present-day systems of this type, such as the system of personal rule in Africa, are examples of neo-patrimonialism.

Nomenklatura is the name of the privileged class (that is, the political, economic, and ideological elite) under the Communist system. In the former Soviet Union, the *nomenklatura* numbers about 75,000 people.

Pacific union is the name Immanuel Kant used to describe his vision of a peaceful world of democracies. The pacific union would be based on three elements: first, the mere existence of democracies with their culture of peaceful conflict resolution; second, the common moral bonds that are forged between democracies; and third, the democracies' economic cooperation toward mutual advantage.

In **patron-client relationships,** a patron provides services, rewards, or protection to a number of clients in return for their personal allegiance. The patron controls the resources; the clients are thus in a relationship of dependence.

Personal rule is the name given to the African system of government based on personal loyalty toward the leading figure of the regime, the strongman. The important positions in the state are filled with followers of the strongman. Their allegiance is reinforced by their sharing of the spoils of office.

In a system with **plural voting,** some members of the electorate have more votes than others. J. S. Mill suggested that the "wiser and more talented" should have more votes than "the ignorant and less able."

Political conditionality is the code word for the demand by donor countries that recipient countries show a respect for human rights and promote democratization as preconditions for receiving economic aid.

Political culture, following Samuel Huntington's definition, refers to the system of values and beliefs that defines the context and meaning of political action.

Political pacts are agreements between elite groups that restrict democracy by defining vital areas of interest for the elites. Often the elite groups will not support the new democracy unless it respects these pacts.

Polyarchy is a word used by Robert Dahl to describe systems that are called democracies in this book. Dahl outlines eight conditions that must be met in order for a system to qualify as democratic. No country satisfies all of these conditions perfectly. Therefore, Dahl uses the term polyarchy for these systems.

Realism, as used in the context of this book, is a theoretical perspective on international relations that purports to analyze the world as it really is, not as it ought to be. In the real world, conflict is imminent due to forces inherent in human nature and due to the way the world's populations have chosen to organize in the form of independent, sovereign states that respect no authority outside or above themselves.

Restricted democracies are political systems with some democratic elements but also with restrictions on competition, participation, and liberties.

A **security community,** according to Karl Deutsch, is made up of groups of people having attained a sense of community and has institutions and practices strong enough and widespread enough to assure dependable expectations of peaceful exchange among its populations. "Sense of community" is a belief that common social problems must and can be resolved by processes of peaceful exchange.

Security complex is the name used by Barry Buzan to describe a group of states whose primary security concerns are linked. Examples of security complexes are Europe, the Gulf, and South Asia.

Soft authoritarian is Chalmers Johnson's label for the Japanese democracy, which has retained some mildly authoritarian features in its governmental institutions, including single-party rule, which has been a part of the system for more than three decades, and an extremely strong and comparatively unsupervised state administration.

A **totalitarian** system is an authoritarian form of regime that is characterized by the attempt of the state to control every aspect of its citizens' lives.

□ □ □

About the Book
and Author

Is the world experiencing a "springtime of democracy," now that the Berlin Wall has crumbled and many formerly communist states have begun to reconfigure their governments and economies? And if democracy is "bursting out all over," is it doing so in a sustainable fashion? Are there pitfalls as well as positive potentials in the recent trends toward democratization?

This book examines the prospects for democracy in the world today and frames the central dilemma confronting all states touched by the process of democratization. The author clarifies the concept of democracy, shows its application in different contexts, and questions whether democratic advancement will continue—and if so, at what price. The consequences of democracy for economic development, human rights, and peaceful relations among countries are illuminated in both their positive and negative aspects.

Professor Sørensen is uniquely qualified to give students and general readers a sense of the long, slow process that democratization entails—both from the inside out (at national and local levels) and from the outside in (international causes and effects). He draws on a wealth of case studies, examples, and anecdotes to illustrate historical as well as contemporary instances of democratic transition.

Democracy, as he convincingly portrays it, is a value in itself as well as a potential promoter of peace, prosperity, and human well-being. But democracy is not inevitable, and actions at every level—from the individual to the international—are necessary to ensure that frail or "frozen" democracies do not founder and that established democracies flourish.

Georg Sørensen is senior lecturer in international politics at the University of Aarhus, Denmark. He has written numerous books and articles on international relations and development issues.

Index

The Women's
Heart Book

The Women's
Heart Book

The Complete Guide to
Keeping Your Heart Healthy

FREDRIC J. PASHKOW, MD,
AND CHARLOTTE LIBOV

NEW YORK

Library of Congress Cataloging-in-Publication Data

Pashkow, Fredric J., 1945-
    The women's heart book : the complete guide to keeping your heart
healthy / Fredric J. Pashkow and Charlotte Libov.—Updated ed.
        p.   cm.
    Prev. ed. published with title: The woman's heart book.
    Includes bibliographical references and index.
    ISBN 0-7868-8428-2
    1. Heart diseases in women.   I. Pashkow, Fredric J., 1945– Woman's
heart book.   II. Libov, Charlotte.   III. Title.

RC682.P353 2001
616.1'2'0082—dc 21
                                                                00-058056

FIRST EDITION

Designed by Cassandra J. Pappas

10   9   8   7   6   5   4   3   2   1

This book is dedicated again
In loving memory of
Laura and Ben
Sister and Brother

A Note to Readers

The Women's Heart Book is the result of a unique collaboration between Dr. Fredric J. Pashkow and Charlotte Libov, a journalist who underwent open-heart surgery. To best convey her own story, Charlotte speaks directly to readers in italics throughout the book.

Contents

Preface by Dr. Fredric J. Pashkow

FOR ME, it was a typical Saturday on call. I had just walked into the kitchen from the garage after making rounds at the hospital almost all day, and the phone was already ringing. "Yes?" I said, knowing it would be the answering service. "Dr. Pashkow, the ER called; they need you back right away. They have a lady with a heart attack and the ER doctor thinks she's unstable."

I didn't even bother yelling "Hello . . . Good-bye!" to my unseen family. I just got back into the car and sped back to the hospital. I found the woman on a mobile cart in the cardiac room of the ER. Nurses were hovering, their hands busy. An ECG technician was running a second tracing. The patient was in obvious pain. The ER doctor looked relieved to see me. He handed me the first tracing: The heart attack was a big one. I started to gently question the patient about her past history and any recent symptoms. I noticed that she was lying stiffly with her fists clenched and her lips tightly pursed. I thought at first it was the discomfort. Wrong! She was grievously irate!

"This really stinks," she finally blurted out. "He's the one who should be here." By "he," I knew instantly she meant her husband. "He smokes like a factory, and I quit ten years ago. He eats everything and anything he wants, usually garbage, and all I eat is rabbit food. I'm always on a diet." She continued her angry soliloquy. "He works day and night in that crummy car dealership of his and he never exercises. Bend-

ix

ing over to tie his shoelace for him is a big-time workout while I slave away at Gloria Stevens three days a week." By this point, she was seething with the injustice of it. I was preoccupied with the details of getting her medically stabilized, so I nodded absently while a nurse tried to placate her. "You're absolutely right, it should be your husband here instead of you." "Well, if that's the case," the patient shot back, getting my full attention, "why isn't he?"

She had a point. Her husband, Ralph, wasn't on that cart where we all expected him to be; he was anxiously waiting in the adjacent waiting area. Josephine had had the heart attack. But women don't have heart attacks, according to the prevailing medical misbelief of that time. Heart attacks happen only to "old" women, and she wasn't old. She was in the prime of her life. What had happened?

What had happened was that the odds had caught up with Josephine. Her individualized risk of a heart attack was about half that of her cigarette-smoking, coffee-swilling, couch potato of a husband. But since *his* risk of a coronary event was about one in six, *her* risk, based on her age and gender, was about one chance in 12. That may not sound like heavy odds, but if you play the lottery, where the chance of winning is one in four or five million, one chance in 12 seems like almost a sure thing. The point is, heart attacks happen to women as well as men— only a little less frequently, and usually at a slightly different point in their life cycle. Ironically, despite the hundreds of women with heart disease I'd treated up to that point in my career, particularly women with the coronary variety, I had considered each and every case of a young woman (under age 45) so afflicted "unusual."

It took about 10 years for me to fully awaken to my bias. Once that happened, however, I became increasingly sensitive to the similarities and differences in the comprehensive manifestations of my female patients' heart disease. When a woman has heart disease, for example, her ancillary problems are often different from a male's. Often, she doesn't get "disability" compensation or much time off from her responsibilities to family and home. To many men, care of a recovering spouse means ordering out for pizza.

What this book means to do is to provide women with the knowledge they need to obtain the best of care for their hearts. This book doesn't pretend to offer all of the answers. But when a woman is told "Forget about it," and she can't, or "We'll take care of it, you don't need to worry about a thing," and she wants to know more, she'll have this book to help her. I owe it to Josephine and to all of her sisters.

Preface by Charlotte Libov

SINCE IT WAS November, it was already growing dark outside, though it was still afternoon. I watched the deepening dusk from the window behind the cardiologist's desk. Before this afternoon, I'd never been to a cardiologist. In fact, I'd never anticipated having to see one, not for 30 or 40 more years, anyway. Only old people get heart problems, right?

Wrong, I was to learn. Even a baby boomer of 40 years of age can have something go wrong with her heart. What was wrong with mine had happened before I was born, I heard the cardiologist saying. The problem was an "atrial septal defect," a hole in the wall separating the chambers of my heart. It had to be fixed. To do that, I would have to undergo open-heart surgery.

I only half listened. I was wondering how I'd manage the drive home without steering my car into a tree.

The news that there was something wrong with my heart came as a complete shock. I'd always considered myself to be robustly healthy. Over the years, whenever I'd had a routine physical, the doctor performing it would usually mention that I had a heart murmur, then hasten to assure me that the murmur was "innocent," that there was nothing whatsoever wrong with my heart.

That is what I believed, until I arrived at the Waterbury, Connecticut, office of Dr. Jeffrey Stern for a routine exam. Unlike all the doctors I'd ever seen, Dr. Stern (a superb diagnostician who never assumes anything) paused when he came across that murmur. "You do have a heart murmur, but I don't know whether or not it's harmless," he said.

He sent me for an echocardiogram, which clearly identified the problem. Six weeks later, I underwent open-heart surgery. Physically, I was fine. Psychologically, I was shaken. I was nagged by the thought that if I had not stumbled upon a truly astute doctor, my heart problem might never had been identified in time. For although this type of heart defect can be corrected relatively easily, if it goes untreated too long, it can irrevocably damage the heart. This was too close a call.

So I set out to find out more about women and their hearts. At first, seeking answers to my questions was a means of dealing with my own anxiety. Before my surgery, I searched for every bit of information I could find. I arrived at the Cleveland Clinic lugging a satchel filled not with toiletries, but with medical books. You would have thought I was going to perform the surgery rather than undergo it.

After my surgery, I fully expected my interest to wane, as I went back to my life as a freelance writer, which includes writing about everything from the economy to the environment to circus sideshows. Instead, my interest in women's hearts continued to grow. The more I learned, the more there was to learn. Before long, I had teamed up with Dr. Fredric Pashkow to write this book.

I was to spend some two years learning the answers to all my questions about women's hearts. My research took me to women's bedsides, to heart support groups, to cardiology conferences. Before the book was done, I'd even had the opportunity to observe open-heart surgery being performed on a 64-year-old woman. I am truly grateful for this unique "insider's" view of women's hearts, from both sides of the bed!

My hope is that this book will convey information. That may not sound dramatic, but information can be powerful, as was illustrated to me a few months ago. I received a telephone call from a woman named Marie. We'd never met, but I was instantly drawn to her, as we had been born with the same type of congenital heart defect. At age 62, Marie's heart defect had just been diagnosed. Her doctor had declared she was not a candidate for surgery (she wasn't certain why, but she thought her age must be a factor). Her situation was hopeless, she'd concluded. She'd been sent home to eventually die.

From my research, I knew that surgery to correct this heart defect had been performed on women older than Marie. That was all Marie needed to hear. She sent her test results to a major heart center for a second opinion. This past summer, she underwent surgery. The operation went fine. Marie comes from a line of indomitable Minnesota farmers. Her parents are in their 90s, and Marie is now looking forward to reaching that age herself. All she'd needed was information; information that was available in medical textbooks and journals, but had never filtered down to her.

Although I didn't realize it at the time, this book began that November afternoon I spent in my cardiologist's office. That day, which at the time seemed the gloomiest of my life, turned out to be the day I began seeking out information about every woman's heart.

Acknowledgments

A book is far more than the worth of its authors. Many people gave generously of their knowledge and expertise to assist us in the preparation of this book.

Special thanks go to the Cleveland Clinic and the following former and current members of its staff: Anita Arnold, DO, Milwaukee, WI; Delbert L. Booher, MD, Davenport, FL; Paul N. Casale, MD, Lancaster, PA; Betty Ching, RN; Michael Cressman, DO; Fetnat M. Fouad-Tarazi, MD; Maria Geraci; Sharon Harvey; Cheryl Jensen; Sally Koulousek; Larry Latson, MD; Bruce W. Lytle, MD; Pam Marinelli; Douglas Moody, MD; Daniel J. Murphy, Jr., MD; Eliot R. Rosencrantz, MD, chief, pediatric cardiovascular surgery, Children's Hospital of Buffalo, Buffalo, NY; Loretta Isada, MD; John Royer, RN; Elena Sgarbossa, MD, Rush Presbyterian Medical Center; William Stewart, MD; Betsy Stovsky, RN; Michelle Tobin, RN; Eric Topol, MD; Cheryl Weinstein, MD, Shaker Heights, OH; Deborah Williams, MD, Howard University Hospital, Washington, DC; and Randy Yetman, MD.

Many other experts gave of their time and knowledge as well. They include Susan J. Blumenthal, MD, Georgetown University and Tufts University Schools of Medicine; Trudy L. Bush, PhD, Johns Hopkins University; Bernard R. Chaitman, MD, St. Louis University Hospital;

Margaret A. Chesney, PhD, University of California, San Francisco; Richard P. Devereux, Weill Medical College of Cornell University; John A. Elefteriades, MD, Yale-New Haven Hospital; Erica Frank, MD, Emory University; Shiriki Kumanyika, PhD, University of Pennsylvania; Florence P. Haseltine, PhD, MD, National Institutes of Health; Irma L. Mebane, PhD, National Institutes of Health; Charles Maynard, PhD, University of Washington School of Medicine; Catherine A. Neill, MD, FRCP, The Johns Hopkins Hospital; Lynda Powell, PhD, Rush Presbyterian/St. Luke's Medical Center; Lynda E. Rosenfeld, MD; Carol Shively, PhD, Wake Forest University School of Medicine; Judith S. Stern, ScD, University of California, Davis; and Nanette K. Wenger, MD, Emory University School of Medicine.

While a large part of the research for this book was done at the Cleveland Clinic Foundation, thanks also go to Yale-New Haven Hospital.

A very special thank you to Joanne Kraynack, for her help in so many ways. Special thanks also go to Jeffrey Loerch, manager of the medical illustrations department of the Cleveland Clinic Education Foundation, for his cooperation, and very special thanks to Nancy Hein, senior medical illustrtaor, who created the drawings that enhance this book. And thanks to Della Lin, MD, Queens Medical Center, Honolulu, Hawaii.

We are exceedingly grateful to Carole Abel, our literary agent, for her wisdom and support in all of our endeavors over the years.

Special thanks to Jane and Michael Eisner who were instrumental in enabling an updated edition of this book to be published. Thanks also to Wendy Lefkon, our former editor at Hyperion, and to our current editor, Anne Cole.

Dr. Pashkow offers very special thanks to Peg, the woman who shares his life. It was her willingness to share what little time was left over that allowed this book to be written. It was also through her experience with "cardiacs" that Dr. Pashkow realized the potential of exercise, education, and psychological support.

Charlotte Libov would like to thank all of her colleagues and friends for their support in innumerable ways. Special thanks go to France Chamberlain and Sheila Hogan.

Most of all, the authors owe a great debt to the women who helped us by sharing their stories. These included those interviewed at the Cleveland Clinic and, in Connecticut, the Norwalk Hospital's Cardiac Rehab Second Chance Association and the Greater Waterbury Heart Club. A heartfelt thanks to all of you.

Foreword

THE PRACTICE OF evidence-based medicine is a hallmark of the new millennium. Evidence-based information for women about their health—and, in particular, heart health—is a requisite for becoming educated and respected partners in decisions about one's health care. What should women know to enhance our heart health? Dr. Fredric Pashkow and Charlotte Libov intensively and extensively explore the landscape in this second edition of *The Women's Heart Book*.

It is important to emphasize that women are not a homogeneous group—their heart disease risks and their occurrence of heart disease vary widely with age and ethnicity. As research studies about heart disease and heart disease risk factors have increasingly enrolled women, and the resulting new knowledge has been examined for gender differences, physicians are beginning to acquire a database specific to women. Raising questions about gender differences is a giant step forward but much remains to be learned. As you read this excellent monograph, remember that the heart health information specific to women was derived from our many sisters who volunteered as participants in clinical research studies. "Some things only a woman can do," as noted by the Society for Women's Health Research, are, whenever possible, to become involved in clinical research trials, to help provide for our daughters and granddaughters the information now available for our sons and grandsons.

Highlights of this book include a summary of normal heart function, information one needs to understand the abnormalities of heart diseases and the risk factors for coronary disease. Did you know that a recent poll showed that four of five women surveyed were not aware that heart disease was the leading cause of death for American women? Women must realize their vulnerability to heart attack in order to be motivated to undertake preventive interventions. Both lifestyle changes and drug treatments are carefully reviewed, citing the evidence for each aspect and identifying myths and fads. Note also the special sections on diet and exercise. Know the warning symptoms of heart attack! Chest pain requires evaluation—never assume that chest discomfort is indigestion or anxiety.

The book also reviews noncoronary heart diseases, describing their characteristics, their presentations, and their management. Pregnancy and heart disease is addressed in detail—many women with heart disease can safely undertake pregnancy; any medication taken during pregnancy should be carefully reviewed with your physician regarding its safety.

What about cardiac tests? Their descriptions and the diagnostic information they provide are clearly displayed. A presentation of newer treatments, involving both drugs and devices, provides background knowledge for understanding recommendations offered by your physician and to help one formulate appropriate questions. Explanations can help diffuse frightening terms. For example, the term "heart failure" does not mean that the heart has stopped beating; it refers to an abnormality of the pumping function of the heart, with a sizable array of therapies currently available to improve symptoms and outcomes.

Heart surgery is commonly undertaken in women both young and old—and even very elderly—to correct congenital heart defects, valve abnormalities, and coronary artery blockages, as well as cardiac transplantation. There is information about results specific for women because the outcomes of surgery are now described based on gender and age. Heart surgery in the 21st century is done for octogenarians and, on occasion, for nonagenarians. Reading the details about the positive hospital experiences of these women, and others, can be reassuring.

Lastly, there are references and resources to expand your learning about the issues that are of specific interest to you. Read, learn, question—and take charge of your heart health.

NANETTE KASS WENGER, MD
Professor of Medicine (Cardiology)
Emory University School of Medicine
Chief of Cardiology
Grady Memorial Hospital
Consultant, Emory Heart & Vascular Center

1

~~~~~nnnnnΩnnnn~~~~~

Female Hearts at Risk

LOIS ZEALOUSLY ELIMINATES every gram of cholesterol from her husband Dan's favorite dishes, convinced him to give up smoking, and surprised him with membership in a health club for their anniversary. So the 52-year-old homemaker is stunned when her doctor tells her that she, not Dan, will soon face coronary bypass surgery.

Allison, a 39-year-old financial analyst, lies on the table in a New York hospital emergency room as waves of unbearable chest pain sweep over her. Tucked into her green leather shoulder bag, among her keys, lipstick, and electronic planner, are packets of birth control pills and cigarettes. With her unusually strong family history of heart disease, this combination is potentially deadly. But no one ever warned Allison.

Formerly a strong swimmer, Joan, age 63, must now be content to paddle slowly up and down the pool. Her enlarged heart has grown so weak that it can't keep up with the demands of much exertion. Early medical treatment could have allowed her to remain active longer, but her family doctor scoffed at her complaints of chest pain for years, telling her, "It's all in your head."

For years, women, and too often their doctors as well, have shared these assumptions. Health care books, articles in women's magazines, and even television commercials convey the impression that heart disease strikes men, not women. "I worried about my husband's cholesterol, but now it's down to 168," exults a woman in a TV commercial about the joys of switching to vegetable shortening. "My husband eats right, works out, and he's feeling great," says another beaming TV commercial wife, shown picking up her husband from the gym.

These assumptions fly in the face of reality. Coronary heart disease is the number one killer of American women, far outranking stroke, lung cancer, and even the disease most dreaded by women, breast cancer. However, women remain largely unaware of their risk. Repeatedly, they voice their fears about breast cancer, never dreaming of a threat that looms much larger.

Since this threat has been so widely overlooked for so long, even now, most women remain unaware of how vulnerable their hearts are. This is tragic, because many of these risks can be avoided or their impact lessened.

Furthermore, although the past few decades have been marked by dramatic progress against heart disease, these innovations often are denied to many women. Such potentially lifesaving procedures as coronary bypass surgery, balloon angioplasty, and thrombolytic therapy (the administration of "clot busters" to minimize damage after a heart attack) are still performed less frequently on women. While experts argue among themselves whether this is scientifically justified, the fact remains that as a woman, it's less likely these procedures will be offered to you.

Also, even though there is now a new awareness of heart disease in women, other problems that affect women's hearts remain too often overlooked. This includes such problems as arrhythmias, or irregular heart rhythms, mitral valve prolapse, and congenital heart defects, all of which more often affect or manifest symptoms in women.

HEART DISEASE: THE "MALE" DISEASE?

Each year, about a one half million American women die of cardiovascular disease, which includes all diseases of the heart and blood vessels, including stroke. Of this number, 235,000 women die from heart attacks. By comparison, 68,000 women die each year from lung cancer, 43,300 from breast cancer, and 28,800 from colon cancer, the three leading cancer killers of women. These other devastating diseases must not be overlooked, but the numbers make it clear that, for women, preventing heart disease is of utmost importance. Still, polls repeatedly show that when women are asked to rank their biggest health worry, breast cancer comes out on top, with heart disease listed far below. This is the case, even though one in 27 deaths in women is from breast cancer compared to one in two from cardiovascular disease.

Faced with this threat, the best way for a woman to safeguard her heart is through knowledge. You must learn about the changing risks that may damage your heart over the course of your life.

As you age, your risk of heart disease increases. Typically, women develop heart disease 15 to 20 years later than men, although once they reach menopause, their rate of heart disease begins to climb.

Once past the age of 65, every woman is a candidate for heart disease, no matter what her state of health: She may be a nonsmoker, get regular exercise, and be a health food enthusiast. At this stage of life, any woman's heart becomes as vulnerable to heart disease as that of her male counterpart.

ARE YOUNG WOMEN "IMMUNE" FROM HEART DISEASE?

The fact that older women have a higher risk of suffering a heart attack than younger women contributes to another dangerous belief: that only older women are in jeopardy. While it's true that heart attacks are more likely to be fatal to elderly women, young women are not necessarily immune. An estimated 74,000 women under age the age of 65 will suffer a heart attack this year.

In fact, heart disease in middle-aged women is far from uncommon. Such women are seen daily in cardiology clinics across the country. There are many reasons why a middle-aged woman is at risk for developing heart disease. She may be diabetic, a factor more strongly related to heart disease in women than in men. She may have gone through menopause early, resulting in a loss of estrogen, which may turn out to be the most important contributor to the development of heart disease in women. She may have inherited abnormal blood cholesterol levels. Or she may develop heart disease for no obvious reason at all.

Some women can appear deceptively robust, like Linda, a nonsmoking gym teacher who suffered a heart attack in her early fifties. In her gym shorts with her whistle hanging around her neck, she once seemed the very picture of good health. But her body harbored two hidden time bombs. The first was hyperlipidemia, a metabolic disorder that results in abnormal levels of blood cholesterol. The second was that her ovaries had been removed years earlier, propelling her body into premature menopause.

Although it's unusual for a woman under the age of 45 to suffer a heart attack or develop heart disease, this happens more often than doctors suspect. Sometimes the risk factors go unrecognized until it's almost too late. That was the case with Randi, 35-year-old mother of two, who was unaware she had hyperlipidemia. When she complained to her doctor of chest pain, he brushed her worries aside. He did reluctantly order a treadmill exercise test, a diagnostic measure commonly used to help diagnose heart disease; but because he ordered a type that is less accurate when used on women than on men, Randi's results were interpreted as normal. Randi's doctor told her she was "too nervous" and that if she worried less, her symptoms would disappear. Fortunately, she saw another doctor who used a more sensitive version of the test. The results clearly showed that two of her three coronary arteries were seriously blocked. If her condition had remained undiscovered, she most likely would have suffered a major heart attack.

Because heart disease is so rarely suspected in young women, if you're a young woman suffering cardiac symptoms for which there is no other explanation, it's up to you to make certain your doctor investigates the possibility of heart problems. It may save your life.

SOCIETY'S RISKS TO WOMEN'S HEARTS

Over the years, women's place in society has changed, in most ways for the better. However, there has been one dangerous change: In recent years, more and more women have taken up smoking, a deadly habit for a woman's heart.

Stress also poses a risk for women and their hearts. Although the link between stress and heart disease is not as clear as the connection between smoking and heart disease, some studies show that stress can present risks to your general health and to your heart. Some say that women's new roles in the workplace may lead to heart attacks, but this is not necessarily so. As we discover more about stress, it appears that it's not the typical, hard-driving type A personality that contributes to heart problems, but anger, frustration, and powerlessness that may be unhealthy. Women trapped in dead-end jobs or workplace discrimination may be the ones who find their emotions tied up in knots, under just the type of stress that may contribute to damaging their hearts.

Heart Attack: High Risk for Women

Some studies have found that when women suffer heart attacks, they often fare even worse than men do. Research finds that younger women who have heart attacks are more likely to die from them than men of the same age—and the younger the woman, the greater the risk, according to a study published in 1999 in *The New England Journal of Medicine.* Researchers analyzed data from 380,000 male and female heart attack victims, aged 30 to 89, and found that younger women who suffered heart attacks were at especially high risk and, the younger the woman, the higher the risk.

Also, women are more at risk during the period right after their heart attack, researchers have found. A study published in 1997 in the *Journal of the American College of Cardiology* found that 13.1 percent of women died during the first month after their heart attack, compared to 4.8 percent for men. Furthermore, the American Heart Association statistics find that nearly double the number of women (42 percent versus 24 percent for men) die during the first year after having a heart attack and 33 percent of women, compared to 21 percent of men, suffered a second heart attack within six years. Also, about 30 percent of women, compared to 21 percent of men, will become disabled by congestive heart failure.

The picture is not completely bleak. Most of the time, women do survive heart attacks. But even if they recover, they tend to suffer more than men do from such symptoms as disabling chest pain. This makes them less likely to be able to return to work or fully enjoy their lives. Mary, a supervisor for a high-tech computer company, had a heart attack when she was 57 years old. Afterward, she still suffered chest pains that forced her to quit her job. Her pains persisted, even after coronary bypass surgery and despite her use of a variety of cardiovascular medications. Although her case was extreme, it's not uncommon for women to be plagued with chest pain and other symptoms even after the physical causes of their heart problems appear to have been resolved.

The social revolution notwithstanding, American women still bear the greater part of household and child care burdens. These responsibilities don't disappear if a woman has a heart attack or undergoes heart surgery. Many women feel compelled to be up and about managing the household when they should rest. Or they may try to return to their jobs outside the home too early because they can't afford not to or feel anxious about losing their hard-won place on the corporate fast track.

Heart Surgery for Women: Risky Business

Coronary bypass surgery is now one of the most common operations in the United States, and the risk factor has decreased sharply over the years. Still, despite some three decades of experience, studies nationwide persist in showing that coronary surgery remains riskier for women than men. This is also true of balloon angioplasty and similar interventional procedures used to treat coronary heart disease. Although the success rates for women have vastly improved, some discrepancies persist.

A "Gender Bias" in Heart Disease?

"Can't I count on my doctor to recognize a heart problem?" you might very well wonder. The unfortunate answer to this is, "Sometimes, but not always." The truth is that while women have mistakenly believed they're not vulnerable to heart problems, this belief is also shared by their doctors.

"Gender bias" refers to the concern that women are less likely than men to be correctly diagnosed or properly treated because of the underlying myth that we don't get heart disease. In years past, for example, research has revealed striking differences between the use of cardiac procedures in men and women. Women underwent far fewer cardiac catheterizations (a definitive test to determine the extent of heart disease), balloon angioplasties, and bypass surgeries.

Although women visit doctors more often than men, their problems are often given short shrift, especially when it comes to their hearts. Doctors once were taught to act and respond differently to women. If a medical student approached an instructor to discuss a case of a woman with chest pain, he or she would almost always be told to dismiss it. "She must be psychosomatic. It's all in her head," was the standard line. Studies found that when doctors are asked to diagnose women with chest pain, the problem is more likely to be attributed to "psychiatric" causes.

Times are changing. As more women have become doctors, many have led the drive to foster awareness of heart disease in women. But misconceptions still exist. A 1996 Gallup survey revealed that half of the primary care physicians polled cited breast cancer and osteoporosis as greater health threats for women over age 50 than heart disease. The survey also showed that one third of the doctors were not aware of the important gender differences in the symptoms of heart attacks and in diagnostic testing for heart disease.

Not all studies find this to be the case. For instance, a study performed at the Cleveland Clinic found that although women were less likely than men to undergo coronary catheterization, an invasive test to determine the extent of blockages from coronary heart disease, they were also less likely to have had earlier abnormal test results or turn out to have severe coronary heart disease. Also, during the next two years, there were half as many deaths among the women. However, some studies show that differences do persist. A 1998 study reported in the *Journal of the American College of Cardiology* found that exercise stress tests were used nearly twice as often in men as in women. Also in 1998, a study in the *Archives of Internal Medicine* compared the treatment of more than 350,000 male and female patients at 1,234 hospitals across the country. Data showed that women were significantly less likely to receive state-of-the-art treatment, such as angioplasty, bypass surgery, or thrombolytic (clot-busting) drugs, after a heart attack.

Also of concern are studies that find that gender bias also exists in how doctors treat female patients. A 1999 study in *The New England Journal of Medicine* tested for hidden bias in how doctors make clinical decisions. Researchers at Georgetown University enlisted 720 primary care physicians, who viewed videotapes of actors in a hospital setting relaying symptoms characteristic of heart disease. The doctors were asked to decide which "patients" should be referred for heart disease testing and treatment. Female patients were referred for diagnostic testing only 60 percent as often as male patients with the identical complaints of chest pain. (African-Americans experienced a similar bias).

Over the years, some studies have intimated that coronary bypass surgery and other "aggressive" treatments may be overused. If these procedures are indeed being performed too often on men, women certainly don't want to fall into the same trap. Still, recognition of the differences between the way men and women are treated has generated an important discussion.

OUR UNDERSTANDING OF HEART DISEASE

Such treatment differences may not be surprising when you consider that coronary heart disease has been viewed as a man's disease, from the early days of modern cardiology. Our modern understanding of coronary disease was shaped, in part, in the 1950s, when pathologists examining the corpses of young Korean War soldiers discovered, to their amazement, the fatty streaking that is the first step on the path to clogged arteries. Since then, coronary heart disease has been perceived as a male problem. In the ensuing years, this emphasis on men has not only persisted, but has helped to shape our national health policy.

A major example is the Framingham Heart Study, the nation's largest continuing study of coronary artery disease that began in 1948 and has very much shaped our thinking about heart disease. While women were included in this major study, the early results concluded that chest pain in women was not a serious problem. Even though this was later found to be wrong, the damage had been done. "The myth that 'women don't get heart disease' had taken root," says Dr. Nanette K. Wenger, a cardiologist and professor of medicine at Emory University School of Medicine in Atlanta. However, she notes, times are changing. "Years ago, older women were less visible. There were less of them, they had retired from the workforce, and they had fulfilled their family duties. Heart disease in women was not seen as a major problem. But now that the life span of women has increased, and they live on average six or seven years longer than men, we are seeing a tremendous change."

The emphasis on men and heart disease has also meant that far less clinical research has focused on women; some believe that potential treatments may have been overlooked. "If we had a disease like breast cancer and most of the research had been done on men, we would not use the male model and say, 'Oh, let's see how we can adapt it to women.' We would want to take a fresh approach," says Dr. Erica Frank, associate professor of family and preventive medicine at Emory University.

This male perspective has also shaped the methods by which drugs are tested in this country. Cardiovascular drugs, the medications that control blood pressure, reduce cholesterol, and ease the symptoms of heart disease, are of particular concern because they're prescribed for women as often as for men, yet have been tested almost exclusively on men. Traditionally, women have been excluded from medical research because of the concern that if they're young, they might become pregnant, or if they're older, they most likely have developed other diseases, which will complicate the results.

"The argument is spurious. It says we cannot study women because they are so different, but yet they should take medicines developed on the basis of work done on men," says Dr. Florence Haseltine, a founder of the Society for Women's Health Research in Washington, DC.

"There has been a general awakening to the fact that all too many articles published in the medical research literature and publicized by the mass media have been based on studies of men. This is unfortunate, as coronary heart disease is the major killer of both men and women," notes Dr. Bernadine Healy, a cardiologist who served as the first female director of the National Institutes of Health.

Another recent development is that more members of minority groups are being included in such clinical studies. The vast majority of medical research in heart disease targeted on not just men, but white men. If information on how heart disease affects women is slim, information on how heart disease affects women of different racial groups, such as African-Americans and Hispanics, is far scantier.

Because of this past lack of emphasis on heart disease and women, women are only now discovering the importance of caring for their hearts. Such urgency extends not only to older women, who make up the majority of heart disease patients, but to younger women as well. The most "heartening" news of all is that women of all ages can benefit from taking care of their hearts.

2

~~~~~nnnnOnnnn~~~~~

How Your Heart Works

My heart stopped at precisely 4:55 P.M. on a Monday in November. Or, at least, that's how it felt. I remember the moment vividly. I was seated across from my cardiologist, who was telling me I would need heart surgery. And that's when I could have sworn I felt my heart momentarily stop beating. Actually, my heart was performing its assigned duty; beating as it had for the 40 years of my life. But, because I was so stunned, for a moment, it seemed to me my heart literally stopped.

This dual role played by our heart, the way its beating keeps us alive, and how it seems to reflect our emotions, is why our hearts seem so fascinating. On one hand, our heart is a biological organ. Unless something goes wrong, we are usually unaware of its tireless beating. But in times of high emotion, of deep sadness, fear, or even joy, our hearts seem to take on a life of their own. They jump, skitter, ache, pound, and sometimes they even seem to sing!

Today's scientists know that such heartfelt reactions are the result of hormones that act on our hearts in times of crisis. For centuries, though, this response has led us to see our hearts in a dual role in our lives; a role that is not only biological, but deeply symbolic as well.

Since prehistoric times, people have puzzled over the mysterious workings of our body. A prehistoric drawing of a mammoth is believed the earliest anatomical drawing of an animal. Drawn on a cave wall some

25,000 years ago, the artist showed the animal with a mass of paint located below its back, roughly shaped like a heart. In different cultures, throughout history, the greatest thinkers of the day all subscribed to the belief that the heart was the powerful source of life. Ancient Babylonians believed a sharp pain in the chest signified the presence of demons. The ancient Egyptians ascribed to the heart many purposes; they believed it not only the seat of intelligence and the central force of life, but the source of love as well. Aristotle thought along similar lines, concluding that the heart was the body's vital source of life as well as the seat of the soul as well.

It was around the first century A.D. that medical knowledge of the heart began to be pieced together. It was a gradual process, though, that took centuries. Great anatomists, such as Claudius Galen, a Greek renowned as the greatest physician of his day, and Leonardo da Vinci, who dissected human bodies to learn how to illustrate them more accurately, gradually pieced together how the heart worked. In the 16th century, the brilliant English doctor, William Harvey put it all together.

Since then, modern science has unlocked many mysteries about the heart. We recognize now that it is not just our heart but our brain where what we consider our "soul" resides; yet, those primitive beliefs remain. We exchange cards on Valentine's Day; festooned with images of hearts not unlike those found on that caveman's wall. We can all understand the yearnings of *The Wizard of Oz*'s Tin Man, who wanted a heart to be able to feel love. We shed tears over sonnets that talk of our heart's losses, and we write songs that sing of our heart's joy. Despite medical evidence to the contrary, this is still how we feel, well, down in the bottom of our hearts.

These feelings help explain why we find any threat to our hearts not only physically threatening, but emotionally frightening as well.

About Your Heart . . .

The heart is one of the main organs that make up your circulatory system, the network of vessels whose job it is to deliver oxygen and nutrients to your body's organs and to remove from your body the carbon dioxide generated during the process known as metabolism. Your circulatory system includes your heart, lungs, arteries, and capillaries (extremely small blood vessels). Your circulatory system also includes veins, the blood vessels through which blood flows on its returns to the heart.

Anatomically speaking, scientists believe the heart of a woman is virtually the same as that of a man's, except for its size. An adult male's heart weighs about 10 ounces; a woman's heart about two ounces less. The size of the heart varies with the size of the individual. If you want a rough idea of the size of your heart, make a fist. Your heart is about that size, or a little larger if you have unusually small hands.

A cone-shaped organ, your heart is situated centrally in your chest. It fits snugly in an area known as the mediastinum of the thoracic cavity, just behind your breastbone and between your lungs. If you want an idea of how the major part of how your heart's left ventricle is shaped, hold a Styrofoam cup with its bottom tilted towards the left. This may not seem very scientific, but it is a reasonable approximation of how the left ventricle or main pump of your heart is shaped. Although your heart is located centrally, between your lungs, the bottom corner juts forward a bit from beneath the breastbone, coming closest to the surface of the chest. This position accentuates the sounds your heart makes as it beats, and makes it appear as if your heart is located on the left side of your body.

Your heart is a strong muscular organ, which is comprised of a special type of tissue known as cardiac muscle, or myocardium. A translucent sac called the pericardium envelops both the heart and the roots of the major blood vessels that emerge from it, the vena cava and the ascending aorta. The myocardium differs from other types of muscle in your body in that it can contract rhythmically when stimulated by the currents of your heart's electrical system. This rhythmic contraction is the origin of your heartbeat.

YOUR HEART'S JOB

Even if it seems like you studied biology ages ago, you probably recall learning that your heart is a pump. This is indeed true. A "pump" is defined as a machine for the raising, driving, or compressing of fluids. Your heart is such a pump; such an efficient one, in fact, that engineers have borrowed from its design.

Your heart is also quite specialized in its purpose. Some of your other organs perform a variety of functions. Your kidneys, for example, have a multitude of jobs. They filter your blood, excrete waste products, control your blood's acid-base balance, and excrete or conserve fluid. Scientists are still learning new things about the heart, but when it comes down the heart's main function, that remains one crucial task. The heart is a pump.

Actually, to be more accurate, your heart is two pumps, which act separately but in concert. The left side of your heart acts as a high-pressure pump that forces oxygen-rich blood out into all the parts of your body. The job of the right side of your heart is to receive the oxygen-depleted blood and pass it into the lungs, where it is replenished with oxygen. The blood then flows into the left side of the heart, to begin its journey again. Every organ in your body needs this blood to live. This is why, if your heart is not working properly, the resulting lack of oxygenated blood can damage your brain, kidneys, and all other organs, which depend upon it.

As the blood makes its journey through the heart, it is very important that it flow only in one direction. You have four heart valves, which ensure this proper flow and see to it that blood enriched with oxygen, does not get mixed with unoxygenated blood.

Your Heart's Structure

Each area of the heart is called a chamber. Each of these chambers is also divided vertically, into lower and upper chambers. This is what is meant when the heart is referred to as a four-chambered pump. The left side of the heart is divided into the left atrium (the upper chamber on the left side) and the left ventricle (the lower chamber on the left side). The right side of the heart is divided into the right atrium (the upper chamber on the right side) and the right ventricle (the lower chamber on the right side). These four chambers have similar jobs to perform.

The atrium and the ventricle on each side of the heart act together. The atrium feeds blood to the ventricle, which then pumps the blood out. The atrium's job is very important, however, because it is this chamber of the heart that supplies a consistent amount of blood flow to the ventricle. In this way, the atrium forms a buffer for the ventricle, making certain that the pump never runs dry. This flow of blood acts to "prime the pump," and explains why, even if you change position, your heart's ventricles are always assured a constant supply of blood to pump. This is one reason why your heart can perform its job so steadily, without you even being aware of it. It is one of the many brilliantly evolved features of the heart.

To enable the two sides of your heart to perform their separate but critically important functions, your heart is divided vertically into right and left sides by the septum, a thick central muscular wall. You also have large blood vessels that emerge from the top and sides of your heart.

These vessels deliver blood to and from your heart. The superior vena cava returns blood to the heart from the upper part of the body, while the inferior vena cava returns blood to the heart from the lower part (the legs, abdomen, torso, etc.).

YOUR CARDIAC VALVES

The proper functioning of your heart is dependent on your four valves, which "control traffic" to the individual chambers of your heart, making certain your blood flows in the right direction. These heart valves are fascinating structures in themselves. The four valves of your heart are the tricuspid valve, which is located between the right atrium and the right ventricle; the pulmonary valve, between the right ventricle and the pulmonary artery; the mitral valve, between the left atrium and the left ventricle; and the aortic valve, between the left ventricle and the aorta. The mitral valve was so named, by the way, because the shape of the valve reminded the anatomists who were studying it of the tall, clamshell-like hat worn by bishops, the bishop's miter.

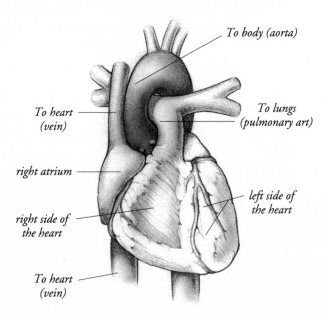

The Heart. The heart pumps blood to all the organs of the body through arteries. The sequence starts when the right side of the heart pumps blood to the lungs through the pulmonary artery. The oxygen-rich blood returns to the left side of the heart and is then pumped through the aorta out to the body. Oxygen-depleted blood returns to the heart's right atrium through the veins, completing the sequence.

Although the word "valve" may conjure up images of a mechanical device with gears and such designed to control the flow of liquid, that image does not truly capture what these structures look like. Actually, your heart valves more resemble the petals of a flower, which move and flow in a sort of orchestrated ballet, following the changes of pressure in the heart. They function like sails moving in a gentle breeze. Each valve is outfitted with a set of "flaps" (also called leaflets or cusps). The mitral valve normally has two leaflets; the others have three. Actual slow motion photography taken within the heart reveals the gentle motion of these leaflets. They billow open gently, like sails do on a sailboat, allowing the blood to pass. As the blood flows out, these leaflets fold down against themselves, effectively sealing the passageway shut. Valves normally do leak a tiny bit, and this can show up on an echocardiogram, but they should not leak significantly. Blood flow occurs only when there's a difference in pressure across the valves, causing them to open and close.

Considering the delicacy of these fragile leaflets, it is easy to understand why, if, one becomes stiff due to valvular heart disease, it becomes impossible for the heart valve to perform its vital function. Although valve disease usually progresses gradually, there are exceptions. With the aortic valve, there are circumstances that, although rare, can result in disaster. If the aorta tears, which is called aortic dissection, or if the aorta balloons out and bursts, which is called an aortic aneurysm, the aortic valve can fail and death can come quickly, because the blood cascading back into it overwhelms the heart.

The tricuspid and mitral valves, which are located within the heart, are the largest of the four valves. They are also more delicate in structure, with leaflets that are larger in area and need to be mechanically supported. Just as cords support a parachute or tent, so are these valves in the heart. These delicate cord-like structures, known as the chordae tendineae, are attached to the papillary muscles. They hold the valves' leaflets to the walls of the ventricle. Sometimes, in the mitral valves, these leaflets can be oversized, so they billow too much, similarly to drapes sewn with too much material. In such a case, the leaflets cannot snap shut properly. When this occurs, as it sometimes does in women, it results in the condition known as mitral valve prolapse.

How Your Heart Pumps Blood

Blood is pumped to the lungs and all of the tissues of the body with a highly organized sequence that involves all four of the heart's chambers.

Your heartbeat has two phases; diastole and systole. Diastole is the period when the heart is said to be predominately relaxed. Systole is the phase when the ventricles contract, and blood is ejected. Together, these two actions, squeezing and relaxing, make up your heartbeat. A heart normally goes through this cycle an average of 60 to 100 times per minute, with adults averaging 70 beats per minute. That's 100,000 times a day!

The purpose of the cardiac cycle is to guide your blood through its journey from your heart into your lungs, where it receives oxygen, and then eventually, through your arteries to every cell in your body. Your blood then returns into your heart, where the cycle is repeated over and over again, for the rest of your life.

Your heart never stops its cyclical pumping, but, to visualize how the process works, let's interrupt one cycle. We'll interrupt it just as the right atrium is receiving blood returning from the body via the veins. This is blood that is oxygen-depleted and loaded with carbon dioxide,

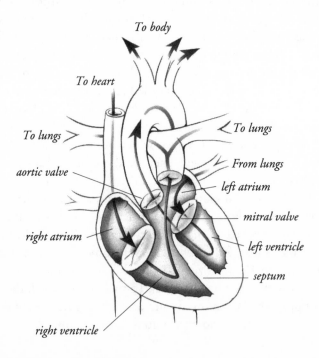

Blood Flow Through the Heart. The heart with its front walls removed, revealing its four-chambered structure: the right and left atria and the right and left ventricles. Valves control the flow of blood from the atria to the ventricles and out of the heart. A tissue-like divider, the septum, separates the heart's two halves.

called venous blood, and it is darker in color than bright red arterial blood, the oxygenated blood that flows through your arteries. At this point, your heart is relaxed. The deoxygenated blood flows through your open tricuspid valve and starts to fill your right ventricle. This causes your right atrium to contract, completing the priming of the ventricle. The tricuspid valve closes, and the deoxygenated blood is pumped through the pulmonary valve into the pulmonary artery and on into the lungs.

Once in the lungs, a very important exchange takes place. The pumping action of your right ventricle spreads the blood through a vast and numerous network of alveoli, the tiny grape-like air sacs within the lungs. Here, the carbon dioxide in the deoxygenated blood is exchanged for a fresh supply of oxygen, which is part of the air you breathe. The addition of fresh oxygen turns the blood bright red. This so-called oxygenated blood is now ready for its trip to nourish the rest of your body. It returns to the left side of the heart filling the relaxed atrium. The left atrium contracts, sending blood past the mitral valve into the left ventricle. Then, once filled, the left ventricle contracts, pumping the blood through the aortic valve. The blood immediately enters the aorta, your body's largest artery. From the aorta, the blood then flows through a branching system of arteries throughout your body.

As your blood travels throughout your body via your circulatory system, it flows through vessels, that become progressively smaller until your blood reaches the tiniest vessels of all, the capillaries. These are tiny, thin-walled blood vessels located in your body's organs and tissues that play an important role in your body's functioning. They are so tiny that the oxygen-carrying red cells move through them in a single file! It is in the capillaries where another important exchange takes place. This process is basically the opposite of what occurred in the lungs: It is at this point that the red cells of the blood give up oxygen in exchange for carbon dioxide.

This is only part of the story, however. Now transformed into venous blood, the blood must make its return trip back to the heart so it can obtain a fresh supply of oxygen. This deoxygenated blood travels back to the heart through a network of veins that rejoin each other and grow progressively larger, until this swelling stream of blood empties into the vena cava, the two major veins that are interconnected to the right atrium leading back into the heart. Then the journey begins again. It is estimated your blood makes this trip a mind-boggling estimated two and one-half *billion* times over a lifespan of 70 years.

YOUR CORONARY ARTERIES

It is very important for the functioning of your body that blood reach every organ in your body, including the heart itself. Your heart, after all, is composed of living tissue that requires oxygenated blood to survive. Since your heart is so busy pumping, you might wonder how the heart gets enough blood for itself. Some oxygen and carbon dioxide are exchanged with the superficial cells adjacent to the inner lining of the heart, but this is not nearly enough to supply your heart with the amount of oxygen it requires. The answer to this riddle shows how cleverly the heart has evolved. To provide for itself, your heart is equipped with its own specialized vascular system, the coronary arteries.

These arteries appear to crown the heart as they branch from the ascending aorta. The Latin term for "crown" is *coronare*, which is most likely how the coronary arteries got their name. Although they are actu-

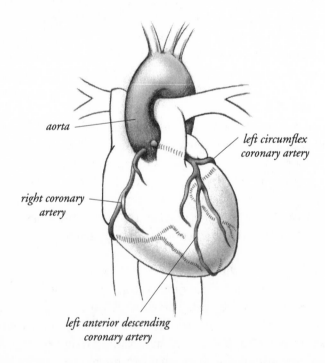

aorta

left circumflex coronary artery

right coronary artery

left anterior descending coronary artery

Coronary Arteries. The heart has two main coronary arteries, the left and the right. The left coronary artery branches off into the left circumflex and the left anterior descending arteries. Collectively, they are referred to as the heart's "three" coronary arteries.

ally two arteries, the left one quickly divides into two, which is why they are sometimes referred to as your heart's "three" coronary arteries.

This action takes place mostly on the left side of your heart, which is responsible for propelling oxygenated blood through your body. The coronary arteries lie on the surface of your heart muscle. They branch from the aorta, right above the leaflets of the aortic valve. Once your blood is pumped by the left ventricle through the aorta, a portion of it flows back directly to the heart via the coronary arteries. This occurs during the diastolic part of the heart's cycle, while the heart is momentarily relaxing. This incredibly well-designed system has evolved over millions of years. Your coronary arteries, by the way, are only the width of a strand of spaghetti, which is why any narrowing that occurs, as it does during atherosclerosis, the process known as coronary disease, can be devastating.

As we mentioned, the hearts of women on average are smaller than those of men. What holds true for the heart as a whole applies to the coronary arteries as well. This means that the inside diameter of the artery is smaller, which means it can clog more easily and is more difficult to operate on.

Until relatively recently, the coronary arteries were considered mainly from the perspective of their role as tubes to deliver blood laden with life-sustaining oxygen and fuel to the heart muscle. However, over the last decade the importance of the coronary artery as a vital and dynamic organ is being recognized. The inner lining of the artery, the endothelium, secretes substances that dynamically control the diameter and flow of blood through the artery. On the other hand, once the artery is damaged by even the early stages of coronary heart disease, this inner lining may secrete substances that cause the artery to narrow and promote blood clots. The hormone estrogen has been identified as an agent that promotes the normal functioning of this inner lining in women. This is discussed in greater detail later in the chapter on hormone replacement therapy.

YOUR HEART'S ELECTRICAL SYSTEM

Your heart's cardiac cycle is coordinated by an intrinsic electrical system, which began operating in your heart even before you were born. This system has its own "timers" and "wiring" that stimulate it to contract an average 100,000 times per day, as mentioned earlier. Each heartbeat originates in a specific area of the right atrium called the sinoatrial node. This is often referred to as your heart's "intrinsic" pacemaker. If anything goes wrong with this electrical system, the result can be some heart rhythm disruption, also known as an arrhythmia.

YOUR BLOOD PRESSURE

Just as the chambers of your heart respond to the electrical signals generated by your heart's electrical system, your heart also responds to changes in the pressures within it. Since your heart is not actually one pump but two, there are also two systems of blood pressure involved. The left side of your heart, which is responsible for pushing the blood out through your entire body, functions as a high-pressure system. The right side of your heart, which is responsible for spreading your blood out into your lungs so the exchange of carbon dioxide and oxygen can occur, functions as a low-pressure system. If your blood pressure is elevated, it indicates your heart is working harder than normal, putting both your heart and arteries under great strain.

YOUR HEART AND YOUR NERVOUS SYSTEM

You may wonder why when you're startled or surprised—say you suddenly realize your wallet is missing—your heart may pound or even seem to stop beating momentarily. Or why it may feel like your heart is bursting when you receive joyous news, such as learning that you have a new grandchild or you've received an award. These responses have to do with the workings of your nervous system.

The function of your nervous system, which is located mostly in your brain, is to act as your body's overall information-gathering center. Based on the information your brain collects, it sends out messages to all the parts of your body. Some of these messages can be voluntary, such as the message to rise when the alarm clock goes off. Other messages can be involuntary, such as when your body jerks as a car backfires or a firecracker explodes. The latter is an example of a spinal cord reflex.

Chemicals called neurotransmitters relay messages between the nervous system and the cardiovascular system. These chemicals travel between cells and can provoke a response in the target organ. There are different types of neurotransmitters. Norepinephrine, an adrenaline-type substance, can increase your heart rate and the force of your heart's contractions in response to a threat, causing more blood to be pumped out by our heart to our muscles so that you can fight or run (hence the reference to adrenaline's effects as the "fight or flight" response.)

This response is believed to stem from our primitive beginnings, when "fight or flight" was an everyday dilemma.

Thus, this link between our heart and our brain was not totally a figment of the imaginations of early scientists. Your heart is more than unresponsive pump; it does beat in step with your emotions. Since those early days, though, scientists have learned a great deal about how you can keep your heart functioning well.

3

~~~~ᴠᴠᴠᴠ∩Ⓞ∩ᴠᴠᴠᴠ~~~~

What's Your Heart Disease Risk?

AFTER SPENDING 15 years in the secretarial pool, Helen was finally promoted to supervisor last year. At first she was delighted, but lately she's been having second thoughts. She's caught in the middle. Her boss is pressuring her to pile the work onto her staff, but these are the same women who used to be her coworkers and friends. Now she sees them glaring at her as if she's the enemy. Helen doesn't know what to do. She's started smoking again, she finds herself grabbing for doughnuts and putting on weight, and her blood pressure and cholesterol are sky-rocketing.

Helen is a heart attack waiting to happen. But you don't have to be exactly like Helen to be at risk for coronary artery disease or a heart attack. Take Melanie, a 36-year-old lawyer. She exercises regularly, enjoys meditation, and is the envy of her friends, who think she's got it all under control. Yet she is at high risk for a heart attack because she is unaware that she has inherited hyperlipidemia, which causes abnormally high blood cholesterol levels. Carolyn, 31, whose mother died young from a heart attack, unwittingly adds to the risk of her family history by combining cigarette-smoking with birth control pills.

Only by learning about risk factors can you realistically determine your individual risk profile. Then you can decide which changes will bring you closest to your goal of preventing heart disease.

Coronary Heart Disease

Coronary heart disease is commonly referred to as "heart disease," but that's like referring to all forms of cancer simply as cancer. Coronary artery disease refers to a particular type of disease process known as atherosclerosis, the formation of fatty deposits (or plaque) on the walls of your heart's three major coronary arteries.

These coronary arteries deliver oxygenated blood to your heart. Your heart needs this oxygen to survive. When the arteries are narrowed by atherosclerosis, the result may be angina pectoris, or chest pain from coronary artery disease. If the arteries suddenly become completely blocked, the result is a heart attack.

Over the decades, coronary artery disease has changed from something fatal to something you can survive—and now, under some circumstances, something you may be able to beat. Currently, there are four methods of treatment. One or a combination of them can be your key to conquering this once-fatal disease.

- Identifying your risk factors and reducing them by making lifestyle changes
- Cardiovascular drugs
- Angioplasty and similar techniques
- Coronary bypass surgery

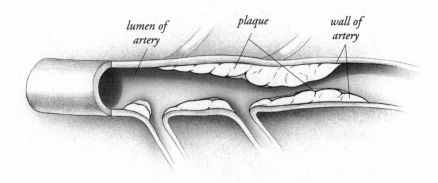

Atherosclerotic Artery. Fatty deposits called atherosclerotic plaque narrow the artery, impeding the flow of blood to the heart and possibly causing a blood clot, which may result in a heart attack.

Identifying and reducing your risk factors are covered in this chapter and the next. Throughout this book, you'll find chapters on cardiovascular drugs, angioplasty, bypass surgery and similar techniques. By putting this information to use, you can reduce your coronary heart disease risk or find the best treatment for it.

IMPORTANT RISKS

A risk factor is an element proven to contribute independently to the development of heart problems. Smoking and diabetes together, for example, increase your chance of developing coronary artery disease, but studies show that women who smoke but are not diabetic and those who are diabetic but don't smoke also are at increased risk.

Traditionally, risk factors have been divided into two groups: those that are considered changeable and those that are not. This is misleading; even though you may think a risk is nonchangeable, such as your age, race, or family history of early coronary artery disease, that is not really the case, as you'll see.

The impact of risk factors cannot be overstated. Although all of the known risk factors for heart attacks have not been identified, at least one half the number of all heart attacks is attributed to known risk factors. This is true no matter how old you are. For instance, even though the risk of heart disease mounts as you grow older, researchers looked at female heart attack victims in their 30s and found that many had risk factors such as high blood pressure, a family history of coronary artery disease, diabetes, or smoking.

MAJOR HEART DISEASE RISK FACTORS

Here are the risk factors for coronary artery disease and heart attacks:

- Your age
- Your family medical history
- Your race
- Smoking
- Oral contraceptives (if you're a smoker)
- Abnormal cholesterol pattern
- Diabetes

- Sedentary lifestyle
- Weight
- High blood pressure/hypertension

Emerging Risk Factors

- Stress
- Depression
- Homocysteine
- Infection
- Iron

In evaluating your personal risk factors for heart disease, it's useful to bear in mind that risks indicate that you have an increased probability of developing heart disease, but they are not necessarily definite predictors.

My father died at the age of 59 of a heart attack. For me to throw up my hands and say, "That's it—there's nothing I can do about it. I'll probably die young of heart disease," is neither correct nor useful. Although my father did have coronary artery disease, his having diabetes contributed to its development. Since I may have inherited a tendency towards diabetes as well, this motivates me to control my weight and exercise, which lessens the probability that I will become diabetic. This in turn reduces my risk of developing coronary artery disease.

You can evaluate your risk factors in much the same way. If you are an African-American woman, knowing you have a greater risk of developing high blood pressure can motivate you to watch your blood pressure carefully. If you have several risk factors for heart disease and you're approaching menopause, knowing your risk factors will help you evaluate whether to begin hormone replacement therapy, which some studies show can help prevent coronary disease.

Consider the case of Rhonda. Her mother, Alice, was overweight and had not been to a doctor in 20 years, so she didn't realize she was diabetic and had high blood pressure when she suffered a heart attack. Shaken by her mother's experience, Rhonda quit smoking, lost weight, and began exercising. In fact, she and her mother now walk two miles a day together.

The impact of risk factors increases when combined. So having two risk factors more than doubles your total risk of developing coronary artery disease. Unfortunately, the number of women in the United

States with multiple risk factors is increasing, despite growing awareness of the importance of this topic.

YOUR AGE

As you grow older, your risk of developing coronary artery disease increases. This is true for both men and women. By virtue of simply being a woman, though, you have a substantial "grace period" over men—for most of their lives, women develop coronary artery disease about 15 years later than men. After menopause, though, your natural protection against heart disease begins to disappear. If you're 55, your risk of dying from heart disease is about equal to that of a man about 10 years your senior. By the time you reach 70, this drops to only five years. By age 75, your chance of dying from heart disease is equal to that of a man your age.

YOUR FAMILY MEDICAL HISTORY

If you have a parent, grandparent, brother, or sister who suffered a heart attack or developed coronary artery disease at an early age, your chance of developing it increases. However, exactly how much it increases remains unknown.

Any discussion of family medical history revolves around genetics, the study of how traits are passed down from one generation to another through the genes; the units of inherited material contained in the body's cells. While coronary artery disease is not considered an inherited trait, it does appear to run in families. This was demonstrated by a Swedish study published in 1994 in *The New England Journal of Medicine*, which found that identical twins whose sibling died from a heart attack had a greatly increased risk of suffering a heart attack themselves. This study found that the men whose identical twin died of heart disease before the age of 55 had an eightfold risk of dying from the ailment themselves; for fraternal (non-identical) twins, the risk was weaker, but still nearly fourfold. Women whose fraternal twins had died had two to three times the risk of the men but for identical female twins, the risk was fifteen times higher. The study also indicated that the effect of genetics was stronger for those who developed heart disease at a younger age and declined as the subjects grew older.

Some of this increased risk might be due to inheriting contributing underlying disease, such as diabetes and abnormal blood cholesterol patterns. Lifestyle may also play a role, since twins are usually raised in the same environment.

If you have a family history of heart disease, the age at which your relatives developed it offers a very important clue to your own risk. If your relatives developed heart disease at a relatively young age, this increases your risk as well. This is the case if your father or brother was diagnosed before the age of 55; and/or your mother or sister was diagnosed before the age of 65. What about grandparents, aunts, and cousins? Their medical history increases your risk, but the evidence is far less strong than with parents or siblings. Remember, though, heredity is not necessarily destiny. This indicates a tendency, not a certainty. Use your knowledge of a negative family medical history to motivate you to make the necessary changes that can make your heart healthier.

YOUR RACE

The frustrating lack of research about women and heart disease is even greater when it comes to race. Still, there is enough known to draw some conclusions. Devastating as heart disease is to African-American males, the disease is even more deadly to African-American women.

Heart disease is the biggest killer of women no matter what their race or ethnic group. However, for most of their lives, African-American women are more vulnerable; they are about one third more likely to die from heart disease than caucasian women. Between the ages of 35 and 74, their risk doubles. This difference evens out by the age of 75, when an equal number of caucasian women are afflicted. It is believed that this difference is due to the fact that African-American women are more likely develop multiple risk factors for heart disease, including high blood pressure, diabetes, and obesity, at a younger age.

Furthermore, the incidence of heart disease in African-American women is even higher than that when compared to men. A 1997 study in the *Archives of Internal Medicine* found that African-American women have a higher rate of heart disease than caucasian women, despite the fact that African-American men have a lower rate of heart disease than their caucasian counterparts. The issue of race brings up a troubling problem similar to that of gender bias. Studies have found that heart disease may be treated less aggressively in both African-American women and men. For instance, that 1997 study found a "markedly lower" number of coronary procedures performed on the African-American patients following hospitalization. Remember that 1999 study in *The New England*

Journal of Medicine cited in Chapter 1, in which primary care doctors viewed videotapes of actors posing as patients and referred women for testing and treatment only 60 percent as often as men? That same study found a similar bias against referring African-Americans for cardiac testing and treatment as well.

♥ **Lifesaving Tip: If your age, race, or family's medical history seems to put you at a disadvantage, make this knowledge work for you. Use it to motivate you to make the changes that can lower your risk. In the long run, you can become healthier than women who don't have these particular risks but don't live as healthy a lifestyle.**

SMOKING: THE BIGGEST RISK FACTOR YOU CAN CHANGE

Estelle, who was diagnosed as having angina pectoris (chest pain caused by coronary artery disease) didn't realize for months that she might have a heart problem. Although she was experiencing shortness of breath and chest pain, she was unaware that her two-pack-a-day habit was ruining her heart. "I just assumed the shortness of breath was from my lungs," she said, "I always figured lung cancer would kill me."

Estelle is not alone. Polls show that women believe cancer is their number-one health risk. Women surveyed usually believe that it's not even lung cancer, but breast cancer that will kill them. As we noted earlier, they're wrong: Cardiovascular disease is the biggest killer of women. Cigarette smoking is the single biggest preventable risk factor; it is considered responsible for more than one in five deaths from cardiovascular disease in women, as well as one half of the heart attacks in women under the age of 55.

But because women don't realize this, they continue to smoke, says Dr. Margaret Chesney, professor of medicine and epidemiology at the University of California, San Francisco.

"Women know that cigarette smoking is unhealthy," says Dr. Chesney. "They have a general idea that it is unhealthy, but they do not realize the very powerful link between smoking and their leading cause of death, heart disease. That is because they think their leading cause of death is breast cancer. So, although they know that smoking is unhealthy, that doesn't give them a compelling reason to quit."

Studies convincingly demonstrate that female smokers are up to five times more likely to suffer a heart attack than their nonsmoking counterparts. Not only that, the Nurses' Health Study has shown that for women who started smoking before the age of 15, the risk is 10 times greater. The studies also showed that the risks are significantly improved after quitting.

You don't have to be a heavy smoker to damage your heart. Although heavy smoking will cause more damage, a nationwide study of nearly 120,000 nurses showed that smoking as few as one to four cigarettes a day increased their risk of a heart attack two to three times. This study also found that smoking was an independent risk factor that accounted for 40 percent of the heart attacks, and this figure climbed to an incredible 90 percent for women who smoked more than 45 cigarettes a day. Nothing erases your natural gender protection against developing heart disease early in life more thoroughly than smoking.

Smoking takes a toll in women no matter what their age: A study published in 1993 in the *Cleveland Clinic Journal of Medicine* found that, of women who suffered heart attacks in their early 30s, 72 percent smoked. Two years later, researchers at an American Heart Association meeting reported on a study of 105 apparently health women in their 30s and 40s. The women in this study who were found to have early signs of heart disease were much more likely to be smokers.

Quitting smoking pays off big. In an Australian study, women who were current cigarette smokers were nearly five times more likely to suffer a heart attack than those who had never smoked. This fell to 1.6 times for women who had quit up to three years ago. Those who quit smoking for four to six years had no more risk than those who never smoked. The Nurses' Health Study also found that women who quit smoking experience an immediate benefit and that their excess risk for coronary heart disease declined eventually to the level of those who had never smoked.

How Cigarette Smoke Damages Your Heart

Each time you inhale cigarette smoke, you're drawing into your body a mixture of 4,000 chemical substances, many of which are poisonous. Cigarette smoke contains carbon monoxide, one of the deadliest of substances. When you inhale cigarette smoke, sulfuric acid not only eats away at the tissue of your lungs, but damages the blood vessels of your heart as well . . . and the toxic list goes on.

Researchers believe that cigarette smoke damages your heart in two ways. First, the toxic materials injure the walls of your coronary arteries and, in attempting to repair them, your body inadvertently creates conditions that make it easier for atherosclerotic plaque—the fatty deposits that cause coronary artery disease—to develop. It's also believed that tobacco smoke works independently to activate your body's blood-clotting system, promoting clots that can block your arteries and cause a heart attack. Substances in some birth control pills can do the same thing; that is why the combination of taking oral contraceptives and smoking can be particularly dangerous.

Besides promoting conditions that can lead to coronary disease, smoking has been linked in women to coronary spasms, a potentially dangerous constriction of the heart's blood vessels. In some cases, even women with apparently healthy hearts can experience chest pain leading to heart attack and death. Cocaine is known to cause coronary spasms, but cigarette smoking has been linked to this problem as well.

Smoking can also lead to the development of high blood pressure, another major risk factor for coronary artery disease. You know nicotine as the substance that causes addiction to cigarettes. What you may not know is that nicotine stimulates the release of the hormone epinephrine, which can raise blood pressure, into your bloodstream.

As if this were not enough, smoking is also one of the biggest risk factors for peripheral vascular disease, a narrowing of the blood vessels that carry blood to the legs, kidneys, and brain, which is often found in people with heart disease. In fact, peripheral vascular disease occurs almost exclusively in smokers.

These dangers to your health exist even if you choose "low-tar" and "low-nicotine" cigarettes. Choosing such cigarettes may lead to your smoking more under the misguided notion that they're safe. Also, the recent fad for cigar smoking by women is harmful as well; cigar smokers are more likely to develop heart disease than nonsmokers, as well as cancer of the lung, mouth, and throat.

♥ **Lifesaving Tip: If you smoke, and do nothing more upon reading this book than quit, you will sharply decrease your chance of developing coronary artery disease. Giving up smoking is the healthiest thing you can do for your heart.**

How Many Women Smoke?

Take a look around at the shopping mall, the office, and the neighborhood restaurant: Women are lighting up.

When they first began smoking, decades ago, women started later, and smoked fewer cigarettes than men, and did not inhale as deeply. As time went on, women began smoking more like men: younger, heavier, and inhaling deeply—and their health risks climbed.

Learning of the harmful effects of cigarette smoking has had some effect. Since 1964, when the landmark warning on the hazards of cigarette smoking was issued, the number of smokers dropped from 40 percent to about 25 percent, according to the federal Centers for Disease Control and Prevention in Atlanta.

Still, women make up a large portion of America's smokers. In fact, between 1930 and 1967, the proportion of adult women who smoked rose from 10 percent to 35 percent. Since then, the percentage of women smokers has declined, but one quarter of the female population still smokes. Young women are starting to smoke earlier, and are less likely to quit than are men. Some young people are still taking up the habit in junior high or even elementary school.

Why Women Smoke

Given the tremendous detrimental effect that smoking has on their health, why do women smoke? They may not realize just how hazardous it is. Not surprisingly, the tobacco companies don't tell them. On the contrary, the tobacco companies have worked hard for years to convince women that smoking is glamorous and slenderizing.

Consider Nina, who underwent a balloon angioplasty because of coronary heat disease at the Cleveland Clinic.

"When I was growing up, smoking was oh-so-glamorous. All the Hollywood stars smoked," said Nina, as she pantomimed smoking a cigarette in a long cigarette holder.

To appeal to women, the tobacco companies have even co-opted the flag of feminism. The famous Virginia Slims motto, "You've Come a Long Way, Baby," seemed to promise female equality, but delivered disease and death. Tobacco companies are big supporters of not only athletic and sports activities, but women's events as well.

If smoking is so dangerous to a woman's health, you might wonder why you don't read more about it in women's magazines. An answer to that question comes from Dr. Kenneth Warner of the University of Michigan School of Public Health. He conducted studies that showed magazines that accept cigarette advertising are less likely to run articles publicizing the health risks of smoking. He found this "censorship phenomenon" very prevalent in women's magazines.

If you smoke, you may also believe it is not that dangerous because your doctor has not advised you to quit. Erica Frank, MD, of Emory University, conducted a study that found that only about one half of the smokers had ever been told by their doctors to quit. This is not because doctors do not believe smoking to be unhealthy, but more likely because they view it as interfering with their patient's private lives. These doctors are wrong, believes Dr. Frank, who adds, "I believe it is a physician's obligation to advise their patients to quit, because quitting smoking is the most important thing people can do to improve their health."

Smoking and Pregnancy

Smoking is one of the most harmful things you can do to your unborn child. According to the Surgeon General, smokers give birth to babies who are, on average, one half inch shorter and seven ounces lighter than babies of nonsmokers. Babies born to smokers are more likely to have birth defects, chronic breathing problems, and learning disabilities.

❤ Lifesaving Tip: If you quit smoking before you become pregnant, or even during your first trimester, you reduce your risk of a low-birth-weight baby to that of a woman who has never smoked.

Smoking and Weight Control (and Wrinkles!)

Most health professionals hate to admit it, but cigarette smoking does keep your weight down. You may naturally assume that this is because when you smoke, you are less likely to snack. While this is true, research also shows that nicotine affects your metabolism, keeping your weight unnaturally low. Studies have found that excess weight gain can be avoided by exercise, such as an aerobic workout for 45 minutes a day, three times a week. However, if smoking has compromised your lung function, making exercise more difficult, you may have to start out more gradually.

If you are so concerned about your appearance that you smoke to keep slim, think of what you may be doing to your face! Most doctors say they can pick out the longtime female smokers in their waiting rooms by the crow's-feet and age lines above their upper lips. In fact, a study published in the *American Journal of Public Health* in 1995 correlated the amount of facial wrinkling with the number of years of smoking.

❤ Lifesaving Tip: Remember, quitting smoking pays off big. It's estimated that, after one year, you'll decrease by 50 percent the risk to your heart that smoking had produced. After 15 years, your risk will be the same as that of a woman who never smoked.

Nonsmokers, Take Note!

Even if you don't smoke, your health is at risk from the deadly fumes around you, which curl from the cigarette dangled by your spouse, your best friend, coworker, or even a stranger seated at the restaurant table across the way.

It was once thought that smokers only endangered themselves, but studies indicate that this is not the case. Researchers are finding that passive smoke, also known as "environmental" or "secondary" smoke is a culprit in the development of heart disease and heart attacks.

Sitting in a smoky room increases your heart rate and blood pressure. Inhaling passive smoke also increases your demand for oxygen during exercise, which can be harmful if you have heart disease. Because your body adjusts to chronic exposure of cigarette smoke, you may be at an even higher risk from ingesting passive smoke than are smokers. So, even if you do not smoke, this is not necessarily one less risk you have to worry about.

Oral Contraceptives

Since their introduction over 25 years ago, oral contraceptives have become widely used. For most women, they are safe, but if you smoke they may pose a threat to your heart.

Birth control pills are generally made up of two hormones, progesterone and estrogen. Taken orally, they act to prevent pregnancy. When they were first developed, it was discovered that women taking them faced a higher risk of cardiovascular problems, including heart attack, stroke, blood clots in the lungs (pulmonary embolism), and cardiovascular disease. Since most birth control pills have been reformulated, this has reduced most of the risk. However, oral contraceptives have implications regarding blood pressure, notes Suzanne Oparil, MD, director of the vascular biology and hypertension program at the University of Alabama School of Medicine and a past president of the American Heart Association.

"The entire population of women taking oral contraceptives, most of whom have normal blood pressure, experience a small but detectable increase in blood pressure during the course of contraceptive therapy," she noted.

Most of the time, this does not prove to be a problem. Only a small percentage of these women develop high blood pressure because of the pill, and their blood pressure generally returns to normal within three months after discontinuing its usage. However, it's possible for this high blood pressure to prove dangerous, so you should bear this in mind, particularly if you have a family history of high blood pressure, experienced high blood pressure when you were pregnant, are overweight, over the age of 35, or have kidney disease. Also, if you have high blood pressure and take oral contraceptives, you are at increased risk of blood clots in the veins and for cardiovascular disease and stroke. So, if you have any of these conditions, or are over the age of 35, you and your doctor should review your medical history before making this decision.

♥ Lifesaving Tip: If you smoke cigarettes, you should definitely use another form of birth control. Studies show that taking birth control pills and smoking, in combination, can increase your risk of suffering a heart attack up to 39 times. This is because both smoking and oral contraceptives increase your blood's tendency to clot, which can lead to heart attack or stroke.

ABNORMAL CHOLESTEROL PATTERN

"What's your cholesterol number?" In the 1980s, this question echoed through doctor's offices, shopping malls, and fitness centers. Cholesterol watching had become a fad. As so often happens, confusion reigned. What was the best way to bring down cholesterol? Oatmeal? Rice cakes? Critics also emerged, charging that Americans were being unduly frightened about cholesterol.

So what's the truth? Studies have shown that high blood cholesterol levels are associated with coronary artery disease.

A pearly, fat-like substance, cholesterol, is an essential component of our body. It's found in the membranes of cells, is used in the formation of the bile acids that help digest our food, and even contributes to sex hormones.

The important news about cholesterol for women is that recent research shows that if you have other risks for coronary heart disease, just knowing your total cholesterol level is not enough. You need to know how your levels of the two different types of cholesterol are represented within your total level. This is your blood cholesterol or lipid pattern. An abnormal lipid pattern is a risk factor for coronary artery disease. There are different ways in which these patterns can be abnormal. For example, one inherited lipid disorder (hyperlipidemia) results in a blood cholesterol pattern of too much low-density lipoprotein, or LDL cholesterol, when compared to high-density lipoprotein, or HDL cholesterol. Women may also develop an abnormal cholesterol pattern after menopause.

If you are concerned about your cholesterol, you should know the following levels, as opposed to just your total cholesterol number:

- High-density lipoproteins, or HDL cholesterol
- Low-density lipoproteins, or LDL cholesterol
- Triglycerides

Low-density lipoprotein (LDL) is the so-called "bad" cholesterol. This substance contributes to the development of heart disease by depositing cholesterol in the arterial wall, which can form the fatty streaks that result in the narrowing of arteries. High levels of LDL increase your chances of developing heart disease.

Triglycerides are fatty compounds found in combination with LDL and low levels of HDL cholesterol, and are increasingly being implicated as important in causing coronary artery disease in women.

High-density lipoprotein cholesterol, or HDL, reverses the accumulation of cholesterol by transferring it away from the artery. In a sense, it does for your arteries what drain cleaner does for your plumbing. Studies have found that, for women, a high HDL level is probably the most important indicator of a low risk of heart disease. On the contrary, women who have low HDL are at significantly higher risk. In fact, follow-up research done by the Framingham Heart Study has shown that those with the highest HDL were found to have half the coronary heart disease risk as those with the lowest, no matter what other risk factors they had.

Here is how total blood cholesterol levels stack up. (Cholesterol is measured in milligrams per deciliter of blood (mg/dl).)

TOTAL BLOOD CHOLESTEROL
Desirable   200 mg/dl
Borderline High   200 to 239 mg/dl
High   240 or over mg/dl

A simple, finger-prick blood test will give you your total cholesterol level, which may be enough if you have no other risk factors for coronary disease. But this can be tricky; a total cholesterol level over 200 does not necessarily indicate high risk. If it's high because your HDL cholesterol level is high, the total may be nothing to worry about; it's probably good, in fact. Women, particularly prior to menopause, are more likely to have these high HDL levels.

HDL CHOLESTEROL LEVELS
Desirable   35 or greater (many doctors
                                     prefer 45 or higher)
Not desirable   Under 35

Sometimes, a ratio instead of a number is used to explain the HDL cholesterol level. The ratio is obtained by dividing the HDL cholesterol level into the total cholesterol number. For example, if you have a total cholesterol level of 200 and a HDL cholesterol level of 50, the ratio would be stated as 4:1 (four-to-one). The highest desirable cholesterol ratio is 5:1.

LDL CHOLESTEROL LEVELS
Desirable   Under 130 mg/dl
Borderline to high   130 to 159 mg/dl
High   160 or over mg/dl

TRIGLYCERIDES
Normal   Less than 200 mg/dl
Borderline-high   200 to 400 mg/dl
High   400 to 1,000 mg/dl
Very high   Greater than 1,000 mg/dl

Getting a cholesterol lipid profile that shows your LDL, HDL, and triglyceride levels provides enough information for most women. However, there is more sophisticated cholesterol testing on the horizon, and you may wish to investigate this further.

Because nearly one half of the people with heart disease have normal cholesterol levels, its becoming more and more evident that this measurement is far too broad an indicator. In fact, there are many different cholesterol patterns—more than a dozen have been identified so far, and it's not necessarily their components, but the way in which they are arranged, that determines their danger. Research is underway, but in the meantime, here are some examples of the patterns that are garnering interest: Lipoprotein (a), LDL pattern A, and LDL pattern B.

Although it was initially assumed that all LDL cholesterol patterns are harmful, some are more dangerous than others are. LDL pattern A, for example, so far seems to be one of the less dangerous forms of LDL cholesterol because its larger, fluffier particles don't seem to have the talent for clogging up arteries that some of the other patterns do. For instance, Lipoprotein (a), known also as Lp(a), appears to be double trouble; this form of LDL cholesterol not only aids in the formation of heart-attack-causing blood clots, but also contributes to atherosclerosis by leading to the overgrowth of smooth muscle tissue inside the coronary artery's walls.

Another deadly pattern is LDL pattern B. Studies have identified this pattern in one of every three men, and one of every five to six postmenopausal women. In this type of cholesterol pattern, the particles are small, dense, and particularly effective in packing the arteries. Additionally, people with this pattern also have less protective HDL "good" cholesterol and higher triglycerides. So studies indicate that people with LDL pattern B have a threefold higher risk of heart disease, even if they have high HDL cholesterol and a low LDL level generally.

It's being learned that these different cholesterol patterns carry different treatment implications. For instance, some small studies indicate that a diet low in fat, while effective in people with LDL pattern B, may be less useful, possibly even harmful, for some people with LDL pattern A. But this work is still in the research stages. Still, it eventually may explain why some people cannot lower their cholesterol levels despite diet and exercise and may also lead to cholesterol-fighting strategies that can be individually tailored. This is an exciting field; before long, a wider range of tests to uncover particular cholesterol patterns—and a larger variety of treatments—may be available. For more information on cholesterol testing, see Chapter 10.

If your blood cholesterol level is undesirable, your doctor will most likely have you try lowering it though diet and exercise. If you have coronary heart disease or have more than three risk factors for it, cholesterol-altering medication should be prescribed right off the bat, along with an individualized nutrition and exercise program that is based on your own personal cholesterol profile.

DIABETES

A powerful risk factor for heart disease in men, diabetes is even more deadly to women's hearts. Studies show diabetes doubles the risk of heart disease in men, but triples it for women. Furthermore, diabetes, like smoking, effectively erases the "grace period" for heart disease afforded by gender. Studies show that if you develop diabetes before menopause, your risk of getting coronary artery disease rises to a level equal to that of a man your age. Diabetes also raises the risk of other risk factors associated with heart disease, including high blood cholesterol and high blood pressure.

What is diabetes? If your pancreas doesn't produce enough insulin, the hormone that metabolizes sugar into energy, or if your body doesn't react correctly to the type of insulin you have, the resulting condition is called diabetes. Diabetics are grouped into two major categories. Type 1, formerly known as juvenile-onset diabetes, is an inherited disorder that usually appears before the age of 40. Type 2, formerly called adult-onset diabetes, is the type that develops usually after age 40 and is by far the most common type. To simplify, both types will be termed here "diabetes." A third type, gestational diabetes, may occur while you're pregnant and disappear afterwards. It's an important warning sign, however: If you have gestational diabetes, your chances of developing diabetes later increases.

The exact reason why diabetes is so damaging to women's hearts is now better understood. Diabetic women tend to have more of the undesirable LDL cholesterol and triglycerides and less of the so-called "good" HDL cholesterol in their blood. In addition, insulin is not utilized as effectively in diabetics, resulting in a condition known as insulin resistance. The adverse effect of diabetes is made worse by the presence of other risk factors such as obesity.

If you have coronary artery disease, diabetes poses an additional danger. Diabetes causes changes in the nerve cells, which can result in your body's misinterpreting pain signals, such as chest pain. You might even suffer a "silent" heart attack, one you don't realize you're having.

Your probability of developing diabetes increases if you're overweight. Being overweight makes it more difficult for your body to properly metabolize sugar and fat. Keeping your weight under control and exercising helps prevent diabetes.

A frightening fact about diabetes is that one half of those who have diabetes don't realize it. This is because, on average, there is a seven-year gap between the onset and the diagnosis of the disease. During this time, diabetes silently damages the body, including the blood vessels that nourish the heart. Most of the risk factors for diabetes are the same as for coronary artery disease, including growing older, having a family medical history of diabetes, being overweight, inactivity, high blood pressure, and smoking. In addition, if you became diabetic temporarily while you were pregnant, a condition known as gestational diabetes, you may have a greater risk of becoming diabetic later in life. If you are approaching menopause, or you have these risk factors, you should be screened for diabetes. See Chapter 10 for more information.

OVERWEIGHT

Most women believe they weigh too much. In discussing overweight as a risk factor for coronary disease, though, we are talking about obesity. If you are obese, which is defined as weighing 20 percent or more above your desirable weight, your risk of coronary artery disease is tripled.

However, nowadays, experts are finding that it's not what you weigh; but the way your weight is distributed (your body mass index, or BMI) that is the key factor. Research has shown that if your fat is concentrated in your stomach, making you "apple"-shaped, you are worse off, in terms of health, than your pear-shaped friends. The fat around your middle makes you more vulnerable to such ailments as hypertension, diabetes, and coronary artery disease.

Eventually, the scale in the doctor's office may become a thing of the past as more doctors pull out a tape measure instead. To learn whether you are apple-shaped (technically, android), or pear-shaped (gynoid), you need to determine your waist-to-hip ratio.

Take a tape measure and measure around your waist at the navel level (no cheating—don't pull in your stomach). Then measure your hips at their widest. Divide the waist measure by the hip measure for your "waist-to-hip" ratio. For example, say your waist is 38 inches and your hips are 43 inches. Divide the 43 into 38 and you'll get 0.88. That's too high. What you're after is a waist-to-hip ratio of 0.80. If you're curious about the man in your life, his waist-to-hip ratio should be 0.95 or less.

HIGH BLOOD PRESSURE/HYPERTENSION

Nearly one half of the estimated 50 million Americans who have high blood pressure are women. High blood pressure, or hypertension, is known as the "silent" killer because, if undiagnosed, it can damage your heart, brain, and kidneys before you notice any symptoms.

Just as gender provides women with protection against coronary artery disease, women are afforded a similar "grace period" in the development of high blood pressure. Men are at greater risk for high blood pressure until the age of 55, when the rate becomes equal. After age 75, women are at greater risk than men are. However, as you age, you become as vulnerable as men are to hypertension and its deadly complications: heart attack and stroke.

This premenopausal gender advantage doesn't apply if you're African-American. As are African-American men, women are at higher risk for hypertension. Studies have shown that African-American women over the age of 25 are twice as likely to have high blood pressure.

No matter what your race, you're much more likely to develop hypertension if you have risk factors. These risks are similar to those of heart disease: a family history of early hypertension, growing older, smoking, obesity, and diabetes.

How Hypertension Damages Your Heart

With each contraction, your heart pumps a small amount of blood into your coronary arteries, which in turn distribute the blood to your heart muscle itself. Oxygen-rich blood similarly nourishes all of your body's organs, including your heart, kidneys, and brain.

Hypertension damages your heart in two ways. If undetected, high blood pressure can result in a form of heart disease called "hypertensive cardiovascular disease," in which your heart becomes enlarged and eventually weakens. While most people are screened for high blood pressure, this disease is still quite common. High blood pressure can damage your heart by contributing to atherosclerosis, the buildup of fatty deposits within your arteries that narrows them, resulting in coronary artery disease.

Think of your circulatory system as a river. At some places, where the river is narrow, pressure can build up and create turbulence, which can damage the banks of the river. The same thing can occur within your body. If your arteries are too narrow, blood pressure can build. High blood pressure can damage the walls of your arteries and, as your body attempts to repair the damage, atherosclerosis, or coronary artery disease, can result.

In most cases, high blood pressure occurs for no discernible reason. This is called essential hypertension, and accounts for about 90 percent of hypertension cases. Much less often, hypertension can stem from an underlying disorder. Some originate in the kidneys, the adrenal glands, or, in rare cases, a congenital disorder. This type of high blood pressure, called secondary hypertension, occurs far less often than essential hypertension. But if you have secondary hypertension, it's imperative that the underlying cause be diagnosed so that it can be corrected.

💙 **Lifesaving Tip: Although uncommon, secondary hypertension occurs more frequently in women. So, if you are diagnosed with high blood pressure, be certain your doctor checks for secondary causes.**

Hypertension in Pregnancy

A third type of hypertension can occur during pregnancy. Such hypertensive disorders, which are among the most serious complications of pregnancy, are discussed in Chapter 8.

White Coat Hypertension

Some people become so anxious when visiting the doctor that their blood pressure may rise, and they may be mistakenly diagnosed as having high blood pressure. This is called white coat hypertension. Stephanie was treated for high blood pressure for two years. When she switched physicians, her new doctor noticed that when she first arrived at the office her blood pressure was elevated. As the visit continued and Stephanie felt more relaxed, her blood pressure returned to normal. After evaluating Stephanie further, her doctor became convinced she did not have high blood pressure after all.

Your doctor may suggest careful home blood pressure checks using a home monitoring system to see what your pressure is like away from the hospital or clinic before deciding that you have high blood pressure, especially if medication is being considered.

If you have borderline high blood pressure, your doctor may advise you to control it by losing weight, exercising, quitting smoking, and cutting down on salt and caffeine. If you have more severe hypertension, these steps, plus medication, will most likely be prescribed.

SEDENTARY LIFESTYLE

An inactive lifestyle has been found to independently contribute to the development of coronary heart disease. In part, this is because inactivity contributes to developing diabetes, obesity, and abnormal cholesterol levels, but being sedentary alone has been found to increase risk, even in the absence of these other risk factors.

EMERGING HEART DISEASE RISK FACTORS

It is estimated that known risk factors are responsible for about one half of all heart attacks. Although they don't account for all heart attacks and cases of heart disease, that 50 percent is a hefty figure, especially when you consider that known risk factors, with heredity predominating, are responsible for only about 15 percent of all cases of breast cancer.

Obviously, though, much more needs to be known about heart disease. For instance, although the disease process that initiates coronary artery disease is believed to be fairly well understood, the event that initiates that process is not. So research continues to investigate what these causes might be.

For instance, the narrowing of the heart's coronary arteries is the result of heart disease. It is known that LDL cholesterol plays a role in this. But what occurs to make LDL cholesterol bind with white cells and other substances to form plaque, the dangerous material that narrows the arteries? Many scientists believe the answer to these question lies in a process called oxidation. Research indicates that cholesterol must be oxidized—combined with oxygen—before it becomes damaging. Once the LDL is oxidized, it attracts white cells and other fibrous substances that lead to the dangerous plaque. This process of oxidation is at the core of some theories discussed in the next section involving homocysteine, infections, and an excess of iron, which may be found to cause heart disease.

In reading about emerging risk factors, it's wise to keep in mind that the American Heart Association's list of major risk factors was compiled only after extensive research led to a consensus as to which items independently cause heart disease. On the other hand, we are inundated daily with health news reports that tout the latest studies with great fanfare. Remember, sometimes risk factors that receive a great deal of attention do not necessarily pan out to be as important as once thought. On the other hand, factors once dismissed are sometimes later found to be important.

This intense attention given to studies relating to heart disease brings up a much broader topic: how much attention you should pay to medical studies and other health news reported in the media.

STRESS

Although there is not yet enough evidence to indict stress as a direct cause of heart disease, a growing body of research indicates that it is a contributing risk factor. Stress, however, is a complicated topic, so we've devoted Chapter 16 to it.

DEPRESSION

Several studies find that women who have heart disease or who suffer heart attacks are at greater risk of dying from cardiac causes. In addition, researchers are now focusing on whether depression is a risk factor for developing heart disease as well. This topic is also covered in more detail in Chapter 16 on stress as well as in Chapter 5 on heart attacks.

HOMOCYSTEINE

A chemical in the blood known as homocysteine first made headlines in 1997, when a *New England Journal of Medicine* study of 587 men and women with heart disease reported that those with elevated homocysteine levels were four and one-half times as likely to die of heart disease as those with normal levels. Even after taking into account other risk factors, such as high cholesterol, high blood pressure, and smoking, homocysteine levels remained the strongest predictors of survival.

When we metabolize methionine, an amino acid found in protein-rich foods, our bodies produce homocysteine. The B vitamins folic acid (folate), B6, and B12 then convert homocysteine into other amino acids. When we don't consume enough folic acid and, to a lesser extent, vitamins B6 and B12, homocysteine accumulates in the blood. Some homocysteine in the blood is normal, but too much can damage the lining of arteries, setting the stage for the accumulation of fatty deposits. It may also accelerate blood clotting.

Some experts have speculated that homocysteine as a risk factor for heart disease is as significant as high cholesterol. Current data suggest that about 10 to 20 percent of heart disease cases are associated with high homocysteine levels. However, not all studies have linked homocysteine to an increased risk of heart disease. This has led to speculation that the amino acid may not be the actual risk factor but rather a marker for the real culprit, possibly low levels of B vitamins.

Homocysteine levels can be measured with a blood test that your doctor sends to a specially equipped lab. Although it is too soon to recommend that everyone get tested, it may be worthwhile for people who already have heart disease or have a strong family history of premature heart disease in the absence of other risk factors.

INFECTION

Although the risk factors that contribute to coronary artery disease are well documented, it isn't known what initiates atherosclerosis, the actual disease process itself. It is known, however, that the process that leads to this disease begins with an injury to the lining of an artery. This damage stimulates an inflammatory response by the body, which sets the stage for the build up of plaque along the vessel wall. Some researchers are looking into the possibility that a bacteria or virus may be the culprit, since even chronic low-grade infections of which you are unaware can set off this inflammatory response.

Research has recently identified several types of bacteria that might cause such inflammation. These include Chlamydia pneumoniae, which causes respiratory infections; Helicobacter pylori (H. pylori), which causes most ulcers; and the various bacteria associated with gum disease. A member of the herpes virus family, cytomegalovirus, has also been linked to heart disease.

Studies of both men and women show that high blood levels of C-reactive protein, a byproduct of the inflammatory process, increase heart attack risk. Furthermore, a 1999 study published in the *Journal of the American Medical Association* found that people who had been treated with certain antibiotics were at lower risk for heart attacks. At this point, taking antibiotics to prevent heart disease is premature; but a study of 4,000 people with heart disease, who will be tracked for three to four years to monitor their incidence of heart attack and other heart conditions, is currently under way.

The bacteria that causes gum disease is another suspect in the infection theory. Over 400 types of bacteria exist in the human mouth. When the gums become infected, these bacteria can easily enter the bloodstream and travel to infect other parts of the body, increasing the risk of heart attack and stroke. Research shows that people with gum disease are one and one-half to two times as likely to suffer a fatal heart attack, and nearly three times as likely to suffer a stroke, as those without gum disease. Scientists now believe that byproducts of oral bacteria that enter the bloodstream may start a chain of reactions that makes bad LDL cholesterol more susceptible to oxidation, the process that leads cholesterol to stick to artery walls. Some species of bacteria have also been found to precipitate the formation of blood clots. Regular brushing, daily flossing, and one or two professional cleanings a year can not only prevent gum disease but can reverse gingivitis, the mildest form of the disease.

IRON

Evidence is building that having high amounts of iron in the blood increases heart disease risk, a hypothesis that also would explain some of the gender differences between heart disease in men and women. Several studies have found that men with more ferritin, a protein that binds iron in the blood, are more likely to have heart attacks. This theory has captivated some researchers since it was first posed in 1981 and most recently in 1999, when it was the topic of a review article published in the *Archives of Internal Medicine*. Proponents of the iron theory contend that stored iron facilitates the oxidation process, which may lead to coronary artery disease. The theory goes onto conclude that since excess iron is shed during menstruation in premenopausal women, it is the depletion of this excess iron, rather than the presence of estrogen, that explains why younger women are generally protected from heart disease and why women develop heart disease later than men do. Studies that have investigated the effect of iron have found that, in women, iron stores remain low and begin to rise only after age 45, while in men, stored iron is at its highest level at 45, an age when heart attack risk is high. The review article notes that in addition, a Canadian study found that men and women with high levels of stored iron both were at elevated risk for fatal heart attacks. Two studies also support the theory in finding that blood donors had a reduced risk of heart disease: One found that this was true in men, but not in women; but the review article notes that this result would not be surprising, because men have higher levels of iron in their blood to begin with, so a statistical reduction in heart disease in men would be more apparent.

However, not all of the studies have found that effect; some have been inconsistent and others have even found an inverse effect of iron on heart disease risk. More studies need to be done to determine whether it is the excess iron, and not some other factor, that has the effect. If the iron hypothesis is proven, it also needs to be determined whether the threat is posed by excess iron normally in the blood or only by elevated levels that are due to certain medical conditions, and whether measures such as blood donation are beneficial. In the meantime, people who take iron supplements on the advice of their doctors are advised to continue doing so.

THE FUTURE

Although a great deal is known about the risk factors that contribute to coronary artery disease, research is ongoing to find out what other factors may be at play. This, however, should not obscure the fact that there are major risk factors that cause coronary artery disease that are within our power to change. Read the next chapter to learn how you can make these lifesaving changes.

4

~~~~~~ΛΛΛΛΛΟΛΛΛΛΛ~~~~

Beating the Odds

"I'M EXERCISING three times a week, but it's trying to stay on a diet that's driving me nuts. Friday night is pizza night at our house and it's hard to eat only one piece," said Lindsay with a sigh. She was examined at the Cleveland Clinic two months before, after her family doctor brushed off her worries about chest pain. Because of her family's strong history of early heart disease, she had refused to take the doctor's word for it when he told her, "Don't worry. Women you're age don't get heart disease." Good thing, too. Lindsay's test results showed that, although she is only 36, fatty deposits are already narrowing her coronary arteries. If untreated, this could someday result in a heart attack.

Lindsay had hoped for some easy answers. She was prescribed medications to relieve her chest pain, but that's only a symptom of her problem. The real job is up to her. To improve the odds that she won't end up with a heart attack, Lindsay learned at the Clinic, she should lose 30 pounds, follow a low-fat diet, and participate in regular aerobic exercise. In that way, it's hoped, Lindsay can bring her cholesterol level down enough to halt, or at least significantly slow, the progression of coronary disease. So, since then, Lindsay had been faithfully going to an aerobics class. But oh, that pizza!

Lindsay, this chapter is not only for you: It is for all of us at risk of developing coronary disease. Most of us have at least some risk factors for heart disease. Transforming ourselves from chip-munching couch potatoes to health club devotees is not easy. But it can be done.

The goal is worthwhile, says Dr. William P. Castelli, former director of the Framingham Heart Study. The silver-haired, distinguished-looking Dr. Castelli fairly bursts with enthusiasm when he talks about our ability to protect ourselves against heart disease. "Women have to understand that we are saying that half of them in America are going to die of atherosclerosis, and they could prevent it!" Dr. Castelli says.

A key way to do that is to adopt a diet that is lower in saturated fat. For Dr. Castelli, this presents no problem. "Just give me your 10 favorite recipes and I could take you on a shopping trip and show you how you could make them healthier."

But when you go to the supermarket, you don't have Dr. Castelli at your side. What you do have is a pizzeria on nearly every corner. How can we fight back such temptation? Much of our problem is that we tend to sabotage ourselves by clinging to long-held beliefs that are, in reality, self-defeating myths. For example:

The Myth: I must attain some "ideal" weight that seems impossible to achieve.

The Truth: The latest research shows that even if you are very significantly overweight, a loss of as little as 15 pounds can improve your self-esteem, improve your health, and reduce the probability of your developing heart disease.

The Myth: "No pain, no gain" is the motto in order to exercise enough to strengthen my heart and cardiovascular system.

The Truth: Studies have shown that moderation is the key. Doing nothing more strenuous than walking can lower your heart disease risk.

The Myth: To improve my heart's health, I'm going to have to make dramatic changes in every single part of my lifestyle.

The Truth: Just turn the myth around. It's true that because many heart disease risks are related, you may have to make more than one lifestyle change to significantly reduce your risk of heart disease. But the rewards are interrelated as well. Take exercise, for example: If you undertake a regular exercise program, not only will you become fit, but you will also increase your chances of losing weight or maintaining a weight loss, and you'll reduce your level of stress level. That's a lot of benefit from just one change!

❤ Lifesaving Tip: The more risk factors you have for developing heart disease, the more important it is to reduce them.

Changing Risky Habits

As we noted in the preceding chapter, there are several risk factors for heart disease in women. One is your genetic makeup. Obviously, you can't change your biological parents. African-American women are more at risk for heart disease. So are women with a close family member who suffered a heart attack under the age of 55.

But some of the most powerful heart disease risk factors are within your power to change. If you're at risk for heart disease, or if you simply want to live a healthier lifestyle, these are the risks you should modify.

- Smoking
- Overweight
- Sedentary lifestyle
- Stress

Because heart risk behaviors are related, it is futile to consider them independently of one another. For example research shows that a woman who is under stress, often is overweight, has a sedentary lifestyle, smokes, and feels angry most of the time. All of these are risk factors for heart disease. Sometimes, just learning about these risk factors is enough to help you reform, but if it is not, berating yourself won't help. "Self-control is not a personality trait. You can have good self-control in some aspects of life and poor self-control in others," says Dr. Michael McKee, vice chairman of the department of psychiatry and psychology at the Cleveland Clinic. "The secret is to learn self-control in the important things."

❤ Mindsaving Tip: Ridding yourself of self-destructive thinking is a good place to start making changes. If you smoke, weigh too much, or exercise too little, don't hate yourself. You are still a worthwhile person; your value has nothing to do with these habits. These are nothing more than unhealthy behaviors that you can change.

Quitting Smoking

If you have tried to quit smoking and failed, successfully staying away from cigarettes may seem impossible. In fact, studies show women sometimes find it more difficult than men do to envision life without a cigarette. But there is plenty of hope. Each year, about 1.3 million Americans quit smoking. All you have to do is become one of them.

If you have suffered a heart attack or have just learned you have a heart problem, you may think it will be easy to quit. This is not necessarily true. A study published in 1999 in the *Journal of Women's Health & Gender-Based Medicine* found that, a year after bypass surgery, 10 percent of the 17 women who had been smokers before the surgery still smoked.

Here are some tips for quitting smoking, compiled with the help of Dr. Judith Ockene, director of preventive and behavioral medicine at the University of Massachusetts Medical School:

- Whether it's better to quit cold turkey or to taper off depends on the individual. Contrary to popular belief, tapering can work, but it's important to set goals. For example, you can say, "Next week, I'll smoke half of what I'm smoking now, and then the next week half of that, and then zero."
- Whether you design your own plan or join an established program, the important thing is to figure out what works for you. Talk to your friends about programs they like. Studies show that women tend to prefer small groups as opposed to larger, lecture-type settings.
- No matter which method you choose, make sure it includes ways to prevent weight gain and to handle stress. Both are key reasons women smokers tend to backslide. Be prepared to gain a modest amount of weight (some studies show an average of eight pounds) as your body adjusts to going without the metabolic changes brought on by nicotine. Some women find that exercise helps them prevent this gain in weight; however, others may find that smoking has compromised their lung function, so they may have to wait awhile after quitting before starting an exercise program.
- Cigarette smoking is a complex addiction. Some people can smoke rather heavily and not become dependent, while some light smok-

ers can suffer extreme withdrawal symptoms, such as restlessness, irritability, nervousness, anxiety, stomach disorders, and even seizures.

• Some research shows that nicotine may be even more addictive for women than for men. If you have tried unsuccessfully to quit before, you may want to consider a smoking cessation aid, such as nicotine gum or patch, or the medication buproprion (Zyban). A study published in *The New England Journal of Medicine,* for instance, found that smokers taking such medicines were more likely to quit smoking and gained less weight.

Here's our favorite tip for quitting smoking:

Set aside the money you've spent on cigarettes each day and indulge yourself in something frivolous when you've saved enough. If you backslide, donate the money to your local lung or heart association or favorite charity. This type of incentive system provides the little extra "oomph" you may need to stay with the program. By the way, some people find this system even more effective if they pledge to donate the money to a cause to which they are strongly opposed if they fail to quit!

❤ Lifesaving Tip: If you've recently suffered a heart attack, nicotine in any form can be dangerous, so check with your doctor before using such a patch, gum, or other products containing this substance. Also, wearing the patch while you smoke may put you at risk for a heart attack.

A GUIDE TO WEIGHT LOSS AND EXERCISE

"I can lose weight! I've done it a thousand times," goes the old joke. As most unsuccessful dieters will tell you, losing weight is easy; it's keeping it off that is hard. Our country's obsession with weight loss has fueled a multibillion dollar diet industry.

But you don't have to shell out big bucks to lose weight. Dr. Judith S. Stern, a professor of nutrition at the University of California at Davis, studied women who had successfully lost weight and kept it off. She found, for example, that besides eating less, the women who maintained their weight loss had developed a whole new set of habits, such as exercising regularly and handling stress and problem-solving more effectively. The women who lost weight initially but gained it back had tried to change only eating habits. These "relapsers" exercised little, ate unconsciously in response to their emotions, avoided problems by overeating or sleeping, and took on too many tasks themselves.

Dr. Stern's study also found the women who were most likely to be successful were those who had designed a weight loss program to suit themselves. This doesn't mean that a formal weight loss program might not help you. It does indicate that you can lose weight by yourself. If you do decide to join a program, you should choose one well suited to your individual needs. "Most diets work initially, but you have to think about long-term success," says Dr. Stern. Experts are now telling us that success should be based upon weight loss not six or 12 months later but two years down the road!

For some more of our tips on losing weight, see Chapter 18, "Every Woman's Eating Plan for Life."

DON'T FORGET EXERCISE!

If you could buy a pill that could help you not only lose weight, but also keep it off, stay off cigarettes, cope with stress, avoid osteoporosis and diabetes, and even sleep better, wouldn't you buy it? Unfortunately, there is no magic pill that can do this all for you. But exercise can. To learn how you can build exercise into your daily schedule, see "Every Woman's Exercise Plan for Life" in Chapter 18.

LOWERING CHOLESTEROL

Many women can lower their cholesterol levels through eating healthily and exercising. Research shows that even taking a daily walk at a comfortable pace of three miles per hour can boost HDL levels. Regular exercise also helps keep your weight down. Losing just 10 pounds can lower cholesterol by 20 or 30 points. Eating wisely also helps. Staying away from saturated and "partially hydrogenated" fats is an important step. These are discussed further in Chapter 18. If you are past menopause, hormone replacement therapy can help as well.

For some women, however, these steps are not enough, and drug therapy, particularly with the newer anti-cholesterol drugs called "statins," is indicated. This is discussed further in Chapter 13.

Beating Stress

Among cardiologists, current debate rages on whether stress is a major cause of heart disease and heart attacks. But most researchers agree that it's at least a contributing factor. For this reason, we've devoted an entire chapter—Chapter 16—to the types of stress that can affect a woman's heart and what you can do about it.

Age

Growing older is a major risk factor for women. In the past, the process of aging was viewed as a fact of life we couldn't do much about. However, with estrogen replacement therapy, studies have shown, women can actually delay some of the adverse affects of aging on their hearts. Whether or not you should opt for such therapy is a decision more and more women are facing. The topic is discussed in depth in Chapter 15.

African-American Women and Heart Disease

It is generally acknowledged that African-American women face a higher risk of cardiovascular disease than do Caucasian women, probably because of their tendency to have high blood pressure.

Dr. Shiriki Kumanyika, associate dean for health promotion and disease prevention at the University of Pennsylvania, has published several papers on African-American women and overweight.

According to Dr. Kumanyika, African-American women are more likely to be overweight than Caucasian women, a fact that has serious ramifications when you consider that excess weight can increase the probability of high blood pressure, diabetes, and such disabling problems as osteoarthritis in the knees.

In one study, Dr. Kumanyika and her colleagues examined the results of two weight loss trials that found that, on average, African-American women lost an average of four and one-half pounds less than their white counterparts. In trying to seek out why this might be so, Dr. Kumanyika noted that studies have shown that there is a more tolerant attitude towards overweight in the African-American community. Also, she noted, cultural food preferences may have played a role. In general, African-Americans consume more meat, especially pork, and fried foods, and certain beloved traditional southern and African-American foods are very high in fat. African-American women may be less successful in losing weight and keeping it off because they tend to exercise less. But here, she cautioned, research is scant.

One problem facing African-American women seeking to lose weight is the same as that facing others: Conventional weight loss programs are not highly effective. One way to increase the chances of losing weight and keeping it off is by joining a church-based or community-based weight loss program. She studied a church-affiliated program in Baltimore known as "Lose Weight and Win," a behaviorally oriented eight-week course of diet, counseling, and exercise designed for moderately overweight adults. A specific diet is not prescribed; participants eat the food they are accustomed to, but make small incremental chances to reduce the fat and calorie content. They also learn strategies to avoid overeating. Participants during the two-month program that was analyzed lost an average of six pounds, and, after six months, 65 percent of the women who returned for follow-up had maintained their weight loss.

According to Dr. Kumanyika, programs like "Lose Weight and Win" are models that could be initiated by women in their own communities, no matter what their race. The key, she believes, is making such groups a part of the local community. To get started, she suggests contacting the local health department, to find someone who could lead the group and distribute proper nutritional information.

"People see an ad for Weight Watchers or Overeater's Anonymous and they go across town for awhile until their interest peters out. Most people in the African-American community know how to create programs for other needs. If they were aware of this need, they could probably create these programs for themselves," she said.

To Sum Up

Reducing your heart disease risk is a valuable goal. If you do not have heart disease and are working to prevent developing it, this is called primary prevention. If you have known heart disease and want to try to slow or halt its progression, this is what is known as secondary prevention. Either way, working to beat the risks of heart disease is a very worthwhile goal.

5

~~~~rrrՈՌ◯ՄՈՈ~~~~

Heart Attack:
A Woman's Worst Enemy

OF THE NEARLY one half million Americans who will die from heart attacks each year, about half of them will be women. This makes heart attack the number one cause of death in women, with about 235,000 women projected to die of them this year alone. Yet, despite this, most women remain unaware of the danger heart attack poses them.

Consider Helen, for instance. It was a November morning as Helen drove down the highway in her yellow school bus filled with kids. At the age of 45, Helen knew her blood pressure and her cholesterol were "on the high side," but she'd been feeling pretty satisfied with her health lately. She'd quit smoking a few years ago, and, feeling stressed out, had just cut back on her work hours. Just in time, too; it was just two days before Thanksgiving, and Helen had a big Thanksgiving dinner to cook.

Suddenly, a car swerved into her lane, nearly colliding with the bus. The scare left Helen with a sudden cramping in her chest, but it quickly disappeared. Greatly relieved over avoiding the accident, Helen finished the route, and returned home for lunch. After eating, she recalls, "I had this gassy sensation I thought was indigestion." By dinnertime, she was feeling worse. She figured it was "an unusually severe gas attack." But nothing she did would relieve it. She cooked dinner, but was feeling worse and worse. "By this time, I'm realizing there's more to this than I'm admitting to. I was beginning to feel pain creeping up into my neck and my jaw."

Helen's son and daughter begged her to call a doctor. Helen refused, and they got into a fight. Helen grabbed her purse, stormed out of the house, and jumped into her new car. "Then I came to my senses and thought to myself, "What are you doing? If you don't kill yourself, you could kill somebody else." She slipped back into the house, unnoticed, and lay down on her bed. But no matter how much she tossed and turned, the pressure bearing down on her chest would simply not let up. Finally, she emerged from the bedroom. "My daughter said to me, 'Ma, I only wanted to know what was the matter,' and I said, 'It hurts.' And then I started to cry. They called 911, and the ambulance came."

On the way to the hospital, Helen still insisted nothing was wrong. Even as the emergency medical technician was giving her oxygen, she told him, "I don't know what everyone is making such a fuss about; it's only gas."

Helen was admitted to the hospital. The next day, when her doctor arrived to tell her she'd suffered a heart attack, she burst into tears. "I just about lost it right there in the bed. I was hysterical. I yelled at the doctor, 'I don't have time for this!' "

Helen's reaction is not unusual. Despite all of the publicity about the importance of people seeking help if they suspect they may be having a heart attack, both men and women often deny it. In fact, studies have shown that women delay even longer, with dangerous consequences.

Medically known as a myocardial infarction (MI), a heart attack occurs when the blood flowing to your heart is cut off completely. Your blood carries oxygen, among other important things, which your heart needs to survive. Thus, a lack of oxygen results eventually in injury to the heart muscle. When your heart muscle is damaged severely, your heart cannot pump the needed oxygenated blood to the rest of your body.

Although most heart attacks are caused by coronary artery disease, some are the result of cardiac spasm, a potentially dangerous constriction of the heart's blood vessels. There is some evidence that cardiac spasms are more common in women, according to a study published in 1999 in *The New England Journal of Medicine.*

Ideally, it's best to treat coronary artery disease before a heart attack occurs. But the fact remains that, for many women, it is a heart attack that leads to their diagnosis.

For some women, a heart attack may occur in the absence of symptoms. But often, if women do experience chest pain or pressure, they may attribute it to other causes, like heartburn, or even anxiety. Another reason why women tend to put off getting help is that they apparently experience heart attack symptoms differently than do men. "Men, when they come to the hospital, come in and talk about severe pressure in the middle of their sternum. Women, on the other hand, tend to have more nausea or other nonspecific signs," says Dr. Eric Topol, head of the Cleveland Clinic's cardiology department. People who are less sensitive to their bodily sensations, and thus less likely to recognize or correctly interpret symptoms, also delay getting medical help, and this goes for both men and women. "This lack of recognition is especially sad because it leads to a delay in getting the newest therapy that has proven effective in saving heart muscle," Dr. Topol added.

Women, like men, are sometimes unwilling to seek help because they simply feel they cannot take the time to be sick. Like Helen, they try to ward off a heart attack with sheer willpower. If you ignore heart attack symptoms, you're not only risking your life, but you are also forfeiting the opportunity to minimize the damage to your heart with prompt emergency treatment. Not long ago, once a heart attack began nothing could be done to affect its course. Today, there are treatments that can halt and, in some cases, even lessen the damage to your heart. But to benefit, you must get to the hospital quickly.

_____

❤ **Lifesaving Tip: If you are at high risk for heart attack, have suffered one, or have had a "silent heart attack," you should have an emergency plan worked out so you can get to the hospital without delay.**

_____

How Do Women Fare After a Heart Attack?

Studies show that women do not fare as well as men after a heart attack. Researchers also have found that more women than men die during their initial hospitalization and after the first year and are more likely to suffer a second heart attack. Some of these figures may reflect the fact that women are generally older at the time of their first heart attack and are more likely to have other existing diseases, such as diabetes.

However, a 1999 study demonstrated that heart attacks are particularly dangerous to younger women. Researchers reported in *The New England Journal of Medicine* that although heart attacks in people under

50 are far less common in women than in men, when they do occur, women are more than twice as likely to die. The difference between women and men who have heart attacks diminishes with age, as men's risk goes up, but women's risk of death stays higher than men's until the age of 75. The study results, based on the hospital records of 155,565 women and 229,313 men who had heart attacks and were treated at 1,658 hospitals, indicates that younger women who suffer heart attacks are a high-risk group needing special study and attention.

❤ **Mindsaving Tip: If you have a heart attack, the odds are great that you'll survive. In fact, every day, women suffer major heart attacks and still go on to fully recover.**

HEART ATTACK SYMPTOMS

How do you know if you're having a heart attack? You may suffer chest pain so severe that it couldn't be anything else. But often the symptoms of a heart attack are subtler, such as annoying chest discomfort, pressure, and nausea. Such symptoms can come on suddenly, or you may have been feeling out of sorts for some time.

"Recognizing symptoms and getting to the hospital is very important," says Charles Maynard, research associate professor, with the department of health services at the University of Washington in Seattle. "Especially if women are elderly, they may get their symptoms confused with other health problems they have." Since symptoms in women are often misdiagnosed, having a doctor who's familiar with you and with whom you can talk freely increases the possibility your heart attack will be accurately diagnosed and treated, Dr. Maynard said.

Fifty-eight-year-old Roberta, a psychiatric nurse, was feeling, as she put it, "lousier and lousier." She thought it was indigestion. One night, her symptoms got worse: She had pressure and burning in her chest, and felt unable to breathe. Upon awakening the next morning, she walked into the kitchen and fainted. The previous night, while she paced back and forth, worrying about her discomfort, she was actually suffering a heart attack. "My first husband died of a fatal heart attack," she says. "It was just like a heart attack you see in the movies; he clutched his chest and fell right to the floor. Since that didn't happen to me, I assumed I couldn't be having a heart attack," she said.

You may be having a heart attack if:

- The chest pain comes on over a minute or two and builds in intensity.
- The pain occurs near the center, not the extreme left side of your chest.
- The pain lasts at least twenty minutes and is usually not relieved by rest or by changing position.
- The pain ranges from mild to severe, and usually feels like pressure or heaviness.
- The pain may radiate up into your jaw or your back or down your left arm.
- You may experience nausea, shortness of breath, or a sense of impending doom. Women often experience these symptoms when having a heart attack.

❤ **Lifesaving Tip: These signs of a heart attack are the most common ones that manifest themselves in both men and women. But studies show that women often experience more subtle symptoms, such as indigestion, discomfort, or difficulty breathing.**

It's also possible to suffer a "silent heart attack." A silent heart attack is one that you may have without even realizing it. Usually, you become aware of it when the resulting changes in your heart's functioning show up on a later cardiac test. If you've suffered a silent heart attack, you are at great risk of suffering a heart attack again. Diabetic women are prone to missing the important sign of chest pain because their bodies sometimes misinterpret pain messages.

GETTING HELP

If you think you may be having a heart attack, dial 911 for help. Do not attempt to drive yourself to the emergency room. Besides the fact that you're risking an accident, emergency measures that could save your life can be started right away by the EMS personnel. Try not to be vague or uncertain in describing your medical history and symptoms. Because in the past women have not been recognized as being at risk for a heart attack, it is important you state your concerns.

After you are evaluated at the hospital, if it appears you may be having a heart attack, you'll probably be taken to a special intensive care unit, in some places called a coronary care unit. During a heart attack, your blood pressure can shoot too high or fall too low. The internal electrical system that regulates your heartbeat can go haywire, sending your heart racing irregularly or slowing it down too much. Today's coronary care units have equipment and staff to counteract such occurrences and stabilize your condition.

You will also undergo further tests to determine whether you are indeed having a heart attack. Your heartbeat will be monitored continuously, although, even in the midst of a heart attack, the heartbeat may appear normal. The diagnosis of a heart attack may not be definite for several hours, or until the results of a particular blood test are available. This is because your doctor will be awaiting the results of one particular type of test. This is a blood test that can detect certain enzymes in your blood. When you are having a heart attack, a portion of your heart muscle is injured. As the muscle is damaged, it produces enzymes, one of which is called creatine kinase, or CK. After a few days, that enzyme level drops. While it is present in high levels in your bloodstream, however, it is a telltale indicator of a heart attack.

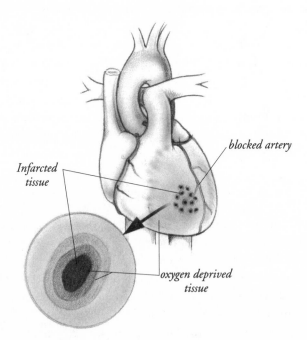

Heart Muscle Damaged by Heart Attack. "Infarcted" tissue (irreversibly injured heart muscle) resulted from the loss of coronary blood flow for too long. Surrounding the area of injury is muscle with varying degrees of oxygen deprivation, which can recover if blood circulation is restored.

Your heart muscle is not the only muscle that gives off CK; the enzyme is present in some of your other muscles as well. Let's say you spend the day playing tennis and then begin suffering chest pains. At the hospital, tests may show you have an elevated level of that enzyme in your blood. If your doctor suspects you did not have a heart attack, another test can be ordered to determine whether the elevated level of this enzyme was due to physical exertion, or indeed did result from damage to your heart muscle.

Another enzyme test now being used to confirm a heart attack involves an enzyme called troponin. This state-of-the-art test has major advantages over using CK for a diagnosis. It is more sensitive, and its availability at the facility where you're being treated can be an indicator of the facility's progressiveness.

❤ Lifesaving Tip: Should you arrive at the hospital only to learn later that you did not suffer a heart attack at all, don't be embarrassed. It's far better to assume the worst and find out the problem isn't serious than to underestimate it and risk serious damage to your heart or even death.

Clot Busters

Not many years ago, if you suffered a heart attack, lifesaving measures could be administered, but nothing could be done to prevent damage to your heart. Happily, this is no longer true. Thanks to a type of drug commonly known as clot busters, damage to your heart can be stopped, and, in some cases, even lessened. These powerful drugs act to dissolve the clot, enabling the flow of blood to resume.

Miraculous as these clot busters seem, they're useful only when administered within a few hours after the heart attack begins. "The early time frame is important. That is, the earlier we get to patients, the more chance there is that we can do something positive," says Dr. Eric Topol, who has pioneered this type of therapy, known formally as thrombolytic therapy.

But although studies have shown these drugs work equally well in men and women, it is women who may be more at risk for complications. Still, there is concern that some women may not be getting these medications often enough, according to Dr. Maynard. "Thrombolytic therapy has been shown to be a very effective means of affecting mortality and my concern is that women are being under-treated," he said.

There are different types of clot dissolvers. Tissue plasminogen activator, or tPA, is a genetically engineered drug. Another popular clot buster is called retaplase. Streptokinase was popular, but is used less often now. If you've had streptokinase during a heart attack before, it should not be given again. Streptokinase contains trace substances which are potentially sensitizing, meaning a second administration of the drug could result in a severe allergic reaction. In this case, tPA or another clot dissolver would be the drug of choice.

There's another consideration as well. If you are African-American, your blood tends to clot more readily than if you are caucasian, raising the threat of heart attack or stroke. While both tPA and streptokinase are effective in African-Americans and in caucasians, research has shown tPA to be more effective in African-Americans. In fact, according to Dr. Topol, if you're an African-American woman, you have about a 90 percent probability of your blood clot being dissolved with tPA compared to about 75 percent if streptokinase is used.

Sometimes, angioplasty is used instead of clot busters to dissolve a clot, or a combination of both a clot buster and angioplasty may be used. Some studies indicate angioplasty may be preferable, but it depends on the individual patient's needs.

♥ **Lifesaving Tip: Clot busters are powerful drugs that can cause serious bleeding complications, so they should be administered only under a doctor's supervision. In several communities, administration of these drugs is done by specially trained paramedics.**

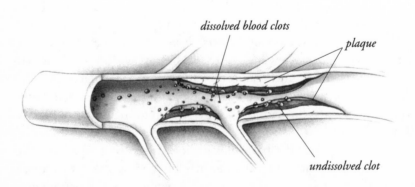

dissolved blood clots

plaque

undissolved clot

Clot Busters. Blood clots normally form and dissolve naturally. However, when a blood clot causes a heart attack, a type of drug therapy called thrombolysis may be used to break up the clot.

Are Female Heart Attack Victims Treated Differently?

Since studies generally find that women heart attack victims do not fare as well as men, any differences in how men and women are treated are important. Many, although not all, studies also find that women are treated less aggressively after their heart attacks. A national study published in 1998 in the *Archives of Internal Medicine,* which examined the records of 354,435 patients from 1,234 hospitals, found that women were less likely to undergo cardiac catheterization, balloon angioplasty, or bypass surgery. A smaller study, published a year earlier in the same journal, noted that although women were prescribed cardiac drugs after a heart attack, they were less likely than men to have undergone treadmill testing and catheterization.

Dr. Maynard speculates that gender bias may be involved. This can occur when these procedures are presented to the patients, he noted.

"Cardiologists, when they talk to a guy, say, basically, 'You've got have this thing done.' With women, I think there may be reluctance. It's a cultural, subtle thing, which is very hard to study. But I've heard too many cardiologists say that the men are stronger than women and more able to withstand the rigors of the procedure when, medically, that assumption is not borne out at all," Dr. Maynard said.

The debate over whether there is a gender bias in the treatment of men and women after heart attacks will continue. Regardless, women are less likely than men to undergo arteriography. Ten years ago, the ratio was about 10 to one, men to women. Now the ratio has improved to about two to one. It is worth noting, however, that cardiac catheterization is an expensive, uncomfortable, and sometimes risky procedure that is not always necessary. As with men, when a woman has a heart attack, sometimes a carefully selected program of other cardiac tests may provide all the information required for her proper diagnosis and treatment. The important thing for women and their doctors to keep in mind is that when a woman has a heart attack, she is entitled to a careful, thorough evaluation to meet her individual medical needs, and the standard of her care should not be any lower than that afforded to a man.

On to Recovery

If tests confirm you have suffered a heart attack, you can expect to spend the next few days in the intensive care unit, being monitored and undergoing diagnostic tests. These tests will seek to determine the cause of your heart attack, how severely your heart was damaged, and what steps need to be taken to ensure your full recovery. This may be balloon angioplasty or coronary bypass surgery, depending on your individual case.

Years ago, total bed rest for several weeks was the rule for treating heart attack patients. How times have changed! Once you're transferred to a regular room, you'll rest, of course. But before long, you'll be encouraged to begin taking care of your personal needs. At first, a nurse will be on hand to assist you, but soon, you'll be doing your personal care yourself.

You'll probably be amazed to learn how quickly you're advised to make exercise part of your recovery plan. You'll be taught exercises to do at first in bed and while sitting down. Before being discharged, you may undergo a short form of an exercise stress test to make certain your heart is strong enough to deal with the demands of living outside the protective environment of the hospital. About six weeks later, you'll probably return for a regular exercise stress test, which gauges the amount of activity your heart is capable of performing with safety. Not only does this provide your doctor with information about your medical condition, but it will also provide you with confidence that you can depend on your heart to get you through the daily work of living.

ONCE YOU'RE HOME

"Recuperation! What recuperation?" hooted Helen. "When I went home, my doctor told me, 'I want you to come home and do what you've done here,' which was nothing but walk the halls. He gave me a schedule, which said, 'Next week, you can dust the furniture, and the following week, you can sweep the floor, and four weeks down the road, you can run the vacuum cleaner.' I said, 'Fine,' but what I was thinking to myself is, 'Are you out of your mind?' "

When a man returns home from the hospital, he may not have anything to do but rest. If you are a woman, you may be a homemaker and a mother, and feel that all the responsibilities in the world are on your shoulders. You need to treat the challenge of recuperating seriously!

❤ Mindsaving Tip: Right after a heart attack, it's normal to be keenly aware of every flutter of your heart and every stab of pain in your chest, heart-related or not. You may very well feel that your heart, which you always depended upon without a thought, has betrayed you, and you cannot imagine living a normal life. That feeling usually fades with time.

———

Just how much you try to do when you return home will depend, of course, on how you feel. If you're an elderly woman, it may take much more time for you to begin getting back even a small portion of your energy. No matter what your age, you must take care of yourself. Your heart needs time to mend, and you must provide it. Leaving the protected environment of the hospital for home will take preparation. Since your recuperation will be similar to that of patients who are recovering from open-heart surgery, that topic is also covered in Chapter 14.

RIDING THE EMOTIONAL ROLLER COASTER

Although it is your heart that suffers the attack, your emotions receive an enormous jolt as well. After a heart attack, many women feel like they are on an emotional roller coaster, feeling lucky to be alive one moment and in tears the next. Some women continue to deny the heart attack, like Helen, who two years later says she still has a difficult time believing her heart attack ever happened. Others, though, find themselves in one of the most emotionally charged times of their lives.

HEART ATTACKS AND DEPRESSION

A catastrophic event, such as a heart attack, the need for heart surgery, or even the diagnosis of coronary artery disease, can render the most cheerful of women depressed. While some depression is normal, many women fall into a serious depression from which they cannot emerge without help.

Just ask Lucinda, who at 47 was divorced, had grown children, and worked full-time. Juggling home and a job never seemed to bother her; in fact, she seemed to thrive on it. She seemed to have it "all together"— at least, until she suffered a heart attack.

"I was always the iron woman in my family. I was never sick. I worked all the time. I was very productive. I don't imagine anyone takes a heart problem lightly, but I never expected it. All of a sudden, from a very healthy woman I went to being a heart patient. Everything in my life had changed. It was too much to handle."

As a result, she drew into herself. "When I was in the hospital, I didn't want to talk to people. I didn't answer my phone; I didn't see anyone outside my immediate family. I didn't want to hear people say 'How are you doing,' or 'How are you feeling,' or, especially, 'I know how you feel.' That expression, 'I know how you feel,' just sent a shiver down my spine, because they didn't know how I felt. Only I knew how I felt."

When she returned home from the hospital, Lucinda felt even worse. "I wasn't eating. I wasn't sleeping. When my friends called, I wouldn't answer the phone. I didn't care about anything. It just got progressively worse."

Finally, at the urging of her family, Lucinda decided to see a psychiatrist. She was put on an antidepressant and went for counseling. Now the future no longer looks bleak. "I have days which are difficult, but days which are also joyous. I won't lie to you and say things changed overnight. But I am feeling better," she says.

Susan J. Blumenthal, MD, is U.S. assistant surgeon general in the department of health and human services and clinical professor of psychiatry at the Tufts University School of Medicine. "One of the important things that both depression and heart disease have in common is that they are both often misdiagnosed and inappropriately treated in women," Dr. Blumenthal says. "Some health care providers may detect anxiety or depression in women but minimize symptoms of heart disease. The opposite can happen as well. Additionally, women themselves often do not know that heart disease is a major threat to their health. Furthermore, depression and heart disease can co-occur with negative health effects."

Certainly, some sadness or worry is normal after a heart attack or heart surgery. But if you are unable to shake feelings such as anger, worthlessness, despair, or if you are entertaining thoughts of suicide, it is important to seek help from your doctor, a hospital social worker, or a psychiatrist. Sometimes, people fail to realize that cardiac medications themselves can magnify depression. In the past, women have also been treated too often with tranquilizers, instead of antidepressants. This is also an important issue because research shows that patients who are depressed after a heart attack fare worse. For instance, a study published in 1999 in the journal *Psychosomatic Medicine* looked at 896 patients, 283 of them women who were evaluated for depression following their heart attacks. The survey found that 133 of the women tested as being mild to moderately depressed. After a year, 8.3 percent of the depressed women had died from cardiac causes, compared to 2.7 percent of those who weren't depressed. The depressed men were also more likely to die

(7.0 percent compared to 2.4 percent), but the numbers also clearly show that it is women who are also far more likely to be depressed, making this a very serious problem.

Signs of depression include:

- Feeling your life is hopeless and not worth living
- Feelings of fatigue not related to your physical condition
- Feeling distant or unable to relate to others
- Suicidal thoughts

There are many ways to treat depression in women who have heart problems. Sometimes, just talking to someone can make you feel better, but if you are seriously depressed, antidepressant drugs can be very effective, as can psychotherapy, or their combination. The important thing is to get help!

💟 Lifesaving Tip: If you are depressed, you may lack the energy or resolve to try to do something about it. But it is very important that you talk about it to someone who can facilitate your getting help, be it a family member, a nurse, or your doctor.

Resuming Sex

"After I had my heart attack, my husband treated me as if I was breakable. I was afraid, and so was he. It did not make for a passionate sexual encounter," Roberta said. When asked if she'd talked about the problem with her doctor, she shrieked with laughter. "My doctor! He's just a baby! He's the same age as my daughter. I could never talk to him about sex!"

Roberta's dilemma is not unusual. Some doctors make it a point to bring up the subject of sex. If your doctor doesn't, you do it. If you feel uncomfortable, perhaps you can ask your doctor's nurse to tell him you want to broach the subject, or change to a female doctor. What you need is the reassurance that resuming sexual activity will be no more stressful to your heart than other activities you're able to do.

Some of the most common reasons for sexual problems after a heart attack or heart surgery are depression and fear. Depression can manifest itself as a loss of sexual desire. It's also very understandable that either partner may fear that intercourse will overstress your heart.

Above all, be frank. "What was most helpful to me was that my husband and I were able to discuss it," Roberta says, "We knew what the problem was; we knew we were both scared, and that gave us the opening to talk about it."

❤ **Mindsaving Tip: Some cardiovascular drugs or medications used to combat depression can result in a loss of sexual desire or your ability to reach orgasm. If you think this may be true in your case, talk to your doctor.**

A WORD ABOUT FAMILY AND FRIENDS

In a crisis, nothing can count more than the support of family and friends. If you have had a heart attack, some of their reactions may surprise you. "After my heart attack, I found some of my friends seemed to back away from me, almost as if I'd done something wrong," says Helen.

Helen found help from a heart support group. The leader explained to her that this reaction was not uncommon. "She made me realize my friends were scared. That they thought, if I, a relatively young woman, could have a heart attack, they could too. It's taken some time, but now everything is back to normal," says Helen.

Having a heart attack is a very frightening experience, but many women, to their surprise, later discover they have emerged from this experience feeling stronger than before.

6

~~~~~⌒~~~~~

Mitral Valve Prolapse

A YOUNG ATTORNEY, Nancy was well on her way to a promising legal career until she began developing excruciating chest pains every time she headed into court. Two cardiologists found nothing wrong, and attributed her chest pains to job stress. One even put her on Valium, but she feared a tranquilizer would interfere with her ability to perform at her legal best. Desperate she might have to give up the job she loved, she visited a third cardiologist. Additional cardiac testing revealed that she had mitral valve prolapse.

Although Nancy required medication, many women with mitral valve prolapse require no treatment at all. Mitral valve prolapse affects a large number of young women, so many that it is their most common heart complaint. While rarely life-threatening, their symptoms can be disturbing.

Symptoms Associated With Mitral Valve Prolapse
• Chest pain
• Palpitations (a "pounding" heartbeat)
• Dizziness
• Fainting

Mitral valve prolapse was first described in medical journals in the 1960s. Doctors differ in their view of it. Some term it a syndrome, which is a collection of symptoms and signs (medical findings) that occur together. Some call it a disorder, referring to it as a physical impairment, while others consider it nothing more than a harmless curiosity. We prefer to describe mitral valve prolapse as an anomaly involving the heart valves. It is more a condition, like being nearsighted, rather than a disease such as cancer. Although it's sometimes difficult to convince a woman who is experiencing symptoms linked to mitral valve prolapse, recent studies verify that this anomaly is almost always harmless. Even women who experience severe symptoms virtually always live out their lives without ever developing serious heart problems.

A study published in 1999 in *The New England Journal of Medicine* notes that it was previously believed that mitral valve prolapse affected 10 to 15 percent of the population, but that new data indicate that it occurs in only about 2 percent of the population and affects men and women equally. The change in the numbers stems from more accurate methods of diagnosing mitral valve prolapse.

Also, although most cardiologists consider mitral valve prolapse to be generally harmless, some studies had linked the anomaly to an increased risk of heart rhythm disturbances, heart failure, stroke, and bacterial endocarditis. However, people with mitral valve prolapse were not at increased danger for any of those problems, the newer studies find.

WHAT IS MITRAL VALVE PROLAPSE?

Your heart is a pump with four chambers. The upper two chambers, the atria, feed blood to the lower two chambers, the ventricles. The ventricles then pump the blood throughout the body. To control the blood flow, there are four valves that open and close to keep the blood flowing in the proper direction.

Oxygenated blood returns to the heart from the lungs through the left atrium. Once filled, the left atrium squeezes, and the blood goes from the left atrium through the mitral valve into the left ventricle. From there, blood is pumped through the aortic valve and through the circulatory system. The mitral valve serves as the gate into the left ventricle, the main pump of the heart.

If you have mitral valve prolapse, however, this means that one or both of the leaflets of your mitral valve are larger than they need to be, and that this prevents the valve from snapping tightly shut. Sometimes a small amount of blood regurgitates, or leaks back into the left atrium.

Usually, this amount of blood is not significant. If it is, it results in a problem called "mitral regurgitation."

Mitral Regurgitation

Usually, mitral regurgitation is not serious. However, in an estimated 5 percent of cases, women with mitral valve prolapse develop a serious leakage problem. This is severe mitral valve regurgitation. In serious mitral valve regurgitation, the leaflets that help close the mitral valves become even less effective, resulting in a greater backwash of blood back into the atrium. This backward flow of blood can eventually lead to pulmonary congestion and eventual enlargement and weakening of the left side of the heart, and progressive heart failure. Before that point, however, the problem can be discovered and the mitral valve can usually be surgically repaired or replaced.

It is interesting to note that although more women than men are bothered by the symptoms of mitral valve prolapse, studies have shown that men more frequently develop complications such as serious mitral regurgitation. Again, when it comes to mitral valve prolapse, it's important to stress that this is a very, very rare complication.

Symptoms of Mitral Regurgitation
• Weakness
• Difficulty breathing while lying down
• Shortness of breath during mild exercise

❤ **Lifesaving Tip: Complications such as mitral regurgitation occur very rarely in those with mitral valve prolapse. That said, however, if you are diagnosed with mitral valve prolapse and notice progressive shortness of breath, fainting, or other unusual symptoms, be sure to check with your doctor.**

Is There a "Mitral Valve Prolapse Syndrome"?

It is generally acknowledged that mitral valve prolapse is a biological entity involving a malformation of the mitral valve's leaflets. However, whether or not this condition accounts for the symptoms suffered by many of those with mitral valve prolapse is a matter of debate.

Initially, mitral valve prolapse was considered to affect only the functioning of a heart valve, but some believe it to be a more generalized disorder, and may affect other parts of the body's functioning as well.

Mitral valve prolapse also is often associated with an impairment of the body's ability to respond properly to adrenaline. This may account for the panic syndrome, palpitations, dizziness, and chest pains commonly experienced by those with mitral valve prolapse.

Another factor that may play a role in awareness of the intensity of mitral valve prolapse symptoms in some individuals is their cardiac sensitivity. Cardiac sensitivity, or nociception, is discussed in more detail in the chapter on chest pain. It refers to the way your central nervous system perceives and processes pain messages, and may be the reason why some people with mild mitral valve prolapse may suffer from severe symptoms, while others with severe prolapse may be scarcely, if at all, aware of the condition.

Some studies have found that women with mitral valve prolapse seem to experience such symptoms as chest pain, palpitations, fainting, and dizziness more than do others. These studies bear out what doctors see in their patients. They find that not uncommonly, women experiencing these symptoms, particularly those in the 20 to 40 age group, are found to have mitral valve prolapse.

There are some experts who question whether these symptoms are really a result of the mitral valve prolapse. They point out that younger women do often suffer such symptoms as chest pain and palpitations, and often no cause, cardiac or otherwise, can be found. Thus is the crux of the controversy: Does mitral valve prolapse cause these symptoms, or is it merely a coincidence that these symptoms appear to occur in combination with mitral valve prolapse?

Adding to this dilemma is the fact that, in the past several years, mitral valve prolapse has received increasing attention in the media, and has become the "chic diagnosis" of the 1990s. Since the symptoms ascribed to mitral valve prolapse can sometimes be baffling, and mimic symptoms of other disorders, some are now claiming mitral valve prolapse is associated with a whole laundry list of symptoms, including vague body aches, difficulty urinating, insomnia, diarrhea, poor memory, allergies, and excessive gas. It is rare we do not suffer from one or another of these vague symptoms.

Among those who doubt whether a "mitral valve prolapse syndrome" actually exists is Dr. Richard B. Devereux, a professor of medicine at Neill Medical College of Cornell University. He interviewed and performed diagnostic tests on thousands of men and women and failed to

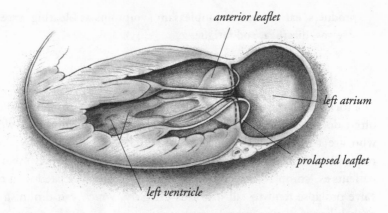

Mitral Valve Prolapse. Dotted lines show where the leaflets are in a normal valve; the solid lines show the leaflets in mitral valve prolapse. The configuration of the leaflets prevents the valve from closing as it normally should.

find a significant association between most of their symptoms and mitral valve prolapse. These included chest pain, palpitations, anxiety, and symptoms associated with a surplus of adrenaline. However, Dr. Devereux did find that women with mitral valve prolapse did more often tend to have low blood pressure, which could account for dizziness and fainting. "There seems to be a real connection there," he says.

His observation is consistent with the findings of Dr. Fetnat Fouad-Tarazi, director of the Syncope (fainting) Clinic at the Cleveland Clinic Foundation. Mitral valve prolapse appears to be commonly associated with abnormalities of autonomic function that help maintain a normal blood pressure when you change your body position.

If you have mitral valve prolapse or experience the symptoms described in this chapter, you may find it frustrating to learn a debate over the significance of mitral valve prolapse exists. It's worthwhile to remember that, in medicine, there are sometimes not as many hard-and-fast answers as you may think. Medicine is an ever-changing field and today's medical "truth" may, with research, not hold true tomorrow. However, bear in mind that the information contained in this chapter has been found to be extremely valuable to a large number of women whose symptoms may (or may not) turn out to be linked to their having mitral valve prolapse.

❤ Mindsaving Tip: Some of the vague complaints that have been "lumped in" with mitral valve prolapse may have other causes. For example, lactose intolerance, which is the inability to digest dairy products, can cause such unpleasant symptoms as bloating, excessive gas, diarrhea, and fatigue.

————

IF YOU HAVE SYMPTOMS ASSOCIATED WITH MVP

Doctors are accustomed to being able to "fix" heart problems, and too often do not have the patience to deal sympathetically with women who are troubled with vague complaints, especially if they do not respond to immediate treatment. Too often, they privately label such patients as "complainers." Women with symptoms associated with mitral valve prolapse tend to fall into this category, which can diminish their probability of getting effective treatment.

This is what happened to Jean, a 45-year-old woman whose lightheadedness had been dismissed by doctors for years. She was sometimes so dizzy that she could barely walk. She was evaluated by doctors for vertigo, with negative findings, so she was told the problem was "all in her head." But virtually every time she got up to walk on some days, she nearly fell down. She even saw one cardiologist who told her to "hang on every time you stand up." Obviously, this was not a very good solution! It turned out she did have mitral valve prolapse. Her symptoms responded to a cardiovascular medication, and she was able to resume her normal life.

If you have mitral valve prolapse, treatment by a cardiologist isn't required. But a cardiologist should treat you if you experience cardiac disorders such as a mitral regurgitation or a serious cardiac arrhythmia. If you do not, however, you may find being treated by your regular doctor (such as a primary physician, internist, or family doctor) may be perfectly satisfactory, providing other heart-related causes have been eliminated for your symptoms, and your doctor is willing to treat the symptoms that cause you discomfort.

COMMON QUESTIONS AND ANSWERS ABOUT MVP

Q: How did I "get" mitral valve prolapse?
A: Mitral valve prolapse is genetically transmitted. This can be seen unusually clearly in the case of the 11-year-old Colorado girl who suffered from chest pains when she competed in school sports. It turns out that her mother, who experienced feelings of extreme lightheadedness and abnormal heart rhythms, had mitral valve prolapse as

well. So, it turns out, did her maternal grandmother, who suffered from fainting spells, and her great-grandmother, who also had a history of chest pains. Although this example shows MVP being passed down only to females, either parent can pass it down to either gender of their offspring.

Q: Do people with MVP always have the same symptoms?

A: Not at all. Some persons with mitral valve prolapse may experience no symptoms, only one symptom or sometimes, many symptoms. The symptoms can change over the course of time or occur intermittently. This is most likely connected with normal changes in blood volume related to the endocrine system, which secrete hormones into the body. Since a woman's hormonal system is more active and changeable than a man's, this is one reason why women may be aware of the symptoms of mitral valve prolapse more frequently and acutely than men.

❤ **Mindsaving Tip: If you have what you believe are severe symptoms associated with mitral valve prolapse, bear in mind that usually there is no correlation between the severity of the symptoms and the severity of the prolapse.**

Q: How is mitral valve prolapse diagnosed?

A: The cardiologist can sometimes make a tentative diagnosis of mitral valve prolapse with the aid of nothing more than a stethoscope. Not uncommonly, however, mitral valve prolapse can be extremely difficult to pin down because its symptoms can be identical to those caused by other ailments. Sometimes, a tentative diagnosis can be made by taking the following factors into consideration:

AGE

Although the malformation of the mitral valve occurs during gestation, when the heart is formed, it usually remains unnoticed until young adulthood. Women usually become aware of such symptoms suddenly, and can often pinpoint the day and even the hour when they first occurred. For example, Nancy recalls a sunny day in June, when she was outside washing her dog. Suddenly, she felt pain in her chest, which she experienced every few weeks from that point on.

BODY TYPE

Body type is often another clue to diagnosing mitral valve prolapse. This condition is most often seen in women with a thin body build, possibly because they lack the extra fat that acts as a blood volume buffer. Blood can move from the tiny blood vessels to the large blood vessels and smoothe the alteration of blood pressure that accompanies changes in body posture and may account for such symptoms as dizziness. Of course, there are exceptions, and women of all shapes and sizes can suffer real discomfort from mitral valve prolapse.

It is not that uncommon for women with mitral valve prolapse to turn out to be dancers, gymnasts, and women athletes of slender build. Sometimes, the symptoms occur during the spurt of adrenaline that accompanies a performance, like the case of a 45-year-old exotic dancer who used to faint while removing her G-string!

THE CLASSICAL CLICK

In many cases, heart sounds comes into play when making a diagnosis of mitral valve prolapse. By carefully listening with a stethoscope, a doctor may discern, in addition to normal heart sounds, a characteristic high-pitched, snapping sound produced near the middle of the heart's ventricular contraction. This is the so-called classical click. This click is often followed by a characteristic murmur heard in the heartbeat cycle caused by the leakage of blood back through the mitral valve into the left atrium.

This click has the tendency to change when you change position, so the cardiologist may listen to your heart as you stand, lie down, squat or sit. But remember that although the click and murmur is characteristic of most prolapse patients, it's not always present in everyone. The click can also come and go, depending on the movement of the person. It is also not uncommon for the heart of a woman with mitral valve prolapse to sound perfectly normal.

CHEST PAIN

The type of chest pain associated with mitral valve prolapse is termed by cardiologists as "atypical," to differentiate it from "typical" chest pain, the type of chest pain associated with coronary artery disease.

Typically, with heart disease, the chest pain is felt underneath the breastbone, and is a squeezing or pressure-like sensation. This pain usually, but not always, occurs after exercise. If not exercise-related, it may come during other activities that increase the workload of the heart, such as eating a heavy meal.

In contrast, the chest pain associated with mitral valve prolapse is usually felt to the left of the breastbone, is sharp, and lasts usually only several seconds. It's an intermittent type of pain, and can, for example, be experienced frequently for a few weeks at a time, disappear completely, and then return.

But such "atypical" chest pain as found in mitral valve prolapse can also occur with other diseases commonly seen in young women. One example is esophagitis, a commonly seen inflammation of the esophagus. The problem may be due to neuromuscular chest pain, for example, pinching of the nerves of the neck as a result of osteoarthritis. Symptoms of gall bladder disease and stomach ulcers can also manifest themselves as chest pain.

As noted earlier, it is a matter of controversy whether there is something inherent in having mitral valve prolapse that "causes" chest pain, whether those with mitral valve prolapse have a heightened sensitivity to such pain, or whether mitral valve prolapse is associated with such chest pain at all.

PALPITATION (THE "POUNDING" HEART)

Women with mitral valve prolapse often suffer from palpitations, or a pounding of the heart, which can be truly frightening. It is believed that women with mitral valve prolapse may be overly sensitive to the secretion of adrenaline, one of the several hormones released by the adrenal glands, which are situated on top of the kidneys. Known as the "flight or fight" hormone, adrenaline, among other things, increases the heart rate. This hypersensitivity to adrenaline may ultimately result in lightheadedness, dizziness, and fatigue. Drinking coffee or other beverages with caffeine may aggravate it.

Some arrhythmias, however, are serious and in extreme and very rare cases, can lead to sudden death. An example of this is ventricular tachycardia, which results in an abnormally fast heart rate. If you have potentially serious ventricular tachycardia, your doctor will most likely prescribe a cardiovascular medication.

Q: What diagnostic tests can confirm whether or not I have mitral valve prolapse?

A: A doctor usually can make a tentative diagnosis of mitral valve prolapse based on your medical history and listening to your heart. Additional tests may be recommended to confirm the diagnosis or evaluate whether it is likely to cause you any serious problems later on. These tests are also used to rule out any other cardiac-related cause or your symptoms.

The following diagnostic tests may be used to diagnose mitral valve prolapse:

- Physical examination: By performing a physical examination, a cardiologist can determine whether you have a heart murmur or whether your heart makes the characteristic click sound associated with mitral valve prolapse.
- Electrocardiogram and/or Holter monitor: An electrocardiogram can show if your heart is generating the proper electrical impulses to keep it functioning regularly or whether you have any heartbeat irregularities, or arrhythmias. An electrocardiogram is used to study your heartbeat at rest, while a Holter monitor records your heartbeat as you go about your daily activities.
- Exercise stress test: If you have chest pain, an exercise stress test or exercise echocardiogram can determine whether you may have coronary artery disease. An exercise stress test is also useful to objectively evaluate your exercise capability.
- Echocardiogram: An echocardiogram is often extremely useful in the diagnosis of mitral valve prolapse because, with this image of your heart, your doctor can actually see if any of your valve leaflets are malformed. Useful as this is, though, mitral valve prolapse is only visible on an echocardiogram image about 50 percent of the time.
- Tilt study: If you are suffering from dizziness or lack of balance, a tilt study may be very useful.

All of these cardiac tests are virtually risk-free and pain-free and are done on an outpatient basis. They are explained in more detail in Chapter 10.

Q: Does mitral valve prolapse cause problems during pregnancy?

A: In an of itself, mitral valve prolapse does not cause problems in pregnancy. For more information, see Chapter 8, "Pregnancy and Your Heart."

OTHER CONSIDERATIONS FOR WOMEN WITH MITRAL VALVE PROLAPSE

Bacterial Endocarditis

Some doctors believe women with mitral valve prolapse may be at increased risk for developing bacterial endocarditis, a dangerous infection of the heart valves caused by bacteria entering the bloodstream. In its most recent recommendations, updated in 1990, the American Heart Association said preventive antibiotics were unnecessary for persons with mitral valve prolapse unless they have a "leaky" mitral valve. For more information, see Chapter 11.

Stroke

Over the years, some studies have found that a stroke may occur in a very tiny percentage of people with mitral valve prolapse, although conclusive evidence of this has not been found.

LIVING WITH MITRAL VALVE PROLAPSE

In most cases, simply being reassured that you do not have a serious heart problem is enough to make the symptoms of mitral valve prolapse seem easier to bear. However, if your symptoms are uncomfortable or disabling, there are some medications that may be useful. Often, a type of cardiovascular drug called beta-blockers are used. Such drugs "muffle" the actions of the sympathetic nerves to the heart, and are very effective in decreasing chest pain and irregular heart beats. Apparently for the same reason that those with mitral valve prolapse appear hypersensitive to adrenaline, they also often appear to experience an exaggerated response to heart medications, so starting out with a low dosage is usually the wisest course. Your doctor may try different drugs before finding the most effective.

Also, you may want to try sharply limiting your caffeine intake by avoiding coffee, tea, chocolate, and other caffeine-rich foods. Caffeine stimulates the production of adrenaline. Since women with mitral valve prolapse appear to be often overly sensitive to adrenaline, eliminating or limiting your caffeine intake may prove a very good idea. Drinking a lot of fluids reduces exaggerations in the fluctuation of blood pressure related to bending or other sudden changes in body position.

And don't neglect your physical condition. It's only natural, if you are suffering from such symptoms as fatigue and shortness of breath, to limit your physical activity. You may not even realize you are doing such things as avoiding stairs, hopping in the car instead of walking, or parking your car closer to stores when you shop. As a result, your body is not conditioned, which may make you even more tired and short of breath than you would be ordinarily. If your doctor has not placed any physical limitations on you, you'll find becoming more active will improve your general health.

Although learning that you have mitral valve prolapse will initially be upsetting, there is another way to look at it. Unlike many women who neglect their hearts when they are young and develop heart disease later in life, you are now more conscious of the importance of maintaining your heart's health. By developing heart-healthy habits now, you may even end up living a longer, healthier life.

If You Have Mitral Valve Prolapse
- Avoid caffeine if you find it worsens your symptoms.
- Eat a nutritionally balanced diet.
- Drink eight glasses of water daily.
- Improve your general cardiovascular fitness level.
- Learn to control your stress and anxiety.
- If you find your symptoms disabling, discuss medication with your doctor.
- Contact your doctor right away if you develop shortness of breath with marginal exertion or change in your chest pain pattern or frequent palpitation (a "pounding heart").

To Sum Up

Mitral valve prolapse is not a disease, but a condition that occurs commonly in women. Complications occur only rarely. Treatment is usually not necessary, except in cases where symptoms are severe. In almost all cases, you will be able to enjoy a normal, active life.

7

~~~~~~ᄋ~~~~~

Congenital Heart Defects:
Hidden Time Bombs

When my doctor told me I had a congenital heart defect, I stared at him in disbelief. I was 40 years old! Whoever heard of a 40-year-old with a birth defect? Certainly not me! I had always assumed that such defects were diagnosed when you were born, or certainly in childhood.

I was to learn later that over one half million Americans are living with some type of congenital heart defect. Yet sometimes even doctors do not realize this. When my friend Pat, whose similar defect, an atrial septal defect, was diagnosed when she was 36, told her children's pediatrician, he replied, "You can't have an atrial septal defect! You must have heard wrong." Not only had Pat heard right, but her mother was diagnosed with the same problem when she was in her late 50s.

Symptoms and Signs of Congenital Heart Defects
- Exercise intolerance
- A heart murmur
- Palpitations
- Symptoms of congestive heart failure
- Blood pressure irregularities

Before the era of open-heart surgery, babies born with serious congenital defects died at birth or shortly thereafter. If the defect was not severe, the child sometimes survived until adulthood, but often died young. Sometimes, the reason for the death was mysterious, or it was said that the person had a "heart condition," although no one exactly knew what the problem was.

That's now ancient history. The correction of congenital heart defects is one of the cheeriest chapters in modern cardiology. Nowadays, the vast majority of children who are born with heart defects are treated and go on to live out a healthy, normal life span. That holds true for most adults as well, since these problems are usually discovered in time. If they are not, however, serious heart problems can result.

If you have such a defect, you may very well have known about it for years. Perhaps it was diagnosed and corrected when you were a child. Or perhaps the defect is so mild it doesn't need correcting, and you visit a cardiologist for periodic check-ups. If your defect is very mild, you may live out your whole long life this way.

But congenital heart defects can be sneaky. That's why we call them hidden time bombs: You can have one without knowing it for years, but remain oblivious as it inflicts serious damage to your heart.

WHAT IS A CONGENITAL DEFECT?

The word "congenital" means inborn or existing at birth. The heart begins to form from a single tube-like structure during the fourth week after conception. As the weeks progress, the tube lengthens and eventually forms the chambers, dividing wall, or septum, and valves that make up a functioning heart. If anything occurs that interferes with this developmental process during the first eight to 10 weeks of pregnancy, a congenital heart defect is the result.

An estimated eight out of every 1,000 babies born alive have some form of congenital heart defect. In general, congenital defects occur more commonly in females, although some types occur more frequently in male babies. In most cases, the reason for this gender difference is not known.

WHAT CAUSES CONGENITAL DEFECTS?

The reasons for most congenital defects are not known, so there's no way to prevent them. Only about 10 percent of the time these defects are caused by genetic abnormalities, including the heart defects commonly associated with Down's syndrome, which also causes mental retardation. Marfan's syndrome, discussed later in this chapter, is also an inherited defect.

In some cases, environmental factors also contribute to congenital defects. But again, the percentage is small. These include the mother's exposure to German measles (rubella), herpes simplex virus, influenza, or mumps. The heavy use of alcohol has been linked to birth defects as well, as has the use of some drugs, including some antidepressants, opiates, and some cardiovascular medications including Coumadin, generically known as Warfarin, a powerful anticlotting drug.

Why Do Adults Have Congenital Defects?

Adults who have congenital heart defects generally fall into three categories.

- Those whose defect was discovered in childhood and was surgically corrected. They are among the large number of adults who are living healthy, normal lives with their repaired hearts, or whose defect may have been so slight that only monitoring is needed.
- Those who were told as children they had a heart murmur or a congenital defect, and perhaps they were even monitored by a pediatric cardiologist for a while. They were not bothered by any symptoms, though, and eventually forgot about it. Now, as they reach their 20s and 30s, they suddenly find themselves dragging. Particularly when they're active, they may become short of breath or experience palpitations.
- Those who assumed they were healthy until they learned, to their surprise, that they have a congenital heart defect. They may have gone to the doctor because they were experiencing symptoms. But, more likely, the defect was discovered through tests for another problem. With the sophisticated tests available today, you may wonder how any cardiac defect in a baby could escape detection, but it still happens, although rarely. Most of the adults who today are discovered to be living with congenital defects were infants 20 or 30 years ago, when diagnosing such problems was much more difficult.

Most of the adults with congenital defects seen at the Cleveland Clinic's Adult Congenital Heart Disease Clinic fall into one of these two last categories, according to clinic director Dr. Daniel J. Murphy.

"Some people have congenital heart defects which were not recognized by their family doctors, but there are probably just as many who knew they had a heart murmur or problem with a valve but they haven't seen a cardiologist since childhood. So, by the time they come here, they may have developed a lot of symptoms," Dr. Murphy said.

How Congenital Defects Damage Your Heart

For your heart to properly perform its job, it is very important that all your blood flows through your heart in the correct direction, as noted in Chapter 2. A congenital defect can disrupt this flow. Many defects are structural problems that can result in some of your blood flowing back the wrong way, or your heart valves may be malformed or narrowed, which prevents your blood from flowing unobstructed. Such problems damage your heart by forcing it to overwork. Over the years, your heart may become enlarged or weakened, and the blood pressure within your heart and lungs can build up. The eventual result can be heart failure.

Even if they are overlooked, most congenital heart defects are detected by the time people reach their 20s and 30s, sparing their hearts from irreversible damage. If they are not, however, their hearts can still be corrected, but any damage already done may be irreversible.

How Do I Know if I Have a Congenital Defect?

Unfortunately, the answer is, often you don't. Congenital heart defects are not that common and about 90 percent are diagnosed in childhood, Dr. Murphy estimates. This means that it is unlikely, though by no means impossible, that you've reached adulthood with an undetected congenital heart defect. Because these defects can be missed until adults are in their 40s, 50s, and even 60s, some experts believe that the number of people with undiagnosed heart defects is larger than generally assumed.

Symptoms of congenital defects are discussed below.

Exercise Intolerance

This is the most common symptom of a congenital heart defect. Exercise intolerance manifests itself as fatigue and shortness of breath when you attempt to be active. But this is tricky to recognize. Exercise intolerance usually develops so gradually and insidiously that it can become quite severe before you realize anything really serious is wrong. Another problem is that people with congenital heart defects often do not even notice they're growing less active.

I can certainly vouch for this. As an adult, I always seemed slightly short of breath. I attributed this to allergies. It also seemed that, no matter how hard I tried to exercise, I never built up any endurance. This, I attributed when I was young to being on the plump side and later to growing older. My discomfort was so minor that the idea anything could be seriously wrong with me would have struck me as ludicrous. According to Dr. Murphy, I fit the picture of an adult with an unrecognized congenital heart defect perfectly.

But not everyone with a congenital heart defect tends to be inactive. Pat, for example, was a runner before her congenital heart defect was discovered. Since her surgery, though, she has noticed a big difference. "I was always frustrated by the fact that I was never able to put on any speed. It would drive me crazy that I was working so hard and never getting anywhere. So, after the surgery, I started checking my time, and I was really surprised. Overall, I've shortened my one-mile running time by quite a bit," she says.

Heart Murmur

A heart murmur sometimes occurs with congenital heart defects and sometimes does not.

It is not at all unusual for a girl to have a heart murmur that she eventually "grows out of." Pregnant women often have heart murmurs as well because of their normal increase in blood volume. The blood volume decreases after giving birth and the murmur disappears.

If you are not pregnant, and you have a heart murmur, you should ask your doctor to determine the reason. As an appropriate test, your doctor may suggest an echocardiogram, a noninvasive test that provides an image of your heart's structure. On the other hand, if your family doctor says it is nothing to worry about, be diplomatic, but persistent. If your doctor declines to check further, consider going to a cardiologist, preferably one with experience in congenital heart defects. Sometimes, because the patient appears healthy, a doctor can assume a heart murmur is "innocent," or does not signify a problem, when that is not actually the case. If your heart murmur does indeed turn out to be innocent, so much the better. This is far preferable to having a potentially serious problem overlooked.

Palpitations

If your heart defect has gone on undetected (or uncorrected) for a long time, you may begin to suffer from palpitations. Sometimes, the pounding of your heart can become so severe it can cause fainting. Palpitations indicate a problem with your heart's electrical system and may indicate your heart is suffering because of the defect. By the time palpitations usually appear, your heart has been overcompensating for quite a while. Unfortunately, even though your heart may benefit greatly from having the defect corrected, the problem leading to the palpitation may be irreversible.

Symptoms of Congestive Heart Failure

This serious syndrome rarely occurs in the case of congenital defects, but it can if the problem has gone undetected for years, or even decades. These symptoms occur more commonly in people who are over 50. Congestive heart failure (often referred to simply as "heart failure"), indicates your heart has been overcompensating so long it can no longer adequately perform its major function of supplying blood to your body. See Chapter 11 for symptoms of congestive heart failure.

Blood Pressure Unevenness

Often with congenital defects, blood pressure can remain normal as measured in your doctor's office, even though you may have developed pulmonary hypertension, which is high blood pressure within the right side of your heart and lungs. People with a certain type of congenital heart defect called coarctation of the aorta are found to have abnormal blood pressure readings. These people have high blood pressure in their upper body, but low blood pressure in the legs. Most doctors don't routinely measure blood pressure readings in both the arms and legs, so this highly suspicious finding is often missed.

❤ Lifesaving Tip: Having a blood pressure reading within normal range is not a guarantee that you don't have pulmonary hypertension. This dangerous condition can build up within your heart and lungs and cause damage even while your regular blood pressure reading remains normal or even low. It can be diagnosed during a physical examination and with the help of an electrocardiogram and an echocardiogram, both commonly performed types of cardiac tests.

DIAGNOSING CONGENITAL DEFECTS

If you suspect that you might have a congenital defect, you should see a cardiologist, preferably one who has experience in congenital heart defects. Although it may seem odd for an adult to visit a pediatric cardiologist, this is the doctor with the most specialized type of training in this field. Many pediatric cardiologists prefer not to see patients older than 16. If this is the case, seek out a cardiologist with special training in congenital heart defects. In many communities, though, such a physician is difficult to find. In that case, consider choosing a general cardiologist who is experienced in treating adults with congenital defects, and who can refer you to a large center where such expertise can be found, should the need arise.

The cardiologist will begin with a physical examination, and, if there is reason to believe you may have such a defect, recommend cardiac testing. Such tests would most likely include an electrocardiogram, chest X ray, echocardiogram, and, possibly a cardiac catheterization. These tests are discussed in Chapter 10.

The types of congenital heart defects found in adults are discussed below.

ATRIAL AND VENTRICULAR SEPTAL DEFECTS (ASD AND VSD)

Septal defects, which are commonly referred to as holes in the heart, occur when the opening in the wall that divides the heart into left and right chambers fails to close before birth. They are among the most common forms of heart defects. Atrial septal defects (ASDs) occur in the upper chambers of the heart. Ventricular septal defects (VSDs) occur in the lower chamber of the heart.

If you have a significant septal defect, it should be corrected as soon as possible. If it persists for too long, an irreversible and potentially deadly complication known as Eisenmenger syndrome can result. This problem occurs when the small blood vessels of the lungs are damaged by the prolonged high blood pressure that has built up within the heart and lungs. Symptoms of this problem include shortness of breath, fainting during exercise, and cyanosis (blue skin, lips, or nail beds caused by

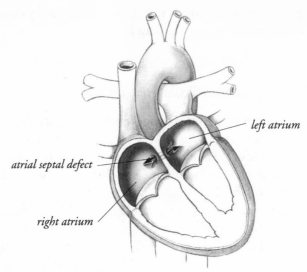

left atrium

atrial septal defect

right atrium

Atrial Septal Defect. The defect in the tissue separating the two upper halves of the heart results in a portion of the blood flowing improperly back through the heart.

lack of oxygen in the blood). The damage caused by this complication is irreversible and will likely shorten your life, even if your septal defect is corrected.

Although open-heart surgery is not 100 percent risk-free, the risk to an otherwise healthy adult is relatively low. According to a study done by the Mayo Clinic of 123 patients who underwent surgery at the Mayo Clinic some 30 years earlier, it was found that patients whose ASDs had been repaired prior to their reaching the age of 25 lived the rest of their lives in excellent health. Patients whose surgery was performed later still enjoyed quite good results, but were more likely to develop heart problems as they grew older. Still, doctors today occasionally find adults whose congenital defects were diagnosed and should have been corrected years ago, but never were.

Typically, septal defects are corrected surgically. If you need to undergo this type of surgery, all the steps are described in Chapter 11. Once you are placed on the heart-lung machine, the surgeon will open the heart and repair the defect, using either a piece of pericardium (the cellophane-like sac covering the heart) or a synthetic patch to cover the hole. No matter which type of patch is used, the heart tissue soon grows over it, sealing it even more permanently. In uncomplicated cases, this procedure essentially cures the problem.

Recently, several new nonsurgical devices to fix such holes have been developed. The advantage to using these devices is that they can be implanted in an outpatient procedure and you do not have to have a surgical scar on the chest. As of this writing, none of these devices has received full governmental approval for use by any physican, but most major pediatric cardiology centers are participating in the use of one or more of these devices. Some of the devices have over 10 years of human experience and full approval for some of the devices is expected in the next year or two.

These nonsurgical methods involve devices that can be folded into a catheter that is guided through a vein from outside your body. When the devices are pushed out of the catheter, they form a plug or one or two relatively flat surfaces that straddle the hole. "In the near future, most but not all, atrial septal defects will be treated with these types of devices," said Larry A. Latson, MD, chairman of pediatric cardiology and medical director of the Center for Pediatric and Congenital Heart Disease at the Cleveland Clinic Foundation.

PATENT DUCTUS ARTERIOSUS

Every baby is born with a ductus arteriosus, an open passageway between the pulmonary artery and the aorta, the heart's two major blood vessels. Normally, this passageway closes within a few hours of birth. If not, the passageway remains open, it creates a shunt, or pathway in which blood flows the wrong way, from the aorta back into the lungs, instead of out into the rest of your body. This problem causes the heart to work too hard, and can result in serious complications.

Patent ductus arteriosus occurs more often in females. This defect can occur alone, or along with such other defects as a VSD or coarctation of the aorta.

Traditionally, surgery through the left side of the chest was required to correct this defect. However, most of these defects can now be closed with the use of a device that can be placed through a catheter to plug the vessel. In this procedure, a catheter is inserted into a vein or artery and pushed through the circulatory system until it is correctly positioned in the heart. Then one of the devices (usually called a coil) is pushed out of the end of the catheter. When the device comes out of the catheter, it forms loops that fill up the vessel and block the abnormal passageway. Some of these devices have full governmental approval, and improved devices specifically designed for closure of patent ductus arteriosus are being studied.

AORTIC STENOSIS (CONGENITAL BICUSPID VALVE)

The term "aortic stenosis" is somewhat misleading. Pinching of the aortic valve can be caused by a congenital defect or rheumatic heart disease or be related to the normal aging process. When it occurs as a congenital heart defect, the term "bicuspid malformation of aortic valve" is more precise.

Normally, your heart's aortic valve has three leaflets that help it open and close properly, allowing blood to exit the heart without interference. People with a bicuspid aortic valve are born with only two leaflets, which are often partially fused together. Instead of opening fully the leaflets obstruct blood flow, making it more difficult for the heart to pump blood through the body. When this defect is severe, surgery may be required, although, under many circumstances, a procedure known as balloon valvuloplasty can be used. This is usually done in the very old or young or on someone who is otherwise a very poor candidate for surgical repair. Since surgical valve replacement can have such a great impact on quality of life, such surgery is increasingly common in patients up into their 90s.

Ninety-five percent of those born with this defect have only the valve problem. In about 5 percent of the cases, people born with this problem may also be missing one of their heart's coronary arteries.

PULMONARY STENOSIS

This congenital heart defect is also termed "valvular pulmonary stenosis" because it affects the pulmonary valve. In a normal heart, the pulmonary valve opens to allow the blood to flow from the right ventricle into the lungs, where it exchanges carbon dioxide and oxygen. If you are born with a malformed valve, which is too narrow, it can partially or completely obstruct the flow of blood, causing your right ventricle to pump too hard. Over the years, this overcompensation causes the valve to become thickened and calcified, increasing the obstruction. Pulmonary stenosis can occur by itself, or as part of a complex of heart defects called tetralogy of Fallot, which is explained below. Traditionally, surgery to repair or replace the valve was required, but this defect is now most often corrected with balloon valvuloplasty.

Coarctation of the Aorta

In people with this congenital heart vascular defect, the aorta, the main artery that carries blood from the heart to the rest of the body, is pinched, crimped, or constricted; obstructing the flow of blood from the heart to the lower part of the body, including the legs. To compensate, the heart works harder, raising the blood pressure in the upper part of your body. This problem should be corrected as early in life as possible, otherwise, the blood pressure may remain high after the coarctation is fixed.

If surgery is required, the surgeon reconstructs the aorta by removing the narrowed segment and reconnecting the normal parts of the aorta. Sometimes, a graft made from synthetic material is used. Sometimes, years after such a repair, the segment can again become narrowed. In such a case, balloon angioplasty with or without a stent (a tiny tube that props the aorta open) usually can be used to dilate it.

Ebstein's Anomaly

This is a defect in which the tricuspid valve of the heart is malformed and displaced, leading to some degree of regurgitation from the right ventricle to the right atrium. If you were born with this as a mild condition, you may not develop any symptoms for years. Open-heart surgery to repair or replace the valve is usually indicated. Often, people born with this condition also have an atrial septal defect, which can be repaired at the same time.

Tetralogy of Fallot

Tetralogy of Fallot, or "the tetralogy," is really a quartet of separate congenital defects. The two major components are a large ventricular septal defect (VSD) and pulmonary stenosis. This narrowing or pinching of the pulmonary valve partially blocks the flow of blood into the lungs. In addition, the right ventricle is more muscular than normal, and the aorta is displaced, lying directly over the VSD.

Tetralogy of Fallot is termed a cyanotic defect because it results in cyanosis, a bluish discoloration of the skin or, in mild cases, a ruddy complexion. This occurs because the blood being pumped through the body does not contain enough oxygen.

Surgery is required to fix the multiple defects associated with this condition. In most cases, surgery effects a cure; in some cases, however, this condition may result in a weakening of the right side of the heart or in heart rhythm disturbances, necessitating additional treatment.

MARFAN'S SYNDROME

Although it is not technically a congenital heart defect, Marfan's syndrome is an inherited congenital disorder that can manifest itself as potentially deadly heart problems. Also, if mild, this potentially very serious problem can be overlooked, with sometimes fatal results.

Some believe President Abraham Lincoln suffered from Marfan's. If you follow sports, you will certainly have heard of Marfan's syndrome. It was the cause of the unexpected death of Flo Hyman, one of the world's leading female volleyball players. Marfan's syndrome is an uncommon genetic disorder of the connective tissues, especially of the heart, eyes, and musculoskeletal system. One of every two children of an affected parent inherits the syndrome. Recently, the gene responsible for the syndrome was located; it is hoped that research will eventually result in a laboratory test to diagnose and correct it.

Marfan's can cause potentially serious eye disorders as well as changes in the musculoskeletal system, creating a characteristic "Marfanoid" appearance. Physical appearance provides the main clue to the presence of Marfan's. People with Marfan's are often tall and thin, with slender, tapering fingers and unusually long arms and legs. However, appearances can be deceiving, and sometimes people who do not have outward physical characteristics of Marfan's can develop serious medical problems.

How Marfan's Affects the Heart

Marfan's usually threatens the heart in two ways: by affecting the aorta, the large artery that carries oxygenated blood from the left ventricle to the rest of the body, and by affecting the heart's major valves. The connective tissue in the aorta weakens and begins to stretch. By early adulthood, this weakness may swell into an aneurysm, a bubble-like formation where the aorta is weakest, which can cause the aortic valve to leak or even the aorta to burst. About 60 percent of the people born with Marfan's also have a leaky mitral valve, which also can reduce their heart's ability to pump. People with Marfan's require treatment as problems develop. Someone with a weakened aortic artery may need to avoid vigorous exercise. This is why diagnosing this ailment is particularly important when it occurs in young, competitive athletes.

❤ **Lifesaving Tip: Marfan's syndrome can be a very dangerous hidden time bomb. It may go completely unnoticed until the afflicted person dies suddenly of a ruptured aortic aneurysm. If one of your parents had Marfan's, you should be examined for it. You should also be examined if you have a family history that includes an unusually large number of tall young men or women who died suddenly at a young age.**

OTHER CONGENITAL HEART DEFECTS

There are other extremely unusual congenital heart defects that, while quite commonly now associated with survival into adulthood, are unlikely to remain undiscovered until adulthood. These anomalies include being born without a tricuspid valve; being born without a pulmonary valve; transposition of the great vessels, in which the pulmonary artery and the aorta are reversed; and various absences or anomalies of the coronary arteries.

❤ **Lifesaving Tip: A congenital heart defect can make your heart more vulnerable to infection. That is why, if you have such a defect, even after it has been corrected, your doctor may recommend you take antibiotics before a routine dental cleaning and some other medical procedures. This is discussed in Chapter 11.**

SURGICAL CONSIDERATIONS FOR CONGENITAL HEART DEFECTS

The correction of congenital heart defects has changed dramatically. Years ago, if your defect was very serious, you died at birth or shortly thereafter. After the development of the heart-lung machine, open-heart surgery became possible, but was risky. Over the past few decades, such surgical techniques have become much safer.

Remember, though, that although risks of open-heart surgery have fallen dramatically, such operations entail at least a 3 to 4 percent risk of death for women, the same as for a coronary bypass operation. However, the risk of suffering a stroke during surgery for correction of a congenital heart defect is slightly higher than that during a bypass because the chamber of the heart must be opened, increasing the possibility that air will get in, travel to the brain, and cause an injury. While the danger of not having the surgery performed seriously outweighs such risks, if you must undergo such surgery, you should choose a surgeon who is experienced in the repair of congenital heart defects. Open-heart surgery is discussed in Chapter 14.

Am I too old to have my defect corrected? In the past, doctors subscribed to the belief there was a cutoff age for the correction of congenital heart defects. This is no longer the case; studies have shown very good results can be obtained in women well over the age of 60 and even older, unless the defect has affected the heart to such an extent that surgery would not be beneficial.

If a doctor says your congenital defect should be corrected, but you are "too old" for surgery, be certain that conclusion is based on sound medical reasoning. Strongly consider getting a second opinion from a physician who is very experienced in treating congenital heart defects in adults. You may have to seek out a major medical center, but often you can send your records ahead of time to learn if further evaluation could help you.

What about cardiac rehabilitation? Cardiac rehabilitation traditionally has been seen as benefiting people who have undergone treatment for coronary disease or for those who have suffered a heart attack. Increasingly, its benefits are being seen in a broader context. Nowadays, many cardiac rehabilitation programs have people trained to work with patients who have congenital heart defects. If you are in otherwise good health, and you undergo surgery to correct your defect, you may not need such a program. On the other hand, if you are in need of physical conditioning, you might benefit a great deal. For the program to be covered by your insurer, your doctor will have to attest that you are in need of this type of therapy. Cardiac rehabilitation is discussed in Chapter 13.

If I have a congenital heart defect, should I become pregnant? If you have a defect, whether or not you should become pregnant, and how that pregnancy should be managed, depend generally on the seriousness of the defect and the condition of your heart. Congenital defects associated with pulmonary hypertension (such as Eisenmenger syndrome or tetralogy of Fallot) carry a risk of maternal death such that pregnancy should be avoided. For more information on congenital heart defects and pregnancy, see Chapter 8.

❤ **Lifesaving Tip: No matter what type of congenital heart defect you have, whether it is corrected or not, the best advice regarding pregnancy is "plan ahead." Discuss the possibility with your doctor before you become pregnant. If you are already pregnant, discuss your heart problem with your doctor as soon as possible. This is especially important if you're taking Coumadin or certain other cardiac medications.**

Will my children's hearts be normal? If you were born with a congenital heart defect, you are probably very concerned about the probability of passing the defect on to your children. The good news is that this is not very likely, unless you have a defect with a strong genetic link, such as Marfan's syndrome. With other congenital heart defects, your risk of having a child with a heart defect goes up slightly above normal, possibly 3 to 4 percent, although in some cases the figure could be as high as 10 percent. "There is no guarantee any time you have a child. For someone with a congenital heart defect, there is going to be an increased risk, but it is generally not significant," notes Dr. Daniel Murphy.

Still, if you have a congenital heart defect, you should consider having a special diagnostic test called a fetal echocardiogram done after you have completed your 16th week of pregnancy. This test, which is identical to an echocardiogram, will usually show if your baby's heart is developing normally. While such a test sometimes cannot detect a relatively mild heart defect, it usually can diagnose serious problems. In about 95 percent of the cases, the ultrasound will be negative, so if you are very concerned about your baby's heart, this test can provide you with peace of mind. Some doctors question the value of the test, reasoning that if there were a defect that requires correction, this would be done after birth.

You should undergo a four-chambered fetal echo sonogram if:

- You were born with a congenital heart defect.
- Your baby's father was born with a congenital heart defect.
- There is a history of congenital heart defects in either of your families.
- You have given birth previously to a child with a congenital heart defect.

❤ Lifesaving Tip: Four-chambered fetal echo sonograms have become routine. As with other diagnostic tests, they are only as good as the person performing and interpreting them. Make sure your test is done in a hospital or clinic that specializes in fetal cardiology.

Still, for women with heart defects who do become mothers, the possibility that their child may have a similar defect lingers in their minds, even after they give birth to apparently robust babies. Even taking their youngster to a pediatric cardiologist and getting a clean bill of health does not always quiet the worry felt by women like Pat, who notes her *own* congenital defect was not discovered until she was in her mid-30s.

Today, though, things are different. Thanks to sophisticated diagnostic tests, such defects are hard to miss. "If your baby has a cardiac sonogram somewhere between 16 and 22 weeks, and then the baby is checked again shortly after birth, I think the parents can be very confident that their child is normal," says Dr. Catherine Neill, professor emeritus of pediatrics at The Johns Hopkins Hospital in Baltimore.

In fact, it is hoped that all adults with congenital heart defects that were not diagnosed until adulthood will eventually become part of a vanishing group.

8

~~~~∿∿∿∿∿Ο∿∿∿∿∿~~~~

Pregnancy and Your Heart

"I LEARNED I had heart disease when my son was two years old. I didn't anticipate getting pregnant again. When I did, I was really scared. But my doctor said he was sure I could handle the pregnancy," says Sandra.

Sandra, who is 37, gave birth to a healthy daughter. At the time, her pregnancy was complicated by two potentially serious problems. She had both coronary artery disease and mitral regurgitation, otherwise known as a leaky heart valve. Throughout her pregnancy, Sandra was watched carefully by doctors skilled in treating high-risk pregnancies. Her heart was carefully monitored. Special ultrasound tests were also done to make sure her baby was developing properly. Was the result worth it? Just ask Sandra.

"When I look at my little girl and see how healthy she is, it's wonderful. I just can't believe it," she says.

Sandra is one of a growing number of women with heart problems who are able to carry a baby safely to term. Years ago, such women risked a further deterioration of their condition, or even death. Nowadays, thanks to advances in cardiology, the probability that such a woman will enjoy a safe pregnancy and give birth to a healthy baby is much higher.

Not every heart problem is cause for great concern during pregnancy, but most require some extra care. Just how much additional care you will need depends upon what type of heart problem you have, whether the problem is mild or severe, and whether it has damaged your heart. Only a few heart problems can endanger your life or the life of your unborn child; unfortunately, though, these can be deadly. After obstetrical causes, heart and cardiovascular problems account for the highest number of maternal deaths during pregnancy. Happily, most pregnancies of most women like Sandra turn out well. With planning and careful consideration, you can help ensure your outcome will be a joyous one, like hers.

Before You Become Pregnant

If you are concerned about your own personal health or a problem in your family's medical history, no matter how frivolous it seems, you should talk to your primary physician or obstetrician about it before you become pregnant, or as soon afterwards as possible. If your pregnancy is not planned, and you find yourself pregnant, you should discuss your heart problem with your doctor as soon as possible.

If you're aware you have a heart problem, a cardiologist should evaluate you before you become pregnant. The more potentially serious your problem, the more important this is. Although a general cardiologist may initially evaluate you, it is important that the cardiologist following your case be experienced in treating pregnant women with your type of heart problem.

There are some key reasons why this pre-pregnancy evaluation is so important. During pregnancy, the sounds your heart makes differ from those when you are not pregnant, rendering a problem found during pregnancy more difficult to evaluate. Also, when you're not pregnant, your doctor has the freedom to do any type of diagnostic tests necessary without fear of harming the baby.

If you do have a heart problem, how closely you should be watched by a cardiologist during your pregnancy depends on the extent of your problem. Sometimes, an evaluation before, during, and after your pregnancy is all that is needed. If you have a potentially dangerous problem, though, you may need to be closely monitored by a team that includes a cardiologist and an obstetrician very experienced in high-risk pregnancies.

If you do have a heart problem, such as a congenital defect, you may find your cardiologist is unduly pessimistic about your chances for a successful pregnancy. A good, conscientious doctor who has had two or three patients do badly, and so has lumped patients with congenital heart defects together, may cautiously advise you not to get pregnant, based on previous experience instead of your specific conditions. So if you have a heart problem and you want to have a baby, but your cardiologist is concerned about it, consider seeking a second opinion at a major medical center from a cardiologist who specializes in dealing with such pregnancies. This way, you'll be certain you have an accurate idea of the risks involved to make your decision. If you live in a small town, you may have to travel to such a center, but you're well advised to do so, considering the importance of your decision.

❤ Lifesaving Tip: If you have a heart problem, in addition to seeing a cardiologist *before* you become pregnant, it is equally important that your heart be examined about six or eight weeks *after* you deliver your baby, to make sure your heart has returned to normal.

PREGNANCY AND THE NORMAL HEART

Everyone is familiar with the outward signs of pregnancy: You suffer bouts of morning sickness, your stomach expands to the size of a watermelon, and your feet swell. These reflect the many changes going on within your body. During your pregnancy, your body must adapt to the changes involved in nurturing a developing baby. None of your body's organs is called upon to work harder than your heart.

Even if your heart is perfectly normal, pregnancy places a heavy burden upon it. When you're not pregnant, your heart already must perform the herculean task of pumping blood throughout your body, day in and day out, without tiring. During pregnancy, several changes in your body take place to make this already tough task even tougher.

During pregnancy, you go through hormonal changes that apparently result in the retention of both salt and water. This accounts for a lot of your weight gain. By the fifth month of your pregnancy, your blood volume has increased by 40 to 50 percent. That represents a vast increase in the amount of blood your heart has to pump. Your heart also beats 10 to 20 times more per minute than before you were pregnant, contracting more strongly with each beat.

During labor, the demands on the normal heart increase even more. With each uterine contraction, your heart's workload increases by about 25 to 30 percent. During delivery, your heart may be called upon to work four to five times as hard is it did before you were pregnant. While the normal female heart can take this in stride (with some huffing and puffing of course), such a workload can place a dangerous strain on a heart that is weak.

As your baby grows inside you, it needs more and more oxygen and nutrients. If you have a heart problem that makes it difficult for your heart to supply enough oxygen to your body, this problem only worsens when your heart is faced with supplying oxygen to your enlarging uterus and developing baby as well.

Also, in pregnancy, many women have a tendency to develop high blood pressure. Hypertensive disorders are among the most dangerous problems of pregnancy. If you have a heart problem, the probability of developing high blood pressure increases.

With all these biological changes going on, it is not surprising that pregnancy can place a burden on a heart that is not perfect. It is the type of heart problem you have, however, that determines how risky your pregnancy will be.

What is a "high-risk" pregnancy? A high-risk pregnancy poses dangers to you, your baby, or both. You'll need to be closely monitored, you may have to undergo special tests, and you may need to schedule your delivery in advance to make certain you have the most experienced doctors and staff. In a high-risk pregnancy, such planning can literally make the difference between life and death.

DIAGNOSTIC TESTING: SAFE OR DANGEROUS?

The best way for a cardiologist to evaluate the likelihood of danger to your pregnancy is with a thorough, up-to-date evaluation of your heart. If you consult the cardiologist about your plans before you become pregnant, all necessary diagnostic tests can be performed safely. If you are already pregnant, the choice of tests is more limited.

One reason that diagnostic tests do not pose the danger to your unborn baby that they formerly did is that of the development of echocardiography, which is discussed in Chapter 7. This type of imaging has amassed a huge safety record over several years. The type of echocardiogram called a "four-chambered sonogram" can provide images of your unborn baby's heart.

In most cases, echocardiography can provide your doctor with most of the information required to evaluate your heart. Other diagnostic tests generally considered safe during pregnancy include monitoring your heartbeat by electrocardiogram or Holter monitor. Some other tests that may be indicated don't have such a safety record. For example, the radiation from a chest X ray can be hazardous to your unborn child during the first three months of pregnancy. In the later stages of pregnancy, a chest X ray can be safely performed if special precautions are taken, such as your belly being shielded with a lead apron.

Some tests used to evaluate your heart make use of radioactive isotopes, such as the thallium used in the diagnostic test known as the exercise nuclear scan, or the isotope called technitium used in a multiple gated acquisition test (MUGA). Whether or not these tests are safe during pregnancy depends on the type of chemical used, so discuss it with your doctor.

In rare cases, your doctor may want you to undergo a cardiac catheterization. Cardiac catheterization uses more radiation than a chest X ray, so ordinarily your doctor would avoid it during pregnancy. But in some cases the need for such tests may outweigh the risk to the baby. If your doctor suspects you may have a potentially life-threatening condition such as a clot in a coronary artery, the use of such radiation may be very warranted. Such circumstances require careful discussion between you and your doctor.

CARDIOVASCULAR DRUGS DURING PREGNANCY

It was once believed that the placenta, the organ within the uterus through which a fetus receives its nourishment, protected the unborn baby from dangerous germs and chemicals. Today, it's recognized that this is untrue, and dangerous chemicals can reach your unborn baby. This is why pregnant women who are pregnant are advised not to take any drugs unnecessarily during their pregnancy.

With some types of cardiac problems, you will be prescribed cardiovascular drugs. This is an area where much caution must be exercised. To gain FDA approval and be marketed in the United States, drugs must go through a rigorous testing process. However, there have never been any animal tests that could prove, with certainty, that a drug is safe for a pregnant woman. Since pregnant women are, quite rightfully, barred from inclusion in such testing, there is a lack of information on the safety and sometimes a time lag. Some drugs once believed safe are later found to cause birth defects. An example was the discovery that angiotensin converting enzyme inhibitors, known as ACE inhibitors, an important class of blood pressure reducing drugs, could cause serious birth defects. Until that warning was sounded, ACE inhibitors had been one of the drugs used by doctors to treat pregnant women with high blood pressure.

To be on the safe side, when you're pregnant, you should take drugs only if they're absolutely needed. If you do require medication, there are many drugs now on the market that have established safety records so your doctor will be able to recommend the right medication for you.

❤ Lifesaving Tip: It cannot be stressed too strongly that any medication during pregnancy, including nonprescription drugs, needs to be cleared by your doctor. If there is a question on a cardiac medication, you or your doctor should consult a cardiologist. If you are taking medications for a heart problem, abruptly stopping can also be risky, so contact your doctor immediately for guidance.

TYPES OF HEART PROBLEMS THAT CAN OCCUR DURING PREGNANCY

One type of heart disease that occurs during pregnancy involves heart problems you've had since before you became pregnant, but of which you may or may not be aware. These include congenital heart defects and cardiac problems caused by rheumatic heart disease. Other heart problems can occur in pregnancy whether you have a heart problem or not. These include blood pressure disorders that occur only during pregnancy and peripartum cardiomyopathy, a rare disease of the heart muscle.

Every woman is an individual and every pregnancy is different. The information in this chapter is designed to give you an idea of what to expect when you have different types of heart problems, and the kinds of treatment available.

CORRECTED CONGENITAL HEART DEFECTS

Over the years, an estimated 300,000 women in the United States have been treated for congenital defects, and many of them are now in their childbearing years. If your heart defect has been corrected, you should still discuss your plans to become pregnant with your doctor. In the vast majority of cases; a corrected heart defect does not present any problem at all. If you've had surgery for a very complex problem, such as tetralogy of Fallot, you may still have a residual problem, such as a leaky heart valve, or perhaps a tendency to develop irregular heart rhythms.

Uncorrected Congenital Heart Defects

A congenital heart defect may or may not pose a problem during pregnancy. This generally depends on the type and severity of the defect and whether it has compromised the function of your heart. Congenital heart defects are not commonly discovered during pregnancy, but sometimes the extra load on your heart can result in your experiencing cardiac symptoms or exhibiting clinical signs for the first time. Congenital heart defects are discussed further in Chapter 7.

❤ **Lifesaving Tip: In adults, a heart murmur may indicate a heart problem, such as a congenital heart defect. However, it is not uncommon for pregnant women to develop heart murmurs. If your heart murmur appears during your pregnancy and doesn't go away after delivery, it should be checked by a cardiologist.**

Whether or not your heart defect should be corrected during pregnancy depends on its type and its severity. Nowadays, even open-heart surgery can be performed safely on a pregnant woman, but usually less risky measures can be used.

The following congenital heart defects are unlikely to cause problems during pregnancy, even if they have not been corrected:

- Small, uncomplicated ventricular septal defects
- Uncomplicated patent ductus arteriosus
- Mild to moderate pulmonary stenosis

The following uncorrected congenital heart defects are those that may cause problems during pregnancy. Again, their impact depends on their severity. If they are not severe enough to cause symptoms during pregnancy, it is unlikely they will cause problems during pregnancy; but a doctor who specializes in congenital birth defects should follow your progress.

Atrial septal defect. An atrial septal defect (ASD) is a so-called "hole" in the atrium, between the upper chambers of the heart and is one of the most common congenital heart defects found in women. Most of the time, an ASD does not pose problems during pregnancy. On rare occasions, though, complications can develop, particularly if you have a large shunt, or abnormal blood flow, through your heart, allowing a significant amount of blood to wash back toward your lungs. Extremely serious problems can develop if your ASD has caused you to develop a condition called Eisenmenger syndrome, an irreversible condition in which the small blood vessels of the lungs are damaged by prolonged high blood pressure within the heart and lungs. This problem is discussed in Chapter 7.

Coarctation of the aorta. Whether coarctation of the aorta will cause complications depends on the severity of the narrowing of your aorta. Your doctor may recommend you have it surgically corrected before pregnancy. If you don't, your blood pressure may become very difficult to control during pregnancy and delivery. This can occur particularly during labor. If your defect is not corrected, your doctor may want to induce delivery before your due date.

Cyanotic congenital heart defects. Some congenital heart defects are known as cyanotic because they can cause your lips and the beds of your fingernails and toenails to take on a bluish hue. The color indicates that the blood going to your skin has a lower than normal amount of oxygen.

Congenital heart defects that cause such problems include:

- Tetralogy of Fallot
- Transposition of the great arteries
- Ebstein's anomaly

The cyanotic effect of these defects also results from the formation of a shunt, the pathway by which some of your blood flows in the wrong direction. This is dangerous because the abnormal blood pathway prevents your body's vital organs from receiving enough oxygenated blood. When you're not pregnant, your heart can compensate for this deficiency by increasing the number of oxygen-carrying cells in your blood. Because of the changes in your blood that occur during pregnancy, your body is no longer able to compensate. As your heart struggles to deliver oxygenated blood both to your body's organs and to the baby, it can become overworked and weakened.

If your defect is mild, it probably will not cause a problem during pregnancy. If it's severe enough to cause symptoms either before you become pregnant or early in your pregnancy, this is a forewarning you may experience problems during your pregnancy. Generally, these are not the serious types of problems that can doom a pregnancy, but doctors skilled in handling high-risk pregnancies must very carefully monitor your pregnancy.

Will My Baby Inherit My Congenital Heart Defect?

Congenital heart defects are very uncommon, and the chances of your baby inheriting your defects are slim. Some types of congenital heart defects, however, do tend to run in families. For more information, see Chapter 7.

❤ **Lifesaving Tip: If you have a congenital heart defect, you should be followed by a cardiologist who is specifically trained in congenital heart disease.**

Heart Valve Problems in Pregnancy

Most women with valve problems in the United States are past the age of childbearing. Their problems usually result from aging or from rheumatic fever, but there are heart valve problems that can affect younger women; they're discussed below.

Mitral Valve Prolapse

Mitral valve prolapse, an anomaly commonly found in women, generally causes no problems during pregnancy. Indeed, the increase in your blood volume may result in the temporary disappearance of symptoms. Such symptoms usually reappear within a few weeks to a few months after the baby is born. Rarely, women with mitral valve prolapse develop a complication called mitral regurgitation. For a further discussion of mitral valve prolapse and mitral regurgitation, see Chapter 6.

Rheumatic Heart Disease

There is a faulty belief that rheumatic fever is an old-fashioned disease that has gone the way of high button shoes and bustles. Unfortunately, this is only partially true. While it is becoming less common for women of childbearing age to exhibit signs of rheumatic heart disease, which is often the aftermath of rheumatic fever, it's not impossible to find it, particularly in women who have immigrated to the United States from countries where rheumatic fever is still prevalent.

Most commonly, women who have suffered rheumatic fever develop either mitral stenosis (blockage) or mitral regurgitation (leakage), or a combination of both. Frequently, women with such problems can also develop atrial fibrillation, a type of heart rhythm irregularity that can lead to serious problems. Atrial fibrillation is discussed later in Chapter 11.

Mitral Stenosis

Mitral stenosis, a stiffening and thickening resulting from to calcification of the heart's mitral valve, can be very worrisome in pregnancy, particularly if it has remained heretofore undetected. Symptoms of mitral stenosis include shortness of breath and bodily swelling.

If you have a mild version of this problem, you may need to do nothing more than follow a salt-restricted diet and possibly take a diuretic or "water pill" to prevent your body from retaining fluid during your pregnancy. If your valve is considerably damaged, however, you could develop major problems such as congestive heart failure or pulmonary edema, a dangerous buildup of fluid in your lungs. In this case, your doctor may recommend valvuloplasty, a nonsurgical method of widening the valve. Even during pregnancy, open-heart surgery can be done to replace your heart valve, but it's obviously not the first choice if there are other options available.

Aortic Stenosis (Congenital or Rheumatic)

A normal aortic valve has three valvular cusps, that enable it to function properly. If you were born with aortic sterosis, you have one or two cusps, which prevents the valve from working properly. Damage to your heart valve caused by rheumatic heart disease can also prevent it from working properly. This valve problem means that your heart must work extra hard to pump enough blood through your body, and during pregnancy, your heart can become very seriously overburdened.

If your defect is mild and you have no symptoms, the chances are good you will not experience problems during pregnancy. However, fainting, chest pain, or symptoms of congestive heart failure portend significant problems during pregnancy. In this case, your cardiologist may advise you to have your aortic valve replaced early in your pregnancy. If you are in the later stages of pregnancy, your doctor will take measures to reduce the demand on your heart, such as ordering bed rest and prescribing cardiovascular medications.

What if I need a heart valve replaced? If you have a valve disorder that may eventually require surgical repair, your doctor may recommend that you have the surgery before you become pregnant. If you are in the early stages of pregnancy, and in urgent need of a valve replacement, your doctor may recommend open-heart surgery. If you are in the later stages of pregnancy, your doctor will probably recommend that surgery be postponed until the baby is delivered. Eventually, though, you'll probably face valve surgery.

Cardiac valve replacement in women of childbearing years raises difficult issues. If your heart valve needs to be replaced, the major question is whether or not you plan to have more children. Your decision has a direct bearing on what type of valve replacement you choose.

Two types of heart valves are currently available. One type, called a biological valve, is made from animal tissue, most often taken from a pig. The other is a mechanical valve. Biological valves may deteriorate quickly and need to be replaced, sometimes after only several years; some experts believe that these valves wear out even more quickly during pregnancy. Because they last longer, mechanical valves are generally the choice for younger people. Although the mechanical valve would seem to be the logical choice, this is not true in women who plan to become pregnant. Mechanical valves are more vulnerable to the formation of blood clots, so those who have them must take a powerful anticlotting drug called Warfarin, known popularly under the trade name of Coumadin, which has been linked to birth defects and other complications.

Hence the dilemma: If you do have a biological valve implanted while you are still young, there's a strong probability it will need to be replaced sometime. Most cardiovascular surgeons don't balk at the prospect of performing an operation to replace a biological valve once, but consider having to do the surgery twice, or even more, increasingly hazardous. If you need a valve replaced, your surgeon may advise you to have a biological valve because it poses less risk to your unborn child should you become pregnant. However, if you want more children, you'll probably also be advised to have your family quickly so that when your biological valve wears out, it can be replaced with a mechanical version.

In some cases, it may be possible to repair the aortic valve. This type of "plastic" surgery of the valve has become commonly performed on the mitral valve and is being found suitable for some patients with aortic valve problems. Repair has fewer of the problems associated with either mechanical or biological tissue valve replacement. Since this is your own, "native" valve, blood clots rarely form after surgery, so you do not need to take a powerful blood thinner. Also, the durability of the repaired valve probably exceeds that of a valve made from animal tissue.

What if I already have a replaced valve? Most women whose valves have already been replaced usually suffer no problems during pregnancy. If you become pregnant and you have a mechanical valve, your doctor will want to switch you from Coumadin, which is taken orally, to a safer blood thinner, most likely heparin, which you must inject yourself. This issue underscores why, if you have such a problem, your doctor should be experienced in treating it. Such a physician will have a staff who can teach you to inject the heparin.

Cardiac Arrhythmia During Pregnancy

During pregnancy, women sometimes develop arrhythmia, or an abnormal heart rhythm. Usually, this does not signify anything worrisome. However, an arrhythmia that develops during pregnancy should be evaluated. If it is caused by an underlying heart problem, it may require treatment. In a few cases, an arrhythmia may be life-threatening.

Treatments for arrhythmias vary depending on the type of rhythm disturbance. Most methods for treating arrhythmias, such as drugs, pacemakers, low-frequency radio wave ablation, and even portable defibrillators, have been used successfully in pregnant women.

If an antiarrhythmic medication is indicated, your doctor should try to choose one that has been on the market long enough to acquire a safety record when given to pregnant women. This is an area where you should expect your doctor to be cautious, as some antiarrhythmic medications can be dangerous. See Chapters 11 and 13.

VERY SERIOUS HEART PROBLEMS IN PREGNANCY

Marfan's Syndrome

Marfan's syndrome technically is not a congenital heart defect, but a disease of the connective tissue. If you have Marfan's, but have not experienced problems, you most likely will have no complications during pregnancy. However, if before becoming pregnant you experience cardiovascular problems, they can become life threatening during pregnancy. Such problems can include dissection or tearing of the aorta, a dangerously leaky mitral valve, or congestive heart failure. There is also a 50 percent risk of passing the genetic disorder to your children. Under these circumstances, choosing to have a baby is a difficult decision. Before deciding, consider consulting a genetic counselor.

Pulmonary Hypertension

Pulmonary hypertension, or high blood pressure that builds up in the vessels that carry the blood from your heart to your lungs, is a threatening condition for both you and your unborn baby. This condition should not be confused with ordinary high blood pressure.

Sometimes, pulmonary hypertension can occur for no underlying reason, but other times, there is a medical cause, such as Eisenmenger syndrome, discussed previously. If you have pulmonary hypertension, your doctor may advise you not to become pregnant or to consider terminating the pregnancy. If you choose to continue your pregnancy, you and the fetus will have to be closely monitored, and may spend most of your pregnancy on bed rest and possibly on oxygen. The baby will be delivered as soon as it is judged safe to do so.

Pulmonary hypertension is by no means a common disease, but it does tend to afflict women more than men. The average age of women when they are diagnosed with it is 35. If you have pulmonary hypertension, you may be able to successfully bear a child, but you should consider yourself at extremely high risk and seek out very highly expert medical care.

Peripartum Cardiomyopathy

Peripartum cardiomyopathy is a rare but very serious disease that results in heart failure. It may appear for no apparent reason during the last month of pregnancy or shortly after delivery. Estimates vary, but it is thought to occur once in every 1,300 to 4,000 deliveries. Although it seems to occur for no apparent reason, there often turns out to be an unrecognized underlying cardiac disorder.

Signs and symptoms of peripartum cardiomyopathy are:

- The inability to breathe comfortably without being propped up
- Coughing
- A "pounding" heart beat, or palpitations
- High blood pressure

Peripartum cardiomyopathy appears most frequently in:
- Older women
- African-American women
- Women who have given birth before
- Women who are carrying multiple babies
- Women who experience high blood pressure disorders in pregnancy
- Women who develop high blood pressure after giving birth

There are cases where, with careful management, and sheer good fortune, women do give birth to healthy babies. If you develop this disease before you go into labor, however, the baby may be stillborn. There is also a 25 to 50 percent chance you will die during pregnancy. The causes of death include congestive heart failure, blood clots, and infection. Sometimes, after delivery, a woman recovers completely and her heart apparently returns to normal. But, if she becomes pregnant again, the condition can return, with even more disastrous results. This does not always occur, but it is the reason why doctors generally advise women who have experienced peripartum cardiomyopathy not to have more children.

♥ **Lifesaving Tip: Although peripartum cardiomyopathy is a disease that develops during pregnancy, its symptoms may show up even in the several weeks following delivery. If you experience such symptoms, contact your doctor immediately.**

Bacterial Endocarditis

This potentially deadly inflammation of the heart is rare during pregnancy, which is fortunate because it can be very difficult to treat. If your heart is already weakened, this disease can push you into congestive heart failure. The drugs used to treat it must be chosen with care because of potential harm to the unborn baby. The best precaution is to guard against developing endocarditis if you have a heart problem that puts you at risk. See Chapter 11.

Heart Attack

Because coronary artery disease more commonly occurs after menopause, heart attacks are unusual in women of childbearing years. They appear to be occurring with more frequency, however, particularly in pregnant women who are older, smoke, or have hyperlipidemia, a metabolic disease that causes abnormally high cholesterol levels. Heart attacks can also occur in women with mitral stenosis, in women whose heart valves have been replaced, and in women with certain types of heart rhythm disturbances.

While suffering a minor heart attack during pregnancy does not necessarily pose a danger to either mother or unborn baby, it can be dangerous if it occurs during labor or delivery.

HIGH BLOOD PRESSURE DISORDERS IN PREGNANCY

Hypertensive disorders are not directly heart-related, but are a major type of cardiovascular disorder in pregnant women. Because of the cardiovascular changes pregnant women undergo, such problems are not uncommon. Whether high blood pressure is pregnancy-induced or not, it can be very dangerous to a woman and her unborn baby.

Pregnancy-Induced Hypertension (PIH), Preeclampsia, and Eclampsia

Hypertensive conditions in pregnancy used to be called by one name, "toxemia." Nowadays, the terminology is a little more complicated. Some researchers like to classify hypertensive disorders of pregnancy into three distinct, progressive stages: pregnancy-induced hypertension, preeclampsia, and eclampsia. Others prefer to use "pregnancy-induced hypertension" as an umbrella term for all. Whatever the term used, such hypertensive disorders can mean serious problems for a woman and her unborn baby. The risk mounts in each progressive stage of hypertension.

An estimated one quarter of all women who give birth in the United States develop abnormally high blood pressure, or pregnancy-induced hypertension (PIH), by the end of their pregnancies. Between 6 and 7 percent of women with PIH go on to develop preeclampsia and about 5 percent of that group develops eclampsia. This is the most severe stage, and can result in seizures, coma, and even death.

A substantial list of factors is considered to put women at increased risk for developing this problem. Women at risk include:

- Teenagers and women over the age of 35
- African-American women (according to some studies)
- Women who are having their first pregnancy
- Women who have high blood pressure, diabetes, or kidney disease
- Women who have heart problems
- Women whose mothers had a hypertensive disorder in pregnancy

Any high blood pressure disorder is dangerous during pregnancy because your heart must work harder. This results in your blood vessels becoming constricted, reducing the amount of blood and nourishment the unborn baby receives. Hypertensive disorders also cause your body to manufacture less blood than it requires, making blood loss during delivery dangerous. For the unborn child, the chance of premature birth is greatly increased, as well as the chances of life-threatening disorders that can lead to death or severe permanent disabilities.

If you have PIH, you will probably not notice any symptoms. This condition is diagnosed by finding both high blood pressure and protein in the urine. If you are at risk for hypertension, your doctor may recommend you monitor your blood pressure at home.

Among the many mysteries of pregnancy, none is more baffling to doctors as to why some women get such hypertensive disorders and others do not. Speculation currently is centering on the cause being an abnormality that occurs as the placenta is being formed. Genetic factors are also being studied.

Preeclampsia is a very serious disorder during pregnancy, and currently there is no treatment for it. If a woman develops preeclampsia late in her pregnancy, the ideal treatment is to deliver the baby. If the disorder occurs too early in pregnancy for this to be considered, bed rest is often prescribed. While bed rest is not considered a treatment for preeclampsia, it may (with the emphasis on "may") potentially retard the disease's progression. Bed rest is also used for another reason: By lying in a certain position, you maximize the flow of the blood to the baby.

Since the cause of such hypertensive disorders is not known, there is no certain way to prevent it. However, several studies have shown that low-dose aspirin may prevent the development of such problems in women who are at high risk. The results of these studies are still preliminary, so a pregnant woman should discuss the pros and cons of such aspirin usage with her doctor. Of course, one should be sure to check with one's doctor before using any medication, including over-the-counter, vitamins, and herbal supplements.

❤ **Lifesaving Tip: If you are at risk of developing a hypertensive disorder in pregnancy, make sure your blood pressure and urine are tested frequently on a regular basis. If you develop this condition, even if you feel fine, follow your doctor's instructions to the letter. This is a condition that, if untreated, can worsen, gravely endangering both you and your unborn baby.**

A Word About Smoking and Pregnancy

There are plenty of excellent reasons to quit smoking if you are not pregnant. If you are pregnant, your need to quit becomes even more urgent. In addition to the hazard cigarette smoking presents to you, babies who are born to mothers who smoke are more likely to be born prematurely. Such babies are in danger of being born with such life-threatening lung conditions as respiratory distress syndrome and hyaline membrane disease. In addition, scientists have also found a possible link between mothers who smoke and sudden infant death syndrome. Studies have also shown that children of smoking parents have health problems as well, such as respiratory illness.

Many women find pregnancy a highly motivating time to quit smoking. If that is true in your case, congratulations. You may find it useful to consider how you will handle life without smoking after the baby is born. This way, you'll be less likely to turn to cigarettes if you are under stress of finding yourself in a situation where you are accustomed to smoking.

If You Are Advised Not to Have Children

It is very rare that a cardiologist advises a woman that, because of her heart problem, she should not become pregnant or that a pregnancy be terminated. If a cardiologist should tell you this, make certain the doctor is very experienced in dealing with your particular problem.

To Sum Up

If you have a heart problem, you may be concerned it will cast a shadow on the family you've been hoping for. But in the vast majority of cases, women with complicated heart problems who years ago could never hope to safely bear a child now can. It's very likely you will be among them.

9

~~~~~~~ΟΛΛΛΛΛ~~~~~~

When to See a Doctor

A STURDY-LOOKING WOMAN of 38, Maggie was determined not to let this bout of indigestion interfere with the church supper she had promised to oversee. True, her vague intestinal discomfort had intensified lately; handfuls of antacids didn't help anymore. But no one was going to call Maggie a wimp. After all, her mother had never shirked her responsibilities because of her health problems; the family still talked about the time Bridgett had refused to go to the hospital, and had delivered Maggie, and her twin brother, Patrick, at home. So no one was going to call her daughter a weakling.

Maggie did indeed finish working at the church supper, but, when she got home, she collapsed on the bed. When she could scarcely struggle out of bed the next day, she finally agreed to let her husband, Michael, take her to the doctor. He'd been begging her for months.

Tests showed Maggie did have a heart problem; in fact, she'd come within a hairs breadth of suffering a heart attack.

There are many women like Maggie. In a way, I was somewhat like her myself. When my physician first recommended I undergo a cardiac test at a local hospital, I managed to put it off until the fall. Things just came up; the car broke down, I had a magazine article to finish, we were going on vacation. I was so certain that my heart was fine, I actually felt sheepish when I finally did go to the hospital for the test. An old pal of mine from college was too terrified to tell anyone about her chest pain for over a year, so convinced was she that she had coronary artery disease. She finally spilled out the story to me in tears after learning about my surgery.

You should seek professional medical advice if you have any of the following signs or symptoms:

- Exceptional (for you) chest pain
- Frequent or severe palpitations
- Unexplained fainting
- Severe shortness of breath
- Overwhelming fatigue
- Bodily swelling

———

❤ **Lifesaving Tip: If you are experiencing what may be a heart attack, seek immediate medical help. The symptoms of a heart attack are dealt with in detail in Chapter 5. If you have other symptoms, make an appointment with your doctor. The information in this chapter is not offered to enable you to diagnose yourself, but is designed so you can help your doctor arrive at a correct diagnosis.**

———

Choosing a Doctor

If you experience chest pain or the other symptoms described in this chapter, start off with a visit to your family doctor. This can be an internist, a family practitioner, or primary care physician, the doctor to whom you turn for the majority of your health care needs.

Every woman should have a primary doctor who specializes in the health problems of adults. Too often, women rely on their gynecologist for all their medical advice. Remember, you're total well-being involves more than your reproductive system. Querying your husband or mother's doctor or your child's pediatrician is not good enough. Certainly, you and your family can share the same doctor, but the physician should be familiar with your individual medical history and physical health as well.

Primary Doctor or Cardiologist?

The reason for beginning with a visit to your primary physician, rather than a cardiologist, is that, especially in women, even symptoms such as chest pain usually turn out to be unrelated to the heart. If necessary, your primary physician can refer you to a cardiologist, or, if you don't receive what you consider adequate diagnosis and treatment, you can always decide to see a cardiologist on your own.

But we cannot stress this more strongly: *Never* overlook the importance of choosing an astute primary doctor. Some people carefully select a specialist but when it comes to their primary doctor, they aren't so choosy. They figure that if they do have a serious problem, their physician will refer them to a specialist. The fallacy in this thinking is this: If your primary doctor overlooks a problem, you may not be referred to the appropriate specialist until the problem has become severe.

Choosing a good doctor, though, is far from foolproof. Jeffrey T. Stern, a physician in Waterbury, Connecticut, enjoys asking his new patients this riddle: "What do you call the person who graduates last in their medical class?" The answer, of course, is "doctor." The meaning behind this humorous riddle is all too serious: When everyone is called "Doctor," how do you know who's good and who's not?

If you do not have a primary doctor, find one now, while you are well. This provides a "baseline" by which to measure what your health normally is like so that your physician can see more easily if something is amiss.

One place to start is by asking friends for a recommendation. If you're older, your friends probably have plenty of knowledge about doctors in your area, but if you're younger, this is usually not the case. If you are new to your area, contact your county medical society or local hospital for names of local doctors. Large libraries and many hospital libraries have directories containing the names of doctors along with their credentials. Nowadays, most people are covered by managed care companies that restrict their choice of doctors. Using the list of doctors supplied by your managed care company, you can go through the same steps to find the doctor of your choice. See Chapter 17.

Some doctors are willing to schedule a brief appointment in which to meet a prospective patient free of charge, but many doctors do not prefer to do this or are too busy. Still, you can tell a lot from your first visit.

Here are tips on choosing a doctor. Many of these tips hold true whether you're seeking a primary physician or a specialist.

Be a diploma reader. Make sure the doctor graduated from a reputable medical school and performed his or her residency at a major hospital. One way to find the top hospitals is to check the annual *U.S. News &*

World Report issue on the best hospitals in the country. If the medical school degree says "Alpha Omega Alpha" even better; it means your doctor was in the top 10 percent of the class!

Is the doctor board-certified? This is an added assurance of quality; it means the doctor has successfully completed an intensive training and testing program in one of 24 medical specialties, such as internal medicine or family practice. This is obviously important if you're seeking a specialist, but it also insures minimum competency if you are seeking a primary physician. A doctor might be "board-eligible," which means he or she has had the requisite training but has not passed necessary examinations. If the doctor is young, this is certainly understandable. In some specialties, certification regulations can change; a good cardiologist, for example, might not be board-certified, but have considerable experience and a solid professional reputation.

What hospital is the doctor affiliated with? You're healthy now, but eventually you may need a hospital stay. Doctors receive "privileges" to practice only at certain hospitals. Bear in mind that, in choosing your doctor, you may also be choosing a hospital.

Does the doctor respect your time? Any doctor may have an emergency that keeps you waiting, but this should not be the norm. Your doctor's time is valuable, but so is yours.

When does the doctor return calls? Being able to reach your doctor by telephone is important; ask when the doctor returns calls. The correct answer should be "as soon as possible" or during a specific time of the day set aside for answering patients' telephone calls. Who wants to find out she needs a prescription long after the pharmacy has closed?

Does your doctor invest in laboratories or services you might be referred to? Your doctor should earn a fair fee for treating you; you should not have to wonder if the tests or treatments being ordered for you are designed to line his or her pockets.

Does the doctor communicate well? Two-way communication is an essential part of keeping you well. You should never be made to feel stupid by asking a question. It's important to feel comfortable asking questions and you should receive answers in terms you can understand. If you feel comfortable talking to your doctor, you can ask about information you may have heard in the media about new diagnostic tests or treatments. Even if the information isn't applicable to you, this can open an important dialogue between you and your physician. You should never feel that there is something you cannot discuss with your doctor.

♥ **Lifesaving Tip: Your doctor is most likely a busy person, but you should feel as if your visit, your concerns, and your well-being are the major focus of his or her attention.**

Changing Doctors

Some people are "doctor shoppers" and go from one to the other. Others tend to stick to the same doctor out of loyalty, long after their confidence has evaporated. Doctors are not infallible. If you cannot talk comfortably to your doctor about your problems, think your doctor doesn't take your problems seriously, or lack faith in your doctor's expertise, by all means consider a change.

♥ **Mindsaving Tip: Remember that you and your doctor are members of a team whose goal is to keep you in good health.**

The All-Important Second Opinion

Yvette's face glows as she watches her mom, Esther, run across the road to greet her. "Isn't that wonderful? I never thought I would see that again," beams Yvette. After her mother's heart attack, Yvette was told that her mother would die. She bitterly recalls the day the doctor told her and her sister that "we should take Mom home and make her comfortable, because there was nothing more that could be done for her."

Fortunately for Esther, her daughters took their mother to another doctor, who recommended a coronary bypass operation. In Esther's case, getting a second opinion literally saved her life by enabling her to obtain the surgery she needed. A second opinion can also be very important in keeping you from undergoing unnecessary surgery.

When to Get a Second Opinion

Unfortunately, there's often no clear-cut answer as to whether or not you should seek a second opinion. Certainly do so if there is any doubt in your mind that your doctor's recommendation is the wisest course. Examples of situations for which you might seek a second opinion include:

- If you're troubled about symptoms that seem cardiac-related, but your doctor brushes off your concerns.
- If you're taking cardiovascular drugs but your symptoms are getting worse, and your doctor is not inclined to investigate further.
- If the doctor seemed to quick to recommend open-heart surgery, or there was disagreement among consultants regarding its appropriateness.

❤ **Lifesaving Tip: It sometimes seems that a person is more willing to seek out a second opinion about a problem with their car than their heart. You should consider a second opinion if you have *any* serious doubts about your doctor's recommendation.**

How to Get a Second Opinion

Sometimes, people are very afraid they'll hurt their doctor's feelings, but if your doctor is angry about your wanting another opinion, or a consultation, then he or she really should not be your doctor.

If you value your relationship with your doctor, you'll want to maintain it. So be diplomatic about your request for a second opinion.

Consumer advocates disagree on how to find a doctor for that second opinion. Some contend that doctors tend to stick together, so someone recommended by your doctor is likely to be only a "rubber stamp." Others contend that since your doctor knows your medical problems best, asking him or her for a recommendation is only logical. It's best to obey your instincts. If you're confident your doctor's recommendation will be objective, follow it. If you are uncertain, contact your county medical society for a list of names, or check your library for a multivolume reference set called *The Directory of Medical Specialists*.

And a third opinion? You've gotten your second opinion, and it's the opposite of the first. This can happen, especially in an area such as heart problems, where experts sometimes disagree. You may have to seek out a third opinion to get a tiebreaker. Once you have three opinions, it's probably time to make a decision. Some people will keep going until they find a doctor to agree with them; eventually they may, but there's no guarantee that they're getting the best medical advice

If you have any doubt about the wisdom of seeking a second opinion, here's what Esther, Yvette's mother, who is now fully recovered from her surgery, has to say. "I remember asking my doctor if I'd be feeling good in time to put up my winter storm windows. He said 'Sure.' It turns out he didn't even think I'd live that long! Now, whenever I put those windows up in the fall and take them down in the spring, I think of that."

ALL ABOUT CHEST PAIN

- Joanne, 43, is a crackerjack realtor who thrives on the pressure of meeting sales deadlines. When she wasn't working, she enjoyed going out to dine on her favorite meal, a cocktail followed by a well-marbled steak. Lately, though, she'd been having chest pains, attacks that left this usually fearless woman scared to death. "It was a very sharp pain and seemed to be coming right from the center of my heart," she says. "I was terrified. I was sure I was having a heart attack."
- Roberta began feeling lousy when she was vacationing in the Caribbean. After dining, she became conscious of "an odd feeling in my chest." The pain seemed so mild, she thought it was indigestion.

The chest pain Joanne was convinced was due to a heart-related cause turned out to stem from a problem in her esophagus, while Roberta's mild "indigestion" was her first warning sign of coronary artery disease.

Confused? You're not alone. Especially in women, heart problems can be tricky to diagnose from the symptoms of chest pain alone. When certain characteristic chest pain occurs in men, the chances are greater that the problem is heart disease. Chest pain in women, particularly in younger women, is often unrelated to the heart.

❤ **Mindsaving Tip: Symptoms of heart problems can be very worrisome, but remember that many nonserious conditions can manifest themselves as truly frightening symptoms. Only your doctor can decide whether they are cause for concern.**

Chest Pain in Women

Virtually all women experience chest pain at some point in their lives. Because men are more likely to develop coronary artery disease, their chest pain often turns out to be from blockage of their coronary arteries. Women are at least as likely as men to suffer from chest pain, but it is less likely your ache stems from heart disease, and pinpointing the cause of your chest pain may prove either straightforward or infuriatingly difficult. That said, however, if you are experiencing chest pain that is unusual for you, discuss it with your doctor.

Historically, women who complained of chest pain were not taken seriously. Such pain in women was initially interpreted as not dangerous, and though this was later proved false, the conclusion stuck, and a doctor might be too quick to assume that the woman seated before him did not have heart disease because "women just don't get heart disease." Although much of that thinking has changed, some doctors still seem chained to it.

That cardiac tests cannot always pinpoint the cause of all chest pain only adds to the problem. Your doctor may tell you your chest pain is "all in your head." Since chest pain is sometimes caused by anxiety, this can compound the confusion. Further complicating matters is the fact that, of all possible cardiac symptoms, chest pain is the scariest. Pain in the chest makes the phrase "heart attack" leap automatically to mind, in a similar way that finding a lump in the breast raises instantaneous fears of breast cancer. But just as most breast lumps are not malignant, chest pain usually doesn't mean you have a heart problem. Read on; you'll discover there are ailments that manifest themselves as chest pain but aren't related to your heart at all.

Diagnosing Chest Pain

Your own observations can provide your doctor with the most useful clues of all. Doctors often forget this and order uncomfortable, expensive, and sometimes risky tests in lieu of spending the time listening to you.

One Person's Pain Is Another's Discomfort

To understand chest pain, let's talk about how you perceive pain. You feel pain not directly, but as it is interpreted through your central nervous system. Your central nervous system is made up of your brain and spinal cord, and your peripheral nerves, which contains nerve cells, or neurons, within every part of your body. These neurons can be stimulated by an outside force; when stub your toe, for example. Any stimulation along the pain pathway from your toe to your brain may also be perceived as "stubbed toe."

Another system of your body also comes into play here: your autonomic nervous system. This system regulates the functions of your body without your being aware of it, and can modify your perception of pain as well. The autonomic nervous system does some of its work through hormone-like substances, chemicals that your body secretes and that keep your body functioning smoothly.

Individuals vary in their response to these substances. Take the hormone adrenaline. Caffeine serves as a stimulus for the production of adrenaline, but some people are more sensitive to the effects of this hormone than others. So, while one cup of coffee is enough to give one person the jitters, another may guzzle cup after cup without much effect.

How you perceive cardiac pain depends in part on your sensitivity to adrenaline and the chemical mediator, adenosine. Those who are more receptive may be hypersensitive to chest pain and feel rapid or skipped heartbeats more intensely.

Think of pain sensitivity as a continuum. On one end are people with heart disease so advanced they should feel excruciating pain, yet they feel nothing, a condition known as "silent ischemia." On the other end of the continuum are those who experience severe chest pain for no known clinical cause. Both these groups suffer from malfunctions in their cardiac pain sensitivity. This sensitivity may affect the quality and intensity of pain you feel, whether it's caused by heart problems or something that has nothing to do with your heart.

CHEST PAIN FROM CORONARY OBSTRUCTION

Heart Attack

A heart attack, medically known as a myocardial infarction, occurs when the flow of oxygenated blood to the heart is completely cut off, resulting in the injury of all, or part, of the heart muscle. Coronary artery disease leading to a coronary blood clot is the most common cause of heart attack. A rarer cause is a sustained coronary spasm, which pinches off blood flow in arteries that appear otherwise healthy. For a detailed discussion of a heart attack, see Chapter 5.

Angina Pectoris: "Classic" Heart Pain

Angina pectoris is the classic type of chest pain, which occurs when your heart muscle does not receive enough oxygen because of a narrowing in the coronary arteries. It most often occurs during physical exertion or stress, and is similar to, but less severe than, the chest pain from a heart attack. Since the arteries are narrowed, but not blocked, the pain is relieved when the need for increased blood flow subsides.

Such pain is usually the result of coronary artery disease. If you are a young woman, it's unlikely, but by no means impossible, that you're experiencing it. Such pain can also result from coronary spasm, elevated pressures within the heart from malfunctioning heart valves, or from a congenital birth defect, although the mechanism that causes the pain is slightly different.

You may be having angina if:

- You experience tightness, squeezing, heaviness, constriction, or a sensation of pressure. You may instinctively clench your fist close to your heart when describing it.
- The pain sometimes moves from where you felt it at first, radiating from the middle of your chest, to the base of your neck, or to your left shoulder, down either your left or right arm, or into your jaw and sometimes your shoulder blade.
- The pain lasts at least a few minutes and is relieved by rest, or by taking a nitroglycerin tablet under the tongue.
- The pain comes on when you are exerting yourself—running for a bus, exercising, carrying heavy packages, walking in the cold or climbing stairs. Or you may feel it in times of emotional stress—during arguments or in an atmosphere of tension.
- With the pain, you may also feel anxious or unable to breathe.

❤ **Lifesaving Tip: If you've only just begun experiencing it, the pain from angina can be a signal that you may be close to suffering a heart attack. Do not delay; make an immediate appointment with your doctor.**

Vasospastic Angina

Lately, almost every night at midnight, Irene's heart begins racing and keeps her up most of the night. The dull pain, which radiates to her back and down her arm, scares her because it's "just like the warning sign of a heart attack." When she manages to fall asleep, the chest pain awakens her. Her symptoms never come on when she's active; only when she's resting. Irene is experiencing the symptoms of vasospastic or variant angina, known also as Prinzmetal's angina, named after the doctor who first described it. This type of angina results from a blockage of blood flow to the heart caused not by permanent narrowing of the coronary arteries but by a spasm of the coronary artery.

You may have vasospastic angina if:

- The nature and the location of the chest pain is similar to that of angina pectoris, but the pain occurs when you're at rest or in the early hours of the morning, sometimes repeatedly each night.
- The pain lasts longer, sometimes up to a half hour, and intensifies quickly.

Variant angina seems most often (but not always) to affect women who are relatively young and heavy smokers. Sometimes, episodes seem to be brought on by stress; in Irene's case, she suspects that the burden of caring for her aging mother contributed to her condition.

❤ **Lifesaving Tip: If you are suffering from what appears to be angina, no matter what type it seems to be, be seen by a physician.**

Atypical Chest Pain Syndromes

Sometimes, women experience chest pains that are caused by their heart, but don't fall into these two larger categories of angina. These are known as atypical chest pain syndromes, and they can be among the most difficult problems to diagnose. A syndrome, by the way, is a group of symptoms that occur together and constitute a specific condition.

Microvascular Angina

This is a type of chest pain that is not caused by disease of the larger coronary arteries or coronary spasm. It affects mostly women; according to one study, 72 percent of 200 patients suffering from this kind of pain turned out to be female. They weren't old, either; they ranged in age from 28 to 65, and their average age was 49.

There are no specific types of tests to pinpoint this problem, and it doesn't turn up on X rays, which is why it can be so difficult to diagnose. The chest pain in this case results from problems in the functioning of the microvascular circulation system. This problem also goes by the somewhat mysterious-sounding name, "Syndrome X."

Ever since the mid-1960s, when the existence of such a problem was first raised, the existence of Syndrome X has been hotly debated. Some believe this chest pain is psychological, but, more and more, evidence is mounting that this type of pain does come from the heart. In the last several years, multiple studies have been published confirming that angina can occur as a result of spasm of the microscopic blood vessels of the heart.

Your heart receives blood from the large coronary blood vessels, which are part of your cardiovascular circulatory system. But you also have a microcirculatory system, a network of tiny blood vessels that branch from the large coronary vessels and that in turn feed oxygen to each of the millions of cells that make up your heart. If these tiny vessels go into spasm, and the blood flow is impeded, anginal chest pain would result. If you're a person with heightened cardiac sensitivity, the pain would feel even worse.

This chest pain sometimes comes on during or after exertion and, in terms of feeling, can be indistinguishable from the pain of angina pectoris. It usually lasts at least 30 minutes or even longer. Diagnosing this problem is largely a matter of eliminating the most common cause of such pain, which is coronary artery disease. Sometimes, if you suffer from angina-type pain but have *absolutely* no risk factors for coronary heart disease, your doctor may decide to treat you for microvascular angina without ordering further tests. If there is a reason to suspect you might have coronary artery disease, you'll probably undergo further testing.

Although microvascular angina may not lead to serious heart problems, it can be very disabling. Susan, a 29-year-old secretary, suffered chest pain so severe she often ended up in the emergency room before her problem was diagnosed. Fortunately, using commonly available cardiovascular medication can often relieve the chest pain of microvascular angina.

Chest Pain From Mitral Valve Prolapse

Mitral valve prolapse, a common heart valve anomaly, sometimes results in chest pain, although the reason for this is not clearly understood. For more information, see Chapter 6.

You may have an atypical chest pain syndrome if:

• The pain is angina-like but isn't predictably related to effort.
• The pain can be achy, sharp, "knife-like," or stabbing. If dull, it may last hours; if sharp, only seconds.
• The first time you feel the pain it starts so suddenly you can remember what you were doing when it began; after that, it comes and goes.
• You may experience additional symptoms such as a pounding heart beat, dizziness, and fatigue.

OTHER CARDIAC CAUSES OF CHEST PAIN

Chest pain from other causes related to your heart can sometimes occur. Two, which are uncommon but serious, are pericarditis and pulmonary hypertension.

Pericarditis

"It felt like a knitting needle was sticking in my chest every time I took a breath," said Diane of the chest pain, that suddenly appeared soon after she recovered from a bout with the flu. It turned out she had pericarditis, an inflammation of the delicate sac that encloses your heart. Pericarditis is usually caused by a viral infection, but it can also occur following a heart attack or open-heart surgery. On occasion, pericarditis occurs for no specific reason. Pericarditis is treated by bed rest and anti-inflammatory drugs, or if required, steroids. If untreated, pericarditis can become very serious.

You may have pericarditis if:

- The pain comes on suddenly, sometimes after an upper respiratory infection.
- The pain is usually sharp and worsens if you take a deep breath.
- The pain worsens, or is relieved, if you change your posture.
- Your pain may be accompanied by fever.

Pulmonary Hypertension

This very serious type of high blood pressure develops within the blood vessels of your lungs and, if untreated, can lead to heart failure. It sometimes develops in the presence of lung disease or some types of congenital heart defects. A symptom of heart failure from pulmonary hypertension is a generalized swelling of the body, especially noticeable in the abdomen. Pulmonary hypertension is discussed further in Chapters 7 and 8.

NON-CARDIAC CHEST PAIN: A CASE OF "MISTAKEN IDENTITY"

Remember Joanne, whose story was related early in this chapter? She learned that chest pain can be deceiving. Sometimes, although the pain you feel seems to come directly from your heart, that may not be the case at all.

How can this be? Since you perceive pain only as your brain interprets it, your brain may misinterpret or "confuse" these signals, according to one theory that seeks to explain how some common non-cardiac disorders can result in chest pain. Imagine your central nervous system as a telephone system, with a bundle of nerves encased by the spinal cord as the telephone lines, and your brain acting as the switchboard. Pain messages travel along the telephone lines, sometimes sharing them, as would callers on a party line. With all these messages traveling back and forth, occasionally the lines can get crossed. The result is pain from "signal confusion," or "mistaken identity."

Non-cardiac causes of chest pain:
- Esophageal irritation and spasm (dysfunction)
- Osteoarthritis of the neck
- Gas in the colon
- Peptic ulcers and gallbladder disease

Esophageal Dysfunction

Because your esophagus and your heart are so near one another, the theory of "signal confusion" explains why pain signals from your esophagus may be misinterpreted by your brain as coming from your heart. In fact, the symptoms of this disorder often mimic the symptoms of pain from coronary artery disease. Such malfunctions can occur as esophageal spasms, or as esophageal reflux, an inflammation of the esophagus caused by regurgitation of some of your stomach acid into your esophagus.

Your esophagus is a muscular tube that carries liquid and chewed food from the back of the throat to the stomach. Its function is to propel food downward into the stomach where it is readied for passage into your small intestine. Your esophagus has muscular valves on each end that relax, allowing the food to pass through.

Normally, when food is not passing through, the lower valve remains closed. But if this lower valve does not shut tightly enough, some of the acidic contents from your stomach may splash back, irritating your esophagus and causing inflammation or, sometimes, spasm. The result can be chest pain.

Often, but not always, esophageal reflux is seen in women who are overweight. Carrying packages against your stomach can cause extra pressure that aggravates this condition. So can smoking, anxiety, alcohol, and heavy meals. Some people with a hiatal hernia have this problem as well.

If your doctor suspects you have esophageal dysfunction, you will probably be referred to a gastroenterologist, a physician trained in the management of digestive system disorders. This specialist can perform a test called an esophagogastroscopy, an examination of the esophagus by means of a long, flexible fiberoptic viewing tube inserted through your mouth, which can determine if the lining of your esophagus is inflamed. Even specialists have their preferred sub-specialties, so ask your doctor to refer you to a gastroenterologist who prefers to concentrate on the esophagus.

Usually, just being reassured you do not have a heart problem, watching your diet, and using antacids will ease these symptoms. If not, such medications as Zantac, Pepcid, or Prilosec may provide relief. Nitroglycerin will sometimes relax esophageal spasm, but may further confuse you and your doctor about the source of the pain. People who have increased cardiac sensitivity can suffer severely from this problem, while others may not notice anything amiss.

Osteoarthritis of the Neck

Another type of chest pain that's tricky to discern may occur if you have osteoarthritis of the neck. There, pain that actually originates in your neck may be interpreted as coming from the chest. In fact, this is one of the most common causes of chest pain in women, and may feel just like angina pectoris, the pain from coronary artery disease.

Known as wear-and-tear arthritis, osteoarthritis is the degenerative type of arthritis that occurs at various joints in your body. If this inflammation occurs in your neck, your body responds by forming calcium deposits, or "bony spurs," which are situated next to the pain neurons that carry pain messages from your chest. These spurs dig into the nerve, and the result is "signal confusion," as your brain misinterprets these pain signals as radiating from your heart.

Although osteoarthritis is thought of as an elderly person's disease, it sometimes occurs in younger people, and it tends to be inherited. You may have osteoarthritis of the neck if your chest pain occurs when you're carrying a briefcase or doing activities such as rearranging furniture, that may strain your neck, or after such activities. Anti-inflammatory drugs, heat, neck traction, or other types of physical therapy may provide relief. A diagnosis of osteoarthritis of the neck can be confirmed by the presence of bony spurs seen on a neck X ray.

Gas in the Colon

An old-fashioned problem like gas can occasionally manifest itself as chest pain. In this case, gas becomes trapped in a loop of colon, or large bowel, located just under the left side of your diaphragm, the muscle that divides your abdominal and chest cavities. Distension of the loop of bowel and spasm probably produce the pain. This pain can be mistaken as coming from the heart because of the signal confusion discussed earlier.

If gas is a persistent problem, try and find out the cause. Excessive gas can be caused by irritable bowel syndrome (also called spastic colon), which is accompanied by alternating diarrhea and constipation. Another source of excessive gas is lactose intolerance, in which your body is unable to digest the lactose, or milk sugar, found in dairy products. This condition also causes cramps, bloating and diarrhea. Eating a dairy-free diet is the best way to ease symptoms from lactose intolerance.

Ulcers and Gallbladder Disease

Peptic ulcers or gallbladder attacks can sometimes cause pain that mimics that associated with angina or a heart attack. To add to the confusion, heart attacks may often be associated with nausea and even vomiting, symptoms that are also associated with the gastrointestinal illness cited above. It's useful to note that pain from peptic ulcers generally occurs more in the lower central area of the chest than does the pain from coronary artery disease, and gallbladder pain more often occurs on the right side of the upper abdomen after meals.

Pain From Your Chest Wall

Shingles

Anna, a 69 year-old woman, was brought to the doctor's office by her worried daughter, Ellen. Over the past several days, Anna had been suffering from sharp chest pains. Anna's husband of 45 years had died recently of a heart attack, and Ellen was terrified her mother was going to die soon too.

The pain Anna was experiencing did indeed resemble pain from coronary artery disease, but the cause was shingles, known medically as herpes zoster. The same virus that causes chicken pox causes shingles. Anna had chicken pox as a child and a few of the viral organisms remained dormant in her nervous system for years. The aging of Anna's body, coupled with the stress of her husband's death, provided the virus with the perfect conditions to become reactivated. The excruciatingly painful disease of shingles was the result.

Shingles manifests itself in a telltale rash, but it may not occur until several weeks after the chest pain has begun. An astute doctor can often diagnose shingles based on hearing details about the pain and when it occurred. For example, the pain of shingles characteristically begins underneath the left arm and radiates around the back. It may start off as vague discomfort; the sufferer may think she's pulled a muscle, but, instead of disappearing, the pain gets worse.

Shingles is not easy to treat, can cause unbearable pain, and can recur. An anti-viral treatment called acyclovir (Zovirax), if started early enough, can be helpful. Until recently, there was no treatment for the painful rash; however, an ointment called capsaicin, made from a derivative of hot peppers, has been found to help. An anti-depression drug called amitriptyline can also relieve the pain.

Muscular Pain

Very buxom women may suffer chest pain from the weight of their breasts. Sometimes, chest pain can arise from problems with the muscular and skeletal structure of the chest.

Your rib cage is connected to the breastbone with cartilage, a type of hard, rubbery tissue which enables your ribs to flex against the other bony structures of your rib cage. If these rib joints become inflamed, a painful condition called costochondritis can result. It can cause chest pain and lead you to fear you may have breast cancer. Sometimes, costochondritis is caused by a virus and follows a respiratory flu-like illness, but it can also occur for no apparent reason. A doctor can often diagnose this problem because of a characteristic tenderness. Costrochondritis is treated similarly to arthritis, with heat, anti-inflammatory drugs such as aspirin and, in severe cases, steroids. For persistent problems, a long-acting steroid is sometimes injected. Tietze syndrome, a similar type of pain and swelling of the rib joints is treated with heat and anti-inflammatory drugs.

Chest Pain From Anxiety

From an era when too many women were told their chest pain was "all in their head" and too many tranquilizers were swallowed, we've moved into an area when the pendulum is in danger of swinging too far over to the other side. The simple fact is that there are many different causes for chest pain, and anxiety remains one of them.

In the same way that anxiety can cause a tension headache, it can also tighten the muscles in your chest wall. Tension can also contribute to spasms of both your large coronary blood vessels and the vessels of your microvascular circulatory system. The result can be chest pain.

If your doctor tells you that your chest pain stems from anxiety, don't immediately dismiss the idea. Think about it. Sometimes, we don't recognize anxiety in ourselves, so it might be worthwhile to seek an evaluation from an expert, such as a psychologist, a psychiatrist, or a psychiatric social worker. Avoid a self-proclaimed therapist or someone who tends to view all problems through a favorite therapeutic prism, such as believing all symptoms are related to allergies that can be cured by dietary changes. If you are convinced anxiety is not the cause, you can choose to return to your original doctor and request a further evaluation. If you are rebuffed, or you feel your symptoms are not being taken seriously, go to another doctor.

OTHER SYMPTOMS

While chest pain is the most common, and usually the scariest, of symptoms that may seem to be originating in your heart, other symptoms can accompany heart problems as well. They can be caused by coronary artery disease or occur in the presence of other heart problems, such as valvular disease or congenital defects. Such symptoms can occur alone, or you may suffer from two, three, or even all of them.

Palpitations

Alicia, the 29-year-old owner of a fashionable women's clothing shop, was in the midst of compiling her monthly inventory report when her heart began to pound. It happened again a few weeks later, while she was reading, then again the following week, while she was window-shopping after work. "I just felt like my heart was beating so hard, it was coming out of my chest," she recalls. It turns out Alicia had an arrhythmia, a disturbance of her heartbeat rhythm.

Most of us experience some arrhythmia all the time, and don't even notice them. When you become aware of them, they're called palpitations, which is a sensation that has been described as a heart that seems to bump, pound, jump, flop, flutter, or race.

There are different types of arrhythmias, ranging from harmless ones to some that are very serious and can even result in death. If you have an arrhythmia, your doctor will want to determine what type it is and whether it requires treatment.

You may have a serious type of palpitation when:

- The palpitation occurs in association with pain or causes severe shortness of breath.
- The palpitation is associated with fainting or severe lightheadedness.
- The palpitation lasts for many hours.

- There is a history of unexplained sudden death of young people in your family.

Arrhythmias are discussed further in Chapter 11.

Fainting

Laura, a 22-year-old who was working in her first advertising job after graduating from college, passed out in a Manhattan bar with some friends after work. She regained consciousness within minutes and forgot about it until a few weeks later, when she passed out again at work and was brought to a hospital emergency room. Her parents were beside themselves with worry, as was she. "I know there must be something wrong with me, because I've never had fainting spells before," she said.

Fainting can be one of the most frightening of symptoms. It can also be very dangerous if you fall and hurt yourself or faint while driving. But the reason behind most fainting spells is usually not serious.

Medically known as syncope, fainting is a temporary loss of consciousness due to insufficient oxygen reaching the brain.

Vasovagal Syncope

Laura's case, frightening as it was, turned out to be from a usually harmless syndrome called vasovagal syncope. Typically, vasovagal syncope is caused by overstimulation of the vagus nerve, a major nerve that runs from the brain to the stomach and helps control breathing and blood circulation.

This type of fainting condition can be triggered by many conditions. Fear or anxiety brings it about in some people; they faint when they hear bad news, or visit the dentist, or see blood. Being in a hot, stuffy room, eating a large meal, taking a hot bath, exercising if you're dehydrated or have been hyperventilating or even straining to have a bowel movement can also bring on such fainting.

A brief feeling of warmth, lightheadedness, nausea, and impending collapse usually precedes episodes of syncope. Fortunately, such fainting spells are relatively harmless and leave no ill effects.

Sometimes, women suffer from fainting if their blood pressure falls when they change position abruptly, such as standing up after sitting or lying down. Such episode can also be a side effect of some forms of antidepressants or drugs to control high blood pressure, or can be caused by nerve damage from diabetes. This type of syncope is called postural hypotension.

While many women occasionally suffer a fainting spell, others can faint with such frequency that their lives become disrupted. This was the case with Mary Ann, a 23-year-old who adores riding roller coasters, but has been known to faint when doing nothing more strenuous than fixing her hair.

Because of her fainting spells, Mary Ann is participating in a research project run by Dr. Fetnat M. Fouad-Tarazi, who specializes in syncope at the Cleveland Clinic. Dr. Fouad-Tarazi is one of the developers of a new type of study that is becoming a standard in the evaluation of syncope, the head-up tilt. When Mary Ann's feet are tilted downward on a tilt table, the response of her blood pressure and pulse provide hints regarding her diagnosis and the underlying circulatory abnormalities can be identified. By studying patients like Mary Ann, Dr. Fouad-Tarazi is finding information to help patients like her.

FAINTING FROM CARDIAC CAUSES

Some heart problems can manifest themselves as fainting. You may have a serious form of fainting if you pass out suddenly, without the warning period of lightheadedness, dizziness and nausea—one instant, you're fine, and the next instant, you're on the floor. This type of fainting can indicate a problem with your heart valve or can be a sign of a dangerous arrhythmia, or heart rhythm malfunction. Such problems can even result in sudden death.

❤ **Lifesaving Tip: If you are in good health, and you faint in a hot, crowded room, or if you are anxious or scared, check with your doctor, but don't be unduly alarmed. If, on the other hand, you suffer an unexplained fainting spell, or faint repeatedly, and you have heart or circulatory problems, or have risk factors for a heart attack or stroke, contact your doctor immediately.**

Shortness of Breath

Pearl, a 62-year-old town librarian, enjoyed walks with her friend along the shore. Lately, though, she's had to stop frequently to rest. Her husband noticed her huffing and puffing and insisted she see a doctor. Her doctor determined that her shortness of breath stemmed from a failing heart valve, the result of a bout of rheumatic fever she'd suffered as a child, and the valve had to be replaced. "My shortness of breath came on so gradually I barely noticed it. I just assumed it was because I was getting older," said Pearl.

As a sign of cardiac problems, shortness of breath, or, as it is termed medically, dyspnea, can be difficult to pin down. It can come on suddenly or gradually. It can stem from a problem with the heart or with the lungs.

But shortness of breath doesn't always indicate a health problem. Sometimes, it's a problem of perception. For example, if you were a star tennis player in college, when you pick up a racket again five years after you graduate, you may find yourself short of breath. Most likely, this simply means you are out of condition. Or, if you're an older person, your body is unable to transform oxygen into energy as efficiently as it used to, so you probably can't walk to the store as briskly as you once did.

Since everyone can become short of breath under certain circumstances, you need to figure out whether your shortness of breath is normal. One way to do this is to see how you feel if you climb one, two, or three flights of stairs. Virtually everyone, no matter their age, should be able to climb one flight of stairs and feel only slightly winded, if at all. If you can't, you should tell your doctor. Another form of shortness of breath that may indicate a heart problem occurs when you are lying down, or can awaken you from sleeping. If this occurs, and you don't have allergies or asthma that can make sleeping uncomfortable, see your doctor.

If you are short of breath, ask yourself:

- Could your shortness of breath be due to overweight, poor physical conditioning, asthma, or respiratory allergies?
- Under what conditions do you get short of breath? Exercising? Relaxing? Sleeping?
- Try to quantify your shortness of breath. Can you climb one flight of stairs without becoming uncomfortable? Two?

❤ Lifesaving Tip: You should contact your doctor if just walking up one flight of stairs makes you very short of breath, if you awaken from sleep short of breath, or if you have a heart problem and become very short of breath.

Fatigue

Ellen, a 34-year-old divorced mother of three, juggles her freelance writing assignments with teaching and research jobs. She's so tired, she's tempted to fall into bed right after dinner. Her friend, Pam, a newly minted accountant, works 60-hour weeks trying to become a partner in her national firm. Pam's sister, Sally, a medical secretary, works full-time, makes a gourmet dinner for her husband when she comes home, then cleans the house. She's exhausted, too. Such instances are so common, its no wonder "chronic sleep deprivation" is becoming our new national malady.

Given all this, it's important to remember that there are plenty of reasons for being tired besides problems having to do with your heart. But since cardiac problems can manifest themselves as fatigue, it's important to determine whether you're just plan tired or may be sick.

As with shortness of breath, perception can come into play here. If you were once an avid ballroom dancer and start whirling around the floor after an absence of ten years, it's normal to be tired quickly. But if you're accustomed to dancing the night away every Saturday and suddenly find yourself spent after a dance or two, that could signal a problem.

If you're always tired, ask yourself:

- Are you sleepy? If you're working very hard or juggling many activities, and you're ready for bed at 6:30 P.M., you probably are suffering from a shortage of sleep.
- Are you depressed? Depression is a common cause of fatigue, and may come upon you without your realizing it. Some other signs of serious depression are insomnia, crying spells, and suicidal thoughts. If this is happening to you, or you realize you're seriously depressed, seek help.
- Are you eating right? If you're too busy, it's also very likely you're skipping meals or eating on the run. A faulty diet may be the cause of your fatigue.
- Is your hair coarse and brittle and your skin dry, and has your sex drive gradually disappeared? If so, you may have an underactive thyroid gland.
- Do you have other symptoms, such as fever, unexplained weight loss, and loss of appetite? While you may not have a heart problem,

you may have another serious illness, such as mononucleosis, hepatitis, or even cancer. Make an appointment to see your doctor immediately.

- Have you suddenly become exhausted by doing the things you're accustomed to doing? If so, again, seeing your doctor is in order.

Swelling

Edema, or swelling, can occur throughout your body. In women, the most common cause is the type of bloating you can experience just before your menstrual period. Peripheral venous disease, in which the veins of the leg become all stretched out and sometimes plugged, can result in swelling. However, edema can also be a sign of congestive heart failure. In this case, it's usually first noticed in the feet and ankles and progressively worsens. If you have this type of progressive swelling, see your doctor.

Heart Murmur

Technically, a heart murmur is not a symptom that you feel; it is a clinical finding that is discovered by listening to your heart with a stethoscope. However, we are including heart murmur in this chapter because it is sometimes an important clue whose significance is sometimes overlooked.

Normally, your heartbeat consists of two sounds, which are made by the opening and closing of your heart valves as blood passes through them. This sounds basically like "lub" followed by "dub," or together, "lub-dub." Using a stethoscope, these sounds can be heard more clearly, along with any abnormal additional sounds, some of which are called "heart murmurs." When they do not represent a significant problem, they are termed "innocent" murmurs. However, murmurs sometimes can indicate such problems as a malfunctioning heart valve or a congenital heart defect.

Years ago, doctors were often reluctant to mention to patients that they had heart murmurs because they were concerned such news alone would turn otherwise healthy adults into cardiac invalids. Today, diagnostic procedures can determine whether or not your heart murmur denotes a serious problem.

To check out your heart murmur further, your doctor will consider having you undergo an echocardiogram. If your doctor demurs, consider asking for a referral to a cardiologist. Your heart murmur may very well be "innocent" but it is always good practice to know for certain. Notes Dr. Roger Mee, world-renowned Cleveland Clinic pediatric congenital heart surgeon, "A so-called innocent murmur may be the first and only indication that something is awry in the normal development of a person's heart."

💙 Lifesaving Tip: It is very common for children and adolescents to have "innocent" heart murmurs. This is very true for pregnant women as well. If, however, your murmur has persisted into adulthood or past your pregnancy, you should consider having it checked further. If the murmur turns out indeed to be "innocent," so much the better.

To Sum Up

The symptoms discussed in this chapter are the more common ones seen with heart problems, but having such symptoms may not signify a problem with your heart at all. The only person who can determine for certain what's going on is your doctor. Remember, though, that your doctor depends on you for an accurate description what you are feeling.

If you have a problem that may be serious, don't delay in seeking your doctor's advice because you're scared. Heart problems are scary—believe me, I know. But today, virtually all heart problems can be treated. If you develop a heart problem and, like me, learn about it in time, your heart problem can be treated, and possibly even resolved, before your heart has been irreversibly damaged.

10

~~~~~~∿~~~~~~

The Diagnostic Difference

OVER THE YEARS, diagnostic testing has become highly sophisticated, enabling doctors to peer ever more closely into the workings of the human heart. But the best diagnostic tools in the world cannot help you if you are not referred for them. Let us tell you about Hope, an energetic woman with a spunky personality befitting her clouds of red hair. A few years ago, she was treated for cancer and had recovered. Now, she was in despair. She felt poorly, but her concerns were dismissed repeatedly by her family doctor, who kept telling her, "Don't worry, your test results say you're fine."

About six months before, she'd gone to the doctor, complaining of exhaustion, shortness of breath, and an achy feeling in her chest. Her doctor admitted her to the hospital for three days of testing; most of which were aimed at ruling out a reoccurrence of her cancer, although a few heart tests were included. When the results came in, her doctor called her into his office, reeled them off, told Hope she was fine, and sent her on her way. But Hope continued to feel below par, so much so she was even considering canceling a trip to Manhattan to visit her daughter, who lives in a fourth-story walk-up. The thought of climbing all those stairs filled Hope with dread. Then one day, by chance, Hope picked up a magazine article on women and heart disease and began reading. She was shocked. "It was a revelation. I realized I was reading about myself," she recalls.

She immediately returned to her doctor, who, still insisting all her test results were fine, told her that he would reluctantly test her heart further, "if it would make me happy," she recalled. The test results clearly showed Hope was suffering from advanced coronary artery disease. She was admitted to the hospital immediately, where she underwent balloon angioplasty to widen her dangerously narrowed coronary arteries.

"The first time, I didn't question my doctor; in fact, I didn't even know what tests he did," Hope says, "but I ask a lot of questions now."

Visiting the Cardiologist

If you suspect you may have a heart problem, the diagnostic procedure actually starts before you undergo your first test. Today, doctors too often substitute uncomfortable, expensive, and sometimes risky tests for conducting an in-depth interview with you about your complaints. A detailed recitation of your symptoms, and your risk factors for heart disease, can go a long way toward helping an astute doctor arrive at the right diagnosis.

♥ **Lifesaving Tip: Be wary if the doctor, upon your first meeting, sends you off on a round of testing, without taking time to talk to you. A good physician, like a good detective, ferrets out clues. Only then does he or she develop a hypothesis, or a tentative diagnosis, and order tests to confirm it.**

Whatever your problem, important clues to its nature may be hidden in your family's medical history. While it isn't necessary to be a walking encyclopedia of every ailment that ever befell every family member, you should know major illnesses, and the causes of death, of any of your grandparents, parents, brothers, and sisters. If you don't, try to do a little familial sleuthing before you visit your doctor.

Consider your own medical background, taking into account your own risk factors for heart disease, as well as any serious illnesses you had as a child. Childhood ailments that can cause heart problems later in life include rheumatic fever, scarlet fever, streptococcal infections, and Kawasaki disease, an increasingly common disease of unknown origin that occurs mostly in children but can result in heart problems. Answer questions about your lifestyle honestly; whether you smoke, your diet, how much you exercise, or whether you're under unusual stress. All of us (your doctor included) wish we lived a more exemplary lifestyle, but this is not the time to cover up possibly important clues.

On your first visit to a cardiologist, expect an extensive interview and a physical examination. Like creating a picture with broad, fast strokes, these procedures provide the doctor with a general picture of your general cardiac health. Then, if needed, diagnostic tests can be used to fill in the important details.

THE PHYSICAL EXAMINATION

When performed by a skilled physician, even such seemingly casual measures as checking the natural color of your fingernails can yield a wealth of information about the health of your heart. Bluish-tinged lips or nails, swollen feet, warm or cold skin, and erratic pulse provide clues.

About the only diagnostic tool your doctor will employ at this point is the familiar stethoscope, still an unbeatable device for listening to your heart. Abnormal sounds, like a heart murmur, can focus suspicion on such conditions as mitral valve prolapse or a congenital heart defect. At the end of the exam, you should expect your doctor to give you a tentative diagnosis and the course of testing needed to confirm it.

This chapter discusses the most commonly performed cardiac tests, along with a few of the ones that are less often done, but that you may encounter. They're grouped according to the conditions they are most commonly used to diagnose. Many cardiac tests, though, are multipurpose. For example, a cardiac catheterization can be used not only to diagnose coronary artery disease, but also to gauge the blood pressure within your heart if you have a congenital heart defect. We've noted whether the tests include preparation, but it's always a good idea to ask your doctor, or the lab where you'll take the test, to find out if you need to take any preparatory measures, such as fasting.

❤ Mindsaving Tip: No matter what test you're taking, you'll find you'll probably have to wait, so bring along a book or something else to occupy your time.

❤ Moneysaving Tip: If you are seeing a new doctor, or visiting a consultant for a second opinion, you may be asked to undergo tests you've already had performed. Ask whether you can bring those earlier test results with you. There are various reasons why those results may be unsuitable, but, if they can be used, you can save yourself time, money, and inconvenience. Hand-carry your tests to their next destination, rather they relying on their being sent, even if you are going for treatment out-of-town.

A Word About Medications

Whether you should continue taking any regular medications you are on is question to ask your doctor at the time the test is ordered. The answer may depend on the reason for the test. For instance, if you're undergoing a test to find out if your chest pain is from a heart-related cause, you may need to temporarily stop taking your chest pain medication. On the other hand, if the test is being ordered to learn how you're doing on the medication, taking it may be in order. The key here is that you need to talk to your doctor about this before the test is performed. You also need to know how far in advance of the test you should stop taking the medication and whether you should taper off or stop it completely. Also, if you are diabetic, you should ask your doctor beforehand what you should eat, and whether you should take your regular dose of diabetic medications you are on prior to undergoing the test. Again, communication with your doctor is the key.

A Note on Test Terminology

Two phrases you'll often hear when cardiac tests, or any medical tests, for that matter, are discussed are "noninvasive" and "invasive." Noninvasive tests don't involve entry or penetration into your body. Such tests generally carry very little risk and are pain-free. They account for the majority of cardiac tests. Invasive tests do involve such penetration. They generally carry a small degree of risk, can be uncomfortable, and are more expensive. Sometimes, though, there is no substitute for them; cardiac catheterization, the definitive test for coronary artery disease, is one example. In this chapter, you can assume the tests discussed are noninvasive unless otherwise noted.

Basic Tests

Basic tests such as a blood pressure reading, a cholesterol test, a chest X ray, and an electrocardiogram are commonly ordered when you visit a cardiologist; you may be familiar with them from visiting your family physician as well.

Blood Pressure

As the chambers of your heart respond to the electrical signals generated by your heart's electrical system, your heart also responds with changes in the pressures within it. Your blood pressure consists of a top and bottom number representing the pressure of blood exiting the pump. These pressures are recorded when you have your blood pressure taken. The top number describes the highest pressure—after the aortic valve opens to allow blood to rush from the heart through the rest of your body. This is the systolic pressure. The bottom number, the diastolic pressure, denotes the point when your aortic valve closes and your heart is just starting to fill with blood.

Your doctor measures these readings with the help of a sphygmomanometer (blood pressure cuff) and a stethoscope. If your blood pressure is elevated, it indicates your heart is working harder than normal, putting both your heart and arteries under greater strain.

Cholesterol

For years, the government has waged a public education campaign to persuade people to "know their cholesterol number." There are two type of cholesterol tests, a so-called "finger-prick" test, which is often taken at health fairs and shopping malls, and the "lipid profile," a more extensive test taken in your doctor's lab. Lipids, and their significance, are discussed in Chapter 3.

If your physician includes such a test in a routine physical, by all means have it done. If your physician does not include it, should you insist upon having it done? That depends. The American Heart Association recommends that everyone have his or her lipid profile done at the age of 20, and every five years after that until the age of 60, after which it becomes optional. If you have reached menopause and have no other risk factors for coronary disease, knowing your total cholesterol level from a finger-prick test should suffice. Such tests are subject to error, so if you have it done at a health fair or mall, as opposed to a doctor's office, and your cholesterol total is above 220, see your doctor for a lipid profile. There is a common misconception that you have to fast before a simple finger prick total cholesterol level test. You needn't. This test can be performed without any special preparation. If, however, you do have significant risk factors for coronary disease, particularly if your family has a history of early heart disease or abnormal cholesterol levels (known also as hyperlipidemia), or if you are overweight or diabetic, you should have your lipid profile checked. This is a relatively simple blood test, but it does require you to fast for about 12 hours beforehand. This will provide you with your cholesterol profile and your triglyceride level. Also, if you have not yet reached menopause, your high-density lipoproteins, or HDL cholesterol (the so-called "good" cholesterol) reading may be high. Although this is actually beneficial, the total cholesterol number may be misinterpreted to appear too high, so a cholesterol profile is more accurate.

Currently, the American Heart Association's recommendations do not go beyond this level of cholesterol testing. However, it is becoming clear that an expanded number of cholesterol patterns may play a role in the development of coronary artery disease. These tests are certainly not recommended for everyone. However, if you developed heart disease even though you have a normal cholesterol level, you may want to consider having more sophisticated forms of testing done. If so, discuss it with your doctor or contact the Berkeley HeartLab, Inc., at 1-800-HEART-89 for more information. This organization can provide you with the name of a doctor in your region who can administer the test and provide recommendations based on the results. You can also contact a medical center that has a cholesterol research department or a lipid clinic to check on the availability of this type of testing.

Diabetes

Because diabetes can damage the heart's coronary arteries, you should consider being screened for it. Since the rate of diabetes is climbing, and occurring at younger ages, the American Diabetes Association recommends that everyone be tested for it beginning at the age of 45, or earlier if you have diabetes risk factors.

Diabetes Risk Factors
- Being overweight (more than 20 percent above ideal body weight);
- Having a parent, brother or sister with diabetes;
- Being a member of a high-risk ethnic population (African-American, Hispanic, Native American, Pacific Islander);
- Delivering a baby weighing more than nine pounds or having been diagnosed with gestational diabetes;

- Having high blood pressure;
- Having abnormal blood cholesterol levels;
- Being found to have impaired fasting glucose (IFG) or impaired glucose tolerance (IGT) in previous testing.

Although there are newer and more sophisticated ways to screen for diabetes, the ADA recommends the simple fasting plasma glucose test. This is a basic blood test that measures the amount of glucose in the blood following an eight-hour fast. It used to be that a level of 140 mg/dl on this test signified diabetes; however, that level has been lowered to 126 mg/dl in hopes of identifying diabetics earlier, before the disease damages the body.

♥ **Lifesaving Tip: In the past, a routine urine sample, known as a urinalysis, was sometimes used to screen for diabetes. This is not a useful screening tool because once the glucose level is high enough to spill into the urine, the disease is already fairly serious.**

Chest X Ray

Among the oldest of cardiac tests, the chest X ray can provide very revealing information. It can show whether your heart is enlarged, and sometimes can indicate a congenital heart defect is present. Taking the test is an easy matter as well; you just stand against the film cassette and pictures of your chest are taken from different vantage points.

The amount of radiation exposure you receive from a chest X ray is considered minimal and within a safe standard, with one important exception: if you know you are pregnant or think you may be. The amount of radiation exposure you receive from a chest X ray might harm your unborn baby. Inform your doctor if there's any chance you may be pregnant, so other, lower-risk tests can be substituted.

Electrocardiogram

Picture the busy emergency room portrayed in any television medical drama: Most likely, there's a patient being wheeled in on a stretcher, while a doctor barks "get me an EKG." The doctor is talking about an electrocardiogram, referred to most commonly as an EKG or ECG.

For this test, a technician dabs a bit of conductive jelly on various points along your bare arms, legs, and chest, and painlessly applies stick-on electrodes. Each electrode conveys a signal from your heart, which is then displayed on a graph. Together, the signals provide such information as the size of your cardiac chambers, whether you have reasonably normal heart rhythms, and whether your heart may have suffered any muscle damage from a previous heart attack.

Often, a resting EKG can indicate that an abnormality exists, but cannot pinpoint the exact cause. An EKG generally records heart activity while you are at rest, so it may reveal nothing about chest pain or a pounding heart that comes on when you're being active, like hurrying the kids out the door in the morning or running for a cab.

If you are a relatively young woman experiencing heart problems, they are most likely to involve the structure of your heart itself, or its rhythm. The following are tests commonly used to diagnose such problems.

DIAGNOSING STRUCTURAL HEART PROBLEMS

The structures that make up your heart are crucially important to your well-being. To evaluate the structure of your heart, the echocardiogram is an unbeatable diagnostic tool.

The Echocardiogram

If you consider that your heart is a pulsing organ submerged in the fluid-like environment of your body, you can understand how useful a device that reads sound waves can be. A procedure called a transthoracic echocardiogram, or "echo" for short, uses sound waves, some of which come from the heart itself, to create an image of it. If you've been pregnant, you're probably familiar with a sonogram, which is basically the same procedure.

To undergo an echocardiogram, you lie on your side on an examining table while a technician moves a sound probe around your chest to various positions. The probe, called a transducer, transmits and then picks up small pulses of ultrasound, which reflect off your heart. These sounds are then amplified and visually displayed on a screen. The echocardiogram shows how efficiently your heart and its valves are working, the direction in which the blood is flowing, and the size of your cardiac chambers. It draws a picture of the overall health of your heart muscle.

Echocardiograms are relatively reliable in women, although if you have large breasts, they may insulate your heart, producing a fuzzy image that is more difficult to interpret. Even if breast size is not a problem, the probe still has to "see" through layers of muscles and fat; so other approaches have been developed to provide more precise pictures of your heart.

The Transesophageal Echocardiogram

This measurement provides a clearer image than the traditional echo because the sound waves are actually produced from a probe placed inside your body. In most cases, a traditional echocardiogram is sufficient, but if, for example, a hard-to-see part of a valve must be examined, the transesophageal echo is used.

For this type of echo, you actually swallow a smaller version of the probe used in a traditional echocardiogram. You are given a mild sedative to relax you first, and your throat is anesthetized so you don't gag. The probe then rests inside the esophagus, where it is provides a crystal-clear view of your heart. This procedure carries a slightly increased risk, in the slim possibility that you may react to the sedative or that some bacteria may be introduced into your body via the probe.

While extremely beneficial in studying your heart's structure, echocardiograms done at rest are not especially useful in the diagnosis of coronary artery disease. However, doctors are finding the combination of an echocardiogram with a stress test, called an stress echocardiogram, to be quite accurate in women. This test is discussed later in the section "Tests to Diagnose for Coronary Artery Disease." An echocardiogram may also provide useful information in diagnosing and following the clinical course of a heart attack.

Tests to Diagnose Heart Rhythm Disturbances

A broad category of problems that tend to affect women more than men are disturbances in the functioning of the heart's electrical system, which regulates the rhythm of the heartbeat and keeps your heart operating perfectly. Called arrhythmias, these electrical disturbances can produce frightening symptoms such as fainting, palpitations, shortness of breath, and chest pain.

Electrocardiogram

The electrocardiogram, explained at the beginning of this chapter, is most likely the first test you'll have if you experience such symptoms.

The problem, though, is that if you don't experience the symptoms while you are undergoing the procedure, your heartbeat may look normal.

This is what happened to Denise, a school nurse, whose symptoms occurred every time she began rushing around to get her three kids ready for school in the morning. "My heart starts pounding and I feel faint," she says. Since Denise never experienced symptoms while she was lying down, it's no surprise that the resting electrocardiogram results were normal. So her doctor suggested she wear an ambulatory (Holter) monitor, a device that would record her heartbeat for 24 hours, while she went about her normal activities. Sure enough, as Denise was scrambling to get her kids off the next morning, her symptoms returned. The Holter monitor revealed Denise did suffer from an arrhythmia, one that was not serious and easily treated.

The Holter Monitor

The Holter monitor (or ambulatory ECG), a small device like a tape recorder, is worn slung over your shoulder or on a belt at your waist, and can record your heart rhythm continuously over a one- to two-day period. The monitor is attached to your chest by five leads. If you're asked to wear the monitor, you'll also be instructed to keep a diary of your activities, noting when symptoms occur. The diary and Holter monitor measurements are analyzed later by your doctor, to determine if you do have an arrhythmia, whether or not it is serious, and what measures, if any, should be taken to treat it.

❤ **Mindsaving Tip: If you are concerned about others being aware you are undergoing a cardiac test, you should be able to conceal the Holter monitor fairly easily beneath your clothing.**

Tilt Study, or Tilt-Table Test

This aptly named test has proven very valuable in determining why some people experience blackout spells or severe attacks of dizziness.

The test is quite simple. You lie on a special table in a quiet, dark room, and the table is gradually tilted sixty degrees off level, so that your head is tilted upward and your feet downward. Such movement should simulate the imperceptible changes in your body when you shift your body position. During the test, your blood pressure and pulse rate are monitored, and special blood tests are sometimes performed.

The response to being tilted can reveal irregularities in your body's vascular regulating system, and in the way your body automatically adjusts itself to changes in posture, such as standing up after you've been lying down. If your body reacts normally, you can change your position without any thought, but in women with irregularities of blood vessel control such as those sometimes associated with mitral valve prolapse, such changes in posture can bring on dizziness or fainting.

Electrophysiologic Study (EPS)

If your doctor suspects you have a very serious arrhythmia, or rhythm disturbance, an electrophysiologic study, known commonly as an EPS, may be ordered. This is an invasive test that is done in a manner similar to cardiac catheterization, which is described later in this chapter. In the case of an EPS, though, wires instead of tubes are threaded inside your heart to stimulate it electrically in hopes of making the arrhythmia appear. Since this is an invasive test, and not without risk, it is performed only when there is concern you might develop a life-threatening arrhythmia, or in some cases where the rhythm problem is disabling and resistant to treatment. For an EPS study, you're conscious, but sedated. The preparations are basically the same as those outlined in the section on cardiac catheterization.

Tests to Diagnose Coronary Artery Disease

Diagnosing coronary artery disease (known also as coronary heart disease or simply coronary disease) has proved more difficult in women. One reason for this is that the exercise stress test, a tool commonly used to diagnose coronary artery disease, appears less accurate in women than it is when performed on men. Since the stress test is a major method of diagnosing coronary artery disease, you should be very aware of different types of stress tests and their pros and cons when used on women.

Exercise Stress Test

The purpose of the exercise stress test, commonly referred to simply as a stress EKG, is to evaluate whether the heart muscle receives an appropriate amount of blood flow during increasing levels of physical exertion. If not, this could indicate the presence of coronary artery disease. The test also evaluates the way your heart responds to the physical stress of exercise—walking and jogging on a treadmill or pedaling a stationary bicycle. Before the test begins, leads are attached to your chest, as in a regular EKG, so changes in your heartbeat can be monitored. You begin exercising at a slow pace that gradually speeds up. Even if you are unfamiliar with a treadmill, you'll soon get used to it. If you have severe arthritis, or some other condition that makes it impossible to exercise with your legs, a drug can be used alternatively to simulate an increase your heart's workload.

❤ **Mindsaving Tip: If you've suffered a heart attack, have recently undergone cardiac surgery, or are experiencing chest pain or other symptoms, you may be concerned that such exercise could be too much of a strain. Relax: During the test, you'll be carefully monitored and the test is halted immediately if you are in danger.**

Research has shown that, in women, the exercise stress test alone is too inaccurate to be used as the sole determinant of coronary artery disease. Even when most carefully performed, this test has proven to be inaccurate in women about one third of the time. There are better tests to determine whether you have coronary artery disease.

The problem with exercise stress tests being done on women is that this test is too often apt to mistakenly diagnose coronary disease in women, even when they are free of it. This can occur for two reasons. First, although most women and men experience chest pain, in women—particularly in relatively young women—it is less likely that the pain is caused by coronary disease. Second, a healthy woman's EKG may display changes characteristic of a person with coronary disease.

Precisely why this happens is not known, but it may relate to the fact that women respond differently to exercise than do men. Some researchers believe a woman's fluctuating estrogen levels may contribute to the response. "Some studies have shown that, if you study women through their menstrual cycle, at some points in the month, the exercise electrocardiogram tends to be abnormal," says Dr. Bernard R. Chaitman, director of clinical research at St. Louis University Hospital.

In interpreting a test that indicates coronary disease, then, a cardiologist takes into consideration the woman's risk factors for coronary disease, as well as how markedly abnormal the test result is. "If a woman is a heavy smoker, is diabetic, and is 52 years old, and has chest pain and the test is markedly abnormal, you'd pay attention to a test like that. But if it is a 35-year-old woman who does not have risk factors and the test is only mildly abnormal, you wouldn't be as concerned about it," Dr. Chaitman says.

This does not mean that you should refuse to take an exercise stress test at all; rather, you should discuss with your doctor the purpose for which it is being performed. Although a stress test alone is not accurate enough to pinpoint the existence of coronary artery disease, it is more precise in determining that no such problem is present. So if you have chest pain, a negative test result can be reassuring. The test can also demonstrate if you have a normal exercise capacity and physical response to exercise, or that such activity brings about such symptoms as chest discomfort, shortness of breath, or an irregular heartbeat.

♥ **Mindsaving Tip: If you're asked to take a stress test in a health or fitness club, for a purpose other than testing your exercise capability, you should decline. When used as a broad screening tool for heart disease, these tests are notoriously inaccurate in women and can cause you unnecessary alarm.**

Exercise Nuclear Scan

This test, which combines an exercise stress test with a special nuclear scanning agent, such as thallium, is a better way of diagnosing coronary artery disease in women than an exercise stress test alone. Instead of relying solely on an electrical depiction of your heartbeat, the test also produces images of your heart.

Before the test, an intravenous (IV) line is attached to your hand. Just as in an ordinary exercise stress test, you exercise on a treadmill or stationary bike until your heart reaches its maximum rate. Then, the nuclear isotope, such as thallium, a safe, radioactive tracer, is injected through the IV and you are taken over to a special imaging table. You lie perfectly still, on the table, your hands stretched above your head, while the camera encircles you, taking images. Afterward, you'll be required to continue to fast, but you'll be able to get up and may even be allowed to leave and go about your business. Four hours later, you'll return for a second set of images, similar to the first. In some labs, using a combination of different nuclear isotopes considerably shortens the time for imaging, so be sure that you get clear instructions from the imaging staff.

What happens during the procedure is this: Upon entering your bloodstream, the nuclear isotope and the chemical it's bonded to head for your heart. If there is no blockage or narrowing, it flows freely and highlights all of your heart muscle, which shows up on the special x-ray image. If a portion of your heart appears to be "missing" in the post-exercise images, it indicates that the isotope was not distributed to all of your heart because one or more arteries are narrowed or blocked. At the time the rest images are taken, the flow of blood should be adequate, and the images of your heart should look normal.

An exercise nuclear scan is much more accurate than an exercise stress test alone, but it is still not perfect. If you have large breasts, your breast tissue may muffle the radioactive energy of the imaging agent and make it appear that it is not being fully absorbed, leading to the mistaken impression that you have coronary artery disease. But this erroneous impression happens far less often than in exercise stress testing.

If this test is abnormal, the next step is usually a cardiac catheterization.

Pharmacological Stress Test

This approach provides an alternative for women who cannot exercise vigorously enough to provide the diagnostic information needed for exercise stress tests. This test also determines whether the heart muscle is receiving an appropriate blood flow during an increased level of demand, but a pharmaceutical, such as Persantine or adenosine, is given intravenously to make your body think it is exercising. A set of x-ray images is taken before the chemical is administered, and another set afterwards. As with other tests, ask your doctor beforehand whether you should continue taking any current medications you are on. If you will be given Persantine, you can have absolutely no caffeine or caffeine-containing foods or beverages (coffee, tea, cocoa, chocolate, cola beverages, and the like), for at least 24 hours beforehand.

Exercise Echocardiogram

The echocardiogram is a particularly fine device for examining the structure of the heart. But when it is done while you're at rest, as it is ordinarily performed, it cannot determine to what degree your coronary arteries may be blocked. However, exciting research studies have shown that when an echocardiogram is performed in combination with a stress test, the result is a more sensitive and reliable procedure for diagnosing coronary artery disease in women. The exercise echocardiogram becomes a more cost-effective and convenient way of providing a comprehensive overall evaluation of your heart. Most importantly, recent studies show it is equally reliable when used on both women and men, regardless of age or body weight.

The test begins with a technician performing a brief version of an echocardiogram, to obtain images of your heart at rest. Then you undergo an exercise or pharmacological stress test, exerting yourself on a stationary bike or treadmill until your heart reaches its peak rate. At that point, you get off the exercise machine and return to the examination table nearby, where a second echo is performed.

By comparing the images of your heart at rest with that following exercise, your imaging specialist can evaluate any changes that may indicate whether you have coronary artery disease. This test does not furnish images of your actual coronary arteries, so, if you do indeed have blocked or narrowed arteries, cardiac catheterization, an invasive test discussed later, may still needed to assess the extent of the disease.

Stress echocardiography is proving more accurate and less expensive than the exercise nuclear scan. However, since the exercise nuclear scan test has traditionally been more widely used, it may take some time before the stress echo catches on. Whichever your doctor's choice, the important thing to remember is both imaging techniques provide non-invasive, risk-free, and relatively effective means of more accurately diagnosing coronary artery disease in women.

Cardiac Catheterization: The "Gold Standard" of Testing

Think of the morning traffic reports you see on your local television station. Some use graphics that display the roadways with the traffic flowing smoothly or, in the case of an accident or other obstruction, with lines of cars all backed up. Wouldn't it be useful if your doctor could peer inside your coronary arteries to see if there are any blockages caused by coronary artery disease?

Your doctor can. This "aerial" picture of your coronary arteries can be obtained through the use of cardiac catheterization, also called a coronary angiogram. Not only does cardiac catheterization show whether and where such blockages or obstructions exist, but it also provides your doctor with a road map to be used in deciding the best way to widen or bypass the really serious obstructions.

Since this is such an important test in cardiology, it's no wonder that, when major research studies were released in 1991 showing that men were twice as likely as women to be referred for it, a furor erupted. To some, this indicated that coronary artery disease was not being addressed as seriously in women as in men. Also, cardiac catheterization is not only a diagnostic tool, it's an imperative prerequisite if you're being considered for such potentially lifesaving treatments as balloon angioplasty or coronary bypass surgery.

So, since women are referred less frequently for catheterizations, it's not surprising they are underrepresented in undergoing such aggressive procedures as angioplasty and coronary bypass surgery. On the other hand, there has been concern that these procedures are done too frequently in men. Since the concern with women runs in the opposite direction, maybe women are at an advantage in this case after all. If you suspect you may need a cardiac catheterization and your doctor demurs, or if you suspect the catheterization may be unnecessary, you might consider seeking a second opinion.

All the tests we've covered until now are noninvasive. The invasive cardiac catheterization involves some discomfort, is expensive, and does entail a degree of risk. In some places, it also necessitates an overnight hospital stay. But, if you may be a candidate for angioplasty or bypass surgery, there may be no substitute.

Cardiac catheterization is also sometimes used to determine, once and for all, whether coronary artery disease exists, and sometimes provides the needed proof that it does not, as in the case of Diana, a 37-year-old guidance counselor, who, for years, had experienced the type of chest pain characteristic of coronary artery disease. Since Diana's mother had died suddenly at the age of 38, presumably of a heart attack, Diana's doctor was concerned. Diana's stress thallium was abnormal, and the doctor feared she might have one or more blocked coronary arteries. But, much to Diana's surprise, when she underwent the catheterization, her coronary arteries appeared normal. It was found that her chest pain did not stem from the usual narrowing of coronary disease, but, without the catheterization, she and her doctor would not have been certain.

Cardiac catheterizations are performed:

- To determine whether coronary artery disease is present.
- To determine the extent of coronary artery disease and the best way to treat it.
- If you have severe chest pain that seems to be of a cardiac cause.
- If chest pain persists following a heart attack.

These days, most cardiac catheterizations are done on an outpatient basis, but some hospitals still require an overnight stay. Beforehand, you'll undergo some routine tests, such as a blood count, a chest X ray and a resting EKG. You'll fast overnight, or be allowed to eat only very lightly if your test is scheduled later in the day.

For your catheterization, you'll be awake, but sedated. A narrow-diameter tubing, called a catheter, is slid inside your heart via a blood vessel and delivers a special x-ray dye into your coronary arteries. A 35 millimeter motion picture or digital camera produces images that clearly show any blockages.

In a woman, the catheter is usually inserted by way of the femoral artery, a large accessible artery in the groin. An artery in the arm is also sometimes used. No matter which site the doctor chooses, the preparation is pretty much the same, except that if the femoral artery is used, the pubic hair is usually shaved. A local anesthetic is administered, which causes a momentary stinging sensation before the area becomes numb.

Once the catheter is in place, the physician guides it to the vicinity where the coronary arteries branch from the aorta branch. Then the dye is injected and traces the route of the blood flow, pinpointing any obstructions. The doctor and you, yourself, if you wish, can watch as the dye travels through your arteries on a video monitor suspended above you. As the contrast dye is flowing, the x-ray motion pictures are taken.

As the dye infuses your heart, you sometimes feel an intense, momentary, uncomfortable warmth. If you have coronary artery disease, the process of injecting the dye may cause chest pain. There will be doctors on hand to monitor your condition and provide relief. If you feel pain, let them know, but don't be unduly alarmed. Every cardiac catheterization lab has emergency equipment and procedures, but they are rarely needed.

Will I find the procedure painful? The injection of the local anesthetic usually causes a bee sting–like sensation. Many people find this the most uncomfortable part of the experience. The dye infusion producing the motion picture image of the heart can cause a most dramatic hot flash. Overall, the procedure is well tolerated by the vast majority of women experiencing it.

After the procedure is over, you'll most likely spend the next several hours resting under observation. If your arm was used to insert the catheter, you'll be free to go almost immediately. If, as is most likely, your femoral artery was used, heavy pressure will be applied for about 20 minutes to close the artery. For some, this is a very uncomfortable part of the procedure. You'll also have to lie perfectly still for several hours. It's not painful, but since most of us are not accustomed to lying motionless, it can be very trying. A new technique for plugging the puncture point in the artery is just becoming widely available, reducing the need for compression and prolonged bed rest after the procedure. Regardless, you will need someone to drive you home, since you should bend your leg only sparingly afterwards.

❤ **Mindsaving Tip: The sedative, in combination with the local anesthetic, really works. Reading about cardiac catheterization is more painful than the procedure. No one pretends that a cardiac catheterization is pleasant. But it can reveal an enormous amount of potentially life-saving information about your heart.**

A Word About Risk

The vast majority of cardiac catheterizations, say 98 percent, go perfectly. If you are elderly or frail or have severe heart disease, there is an up to 2 percent risk that moving the catheter around in your blood vessels could result in infection, heart attack, or stroke. On the other hand, successful catheterizations are now being routinely performed in patients in their 90s. If you are in a high-risk category, having the catheterization may be far less dangerous than doing nothing about your heart problem at all.

❤ **Lifesaving Tip: If you are a high-risk patient, you should use extra care in choosing the hospital in which you undergo the catheterization. Although it is extremely unlikely, if you suffer a heart attack or need to undergo emergency open-heart surgery immediately after the catheterization, there will not be time to transfer you to another hospital.**

Intravascular Ultrasound: Combining Echo and Cath

Dr. Steven Nissen, director of clinical cardiology at the Cleveland Clinic, becomes very animated when he describes Adele, a 44-year-old woman with chest pains that might be angina. She was hospitalized several times, but her test results showed nothing wrong. In fact, routine coronary angiograms revealed no major blockages of her coronary arteries. He has been involved in the refinement of a procedure that uses a miniature sound probe that is threaded inside of a coronary catheter and then into the coronary arteries during catheterization. Images that accurately reflect the status of the blood vessels can thus be seen. "Sure enough," said Dr. Nissen, "we put the probe in her coronary circulation and found cholesterol-laden plaque all up and down her coronary arteries," indicating that serious blockage was really present. "We now have another powerful means of discriminating a normal from a diseased artery," Dr. Nissen said. In Adeline's case, the information was used to initiate a program of aggressive drug and dietary treatment. Since women experience more "negative" catheterizations, this technique may turn out to be especially valuable for the diagnosis of chest pain.

OTHER CARDIAC TESTS

MUGA

The MUGA, or multiple gated acquisition, is a test that evaluates the overall efficiency of your heart. It is particularly useful in assessing whether your heart has been weakened by a virus or damaged by a heart attack and in measuring your heart's recovery after surgery. The technique is now being combined with perfusion imaging in many laboratories, greatly increasing the value of both tests.

The MUGA uses a special radioisotope that is injected into your arm as you lie on an examining table. On entering your bloodstream, this "tracer" radioisotope mixes with your blood and races through the chambers of your heart, highlighting them. A special camera then takes a picture of your heart.

The results of this very useful test determine the efficiency of your heart as a pump, by measuring the amount of energy present in the course of each heartbeat and doing some arithmetic. The value derived is called the ejection fraction, which is one of the most important indicators of the health of your heart.

THE FUTURE OF DIAGNOSTIC TESTING

One of the reasons heart disease takes such a large number of women's lives is that it is diagnosed at an advanced stage. Screening tests to identify early signs of heart disease in apparently healthy women have thus far proven unsuccessful. But several promising tests are on the horizon.

PET: One of the Best, and Least Used, Tests

There is a very accurate nuclear technique for detecting coronary artery disease and heart muscle viability in women, but you probably will not have the opportunity to avail yourself of it. The test is called positron emission tomography, or PET, for short. The problem is there are relatively few medical centers equipped for PET, and, for political and economic reasons, their number is unlikely to grow. If, however, you are referred for PET testing, here's how it works:

The PET scanner often looks like a huge doughnut. You lie on your back on a table inserted into the donut's hole. A small amount of a radioactive isotope is injected into your body. As the isotope decays, or loses energy, it emits small particles called positrons, which can be detected as they leave the body. PET produces sharp three-dimensional images of your heart. You don't need to exercise, because a drug, usually Persantine, is used to increase your heart's coronary blood flow.

Because of the clarity of the image, a PET scan, in women, is the most reliable noninvasive means of identifying the presence and extent of coronary artery disease.

A PET scan can also provide very valuable information following a heart attack. During a heart attack, the heart muscle is damaged, but some of the muscle that appears dead may actually be viable if the blood flow to that area is increased. A PET scan can identify whether portions of the heart muscle indeed are salvageable.

So why are so few centers equipped for PET? A PET scan is expensive, costing usually several hundred dollars more than a thallium test. The federal government considers PET a "redundant" test, and has discouraged insurers from paying for it. So, if your doctor recommends such a test, you may have to pay for it out of your own pocket.

Ultrafast CT Scanning

Electron beam computerized tomography (EBCT), known also as ultrafast CT scanning, is a new technique being touted as a way to diagnose heart disease early, but that may be overstating the case.

The test involves rapidly scanning the heart with an X ray machine to detect the presence of calcifications, which are present in plaque in the arteries. The test is appealing because it is noninvasive, fast, and simple. But it doesn't provide information about how many noncalcified lesions are present, which would indicate the presence of plaque likely to rupture, resulting in a heart attack. There is also a question of whether the information provided by ultrafast CT is actually more useful than a careful evaluation of risk factors, which is much less costly. Recent studies have shown that people with high calcification levels have gone on to suffer heart attacks, raising the possibility that calcium deposits are not necessarily an indicator of future heart attacks. In short, cardiologists are uncertain of the accuracy of this test. Because of these concerns, the American Heart Association gives lukewarm endorsement to the use of ultrafast CT as a screening procedure in low-risk patients without symptoms.

On a more encouraging note, Israeli investigators from Tel Aviv have found a similar type of ultrafast CT to be very helpful in the evaluation of women with chest pain. The technique appears to be as accurate as stress echocardiography and takes less time.

Magnetic Resonance Imaging

Magnetic resonance imaging, commonly referred to as MRI, is a noninvasive technique that uses superconductive magnets and radio waves to obtain high quality, detailed images of your body's internal organs. MRI had limited use for several years mainly to find cardiac tumors or to look for other structural heart problems. But now this technology is looking more promising as a potential diagnostic technique for heart disease.

Researchers are particularly excited about the ability of MRI not only to find blockages in the blood vessels, but also to discern which ones are more likely to cause a heart attack. The test can determine the composition of plaque in the aorta (the main artery of the heart), and the results can be extrapolated to characterize the plaque in the coronary arteries. This is important because not all plaque is the same. In fact, plaque can be made up of cholesterol, connective fibrous tissue, or calcium. When it is composed of connective fibrous tissue, plaque tends to be relatively solid and stable. As long as the opening in the artery is wide enough, this type of plaque probably won't cause a problem. By contrast, if the plaque is made up mostly of cholesterol, it tends to be soft and more likely to rupture, which can lead to a heart attack or stroke.

Eventually, it is hoped that MRI will be able to replace cardiac catheterization as the definitive means of imaging the coronary arteries. The MRI test can also be used in carotid (neck) arteries. MRI is noninvasive. No radiation is produced, and no special preparations on your part are required. For the procedure, you lie on a scanner table, which is drawn slowly inside a huge doughnut-shaped machine. This machine is basically a large, hollow magnet. You lie motionless during several imaging periods, which last from one to 15 minutes. You can talk to the technician outside via intercom. If you're prone to claustrophobia, ask for a mild sedative beforehand. While you're inside the machine, you often hear loud clanging noises, so ask for earplugs. An average examination takes about one hour, but this can vary from 45 minutes to an hour and 15 minutes.

❤ **Mindsaving Tip:** Since the MRI is basically a magnet, some people worry that if they have a pacemaker, or a mechanical heart valve, or if they have undergone heart surgery and have sternal wires, such items could pose a danger. This is usually not the case, but ask. However, if you have metallic materials in your body, such as steel pins, a pacemaker, or an artifical joint, you may not be able to undergo MRI. Your doctor and the MRI operator will probably have discussed ahead of time whether any such items will pose a problem. It's also a very good idea to leave all of your jewelry at home.

C-Reactive Protein Test

Another promising avenue towards diagnosing early heart disease in women is a test for a chemical in the blood called C-reactive protein (CRP), which is an inflammatory marker that may indicate whether the atherosclerotic process is under way. As noted earlier, atherosclerosis begins when the body perceives an injury to a blood vessel and initiates an inflammatory response to heal the damage. Several studies have found that a high level of CRP predicted an increased risk of a future heart attack in healthy men. Until recently, research in women has been lacking. One 1998 report in the journal *Circulation* did look at baseline CRP levels of apparently healthy women who later went on to suffer heart problems. CRP blood levels were indeed higher among women who developed coronary heart problems compared with those who did not. But while this was a relatively small study, Harvard investigators recently published in *The New England Journal of Medicine* results from the Women's Health Study that show CRP to be the strongest and most significant predictor of risk for subsequent cardiovascular events in this group of women.

A Final Word on Testing

Over the years, doctors have amassed an arsenal of sophisticated diagnostic tools, and more are on the way. It's easy for both you and your doctor to be seduced by this wealth of fancy high-tech stuff. Valuable as these tests are, they're no substitute for the kind of valuable information your doctor can glean by taking the time to talk with you. That type of thoughtful interview, enhanced by the careful, correct use of modern testing, can usually solve the most puzzling of cardiac problems.

11

〰〰〰〰〰◯〰〰〰〰〰

An Encyclopedia of Heart Problems

THIS CHAPTER is designed to provide you with information on many different problems that can befall your heart. The topics are arranged in alphabetical order. Problems relatively more common in women, such as arrhythmias, are dealt with in greater length than rarer problems such as cardiac tumors.

ARRHYTHMIAS

The Case of the Too-Fast (or Too-Slow) Heartbeat

"It's like a hummingbird fluttering in my chest," Joan, a woman in her late thirties said, describing the feeling that was disrupting her life. Often the flutter escalated into a terrifying panic. A doctor gave her tranquilizers, which helped some. One night, she felt a crushing pain in her chest. She was hospitalized, but the tests showed nothing. "The doctor was very patronizing. He gave me a pat on the head, in essence, and told me, 'Go home and don't be such a nervous girl.'"

Joan struggled with her symptoms, frustrated she could not find a doctor to take them seriously. It was not until she went to the Cleveland Clinic for cosmetic surgery that the mystery was solved. Since the cosmetic procedure required an anesthetic, Joan was hooked up to an electrocardiogram. The results sent the surgeons scurrying for a cardiologist. Some simple tests were performed that found that Joan suffers from Wolff Parkinson White syndrome, a type of arrhythmia, or irregular heartbeat.

Joan is not alone. Heartbeat irregularities are a common reason why many women end up in the offices of cardiologists.

Symptoms and signs of arrhythmias are:

- Palpitations (a pounding, fluttering, skipping, thumping, or racing heartbeat)
- Lightheadedness or fainting
- Chest pain
- Shortness of breath

Often, such heartbeat irregularities aren't serious, but they can be truly frightening. As James Thurber once observed, the little innocent things that one hears in the darkness of night are always magnified by our imagination. So it is with the "pounding" or "jumping" that people frequently notice in their chests. This sensation, also often described as "stopping," "flopping," "bumping," or "racing" is collectively referred to by doctors as palpitations. It usually represents some irregularity of the heartbeat.

On the other hand, some types of arrhythmias can be very serious, even deadly. This is especially true if your heart is already weak from coronary disease or cardiomyopathy, a disease of your heart muscle. Cardiac rhythm disturbances associated with these problems account for the sudden death of about a thousand Americans each day.

The number of people with some types of arrhythmia appears to be increasing, particularly those with arrhythmias following heart attacks. Ironically, this is because of improvements in cardiac treatment. "More people are surviving with coronary disease. More people are not dying because of heart attacks," notes Dr. Lynda E. Rosenfeld, a staff cardiologist at Yale-New Haven Hospital. "They are surviving, but are living on with problems associated with having had a heart attack. One such problem is arrhythmias."

♥ **Mindsaving Tip: Having palpitations doesn't mean you have heart disease. Palpitations can have non-cardiac causes such as a hyperactive thyroid or a sensitivity to caffeine. Arrhythmias can** also occur following a chest injury or open-heart surgery, or as a side effect of some drugs. Also, using cocaine can cause heartbeat irregularities, including some serious ones that can be fatal.

———

What Causes Arrhythmias: The ABCs of PACs and PVCs

Although it is referred to as a pump, your heart actually consists of two pumps attached to one another side by side: The right one pumps blood to the lungs where it absorbs oxygen, and the left one pumps this oxygen-laden blood to all the organs of the body. The upper chamber of each side is called the atrium; each bottom chamber, the ventricle.

Your heart's electrical system controls this pump function. This system has its own "timers" and "wiring" that stimulate it to contract 100,000 times per day on average. Each heartbeat originates in a specific area of the right atrium called the sinoatrial node. This is often referred to as your heart's intrinsic pacemaker.

But all the tissue of your heart is capable of originating heartbeats. When this occurs, and the beat comes from tissue in the atrium other than the sinoatrial node, or when signals echo back and reenter the atrium, a premature heartbeat occurs. This is called a PAC, or premature atrial contraction. When a similar event occurs in the ventricle, it's called a premature ventricular complex (PVC). Virtually all of us experience PACs and PVCs every day. Why some people are aware of even one or two a day and others tolerate several hundred an hour remains a mystery.

Types of Arrhythmias

Your heart beats an average of between 60 and 100 beats a minute, with most people's averaging about 72. An arrhythmia is a significant deviation from the normal range. There are two basic types of arrhythmias: tachycardias and bradycardias.

Tachycardias are arrhythmias in which your heart beats too fast. Types of tachycardias include atrial flutter, atrial fibrillation, paroxysmal supraventricular tachycardia (PSVT), Wolff Parkinson White syndrome, premature ventricular contractions, ventricular arrhythmias, ventricular tachycardias, and ventricular fibrillation.

Each of these arrhythmias has different characteristics, such as the rate of the heartbeat, whether it beats in a pattern or is chaotic, and whether the irregularity originates in the atrium or the ventricle. Wolff

Parkinson White syndrome, for example, is caused by the development of an abnormal pathway in the heart that conducts electricity and can produce very fast heart rhythms.

Bradycardia is a heartbeat that is slower than 60 beats per minute. The hearts of well-conditioned athletes often beat more slowly than this. In practical terms, a slow heartbeat becomes abnormal when it results in too little blood flowing to the body, causing symptoms such as fatigue, shortness of breath, and even fainting spells.

Heart Block

This is a disorder of the heartbeat that is caused by an interruption in the passages of impulses through your heart's electrical system. Depending on the degree of the heart block, it can cause dizziness, fainting, or even strokes. Although heart block can occur at any age, it's primarily found in older people. Causes include coronary disease, hypertension, myocarditis (an inflammation of the heart muscle), or aging. It can also be caused by an overdose of the heart drug digitalis. Mild cases do not require treatment. In the case of fainting, a pacemaker can be used. Medication is also sometimes used until the person can be treated with a pacemaker.

❤ **Mindsaving Tip: Sometimes an arrhythmia that causes a lot of symptoms can be harmless, while one that you may not even be aware of can be dangerous. Arrhythmia diagnosis can be tricky and may require you to consult with a specialist.**

Fainting Spells

Some arrhythmias result not in palpitations but in fainting spells, or a combination of the two. When such fainting spells occur, they may be harmful and even potentially deadly. If you suffer from unexplained fainting spells, you should definitely see your doctor. Several noncardiac causes of fainting are discussed in Chapter 9.

Testing for Arrhythmias

The decision whether to treat an arrhythmia depends on what kind it is and whether you have any other heart problems. A strong, healthy heart can withstand an arrhythmia that might push a weakened heart into cardiac arrest.

If you're a healthy woman who experiences only an occasional palpitation, your doctor will probably tell you not to worry. If, on the other hand, you experience severe palpitations that interfere with your activities, or if you have other heart problems, your doctor will recommend you undergo diagnostic tests. These tests are explained in Chapter 10.

If your test results are normal, then your arrhythmia probably is not serious and unless it is very bothersome, you'll probably prefer not to be treated for it. Sometimes such reassurance is all you need to enable you to live with minor flutters. Eliminating caffeine, tobacco, or alcohol, substances that can cause palpitations, can also help. However, if your arrhythmia requires treatment, what is done will depend on the kind of heartbeat irregularity you have.

Treating Arrhythmias

Over the past few decades, tremendous strides have been made in the treatment of arrhythmias. Doctors nowadays can choose among several types of procedures or a combination of several different types of procedures. Thus, it's especially important that your particular arrhythmia be evaluated by a cardiologist who specializes in electrophysiology (your heart's electrical system) and has access to up-to-date hospital facilities.

❤ **Lifesaving Tip: If you suffer from a serious arrhythmia, particularly if it manifests itself as an episode of "sudden death," or cardiac arrest, you should be taken to the nearest hospital for immediate medical attention. After the crisis is over, get a comprehensive evaluation of your heart by a cardiologist who specializes in arrhythmias.**

Drug Treatment

Antiarrhythmic drugs are responsible for saving hundreds of thousands of lives each year. Most of these drugs work by reducing the irritability of the heart cells responsible for the rhythm disturbances. These are strong drugs and should be taken only under close supervision of your doctor. You may also have to undergo periodic testing to make sure your medication is working properly.

Radio Frequency Ablation

In the past few years, this technique has shown excellent results in providing permanent relief for certain types of tachycardias, or runs of fast heartbeats. Some specific arrhythmias it is used to treat include Wolff Parkinson White syndrome, AV nodal reentry tachycardia, and atrial fibrillation.

Dr. Deborah Williams, a former cardiologist at the Cleveland Clinic, recalls attending a conference a few years ago, where surgery was presented as the only definitive treatment for Wolff Parkinson White. Nowadays, ablation is seen as the treatment of choice. "That just shows you how fast things are changing," notes Dr. Williams.

Radio wave (also called radio frequency) ablation is a nonsurgical method in which thin wires are threaded up into your heart by way of your femoral vein, the accessible vessel near your groin. The catheter is then advanced slowly and positioned within your heart and radio waves are aimed at the heart tissue that is causing a problem. The procedure generally lasts from two to four hours, although the trend is towards a shorter period to avoid excessive exposure to radiation. With these kinds of arrhythmias, ablation is proving more effective than medication; drugs typically work for awhile, but then the arrhythmia reappears.

One complication is that in some cases, the radio waves destroy not only the abnormal tissue, but also the specialized tissue, which acts as your heart's intrinsic pacemaker system. How often this occurs depends on the type of arrhythmia. With Wolff Parkinson White, it occurs only rarely, an estimated 5 percent of the time. For AV nodal reentry tachycardia, it occurs about 15 percent of the time. When ablation is used for atrial fibrillation, however, a pacemaker is always required because, in order to eliminate the arrhythmia, the area of the heart that controls the heartbeat is damaged and heart block occurs.

❤ **Lifesaving Tip: If you are planning to undergo radio wave ablation, you should understand that for certain arrhythmias you may require a pacemaker afterwards. Try to minimize this possibility by asking how often patients undergoing these procedures will require pacemakers. If the figures are significantly more than those mentioned here, you might consider consulting another doctor.**

Radio wave ablation also has been used in cases of ventricular tachycardia, but with mixed results, usually a 40 to 50 percent success rate. If it fails, however, ablation with a higher energy frequency (DC ablation) usually successfully eliminates the problem.

Patients who have suffered with arrhythmias for years find great relief after ablation. "Before this technique, I remember seeing patients who weren't doing well on medication," says Dr. Williams. "They didn't feel well and their quality of life was not that great. Nowadays, there is a terrific difference, because the day they walk out after having the ablation, we can usually say, 'You're cured.' "

Undergoing ablation is very similar to undergoing balloon angioplasty; however, because of the length of the procedure, you're usually sedated a bit more. So, while you're not unconscious, you'll probably sleep during at least part of the procedure. According to Dr. Williams, patients are most bothered by having to lie on their back for the several hours of the duration of the procedure. Eventually, ablation may become an outpatient procedure, but currently an overnight stay in the hospital is routine.

❤ **Lifesaving Tip: Ablation is not considered safe if you are or may be pregnant.**

Pacemakers

Artificial pacemakers, small devices used to regulate the heartbeat, were first introduced some thirty years ago. Over the years, they've become smaller, lighter, and more streamlined. Once the size and weight of a can of tuna fish, they are now about the diameter and twice the thickness of a half-dollar.

Who uses a pacemaker? Different types of rhythm disturbances can result in your needing a pacemaker. One type is heart block. Another is bradycardia, which causes your heart to beat too slowly. An example of this is called sick sinus syndrome, which results in a very slow heartbeat or even very short periods of cardiac arrest. Pacemakers are also used to correct certain types of tachycardias known as "refractory." This means that, although your heart seems to be beating very quickly, only some of these beats are functional beats, and the rest are just beats that sort of "echo," so for functional purposes, your heartbeat is actually very slow.

Besides the fact that it's a serious medical problem, the symptoms caused by bradycardia can be frightening. A pacemaker may seem a very welcome alternative to being so tired you can't even drag yourself around or fearing you are going to pass out at any minute. "If you're walking around with a heart rate of twenty beats, you don't feel very good. You don't have a lot of energy, you might feel lightheaded. A pacemaker can make a big difference," says Michelle Tobin, a nurse clinician who works with pacemaker patients at the Cleveland Clinic.

It's more common for older women to require pacemakers, but not that rare for younger women to need them. Sometimes these women require a pacemaker following surgery for the correction of a congenital heart defect.

How Does a Pacemaker Work?

A pacemaker is, in essence, a "chronostat." This is because the device not only regulates the timing of your heartbeat (*chrono* is the Greek word for time), but it also works like a thermostat. A thermostat is set at a certain temperature and is activated when the temperature falls below that. A pacemaker works much the same way; it's designed to start up automatically if your heartbeat falls below a certain point, just like a thermostat does when the temperature falls too low.

Over the years, the image of the pacemaker wearer has changed dramatically. Once the word "pacemaker" engendered images of the elderly but they are now worn by people of all ages.

Different types of pacemakers have been developed to suit different needs. Some work constantly, providing the heart with a constant, regular beat. Others work "on demand," providing beats only when needed. Dual-chambered pacemakers, which replicate a normal heartbeat that starts in the atria and stimulates the ventricles, can vary the heart rate, enabling the wearer to enjoy vigorous exercise. Once implanted, a nurse, using a special transmitter, can reprogram the pacemaker to adjust automatically for various activities. Once reprogrammed, you'll have the correct rhythm whether you're sleeping, exercising, or having sex, for example. Some pacemakers can even provide your doctor with diagnostic information over the telephone. If you need a pacemaker, talk to your doctor about the one best suited for you. There are plenty of choices.

How is a pacemaker inserted? If you are going to have a pacemaker inserted, you'll probably check in to the hospital that day, and stay over

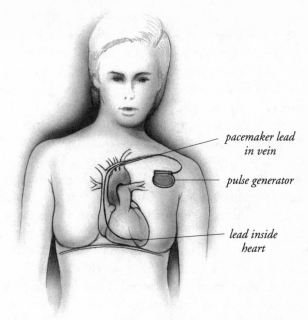

*pacemaker lead
in vein*

pulse generator

*lead inside
heart*

Cardiac Pacemaker. A pacemaker consists of a pulse generator containing the "brains" and the system's battery, as well as an insulated wire (a "lead") that maintains the flow of electricity from the pulse generator to the heart muscle. The lead is inserted into the heart through a vein located underneath the collarbone. The pulse generator is slipped into a small pocket created between the skin and the muscle of the upper chest.

for a day or two, so you can rest after the procedure and so that your pacemaker can be tested to make sure it's working properly.

For the procedure itself, you're conscious, but heavily sedated. A local anesthetic is used so you do not feel any pain. An incision of about two inches is made below your collarbone. Using a device similar to those used to insert a catheter, the wires of the pacemaker are inserted through a vein into your heart. The pacemaker's generator, the coin-sized unit, is implanted where the incision was made. A surgeon or cardiologist usually performs this procedure, which takes about three hours.

What will the pacemaker look like when it's in? How a pacemaker will look once it's implanted is a concern of some women. Through the years, pacemakers have gotten much smaller and lighter, but the device can still be noticeable in bathing suits or low-cut evening gowns, and you can feel them if you brush your fingers over your skin. Talk to your doctor to make sure the pacemaker is implanted as unobtrusively as possible.

♥ Mindsaving Tip: If you're self-conscious, ask your doctor about the possibility of implanting the pacemaker under your left breast, where it is completely hidden. You may need to consult a plastic surgeon for this in addition to the implanting doctor. Don't be surprised if this notion is not greeted with enthusiasm. Doctors sometimes resist deviating from their normal practices. But if it's important to you, it's worth pursuing.

What happens afterwards? You can go home from the hospital within a day after the pacemaker is inserted. You may feel fatigued at first. There will also be a period of adjustment lasting about six weeks while you become accustomed to having a pacemaker nestled beneath your skin. Over this period, the pacemaker's wires will grow into your heart tissue so that the pacemaker is less likely to become dislodged. During this time, you'll need to be careful. Your doctor will probably give you permission to drive, but strenuous sports that involve your arms, like golf and tennis, are out. So is most housework and lifting anything heavier than 10 pounds, including children and grandchildren!

Your new pacemaker also may need to be adjusted so that it provides you with the right heart rhythm for your activities. If your heartbeat is too slow, for example, you'll never have the oomph you need to do aerobics or even take a brisk walk. At the Cleveland Clinic, pacemaker nurses go to great lengths to make sure you are happy with your pacemaker. They can put you on a treadmill and adjust your pacemaker's function properly, to make sure your pacemaker is providing you with enough zip.

"We've even had patients make beds here. One woman told us, 'Every time I make a bed and rustle the sheets just so, I feel funny.' So we had her do it here. Sure enough, we were able to adjust her pacemaker so she'd feel fine," says nurse clinician Michelle Tobin.

There may be other, more subtle adjustments as well. If your heart rate has been very slow for awhile, you may need some time to become adjusted to your new, quicker one. Although you can't hear your pacemaker, you may be very conscious of your heart beating, especially at night, before you fall asleep.

♥ Mindsaving Tip: Some people are unable to become psychologically adjusted to the pacemaker, but this is extremely rare. It's much more likely that before long, you will become so used to your pacemaker it will feel like it was always a part of you.

Some women have difficulty adjusting at first to a pacemaker because they feel as if a device, not their own body, is in control of their heart. "A woman thinks she is invincible, and now she is relying on a device. I've found that men seem to handle that a bit better than women do," says Betty Ching, a pacemaker nurse at the Cleveland Clinic.

Invariably, that feeling subsides when women discover that the pacemaker enables them to do things they haven't done in awhile. Sometimes, Betty Ching says, the change can be very dramatic. She recalled the case of a 41-year-old woman who worked for a local company. She had a heart rhythm problem that caused her to pass out several times a day. While the heart rhythm problem itself was not considered medically serious, it was, for all practical purposes, ruining her life.

"This woman used to faint four or five times a day," says Ching. "Every time she'd stand up, she'd gray out, and all of a sudden, she'd be down. You can't live your life like that. Now, with her pacemaker, she's feeling so much better. She's back at work. She's not afraid to go out anymore."

Common Questions About Pacemakers

How long do pacemakers last? Pacemakers generally don't wear out, but their batteries do. You can expect your pacemaker battery to last at least five years. However, if your pacemaker is the "on demand" type and is rarely needed, it could last years longer. When the battery does wear out, the unit needs to be replaced. No one looks forward to this, but since pacemakers are always being improved, this may provide you with an opportunity to be fitted with one that is even better suited to your needs.

How do I know if the battery is wearing down? You don't need to worry about it. These days, a nurse or technician at the hospital periodically checks on the strength of the battery by using a special device over the phone.

Can I do all the activities I normally do with a pacemaker? Absolutely! Once the incision is healed and the pacemaker firmly in place, it's not likely to dislodge, so you can perform all the activities you normally do.

When pacemakers were first developed, people had a lot of misconceptions about them. Some would be laughable if they hadn't been so worrisome. For example, for awhile, nuclear-powered pacemakers were once available until they were replaced by the lithium-cell powered devices that are now favored. One patient at the Cleveland Clinic was delighted when her nuclear pacemaker was removed. "Can I take my honeymoon now?" she asked. The poor woman had waited 20 years to take the trip because when her nuclear-powered pacemaker had been implanted, she had been warned not to leave the state without notifying the Atomic Energy Commission. She had tried to call the commission without success, not knowing it had been dismantled!

♥ **Mindsaving Tip:** The most widely held myth about pacemakers is that you must not go near a microwave oven if you're wearing one. Modern pacemakers are well shielded, so you can even operate a microwave (unless it is a really old model) without a second thought.

How do I know my pacemaker is working okay? Problems with pacemakers, and the wires that connect them to your heart, are uncommon, but they can occur. If you experience the symptoms that resulted in your getting a pacemaker, call your doctor. Sometimes, though, you may not have experienced anything more than subtle symptoms, so ask your doctor to review with you symptoms that may indicate your pacemaker or its wiring may not be working right. You'll also be taught to take your pulse. Usually, minor pulse irregularities don't indicate a problem but if, for example, your pacemaker is set to give you 70 beats per minute, and you carefully check your pulse and discover it has fallen to below 60, this could indicate a problem. Likewise, if, while you are resting, your pulse is consistently over 100, this may indicate your pacemaker is not working appropriately, and you should call your physician.

♥ **Lifesaving Tip:** Problems with pacemakers are uncommon. However, if you've suffered a fainting or near fainting spell, or if you have reason to believe your pacemaker is not working properly, contact your doctor immediately. In most cases, nowadays, whether or not the pacemaker is working properly can be determined over the telephone.

If you have a pacemaker, you are wearing a piece of artificial material in your heart, which can make you more vulnerable to bacterial endocarditis, discussed later in this chapter. Some doctors recommend taking antibiotics as a protective measure but others don't believe it is warranted. Discuss this with your doctor.

Over the years, there have been other misconceptions about pacemakers. Here are the most common:

Myth: If you wear a pacemaker, your hair permanent won't hold.
Truth: A pacemaker has no effect on your hairstyle.

Myth: You can't go through the metal detector at an airport without setting it off.
Truth: Again, untrue. But pacemaker wearers are issued identification cards so, if you are concerned about metal detectors, you can show it to the security guard in airports or stores.

Myth: A garage door opener can turn off or reprogram a pacemaker.
Truth: Again, not true. A lot of folks worry about it, though.

Myth: If I'm wearing a pacemaker, it's unsafe to use an electric blanket or heating pad.
Truth: Nope. It's perfectly safe for you to use any home electrical appliance while wearing your pacemaker.

Implantable Defibrillators

One of the most dangerous heart conditions is the type of arrhythmia that can cause cardiac arrest, usually when the heart goes into such a quick, erratic rhythm it can no longer pump blood effectively. The result is called "sudden death," or cardiac arrest. In cases such as these, a portable device called an implantable cardioverter defibrillator (ICD) is implanted in the body. It uses electric shock to restart the heart rhythm.

This device, which became available in the late 1980s, is made up of two electrodes, implanted in or on the heart, connected to a sensing unit implanted in the abdomen. A typical ICD senses arrhythmias in 10 to 35 seconds, then delivers an electric jolt to the heart. ICDs are used in cases of life-threatening arrhythmias that don't respond to other types of treatment.

While most people adjust to wearing a pacemaker quite easily, the ICD is significantly larger, about the size of a small cassette player, and heavier as well. The sensing unit is implanted under the skin of the abdomen, where it can be seen and felt fairly noticeably. So, its cosmetic appearance can be a big issue for women.

"Less than 20 years ago, pacemakers were the size of defibrillators and now they're the size of a tiny eye shadow case. That's what's going to happen to defibrillators. They've already gotten smaller," says Dr. Lynda Rosenfeld. Until then, she is experimenting with different positioning in order to make their implantation as unnoticeable as possible.

Obviously, if you are concerned about your appearance, an ICD is an issue. But it's worth remembering that, if you have been revived after an episode of sudden death, the chances are very great it could occur again, this time with deadly results. So this device, cumbersome as it seems, is truly a lifesaver and any cosmetic considerations should be secondary.

Surgery

Today open-heart surgery is rarely used to correct arrhythmias; it is resorted to mainly when other types of treatments have failed, or when a person is slated for heart surgery for another reason and such treatment for an arrhythmia at the same time is deemed beneficial.

Different surgical procedures are used for various types of rhythm disturbances. Sometimes, surgery is done following a heart attack. In this case, the surgical procedure involves cutting away, or even freezing, the area of scar tissue, which may be causing a ventricular arrhythmia. In the case of atrial fibrillation, when all else fails, another type of surgery may be used. This operation, called a maze procedure, is quite a radical one in which the atrium is actually taken apart and reassembled. In general, though, other techniques discussed earlier in this chapter, such as radio wave ablation, have largely supplanted surgery for many other arrhythmias.

♥ **Lifesaving Tip: If your doctor is talking about surgery before other techniques have been tried, consider getting a second opinion. It's always preferable to correct a heart problem nonsurgically if possible.**

♥ **Mindsaving Tip: If you have a rhythm disturbance that requires treatment, but that is your only heart problem, medication or mechanical devices such as a pacemaker or ICD will benefit you greatly. But if you have a heart that has been damaged or greatly** weakened by coronary disease, such devices can be helpful, but are not a cure-all.

———

BACTERIAL ENDOCARDITIS

Throughout this book, you will find many references to bacterial endocarditis. This is because bacterial endocarditis (also referred to simply as endocarditis) is a potentially deadly heart infection that many people with heart problems are at risk of contracting. Although it is easily prevented, endocarditis is difficult to treat, and can result in death or a seriously damaged heart. Even procedures used to correct a heart problem, the most noticeable example being an artificial heart valve, can make your heart vulnerable to endocarditis.

What Is Endocarditis?

Endocarditis is an inflammation of your endocardium, your heart's internal lining. Bacteria that normally reside in your body, but safely in your mouth, respiratory system, or gastrointestinal tract, often cause the infection. Such bacteria are dangerous if they escape into your bloodstream and enter organs that are usually bacteria-free, such as your heart and your brain. Usually, your body's immune defenses destroy such bacteria almost instantly, but, if a bacterium lodges in the tissues of your heart's lining or valves, and evades your body's natural defenses, serious damage can be done. If you have certain types of heart problems, this puts you at risk for this potentially fatal and difficult-to-treat ailment.

Although it is not known why some people get endocarditis while others do not, if your heart is structurally abnormal or damaged, you are at particular risk for this disease. This is because the bacteria that cause endocarditis are attracted to areas of the heart that have been damaged or where there is exposure to turbulent blood flow. If you have a leaky heart valve, or your heart valve has been replaced, just such conditions exist. The bacteria can then lodge in your heart, begin to grow, and cause damage.

Symptoms of Endocarditis

Endocarditis can be very insidious. The infection can cause symptoms immediately or it can remain undetected for months. Acute endocarditis comes on suddenly. Symptoms include:

- Severe chills
- High fever (102 to 104 degrees) or in some cases, low fever (102 degrees or less)
- Shortness of breath
- Rapid, irregular heartbeat

Endocarditis can also develop slowly, over a period of weeks or even a few months. Symptoms include:

- General malaise, fatigue, weakness
- Low-grade fever
- Loss of appetite
- Night sweats
- Muscular aches and pains
- Painful joints
- Headache
- Pallor

❤ Lifesaving Tip: Sue Dehner, a Cleveland Clinic nurse who educates cardiac patients about endocarditis, says that too often a person may develop endocarditis, but think she has "only the flu." Bear this in mind if you are at risk for developing endocarditis.

How Is Endocarditis Treated?

When endocarditis is discussed, the focus is usually on prevention, because this ailment is proof of the old adage, "An ounce of prevention is worth a pound of cure." Treatment for endocarditis often involves a lengthy hospital stay, perhaps six weeks or even longer, while the patient is given strong antibiotics by injection.

❤ Lifesaving Tip: Endocarditis is diagnosed by blood culture, but the results may take several days. If your doctor seriously suspects you have endocarditis, you will probably be hospitalized even before the results of the blood culture are received so that treatment can begin.

How to Protect Your Heart From Endocarditis

Even though endocarditis is sometimes difficult to treat with even the strongest antibiotics, it is fairly easy to prevent. If you're at risk for endocarditis, you should take antibiotics before undergoing procedures that could introduce the bacteria into your bloodstream. The American Heart Association has guidelines on how and when antibiotics should be used. (See the Resources section. If you are at risk for developing endocarditis, ask your doctor for a list of the procedures before which penicillin should be used. They range from a dental cleaning to more elaborate medical procedures.)

♥ **Lifesaving Tip: If you are at risk for endocarditis, keep in mind that although antibiotics protect against endocarditis quite well, no method is 100 percent effective. Call your doctor immediately if you have symptoms of endocarditis.**

CARDIAC TUMORS

During the time we were working on the final chapters of this book, I had a visit from my friend, Henry, whom I had not seen in nearly 20 years, and his wife, Shirley, whom I had never met. When we discussed my experiences, Shirley, who was 42, mentioned that she had a heart murmur years before that had not signified any problem. Our conversation stuck in her mind, though, and she decided to request an echocardiogram. The test did show her heart murmur was nothing to worry about. But then, the doctor added, "I'm really glad you came in. The echocardiogram showed you have a mass growing in your heart." Shirley turned to him, shocked. "That's impossible," she said, "I feel fine."

Improbable, yes. Impossible, no. It turned out Shirley did have a benign cardiac tumor. Within a month, she underwent open-heart surgery, the tumor was removed, and she was well on the road to recovery. She was also very lucky, the doctor told her; the tumor, though benign, might have proven fatal.

The good news about cardiac tumors is that they are rare, and often benign. In fact, about 75 percent of primary tumors are benign, and benign tumors called myxomas make up about one half of this group. Although a myxoma can occur in either sex, it's most commonly found in women between the ages of 30 and 60. Benign tumors can also occur in the pericardium, the heart's inner lining.

A myxoma, which can be most easily described as being similar to a polyp, is a benign tumor that grows on a stalk and is composed of mucous-like tissue. It is more common for a myxoma to develop in other parts of the body, such as under the skin in the limbs or neck, or less commonly in the abdomen, bladder, or bone. More rarely, it can develop in the heart, usually occurring in the left atrium, the upper chamber on the left side of the heart.

Although myxomas are benign, it's generally recommended that they be removed. They can grow quite large, sometimes to the size of a golf balls, or even larger. A myxoma often grows on a stalk and can flop back and forth, seriously disrupting the normal flow of blood through the heart, causing such cardiac symptoms as fainting, breathlessness, cough, palpitations, chest pain, and fatigue (although, sometimes, as in Shirley's case, they manifest no symptoms at all). While it is very unlikely that such a tumor would become detached, in an estimated 50 percent of the cases, a bit of material can break off and may travel to the brain, resulting in a stroke. Open-heart surgery is required to remove a myxoma, and usually results in a complete cure. It is often possible to remove other primary tumors that occur in the heart as well.

Heart tumors such as myxomas are called primary tumors, because they originate where they occur. Sometimes, secondary tumors appear in the heart as well. These are tumors that have metastasized, or spread from malignancies located elsewhere in the body. These are usually not considered curable, but are addressed with radiation and chemotherapy to shrink their size.

The diagnosis of a cardiac tumor usually comes as a shock for both doctor and patient, because these tumors occur so rarely. In medical parlance, in fact, my friend Shirley is known as a "zebra." This comes from the old diagnostic saying, "if you hear hoof beats in the average American town, it's a horse, not a zebra." For a doctor, this means that if a relatively young woman is experiencing symptoms such as chest pain or palpitation, the diagnosis is probably something common, like mitral valve prolapse, not a cardiac tumor. Being known as a "zebra" probably would not comfort Shirley, but it does explain her doctor's surprise.

CONGESTIVE HEART FAILURE

"Congestive heart failure" is one of those terms that sounds drastically worse than the condition may actually be. This is not to say that it does not denote a serious heart problem: It does. "Congestive heart failure" (and the equally frightening term, "heart failure") sounds as if the heart could stop beating at any moment, which is only rarely the case. The term simply means that your heart is too weak to adequately perform its pumping function.

Unlike the other cardiac problems discussed in this book, which can occur independently, congestive heart failure is always a manifestation of an underlying cardiac disease. It's a common malady: Some two million Americans have congestive heart failure and 250,000 new cases are diagnosed each year. It's particularly common in people over the age of 70. With proper treatment, however, individuals who have it can often lead reasonably normal lives.

What Is Congestive Heart Failure?

In the most common kind of congestive heart failure (CHF), pressure "backs up" in the pulmonary veins so fluid collects in the lungs and tissues of the legs, causing the telltale shortness of breath and bodily swelling. The inefficient pumping of blood can also result in low cardiac output, which, in turn, causes fatigue, especially with exertion. As the heart strives to compensate for these problems, it usually become enlarged and thickened, and the problem grows progressively worse.

Sometimes, congestive heart failure is caused by a problem not specifically related to your heart, such as severe lung disease, severe anemia, or hyperthyroidism (overactivity of the thyroid gland). But congestive heart failure is most commonly caused by heart problems, such as coronary disease (damage from a heart attack), a faulty heart valve, heart arrhythmias (rhythm irregularities), cardiomyopathy (a disease of the heart muscle tissue itself), bacterial endocarditis, or undetected congenital heart defects. Although congestive heart failure most commonly occurs in the elderly, it sometimes appears in younger people, often caused by an undiagnosed heart ailment.

Symptoms of congestive heart failure are:

- Shortness of breath. This can occur with exertion, or when you're lying flat in bed. You may feel unable to catch your breath. When you go to sleep, you find you sleep more comfortably propped up against pillows. During the night, you may wake up panting or gasping for breath.
- Profound fatigue. Simply walking up a flight of stairs can leave you winded and exhausted.

- Coughing. In the early stages of congestive heart failure, the cough can be nonproductive; later on, you may bring up bloody or frothy sputum.
- Rapid weight gain and/or body swelling. This is caused by an accumulation of fluids in your body, usually in the legs and the ankles.
- Rapid heartbeat.

If you've been diagnosed with a type of heart problem that can lead to heart failure and you experience one or more of these symptoms, it's an important signal that your condition may have worsened. Call your cardiologist right away. If you do not have any heart problem of which you're aware, symptoms such as these suggest a visit to your family doctor or internist is in order. If you suspect you may have a heart problem, and you don't believe your doctor is giving the possibility adequate consideration, consider requesting a referral to a cardiologist.

How Is Heart Failure Treated?

Congestive heart failure is treated in two main ways. In an estimated 5 to 10 percent of the cases, the underlying disease causing the symptoms can be cured. Otherwise, the symptoms of the disease are a major focus of treatment. The milder the symptoms, the better the outlook.

To treat heart failure, your doctor will prescribe drugs, sometimes in various combinations. If you're in an advanced state of heart failure, you may have to be hospitalized.

The medications used to treat congestive heart failure include time-proven digoxin (Lanoxin), which increases the heart muscle's ability to pump, and diuretics, to help rid your body of excessive fluid. Recently, beta-blockers joined ACE inhibitors, a type of vasodilator that helps relax the arteries, as being recognized as the best treatments for preventing the onset of symptoms as well as being the major forms of therapy for reducing mortality from heart failure. Cardiovascular drugs are discussed in more detail in Chapter 13.

♥ **Lifesaving Tip: The cardiovascular drugs used to treat heart failure are powerful and periodic follow-ups with your doctor are necessary.**

If you have congestive heart failure, you should take care to avoid contracting infections. You should also try to maintain your ideal weight and eat a low-salt diet. Following these guidelines can prevent the condition from worsening, and ensure that you will have many productive years ahead. Weigh yourself at home every day and if you notice a sudden weight gain, say five pounds over a few days, get in touch with your doctor.

❤ **Mindsaving Tip: Many people lead active lives long after their congestive heart failure problem has been diagnosed, particularly since the introduction of ACE inhibitors. In fact, although you may not be aware of it, some of the people you may see at work every day may be living proof that it is possible to lead a reasonably normal life with congestive heart failure for years.**

Hypertensive Cardiovascular Disease

Untreated high blood pressure can lead to a serious problem known as hypertensive cardiovascular disease, which is a leading cause of congestive heart failure in adults. This deadly problem is preventable, but very often unrecognized even in today's sophisticated medical environment.

One reason why high blood pressure is so dangerous is that over time it can lead to changes in your coronary arteries that make them more vulnerable to atherosclerosis, the deadly buildup of fatty deposits and other materials that narrows the vessels and can impede the flow of blood.

But high blood pressure can also lead to hypertensive cardiovascular disease. When this occurs, the high blood pressure, besides accelerating the damage to the coronary arteries, can also damage the heart itself by causing the heart's muscular walls to thicken and stiffen. The resulting stress on the heart can cause it to dilate, eventually leading to heart failure.

Fifty years ago, hypertensive cardiovascular disease was the most common cause of heart failure. Today, with the emphasis on the importance of having high blood pressure diagnosed and treated, this ailment is found less often, but it is still far from uncommon. Marie is a 62-year-old woman whose electrocardiogram showed changes indicative of hypertensive cardiovascular disease. She'd been increasingly short of breath and suffering other symptoms of congestive heart failure, too. "I was diagnosed several years ago with high blood pressure, and I took medication for awhile. But it seemed to go away. So, I stopped taking the medicine and assumed everything was fine," she recalls. Since high blood pressure usually has no symptoms, she felt fine and stopped going to the doctor. So she was unaware her blood pressure had started climbing again.

Fortunately, if a person with hypertensive cardiovascular disease has not yet experienced heart failure, the cardiac changes from this problem can be largely resolved when the person goes back on the proper high blood pressure medication. Damage from hypertensive cardiovascular disease is not irreversible, as is damage to the heart muscle caused by a heart attack.

❤ **Lifesaving Tip: Until it causes heart failure, hypertensive cardiovascular disease has no symptoms. The best way to prevent this complication it is to take your blood pressure medication as prescribed.**

LUPUS: CARDIAC COMPLICATIONS

Systemic lupus erythematosus (SLE), or lupus, is a chronic disease of unknown cause that occurs predominantly in women, resulting in episodes of inflammation in the joints, tendons, and other connective tissues and organs. Bear in mind, however, that lupus-related heart problems occur only in those with this form of the disease. There is a less serious form of lupus, discoid lupus erythematosus, a chronic recurring rash on the skin, which doesn't affect the heart. Even in those with the SLE form of the disease, the impact on the heart can vary. Some people with lupus will develop heart-related complications, but others may not.

Lupus pericarditis, an inflammation of the sac around the heart, is the most common disease involving the heart caused by lupus. Symptoms include sharp chest pain underneath the sternum, fever, rapid heartbeat, and occasionally, shortness of breath. The pain can change with changes in position and is often relieved by leaning forward slightly. The chest pain can feel like a heart attack. Sometimes, though, there may be no symptoms. Because pericarditis can be caused by conditions other than lupus, the cause must be determined before treatment begins.

Lupus can also cause inflammation of the myocardium, which is the muscular mass of the heart. This is a less common complication caused by lupus. Symptoms include an unexplained rapid heartbeat, an abnormal electrocardiogram, an irregular heartbeat, and heart failure. Myocarditis can lead to tissue damage and replace heart tissue with scar tissue.

Another heart-related complication of lupus is endocarditis, an inflammation of the lining of the inside of the heart. When this occurs, the heart valve can be damaged, but the function of the valve is usually not affected. But if bacteria lodge in the valves, this can lead to bacterial endocarditis, an uncommon, but potentially deadly, complication discussed earlier in this chapter. All of these heart-related problems of lupus can be treated with various types of drugs.

Lupus can also cause coronary heart disease, or atherosclerosis, which can lead to heart attacks. This can be due to the disease itself, in which the artery walls become inflamed and prematurely narrowed, and also possibly due to the side effects of steroids, which are used in the treatment of lupus. So if you have lupus, it's important to reduce your risk of coronary heart disease and make sure your doctor monitors your use of steroids.

Although heart problems do pose a serious threat to those with lupus, early diagnosis of complications and prompt treatment can help prevent these problems from becoming life threatening or even fatal.

STROKE

What is a section on stroke doing in a book about your heart? The answer is that heart problems and stroke are very closely linked.

A stroke is a form of cardiovascular disease that affects the brain. Some forms of stroke have many similarities to heart disease. For example, a heart attack is a form of cardiovascular disease that damages the heart muscle. A stroke is similar, but it causes damage to the brain. Your brain, like your heart, needs oxygenated blood to thrive. If, for any reason, this blood supply is cut off to the brain, the result may be a stroke.

Possible symptoms of stroke are:

- Sudden weakness or numbness of the face, arm, or leg on one side of the body
- Sudden difficulty speaking or understanding others
- Sudden dimness or impaired vision in one eye
- Loss or near loss of consciousness
- Confusion
- Unexplained dizziness or sudden falls, especially with any of the above symptoms

TIAs or "Mini-Strokes"

A stroke can have warning signs, just as can an impending heart attack. Before a heart attack, a person may experience attacks of angina pectoris, the chest pain of coronary artery disease that signals that the heart muscle is temporarily not getting enough oxygen. Similarly, a person who is in danger of suffering a stroke may suffer what is called a TIA, a transient ischemic attack. This is sometimes called a "mini-stroke." The symptoms are the same as a stroke, but their duration is brief, usually lasting from several minutes to a half-hour.

Types of Stroke

Strokes can come at any age, but most commonly, they occur in elderly people or those who have high blood pressure or certain types of heart problems, such as valvular heart disease. As with a heart attack, damage, from very mild to devastating, can occur. There are three types of stroke.

Cerebral thrombosis, or "brain attack." This is most analogous to coronary thrombosis, another name for a heart attack caused by a blockage in the coronary arteries. In this case, the blockage is due to a thrombosis, or clot, that has built up on the wall of a neck or brain artery. Often, this is due to atherosclerosis, the same gradual narrowing of the artery that occurs in coronary artery disease. Since it's uncommon for a person's arteries to be narrow in just one place, a person with coronary artery disease may very well have such narrowing in the arteries of the brain as well. Thrombosis accounts for most strokes.

Cerebral hemorrhage. A stroke can occur as the result of a rupture of a blood vessel in or near the brain. People with high blood pressure or congenital abnormalities of certain blood vessels of the brain are predisposed to this type of stroke.

Cerebral embolism. This type of stroke occurs when a clot, or embolus, carried in your bloodstream from elsewhere in your body is swept into an artery of the brain and causes a blockage in the blood flow. Causes of this type of stroke include coronary artery disease or valvular disease. For example, a blood clot may form in the inner lining of a heart that has been previously damaged from a heart attack and may travel in the bloodstream to your brain.

Another major cause of this type of stroke is cardiac valvular disease. Your heart has four cardiac valves, all which must function well for your heart to pump blood properly throughout your body. For various reasons, such as aging or rheumatic heart disease, one of your valves may become stenotic or stiff. This can result in your blood's flowing too sluggishly through the valve, which can lead to the blood forming a clot. Atrial fibrillation, a type of heartbeat irregularity, can make it more likely that a clot will form as well.

These types of strokes can also occur during or after open-heart surgery. The source is usually an aorta that is severely atherosclerotic. When the surgeon inserts the large tube from the heart-lung machine into the aorta, emboli are dislodged. Intraoperative echo is now used to reduce the risks of this complication. Rarely, a tiny bubble of air enters the bloodstream during the procedure and travels to the brain, with devastating consequences.

A stroke occasionally signals an undiagnosed heart problem. Mona, a 64-year-old woman, suffered a stroke. When she underwent diagnostic tests, it was discovered that after a bout of rheumatic fever when she was a young girl, she had developed a diseased mitral valve. The mitral valve had grown stiff, interfering with the blood flow through the heart and setting the stage for her future stroke.

How Are Strokes Treated?

The way strokes are treated bears striking similarity to the treatment of heart attacks. Since, as with heart attacks, most strokes are caused by blood clots, the same clot-busting drugs are often prescribed. Because a stroke can damage the brain, leading to weakness and inability to function, rehabilitation also plays a very important role in treatment. The outlook for recovery depends on how much brain damage occurs. About one half of patients recover fully, or nearly so, from their first stroke, and many people who are paralyzed learn to walk and use their arms again.

❤ **Lifesaving Tip: As with heart attacks, the key to successful stroke treatment is getting to the hospital early. This can minimize the damage caused by a stroke. Studies have shown that people** suffering a stroke who called the emergency number, 911, rather than calling their physician, arrived at the hospital sooner. Recently, hospitals have started to develop special rapid-response programs for brain attack similar to those for heart attack.

————

12

~~~~~✹~~~~~

Heart Valve Problems

BERNICE IS A "snowbird," a retiree who winters in Florida and flies home to summer up north. A few years ago, in preparation for her annual southern trip, she stopped in to see her doctor for a routine physical. She felt fine but her doctor detected a heart murmur and sent her for tests. They showed Bernice's aortic valve was becoming stiff. That year, Bernice's doctor bid her bon voyage. When she returned the following year, the usual energetic, cheery Bernice was tiring easily and becoming short of breath. "Can't I just go to Florida for the holidays?" she asked. "No way," her doctor responded. "Not before you have that valve replaced." Bernice did as her doctor instructed. The following year, she was winging her way back to Florida.

Your heart has four valves (tricuspid, pulmonary, mitral, and aortic) and all four must function properly in order to circulate blood effectively through your heart. The right atrium and ventricle of your heart receive oxygen-depleted blood as it arrives from your circulatory system and pumps it into your lungs, where it is replenished with oxygen. Then this oxygenated blood flows into the left side of your heart, where it is pumped back into your circulatory system and to the rest of your body. That process is repeated over your entire life.

For this to work smoothly, all of the blood must flow in one direction. The efficient opening and closing of your valves keep it that way. But problems can arise with your valves.

Years ago, if you had valve problems, little could be done for you. These days, valve surgery accounts for one third of all open-heart surgeries in the United States. Not only are surgeons replacing valves at a record pace, but they are also discovering new ways to repair your own valves as well.

A heart valve can fail in one of two ways. The valve can become stiff, no longer opening and shutting freely. When such stiffening occurs in the aortic valve, it is called aortic stenosis. When this occurs in the mitral valve, it is called mitral stenosis.

The other type of problem occurs when a valve becomes "leaky" and allows blood to flow backwards, in the wrong direction. This happens more commonly in the mitral valve and is called mitral regurgitation or mitral insufficiency. This problem can also occur as a complication to mitral valve prolapse, and is discussed in Chapter 7.

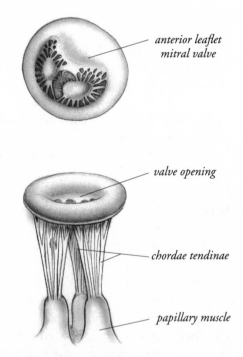

anterior leaflet mitral valve

valve opening

chordae tendinae

papillary muscle

Mitral Valve. Blood flows down through the opening of the valve past the chordae tendinae, which support the valve leaflets. The finger-like protrusions of the heart muscle, the papillary muscles, connect the chordae tendinae to the interior of the heart's muscular pump.

Stiffening and leaking can occur in more than one valve and both conditions can also occur in the same valve. If this sounds confusing, just think about a house that you might have lived in, say a summer cottage, perhaps, which had an old screen door. If the door were repainted several times, the paint would build up. Eventually, the door wouldn't shut tightly enough. In fact, it would be both hard to open (stiff) and hard to shut (leaky). This is a useful analogy when considering how these seemingly opposite problems can occur in the same heart valve.

No matter which type of valvular disorder you have, the result is the same: Your heart is forced to work to overcompensate. The result is an enlarged, weakened, and, eventually failing heart. An abnormally functioning valve also makes you vulnerable to a heart infection, and can lead to the formation of blood clots, which can cause heart attacks and strokes.

Causes of Heart Valve Problems

Most female valve patients are older, like Bernice. But young women are not necessarily immune. You can be born with a heart valve abnormality or you can develop such a problem at any age.

- Coronary disease or a heart attack. Either can result in damage to one or more of your heart's valves.
- Congenital defects. You can be born with a heart valve abnormality, which may be discovered while you're young, or later, when you're an adult. For more information, see Chapter 7.
- Aging. As we age, our heart valves sometimes stiffen. With more women living longer, often well into their eighties, it's not surprising that this problem is among the fastest-growing type of heart disease among women.
- Rheumatic heart disease. Years ago, rheumatic fever resulted in a large proportion of valvular heart problems, particularly in women. Nowadays, that threat is seen as the vestige of a bygone era by some, but not by cardiologists, who have noted an increasing number of patients among new immigrants.
- Mitral valve prolapse. In the vast majority of cases, mitral valve prolapse poses no serious threat to our heart. In about 5 percent of those who have it, however, it can develop into a "leaky" mitral valve.

SYMPTOMS OF VALVE PROBLEMS

Some people with a valve problem experience no symptoms, and don't know about the problem until it is discovered during a physical examination. Others experience exhaustion, shortness of breath, dizziness, fainting, lung congestion, irregular heart rhythms, or chest pain.

DIAGNOSING VALVE PROBLEMS

Sometimes a problem with a heart valve is noticed first by a physician, who, upon listening to your heart with a stethoscope, notices a heart murmur and orders an echocardiogram, which shows the structures of your heart. Cardiac catheterization is often performed as well. These tests are discussed in Chapter 10.

WILL I NEED VALVE SURGERY?

A few decades ago, if you had a bad heart valve often not much could be done for you. Your heart, forced to overextend itself, would gradually weaken and eventually fail. But those days have vanished. The development of the heart-lung machine ushered in the advent of modern valvular heart surgery. Such surgery can restore those with failing valves to an active, healthy life.

If you have a valve problem, you may only need to be monitored regularly by a cardiologist. But if you begin to suffer from symptoms or tests show your heart is overworking, surgery may very well be the recommended course.

VALVE REPAIR VS. REPLACEMENT

Both valve replacement and valve repair necessitate open-heart surgery. The goal of valve repair is to improve the function of the valve you already have, either aortic or mitral. The more commonly repaired valve of the two is the mitral valve. The surgeon accomplishes the repair with a combination of trimming, sewing, and reinforcing the affected valve. Repairing a leaky aortic valve is much more unusual, so it may be very difficult to find a hospital where it is being done. This type of surgery is done at a few major heart centers.

If you've been told you have a valve problem that must be corrected, be sure to select a surgeon who is comfortable with both replacement and repair. If at all possible, it is preferable to retain your own heart valve. Repair versus replacement has fewer of the problems associated with most types of valve replacement. Since with replacement, you retain your own, "native" valve, blood clots rarely form after surgery. Also, if the repair works, the durability of the repaired valve will probably exceed that of a valve made from animal tissue.

Sometimes repairing a valve is not feasible. Experienced cardiologists and surgeons can make an accurate evaluation from the findings of the echocardiogram, but this decision sometimes has to be made during surgery.

❤ **Lifesaving Tip: If the surgeon you select rules out the possibility of repair on the grounds that he or she is not familiar with performing it, you have good reason to seek a second opinion. At the very least, you want the possibility of valve repair considered.**

There are two alternatives to valve repair: balloon valvuloplasty and valve replacement.

Balloon Valvuloplasty for Mitral Valve Problems

With balloon angioplasty becoming increasingly useful in the widening of coronary arteries without surgery, it's not surprising that this technique should also be used also to help open valves that have become stiff, or "stenotic," without the need for open-heart surgery.

The balloon valvuloplasty procedure is very similar to the angioplasty procedure in that you are given a sedative to make you drowsy and

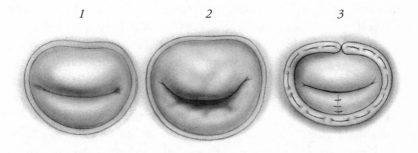

1   *2*   *3*

Mitral Valve Repair. The first sketch represents a normal closed mitral valve. The second shows an abnormal valve where the leaflets don't close properly. The third shows the repaired valve with leaflets that now come together tightly.

relaxed. A catheter with two balloons is inserted through your right femoral vein, near your groin. Once that is accomplished, the balloons are inflated to open the valve.

Valvuloplasty is usually not recommended:

- For the aortic valve, as reclosure is inevitable
- If the valve is too thickened or stiff
- If you are at risk for blood clots
- If you have a leaky valve that requires correction as well

Even if balloon valvuloplasty is not useful in all cases, it's worthwhile to explore. The preparation, procedure, and recuperation are similar to what you would experience undergoing balloon angioplasty, which is described in Chapter 13.

Valve Replacement

If you have a problem that requires valve replacement, you'll want to give careful consideration to the type of valve used. There are two categories. The first is a biological valve, usually taken from a pig. Surprisingly, a pig's circulatory system is very similar to a human's, and the pig valve is used intact. The second category is a mechanical valve, made from metal, plastic, and carbon fibers. Some heart centers may use a valve from a human cadaver, but this is not often done.

The main argument in favor of using a biological valve is that if you have this type of valve, you probably won't need to take a powerful anti-clotting drug such as Coumadin. Because this medication can cause bleeding, the amount you take must be very precisely measured and you must undergo regular blood tests to monitor it. The main drawback of a biological valve is that it does not generally last as long as a mechanical valve. The average life span of a biological valve is about 10 to 12 years. So, if you are a younger woman who undergoes biological valve replacement, it's more likely your new valve will not last as long as it would if you were older. Although it is not known precisely why, biological valves tend to wear out more quickly in younger people.

In elderly people, the decision to opt for the biologic valve is usually easy. If you are a middle-aged woman, the mechanical valve would seem the logical choice. But if you are women of childbearing years, the choice becomes more complicated. This issue is discussed further in Chapter 8.

Can a Mechanical Valve Break?

Although this is not likely, it can occur. The replacement valves used today have a track record of at least several years, but there's no way to make 100 percent certain that a manufacturer's defect will not occur. A case in point is the well-publicized problem that occurred with a type of heart valve manufactured by Shiley, Inc. While not all Shiley valves were defective, studies here and abroad have found that the wire frame of some Bjork-Shiley Convexo-Concave (BSCC) valves occasionally fracture without warning. The valve was withdrawn from the market in 1986 and no such problems have been reported in recent years. But if you have this model valve that was implanted during these years, you should discuss it with your doctor. If you have a mechanical valve, but don't know the type, your doctor should be able to tell from your medical records and a chest X ray.

Valve Surgery

The preparation and most of the recuperation for a valve procedure are essentially the same as for open-heart surgery. This is discussed in Chapter 14.

After the heart-lung machine has taken over the functions of the heart and lungs, the surgeon gently opens the pericardium, the membranous sac around the heart, to expose the inside of the heart. If the valve is not repairable, the surgeon carefully cuts the old valve away. Then, the new valve, either mechanical or biological, is sewn into place using numerous stitches. Then, the process of taking the patient off the open-heart machine begins.

As for what you do after the surgery, every single doctor and nurse who works with heart valve patients stresses this command: Protect your valve from future infection!

Whether you've had a valve repaired or replaced, you must vigilantly guard yourself against valvular infection for the rest of your life. Even if it has only been repaired, your heart now includes material that is foreign to your body, making it a target for infection. Bacterial endocarditis, an infection that can be life-threatening, was discussed in Chapter 11.

❤ **Lifesaving Tips: When you first have a new heart valve, you may be overly conscious of it. In time, that feeling will fade. It then** may be tempting to forget about the valve completely. This can be dangerous. There are some important things to keep in mind: If you have a mechanical valve, know the type of valve, the manufacturer, and the serial number of the valve. Although it is unusual, malfunctions and recalls do occur. If this happens, it doesn't necessarily mean you will need to have the valve replaced, but there may be important medical recommendations you need. Also, if you experience dizziness, shortness of breath, or fainting, contact your doctor immediately. If you have a biological valve, remember that they don't last forever. If you start feeling the way you did before your own valve failed, experiencing such symptoms as chest congestion, chest pain, unusual fatigue, fainting or shortness of breath, contact your cardiologist. If your cardiologist is not available, make sure the doctor you see is aware you have a biological valve. Make sure a heart valve problem is ruled out. If your symptoms persist, consider getting a second opinion.

13

~~~~~nnnΩ∩nnn~~~~~

Treatments

OVER THE PAST FEW DECADES, vast strides have been made in the treatment of heart problems. Thanks to such advances, many cardiac problems that formerly were considered hopeless are now treatable, and some are even curable. What follows is the latest information on treatment techniques.

THE CARDIOVASCULAR MEDICINE CHEST

If you've been told you need to go on cardiac medication, you may not welcome the news. Remember, though, that it's because of such drugs that many people are now enjoying life despite having heart problems that once were considered untreatable. You may have to take cardiovascular drugs for a short period, or indefinitely. You may be put on a single drug or a combination. Even if you undergo balloon angioplasty or coronary bypass surgery, you will probably still be put on one or more cardiovascular drugs.

There are currently several books on the market that can help you sort through the many types of cardiovascular drugs in more detail. Such books are listed in the "Resources" section.

Antianginal Drugs

These drugs relieve angina pectoris, the chest pain that often accompanies coronary disease. These medications include nitrates, beta-blockers, and calcium channel blockers.

Nitroglycerin: An "Oldie but Goodie"

Almost everyone with coronary disease has taken nitrates in some form. They are some of the oldest heart medicines. Nitrates provide temporary relief from chest pain by dilating your blood vessels, effectively enabling more oxygen to reach the heart.

Nitrates come in various forms. Short-acting nitroglycerin can be used to relieve chest pain during an acute episode of angina. It is taken as a small pill under the tongue and works within five minutes, lasting for 10 to 30 minutes. Longer acting nitroglycerin, which can last for several hours, is also available as pills, patches, and ointments. Examples of nitrates include Nitrostat, Isordil, Ismo, Imdur, NitroBid Ointment, NitroDur, and Transderm Nitro Transdermal.

> ♥ **Mindsaving Tip: Most doctors prescribe nitroglycerin tablets for rapid-acting under-the-tongue use. A product called Nitrolingual Pumpspray is more expensive but is more rapidly acting and easy to use even in the dark. The spray is easier if you have arthritis in your hands or if you are wearing gloves.**

Beta-Blockers

Beta-blockers block the effects of adrenaline, lowering your heart rate, reducing the squeezing of your cardiac muscle, and lowering your blood pressure. There are 12 to 15 types of beta-blockers on the market. (Brand names include Lopresor, Sectral, Tenormin and Toprol-XL.) Propranolol (Inderal) was one of the earliest available and is still frequently prescribed because it has more than just cardiovascular effects; some people report that it reduces anxiety.

Calcium Channel Blockers

Calcium channel blockers interfere with the movement of calcium through specialized channels in the cell membranes of cardiac and vascular smooth muscles. These drugs affect the squeezing of your heart and cause your blood vessels to relax. Because of this, calcium channel blockers, like beta-blockers, are excellent drugs for lowering high blood pressure. Calcium channel blockers are also useful in regulating erratic heart rhythms. Calcium channel blockers include diltiazem (Cardizem), verapamil (Isoptin, Calan), and nifedipine (Procardia, Adalat).

Combination Drugs

Nitrates, beta-blockers, and calcium channel blockers can be used alone but, sometimes, they may be prescribed in combination with each other or with diuretic drugs (see below).

Diuretics

For years doctors prescribed diuretic drugs ("water pills") for high blood pressure. Today, experts no longer believe that diuretics are the best first-step therapy for most people with high blood pressure. The development of new drugs—beta-blockers, calcium channel blockers, and angiotensin converting enzyme (ACE inhibitors)—has diminished their role. Now, diuretics are used more often as backup drugs when other medications fail or in combination with other antihypertensive agents. Diuretics, though, are still commonly used to treat heart failure and fluid retention.

❤ **Lifesaving Tip:** Some diuretics, such as furmosemide (Lasix) and bumetanide (Bumex) are extremely powerful and can cause potassium loss, so, you may need to take a potassium supplement in addition to the diuretic. Other less powerful diuretics may not require such a supplement, especially if they are used in combination with a diuretic that causes potassium retention. Some medications combine two types of diuretics: one that tends to cause potassium loss and one that causes potassium retention. They include Dyazide, Aldactazide, and Maxzide.

ACE Inhibitors

Angiotensin converting enzyme inhibitors, commonly called ACE inhibitors, have been found to be highly effective in treating different types of heart problems. ACE inhibitors lower blood pressure by blocking the formation of an enzyme that is a powerful retainer of salt in the kidney. Thus, they are another line of defense against heart failure and high blood pressure. Also, because they may cause potassium retention, you may not need a potassium supplement if you are on a combination of a diuretic and an ACE inhibitor. ACE inhibitors include enalapril maleate (Vasotec), lisinopril (Zestril, Prinivil), and captopril (Capoten).

Cardiac Strengtheners

Some drugs are used to strengthen the heart muscle and improve the squeezing action. Digoxin (Lanoxin) is the only such drug that can be taken orally. In the past, the effectiveness of digoxin for people with heart failure was questioned, but research shows it helps many. It's also used to control certain common types of heart rhythm disturbances. Dobutamine (Dobutrex) also improves the heart's squeezing, but can only be administered in the vein, so it is usually reserved for hospital use, though special home programs are becoming available.

Blood Thinners

Two general types of blood thinners, or anticoagulants, are used to treat a variety of heart problems. One kind blocks platelets from forming a clot, thereby preventing heart attack and stroke. The most popular type of drug in this class is aspirin.

The other common blood thinner, Warfarin (Coumadin and others), interferes with your blood's normal coagulation. Warfarin is commonly prescribed for those whose heart valves have been replaced with mechanical valves, or to prevent stroke in those who suffer from atrial fibrillation, a type of heartbeat irregularity. Warfarin is a very powerful blood thinner. If you're taking it, your blood must be tested periodically. Avoid eating green, leafy vegetables like spinach or drinking alcohol, as these can alter the test results. Heparin is another blood thinner used when quick action is needed. It can only be given by injection.

❤ Lifesaving Tip: When you take blood thinners such as Warfarin, internal bleeding after an injury could prove especially dangerous. You should consider avoiding such potentially dangerous activities as horseback riding, motorcycle riding, and climbing ladders.

Rhythm Stabilizers

These drugs correct an irregular heartbeat or slow one that's too fast. Over the past several years, the thinking about when to administer such drugs, especially after a heart attack, has changed dramatically. It has been discovered that using stabilizers to treat the heartbeat irregularities known as premature ventricular contractions (PVCs) may be more dangerous than the PVCs themselves. Studies also show that people treated with antiarrhythmics after a heart attack may not fare as well as people whose heartbeat irregularities are not treated.

Beta blockers are the only rhythm-stabilizing drugs that seem to lower the probability of dying after a heart attack. Other medications such as procainamide (Procan, Pronestyl), quinidine (Quinidex, Quinaglute), propafenone (Rythmol), and amiodarone (Cordarone) are used judiciously. Nowadays, treatment with antiarrhythmics is usually reserved for patients with severe ventricular rhythm disturbances. If you have a much-weakened heart and potentially deadly rhythm disturbances, your doctor may prefer you be fitted with a device called an implantable cardioverter defibrillator (ICD).

❤ Lifesaving Tip: Many cardiovascular drugs are quite powerful and may have side effects, such as fatigue, depression, fainting, dizziness, and loss of sexual desire or inability to achieve orgasm. If you experience such side effects, contact your doctor. If the medication is causing the problem, the dose or schedule may need to be changed, or you may need to switched to another drug. It is very important, though, that you never start or stop taking a cardiovascular drug without your doctor's approval.

Cholesterol-Lowering Drugs

A class of powerful cholesterol-lowering drugs known as "statins" is revolutionizing the treatment of high cholesterol. Previously, cholesterol-lowering drugs had been reserved for people with heart disease or very high cholesterol levels. These newer drugs have the potential for saving the lives of healthy women with only mildly elevated cholesterol.

Considered 25 times more potent than their predecessors, the statins reduce LDL cholesterol by over 50 percent and increase the amount of HDL cholesterol by 5 to 10 percent. Although this is a small increase, it is significant because this "good" cholesterol is very difficult to raise.

Interest in the statins jumped following the publication of a major study in 1998 in the *Journal of the American Medical Association* that found the drug benefited not only women with heart disease but also those with no history of it and only mildly elevated cholesterol levels. The study included 5,600 men and 1,000 women, aged 45 and older. All participants followed a healthy diet and exercise program, but the experimental group took lovastatin (Mevacor) and the control group took a placebo. After five years, the cholesterol levels in the lovastatin group improved their cholesterol levels and reduced their risk of a heart attack. Previously, statins had demonstrated their value for men and women with heart disease. However, these drugs may not be prescribed often enough for women, according to a study published in 2000 in the *Archives of Internal Medicine*. The study, which looked at data from 16 hospitals across the United States and Canada, found that women were less likely to receive lipid-lowering therapy.

There are several different types of statins. The ones first developed include fluvastatin (Lescol), lovastatin (Mevacor), pravastatin (Pravachol), and simvastatin (Zocor). Atorvastatin (Lipitor) and cerivastatin (Baycol) were added later. They range in cholesterol-lowering power from 27 percent for fluvastatin to 60 percent for atorvastatin, so the prescription can be tailored to the amount of cholesterol lowering needed. The statins may also lower triglycerides, which can be an added risk factor, especially in women.

But should all women take them? Not necessarily. These drugs are not considered necessary for women who have an LDL level of 130 mg/dl (130 being the dividing line between desirable and borderline LDL levels), whose HDL level is at least 40, and who has a healthy lifestyle and few risk factors for coronary heart disease.

Also, taking statin drugs does not eradicate the need for lifestyle changes. Although they lower LDL cholesterol more than diet and exercise alone, all of the studies show they are more effective when combined with these healthy habits.

In addition to the statins, bile acid sequestrants, available in powders and bars, are also used to reduce high cholesterol. These drugs work by ridding the body of bile acids in the intestines. (A major component of bile acids is cholesterol.) This diverts cholesterol from the bloodstream to the liver, where the cholesterol then converts itself into the missing bile acids. These drugs have been shown to reduce LDL cholesterol by about 20 percent, although they have no effect on HDL levels. Many patients complain about the sandy, gritty taste and the side effects, which include nausea, abdominal pain, indigestion, and constipation.

There also are many cholesterol-lowering supplements on the shelves of your local health food store. Niacin is perhaps the most common supplement used to treat high cholesterol. Regular doses (2,000–3,000 milligrams per day) have been shown to decrease LDL cholesterol by roughly 25 percent, while increasing HDL cholesterol by about 20 percent. Yet, despite its effectiveness, niacin is unpopular because side effects include headaches, flushing, nausea, diarrhea, and heartburn. Before trying niacin, consult with your doctor. In excessively large doses, it can damage the liver, activate peptic ulcers, and worsen blood sugar fluctuations in diabetics. Another supplement, Cholestin, contains the same ingredient—lovastatin—as the prescription statin drug. The first U.S. study to test Cholestin was published in 1999 in the *American Journal of Clinical Nutrition*. Among 83 people with high cholesterol, those who took Cholestin for 12 weeks reduced their cholesterol by an average of 16 percent. Long-term safety has not yet been tested, so don't take Cholestin without telling your doctor.

Aspirin

Aspirin appears to prevent heart attacks by thinning the blood and making it less likely to clot. Many doctors put their male patients who are at risk for heart attack on low-dose aspirin therapy to protect their hearts. This practice is based on a 1988 Harvard study, which found that middle-aged men who took an aspirin every other day substantially lowered their risk of a first heart attack.

Unfortunately, it is not yet known whether aspirin therapy is effective at cutting heart attack risk in women. But preliminary data reported in 1991 from the Nurses' Health Study hints that the drug might be beneficial. Researchers tracked 80,000 women for six years. They found that women age 50 and over who took an aspirin between one and six times a week had one third fewer heart attacks than women who didn't take aspirin.

The researchers are now conducting a study to evaluate the efficacy of low-dose aspirin versus a placebo among a group of 40,000 female health professionals. Results from the trial are expected within the next few years. This will provide a more definite answer as to whether women can benefit from regular use of low-dose aspirin.

The standard dose for aspirin therapy is one-quarter aspirin or a baby aspirin (81 milligrams) daily, or half a regular aspirin (162 milligrams) every other day.

Those who already have heart disease are most likely to benefit from taking a daily aspirin, studies find. If you want to take aspirin to prevent coronary artery disease, the American Heart Association recommends you check with your doctor first, since dosages range from 80 to 325 milligrams. Bear in mind that aspirin can cause side effects, such as gastrointestinal bleeding.

❤ **Lifesaving Tip: Although aspirin is likely to be the most familiar item in your medicine chest, taking it is not risk-free. An anticlotting agent, aspirin protects against heart attack and stroke, but taking it daily can be dangerous if you are already on anticlotting drugs or have other risk factors for bleeding. Ask your doctor first.**

BALLOON ANGIOPLASTY AND RELATED PROCEDURES

Nina sat propped up comfortably in her hospital bed at the Cleveland Clinic. Her shoulder-length brown hair fanned out on the pillow behind her, her eyes sparkled, and her smile broadened in response to a visitor's inquiry on how she was feeling this morning. "Fine, I'm really feeling fine," said Nina, "I wasn't expecting to feel this good," said Nina, with a glimmer of surprise in her voice.

Less than twenty-four hours earlier, Nina had been lying on an imaging table. Although she was awake, she was sedated. On a screen above her feet were displayed X-ray images of her arteries. Nina's coronary arteries (like yours) resemble a large river that divides into branches, then tributaries. Normally, the blood flows through this network smoothly, but Nina's left main coronary artery, the one that supplies most of the blood to her heart, was almost completely blocked. If nothing was done, Nina almost certainly would suffer a heart attack.

Working quickly but with great care, Dr. Russell E. Raymond, an interventional cardiologist, began a procedure that, within an hour, had removed the blockage. The blood flow to Nina's heart returned to normal and the threat of an impending a heart attack virtually disappeared. What's amazing about the procedure is that Dr. Raymond accomplished it without even picking up a scalpel. Known formally as percutaneous transluminal coronary angioplasty (PCTA), or, more commonly as balloon angioplasty, this procedure can widen blocked coronary arteries without subjecting your body to open-heart surgery.

Balloon angioplasty, or PCTA, the type of revascularization procedure Nina underwent, is the elder statesman of interventional techniques. Other such techniques include coronary stenting, in which a tiny scaffold is inserted in the artery to prop it open, and atherectomy, in which different types of tools are used to cut away or shave plaque from the coronary arteries. For simplification, all of these procedures will be termed "angioplasty" initially with the specific techniques discussed later in this chapter.

Why Consider Angioplasty?

If you have a blocked or narrowed coronary artery, angioplasty may be preferable to coronary bypass surgery. It can be a lifesaver for patients considered too frail to survive open-heart surgery, and has spared hundreds of thousands of others from the rigors of this surgery. It is also a

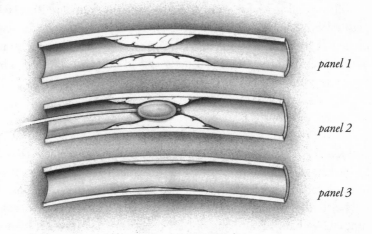

panel 1

panel 2

panel 3

Balloon Angioplasty. The first panel shows an artery narrowed by atherosclerotic plaque. In the second, a special balloon-tipped catheter is inserted into the artery and inflated. In the third panel, the balloon has been removed and blood flow is largely restored.

safe, effective means of treating coronary artery disease. But, as a woman, you need to keep a few points in mind.

Although the medical community has embraced this procedure, it is performed far less often in women. In fact, only 157,000 of the 476,000 patients who underwent angioplasty procedures in 1996 were women.

In the early years of angioplasty, the procedure was more risky and less successful when used on women. A study published in 1985 that reviewed over 3,079 patients found that women had a higher risk of dying or of suffering such complications of tearing of the coronary artery or bleeding. During those early years, use of a balloon that was possibly too large for a woman's smaller arteries was considered the culprit. Today, smaller balloons are used and the overall complication rate has decreased, although the procedure may be slightly riskier for women. However, a study published in 1998 in the journal *Circulation* found that the death rates for women and men are now equal. The study looked at 1,829 people who underwent angioplasty and found that just less than one percent of the women versus 1.2 percent of the men died, meaning no significant difference in the death rates.

"This is good news for women," said Alice K. Jacobs, MD, of the Boston Medical Center, in Boston, Mass., the lead author of the study. She noted this was especially important, since the women in the study tended to be slightly older than the men.

More good news for women comes recently from the Bypass Angio-plasty Revascularization Investigation (BARI). It found that women tended to have procedures for multiple arteries staged over a number of hospital admissions (men almost always had these procedures completed in one session). This leads to better outcomes for the women.

Who Undergoes Angioplasty?

Balloon angioplasty is not for everyone, but the procedure is now per-formed in many instances in which it would have been advised against just a decade ago. Originally, the procedure was used if the patient had only a single vessel narrowed by a single, easily accessible blockage. But times have changed, and angioplasty procedures are now performed even on women with multiple blockages in two vessels. Because angioplasty is so much less stressful than bypass surgery, most doctors are inclined to at least give it a try if it is indicated. Balloon angioplasty is sometimes also performed as an emergency procedure to open clogged coronary arteries after a heart attack. In the case of "three vessel disease," in which all three coronary arteries are narrowed, coronary bypass surgery is still the procedure of choice, because it is likely that one or more vessels would eventually reclose, necessitating repeat angioplasty procedures.

—————

❤ **Lifesaving Tip: To find out whether you're a good candidate for angioplasty, a cardiologist who has considerable experience in performing the procedure on women should evaluate you.**

—————

Before Your Angioplasty: Cardiac Catheterization

If you're been told you're a candidate for angioplasty, you've already had a cardiac catheterization. Sometimes the angioplasty is done at the same time as the catheterization. Often, though, catheterization is done first, and the patient returns at a later time for the angioplasty.

—————

❤ **Mindsaving Tip: It's normal to experience anxiety about any procedure regarding angioplasty. Talking with women who have undergone angioplasty can make you feel better. Visiting a heart support group before the surgery can ease your mind.**

—————

Who Does the Angioplasty?

A hospital should perform at least 200 balloon angioplasties each year, according to a task forum composed of the American College of Cardiology, the American Heart Association, and the American College of Physicians. An individual physician should act as the "primary operator" for a minimum of 75 angioplasties annually. In some large medical centers, a team performs angioplasty, and you do not necessarily get to pick the person who will perform yours. In that case, make certain all the team members meet these minimum qualifications.

It is important that you choose the hospital where you undergo your angioplasty with the same care you would use if you were having open-heart surgery. Although the vast majority of angioplasties go smoothly, sometimes emergency surgery is required. Therefore, you should undergo your angioplasty only in a hospital that is equipped to perform open-heart surgery. "Some hospitals are doing angioplasty without open-heart surgery backup, but use a hospital nearby to cover them. In the event of an emergency, you should never have to be transported to a different building," says Dr. Anita Arnold, an interventional cardiologist at Olympia Fields Osteopathic Hospital and Medical Center.

Your Angioplasty

An angioplasty begins very much as a cardiac catheterization does: In fact, many of the steps are identical. Just as for the catheterization, you're heavily sedated; the doctor will make a tiny puncture in your femoral artery, the artery that leads from your groin to your coronary arteries. Once that is accomplished, the doctor maneuvers a thin guide wire along your arteries until it is just past the point of the blockage. Then a special catheter with a balloon on its tip is threaded over the guide wire and pushed along until it reaches past the area of the blockage. The balloon is inflated and held in that position from several seconds to several minutes. It may be reinflated a couple of times to maintain patency (the opening). The procedure usually takes about two hours, depending on the number and severity of the blockages.

After Your Angioplasty

Your sedation will not wear off after the procedure, so you'll probably be sleeping for awhile. Heavy pressure will be applied to your groin to stop any bleeding, and you'll be ordered to lie perfectly still (a recently approved technique reduces the need for the heavy weights). You'll probably sleep until the next morning. When you wake up, your groin area will be a little sore, but probably not as sore as you expect. You'll be encouraged to get up, and, before long you'll be walking around the floor. If no problems occur, you'll be discharged. You'll be closely watched to make sure no chest pain or cardiac symptoms occur.

Once You're Home:

- If you have a car with a standard transmission, you should probably skip driving it for a few days to rest your leg.
- You won't have any other restrictions related to this procedure, but you'll probably want to take it easy for a few days.
- If you work primarily at a desk job, you can return to work almost immediately. If you work at a job where you use your leg a lot, or do bending or lifting, you should stay out of work at least a few days longer.

- It is likely that you will be placed on some type of blood thinning drug. You need to make sure you understand exactly how long you should take the drug and what to do when your prescription runs out.
- You'll probably be asked to return at six weeks for an exercise EKG test. This is done not only to make sure that your arteries have remained open, but also furnishes results that can be used for comparative purposes if you have any chest pain or other symptoms later on.

❤ **Lifesaving Tip: Once you're home, if your chest pain or other cardiac symptoms return, contact your doctor immediately.**

The Problem of Restenosis

If you're thinking that balloon angioplasty sounds too good to be true, in one respect, you're right. When angioplasty achieves lasting results, it really can seem like a miracle. However, arteries can sometimes become narrowed again, a process called restenosis.

Restenosis of arteries occurs approximately 35 percent of the time within three months of all angioplasties. Although 35 percent may seem high, it does not usually deter doctors from recommending angioplasty once, or suggesting it be repeated once more if restenosis recurs. Sometimes, two angioplasties are needed to achieve lasting results, and you'll still be spared open-heart surgery.

However, restenosis can take an emotional toll on you. Just ask Hope, who underwent angioplasty four times (on two different blood vessels) over a nine-month period. "After the third angioplasty, I was ecstatic. I thought I had absolutely licked it. Then, I began having chest pain again, and the angiogram showed the blockage had returned," she said. Hope may be part of a small minority of women whose arteries have a tendency to become reclogged no matter what. For her, coronary bypass surgery may provide the only long-term solution.

Although it's not known why restenosis occurs, several conditions are known or believed to be known to increase the risk of restenosis after angioplasty: high blood pressure, diabetes, unstable angina (more frequent or intense chest pain), vasospastic angina (caused by blood vessel spasms), and kidney disease requiring dialysis. There is also a theory that revascularization procedures activate cytomegalovirus (CMV), a herpes virus that is common in older people but is usually dormant. According to this theory, CMV is the factor that allows too many cells to proliferate during the artery's healing process and eventually narrows it again.

Researchers are gaining a better understanding of the restenosis process and are experimenting with several different approaches to prevent it. They believe that three complex, interrelated mechanisms are involved. First, within hours after a procedure, the walls of the artery may start to recoil, gradually "caving in" to their original position, reducing the channel that was created sometimes by as much as half. Also, the procedure causes a certain amount of injury to the cell wall, so as the body attempts to heal itself, blood platelets may accumulate, possibly causing a clot. Blood clots create a substance, thrombin, that causes the cells to proliferate and new tissue to form. This is a helpful part of the healing process but, if too much tissue is formed, it can reduce flow of blood through the artery. Thanks to this greater understanding of restenosis, several drugs are now being tested to help prevent it.

❤ **Lifesaving Tip: Consult your doctor if you experience chest pain or other symptoms identical to what you experienced before angioplasty, or if you have had angina or experienced it within six months after angioplasty or any other coronary revascularization process, including coronary bypass surgery. It's important to remember that restenosis is sometimes "silent" (it doesn't always cause symptoms). If you've had any revascularization procedure, it's important to monitor your own well-being and see your doctor for regular checkups.**

❤ **Mindsaving Tip: Even though your first angioplasty will probably be your last, you should be emotionally prepared in case it does not turn out that way. Restenosis can occur, no matter how good a job the doctor did or how model a patient you were.**

Coronary Stenting

Coronary stenting has gained popularity since it was first used in clinical trials in the early 1990s. Stents are now used in combination with angioplasty in 60 to 70 percent of all procedures to help reduce the possibility of restenosis. In this procedure, the stent, or wire mesh tube is used to prop open an artery that was recently cleared using angioplasty. The stent is collapsed to a small diameter, placed over an angioplasty balloon catheter and moved into the area of the blockage. When the balloon is inflated, the stent expands, locks in place and forms a rigid support to hold the artery open. The stent remains in the artery permanently to keep it open. In the Primary Angioplasty in Myocardial Infarction (PAMI) trials, however, stenting was less effective in women. It is likely that this is due to the smaller size of their vessels.

Coronary Atherectomy

Because of the restenosis problem, atherectomy is also used as an alternative to balloon angioplasty. It is also proving very useful in treating blockages that may be too hardened or inaccessible for balloon angioplasty.

An atherectomy is similar to angioplasty, except instead of a balloon compressing the fatty deposits against the walls of your arteries, special instruments are used to destroy the blockages. Types of atherectomy include:

- Extraction atherectomy. This procedure uses a tiny rotating blade that works in much the same fashion as the cutter on a food processor to whisk away blockages inside the artery wall at a rate of up to 1,200 revolutions per minute.
- Rotational atherectomy. This procedure uses a high-speed, diamond-tipped drill to penetrate fatty deposits and is particularly useful on hard, calcified plaque.
- Directional atherectomy. This procedure uses a device that is a combination of a balloon and a shaving blade. The cutting device, usually located on the side, is run back and forth and shaves the deposits away.

❤ **Lifesaving Tip: The interventional cardiologist who evaluates your case should also be experienced in these similar techniques. Some are designed for cases in which the blockages are considered inaccessible or resistant to the balloon methods. But if your doctor does not practice them, you won't be offered them. Hence, you may be slated for bypass surgery without learning whether these newer procedures might have worked for you.**

LASERS: ZAPPING BLOCKAGES

The use of lasers has always intrigued cardiologists, but presents some problems. A laser beam shoots straight ahead, and is unable to follow the winding course of your coronary blood vessels. However, lasers are being increasingly used in these following ways:

Laser Revascularization

Also called transmyocardial revascularization (TMR), this procedure is used to help alleviate severe angina, the chest pain that is due to a lack of oxygenated blood reaching the heart. It is not an alternative to coronary bypass surgery or angioplasty, but is now approved to be used for patients in combination with bypass procedures and whose symptoms aren't relieved by bypass alone.

Sometimes called the "snake heart" procedure, TMR is based on the natural structure of reptile hearts. Rather than having blood vessels connected to the ventricle and heart muscles, reptiles have open channels. In TMR, the surgeon duplicates the design of the reptile heart. Working through a small incision, he or she uses a computer-controlled laser to create 20 to 40 channels in the areas of the heart muscle that are not receiving enough blood. The goal is to get blood pumped directly from the ventricle through the newly created channels for the heart muscle. Following the procedure, the surface of the heart heals quickly, but it seems that newly generated microvessels are left behind to transport blood.

This procedure has produced early promising results in alleviating chest pain, but few long-term studies have been done. Laser revascularization may be suitable for people who are at high risk for a second coronary bypass operation or angioplasty, or those with blockages too widely dispersed to be treated with a bypass operation or angioplasty alone.

A related procedure currently in the experimental stage is called percutaneous transmyocardial revascularization (PMR). PMR also involves using lasers to drill holes in the heart, but the procedure is done using a catheter, thereby avoiding the need for the patient's chest to be opened. This procedure is proving less effective than TMR and is not likely to be approved by the FDA.

These techniques are not designed to replace coronary bypass surgery or balloon angioplasty but might someday be used in conjunction with other standard treatments to achieve even better blood flow. Also, although both these techniques are promising, longer-term studies are needed to establish proof of their benefit.

Intravascular Ultrasound

Another use of lasers that is becoming increasingly important is intravascular ultrasound, a technique that combines echo with catheterization. This technique may have a significant effect on making laser therapy a reality. Dr. Steven Nissen, a cardiovascular imaging specialist at the Cleveland Clinic, believes this technique will revolutionize coronary artery intervention by permitting ultrasound guided therapies. It is the equivalent of having a camera on the tip of a catheter providing clear images of the presence and extent of atherosclerotic blockage, allowing more precise targeting of angioplasty, atherectomy, and laser technique. "This capability is going to change how we diagnose and treat coronary disease, and by the end of the 1990s," predicts Dr. Nissen, "diagnosis and therapy will be combined."

Bear in Mind

When angioplasty and similar procedures work, and in the majority of cases they do, they certainly can seem like a miracle. But these procedures don't correct the underlying condition that caused your coronary arteries to become narrowed in the first place. Because angioplasty is a relatively brief and painless procedure, you can be lulled into thinking you are now cured and do not have to go through the hard work of changing your lifestyle. Before you know it, you're back to work, managing your household and dealing with the other pressures of daily life. It's easy to slip back into old habits. If you do, you could end up back in the hospital, this time as a heart attack victim or surgery patient in worse shape.

To get yourself on the right track, consider participating in a cardiac rehabilitation program. Such a program may have been introduced to you in the hospital but you may have to inquire about it yourself. In addition, joining a support group for those with heart problems can provide you with emotional support and help you make those necessary lifestyle changes.

❤ **Lifesaving Tip: Adopting a healthy lifestyle, which includes quitting smoking, eating a low-fat diet, and undertaking a regular program of exercise, is as important for those who have angioplasty as for people who undergo coronary bypass surgery.**

CORONARY ARTERY BYPASS SURGERY

It was a chilly wet autumn and Beverly was having trouble shaking what she thought was bronchitis. That nagging problem was the only shadow being cast on her happy, energetic life. She had a wonderful marriage, had raised two adoring sons, and loved her job as a customer representative in a telecommunications company. At the age of 56, she was mildly diabetic, but considered herself otherwise healthy. Her only concern was this respiratory problem. But, as the days wore on, Beverly was finding it harder and harder to breathe.

"I went into congestive heart failure around Thanksgiving time, although, of course, I didn't realize it," she remembered, "when I went to the doctor and was literally gasping for breath. My doctor told me, 'You're in heart failure. I'm sending you to a cardiologist.'"

At first, the cardiologist thought a virus had attacked and weakened Beverly's heart. But tests showed her problem was caused by coronary heart disease. Not long afterwards, Beverly was doing fine and already itching to return to work.

What Is Coronary Bypass Surgery?

Coronary artery bypass grafting, known informally as "bypass grafting" (and even more informally among doctors themselves as "CABG," pronounced "cabbage"), is a type of open-heart surgery. The procedure involves taking a vein or artery from your body and grafting it onto the vessels of your heart. This grafted vessel provides an alternative route for blood to reach the heart muscle, literally providing a "bypass" around a clogged vessel that has been narrowed by coronary disease.

When it was developed in the 1960s, this surgery was considered miraculous. Skeptics, however, viewed it as the latest in a parade of procedures devised to counter the devastating effects of coronary disease. Many of those procedures had been hailed as breakthroughs but had later been abandoned. Over the years, however, studies have proved that bypass surgery, although no longer considered a miracle cure, is a very effective treatment. One major study showed that 87 percent of patients with severe narrowing in their three coronary arteries survived at least another five years after bypass, while only 59 percent were alive after being treated with drugs. Besides prolonging the life of certain patients,

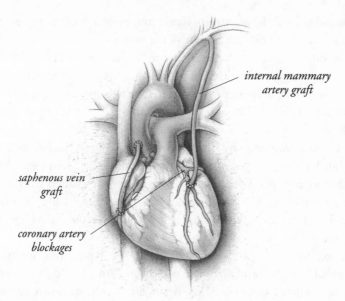

internal mammary
artery graft

saphenous vein
graft

coronary artery
blockages

Coronary Bypass Surgery. This procedure uses "grafts" to route blood around areas of serious blockage. If a leg vein is used as a graft, it is inserted into the aorta on the one end and anchored past the obstruction in the coronary artery on the other end. If an internal mammary artery is used, only the end is freed from the chest wall and attached to the blocked coronary artery, bypassing the obstruction.

bypass surgery also has been shown to relieve the debilitating chest pain of coronary disease that doesn't respond to medication.

When it comes to women, another type of controversy has arisen. Nowadays, bypass surgery is among the most common of operations, with 598,000 performed in 1996 alone. Such high numbers have led some to question whether the surgery is being performed too often. But this is not the worry for women. Only 175,000 of these bypasses were performed on women, resulting in the concern that, when it comes to women, bypass surgery is not being performed often enough.

Bypass Risks for Women

Although coronary bypass surgery is considered, by and large, to be a safe procedure, women used to have double the death rate of men. Thanks to advances in technology and improved surgical techniques, this has changed. A study published in 1998 in the journal *Circulation* found no differences between men and women in terms of both in-hospital deaths and five-year survival rates, even though the women were more often older and had more risk factors.

Although outcomes for women are improving, there are still some inherent risks you should bear in mind. First, women tend to have smaller, more delicate coronary arteries, which makes the surgery more technically difficult. The size of the coronary vessels varies according to height.

"A small woman, say, one who is four feet, 11 inches or five feet tall, can have very, very small coronary arteries and can be technically difficult to do a good job. I've done bypasses on women who were five feet, 10 inches or so, and their arteries were just as big as a man's," notes Dr. John A. Elefteriades, a heart surgeon at Yale-New Haven Hospital.

If you are a petite woman and in need of a bypass, this doesn't mean you shouldn't go ahead with the operation. You should, however, consider yourself at higher risk. "We don't turn a patient down on the basis of body size," Dr. Elefteriades said. "We proceed and do it if there is an important need for it. We worry more about it, and it's definitely more common to have problems."

So it remains important that you wisely choose your surgeon and hospital. Studies have shown that death rates for bypass vary widely according to these factors. For guidelines in making these selections, see Chapter 14.

Treatment, Not Cure

Doctors now know that bypass surgery does not halt the progression of the coronary disease. Over the years, the remaining native arteries can become blocked by disease, as can the newly grafted vessel. This means that, after a bypass:

- You may still need to take cardiovascular drugs.
- You must make lifestyle changes.
- You must quit smoking. Cigarette smoking has a profoundly negative effect on new grafts, and greatly increases the probability they will eventually close up. Dr. Elefteriades even tells patients, "If you cannot decide right here and now never to smoke another cigarette, don't have the operation. It's not worth it."

Should You Have a Bypass?

Ever since bypasses began being performed, the question of which patients benefit most has been hotly debated. Recently, the American College of Cardiology and the American Heart Association issued joint guidelines on which patients are likely to most benefit from a coronary bypass. Their report showed the patients who benefited the most from a bypass were those with the worst prognosis. Whether or not a bypass is your best course is a decision that should be made by you and your doctor. But here are some examples of when a bypass is clearly the best therapy.

You may be a candidate for CABG if:

- Tests show a critical narrowing of your left main artery, the channel that supplies most of the blood to the main portion of your heart.
- You suffer from severe angina, the chest pain of coronary artery disease that does not respond to medication in adequate amounts.
- You suffer from three-vessel disease, which is characterized by blockages affecting your three major coronary arteries. In such cases, bypass is often preferable to angioplasty because, with so many vessels to be opened, there is a high likelihood that one or more of them will close up again, necessitating a repeat procedure.
- If you've had angioplasty repeatedly and the vessels have become closed again.
- If you underwent bypass years ago, and the graft has become clogged.

❤ **Lifesaving Tip: The final decision to undergo bypass surgery can be made only by you. If you have any doubt, by all means, seek a second opinion, or even a third. Coronary bypass is serious surgery, and requires serious consideration. Likewise, you should consider getting a second opinion if you are told you need a bypass, but, for some reason, you are an unsuitable candidate.**

Are You a High-Risk Patient?

In the past, just being a woman put you at a slightly higher risk of dying or suffering a serious complication, but success rates in women are improving. If you are in otherwise good health, a community hospital

with a well-experienced cardiovascular staff may provide you with satisfactory care. On the other hand, if you have additional risk factors, you
would be wise to seek out a medical center that specializes in heart
surgery. For a list of factors that may indicate you are at high risk for
open-heart surgical procedures including CABG, see Chapter 14.

What Type of Bypass Graft: Leg Vein or Chest Artery?

Traditionally, most coronary artery bypass operations were done using a
vein taken from the legs. Most recently, though, surgeries that use the
internal thoracic artery (commonly known as the "internal mammary
artery" in the past), taken from the inside of the chest wall, are gaining in
general popularity, having been previously performed in only a handful
of cases. This is because such grafts are much less likely to develop future
disease. Studies show that using the internal thoracic artery greatly
reduces the possibility the graft will soon become narrow again and even
improves long-term survival.

Since most coronary bypasses today are done to replace more than
one artery, even when the internal thoracic artery is used, a vein from the
leg is often also used. The internal thoracic artery, though, is used for the
more important graft.

Surgeons differ in their preferences, and there are some very highly
regarded surgeons who still maintain that the internal thoracic artery
prolongs the bypass procedure. If your surgery is done on an emergency
basis, you probably won't have a choice. If it is elective surgery, however,
you should make certain your surgeon is willing to consider using your
internal thoracic artery. Whether or not the internal thoracic artery is
suitable for use can usually be evaluated by cardiac catheterization.
Sometimes, using the internal thoracic artery can result in some inci-
sional pain or an increased risk of infection, especially if you are diabetic.

The CABG Procedure

Whether you're undergoing open-heart surgery for a bypass or for
another type of heart repair, many of the preliminary steps are the same,
including hooking you up to the heart-lung machine. They are covered
in Chapter 14.

If the bypass is to be done with your leg vein, that vein is removed
after you are put to sleep. Then, the surgeon makes an opening in your
aorta, which is your main artery, and another in the narrowed artery

beyond the blockage. The surgeon then sews one end of the grafted vein to each opening, creating a new route along which the blood from your aorta can flow. If the surgeon is using your internal thoracic artery, that vessel is freed from your chest wall, then the end is sewn below the blockage in the affected artery.

❤ **Mindsaving Tip: Don't worry about missing either your leg vein or your thoracic artery. You can get along without either. In the case of your leg, other veins will take over its circulation. In the case of your thoracic artery, you were born with duplicate circulation and can easily spare one.**

Although it's by no means minor surgery, coronary artery bypass is very frequently done today, and many women in your circle of friends may have gone through it. To learn our tips for recuperating, see Chapter 14.

Minimally Invasive Coronary Bypass Surgery

Minimally invasive bypass surgery is a new technique designed to minimize the trauma to the body of bypass surgery. As in traditional bypass, the goal of surgery is to reroute blood around clogged arteries, bypassing blockages to improve the supply of blood and oxygen to the heart. But rather than making a chest-length incision, splitting the breast bone and prying open the rib cage, as in traditional bypass surgery, the surgeon operates through smaller openings with miniaturized surgical instruments.

There are two approaches commonly used: port-access coronary artery bypass, also referred to as PACAB or PortCAB, and minimally invasive coronary artery bypass, also called MIDCAB. In PACAB, your heart is stopped with a heart-lung machine, as it is done in traditional bypass, but instead of your chest being opened, the surgeon operates through several small holes, or ports, viewing the procedure on video monitors. The MIDCAB procedure offers even greater advantages, because the surgery is performed while the heart is still beating. This eliminates the need for the heart-lung machine, which has been linked with an increased risk of stroke and cognitive problems after bypass. MIDCAB is intended for less extensive coronary artery disease, when only one or two arteries need to be bypassed.

Not everyone who needs a bypass is a candidate for a less-invasive operation. Your surgeon must consider the location and extent of your coronary artery disease, among other factors, in deciding whether or not to offer the new approach. Blockages of the two "anterior" cardiac arteries (those toward the front of the heart) are the most amenable to beating-heart, minimally invasive procedures. These vessels—the right coronary artery and the left anterior descending artery—are readily accessible with new techniques. If you have blockages in the "posterior" coronary arteries, you may still be a candidate for this type of surgery, but these vessels—the circumflex and posterior descending arteries—are difficult to bypass when the heart is beating.

At the Cleveland Clinic, for instance, MIDCAB patients typically stay 24 hours less in intensive care. For a single-vessel bypass with the new technique, your hospital stay may be as brief as two days, and your postoperative recovery time just two to four weeks. With a traditional open-heart procedure, patients spend about six days in the hospital and six to eight weeks recuperating at home. If you're older and have additional health problems, you may have a longer hospital stay after a minimally invasive procedure than younger patients, but it's still probably shorter than it would be if you underwent a conventional bypass operation.

Since these are new techniques, there are limited data on whether these surgeries will be as successful as coronary bypass. By contrast, traditional bypass has been used since the mid-1960s and has an excellent track record based on large amounts of data. But small studies to date have been encouraging. For instance, one small 1998 study, published in the *Annals of Thoracic Surgery,* looked at the results of both PACAB and MIDCAB in 102 patients, 20 of whom were women. The techniques appeared to work well, although research still needs to compare the success of the new methods with traditional bypass. To get the true picture, though, much more research is needed.

Minimally invasive cardiac surgery is on a fast track that is expected to continue to expand patients' options. Of course, your surgeon should make a recommendation based on how best to treat your particular blockages with the least risk to you, and that may dictate a conventional bypass procedure. Again, the decision should be based on your particular case and your surgeon's expertise.

CARDIAC REHABILITATION

With her masses of red hair, it was impossible to overlook Hope. Clad in black stretch pants and a purple-and-lavender billowy blouse, she pedaled away on her stationary bike to the beat of the jazz classic, "In the

Mood." She was in a mirrored room, filled with exercise bikes and tread-mills. The scene could have been any health club, but Hope was happily pedaling away in the Out-Patient Cardiac Rehabilitation Center at the Cleveland Clinic Foundation. If you have a heart problem, probably your first fear is that you will die. Your second fear is most likely to be that you will become an invalid. Though once rooted in reality, these are now misconceptions.

What Is Cardiac Rehabilitation?

Cardiac rehabilitation (referred to usually as "cardiac rehab") is a spe-cially structured program of exercise, education, and support designed to strengthen your heart's ability to perform exercise and return you to normal health or better. If you've been hospitalized with a heart prob-lem, your program may get underway while you're still in your hospital gown. At the Cleveland Clinic, for example, cardiac patients are given a notebook with an exercise program that begins in the hospital and con-tinues once they've gone home. Cardiac rehab is seen as an integral part of virtually every heart patient's treatment.

New Friends

A good cardiac rehab program provides you with more than just exer-cise; you also get a new set of friends, friends who know what you are going through because they've been there. "After my heart attack, I got very depressed," says Roberta, "Part of it was dealing with the reality that I might have died. I got very low. One of the things that really helped was signing up for the cardiac rehab program. It meant getting up, going out, and also meeting people who'd also had this experience. I learned that I really wasn't alone."

Cardiac rehabilitation may benefit you if:

- You have chest pain (angina pectoris) from coronary disease. By exercising, you condition your heart to withstand physical activity, so you experience less chest pain. You'll also learn ways to make necessary lifestyle changes.
- You've had a heart attack. Studies have shown that cardiac rehabil-itation can reduce the likelihood of your suffering a second heart attack and decrease the likelihood that you will become disabled because of your cardiac problem.

- You've undergone heart surgery or angioplasty. Whether you've had a bypass, valve replacement, or any type of cardiac procedure, such programs can benefit you. Studies show you can experience a 90 percent improvement in your ability to exercise after four months in such a program.
- You are at high risk for developing coronary artery disease: You don't need to have suffered a heart attack or had bypass surgery to benefit from cardiac rehab.
- You have an irregular heart rhythm, a pacemaker, or a weakened heart. Once, people with such problems were not considered suitable for cardiac rehab. But new studies have proven otherwise. Although it depends on your individual case, cardiac rehab may improve your condition.
- You've had surgery to correct a valve problem or congenital heart defect. Cardiac rehabilitation has not traditionally been viewed as necessary for patients with congenital heart defects because most patients recover well without it. However, if your heart defect has interfered with your ability to exercise for some time, you may be in poor physical condition or unsure about your own exercise ability.

❤ **Lifesaving Tip: Cardiac rehabilitation is being to found to benefit people with a whole range of heart problems, but there are some conditions in which exercise is dangerous. No matter what your heart problem, you should check with your doctor before starting any exercise program.**

Finding a Good Cardiac Rehab Program

A good cardiac rehab program must also meet important standards to provide you with a safe environment in which to exercise. Your doctor or local hospital can refer you. To find a good cardiac rehab program, here's a list of things to look for:

- A good cardiac rehab program should conform to guidelines of the American Heart Association, the American College of Cardiology, and the American Association of Cardiovascular and Pulmonary Rehabilitation.
- The program should be supervised by a cardiologist or otherwise qualified physician.

- A qualified nurse should be on hand at all times.
- The exercise instructors should have a college degree in physical fitness or a related field and should also be trained in cardiac rehabilitation.

❤ **Mindsaving Tip: If you've been diagnosed with a cardiac problem, you may suddenly feel very fragile. A cardiac rehab program provides you with a safe environment in which you can improve your strength and endurance to a point you never expected to achieve.**

What's the Program Like?

There are four phases of cardiac rehabilitation. These are the same, whether you've had a heart attack, surgery, or angioplasty. The first phase begins while you are in the hospital, where you'll be visited by a rehabilitation therapist, who will teach you exercises to do while still in bed or sitting down. The exercise pace will initially be slow. Given the trend for shorter lengths of hospital stays, you may be discharged at this point. You'll be given a program to continue at home, which will probably include warm-up exercises and walking. Before you know it, you'll probably be walking a couple of miles a day. You can also exercise in a group setting, at an outpatient rehab center, and become comfortable with such exercise devices as stationary bikes and treadmills. Phases two, three, and four focus on the intensity of your exercise and the amount of supervision and monitoring, which will decrease as your physical condition and confidence improve. Phase three often takes place in an outpatient center, which may be at the hospital, but a community gym, YMCA, or health club setting is fine, as long as the program meets high cardiac rehab standards.

After you "graduate" from phase four, you may choose to exercise at home or continue your program at a health club or exercise facility. While you will no longer need the medical supervision you once did, many people find they miss the company of their friends from cardiac rehab. Some programs are structured so you can continue indefinitely. Charlene, for example, has been attending cardiac rehab faithfully since she had her heart attack seven years ago. "It's not just an exercise group, it's a support group," she says, "We talk over our problems, and exchange recipes or articles. If one of us is in the dumps, we pull ourselves out of it. That's the real important benefit."

❤ **Mindsaving Tip:** As part of cardiac rehab, you may be told to take extra walks outdoors on your own, or given another form of home exercise. If it's cold or inclement, try your walking in an indoor mall. Nowadays, some malls even sponsor walking clubs!

Cardiac Rehab Reaps Big Benefits

The benefits of cardiac rehabilitation are many. They include an improvement in cardiovascular function, an increased ability to exercise, and added confidence. An important component of a good rehab program is also the educational sessions, lectures, group discussions, and fireside chats that are held regularly. Here, you can get support in making lifestyle changes, low-fat cooking tips, ideas on quitting smoking, and share ways to deal with the emotional issues that arise when dealing with heart problems.

Cardiac Rehab and Women

As good as cardiac rehab programs are for women, they appear to have some drawbacks. Studies show that women are less likely to join and more likely to drop out. As much as Hope enjoys her program, such studies do not surprise her. At the moment, she's the only woman in her class. "Sometimes, its hard being the only woman here," she says, "I like the guys, but I miss having a woman to talk to."

Part of the reason for that, or course, is that more men than women are currently undergoing hospital procedures for their heart problems, so they are more likely to be referred to a cardiac rehab program. The cardiac rehab educator may focus the lectures and materials on men's needs and erroneously assume that any woman present must be a spouse, not a patient. Single women, like Hope, sometimes feel even more like outsiders. Also, while doctors usually don't hesitate to refer men to cardiac rehab programs, some believe that women, especially older women, may not be interested in exercise, and miss out on the chance to refer women to the program. Time can also be a factor. Most cardiac rehab programs are conducted during the day. A woman is more likely to have home responsibilities that can interfere with her attendance, or to work in a job from which she cannot get the necessary time off. If this is true in your case, there are some facts that may persuade your employer that cardiac rehab is an important part of your recuperation. You can point to a study done at Coors Brewing Co. in Colorado, where workers who participated in cardiac rehab returned to work sooner, resulting in a savings of over $10,000 in wages and disability expenses per participant.

Who Pays for Cardiac Rehab?

If you have private health insurance or Medicare, you should be covered for cardiac rehabilitation if you have had a heart attack or unstable angina or have had balloon angioplasty or bypass or valve surgery. If there is another reason for you to participate in cardiac rehab, such as a congenital defect or heart failure, your doctor may be able to convince the insurer it will benefit you.

If you do not have insurance, a good cardiac rehab program strives to keep its costs low, so the fee may be less than you think. If you want to continue going to cardiac rehab after your program ends, you'll probably have to pick up the cost yourself but you may find the cost less than joining a health club.

Also, even if you undergo cardiac rehab, remember that is not the end of the road. To continue to accrue benefits, you must continue exercising. Many women don't, as a study published in 1998 in the journal *Nursing Research* pointed out. This study followed 40 women who completed a cardiac rehab program following either a heart attack or bypass surgery. The study found that although 83 percent of the participating women started exercising during the first month, one third of the participants had stopped exercising. During the last week of the study, only 50 percent of the women were still exercising.

Be Your Own Cheerleader

Lack of emotional support may be the most important factor of all in explaining why women take less advantage of cardiac rehab. Typically, a male heart patient has a wife who acts as cheerleader and encourages him to go. As a woman, you may be divorced, widowed, or otherwise living alone, with no one to give you the encouragement you need. If this is so, be your own cheerleader! Cardiac rehab may turn out to be the most important part of your recovery.

❤ **Lifesaving Tip: Even if you had your heart attack or surgery years ago, it's not too late to join a cardiac rehab program. Exercising will improve your health, increase your sense of well-being, add** to your store of knowledge about your heart, and help you make new friends.

HEART TRANSPLANTS

Eleanor strode around a Milwaukee shopping mall, handing out pamphlets about organ donation. Her T-shirt, blue and decorated with fluffy white clouds, read "Don't Take Your Organs to Heaven—Heaven Knows We Need Them Here." Eleanor should know. When she was in her 50s, she found out she had an enlarged heart. Her condition worsened and, when she was in her 60s, she was placed on a list for a heart transplant. Nine months later, she received a donor heart.

"The transplant experience was not easy. It was a very emotional time for me. But I'd made up my mind I had walked into the hospital and I would walk out and I did," said Eleanor, who now works with the Wisconsin Donor Network to encourage people to make arrangements to donate their organs when they die.

It is very rare that a heart becomes so weakened as to require a heart transplant. Much less drastic measures have been developed to treat, and even correct, the majority of heart problems.

In some cases, though, your heart may be so badly weakened and damaged that a heart transplant is your only hope. For these persons, heart transplants have become much safer. In his 1971 book, *Hearts,* journalist Thomas Thompson chronicled several heart transplant cases performed during the period of 1968 to 1971. These were the early, heady days of heart transplants, before doctors fully realized the daunting problems presented by the body's own immune system. As a result, many of early these heart transplants failed.

But doctors learned a great deal from this early, experimental period. Techniques have been refined and important drugs to suppress the body's immune system discovered. In 1997, 2,290 heart transplants were performed in the United States, about three quarters of them on men. Most recent statistics show 70 percent of heart transplant patients were still alive after four years. Many of them are able to return to leading active lives.

Careful patient selection has also contributed to the increased survival rate among transplant patients. Candidates for heart transplants are usually under 60 years of age. They're usually male, as women often develop heart disease later in life (there were 15 men and three women in Eleanor's transplant support group). There is no lower age limit for a heart transplants; indeed, children with very severe congenital heart defects are now receiving them.

In adults, recipients have very little chance of survival without a transplant. They are usually in the final stages of congestive heart failure, caused either by coronary heart disease, or a heart muscle disorder, such as a cardiomyopathy, usually from a virus that attacks the heart. They need to be in otherwise good health, without such diseases such as diabetes or cancer, for example.

One of the biggest barriers to a heart transplant remains the shortage of donor organs. Often, a patient awaiting a heart transplant is placed on a long waiting list or may even have to travel to an area where donor hearts are more available. It's unfortunate, but true, that the odds of receiving a donor heart are better in larger cities, where higher accident rates contribute to the availability of organs for transplant. Health insurers are also increasingly assuming a major role in determining where a transplant patient will be treated.

Heart transplants are similar to other types of open-heart surgery, which is covered in Chapter 14. As in other open-heart procedures, the patient is placed on the heart-lung machine. Although it may sound from the term "heart transplant" as if the entire heart is removed, this is not accurate. In a heart transplant, the major portion of the heart that is diseased—the ventricles—are removed. The vena cavae—the major blood vessels—are left in place, as are the "back walls" of the atria (the upper chambers of the heart). The donor heart is inserted and the major blood vessels reconnected.

Because of the risk that the donor heart may be rejected, patients who undergo heart transplants must remain on strong immunosuppressive drugs, such as cyclosporine, for the rest of their lives. They must guard their new hearts against infection and return to the hospital frequently for tests.

Psychologically, a heart transplant can be a very difficult experience. Often, the wait for a donor heart is an emotional roller-coaster ride, with hopes of a donor heart raised, then dashed again. All of our beliefs about our hearts, even the most primitive, rise to the surface when the topic is a heart transplant. Often, patients may wonder if they will be somehow "different" with another person's heart beating within their chest. If you are a candidate for a heart transplant, patient organizations such as "Mended Hearts," listed in the "Resources" section of this book, can be of tremendous help.

Although heart transplants are relatively uncommon, they have become far safer over the years, and may offer the best chance for some patients to lead a normal life.

What About Artificial Hearts?

During those early days, there was great hope that an artificial heart could be perfected that a person could live with indefinitely. In the 1980s, the whole world followed the story of Barney Clark, the dentist who lived with an artificial heart for 112 days before he died. But researchers had underestimated how perfectly the heart performs, and they discovered that artificial hearts, at least up to now, cannot simulate the work of the heart precisely enough to keep many of the body's organs from eventually deteriorating. Nowadays, artificial hearts are increasingly used, but mainly as a temporary booster-pump to keep the patient alive for a few days or weeks until a human donor heart can be found and a heart transplant performed. However, as the technology improves, the use of such booster-pumps may increase and it is likely that we will see such pumps offered to patients, who are unlikely to receive transplants, as a "permanent" therapy for their advanced heart failure.

ALTERNATIVE MEDICINE

"Alternative medicine" is a term that is applied to a plethora of therapies that don't comfortably fit into traditional medical practice. In some cases it represents a real innovation and an opportunity to achieve comparable or better results, but keep in mind that it has become a multi-billion-dollar business. Also be well aware that most of the therapies offered alternatively have not been submitted to the same scrutiny for safety and effectiveness that are required by law for the traditional ones. Here's a rundown on the pros and cons of the most common alternative treatments for coronary heart disease.

Coenzyme Q10

Coenzyme Q10 (CoQ10), also known as ubiquinone, is a naturally occurring vitamin-like substance present in all living cells of the body but is most prevalent in tissues with high-energy demands—for example, the muscles, the heart, and the liver.

Adherents of coenzyme Q10 believe it is useful in the treatment of heart disease, particularly congestive heart failure, in which the heart muscle progressively weakens, causing deterioration in the heart's ability to pump. Also, because, like vitamin E, coenzyme Q10 is an antioxidant, it is also seen as a heart disease preventive. Oxidation is a cellular process that is believed to contribute to the initiation of atherosclerosis.

Advocates of this vitamin-like substances contend that taking coenzyme Q10 supplements does appear to revitalize heart function and reduce heart disease symptoms. However, to date, data supporting the use of coenzyme Q10 have come from small studies, most lacking the control group needed to compare the health of those taking the substance to those who do not.

One recent careful and rigorous study that evaluated coenzyme Q10 in 30 patients enrolled in a heart failure and transplant program found the results disappointing. During the study, each participant was treated with coenzyme Q10 or a placebo for 12-week periods. However, when the researchers performed tests to search for evidence of some favorable effect, they found none. Nor did coenzyme Q10 appear to improve well-being, according to the study, published in 1999 in the *Journal of the American College of Cardiology*.

This study is not apt to end the controversy over coenzyme Q10. The American Heart Association currently maintains that there is not enough scientific evidence on coenzyme Q10 to warrant an endorsement. But side effects are uncommon and no toxicity has been found in animals even at high doses. If you decide to take coenzyme Q10, be sure to inform your doctor of your decision.

Chelation Therapy

Chelation therapy, an approved treatment for patients with lead poisoning and other types of metal toxicity, has been used for years as an alternative medicine treatment for the treatment of heart disease.

This type of therapy uses intravenous infusions (injections into the bloodstream) of the chemical substance ethylenediamine tetraacetic acid (EDTA) over several weeks or months. Simply put, through such treatment, harmful heavy-metal molecules (such as lead) can be bound with other chemicals and eliminated from the body. Advocates of chelation therapy for atherosclerosis claim that it rids the body of unstable calcium, a component of plaque that binds fat to the wall of the artery. But virtually all of the claims for the effectiveness of chelation therapy have been unsubstantiated. No well-designed clinical trials have shown it to be of any more benefit than a placebo in treating vascular problems caused by atherosclerosis.

Both the American Heart Association and the American College of Cardiology recognize chelation therapy in the treatment of heavy-metal poisoning but do not endorse it as an acceptable method of treating heart disease.

Herbal Remedies

Herbal remedies and supplements are a boom business; current figures show Americans spend as much as $13 billion annually on these products. Can these products lower your cholesterol and reduce your risk of heart attack?

What distinguishes herbal remedies and dietary supplements from conventional pharmaceuticals are the rigorous scientific studies and clinical trials that prescription drugs must undergo before being approved for general use by the Food and Drug Administration (FDA). The FDA's ability to regulate control of herbal and dietary supplements has been repeatedly reduced and, as a result, these products can be sold in formulations like drugs and potencies without any proof of effectiveness and safety.

Some herbal remedies that are being touted supposedly reduce cholesterol. But the most widely prescribed, clinically tested drugs to lower cholesterol are the statins. They are proven to reduce the risk of death from cardiovascular disease, a claim no herbal remedy currently on the market can make and substantiate. Also, some people turn to herbal supplements because they are wary of so-called hazardous side effects. But these side effects are not that common and, during clinical trial of statins, the side effects of the placebo were often as great or greater than that of the lipid-lowering medication. So if you've been prescribed medication to lower your cholesterol, do not stop taking it. If you choose to use supplements, always let your physician know what you are taking.

A major reason many people turn to supplements is that they subscribe to the belief that, because these supplements are "natural," they are safe. This is not always the case. There have been instances were so-called natural substances proved hazardous, such as the diet supplement known as fen-phen. This combination of fenfluramine and phentermine was withdrawn from the market because of possible links to heart disease.

Another example is niacin. In many respects, nicotinic acid (niacin), a B vitamin, is almost the perfect agent for controlling cholesterol. It lowers LDL cholesterol by 20 percent and triglycerides by 30 percent.

When used in high doses of three or more grams per day it can raise HDL levels by as much as 20 percent. It's available over the counter. It's cheap. So what's the problem? Why isn't everyone using it instead of the more expensive statins?

The niacin story is a good example of how something that seemed destined to be a big success can ultimately prove to be a flop. While niacin is highly effective, it also produces the very annoying side effect of skin flushing. While this does improve with time in most people, it still can affect a large number of people taking it.

Further, however, hepatitis-like liver function abnormalities occur in as many as one third of people taking the high doses required to significantly lower cholesterol. It can also aggravate diabetes, gout, and peptic ulcers. So, we believe that niacin should be considered a drug rather than simply a vitamin and that it should not be taken without consultation with your doctor.

A WORD ABOUT RESEARCH

Throughout this book, we often note that information on women's health problems is lacking because they have seldom been included in major research studies. Even when research projects are formulated specifically for women, it can be difficult to find enough female volunteers.

If you are asked to participate and don't wish to, just say no. No one at the hospital will think any less of you, and your care won't suffer in any way. But there are some reasons to consider saying yes.

First, patients who participate in experimental studies get special care. They're very carefully followed according to strict protocols established by committees "watchdogging" the experiment. Second, these studies usually give you the opportunity to receive therapies that won't be generally available for several years. While they're called "experimental," these therapies have been carefully evaluated for safety. Clinical trials need to be performed because unfortunately, there is no way to tell whether or not a new treatment is actually an improved treatment unless you carefully compare them.

Medical science has made tremendous strides over the years in treating cardiac problems, including many formerly considered hopeless. As of this writing, though, that symbol of the bionic age, the artificial heart, remains out of reach. Perhaps that should serve to underscore the tremendous importance of taking good care of the hearts with which we were born.

14

~~~~mmmm∩mmmm~~~~

Open-Heart Surgery

I was sitting across the desk from the cardiologist, but his voice seemed to echo from a great distance. He was telling me I needed open-heart surgery. "Do you want to have it done in Hartford or New Haven? Just let me know and I'll find somebody good to do it," he was saying.

Perhaps he was trying not to alarm me, but I did not feel like being non-chalant. The cardiologist was someone I'd met just that afternoon, and he was giving me news that stunned me! Up until a few weeks ago, I had not known anything was wrong with my heart at all. Now I was being presented with choices regarding open-heart surgery as casually as a waiter might ask what I wanted for lunch! It seemed unbelievable, but, since then, I've found this approach is not unusual.

If you need open-heart surgery, you may find yourself being given the names of doctors and hospitals and being urged to choose quickly, without any consideration at all. Of course, if you suddenly find yourself faced with the need for emergency surgery, you may have little to say in the matter. That's true also if you belong to a managed health care plan, which limits your choice of hospitals and surgeons. But, most of the time, you will have the opportunity to make a choice.

When it comes to making medical decisions about your heart, the choices you make can be among the most important of your life. Just ask Dr. Bruce Lytle, a cardiovascular surgeon at the Cleveland Clinic.

"When you have open-heart surgery, that is one of the most important events in your life. The outcome is very important. Whether you'll be alive, how long you will live, and how well you will do for the rest of your life are the types of things which are at stake," Dr. Lytle notes.

If you are facing a serious heart problem, that may seem like it is enough in itself to absorb, and that making decisions about hospitals and surgeons is the last thing you need to worry about. But by becoming informed, you ensure that you will get the best care.

❤ **Mindsaving Tip: If you are visiting a physician or cardiologist about a serious medical problem, don't go alone. Learning you have a serious heart problem or need surgery is a lot to absorb. Take along your spouse, a grown child, or a close friend to serve as your "listener" so you can be certain what you've heard is accurate. Also, arrange to call back or E-mail the doctor once you've absorbed the news and have formulated a list of questions to ask.**

CHOICES YOU NEED TO MAKE

Choosing a Hospital

In these days of tough competition, hospitals are too often tempted to represent themselves as being all things to all people. Hospitals play up their strengths, but are unwilling to reveal their weaknesses and risk losing "customers." They eagerly recruit new patients with shiny brochures, impressive annual reports, and health fairs. They will almost always claim to be comparable to hospitals that rank nationally in the first tier. But all hospitals are not alike.

Small Hospital vs. Large Hospital

Most people feel more comfortable about being in a hospital that is close to home, even if it's small. There's no problem with that, as long as it can provide you with the care you need. The bottom line in choosing a hospital, no matter what its size, should be "Is this where I will receive the best care?"

❤ **Lifesaving Tip: Many hospitals tout themselves as "heart centers," but have only a cardiovascular surgeon and a cardiologist or two on staff. This can spell danger for you. For your cardiac proce-**

dure, it is imperative that your hospital be a cardiac treatment center in reality, not only in name. At the bare minimum, your hospital should have two well-experienced cardiovascular teams. After all, members need to fill in for each other.

Teaching Hospital vs. Non-Teaching Hospital

Whether or not to select a teaching hospital is another often-debated topic. At a teaching hospital, the doctors tend to be at the cutting edge of their profession and have access to the most advanced diagnostic technology and therapies. On the other hand, if you're in a teaching hospital, you may find that, while your care is supervised by an attending physician, you'll be attended by some doctors who are still in training. You may be attracted to the hospital because someone famous is on the staff, but you probably won't get a glimpse of the medical celebrity unless your case is quite exotic. You can also expect to be periodically visited by troops of student doctors. Such attention can be welcome and a newly minted doctor can sometimes pick up a problem a veteran may miss. But such visits can also be exhausting.

Heart Mega-Centers

Some hospitals are considered among the "best of the best" for heart care. They can be found in such articles such as the one in annual edition of *U.S. News & World Report,* which ranks hospitals based upon selected criteria including a survey that asks leading cardiologists to indicate their choices for the best hospitals in the country.

Should you seek out such a center for your heart problem? If you are not considered an unusually high heart surgery risk and your problem is relatively straightforward, probably not. But, if you are considered high risk, your problem is unusually complex, or you are undergoing open-heart surgery for a second or third time (particularly if you did not do that well before), you should certainly consider seeking out such a facility.

ARE YOU A HIGH-RISK PATIENT?

Just by virtue of being female, you may still be at slightly higher risk for open-heart surgery, but if you are in otherwise good health, this does not necessarily make you a high-risk patient. There are other factors to consider. If you fall into one of the categories below, you should choose your hospital and surgeon with extra care.

Other Factors That Increase Your Risk:
- You are undergoing surgery on an emergency basis
- Your heart is extensively damaged from a heart attack or other cause.
- You have multiple heart problems, for example, if you need a coronary bypass operation but you also have a leaky mitral valve that may or may not require surgery.
- If you underwent open-heart surgery before, most particularly if you did not do well.
- If you already had a heart valve replacement, but need to now have that valve replaced.
- You have other serious medical problems such as diabetes and/or high blood pressure.
- If you are over 65 years of age. Open-heart surgery is now being done successfully on people in their 70s, and even their 80s, but the risk is higher.

Even if you are not considered at higher risk, still chose your hospital and surgeon carefully. In 1998, the *Annals of Thoracic Surgery* published a report based on the records of 345,000 patients, over 97,000 of them women. Surprisingly, the report indicated that the death rate due to complications of surgery, although extremely low to begin with, was actually higher for those considered at low or medium risk for problems compared with those considered at high risk.

BUYER (AND PATIENT) BEWARE!

While it is reassuring to think of hospitals as benevolent institutions, that is not always the case. All hospitals are not created equal, and it pays off to eye them critically. This is what Pat found out when she had her surgery. It turns out that her mother underwent the same procedure just two weeks after Pat did. In her small Connecticut hospital, Pat's every need was attended to, but for her 65-year-old mother, who was in a large, inner-city hospital in another state, it was a different story.

"The accommodations were awful. Soap and towels were in demand. My sister had to bring them from home. She bartered for toilet paper.

My mother had great doctors, but the hospital was a brutal introduction to inner-city life for her," Pat said.

The growing competition between hospitals, coupled with the increasing tendency of patients to view themselves as consumers, has resulted in hospitals responding to this need by offering more information. Beware, though, that these materials may be just glossy public relations offerings. You can expect these materials to play up the institution's strengths, but good ones offer valuable information as well. For example, the Cleveland Clinic now offers a free guide on selecting a doctor and hospital called "How to Choose a Doctor and Hospital If You Have Coronary Disease."

Some Questions to Ask When Choosing a Hospital:
- Is the hospital accredited by the Joint Commission on Accreditation of Healthcare Organizations (JCAHO)? While such accreditation is voluntary, it assures you the hospital meets minimum standards of staffing, equipment, and safety regulations. To find out the status of the hospital you are considering, call 1-630-792-5800 or at the Web site *www.JCAHO.org*, where you can access information about hospitals in your area.
- How many cardiac procedures are performed annually? The hospital you are considering should perform least 200 to 300 open-heart operations annually, the majority being coronary bypass operations, according to joint guidelines published by the American College of Cardiology and the American Heart Association.
- What is the mortality rate? While most hospitals are more than happy to shower you with glossy annual reports and slick magazines, they are often less eager to show off their death and surgical complication rates. That, however, is precisely the information you need. If the hospital won't tell you, that's a good reason to consider going elsewhere.
- What is the morbidity rate? While "mortality rate" refers to the number of deaths that occur as a result of certain treatments or procedures, hospitals also keep track of their morbidity rate, which refers to the number of serious complications that occur. If you are a candidate for open-heart surgery, you want to know how often patients undergoing the procedure suffer strokes or heart attacks.
- Is the hospital in relatively good financial shape? Certainly there is a medical cost crisis throughout the country, but have there been

newspaper articles in your community warning the hospital is deeply in debt or about to go under? If so, you could experience staffing and supply shortages that could compromise your care.

- Is the hospital beset with labor problems? Although it is uncommon for hospital staff to go on strike, you don't want it to happen while you are a patient there. Watch newspapers in the hospital's area for articles about wage disputes or labor unrest. If the staff is underpaid and unhappy, you may not get the quality of care you need.
- How's the nursing staff? Ask former patients (your doctor's waiting room is a good place to find them) about the nursing care they received. Were the nurses well trained and caring? Distracted or unprofessional? Normally busy or hopelessly overworked? Were patients sent home with written follow-up instructions? That's very important.
- What percentage of the staff are temporary employees? As journalist Walt Bogdanich wrote in his investigative book about the nation's hospitals, entitled, *The Great White Lie,* some of the most dangerous slip-ups occur in hospitals that rely on temporary workers.
- What do your friends think of the hospital? Unless you are going to a medical center far from home, you probably have friends who have been hospitalized at this hospital. If not, they may very well have friends who would be happy to share their experiences. Seek them out! First-hand testimonials can count a lot.

Choosing a Surgeon

If you need surgery in an emergency, you will not have time to consider your choice. More likely, though, your decision to undergo surgery will be made after serious consideration. The surgeon is the person to whom you are entrusting your life, so choosing someone you trust is an important matter indeed.

In smaller institutions, a cardiovascular surgeon is a jack-of-all-trades. While such a surgeon generally performs all different sorts of heart surgery, the vast majority of it will be coronary bypass procedures. If you are to have another type of heart surgery, you want to be sure your surgeon does enough of these operations to be proficient. If your problem is unusual, such as a complicated congenital defect or an aortic valve repair, it is wise to seek a surgeon who specializes in this area. This may be a good reason to consider a larger hospital or medical center.

It is important to remember that, in choosing a surgeon, you are, in essence, often choosing the hospital where the surgery will be performed. Most surgeons operate out of only one or two hospitals. Likewise if you choose a hospital you are choosing a limited group of surgeons who have privileges there.

How Important Is It That You Like Your Surgeon?

"When I left my cardiologist's office, I went to see the surgeon he recommended. I liked my cardiologist, but, when it came to the surgeon, he seemed to feel the less the patient knew, the better. He gave me the impression he felt the patient should shut up, let him do his magic, and be appreciative," says Pat, who, at the age of 36, had surgery to correct a congenital heart defect. Still, even though Pat still bristles when she recalls her surgeon, she probably would not have chosen someone else. "This surgeon was presented to me as the best in his field. What should I have done, chosen second best?" she said.

Ideally, the surgeon you choose will embody both a fine personality and a high degree of skill. If it is not possible to have both, the nod should go to skill; but even if a surgeon is a star, that is no reason for a patient not to be treated with respect.

When Should I Meet the Surgeon?

You should certainly meet with the surgeon well in advance of the surgery. Dr. John Elefteriades, a cardiothoracic surgeon at Yale-New Haven Hospital, for example, meets in advance with patients who are candidates for surgery to discuss not only the procedures but any other options they may have as well.

"Every patient deserves to know their condition, what's going on with their heart. Patients also should know what their options are, both surgical and nonsurgical, and they should receive a description of the operation, the risks, the estimated length of their hospital stay and their recovery," says Dr. Elefteriades

If you are having emergency surgery, of course, this is not usually possible. Also, some hospitals keep their "star" surgeons so busy they simply do not have time to meet with patients.

My hospital roommate never even laid eyes on her surgeon at all. I later

learned he was legendary in this respect. In fact, the story goes several of his former patients once turned up where he was giving a lecture, just to thank him! This surgeon may not have succeeded in the realm of patient relations, but his skill with a scalpel was such that his patients were willing to overlook it.

❤ Lifesaving Tip: Your choice of a surgeon will probably come from your cardiologist. Ask for two or three names; this way, if you decide you do not want a particular surgeon, you can choose another more easily.

The Surgical Team

Having heart surgery is something like choosing a package deal vacation: In choosing the surgeon, you are not only selecting the doctor who will perform the procedure, but also the entire surgical team as well. While open-heart surgery has become quite commonly performed, it is still a very complex and precise operation that requires that every member of the surgical team, from the anesthesiologist to the scrub nurse, to perform their job flawlessly. If you choose your surgeon wisely, you can have confidence that this will be so. No top-flight heart surgeon would tolerate an inferior team.

Questions to Ask a Surgeon

Many people feel uncomfortable questioning prospective surgeons. According to Dr. Bruce Lytle of the Cleveland Clinic, they should not. "Your surgeon is working for you, you are not working for your surgeon, and you have the right to ask anything you want," notes Dr. Lytle, who always volunteers information such as his mortality rate. Certainly, you can phrase such seemingly awkward questions diplomatically, or have a family member ask instead. But you should not be reluctant to press for this important information.

A surgeon may not have precise figures on hand to answer your questions, but should be able to give you some idea. If a surgeon is very defensive, or refuses to discuss the topic, you might take that into consideration when deciding whether you want this surgeon to do the operation.

- "What is your mortality rate when you do this type of procedure on a woman of my age and condition?" Of course, mortality rates can vary; it is not surprising for a surgeon specializing in coronary bypass operations on patients with serious kidney failure to have a higher death rate than do others. For open-heart surgery on a woman in otherwise good health, a surgeon should have an overall mortality rate no higher than 3 to 4 percent.

- "What is morbidity rate for patients in my age and condition?" During open-heart surgery, suffering a stroke is among the most threatening complication to your future quality of life, but heart attack, serious lung complications, or bleeding complications can also occur. These major complications are usually called "morbidities." For open-heart procedures, they are usually equal to the mortality rate.

- "Do you offer alternative approaches to treating cardiac problems?" The field of medicine is ever changing. To make sure you are getting the best care, your surgeon should be able to offer you the most up-to-date treatments, such as valve repair instead of replacement or an atherectomy instead of coronary bypass surgery. If your surgeon is not familiar with the latest techniques, you won't be receiving the best in surgical care.

- "How many cardiac procedures do you perform?" Practice makes perfect. According to the American College of Cardiology and the American Heart Association, a cardiovascular surgeon should perform at least 100 to 150 open-heart operations annually. However, while quantity counts, be wary of the surgeon who seems too busy. That surgeon may not have the time to give patients adequate before-and-after surgical care.

❤ Mindsaving Tip: When quizzing your prospective surgeon on such matters, be tactful. You are entitled to this information, but that doesn't mean you have to come on like Attila the Hun.

HAVING OPEN-HEART SURGERY

It was shortly after midnight on the day that I was to have open-heart surgery. I couldn't sleep. I was nervously leafing through a magazine for heart patients when I came across the statement that such operations had become "almost as routine as an appendectomy." "Hah! That's easy for you to say; it's not your heart," I said back at the page. Open-heart surgery is the operation that evokes the most anxiety in us. After all, as a child, we all learned that, if our heart stops, we die. All of the discussion in the world about the marvels of technology will not completely erase that fear. So, if it is your heart for which surgery is being considered, you may not be surprised to find that, like me, you do not consider it routine at all.

If you are going to undergo heart surgery, plenty of people are probably eager to tell you how "routine" a procedure it has become. In a way, they are right. According to the American Heart Association's most recent figures, nearly 760,000 open-heart operations are performed annually in the United States, making it one of the most common surgical procedures in the country.

If it is you, however, who are to undergo such surgery, you undoubtedly do not view this as routine at all, nor should you. Open-heart surgery is very precise, delicate work that must be performed flawlessly. Over the years, the skill in performing this type of surgery has improved and the rate of death and major complications has fallen dramatically.

Before the Surgery: Finding Support

If you are to undergo open-heart surgery, you'll probably discover that there is usually plenty of support and information available afterwards, but not much before.

My cardiologist's advice to "go home, have a cup of tea, and call me with any questions you have" was okay, as far as it went. But what I really needed to do was talk to someone who had gone through the surgery. Fortunately, I discovered my friend Julia had a friend, Pat, who had undergone the exact same surgery I was to have. Thus began our friendship. We never met until after my surgery but during those excruciating six weeks beforehand, Pat was often the last person I talked to by phone at night, and the first person I called in the morning. In retrospect, I would never leave finding such support to chance. Neither should you.

Ask your doctor to suggest a patient to whom you can talk. Contact the hospital too, and ask if there are volunteers who meet with patients undergoing similar surgery. Often, such meetings take place the day before surgery. Trust us, you'll want someone to talk to way before then. Ask to talk to a woman, so you can get as personal as you like. Or contact your local office of the American Heart Association.

❤ **Mindsaving Tip: Many hospitals provide you with educational information about your surgery, but they usually give it to you afterwards. Request such materials ahead of time to help you prepare.**

Before Your Surgery

Ask questions. Back in 1979, when Cheri had open-heart surgery to correct a heart problem caused by Marfan's syndrome, a serious congenital condition, she fumed, because "they told my husband everything, but they kept me totally in the dark." When she had cardiac surgery again several years later, she discovered that such thinking had changed. Nowadays, it is recognized that patients have the right to know what is going to happen to them.

♥ Mindsaving Tip: Be informed: What you are imagining the procedure is like is probably more frightening than it actually is. If you are squeamish, feel free about declining information that's offered, but it should be your choice.

Banking your blood. With the concern these days about AIDS and other blood-borne viruses, you are probably worried about your hospital's blood supply. Surprisingly, open-heart surgery in many hospitals does not currently require blood transfusions. However, complications can arise, and you might need a pint or two. As soon as you've decided to undergo the surgery, ask your doctor if you can bank some of your own blood and check with the hospital to find how this is done. You can also ask your family and friends if they wish to donate blood, but remember, their blood type must match yours.

If you are not medically well enough to donate your own blood, or if you are having surgery out of state, find out what precautions the hospital takes to ensure its blood supply is safe from such problems as AIDS and hepatitis. Unfortunately, this is one of those areas where you can't be 100 percent sure, but the risks of not having needed surgery outweigh the risk of receiving contaminated blood.

Other preparations. Find out if you require any additional tests before the surgery, and whether you should discontinue any medications you are taking beforehand. Doctors may vary in their advice on this; for example, if you take birth control pills, some surgeons suggest you switch to another method of contraception prior to surgery to avoid the danger of blood clots.

Things to Do Before Surgery:

- Recruit emotional support.
- Obtain educational materials about your procedure.
- Plan your recuperation.
- Find out when you will enter the hospital, and about any preparations or tests that need to be done beforehand.
- Inquire about banking your own blood.
- Check about medications.

❤ **Lifesaving Tip: If you have not reached menopause, and your surgery is not an emergency, ask your surgeon if your operation should be scheduled at time you are not menstruating. While you are on the heart-lung machine, your blood is infused with anti-clotting agent, which can sometimes result in bleeding problems.**

The Night Before Surgery

When I had my surgery at the Cleveland Clinic, I was stunned to discover that the procedure was "T.C.I." In hospital parlance, that means "to come in," and it meant that I was to arrive the morning of my surgery. Since I had always checked in the night before for less major procedures, I was amazed. "This is almost like walk-in open-heart surgery," I marveled.

While some large hospitals specializing in open-heart surgery use a T.C.I. system, most hospitals do require you to check in the night before. If you are hospitalized, you'll probably be visited by the anesthesiologist, whose job it is to put you to sleep the next day. You'll probably be asked questions about your health, allergies, medications, and even such lifestyle questions as whether or not you smoke. The anesthesiologist's job is to select the type of drugs that will be used to "put you out" for your surgery. Be honest in your answers; it is very important you receive the right type of anesthesia for you.

❤ **Mindsaving Tip: Wherever you spend it, in the hospital or at home, the night before heart surgery is bound to be anxiety-provoking. Plan some pleasant distractions for yourself, such as inviting a good friend or relative to come see you. Or treat yourself to some long-distance phone calls.**

The Day of Your Surgery

The day of the surgery, you'll be given a sedative to relax you. Preparations vary from hospital to hospital. Sometimes, they are done before you are put to sleep or afterwards. Your body will be scrubbed with an antiseptic. Part of your pubic area may be shaved in case your femoral artery (the one located near the groin) needs to be accessed during surgery. If you do not shave your legs, and a leg vein is to be used for a coronary bypass, part of your leg will be shaved. Some of these preparations may be done the night before.

❤ **Mindsaving Tip: Sometimes, surgery is delayed. You're probably the last person anyone will think to tell. Relax; the delay probably is due to the surgical schedule, and has nothing to do with you medically at all.**

The Surgery Itself

Because of the sedative, some people do not recall being in the operating room, but others do. The following procedures remain the same, no matter what type of open-heart surgery you are having.

First, you'll receive an injection of a premedication such as diazepam (the generic name for Valium), morphine, or a similar drug to relax you. Then, unconsciousness will be induced with a combination of drugs such as hypnotics, sedatives, and narcotics. After you are unconscious, the anesthesiologist will place a breathing tube down your windpipe for the delivery of anesthetic gasses (and oxygen) and to connect you with a machine that will regulate your breathing during surgery. Various tubes and monitors are connected to you as well, so your body's functions can be monitored very closely.

The heart-lung machine is the device that makes open-heart surgery possible. It is a machine that temporarily takes over the function of the heart and lungs. It consists principally of a pump, which does the work of your heart, and an oxygenator, which does the work of the lungs. Your blood flows from your heart's main veins into the machine. There it is cleansed of carbon dioxide, filled with oxygen, and recirculated throughout your body.

For the surgery, your chest is opened, and your heart is exposed. The surgeon places tubes in your heart that enable your blood to begin flowing through the circuitous tubing of the heart-lung machine. This recirculation of your own blood reduces the probability you will need any blood transfusion. It also enables the surgeon access to a "bloodless field," to be able to see and work on your heart more easily.

An important part of open-heart surgery involves the lowering of your body temperature. This is done for two important reasons. The first is that lowering the temperature of your heart slows down its beat. The second is that when your heart is cooled, it requires far less oxygenated blood. Once your chest is opened, though, the surgeon stops the blood flow to your heart by clamping your coronary arteries. A mixture of cold water and saline is applied to your heart to stop it from beating

The particular surgical procedures for a coronary bypass, valve repairs and replacements, and congenital defects differ and are discussed in those specific chapters. Whatever the procedure, once it is completed, the surgeon directs the perfusionist (the technician who operates the heart-lung machine) to gradually begin allowing your heart and lungs to begin taking their familiar functions. Your own rewarmed blood begins flowing slowly back through your heart. This infusion of warm blood is enough to start your heart's beating again. It is not unusual for a heart to begin beating erratically. If this happens, the surgeon applies an electric shock, which gets your heart beating in its own rhythm again. Once your heart is beating satisfactorily on its own, your chest is sewn up and you are transferred to an intensive care ward.

❤ **Mindsaving Tip: During the operation, you'll be administered narcotics to make sure you'll remain asleep. Surveys have shown that many people fear waking up during an operation, but this virtually never occurs. You will be monitored and if it appears you are not sleeping deeply enough, you'll be given more drugs.**

Complications of Open-Heart Surgery

Earlier in this chapter, we dealt with such complications of open-heart surgery as death and stroke. There are some other risks particular to this type of surgery as well.

The risk of stroke is higher if you're elderly, but, no matter what your age, it's also slightly increased in procedures where the cardiac chamber itself must be opened. This is not done in coronary bypass surgery, which is performed on the surface of the heart, but in such procedures as to repair congenital heart defects or replace valves. When the heart chamber is opened, this increases the chance that a tiny air bubble could enter your bloodstream and travel to your brain.

No matter how miraculous this man-made machine is, it cannot do its job as perfectly as your own heart and lungs in providing your brain with perfectly oxygenated blood. One particular type of complication seems related to the use of the heart-lung machine. These are neurological problems, which can range from temporary confusion to, at worse, a stroke. How often such problems occur is difficult to calculate, but a study that appeared in 1996 in *The New England Journal of Medicine,* shed some light. The researchers evaluated 2,108 patients from 24 hospitals who underwent coronary bypass operations. They found that 3.1 percent suffered serious brain complications, such as stroke, and another 3 percent suffered symptoms suggesting milder brain damage, such as confusion, deterioration in intellectual function, agitation, disorientation, memory loss, or a seizure. The study found those most at risk for serious neurological problems were those with severe aortic atherosclerosis, that is, fat-laden deposits in the aorta (the main artery of the body just above the heart). Other risk factors were a history of neurological disease, being age 70 or more, and a history of lung disease. As for the less serious neurological ailments, risk factors included a history of excessive alcohol consumption, prior bypass surgery, abnormal heart rhythms, a history of peripheral vascular disease (blockages in the blood vessels of the legs), and congestive heart failure on the day of surgery.

This study demonstrates that neurological problems, although rare, are very serious for the unlucky patients who suffer them. However, this study should not be construed as an indictment of open-heart surgery, as the vast majority of patients enrolled in the study did very well, both from a cardiac and a neurological perspective.

In addition, there is a new technology being deployed in many hospitals that is likely to reduce the incidence of stroke during open-heart surgery and to improve other aspects of surgical outcomes. The technology involves the use of echocardiographic ultrasound in the operating room.

♥ Lifesaving Tip: Find out if echo ultrasound is used during open-heart operations at the facility where you are going to have open-heart surgery. It can be used during the initial stages of the operation to aid the surgical team in deciding where to insert tubes into the aorta. It can also be used later in the operation to guide the repair of valves or to see if a coronary graft is providing good flow to a segment of muscle that was previously deprived.

How Will I Feel When I Come To?

Once you awaken, you may feel groggy. Your first sensation, though, is likely to be the most unpleasant: You will probably awaken fighting the breathing tube. Try not to fight the machine, but to breathe with it. Most likely, a nurse will be nearby to assist you. The staff is aware the breathing tube is uncomfortable, and it will be removed as soon as possible, but not before you are fully awake and able to breathe normally on your own. This usually means the morning after your surgery, but most people are only aware of the breathing tube for the last hour or two because they are pretty sleepy.

What did I feel like after surgery? After I came to (and got rid of that darned breathing tube!), I recall doing a mental inventory from my feet up to my head. I was surprised to find that I felt, basically, okay. The only annoyance I recall is that everything looked fuzzy. I soon realized that was because I wasn't wearing my glasses!

What Will I Feel Like After Surgery?

When you first regain consciousness, you probably won't feel too great. On the other hand, some women are surprised that they felt better than they expected to. How you feel can all depend on how much anesthesia you were given, how long your procedure was, and the complexity of the procedure. Despite all these factors, there is no simple formula; individuals simply differ in the way their bodies respond to surgery.

But times have changed and, open-heart surgery is not the long ordeal it used to be. Just ask Cheri, who was born with Marfan's syndrome and developed a life-threatening aneurysm (ballooning of the aorta) at the age of 21. It grew slowly until Cheri was 29, when it became so large there was no choice but to remove it. Still, the surgery was deemed so risky at the time she was sent to Texas, where Denton Cooley, the world-famous heart surgeon, performed the operation. She was hospitalized for a month and spent an additional three months recuperating. In 1991, she underwent open-heart surgery again, to correct another aneurysm. After her first experience, she was understandably terrified, but her recent surgery turned out not to be anything like she expected. "There was a big difference. This time, I was home in several days and the recuperation period was much shorter. I felt pain, but not the kind of pain that I remember from 1979. Either I'm fooling myself or it's been fantastic. I have to slow down occasionally because I just get carried away, I feel so good," Cheri said.

Tips on Surviving (and Even Enjoying) Your Hospital Stay

Here are our favorite tips for making a hospital stay not only survivable, but even sometimes fun.

- Appoint an advocate: During your hospital stay, there will be times when you will not be able to look out for yourself. Ask your partner, relative, or a close friend to look out for your interests, and to question any tests, medications, or procedures ordered for you.
- Bring your underwear! Those drafty hospital gowns are a necessity right after surgery but, later on, most hospitals won't mind you wearing underwear. Warm flannel or cotton underwear makes a big difference.
- Bring a few inexpensive mementos from home. This can be a few family pictures or a favorite souvenir or memento. But don't bring anything you could not bear to lose if it were misplaced or even stolen.
- Be pleasant to the staff. It may be unfair, but it's true: Nobody wants to be around a grouch. The old saying "You can catch more flies with honey than you can with vinegar" is as true on the hospital ward as anywhere else. If you're nice, the staff may be inspired to do their best to brighten your stay.
- A bright piece of costume jewelry (perhaps something heart-shaped?) or a whimsical pin can brighten a hospital gown. For one woman, her son's gift of oversized "Snoopy" slippers kept up her spirits, and provided her with a sense of identity as well. Padding up and down, she cheered up the whole floor!
- Tired of TV? Take along an inexpensive tape recorder or cassette players with earphones. This way you can listen to your favorite music, or enjoy that novel you always wanted to read on tape.

❤ **Mindsaving Tip: Heart surgery is serious business, but don't lose your sense of humor. If it will cheer you, bring along comedy tapes or humor books.**

Starting Your Recuperation

Soon you'll begin getting out of bed, at first with a nurse at your side. Before long, you'll be strolling down the hall. Then, you'll be complaining about the hospital food. Hallelujah, you've survived!

A Word About Those Beeps . . .

Although it looks like you're on a regular hospital floor, you'll soon discover all your fellow patients are heart patients. This is because you are in a "telemetry" unit, which refers to the constant monitoring of your heart. You are connected to devices that record your heartbeat, even if you are walking down the hall. One reason for this is that after heart surgery, your heart is prone to such problems as an irregular heart rhythm.

♥ **Mindsaving Tip: If you've had heart surgery, your heart's electrical patterns, while normal for you, may appear abnormal on an electrocardiogram. If this is true in your case, ask your cardiologist for a copy of your EKG to carry with you. This way, if an EKG is ever done on you in an emergency, it won't be erroneously assumed that what they're observing represents an undiagnosed heart problem.**

Once You're Home: Planning Your Recuperation

With costs rising, hospitals are under pressure to release you just as soon as they possibly can. If there are no complications, you will probably stay in the hospital about a week or so. Just at the time you are beginning to feel able to get around, you'll find yourself being discharged.

Just as you plan a successful vacation, you should plan for a successful recuperation. If you leave things to chance, they may not work out the way you want them to.

Despite the women's movement, it remains largely true that men's work takes place outside the home, while women work at a job and then come home to another day's worth of responsibilities. This alone creates extra pressure when you return home from the hospital.

Your needs during recuperation will vary, depending on what stage of life you are in. When Pat returned from the hospital, she had three young children, including a baby, to care for. Eleanor, in her late 40s, had teenagers who relied on her to chauffeur them to school activities. Hope, in her mid-60s, lived alone, with no one to help out.

The best time to make arrangements for your aftercare is before your surgery. Notes Sue Dehner, a nurse at the Cleveland Clinic who provides post-surgical education, "We tell patients they can't lift anything greater than eight to ten pounds for six to eight weeks. That means no vacuuming or lifting of laundry baskets or small children. Often, that poses problems for women. So we encourage them not to be shy about asking for outside help."

Women heart patients may face a special problem. Since women tend to develop coronary heart disease at an older age, they may have husbands who have heart problems as well. Sometimes, one spouse can become too protective of the other. More often, though, the woman will be a widow. This can lead to depression, because her own illness can bring up painful memories of when her husband was ill.

Here are the advantages of planning your recuperation in advance:

- You will be faced with a minimum of pressure and disorganization when you can least cope with it, which is when you first get home.
- You will be sending a message to your family that it won't be "business as usual" when you get home; that you'll need their help.
- You'll be thinking about your life after surgery, a strong, but subtle message that you will survive. This can lessen everyone's anxiety.

♥ **Mindsaving Tip: If your husband or a close friend or relative can take some time off from work, the best time to do it is your first week at home, rather than the week you are in the hospital. That's when you'll need the help and the company more.**

On your return home, you may find you'll still feel some pain. The severity of the pain depends on the individual. For example, women who have had bypass surgery done with mammary grafts appear to feel more postoperative chest pain. Many patients (and sometimes their doctors) erroneously believe they will become addicted to pain medication after surgery. Recently, though, the federal government urged doctors to give such painkillers more freely after surgery because their appropriate use actually speeds recovery.

As you recuperate, you'll discover your energy supply ebbs and flows. It's normal on some days to feel peppier than others, or start the day with a burst of energy, and start drooping around noon. Gradually, the time you feel like your old self should become longer and longer. This can take as little as a few weeks for some, up to a year, or even longer for others. The important thing is to remember you are an individual, and not to compare yourself with others.

"The one thing I resented was people telling me I'd be a new woman," said 58-year-old Ida. "They'd heard of others recuperating within a few weeks. I felt everyone was blaming me because it didn't happen that way for me."

♥ **Mindsaving Tip: Consider keeping a journal of your progress as you recuperate. You can note the day you walked one block, then two, than three. Before long, you'll soon discover that, overall, you are doing better than you realized.**

Back to Work

Studies have shown that more men than women return to work following open-heart surgery. Some differences are that most women patients tend to be older, so they are closer to retirement, or they are homemakers.

After surgery, you can expect to return to your regular activities in about six weeks, although it may certainly take you longer to regain your customary stamina. Before you're allowed to return to work, your doctor may order an exercise stress test. This test not only provides medical information about your heart, but it provides you with the reassurance that your heart is up to the rigors of your everyday life.

If you work, try to return on a part-time basis, at least for the first week or so. You may find yourself eager to go in the morning, but spent by early afternoon.

I recall my own experience years ago after abdominal surgery. I'd returned to my reporting job at a small newspaper part-time, but I couldn't resist the lure of a night editing job at a larger paper. After two days, I discovered I was walking bent over! That was the last time I tried to convince my recuperating body that I knew better than it did!

♥ **Mindsaving Tip: When we talked to women in the course of researching this book, it was surprising to discover how many had** only the vaguest idea what had been done to them. They were dismayed about this as well. After your surgery, ask your doctor for a copy of your "operative report" (made after every surgery) or a written description of your operation.

———

Your Emotions

Depression is sometimes a byproduct of bypass surgery, and can pose a serious threat to your health. After heart surgery, you may also experience some reluctance when it comes to having sex. Women who suffer heart attacks experience similar problems, so these subjects are covered in Chapter 16.

Your Incision

If you are having open-heart surgery, a permanent memento of your experience will be your incision. If you are undergoing bypass surgery, you do not have a choice. You will be the recipient of the famous "zipper" incision, which runs from the base of your neck down to the middle of your chest.

This surgical incision affects many women differently. But, too often, women are given the impression they shouldn't give their impending incision a thought or that they are only entitled to be concerned if they are young. Grace, a 79-year-old impeccably groomed fashion designer, is eager to set the record straight on that misconception. Talking about her reaction after her bypass, she said, "I think the greatest shock was in the morning, when I awoke for the first time, and I saw this horrible scar that started at pit of my neck and went all the way down to my navel," she said. But not all women think that way. For example, Barbara, a bypass patient in her fifties, doesn't mind her incision at all. "When I think of the incision, I look down and say to myself, 'That's why you're alive, kid.' So it's really not a problem," she said.

The horizontal, or submammary incision. If you're having coronary bypass surgery to all three coronary vessels, there is no alternative to the vertical scar. But if you are getting grafts to one or two vessels or having another type of heart surgery, take note! There may be a more cosmetically pleasing alternative. In the case of certain non-coronary operations such as simple congenital heart defect repair or certain types of valve surgery, the "submammary," or horizontal, incision may be appropriate.

With this type of incision, you are opened across your middle, rather than cut vertically down your chest, and most of the incision is hidden in the crease under your breasts. The incision is low enough to be invisible beneath the most skimpy of swimsuits.

Don't necessarily expect to be offered this alternative. Most cardiovascular surgeons spend the majority of their time performing bypasses, and the submammary incision is not suitable for those cases. So, they may not be familiar with it and therefore uninterested in performing it.

"When I asked if there was an option of having a submammary incision done as opposed to an incision down the middle, my surgeon treated me as if I was vain and somewhat simple-minded. He was very sarcastic about it also and implied that I thought cosmetics were more important to me than my life," said Pat.

Dr. Eliot Rosencrantz, formerly of the Cleveland Clinic and now practicing in Buffalo, NY, specializes in repairing congenital defects and uses a submammary incision when it does not compromise other requirements for a safe operation. This incision, he says, "provides the heart surgery patient with a cosmetically more acceptable scar while at the same time providing the surgeon safe, easy access to the heart." However, he adds, it should never be done if there are medical consider-

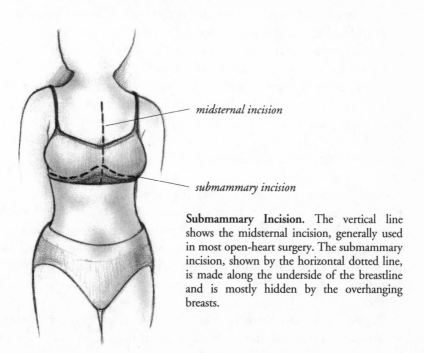

midsternal incision

submammary incision

Submammary Incision. The vertical line shows the midsternal incision, generally used in most open-heart surgery. The submammary incision, shown by the horizontal dotted line, is made along the underside of the breastline and is mostly hidden by the overhanging breasts.

ations that dictate a vertical incision, such as the possibility you may need to undergo surgery again. This is because the submammary incision does not lend itself to being redone. This is also a difficult incision to perform if a woman has very large breasts. Such an incision requires the cutting of some the sensory nerves in the breasts, which can result in a loss of sensation in areas of the breasts. This should eventually return to normal, but sometimes it never does. So this is a factor you should consider.

If you think you may be a candidate for a submammary incision, but your surgeon resists the idea, you might consider seeking out a surgeon who is more receptive, possibly one who specializes in congenital heart defects, for example. Remember, though, your first priority should always be the skill of the surgeon.

In the case of bypass to only one or two coronary vessels, one of the new "mini-bypass" procedures may work for you. In this approach a short (two-to three-inch) incision is made to the side of the breastbone. Special techniques for performance of the bypass procedure are required and not all surgeons are familiar or completely comfortable with the procedure or sure that it in fact results in less discomfort than the traditional sternal-splitting incision. This is discussed earlier in this chapter.

About your incision: No matter what type it is, whether you have a vertical or submammary incision, in time, it should become less noticeable. Unfortunately, many incisions do not heal as nicely as we would like. Many times, they form a noticeable scar: There are two types of abnormal scars; hypertrophic scars and keloids.

A hypertrophic scar is a thick covering that remains within the bounds of the incision. A keloid, on the other hand, exceeds these boundaries, and can even come to resemble a tumor on the skin. Although it is not known why, those of African and Southern European heritage develop keloids more often.

Should a plastic surgeon close my incision? "I don't think having a plastic surgeon close an incision guarantees you a better scar. I think heart surgeons close their wounds very carefully. Unfortunately, it's not who closes the wound, but where the wound is located and the individual patient and how she scars that are usually the determining factors," according to Dr. Randall Yetman, a plastic surgeon at the Cleveland Clinic.

According to Dr. Yetman, scarring can occur no matter whether your incision is vertical or horizontal. When it does, it tends to be most visible in the area of the breast, possibly because of the weight of the breasts on the incision.

During the first weeks after surgery, some doctors recommend massaging the incision, or applying moisturizing oil, with or without vitamin E. While Dr. Yetman finds both measures promote healing, he questions their help in avoiding abnormal scarring. According to him, people who have a tendency to form abnormal scars generally do, no matter how they try to avoid it. If you are unhappy with the way your scar looks, or if it is "symptomatic," that it, is still burns and itches after you should have adequately recuperated, you might consider a procedure called "scar revision."

Scar revision. Sheila, who is in her mid-30s, had surgery when she was only a child to correct a congenital defect. Although her incision has healed quite well, she's always hated it. "The scar made me feel different. It's always bothered me and affected my self-image and self-esteem," said Sheila, who recently made an appointment for a procedure called a scar revision.

Scar revisions are done by plastic surgeons. During the procedure, you are awake, but sedated, and the doctor uses a local anesthetic. When Dr. Yetman does his scar revisions, for example, he uses a combination of methods. He cuts away the thickened part of the scar and applies cortisone, a synthetic corticosteroid drug, to promote better healing. Afterwards, he has found it helpful to have his patients wear a special silicone covering over the incision for about a year. This sheet-like material covers the incision but must be washed and changed every few days.

Dr. Yetman performs most of these scar revisions for patients who complain of burning and itching, but he finds they are usually pleased by the improvement in their appearance as well.

❤ Lifesaving Tip: If you are considering scar revision, find a surgeon who has that type of experience. Don't believe it if you are told the scar will be eliminated. The appearance of scars can be improved, but they cannot be made to completely disappear.

15

~~~~~~୦~~~~~~

Is Hormone Replacement
Therapy for You?

"The Dilemma of Estrogen Replacement," "The Estrogen Question," "Menopausal Hormone Therapy: A New Risk?" These are some recent titles of magazine articles that examine whether women should take hormones to replace those that naturally decline at menopause. Actually, "The Estrogen Question" was used twice. It shows that, when the topic is hormone replacement therapy, there is invariably a giant question mark hanging over it.

Supporters of hormone replacement therapy contend it is a health bonanza for women, bringing them younger-looking skin, stronger bones, healthier hearts, and even better spirits. Critics argue, however, that drug companies are out to brainwash women, convincing them they need a drug to see them through a natural part of life.

The studies on heart disease have further fueled the controversy. But before we get to that, here are some facts about menopause.

WHAT IS MENOPAUSE?

Menopause is the time when a woman's reproductive life ceases. It is usually considered to occur between the ages of 41 and 55, with the average age 51. The onset of menopause begins gradually with a period of subtle hormonal changes called the climacteric. This phase ends with estrogen levels falling so low that eventually the woman has her last menstrual period. This occurs over several years, sometimes beginning when women are in their mid-30s. If you haven't yet reached menopause, you most likely will around the same age your mother did. Studies have found that women who smoke enter menopause a few years earlier than if they didn't smoke.

These changes that women undergo during menopause are primarily due to the decline in our production of estrogen, our so-called "female" sex hormone, which oversees the sexual and reproductive system. This reduction was once thought to primarily affect a woman's reproductive system. While this effect of estrogen is indeed enormous, researchers are only now coming to realize how the decline in this hormone affects the rest of the body as well.

Symptoms include hot flashes, night sweats, moodiness, cloudy thinking, vaginal dryness, loss of sexual desire, and such urinary problems as incontinence. Women can also develop thinning hair or baldness, or unwanted facial hair. Depression is cited by some as a symptom of menopause, but others argue that "feeling blue" during this time can be better explained by the fact that women reaching this stage in their lives may be grappling with other pressures such as caring for an aging parent or dealing with other problems of growing older.

Every woman's experience going through menopause varies. Some barely notice it; others develop debilitating symptoms. Experts estimate 15 percent to 25 percent of women breeze through menopause. On the other end of the spectrum, an equal percentage of women suffer symptoms that can stretch on for years. The majority falls somewhere in between.

Generations ago, when a woman's life span was shorter, menopause was something to be dreaded, as it signaled the approach of old age. Today, nothing could be further from the truth. Currently, a woman's life span is 75 years and, in the absence of disease, experts say that 85 years is a realistic expectation. By the time you reach menopause, your life may only be barely half over.

It's no wonder that these days women wish to consider menopause nothing more than a halfway marker in their busy lives. But the biological changes that come with menopause are far from minor. Just as momentous changes in our body heralded the start of your life as a female capable of reproduction, so do major changes within your body now herald the end of this phase of your life.

How Can HRT Benefit Me?

As of this writing, there are three FDA-approved indications for the use of estrogen in menopausal women. They are:

- For the relief of hot flashes. Although hot flashes are not life-threatening, HRT can seem like a lifesaver to women who suffer from them, as well as drenching night sweats, disrupted sleep patterns, and other symptoms of menopause.
- To prevent vaginal atrophy. As a result of declining estrogen levels, many women experience a thinning of their vaginal tissue, which becomes easily irritated and susceptible to vaginal infection. This can make sexual intercourse painful.
- To prevent osteoporosis. Nearly half of the 40 million women in the United States over the age of 50 have osteoporosis to some extent. This condition results in loss of bone density, particularly in caucasian women. Osteoporosis is blamed for 1.3 million fractures per year. Hip fractures in the elderly are particularly devastating, as they can lead to disability and even death.

Noticeably absent as of this writing is any mention of using HRT as a means of preventing heart disease. But prescribing HRT for that purpose is a practice that can be done now at a doctor's discretion and is referred to as "non-label" prescribing.

Types of Hormone Replacement Therapy

Thanks to a proliferation in menopausal products, there are now several different types of hormone replacement therapy, and more are in the pipeline. Here's a rundown on four of the major classifications:

- Estrogen replacement therapy (ERT)—This refers to the practice of giving pure (also called "unopposed") estrogen, the first type of hormonal replacement that came into use.
- Hormone replacement therapy (HRT)—This combination of estrogen and progesterone, the other hormone produced during the menstrual cycle, is taken by the vast majority of women. There are several such combination preparations on the market, such as Provera and Aygestin. Up until recently, progestin, a synthetic form

of progesterone, was the only type available, but recently, the FDA approved Prometrium, a natural form of oral micronized progesterone derived from yams.

- Selective estrogen receptor modulators (SERMs)—Known also as "designer hormones," these are drugs designed to prevent cardiovascular heart disease and osteoporosis and hopefully prevent breast and uterine cancer.
- Plant-based estrogens—Hormones made from plants, instead of conventionally made from animal hormones, are still another hormonal alternative. For instance, Estratab is a low-dose estrogen synthesized from soy and yams that helps prevent bone loss, although not as much as higher doses of ERT or HRT.

These are only some of the examples of HRT; the choice of menopausal treatments is constantly expanding and changing. So, if you decide to use them, you need to discuss with your doctor the right product and formulation for you. Also, if you are most interested in the cardiovascular effects, you need to make sure that the type you use confers this benefit.

The Checkered History of Estrogen Replacement Therapy

The controversy over hormone replacement therapy is not new. It's been around for half a century, ever since an oral form of estrogen was developed. The debate intensified in the 1970s, a decade when oral estrogen was trumpeted as the veritable fountain-of-youth for aging women. Then, it was found that giving estrogen alone increased their risk of uterine cancer (known also as endometrial cancer). This unwelcome discovery understandably dampened the enthusiasm for estrogen replacement therapy. There is another problem associated with the use of unopposed estrogen for women who have their uterus, and that is known as breakthrough bleeding. Women find it objectionable, and it is impossible for a doctor to discern whether it is due to an estrogen-induced period, or whether it is symptomatic of a precancerous uterine condition.

Since then, hormone replacement therapy has undergone a major change. In the mid-1970s, scientists discovered that combining progesterone, the other hormone produced during a woman's menstrual cycle, with estrogen greatly reduced the risk of uterine cancer. Given together, these hormones more closely approximate a woman's natural reproductive cycle, with estrogen stimulating the growth of the uterine lining during the first part of the menstrual cycle and progesterone responsible for its sloughing off towards the end. This strategy proved quite successful: When the two hormones are used in combination, the risk of uterine cancer is not eliminated, but it fell to the level when no hormones are used. This decrease in uterine cancer, however, does not offset the fact that HRT may increase breast cancer risk, a concern discussed more fully later in this chapter.

THE NEW GENERATION OF HRT: SERMs

Estrogen's beneficial effects on the heart are well-established, but many women are reluctant to take it because they fear it will increase their risk of breast cancer. Selective estrogen receptor modulators, called SERMs, known also as "designer hormones," were created to address that concern.

Although it is not fully understood how estrogen works, it is known that the hormone produces its effect indirectly by stimulating the production of proteins that encourage cell growth and proliferation. In doing this, the hormone locks into a receptor molecule in the nucleus of the cell. In turn, the cell's receptor sends a signal that turns on the gene responsible for making a growth protein, giving estrogen its effect. These receptors are not exclusive, however; they can also pair up with other molecules that bear a resemblance to estrogen. In doing so, though, they don't send the signal for protein production, and, in effect, become estrogen blockers.

Scientists have been able to take advantage of this knowledge to create this new class of drugs. These can be directed to bind to some estrogen receptors but block others. Raloxifene (Evista), approved by the FDA in 1996, stimulates estrogen receptors in the bones and liver, increasing bone mass and reducing LDL (bad) cholesterol, but blocks estrogen receptors in the breast and the uterus, so cancer risk is not increased at these sites.

ERT AND HEART DISEASE

Although estrogen is primarily considered a sexual hormone, it's now being credited with affording the natural protection that women enjoy against heart disease. Since the early part of this century, it has been known that women begin catching up to men after menopause in the rate at which they develop coronary heart disease and suffer heart attacks.

In the 1950s, some classic experiments found that those animals given estrogen were less likely to develop coronary heart disease. In recent years, studies involving not animals, but women, have led to a mounting body of evidence that estrogen is indeed effective in preventing coronary heart disease.

As noted earlier, a great deal of the enthusiasm for HRT stems from the numerous observational studies that found that its use is associated with a reduction in the risk of heart disease by an estimated 30 to 50 percent. This potential reduction represents an enormous number of women, when you consider that more than 250,000 American women die of heart disease each year.

Furthermore, hormone replacement therapy, whether it be ERT or HRT, has been found to have a multiple beneficial effects on the heart disease risk factors. First, hormone replacement therapy improves cholesterol levels. Specifically, research shows that HRT can lower harmful cholesterol by about 15 percent and boost protective HDL cholesterol by about 20 to 25 percent. This is particularly beneficial as there are not many other ways to raise HDL. Second, HRT has been found to cut levels of Lp (a), or lipoprotein "little 'a,' " a dangerous type of cholesterol. Lp (a) is associated with premature, progressive hardening of the arteries independent of the other cholesterol levels.

Estrogen also benefits the walls and linings of the veins and arteries, keeping them smooth, flexible, and elastic, which helps them to expand and contract, better accommodating blood flow.

Finally, estrogen lowers blood levels of fibrinogen, a substance involved in the formation of blood clots. Fibrinogen levels rise as a natural consequence of aging, increasing risk of heart attack or stroke.

In addition, these benefits have repeatedly been shown to benefit women who have known risk factors for heart disease even more so than in women who do not. For instance, the Nurses' Health Study found a 50 percent reduction in the death rate of HRT users who had one or more risk factors for heart disease. This was compared to an 11 percent reduction for those HRT users with no risk factors, according to a 1997 study published in *The New England Journal of Medicine*.

However, even enthusiastic supporters of HRT acknowledge that the largest proof of benefits have come from such observational data as the Nurses' Health Study, which is designed in such a way that it could skew these results. For instance, women who regularly take HRT are more likely to have healthier profiles; they are usually thinner, exercise regularly, see their doctors more often, and so on, which may translate to a lower risk to begin with. Also, a "healthy survivor" factor may exist, because women often stop taking HRT if they become acutely or seriously ill, thus creating a healthy survivor population of current users. Lastly, most studies looked at women taking only ERT, which may have the strongest protective benefit, when it is now known the majority of women must take HRT to protect themselves from uterine cancer.

However, even if it turns out that the large reductions shown in these observational studies do not hold up, it is becoming more and more apparent that there is at least some benefit to the heart from hormone use. After all, not all of the studies have been observational; the Postmenopausal Estrogen/Progestin Interventions trial, known as the PEPI study, found that hormones, no matter which regimen, decreased heart disease risk, although not as much as shown in the observational studies. This randomized study involved 875 healthy, postmenopausal women who were placed on four different hormonal regimens. The results found that all the women taking hormones experienced a 20 percent reduction in LDL (bad) cholesterol, and their HDL (good) cholesterol increased as well. Although the women who volunteered for the PEPI study presumably were more health-conscious than average, those taking placebos instead of hormones did not have as good results.

But researchers puzzle, because not all the studies have turned out as expected. If HRT benefits healthy women, it would seem to follow that HRT would be good for women with heart disease as well. The Heart and Estrogen/progestin Replacement Study (HERS) was designed to measure the effect of replacement hormones on women who already had heart disease. The study was conducted on 2,763 postmenopausal women with heart disease who had a history of heart attacks or angina (chest pain caused by heart disease), or had undergone bypass surgery or angioplasty. To the surprise of the researchers, the study published in 1998 in the *Journal of the American Medical Association* found no significant difference between the two groups. In fact, in the first year, those women randomly assigned to take HRT (estrogen plus synthetic progesterone) suffered more heart attacks than those who didn't take HRT. But by the third and fourth year, the group taking hormones experienced 40 percent fewer heart attacks. In the end, the effects of HRT balanced out, showing no significant differences between the users. Critics of the results contend that, if the study had been conducted longer, a benefit would have been shown. But the study also provided sobering evidence to doctors that HRT may not be as powerful a cardiac disease preventive as originally thought.

Frequently asked questions about hormone replacement therapy:

When should I go on HRT? Some doctors prefer to wait for a year after a woman has had her last period, but others say this unfairly deprives women of the hormone. If you are experiencing menopausal-like symptoms, your doctor can perform a blood test to measure your estrogen levels and determine if your estrogen level is indeed declining.

What are the side effects of HRT? No matter how "natural" replacement hormones are viewed, they're still medication. As can any drug, they can make you feel better or worse. Many women so dislike the side effects of replacement hormones, such as bloating and breast tenderness, so much they stop taking them. Switching to a different type of hormone formula or reducing the dosage may help.

What if I went through menopause early because I had a hysterectomy? A hysterectomy does not always include removal of the ovaries. However, if your ovaries have been removed and your body no longer produces estrogen, you should definitely consider estrogen replacement therapy as a means of securing protection against heart disease and osteoporosis. "If a woman has her ovarian function removed ten years prematurely, she is going to have her hip fracture ten years sooner or her heart attack ten years sooner. These are women who are at particularly higher risk of experiencing problems related to a lack of estrogen because it began earlier in their lives," says Dr. Delbert L. Booher, former director of the Cleveland Clinic's Program for Mature Women.

If you have undergone a hysterectomy, which by definition is removal of the uterus, your choice of hormonal replacement is somewhat easier. Since your uterus has been removed, you have no possibility of developing uterine cancer, so you're a candidate for pure estrogen alone. On the other hand, just because you are no longer at risk for one type of cancer doesn't mean that you are immune from other types, including breast cancer. You should weigh the information on HRT and breast cancer set forth below.

Is it ever "too late" to go on HRT? Doctors who are enthusiastic about HRT contend that women can enjoy such benefits as relief from menopausal symptoms and a decreased risk of cardiovascular disease even if they went through natural or surgically induced menopause years ago. Traditionally the age of 70 has been viewed as an unofficial cutoff date, but some doctors are now prescribing HRT for women over 70 if they are experiencing such postmenopausal problems as urinary incontinence, or to decrease the risk of cardiovascular disease.

How does the method of administration effect estrogen as a protection against coronary heart disease? Replacement hormones are administered in either a tablet or as a transdermal patch placed on the skin. A third option, estrogen cream, works very well in rejuvenating the tissue in the vagina, but doesn't protect against osteoporosis or cardiovascular disease.

- Tablets. In this form, pure estrogen, often made from the urine of pregnant mares, is taken orally. If you were taking progesterone as well, a typical regimen would be for you to take estrogen for most of the month, with progesterone added during the latter part of the cycle. Since this usually results in menstruation-like shedding at the end of the cycle, doctors now vary the schedule to avoid this unwanted side effect.
- The transdermal patch. In this method, estrogen is administered directly into the bloodstream through the skin. The patch is also considered preferable for smokers because of the way in which cigarette smoke affects metabolism. If you're taking combined replacement hormones (HRT) in this manner, the estrogen would be delivered by way of the patch, and you would take the progesterone orally.
- Transdermal estrogen patches (Climara, Estraderm, Vivelle) are growing in popularity because the hormone is absorbed directly into the bloodstream and is less likely to cause side effects such as nausea or headache.

One of the chief effects of HRT is its impact on cholesterol levels. Since the liver manufactures cholesterol, the way in which the hormone is administered impacts this. Estrogen delivered via the patch bypasses the liver, where high levels of the hormone can raise the production of clotting factors, but lessens the beneficial effect on the cholesterol level. On the other hand, taking the tablets maximizes the effect on cholesterol. So if you're taking HRT to lower cholesterol, oral estrogen may be preferable. Since the patch does not affect the liver, it may be preferable for women who have gallbladder disease, those with a tendency toward blood clotting, and those who are prone to gastrointestinal problems because the estrogen does not pass through the digestive tract.

But what happens when you add progesterone? Up until recently, progestin, a synthetic form of the hormone progesterone, was the only kind of that hormone available in HRT formulations (Provera, Aygestin), prescribed for postmenopausal women to lower the risk of uterine cancer. However, research suggests that adding it may blunt some of the cardiovascular benefits of taking HRT. But this picture may be changing with the FDA's approval of Prometrium. In the PEPI study, mentioned earlier, researchers found that the women who took this natural form of progesterone instead of the synthetic type had greater levels of HDL (good) cholesterol.

How good is raloxifene for reducing heart disease risk? Raloxifene, the drug designed to offer the benefits of HRT for osteoporosis and heart disease without increasing cancer risk, has been studied far less than HRT, but data thus far suggest that HRT appears to offer more cardiac benefits.

A study published in 1998 in the *Journal of the American Medical Association* involved 390 healthy postmenopausal women randomly assigned to take raloxifene, HRT, or a placebo. Compared to the placebo group, women who took raloxifene improved several known risk factors for coronary artery disease, including LDL cholesterol, but HRT lowered them even more. If your medical history prohibits you from taking HRT, though, ask your doctor about raloxifene. Even though its cardiac benefits are less pronounced than HRT, they are still significant.

Also, although raloxifene appears safe in the short term, there isn't that much known about long-term results. Raloxifene was approved following clinical trials in which more than 12,800 took the drug for over two and one-half years. But some researchers worry that this wasn't a large enough group, and not a long enough trial period, to rule out any potential increased cancer risks. So only time will tell if SERMs can deliver all that is promised.

The Risks of Hormone Replacement Therapy

Breast Cancer

For many women, the osteoporosis-preventive properties of HRT, along with a healthier heart and other potential health benefits pale in comparison to any increased breast cancer risk. Others, however, find any such increased risk unacceptable.

It's generally estimated that using HRT can increase the risk of breast cancer over a woman's lifetime from 10 percent to 13 to 17 percent, although some critics contend this may be an underestimate. Fears about a possible link between estrogen replacement therapy and breast cancer were sparked by a 1989 Swedish study that found a significant increase in the risk of breast cancer for 23,244 women taking estrogen. Since then, numerous studies have been done, with some finding significantly increased risk, others none at all, and many others in between.

For instance, a pair of studies published a month apart in 1995, found very different results. One study found those women using HRT for over five years increased their breast cancer risk; the second study found no such increase.

The first study, published in *The New England Journal of Medicine*, was from the Nurses' Health Study, and evaluated observational data from over 121,000 participants. The most added risk was found for women over the age of 55 who had been on HRT for over five years. But a study reported one month later in the *Journal of the American Medical Association* compared 537 breast cancer patients with 492 randomly selected healthy women and found no correlation between taking HRT and getting breast cancer. However, it should be noted that this was a much smaller study.

Almost everyone, including those who tout HRT for osteoporosis and heart disease, acknowledge that using hormones for over five years does increase the risk of breast cancer. But experts vary from those who find such risk figures tolerable, given the vast numbers of women who could be saved from heart attacks, to critics such as to Graham Colditz, MD, professor of medicine at Harvard Medical School. His analysis of studies on breast cancer risk posed by hormone replacement therapy, published in 1998 in the *Journal of the National Cancer Institute,* pegged the increased risk at 35 percent for current users who have been taking HRT for over five years.

Two studies published in 2000 added to this controversy. Both found that women using HRT, the combination of estrogen and progesterone, faced a higher breast cancer risk. The first study, published in the *Journal of the American Medical Association,* used data from 46,355 questionnaires filled out by women enrolled in a nationwide 1980–1995 breast cancer screening project. Of these, 2,082 women developed breast cancer. Compared with women who never used hormones, this meant those using estrogen had a 20 percent higher breast cancer risk, but the risk for those using HRT rose to 40 percent. The second study, published in the *Journal of the National Cancer Institute,* also found an added risk for those taking HRT compared to women using just estrogen.

Ovarian Cancer

There is concern that using hormones may raise risk, but definitive proof is lacking. Researchers speculate that the use of postmenopausal estrogen could increase the risk of ovarian cancer by promoting the overgrowth of cells in the ovary, which may then result in cancer. This theory is similar to the way in which it is believed hormone replacement causes breast cancer, but, with ovarian cancer, the tie is much more tenuous because research findings are contradictory.

Blood Clots

Although most of the discussion about the risks of HRT generally center on breast cancer, studies have found there is a two- to fourfold increase in the relative risk of venous thromboembolism, or blood clots that can form in the veins of the legs and travel to the lungs. This is a risk factor for a small number of women, though, not a major risk factor for most.

MAKING YOUR DECISION ABOUT HRT

First, make a distinction between short-term and long-term use of hormone replacement therapy.

Short-Term Hormone Use

The controversy over the potential health risks of hormone therapy stems from studies of women who have used them for several years, not those using them for shorter periods. Menopausal symptoms such as hot flashes, depression and insomnia, can be truly debilitating. If this is the case, consider using them. If you decide to stop taking them, you should taper off over a period of four to six months, though, or those hot flashes and other symptoms will return.

Long-Term Hormone Use

As noted at the start of this chapter, there are so many books, magazines, and discussions surrounding the question of hormone replacement therapy, you may feel compelled to make a decision. You don't necessarily have to. If you are at low or even average risk for osteoporosis and heart disease, this may not even be an issue for you.

On the other hand, if you are at high risk for osteoporosis or heart disease, going on hormones after menopause may be wise. How do you know this is the right decision for you? There really isn't a definite "yes" or "no" answer at this point, although it would be nice if there were. The Women's Health Initiative, a multimillion-dollar randomized study, was designed in part to ferret out what the true benefits and risks of hormone replacement therapy are. However, as more and more menopause drugs are added to the roster, including formulations not included in the studies, the choice may still not be simple. So the best thing to do, the experts advise, is to weigh your personal risk factors, along with other facts on whether or not some form of HRT is right for you.

Next, consider whether you currently do or do not have heart disease.

If You Do Not Have Heart Disease

- Weigh your personal risks and benefits. If you're at risk for osteoporosis, HRT may be a good choice for you. On the other hand, if it's cholesterol-lowering effects you're looking for, one of the cholesterol-preventive "statin" drugs may be a better choice (see Chapter 13).
- Make your decision on a short-term basis and feel free to change your mind later. Many women feel that they need to make an irrevocable decision about hormones that they will stick with for their whole lives. This is usually not the case. You can reevaluate your decision based on new medical findings, changes in your risk factors, or simply because you wish to, anytime you want.
- If you do opt for HRT, make sure you're on the smallest dose that is supposed to afford the preventive effects you are seeking.

- If you opt for HRT, monitor your breast cancer risk by doing regular self-exams, having annual breast exams by a health professional, and having annual mammograms.
- Don't neglect other healthy lifestyle changes. Studies indicate HRT may give you an edge in warding off some diseases, but it's not a "magic bullet" that erases the effects of an unhealthy lifestyle. Research has found, for instance, that combining HRT with exercise provides the most protection against osteoporosis and heart disease.

If You Already Have Heart Disease

The results of the HERS study has made doctors more cautious about prescribing HRT for the purpose of lowering the risk of heart attack. However, if you already have heart disease and have already been taking HRT for several years, it may be appropriate to continue, since the study did show a favorable effect on heart attack risk after a few years. If you are taking HRT with synthetic progesterone, you may want to discuss substituting Prometrium, the natural form, with your doctor. This is because Protetrium may better preserve the anticholesterol benefits.

Which Women Should Not Take HRT

The debate over HRT is of interest to most women. However, there are some groups of women for which hormones are usually not indicated. These are women with:

- Current breast cancer
- Current endometrial cancer
- Current ovarian cancer
- Active liver disease
- Active thrombophlebitis or thromboembolism (conditions associated with blood clots)

Discuss hormone therapy with your doctor if you have any of the following:

- Large uterine fibroids
- Endometriosis
- High blood pressure (that is aggravated by estrogen)

Other Considerations:
- Migraine—Women who suffer so-called "menstrual migraines" may find that hormones can worsen these symptoms. However, adjusting the levels of estrogen and/or progestin can help this problem.
- Gallbladder Disease—Some studies indicate that estrogen may increase the risk of gallstones.

IF YOU'RE A CANCER SURVIVOR

Women who have had certain types of cancer, particularly breast cancer, have long been told they should not take postmenopausal hormones. However, chemotherapy and radiation often propel these women into early menopause, which can be accompanied by severe menopausal symptoms. Studies are currently underway to learn if these women can safely take HRT, so discuss this with your doctor.

ALTERNATIVES TO HRT IN PREVENTING CORONARY HEART DISEASE

There are lifestyle changes you can make to improve your cardiovascular risk without turning to such artificial treatments as replacement hormones. See Chapter 4, "Beating the Odds." Here are some extra points to remember if you are approaching menopause.

Staying Young Without HRT

Exercise. Studies have shown that menopausal and postmenopausal women who exercise can benefit in three ways:

- Middle-aged women who participate in aerobic exercise can increase their level of cardiovascular fitness.
- Performing weight-bearing exercises, such as walking and weightlifting, helps prevent osteoporosis.
- Exercise can improve your ratio of HDL, or "good" cholesterol to LDL, or "bad" cholesterol,

Eat a calcium-rich diet to prevent osteoporosis. See Chapter 18 for a woman's calcium requirements. If you are lactose-intolerant, ask your doctor about calcium supplements.

Quit smoking. Cigarettes increase your risk of coronary heart disease and osteoporosis. Give quitting another try! You eventually will succeed!

To Sum Up

Deciding whether hormone replacement therapy is for you is a subject that requires careful consideration. If your doctor is abrupt with you, that is a signal you may want to consider in deciding whether to see another doctor, perhaps one who specializes in treating the health problems of older women. Going through menopause is a delicate and sensitive process, just as reaching womanhood was when you were in your teens. Menopause should be the start of another vibrant and exciting chapter in your life.

16

~~~~∿∿∿∿⌒∿∿∿∿~~~~

A Woman's Stress

NANCY LOVED her teaching job, but was being pressured by her superiors to switch to a new technique. She was convinced her students couldn't learn as well under the new system, but she had no choice. To keep her job, she had to change her methods. Shortly after the start of the new school year, she suffered a heart attack. "The doctors don't know why I had a heart attack," says Nancy, now 42. "They can't explain it. In my opinion, though, my heart attack was caused by stress from my job. The stress built up until I short-circuited."

Veronica attributes her heart attack at the age of 37 to her hard-driving ambition and the unrealistic expectations she placed on herself, both on and off the job. "I'm a very intense individual. I was a perfectionist," she says, "I never felt like I was accomplishing anything. That's what led to my heart attack."

Roberta, a 58-year-old psychiatric nurse, says there is no mystery why she suffered a heart attack: Her abnormal cholesterol levels resulted in coronary disease. "My high cholesterol level led to my heart attack, I'm sure. But my job had been getting more and more difficult. The last night I worked was particularly hectic. Two days later, I had my heart attack. I really think it was the stress of my job that pushed me over the edge."

Did stress really cause these women's heart attacks? They believe it did. But what does the research show?

Scientists have long pondered why some of us develop heart disease and others don't. Why does someone like Carol, who leads a heart-healthy lifestyle, suffer a heart attack while her neighbor, Penny, a 62-year-old chain-smoking, exercise-phobic pizza-chomper, remain in apparently robust health?

In their search for answers for other causes of heart disease, scientists have turned to issues known as "psychosocial" or behavioral factors. Such factors include stress, poverty, lack of education, social isolation, and discrimination.

But just as there is a lack of studies on women and the diagnosis and treatment of heart disease, so is there a dearth of information on how these other factors may affect a woman's heart. Proving links can be difficult. Some studies have shown that the behavioral factors of hostility and anger are linked to atherosclerosis, but other studies have found no such connection. We agree with the experts who contend that although stress is probably not linked to the development of heart disease in the same major way as risks such as smoking, an early family history of heart disease, high blood pressure, or diabetes, it should be considered a contributing factor. In other words, if you smoke and favor a diet high in fatty foods, blaming your health problems on stress alone may be wishful thinking. But being under continual stress can certainly contribute to such unhealthy behaviors, such as smoking and eating too much, and may damage your health in other subtle ways as well.

What Is Stress?

Stress is the body's response to the perception of threat. As we evolved over millions of years, it was an essential response and had survival value. The sight of a saber-toothed tiger by a woman gathering berries with her infant child strapped to her back would trigger an intricate series of interrelated physiological events: heightening her mental alertness and lowering of her reaction time, increasing her heart rate and blood flow to the large muscles of her legs so she can make her escape, increasing her blood clotting tendency in case she's wounded, and an altering of the amount of circulating sugar and quick-burning fat to energize her escape. The stress response, known also as the "fight or flight" response, thus evolved as a complex and critical reaction with very important implications for survival.

As modern people, this response still has value, say during a mugging or a serious family crisis, but if it is triggered during the micro-crises of everyday life, it can be seriously troublesome. When we feel stress, we are usually referring to the mental or physical manifestations we attribute to it—a state of anxiety or anger, or symptoms such as chest pain or fatigue.

Stress also means different things to different people. Dr. Hans Selye, a leading stress researcher, differentiated between the emotional feelings engendered by two different types of stress. Positive stress, he noted, was associated with joy, exhilaration, and a feeling of a job well done, while negative stress engenders anger, frustration, anxiety, fatigue, and a general feeling that something is amiss. That's the difference between "good" stress and "bad" stress. When Barbara was called upon to give an after-dinner toast at her daughter's wedding, she felt almost paralyzed with fear. "I just sat there during the entire dinner, fearing the moment I would have to get up and say a few words. I wanted to run from the room," she recalls. Her sister-in-law, though, couldn't wait to get her hands on the microphone. For her, being called upon to speak on such an occasion gave her a zip of adrenaline—the same event served "good stress" to her. In our daily lives, it is impossible to escape from some form of stress. Nor would we necessarily wish to. What is draining stress for one person can be energizing for another.

How Stress Affects Your Heart

Although stress is an emotion that you usually "feel" consciously, your response to it activates mechanisms within your body of which you may not be aware. Bodily responses are controlled by our autonomic nervous system, which gathers information about our environment and enables our body to respond without our awareness. When faced with a stressful situation, the autonomic nervous system responds by increasing production of such hormones as cortisol and epinephrine, which increase the heart rate, raise the blood pressure, and speed up the metabolism. As noted earlier, this is the "fight or flight" response. When we respond in such a major way to situations that are chronically stressful, we may be damaging our cardiovascular system.

In coronary disease, stress may be a factor in the development of high cholesterol levels, one of the most important risk factors. Further, stress may accelerate the process of cholesterol oxidation a significant phase in the formation of the plaque that plugs the coronary arteries. Stress also can affect the tendency for the blood to clot, an important step in the event of a heart attack. Stress also may raise levels homocysteine, a chemical associated with the development of heart disease, one small study published in 1999 in the journal *Life Sciences* found.

That stress plays a role in heart attacks can be seen when disasters occur. For instance, an increased number of heart attacks was observed during the week following the 1994 Los Angeles earthquake. On that day, 24 people died from cardiac causes related to coronary heart disease, compared to about five the week before.

In addition to coronary heart disease, stress may manifest itself in other types of heart problems as well. More women than men consult with doctors for chest pain, but after thorough evaluation, only half as many are found to have coronary heart disease when compared to men with similar symptoms. What accounts for this huge discrepancy? The answer, in part, is that females perceive pain differently than males and thus influenced by psychological stress.

One of the other common causes of not-so-serious chest pain in women is mitral valve prolapse, as noted in Chapter 6. Women with this disorder are more likely to experience chest pain, although exactly why remains a mystery. Stress may play a role, though, when you consider that researchers find that up to 50 percent of people experiencing panic attacks have been found to have mitral valve prolapse. Panic attacks are an experience that can be triggered by a stressful event. Although it isn't known how, chest pain in those with mitral valve prolapse may be a related stress manifestation as well.

Another cardiac problem that may be affected by stress is palpitation, a common complaint of women. Most often, it is a heightened awareness of either normal heart rhythm of minor irregularities of the heartbeat. This symptom is often aggravated by chronic sleep deprivation, a common condition in young working women that can result from too much caffeine or certain medications. Rarely, the rhythm abnormality may be so bothersome as to require treatment, and, even rarer still, it can be dangerous. In the case of life-threatening rhythm disorders caused by serious underlying heart disease, such as advanced inflammation of the heart muscle, both acute and chronic stress can play a role.

Another theory in which the way stress may affect women's hearts in particular is one that focuses on estrogen level. Since women usually develop heart disease after menopause, it's very likely that estrogen, the so-called "female" sex hormone, plays a key role in protecting the female heart. So some researchers are looking at how stress may affect a woman's estrogen level. Some of this research is coming from the animal kingdom.

Dr. Carol A. Shively, professor of pathology (comparative medicine) at Wake Forest University School of Medicine in Winston-Salem, North Carolina, studies cynomolgus monkeys, a species that shares many similarities with humans, including the way in which they develop heart disease. Female cynomolgus monkeys have menstrual cycles very similar to women's, and it's believed that the estrogen they produce may protect their hearts, in much the same way as apparently occurs in human females. Dr. Shively studies how behavioral factors affects the hormonal cycles of these monkeys. Dr. Shively and her colleagues found that female monkeys who are subordinate to the dominant females produce less estrogen and tend to have more heart disease. In another study, they looked at social isolation, which has also been connected with a higher rate of heart disease. They also found that monkeys who were socially isolated tended to develop heart disease at a significantly higher rate than the monkeys who were allowed to live together, as they would normally in the wild.

Dr. Shively also looked at the link between depression and coronary heart disease in monkeys. In people, depression is more common in lower socioeconomic classes. Depression is at least twice as common in women than in men and studies show that heart attack victims who are depressed are four times more likely to die of a second heart attack in the next 18 months, she noted. Intriguingly, subordinate female monkeys that develop coronary artery atherosclerosis are also more likely to have depression. This is not because lower socioeconomic status in people and subordinate status in monkeys are equivalent social phenomena, but, Dr. Shively notes "we think they do have one important trait in common; being of low social status, whether in a human or nonhuman primate society, is stressful. It's the stress that leads to depression, and a second fatal heart attack as well." She adds, "You have to be really careful not to think of the monkeys as little people, but to the extent that they function like we do in certain areas, we can study them and determine what type of research to focus on in humans." Perhaps these monkey studies will turn out to be a "missing link" in showing how stress and other behavioral factors influence our female hearts.

IS THERE A TYPE A PERSONALITY, AND DO WOMEN HAVE IT, TOO?

In 1959, two California cardiologists, Dr. Ray H. Rosenman and Dr. Meyer Friedman, first described the "type A personality," which has dominated most of our modern-day thinking about stress. These doctors wondered whether the then-accepted risk factors of smoking, diet, and exercise really explained why people got heart disease, or whether there were other dynamics at work as well. By studying heart patients, they were able to categorize the personality attributes of those more likely to get heart disease. This was dubbed the "type A," the "coronary-prone" personality. According to this theory, someone who was a type A personality embodied a certain set of characteristics, including impatience, anger, hostility, competitiveness, high job involvement, and achievement orientation. The type A person was also assumed to be a white, middle-aged male. Indeed, the type A personality was seen as the possible explanation for what appeared to be at the time to be an epidemic of white, middle-aged men keeling over at their desks with heart attacks. There was a second personality type, type B. Those who fit its characteristics were said to be less driven and competitive and more easygoing. Although both personality types were equally likely to achieve success, it was the type As that most often went on to develop heart disease.

Whether a woman can have a type A personality, and what, if anything, this means for her heart, are much more difficult to determine. Researchers have noted that it is difficult to come to conclusions regarding women because most such studies have been done on men. Some researchers still subscribe to the theory of the type A personality; others disagree, contending that it's not the type A personality as a whole that is harmful, but there are some components that may be damaging. Among these researchers is Dr. Lynda Powell, an epidemiologist at Rush Presbyterian/St. Luke's Medical Center in Chicago, Illinois.

"What we are starting to realize now is that components such as job involvement, achievement orientation, and perhaps even competitiveness really have very little to do with heart disease," says Dr. Powell. "What seems to be important are the characteristics such as anger or hostility and time urgency."

Dr. Powell has found that being a woman certainly does not exclude you from feeling simmering hostility, no matter what your age or whether or not you work outside the home. She and her researchers are involved in a study that is trying to determine what women and men who have suffered heart attacks find stressful.

"In these interviews, a lot of the men are the 'Archie Bunker' types," says Dr. Powell. "They are always doing the traditional type A behaviors, like pounding their fists, flailing their arms, talking fast, and so forth. The women, or at least the women who are 55 and older, don't have these characteristics at all. They have characteristics that are more consistent with resentment. They may be angry inside, but instead of pounding their fists, what they tend to do is say things quietly like, 'I don't expect my husband to pick me up at the airport. He never did that for me in his life. Why should he start now?' So you don't get those overt manifestations of anger, but you know there is a lot of anger inside."

Indeed, women who are hostile, hold in their anger, or feel self-conscious in public, may be more likely to have a thickening in their carotid arteries, the arteries of the neck, an early marker for the development of atherosclerosis throughout the body, according to a study of 200 middle-aged healthy women, according to a study published in 1998 in the journal *Psychosomatic Medicine*.

Younger women also exhibit characteristics of stress, but such feelings seem to be triggered by different factors than those for older women, notes Dr. Powell.

"I have this videotape of a woman with coronary disease who is about 60 years old. She feels abandoned by her husband and kids. The kids are all grown up and they've moved away. Her husband appears only interested in his golf game, and she's resentful of that. Since her kids are grown, she's been stripped of her role as mother. Her husband has a life of his own and doesn't need her to take care of him. Now she doesn't know what to do with herself, and even if she did, she doesn't have the self-confidence to do it."

The stresses felt by older women may be different than their younger counterparts, who came of age during the "women's movement," she has found. "The women in the younger group were trained to have a lot of skills associated with the traditional women's role. On the other hand, they've been told they don't have to be just mothers, that they can really have it all. So what you see now is women involved in demanding occupations, managing houses, raising children, caring for husbands and other family members, and eventually being overloaded with responsibilities. It will be interesting to see if this overload has an adverse effect on the heart as these women begin to pass through the menopause and come of heart attack age," Dr. Powell said.

TYPES OF STRESS WOMEN FACE

Here's a look at some of the stresses women face that we believe can affect a woman's heart. This is not to say these factors can inflict the same type of damage as smoking or diabetes, but they may contribute to the probability of a woman developing heart disease.

The Stress of Work

If you bring up the topic of women and heart disease at a dinner party, it probably will not be long before someone declares, "Well, the reason women are getting heart attacks now is that they are out in the workforce, competing with men, and trying to climb the corporate ladder."

Actually, so far as we know, women have always gotten heart attacks. But is there any truth to the notion that a woman is more at risk of heart disease because she's taking her place in the boardroom, instead of staying home, scrubbing the bathroom? Again, the role work plays in contributing to heart disease is exceedingly difficult to evaluate, especially because of the lack of research on the effect of the workplace on women. Some studies have found that joining the workforce can make a woman more prone to developing heart disease, while others have shown just the opposite.

On the whole, most large-scale studies have shown that working outside the home, in and of itself, is not detrimental to a woman's health. On the other hand, some research has teased out different aspects that may be detrimental. For instance, women who perform low-level jobs over which they have no control have been found to have higher rates of heart disease. This would imply that high-level jobs, such as in law or the corporate upper echelon, would be health-enhancing. But the reality for the majority of working women is much different. They can be found in less glamorous and more physically punishing workplaces, such as factories or in low-paying service jobs. Also, jobs that involve third-shift work have been found to correlate to higher rates of heart disease in both men and women. Yet another factor often not measured by labor studies is the amount and importance of social support some women gain from their jobs. Studies have shown that social isolation is much more stressful for women than for men. So, a woman who is allowed to interact with her co-workers can find her job a much different place than a night cleaning woman who works alone.

"The Stress Sandwich"

Since the research doesn't show that working outside the home is necessarily bad for a woman's heart (and, under some circumstances, could actually be good for it), let's look at some types of stress that may take a toll.

Consider Shirley, a 58-year-old woman who has worked on a factory production line for some 20 years. Last year, she was promoted to line supervisor. The move freed her from monotony, but now she has a new problem. Before, she was just "one of the girls," faced with the same level of responsibility and workload as her friends along the line. Now Shirley is responsible for keeping the production line moving. She isn't supposed to care that her friend Eleanor's arthritis is so painful it keeps her hands from moving fast enough, or that Diane came in late because one of her kids is in trouble with the police. None of that is supposed to matter. Shirley no longer has that camaraderie with her work peers. The boss pressures her, her former friends distrust her, and Shirley is miserable. As a result, she's eating more and smoking more, and is a prime candidate for a heart attack.

Shirley is caught in a "stress sandwich," an emotionally wrenching pressure-cooker of a situation from which she has no way out. In our society, women are particularly vulnerable to being caught in such a situation. Women are socialized to be "pleasers," trying to make everyone they encounter happy. As a result, they're too often torn between loyalties, divided among husband, children, their co-workers, and their boss.

A Woman's Multiple Roles

Today, the vast majority of women do work outside the home, either out of choice or from economic necessity. Whatever the reason, women must cope with multiple roles. The impact of such multiple roles is not necessarily negative. On the contrary, a study published in 1998 in the *Journal of Health and Social Behavior,* found that having multiple roles, such as holding a job and being married, could be positive, by providing additional social and economic support.

On the other hand, though, women can be subject to special stresses when they are carrying out these multiple roles. In the old days, these roles were spread out across a woman's life span. If a woman wanted to work outside the home, she could afford to wait until their youngest child entered school.

"The numbers of women who have to leave their babies every day to work outside the home has grown unbelievably. You used to be able to stay home until your children were in grade school and then go back to work. Now women can't afford to do that," notes Dr. Margaret Chesney, professor of medicine and epidemiology at the University of California, San Francisco, School of Medicine.

Baby boomers are also in the "sandwich generation," caught between the demands of raising children and the needs of aging parents. Studies have shown that it's most often the woman who is actually called upon to minister to these needs.

Because of these multiple roles, the woman's workday, unlike the man's, does not end when she goes home. Indeed, another part of her workday may just be beginning. Dr. Chesney cites a famous 1989 Swedish study which looked at male and female managers at a Volvo plant. The study found that, throughout the workday, most female and male managers experienced signs of cardiovascular arousal, including an increase in norepinephrine, one of the so-called "stress" hormones in their blood. But at the end of the workday, when the men returned home, their norepinephrine levels declined. Not for the women, though; their "stress" hormone level continued to climb into the evening. This indicated that, unlike the men, the women were unable to "wind down," but instead had to gear up to meet the demands of homemaking.

Studies show that the pressure on working women is growing even worse, with more women being forced to take up second jobs.

Unrealistic Expectations

It's not only getting squeezed in "stress sandwiches" and juggling multiple roles that may engender stress in women. Women also are socialized to take too much responsibility upon them.

"Women have very unrealistic expectations. We take responsibility for everything, even the weather," says Dr. Chesney. "If we invite people to a picnic and it rains, we apologize for it."

Women also place unrealistic demands upon themselves. In our society, men tend to compete with one another, but studies show that women tend to compete against unrealistically high expectations they hold for themselves—and naturally come up short.

What About Discrimination?

It's indisputable that some differences in health are found among people of different races and ethnic groups. Still, the relationship between race and health factors remains a sensitive subject. It's known, for example, that African-American women face a higher risk of developing heart disease, which is likely due to their being more prone to high blood pressure. But what accounts for this higher rate of high blood pressure among African-Americans? Some researchers are also looking at heredity. Others are looking at possible biological adaptations to slavery or the day-to-day toll taken by what may be perceived as unfair treatment.

ARE YOU UNDER STRESS?

Some people say they cannot change their response to stress. "Personality-wise, you are who you are," declares Helen, the 45-year-old school bus driver who suffered a heart attack. Even though she was told to try and cut down on her stress, she's found that advice difficult to follow. "Some people can go through life and not have anything floor them, and for some people, everything floors them," she says. "I'm in that category. I let everything bother me," says Helen.

But experts believe there are ways we can learn to make stress more manageable.

STRATEGIES FOR REDUCING STRESS

Leslie, who is 47, suffered a heart attack about a year after her promotion to supervisor of a word-processing department. She'd enjoyed her previous job, but now, she found herself squeezed in a "stress sandwich" between her demanding boss and her former co-workers. Before returning to work, Leslie voiced her concerns to her boss. He offered her the opportunity to keep her supervisory position, but transfer to a new department. Leslie was lucky. The receptiveness she found is rare. Usually, we must learn to change our reactions to stress.

According to Dr. Lynda Powell, those of us who find it difficult to reduce stress have a high degree of "emotional arousability." An event that would mildly annoy another, like having someone cut in front of her in a grocery store, infuriates such a person. When she works with these sorts of people, Dr. Powell tries to get them to see they have a choice whether to respond or not. She tells them to think of such incidents as "hooks."

"Each morning when you wake up, you are like a fish swimming downstream in clear water," she says. "All of a sudden, a baited hook drops." If you rise to the bait and snap at the first hook by becoming upset, the chances are high you'll snap at the next one and the next, and spend the whole day feeling upset, angry, and simmering with harmful hostility. On the other hand, if you let that first hook pass, it makes it easier to let the next ones glide by as well. "If you can learn to say to yourself that one word, 'Hook!' at the time the hook drops, you'll find your anger, irritation, aggravation, and impatience will decrease."

Ways to avoid snapping at "hooks" and channel your stress can be learned in stress management courses, which are offered by local hospitals, community centers, and adult education programs. Techniques used in such courses may include biofeedback, in which you learn to be more aware of and to control your unconscious body responses; relaxation techniques; role-playing, in which you rehearse your response to stressful situations; and "self-talk," where you learn to replace negative thoughts with positive ones.

♥ Mindsaving Tip: Learning to manage your stress can have other benefits as well. Researchers have found that by reducing stress, women who want to lose weight are more likely to stick to their diets and women who want to stop smoking are more likely to be successful quitters.

Here are some short-term ways to relieve tension:

- **Exercise.** Even if it's only going out for a walk. Exercise has been shown to be an excellent way to reduce stress.
- **Pamper yourself.** Take a hot bath, get a massage, lose yourself in a novel (or try to write one) or find other ways to add enjoyment to your life.
- **Get a hobby.** Did you used to paint, sing, or dance? Try it again. Creative hobbies can be great stress relievers—don't worry, you don't have to be a Picasso. For some people, oil painting is relaxing; others find rug hooking or knitting does the trick.
- **Play with your pet.** Studies have shown that stroking a dog or cat is so relaxing it even lowers blood pressure.
- **Work for change.** For those who are easily "emotionally aroused," becoming involved in a political campaign, your company union, or a community group may be inviting more stress. Others, though, may find it personally empowering and stress reducing. Even stuffing envelopes for a candidate you support can be relaxing and can have a positive long-term result.

17

~~~~~⌇⌇⌇〇⌇⌇⌇~~~~~

Paying for Your Heart's Care

As she talked, Laurie busily arranged a display of potpourri jars on some shelves at the gift shop she owns. "I have this jumping and fluttering in my chest. My doctor doesn't think its anything serious, but she wants to do some tests to be sure. The trouble is, the only health insurance I could afford comes with a $1,000 deductible. If I have these cardiac tests done, I won't have enough money to buy inventory for the Christmas shopping season."

Nora, a 35-year-old freelance writer, has health care for her children through her ex-husband's policy. She decided against continuing her own health coverage when the choice came down to that or paying for car insurance. "I live in the country," she says, "Without my car, I can't get to work, so I basically didn't have any choice."

Denise, 53, started her own business after she was laid off, earns a good living, but cannot find a health insurer who will cover her, because of the cardiac valve replacement she had a few years ago. "They say it's a preexisting condition, so they won't cover me," she says. "I'm so worried about it I can't sleep at night."

Hope, a long-divorced artist, developed coronary disease at the age of 62. "Thank God for Medicare," she says, "I had my other hospital stays before I turned 65, so whatever the insurance didn't pay, I had to pay. I used to break out in a rash trying to figure out what I was supposed to pay, what I wasn't, and how to find the money for it."

What's a section on health insurance doing in a book that tells you how to take care of your heart? Frankly, we're tired of seeing health care books that celebrate the latest in medical technology, but make no mention of who pays for it. What good is it to know what an echocardiogram does if you don't have insurance to cover its cost? Why spend time locating the best medical center for your heart problem if your insurer won't pay for your treatment there? As notes Cheryl Jensen, an author who writes about health insurance, "The death or severe illness of a loved one is a tragedy, but it may not be a catastrophe. The catastrophe comes when you cannot pay for it."

As of this writing, there are several plans being debated on how to solve our nation's health care crisis. This is a complex problem we do not expect will be solved by the time this book is published. If it is, just skip this chapter. Unfortunately, we don't think you will be able to do this.

WOMEN AND THE HEALTH CARE CRISIS

Increasingly, the spotlight has been shining on how America's system of health insurance works, and doesn't work. Being unable to afford health care coverage used to be an issue that affected only the poor, but a recent Gallup Poll showed that the cost of health care is now one of the top concerns of all Americans. We're all discovering, much to our dismay, that health insurance coverage no longer provides the type of worry-free guarantee it once did.

The lack of health insurance is a problem that affects both men and women; the plight is worsening for women. According to the Commonwealth Fund 1998 Survey of Women's Health, 26 percent of women under the age of 65, or 21 million women, are either uninsured now (18 percent) or were at some point during the proceeding year (8 percent). While Medicare has achieved universal health coverage for women age 65 and older, low- and modest-wage women under age 65 are at especially high risk for being uninsured, as are minority women and women with health problems. Furthermore, women who had gaps in coverage—as well as women who were currently uninsured—were at twice the risk for health care access difficulties, as women insured throughout the year.

Employment is no guarantee of health insurance coverage. Indeed, most uninsured women are part of a family with at least one full-time worker. Fifteen percent of uninsured women in families had at least one part-time worker and no full-time worker. Less than one fifth of the uninsured women were in families in which no one was working.

Not surprisingly, women without continuous health insurance faced significantly more problems getting access to care. Compared with continuously insured women, those who experienced some time uninsured were about three times as likely to have problems getting access to care. Among those currently uninsured, one half reported difficulty getting care when needed, and one out of five said they had not visited a physician in the past year. They were also more likely to forgo cost-effective preventive care: Two of five had not had a Pap test in the past year, and one half reported not having a regular doctor. Those who experienced gaps in coverage were less likely to have a regular doctor to develop an ongoing relationship with, and were more likely to seek care at emergency departments or busy hospital clinics, the survey found.

There are many reasons built into our society that account for why women are at a disadvantage when it comes to health care coverage. More women than men are listed as dependents on their spouse's health insurance plans, making them vulnerable to losing their coverage if their husbands lose their jobs, or they divorce or become widowed. Also, women are more likely to hold low-paying jobs or to work part-time for small businesses, which makes it less likely they will get health care coverage.

You may think that, if you are older, Medicare will cover your costs, but this is not the total picture. According to a 1999 report by the Older Women's League, an advocacy organization, the majority of Medicare recipients—six in 10 of those receiving benefits from the program at age 65—are women. Medicare has made it possible for these women to have access to health care they increasingly need as they age and otherwise would not be able to afford, but significant gaps in the program exist. For instance, traditional Medicare does not cover prescription drugs unless they are used in a hospital or other health care institution. Almost eight of every 10 women on Medicare use prescription drugs regularly— drugs, such as cardiac medications, that can be costly. Estimates for 1998 showed that older women on Medicare spend more on out-of-pocket costs than do men. The women spent, on average, $2,613 for health care, or 22 percent of their incomes, compared to men, who spent $2,385, or 17 percent of their incomes. Also, the older and poorer the woman, the higher her out-of-pocket costs.

What You Can Do About Health Insurance

Some of the problems of health insurance are built into the system, and will not be remedied until the system is changed. We don't have a solution to this complex problem, but we do have some ideas on how you can become a smarter consumer and increase the possibility that, if you do have to undergo medical treatment, you'll be able to pay for it. That's why, in addition to the Lifesaving and Mindsaving tips in the other chapters, there are some Moneysaving tips in this chapter as well.

> ❤ **Moneysaving Tip: It's not enough to be a smart patient when it comes to taking care of your heart: You also need to be a smart consumer when it comes to shopping for and using health care coverage. It is no longer enough to sit back and assume your health insurance will cover you if you get sick. You need to know for certain beforehand. If you develop a heart problem, the cost of cardiac tests and treatments can mount up very fast.**

This section is not intended to be a full-scale discussion of how to shop for health insurance; we've listed materials in the "Recommended Reading and Resources" section to help you with that. But here are some things you should be thinking about.

The ABCs of Health Insurance

It used to be that health insurance came in one basic type; now there is a veritable alphabet-soup of programs. These include traditional health insurance, where you (or your employer) pay a monthly premium, and the insurer reviews and pays any medical bills after they come in. There are also HMOs, or health maintenance organizations, in which one fee covers the services of primary care physicians and a variety of specialists. There are variations on these two models as well. If you're starting a new job, or are already employed, at some point you may be asked to choose from a mind-boggling variety of plans.

The ABCs of HMOs and Related Health Care Plans

The system of health care in this country is undergoing a major revolution. Despite the failure of the White House–advocated health care reform act a few years ago, change remains the order of the day. The biggest shift has been the growth of HMOs and other managed health care plans. This movement, which began many years ago in California, has now spread throughout the country. According to the Commonwealth Fund, as of 1998, three of four insured women under the age of 65 were enrolled in some type of managed health care plan.

The Managed Health Care Plan (HMO)

An HMO (health maintenance organization) provides comprehensive health care services to its enrolled members for a prepaid, fixed monthly fee. It differs from traditional health insurance in not charging for each service provided. There are limitations, however. Most plans allow you to use only the doctors who are on the HMOs staff, and you may be limited in your choice of clinics or hospitals as well.

Over the years, different variations on the HMO have also sprung up. For example, there is also the PPO, or preferred provider organization. This is a network of physicians who supply care. These doctors are contracted by a third party, usually a self-insured employer, union trust, or insurance carrier. The participating physicians provide care at a discount to the third-party payer, resulting in lower costs. Another variation is the independent practice association, or IPA, in which a group of doctors in private practice contract with the HMO to provide care for subscribers. A point-of-service (POS) costs more than an HMO, but allows more flexibility in choice of doctors.

What Is Managed Health Care?

As health care costs have risen, private insurers have also clamped down more stipulations on consumers too. Currently, insurers throughout the country are adopting a system called "managed health care," which comes into play in two ways. The policyholders are usually required to get second opinions for some procedures, and also must notify the insurer ahead of time for permission to enter the hospital. If you don't follow these procedures, you can be penalized when it comes time for you to receive your benefits. From the insurer's perspective, this plan is designed to minimize unnecessary hospital stays, eliminate unnecessary surgery, and get you home as soon as possible. For you, managed health care usually means restrictions to which you're unaccustomed.

"One of the biggest issues today is what type of health insurance people have," says Dr. Bruce Lytle, a heart surgeon at the Cleveland Clinic. "I can't tell you how many times someone has called me up and said they want me to operate on them, and I'll say, 'Fine.' Then, they'll say, 'Well, my insurance says I have to go to such-and-such a hospital.' So I can't do it. People need to understand what their health insurance covers and what it doesn't."

If you do have a managed health care plan, your insurer may allow you to go elsewhere if you pick up part of the tab yourself. If you are accustomed to thinking you have 100 percent coverage, you may find this unfair. But if you're a high-risk patient with a serious heart problem, you may be better off in the long run seeking out the most expert care you can find, even if you do have to incur part of the cost yourself.

If you have traditional health insurance, here are tips for getting the most out of your coverage.

Know your health insurance plan. In the past, a health care policy was too often stuck in a drawer. Today, you need to know what that health care plan covers. Are the benefits adequate? What is your maximum out-of-pocket cost? Is your health insurance renewable, or can it be canceled if you become ill?

Face facts: No matter what type of private health insurance you have, nowadays, it is more than likely it will not cover 100 percent of your bills. First of all, insurance has gotten so expensive that few people can afford a policy without any deductibles; indeed, many insurers no longer offer such a luxury. Second, although your insurer may imply that you do have 100 percent coverage, that's often not the case. Most insurers use a payment schedule that includes a loophole known as "reasonable and customary charges." Often, this amounts to something like 80 percent of what the insurers consider the prevailing fees for the area where you live. For example, say your cardiologist charges $110 for a physical, but your insurer considers $80 to be the "reasonable, customary charge" for that procedure. Unless your doctor participates in that particular insurance plan, you'll have to convince him or her to accept the lesser figure or pay the difference yourself.

Know your company's policy on "preexisting conditions" and waiting periods. If you have a heart problem, or any other health problem, sometimes insurers can use this as a reason to raise your rate, exclude you from coverage for a given time, or even refuse to cover your problem at all for a certain amount of time. Know the ins and outs of your own heart problem; if it's relatively minor, you may be able to use that information to convince your insurer that the company's practice is not fair. If you take this route, send a copy of your letter to the agency in your state that regulates insurance companies. If your insurance company is not on firm medical ground, it may change its stand.

♥ Mindsaving Tip: Some states have taken steps to ensure that health coverage is denied to no one with the means to pay for it. For example, Connecticut has created a "high-risk pool," similar to a high-risk pool for car insurance. If you have a preexisting condition, an insurer may assign you to such a pool. You may need to pay higher premiums, but at least you can get coverage you need. Find out whether your state has such a system or consider lobbying your legislature to create one.

Know your insurer's appeal process—and use it. When I had my heart surgery, I spent my entire recuperation period checking and double-checking medical bills. This meant reading and rereading my insurance policy, learning to decipher the code numbers used instead of names for treatment, making numerous calls to both hospital and insurer (finding out their toll-free numbers, if available), and availing myself of the appeals procedure. I appealed almost every charge that was denied. This was time-consuming and frustrating, but it turned out well. First, I was able to whittle down the over $1,500 my insurer wanted me to pay to about $165. I'm still not sure what that $165 was for; I finally gave up out of exhaustion and sent in the check. Then I wrote a newspaper column filled with all the errors I found and contradictory information I was given. An example? The day before my surgery, I underwent several tests that were required for my heart operation. The cost of these tests amounted to several hundred dollars. My insurance company later told me my policy covered only the first test when multiple procedures were done on the same day. This sounded bizarre. Sure enough, I checked my policy, and found no such stipulation. I called back, saying that, if this was indeed the case, I would like it in writing. "No problem," I was told. I received a call the very next day and was told there had been a change (just the day before; what a coincidence!). The tests were covered and an amended statement to that effect was already in the mail.

Know whether your health insurer is financially sound. After the booming 1980s, not only banks went bust; some health insurance companies did as well. We've heard heartbreaking stories of people who paid their insurance premiums, only to find out later, when they needed coverage, that it wasn't there. Some even went into bankruptcy or lost their homes. There is no sure-fire way to make certain this will not happen to you, but experts suggest these steps:

- **Check to make sure the insurer is licensed to sell insurance in your state.** This assures you that the company has met certain financial guidelines. In addition, if a licensed insurer fails, your state's insurance guaranty fund can help cover your unpaid claims.
- **Check the insurance company's financial rating.** Insurance companies are rated by such independent rating companies as Standard & Poor's Corporation and Moody's Investors Service, both of New York. You can find such ratings directories in your library. Consider buying from companies with only an "A" rating or better, but keep in mind that such a guarantee today is still not iron-clad tomorrow. Some agencies offer telephone call-in services for a more up-to-date rating.

Think about options for group coverage. If you're self-employed, you may find it difficult or too expensive to get individual coverage. However, group insurance may be available through your labor union, a professional organization, or such groups as the National Organization for Women. You also may be able to obtain group coverage by joining a professional organization, or your local Chamber of Commerce or Council of Small Businesses.

Plan ahead if there is a possibility you may lose your group insurance benefits. There are non-health-related reasons for losing your group insurance coverage, such as leaving your job, getting divorced, or becoming widowed. Whatever the reason, you may be able to continue that insurance by participating in a federally sponsored plan established under COBRA (the Consolidated Omnibus Budget Reconciliation Act). COBRA requires employers with twenty or more workers to provide them and their families with the option of continuing health insurance (18 to 36 months, depending on the circumstances). Continuing the insurance provided by your spouse's employer may be available to you if you are divorcing or become widowed.

WHAT ELSE CAN YOU DO?

If you want to have health care that truly answers your needs, become involved in the debate. Study the pros and the cons of various plans and decide what type of health care you'd like to see. Beware of proposals that have hidden factors that may discriminate against certain groups, such as women. For example, some proposals support keeping health costs down by promoting the concept of health care rationing based on age. While this might seem to make common sense, such plans actually discriminate against women, because the expense of caring for growing number of aging women can create strong incentives to ration health care based on age. Although such policies do not explicitly seek to penalize women, women would be among those most affected because they are likely to live longer.

Although the formal attempt to overhaul our nation's health care system failed a few years ago, the debate continues. The outcome of this debate is terribly important for the well-being of everyone in our country. The solution, of course, is a system that would afford care to everyone but still maintain a system of medical care that has been justifiably called the best in the world. There is no easy answer. But it is important for everyone to take part in the debate. The decisions that are made in the next few years may well shape the future of our country's health care—including the care of women's hearts.

18

~~~~ハⵔⵔⵔⵔ~~~~

How to Keep a Healthy Heart

Every Woman's Eating Plan for Life

Keeping your heart healthy is an excellent reason to eat right. In doing so, you reduce your risk of heart disease. Research finds that eating "wrong," that is, eating a diet loaded with saturated fat and cholesterol, can increase your chances of developing coronary heart disease. On the other hand, eating right can improve your blood cholesterol profile, thus lessening the risk.

Eating right doesn't necessarily mean dieting. You may desire to lose weight; if you're overweight, that's a fine goal, but for many women, these two goals tend to get mixed up, sometimes with unfortunate results. So, even though we talk about losing weight later in this chapter, the emphasis is on eating healthy.

Creating Your Personal Eating Plan

We suggest you compare the way you eat with the recommendations of the United States Department of Agriculture (USDA) for a healthy diet. Your taxpayer dollars paid for it. If you look closely, you'll see it resembles the kinds of plans you have to pay lots of money for when you join diet clubs. Since you've already paid big bucks for this one, take advantage of it. The USDA will send you lots of information on how to use this eating plan, create menus, bag lunches—all kinds of good stuff, for free or at very low cost. For information on ordering, see the "Resources" section of this book.

The following menu comes from the USDA's dietary guidelines. These guidelines are written for both men and women. Since most women require less food than men do, you should use the lower number of suggested servings. Especially, of course, if you want to lose weight.

TYPE OF FOOD	SUGGESTED DAILY SERVINGS
Vegetables	3–5 servings (raw, leafy vegetables, 1 cup; other types, ½ cup)
Fruits	2–4 servings (1 medium-sized apple, orange, or banana counts as one fruit, as does ½ cup diced fruit or ¾ cup of fruit juice)
Breads, cereals, rice, and pasta	6–11 servings (one serving equals one slice bread; ½ bun, bagel, or English muffin; one ounce dry cereal; ½ cup cooked cereal, rice, or pasta)
Milk, yogurt, and cheese	2–3 servings (one serving equals 1 cup of milk or yogurt, or ½ ounce of cheese)
Meats, poultry, fish, dry beans and peas, eggs, and nuts	2–3 servings (Your daily total should be about 6 ounces. Beef should be lean, and chicken cooked without skin. A three-ounce portion is about the size of a deck of cards.)
Fats, oils, and sweets	Use sparingly

Two types of women will read this chapter: those who are close to their ideal weight and want to make their sure their diet is as healthy for their hearts, and those who want to shake the "diet" habit once and for all, lose weight healthily, and maintain their weight. For both groups, many of our suggestions are the same. Much of what we suggest revolves around limiting the amount of fat you ingest each day.

According to research, the best way to reduce your risk of heart disease is to reduce the amount of saturated fat in your diet. Happily, studies also show that limiting fat is a great way to lose weight. Since this is the strategy we follow, we can attest to the fact that limiting fat intake is the best way to lose weight and not feel hungry.

Depending on which statistics you read, Americans derive from 37 to 50 percent of their daily calories from fat, far higher than the current level of 30 percent recommended by the American Heart Association. Now, you may have learned that "a calorie is a calorie is a calorie." Technically, that's true, but the great thing about cutting out fat is you can actually feel like you're eating more, even while consuming fewer calories. One gram of fat contains nine calories, but carbohydrates and protein each contain only four calories. So, every time you choose protein or carbohydrates instead of fat, you're saving five calories per gram consumed.

❤ **Lifesaving Tip: Lowering the fat in your diet reduces your risk of developing not only coronary artery disease, but also diabetes and colon cancer, and possibly breast cancer as well.**

Another "Pyramid" Alternative— the Mediterranean-Style Diet

The USDA's food pyramid, though, is not the only potential healthy eating choice. A variation known as the Mediterranean Diet Pyramid is gaining attention for its potential health benefits. This plan takes its name from the way people eat in Mediterranean countries, such as Greece, which has a lower rate of heart disease and some cancer than Western countries.

Although similar to the USDA Food Pyramid, this alternative places greater emphasis on eating foods from plant sources, including fruits and vegetables, potatoes, breads and grains, beans, and nuts and seeds. The plan also calls for eating daily low to moderate amounts of cheese and yogurt, low to moderate amounts of fish and poultry (with an emphasis on fish), and limiting eggs. Fresh fruit is the preferred daily dessert, and red meat is suggested only a few times a month. A key difference between the Mediterranean Diet and the traditional Food Pyramid is in the amount of total fat. The Mediterranean-type plan is more liberal in the use of fat, providing it is the monounsaturated or polyunsaturated type, such as olive oil, and not saturated fats, such as butter or margarine.

The potential benefits of the Mediterranean-type diet were showcased in a report published in 1999 in the American Heart Association's journal *Circulation*. The study divided patients who had suffered a heart attack into two groups; those who followed the Mediterranean-type diet and those who followed a "prudent" Western-type diet relatively low in fat, cholesterol, and saturated fat. The 219 patients who followed the Mediterranean-type diet cut their risk of a second heart attack by 50 to 70 percent. They also reduced other heart-related risks such as unstable angina, congestive heart failure, and stroke. This was a relatively small study, but others have shown that the Mediterranean-type diet may be very beneficial. For more information, see the "Resources" section.

The Skinny on Fat

The American Heart Association recommends that we obtain no more than 30 percent of our daily calories from fat, and only one third of that from saturated fat. Some experts believe this figure is too high, and should be pared to 25 or 20 percent or even lower. When it comes to fats, all of them contain the same number of calories, but they differ widely in their effect on our body.

Generally, saturated fat raises blood cholesterol more than anything else. Examples of saturated fats include butter, lard, meat fat, shortening, and hydrogenated oils such as palm and coconut oil, palm kernel oil, and cocoa butter. A substance known as "trans-fatty acids" also has been found to increase the risk of heart disease. Trans-fatty acids are found in margarine and also are a major ingredient in packaged baked goods, snack foods, and crackers. Therefore, monounsaturated and polyunsaturated fats are considered preferable.

How Low (Fat) Should You Go?

Since the implication of dietary fat as a culprit in the creation of coronary heart disease, the importance of low-fat eating was emphasized. Lately, though, the pendulum has swung the other way. Looking at the best-seller lists makes it all the more confusing; you can find books authored by low-fat eating advocate Dr. Dean Ornish sharing the honors with books written by Dr. Robert Atkins, who advocates a diet high in fat.

Confused? Let us sound the call for moderation!

Although eating a low-fat diet has been shown to reduce some risk of factors associated with coronary heart disease, the American Heart Association issued a statement in 1998 warning that reducing dietary fat to very low levels may not provide any additional benefit over a more traditional low-fat diet. Very low-fat diets contain no more than 10 percent of total calories from dietary fats, an eating method most easy to achieve by vegetarians. Eating a diet moderately low in fat can reduce levels of LDL-cholesterol, the so-called "bad" cholesterol, but reducing the fat levels significantly further can, at least in the short term, decrease the HDL, or "good" cholesterol levels, and increase levels of triglycerides, a "bad" lipid. Since there are not that many studies done on people following very low-fat diets, unanswered questions remain. Some of the studies combined low-fat eating with other factors, such as food choice and exercise, so it's not known what impact the diet alone had. It's also not known whether these diets provide enough nutrients, such as vitamins and minerals, the AHA said.

In addition, too often, low-fat diets have relied heavily on loading up on carbohydrates. In the quest to follow a low-fat diet, it's easy to eat too much of certain carbohydrates, such as fat-free cookies, pasta, rice, and bread. But any high-carbohydrate food consumed in large quantities can lead to weight gain and obesity, which, in turn, raise heart disease risk. So, although the USDA's food pyramid appears to advocate a diet high in carbohydrates, it's worth noting that the portions are quite a bit smaller than Americans are usually accustomed to eating. For instance, a potato the size of a tennis ball is considered one serving, while a huge Idaho potato, the type most often found on dinner plates, is about two to two and one-half servings.

Is this the last word on what to eat? Not by a long shot. For instance, our understanding of how certain fats are metabolized continues to grow. Remember when eggs were singled out as a cholesterol-raising villain? That's because egg yolks are composed of cholesterol. But it was found out later that eating them didn't necessarily translate into higher cholesterol levels in the body, especially if eaten in moderation. Some saturated fats once viewed as harmful, such foods containing stearic acid, have been found to be less detrimental than once believed. Foods containing this type of fatty acid include chocolate (yay!).

These guidelines on diet will be further refined in the future. Research is underway to identify more particular patterns of cholesterol and learn what type of diet can be used to achieve the best results.

What Else Should You Eat?

So, if you are eating less fat, what are you eating? Here are the types of foods to emphasize:

Fruits and vegetables. Eating at least five daily servings of both fruits and vegetables each day may lower the risk of coronary heart disease and stroke, as well as some types of cancer. Why? It's not known precisely, but they're loaded with antioxidant vitamins, including beta-carotene (which the body converts to vitamin A), vitamin E, and vitamin C.

Here's where to find them:

VITAMIN C	Broccoli, brussels sprouts, cantaloupe, cauliflower, currants (fresh), mango, peppers, kiwi, papayas, oranges, parsley, pod peas, strawberries, red cabbages, grapefruits
VITAMIN E	Dried apricots, mango, pumpkin seeds, fortified cereals, sweet potatoes, wheat germ, sunflower seeds, asparagus, raw kale
VITAMIN A AND BETA-CAROTENE	Broccoli, carrots, sweet potatoes, pumpkin, yellow squash, cooked spinach, tomatoes, kale, red peppers, red chili peppers, parsley, watercress, cantaloupe

Fiber. Fiber, the indigestible part of fruits, vegetables, and grain, deserves a featured role in your diet. Although it has no nutritional value in itself, fiber is credited with an impressive array of positive benefits.

A cholesterol-fighter, fiber apparently helps lowers the risk of coronary heart disease. Fiber is also credited with protecting against colon cancer, and it helps reduce high blood pressure and improves the way diabetics metabolize sugar. As a bonus, because foods rich in fiber stave off hunger, it's a boon to weight watchers.

Most experts recommend you try to eat 25 to 35 grams of fiber a day, but don't go over 35. Since most processed foods don't contain any fiber, and foods rich in fiber contain only a few grams, it's difficult to reach that number anyway. Too much fiber too quickly can also upset your stomach; add it to your diet gradually, a few grams a day, and remember to drink plenty of water.

Fiber-rich foods include most whole grains, oats, oat bran, flakes, rye crisp crackers, popcorn, toasted wheat germ, granola, high-fiber bread, and all types of beans. Also, many fruits, including apples, figs, peaches, pears, prunes, raspberries, and strawberries, as well as many types of vegetables, including asparagus, beets, broccoli, carrots, kale, corn, okra, potatoes with skin, and zucchini.

Here are the government's tips for getting more fiber in your diet:

- Clean fruits and vegetables, but leave the peels on.
- Use oats as filler in casseroles or meat loaf.
- Use whole grains when you bake.
- Snack on raw fruits and vegetables, air-popped popcorn, or low-fat cereal mix instead of high-fat, low-fiber chips.
- Read bread labels carefully. Some whole-grain breads are rich in fiber, but many whose labeling include "whole grain" or "whole wheat" have no more fiber than does white bread.

Soy. There's increasing evidence that soy, a substance made from soybeans, may reduce the risk of heart disease, because it reduces cholesterol. An added benefit is that it may reduce breast cancer risk as well, as it contains phytoestrogen, a substance that chemically resembles estrogen and may block cancer-promoting receptor cells in the breast; and osteoporosis, because it's rich in calcium. How do you incorporate soy into your diet? It's easier than ever, with soy products making their way into the supermarket, disguised as more familiar foods, such as soy burgers. Also, although tofu is bland in itself, it's spongy and soaks up flavor, so it can pinch-hit for chicken or beef in stir-fried dishes, for example. Other soy products include tempeh, a thin cake made from fermented soybeans; isolated soy protein; soy flour; soya powder; textured soy powder; and soy milk.

Calcium-rich foods. It's very important that women consume enough calcium. Calcium can help prevent osteoporosis, the "brittle bone" disease that can come with aging. As noted, your body requires a constant supply of calcium to live; if the supply isn't maintained, calcium is taken from the bones. That's why you need to replenish your store of calcium each day, whether you're at risk for osteoporosis or not. Unfortunately, most women think they can get away with just splashing some milk on their cereal. They're wrong. Studies find that although most women think they're getting enough calcium in their diet, they often fall short.

Get as much calcium as you can from the food you eat. Dairy products are loaded with calcium. To be heart-healthy, choose skim milk, nonfat and low-fat yogurt, and lower-fat cheeses, which have the same, if not more, calcium. Low-fat yogurt is also an excellent calcium source. Besides dairy, broccoli, collard greens, and kale are all rich in calcium. When it comes to vegetables, let color be your guide; the darker they are, the more calcium they contain. The exception is spinach; it contains oxalates, which inhibits calcium absorption. It's virtually impossible, though, to get all the calcium you need from food, so it's recommended that women take calcium supplements. Calcium carbonate is considered a good type of calcium. It is the type contained in Tums, the antacid. Two Tums tablets contain 600 mg of calcium.

Here are the government's recommendations:

- 1,000 mg for premenopausal women between the ages of 25 and 49, or postmenopausal women ages 50 to 64 currently taking estrogen;
- 1,500 mg for postmenopausal women ages 50 to 64 who are not taking estrogen and for all women over the age of 65.

Omega-3 fatty acids. These types of fatty acids are not to be confused with the trans-fatty acids mentioned earlier that raise heart disease risk. Omega-3 fatty acids are "good" acids that have been shown in many studies to protect against coronary heart disease and may also prevent sudden cardiac death. These types of fatty acids are found in tofu, nuts, soybeans, flaxseed oils, and canola oil, as well as in seafood, especially cold-water seafood such as salmon, codfish, and sardines.

What About Wine?

Ever since the television show *60 Minutes* publicized the concept known as "The French Paradox," the health benefits of alcohol have been a hot topic.

The French Paradox refers to the fact that the French traditionally eat a very rich diet, yet they have one of the lowest rates of heart disease in the industrialized world. How can this be so? One possible explanation promulgated is that the French drink wine with their meals.

Numerous studies have found that the moderate consumption of alcoholic beverages—be it wine, beer, or liquor—reduces heart disease risk by 30 to 50 percent. Evidence suggests much of this benefit is due to the fact that alcohol increases the amount of the "good" HDL cholesterol in the blood. There's also evidence that alcohol may favorably affect blood clotting, reducing the risk of heart attack. These protective effects are found no matter whether wine, beer, or alcohol is consumed. However, red wine and dark beer also may have antioxidant effects that can help retard the effects of aging on the heart's vessels. (Teetotalers may get some of this beneficial effect by drinking grape juice.)

However, before you imbibe, there are other factors to take into account.

First, the studies show that these protective effects are true only for those who indulge moderately; for women, this is defined as one drink, a standard drink being 12 ounces of beer, 4 ounces of wine, or 1.5 ounces of 80-proof spirit. In contrast, studies find that women who drink heavily are more likely to develop such serious health problems as cardiomyopathy, a disease that destroys the heart muscle, and potentially deadly liver diseases like cirrhosis and hepatitis, than men are. Heavy female drinkers are also believed more prone to alcoholism, depression, and suicide. There is also concern that alcohol drinkers, especially heavy ones, raise their risk of breast cancer.

So while an occasional drink may not harm your heart, and may have a modest health benefit, adopting a healthy eating plan and exercising are healthier ways to reduce your risk of heart disease.

❤ **Lifesaving Tip: If you have specific health problems, such as diabetes, elevated triglycerides, or heart failure from any cause, you should consume alcohol only with your doctor's permission.**

What About Supplements?

It's amazing how many people distrust doctors, but are willing to down handfuls of vitamins and supplements on the recommendation of their neighbor, their hairdresser, or even the guy on television doing an infomercial. Indeed, this faith in the value of vitamins and nutritional supplements has fueled a multibillion-dollar industry. But do you need to take vitamin and mineral supplements to keep your heart healthy? As long as you're eating a healthy diet, the answer, generally, is "no," says the American Heart Association.

Still, there is interest in the role of the vitamins known as antioxidants, including beta-carotene, vitamin C, and vitamin E, in the prevention of heart disease. Although there isn't complete evidence of it, vitamin E and the other antioxidants show promise in preventing heart disease.

The one that has received the most media attention is vitamin E. Several studies lend credibility to this belief. It's not known exactly why vitamin E may be protective, but the hypothesis is that oxidation, a process that occurs in our body's cells with every breath we take, may contribute to heart disease. Vitamin E and other antioxidants are believed to block this process.

You can't consume vitamin E naturally in the quantities used in the research studies, but you can obtain at least some vitamin E from the food you eat. That this may be beneficial is seen in a study published in 1996 in *The New England Journal of Medicine*. Researchers queried 34,486 women and found that those who favored those whole foods containing vitamin E, specifically nuts, margarine, and mayonnaise, had a lower risk of dying of heart disease. Bear in mind, though, that although the headlines interpreted finding this as "It's okay to eat fatty food after all," the study was not a wholesale endorsement of pigging out on cheeseburgers. Indeed, the women who ate the most foods with natural vitamin E still ate relatively modest amounts of fatty foods, such as salad dressing made with mayonnaise. Another endorsement of moderation!

Another nutrient being explored are the B vitamins, including folic acid, because of their effect on homocysteine, the amino acid that may contribute to heart disease. Although more research is needed before calling for supplements, fruits and vegetables are high in folic acid and you should be eating a lot of them anyway. Even red meat, seen as a scourge by the health food faddist, is a valuable source of vitamin B6.

Over the past few years, a mushrooming number of nutritional supplements have been advertised as heart disease preventives. Don't such claims have to be proven? The answer, alas, is no. That's because of the passage of the Dietary Supplement Health and Education Act of 1994. That law granted makers of dietary supplements and herbal preparations greater freedom to make these claims. You can identify these products carefully by looking for the required disclaimer, which must state that the claim has not been evaluated by the government's Food and Drug Administration; in other words, you're just taking the manufacturer's word for it.

❤ **Lifesaving Tip:** The fact that a supplement is sold in a health food store, or labeled "natural," doesn't necessarily mean it is harmless. Here are a few examples of the dangers of vitamin overuse: Too much vitamin A can cause birth defects if taken by pregnant women; too much calcium can limit the absorption of iron; and too much zinc can impair the immune response and negatively affect cholesterol levels. So if you're uncertain about a supplement you're tempted to take, or if you're considering mega doses, check with your doctor.

If You Want to Lose Weight . . .

Men and women usually react very differently to the idea of going on a diet. Imagine this scenario. Consider the co-authors of this book, for instance. Say it's winter, we've been working hard on this manuscript and we haven't been paying attention to what we eat. In fact, we've each gained 10 pounds. Here are our reactions:

Dr. Pashkow: "I've put on 10 pounds. I'd better start watching what I eat more closely and cut out snacks. It won't take long to lose that weight."

Charlotte: "Oh, my God! I've gained 10 pounds! This is horrible! I hate myself! How could I have let myself get out of control that way? I should go out into the garden and eat worms. No, that's too fattening; I should go out into the garden and eat lettuce!"

Are we exaggerating? Not much. Women in general have so well absorbed our society's obsession with thinness that many can no longer think about eating rationally. More and more American women are dieting, and at younger and younger ages. Eating disorders, formerly rare, have become common. The desire to lose weight has fueled a booming multibillion-dollar diet industry. But most of that money just goes to waste, as studies show that diets don't last. In fact, an estimated 75 to 90 percent of women diet only to gain back the weight they've lost, and often extra pounds besides.

This is not to build a case for being fat; that is neither healthy nor desirable. Obesity is a risk factor for heart disease as well as other ailments. But obesity is generally defined as being 20 to 30 percent above one's ideal weight. Many women far more slender than this are obsessed with losing weight.

Studies have shown that women, more than men, tend to have unrealistic images of their body, invariably for the worse. It is not unusual for a slender woman to look in the mirror and "see" fat that simply is not there. As a result, women often follow such stringent caloric restriction that it's not surprising they become obsessed with food. If they eat anything at all, they feel guilty. For these women, just the word "diet" can trigger an eating binge.

For this reason, we've banished the word "diet" from this book as it is used to connote the limiting of food. (We do use it occasionally as a synonym for "eating plan.")

Reasons we abolished the "D" word
- This chapter is not just for women who want to lose weight. Its suggestions are aimed at women who want to create a healthier way of eating.
- Diets don't work. The word "diet" implies a regime you're adopting for a limited period. People go "on" diets and "off" diets with alarming frequency. Unless you permanently change the way you eat, it's highly unlikely you will succeed in losing weight and keeping it off.
- Over the years, we have observed that dieting seems to trigger a metabolic response that leads to more efficient (i.e., less rapid) burning of calories. This most likely is a mechanism that formerly protected us from starvation in eons past, but now probably accounts for the observation by dieters that they now gain weight consuming the same amount of calories that used to result in weight loss.
- For many women, the word "diet" is so emotionally loaded that it sends them right to the pastry shelf. Both of your co-authors love food. We were raised in families where a table laden with food was seen as a symbol of love. Also, neither one of us is naturally svelte.

By adopting the strategies we've outlined in this chapter, we've been able to maintain healthy bodies and eat our cake (on occasion) as well.

Are You a Compulsive Eater (or Dieter)?

As we've noted, for many women, eating has become a compulsion, often manifested in "yo-yo" dieting. This pattern often begins quite early. A young girl who is slightly overweight decides to lose the weight. That's all well and good, but more often than not, it's difficult to lose the last few pounds because she's dipping below her realistic weight, so to lose that weight and to keep it off, she starves herself. Since she's starving herself, she becomes obsessed with food. Before long, a "starve and binge" cycle can set in.

Are you a compulsive eater? Ask yourself these questions:

- Do words associated with food conjure up feelings of guilt and shame?
- Can you keep anything "good" in the house without devouring it immediately?
- Do you constantly go on diets only to go off them just as quickly?
- Do you hate your body?
- Do your thoughts constantly revolve around food?

Some women are addicted to compulsive eating; others fall prey to another addiction: the addiction of dieting. While some women find the idea of "going on" a diet threatening, others find the idea of "going off" a diet equally scary. For them, dieting is a way of life. Before you consider embarking on any eating plan, you must get this diet "monkey" off your back! Some people find this is easier than others do.

Many compulsive eaters have a poor body image. This works to your detriment if you're trying to successfully lose weight. According to a study headed by Marcia Kiernan, PhD, at Stanford University School of Medicine in Palo Alto, California, overweight women who were dissatisfied with their bodies were among the most unsuccessful dieters.

The study, published in 1998 in the *Annals of Behavioral Medicine*, assigned 132 women who were mildly to moderately overweight and to various weight loss regimens, including diet alone and diet plus exercise. The women who were less dissatisfied with their bodies and didn't have a history of repeated weight loss were the most likely to succeed. Those who were the most dissatisfied with their bodies and had repeatedly dieted were the least likely to succeed, whether they only followed the diet or combined it with exercise. Although exercise is now being stressed as an adjunct to losing weight, this was extremely difficult for women who were unhappy with how they looked in such situations as exercise classes, she noted.

With these findings in mind, it makes sense to try to overcome compulsive eating patterns and also work to accept yourself and your body. This is not easy. There are some books included in the "Resources" section, but sometimes professional counseling is needed.

Strategies for Eating Right

Here is the basic strategy for eating right (drum roll, please).

The eating plan you are most likely to stick with is the one closest to the way you normally eat.

Perhaps it seems like the foods you eat daily are mostly of random choice; for example, "There's a muffin shop across from my office, so I start the day with a muffin." Such choices may actually not be random at all; your food preferences are probably far more deep-seated. After all, when you go "off" a diet, you automatically revert to your old eating habits. So, it follows that, if your eating plan is similar to the one you would normally follow, it is harder to "go off it."

This is one reason we believe that following a "diet" of someone else's creation doesn't work in the long term. Such a plan does not encompass your personal preferences or fulfill your needs. This is why we cannot create an "eating plan" for you: It is you who must create such a plan for yourself, based on the foods you usually prefer. If you're a hard-core dieter, you may have suppressed your own food preferences for so long you don't even remember the foods you used to enjoy eating.

What If I Want to Lose Weight?

Considering our society's obsession with thinness, we suspect many of you reading this chapter for information on how to lose weight are actually at, or near, your desirable weight. If so, relax, follow the guidelines on cutting fat in your diet, and exercise. If you are overweight, however, reducing your weight is an admirable goal. There is only one way to lose weight; you have to ingest 3,500 fewer calories for every pound of weight you wish to lose. It isn't necessary to be a calorie counter to lose weight; you can do it by paring the fat in the foods you eat, choosing fruits, vegetables and fiber, and adding exercise. In this way, you can reduce the number of calories you're eating naturally. Some people prefer to be more precise, though, so if you want to follow a precise eating plan, by either counting calories or fat grams, the following sections explain how.

Losing Weight by Counting Calories

If you want to lose weight by counting calories, here is how to do it:

To calculate how many fewer calories you need to eat, you have to know how many calories you are eating each day in the first place. Then, you need to calculate how many fewer calories you need to eat in order to lose your desired amount of weight. Here's how to do it:

Step 1. Figure out how many calories you are now eating by keeping a food diary. For at least one day, but preferably two or three, write down everything you eat. Using a calorie counter, figure out the exact number of calories you are eating. Figure out the fat grams as well (we'll tell you how to do this below). Knowing what you normally eat is necessary before you can even begin to figure out the dietary modifications that you'll need to make. Also write down when you eat, and why. Were you hungry? Tired? Depressed? Anxious? Most of us eat not only when we are hungry, but for psychological reasons as well. You can use this information to choose alternative activities to eating when you are actually not hungry.

Keeping a food diary is easy to do, but it will only work if you are not on a constant diet already, or if just keeping the diary makes you anxious. If this is the case, it may indicate you need to change your attitude towards food before you consider losing weight.

Step 2. Calculate how many calories you need to maintain your ideal weight. Take your desirable weight (and make sure that is a realistic weight, which is not necessarily what you weighed in high school), and multiply every pound times 15 calories. If you do not use a realistic weight, the resulting calorie count will be too low, dooming your reducing plan to failure.

According to these calculations, a moderately active woman whose ideal weight is 125 pounds would need to eat 1,875 per day. Since women (especially those who are less active) generally need slightly fewer calories than men, some experts advise using a figure of 12 or 13 calories instead. If you use both the upper and lower figures, this can give you a range of, say 1,500 to 1,875. This gives you the number of calories you need to eat to maintain your ideal weight.

Step 3. Calculate the number of calories you need to eat to lose weight. To lose a pound of weight, you need to burn 3,500 more calories. How do you apply this to yourself? If your ideal weight is 125, consuming 1,500 to 1,875 calories a day would maintain your normal weight. If you want to be certain to lose weight, it's probably better to take the lower figure. So, take 1,500 calories each day and multiply that by seven days, to get a figure of 10,500 calories. Then, subtract the 3,500 calories you want to lose and divide by 7, for 1,000 calories a day. If you find yourself too hungry, use the "15-calories-a-pound" figure. This would give you 1,375 calories. If you find yourself not losing weight, you can always pick a figure somewhere between 1,000 and 1,375.

Step 4. Subtract the number of calories you need to lose from the number of calories you are currently eating, and you should be left with the number of calories you need to eat in order to lose weight.

💜 **Mindsaving Tip: In calculating your ideal caloric intake, make certain you use your ideal weight, not some unrealistically low weight our Barbie-doll-conscious society may have instilled in you. If you start off with an unrealistically low calorie goal, it becomes virtually impossible for you to lose weight and maintain the lower weight.**

Losing Weight by Counting Fat Grams

For many women, counting fat grams is easier than counting calories. Determining your caloric intake is fairly easy, as there are many guides to counting calories and many foods list caloric counts on their labels. Evaluating the fat content of your food is not that simple, as fat is expressed in grams.

If you want to maintain your current weight, take the number of calories a day you need to do that and multiply it by the percentage of fat you should be eating in your daily diet. The American Heart Association recommends 30 percent, although many experts now use 25 percent. If the woman in the previous example wants to eat less fat, say 25 percent, she should take the ideal number of calories she needs to maintain her ideal weight (1,875) and multiple that by 25 percent. That comes out to about 47 grams of fat a day. So if she's following a 1,125-calorie-per-day plan, she should be limiting herself to 28 grams of fat a day. You can eat a wide variety of foods, including a moderate amount of meat, as well as carbohydrates and proteins, on such a plan. To make fat gram counting easier, pick up one of the fat gram counters on the market.

❤ **Mindsaving Tip: If you're counting fat grams, here's a tip from Dr. Victoria Clyne, a primary care physician from Ohio. When her patients read food labels, she tells them that for every 100 calories of food, there should be no more than two grams of fat! That ensures that fewer than 20 percent of that food's calories comes from fat.**

Food "Banking"

No matter whether you're counting calories, counting fat grams, or simply "watching what you eat," food banking can be a way of following an eating plan without feeling that you've blown it if you want a special treat.

Now that you've figured out what you're eating, decide what modifications to make. Often, people find the best place to cut down on eating is to eliminate snacks. If that is not enough reduction, limit your desserts to one serving per day, or substitute fruit. Again, eating is a very individual thing. You may find it impossible to cut snacks out, but you may find it relatively painless to substitute, say, sugar-free cocoa and four vanilla wafers for the donut and hot chocolate you normally eat. You'll still be satisfied and you'll save calories too. Women often prefer eating several small meals throughout the day, instead of larger ones. If you stay within your calorie count, this won't make a difference, although it's probably better to limit the amount of calories consumed before bedtime.

Let's face it: The key reason diets don't work is we go off them. You might go on a cruise where you're surrounded by food, or travel to an exotic locale and not want to miss out on the culinary delights. Perhaps you're at a wedding and can't bear to pass up the wedding cake. Perhaps you've been passing up desserts all week and are now dreaming of a chocolate bar. Follow the same principle as you would if you were following a money budget and saving for a special "splurge" like an expensive dress or trip. If you put a little extra money aside, before long, you'll have enough for a special treat. It's the same way with food; if you get into the habit of eating prudently at most times, you can "splurge" for special occasions, like a wedding or dinner party, without feeling an iota of guilt.

How Fast Should You Lose Weight?

According to many nutritional experts, losing a pound a week is too fast. They contend it should be one half pound a week, but most of us would find that excruciatingly slow. Still, losing weight gradually is the only way to accomplish a permanent weight loss. Unfortunately, it's human nature to want to lose lots of weight fast. So, if you adopt this strategy, there is one pitfall of which you must be aware.

Let's say you've changed your eating habits and you have lost about half the weight you want to lose. Invariably, you'll run into a friend. She's lost a great deal of weight and looks terrific! "I went on so-and-so's plan and lost 15 pounds in three weeks!" she exclaims. How depressing! You've been diligently following our eating plan for two months and you've only lost half the weight she lost in two weeks! Now, here's where the *real* test of your willpower comes in. What you must do is smile graciously and congratulate your friend, realizing (to yourself, of course) that by the next time you see her again, you may well have lost all your weight, but the chances are very great she will have regained hers!

❤ Mindsaving Tip: You've been very good all day, but now you're yearning for a piece of chocolate. You've tried carrots, rice cakes, an apple—nothing satisfies you. Eat the piece of chocolate, we say. In the long run, it will not make a difference in your weight, and you'll be more likely to keep your resolve. Also, if you allow yourself a treat now and then, you're less likely to binge.

Be a Label-Reader

During the 1960s, about the only "diet" foods available were low-calorie soft drinks. Since then, there has been an explosion of low-calorie, low-fat foods. Some of these can be a real boon to us food-lovers. There are absolutely delicious low-fat and even nonfat frozen yogurt, puddings, and even cakes available. But watch out! A lot of these foods have loopholes. Some may be low in fat, but high in sugar. Others get their low "calorie" counts by virtue of minuscule portions. To make your way through this caloric minefield, you need to be a label-reader. Here is how the government's food labels work.

The uniform label entitled "Nutrition Facts" provides you with a wealth of information so you can make informed choices about the type of foods you eat, and helps you compare food items. Processed foods include the vast majority of items Americans consume daily, ranging from soups to cereals to frozen pastries.

The labels list the serving size, amount of calories, total fat, total carbohydrates, dietary fiber, protein, saturated fat, cholesterol, sodium, and a selection of vitamins and minerals: vitamin A, vitamin C, calcium and iron. The label also stipulates the serving size and shows how the food fits into a 2,000 and a 2,500 calorie diet. Particularly if you're a woman, this calorie count may be too high. But it does give you some perspective.

The total amount of calories derived from fat is the most important feature on the label. Aim for small numbers here. Under the category "Total fat," you should find no more than 20 percent of the calories derived from fat. The label also lists "Saturated fat." As noted earlier, this is the most undesirable fat because of the role it plays in raising blood cholesterol. Choose foods whose saturated fat number is zero, or very low. This goes also for the next listing, "Cholesterol," which also leads to heart disease. The American Heart Association recommends you eat less than 300 mg per day but recent studies suggest even this may be too high. Another undesirable fat is trans-fatty acids. Unfortunately, this substance was not included in the most recent USDA's food labeling regulations, discussed later in this chapter. But there's a way to detect it. Looking at the label, add up all the types of listed fats; if your total falls short of the "Total fat" listed on the label, the remaining "missing fat" is trans-fatty acids.

❤ **Mindsaving Tip: Skipping breakfast to lose weight is not a good idea. Eating breakfast "wakes up" your metabolism and you burn calories more efficiently throughout the day.**

Why We Eat

Eating can be a complex activity. If you're hungry, eating satisfies you. But eating also has emotional causes. Many of us eat not only when we're hungry, but also often when we are depressed, bored, or lonely, or even happy or excited.

If food has become your way of dealing with your emotions, you're probably misinterpreting your bodily and emotional cues. You leap from your desk to the candy machine automatically, without giving a second thought to what your body is really trying to tell you. Maybe you need a good stretch or a walk around the office. Maybe you're tired, and need to go to bed earlier. Or you may be lonely and really longing to chat with a friend. Keeping track of when and why you eat can help you get a handle on these needs, and provide you with alternate ways to fulfill them. So, instead of automatically heading into the kitchen for something to eat, ask yourself what it is you really need. Maybe it's not a candy bar at all, but a hug!

The Importance of Exercise

To maintain your desirable weight, or to lose weight and keep it off, you must step up your level of physical activity. Being active not only helps you burn more calories, but also improves your self-esteem and alleviates depression. For many women, poor self-esteem and depression can lead to unhealthy eating. To get the most out of our eating plan, use it with its companion section, "Every Woman's Exercise Plan for Life." These two guides together contain our best advice to create a healthier lifestyle.

EVERY WOMAN'S EXERCISE PLAN FOR LIFE

For too many of us, our only exercise is trotting around the aisles of the supermarket, dashing from one corporate suite to the other, or helping our husband or boyfriend search for the TV remote control. That's not good for our hearts. Living a sedentary lifestyle is a risk factor for heart disease.

Want some proof? For a healthy heart, research finds that if you exercise regularly—even if this means just briskly walking three or four times a week—you'll cut your risk of coronary heart disease. You'll also be healthier as a whole—you'll be less likely to develop certain cancers, including colon cancer and possibly breast cancer, as well as obesity, diabetes, osteoporosis, and stroke. In fact, researchers estimate that 250,000 deaths per year in the United States can be attributed to our sedentary lifestyle.

Why don't we exercise? There's a combination of reasons, including lack of time, lack of emphasis, and, most of all, the belief most of us have that exercise isn't fun. But the best exercise is exercise that's fun, a factor we kept in mind when writing this chapter.

This chapter was created with the invaluable assistance of Peg Pashkow. A licensed physical therapist and exercise physiologist, she and her husband, Dr. Fredric Pashkow, this book's co-author, founded HeartWatchers in 1977, an international expert resource group for cardiac professionals. Most importantly, Peg truly exemplifies the benefits of exercise. Vibrant and enthusiastic, she begins nearly every day with a vigorous exercise program. She is also an avid jogger, swimmer, and bicyclist. For Peg, exercising is as necessary and natural as breathing. As a special bonus, along with our usual Lifesaving, Mindsaving, and Moneysaving Tips, there is special exercise advice from Peg, called Peg's Tips.

This chapter truly does contain recommendations for every woman's heart. No matter what your age or physical condition, whether you're young or old, athletic or sedentary, there is information here that you can use to design your own exercise plan. This is also true if you have a heart problem. If that is the case, though, you definitely should check with your doctor before beginning new physical activities.

Before we get down to basics, here are the answers to some questions you may have.

Exercise: What's in It for Me?

Quite a lot. Exercise is a small investment that reaps big benefits. Exercise can

- Help you lose weight and keep it off
- Tone your muscles
- Help you sleep
- Reduce stress
- Enhance your self-esteem
- Help reduce high blood pressure

Exercise and Diabetes

Exercise has great benefits for those who have diabetes or a family history of this disease. For example, regular physical exercise can help control diabetes and increase the probability that someone who is not insulin dependent may be able to stay off insulin. Research also shows that regular exercise can help prevent the onset of the most common form of diabetes.

Exercise and Osteoporosis

Exercise builds muscle mass, a major way of warding off osteoporosis. However, you must carefully choose the type of exercise you do. We'll tell you how in this chapter.

Exercise and Stress

Being physically active has been shown to be a great stress-reducer. As Peg notes, "By exercising, you get a sense of stretching your mind as well as your body. Exercising makes you feel very free."

If You're Older

Studies show exercise can benefit older women tremendously. Of course, you should consult with your doctor before starting a program. Your doctor should be delighted to know that you want to, but if he or she is not encouraging, and there's no medical reason why you shouldn't exercise, it may be that your doctor has some outdated myths about the appropriateness of exercise for older people. You can educate your doctor, or find a new one. Tell your doctor studies show that, by exercising, older people can become more fit than younger sedentary ones. If you have kids, you'll probably enjoy telling that to them as well.

Here are some commonly asked questions and answers about exercise:

Q: I spend a lot of time on my feet just doing my daily activities at work and at home. Isn't that enough?

A: No. To get the most out of exercise, you should choose an activity unrelated to the type of work you normally do. If you're doing housework, chasing after the kids, or trotting from one office to another, your mind is on the task at hand, not on exercising your body. Exercise is something you do for yourself, not for anyone else.

Q: Most books on exercise include six- or eight-week plans. Where's one of those nifty charts that tells me exactly what I should do?

A: We could have included a chart, and a chart might even pay off in the short run, but just as most diets don't work in the long run, neither do most exercise plans. When you talk about a "plan," you're summing up the whole problem. To many people, a plan suggests you are going to do something only for a specific period, then quit. That's how people usually view exercise, as a quick fix. Formulating a plan is fine if it's one you can follow for life. For example, you can plan to go cross-country skiing in the winter and swimming in the summer. That's fine. Or, as this chapter suggests, you can plan to build more activity into your daily life.

Q: But if there's no set plan, how do I know what my goal should be?
A: We live in a very goal-oriented society. We set goals all the time; we'll lose weight in two months, stop smoking in three, and transform ourselves into Jane Fonda in four. Such goals are unrealistic, and unrealistic goals are self-defeating.

Since no one knows you better than you know yourself, you should set realistic goals for yourself. Maybe your goal will be to get into condition so you can walk briskly to work without huffing and puffing, or go dancing without feeling winded. If you'd like a goal from us, here's one: "My goal is to become more active than I currently am."

Now that you have a realistic goal in mind, we'll give you some information on exercise so you can choose the types of activities that are best for your body, including, of course, your heart. We'll also give you the principles of our "Every Woman's Exercise Philosophy," which is designed to transform even couch potatoes into exercise-lovers—or at least exercise-likers.

❤ **Peg's Tip:** Being "physically fit" doesn't mean being an Amazon. Being physically fit means you can accomplish such everyday activities as raking leaves, taking brisk walks, or playing with your kids (or your grandkids). You can maintain this level of conditioning throughout your life.

THE BASICS OF HEART HEALTHY EXERCISE

Here is the basic tenet of our exercise philosophy: Whatever you do is better than doing nothing at all. You need to understand three types of exercise that will strengthen your body in different ways:

- Aerobic exercise (for endurance)
- Weight-bearing exercise (to retard osteoporosis)
- Anaerobic exercise (for strength)

All three of these types of exercise are needed if you want to fully condition and strengthen your body.

Aerobic Exercise

This type of activity is vital if you want to improve the functioning of your cardiovascular system, which includes your heart. Aerobic exercise also improves your endurance and strengthens your musculoskeletal system, the bony skeleton of your body and the muscles attached to it. Aerobic exercise makes use of rhythmic, repetitive exercises that use your large muscle groups. It's a sustained form of exercise during which your heartbeat must remain in an elevated range, which is also called your "target heart range." How to find your target heart range is discussed later in this chapter.

It used to be thought that in order to be beneficial, aerobic exercise must be performed for at least a 20-minute period, three times a week. Some studies have shown, however, that you can also derive benefits from doing aerobic exercises for shorter periods, for example, for ten minutes at the start and end of each day.

Aerobic activities include brisk walking, jogging, race walking, swimming, pool aerobics, bicycling (either stationary or on a real bicycle), aerobic dancing, folk-dancing, using rowing and skiing machines, calisthenics, and using free weights and pulleys.

❤ **Peg's Tip: Playing softball or volleyball is fun, but they don't qualify as aerobic workouts. Some teams solve that problem by doing aerobic workouts before the game. Square dancing is fun, too, but may not be vigorous enough to qualify as an aerobic workout. For a more intense workout, widen the dance circle. For an easier workout, walk, don't skip, around the circle**

Weight-Bearing Exercise

As a woman, you especially need to incorporate weight-bearing exercise into your daily life. Aerobic exercise is marvelous for the cardiovascular system, but alone does not help prevent the loss of bone mineral, which, as you age, can result in osteoporosis. Weight-bearing exercises are those that provide impact on the joints and, in doing so, stimulate the ends of your bones.

There are two ways to build in weight-bearing exercise into your activities. One is by choosing aerobic activities that apply some force to the bones. Swimming provides aerobic exercise but, because your body is suspended weightless in water, there is no force provided to your bones. Walking, jogging, aerobic dancing, and racquet sports qualify as both aerobic and weight-bearing activities.

Anaerobic Exercise (Strength-Resistance Training)

Women especially should be aware of the need to keep up the strength in their upper arms. "Women tend to focus on their hips and thighs, but as we age, we need to build up our arms," says Peg Pashkow. "This enables us carry packages more easily, for example, and keeps the skin on our arms firm."

A good way to strengthen your upper body is to work out with weights. A simple exercise using dumbbells or other weights will accomplish your goal. Most sporting goods stores carry a variety of inexpensive weights and exercise books or videotapes with exercises you can learn. Joining a gym or health club can also provide you with a good program.

❤ **Moneysaving Tip: If you don't want to buy weights, buy some detergent in the type of plastic bottle that has a grip handle. Not only is this inexpensive, but you can lighten the weight, if necessary, by using some of the detergent!**

❤ **Peg's Tip: Some women find the kind of muscles they can build by "pumping iron" quite attractive, but many do not. Should you decide to work with weights, don't worry about becoming muscle-bound. Working with weights will give you a stronger, firmer body, but, unless you perform daily, lengthy workouts, you won't end up looking like a professional weight lifter.**

Here are some basics for getting started.

Before beginning to exercise, you must take the following guidelines from the American College of Sports Medicine into consideration. If you are in *good general health*, and are 50 years of age or younger, and you plan to increase your activity very gradually (the best way to do it), you probably do not need to see your doctor before beginning an exercise program. If you have a heart problem, if you're at risk for coronary heart disease, if you have another medical problem (such as asthma), or if you have any reason to doubt your physical condition, you should check with your doctor before starting a vigorous exercise program. If you are experiencing chest pains or palpitations, you should have a physical examination and exercise stress test before beginning even a moderate exercise program. This holds true whether or not you are at risk for coronary heart disease.

These guidelines are not intended to discourage you from exercising (nor are they an excuse for not exercising!). We just want you to take care.

❤ Lifesaving Tip: If you have heart disease, you must consult with your doctor before starting an exercise program. As you start or increase your level of activity, if you experience any symptoms as chest pain, shortness of breath, dizziness, or undue fatigue, consult your doctor.

❤ Peg's Tip: Before beginning an activity, you should take a medical "inventory" of yourself. Recall any injuries or problems with your back, ankles, arms or legs you may have suffered. Make certain that the activities you choose will not damage, but instead will strengthen, these problem areas. Research shows that higher rates of injury are associated with weight-bearing activities like jogging and running. Those most likely to injure themselves are people who run for long distances, have a personal history of injury, or suddenly increase their exercise schedule.

Whenever you exercise, start with a warm-up and end with a cool-down period. Never overlook the importance of warming up and cooling down. Abruptly throwing yourself into vigorous activity is too demanding for your body. You need to warm up your muscles and stretch joints slowly to avoid strains and cramps. A 10-minute warm-up period also increases the circulation to your heart and muscles in preparation for more vigorous exercise. A 10-minute cool-down period is needed to gradually slow your heartbeat to its normal rate. If you've been exercising vigorously, cooling down will prevent dizziness, lightheadedness, nausea, and muscle cramps. If you exercise in a class, or with an exercise videotape, make certain that warm-up and cool-down periods are included. Even if you're only starting with a brisk 10-minute walk, build in a warm-up and cool-down period. Increasing your flexibility is an important benefit of warming up and exercising in general. Stretching is a great way to warm up, but you need to stretch slowly to avoid the "rubber-band" effect. "If you pick up a new rubber band and stretch it, you'll think you've really stretched it out," explains Peg. "But if you put it around a vise and hold it there for five minutes, when you let it go, it's more likely it will be stretched out. The same is true of your muscles."

Drink plenty of fluids. Be *sure* to drink plenty of fluids before, after, and during exercise. Those water bottles, that look so chic in exercise class actually serve a good purpose. But don't drink a solution with sugar in it, because your stomach will demand priority circulation to digest the sugar instead of sending blood to the muscles you're exercising.

♥ **Peg's Tip: Too often, women tend to believe that if they don't drink water, they'll lose weight more quickly. This is a dangerous fallacy—your body needs water.**

Monitor your heart rate. Whether your vigorous exercise is walking, running, or doing calisthenics, if you want to be certain you're benefiting aerobically, you need to monitor your heart, making sure it stays at target rate. By monitoring your heartbeat at various points during your exercise, you can make sure the exercise is not too mild or too intense. Some people mistakenly think that, if pushing your heart rate to its target rate is good, pushing it higher is even better. This is definitely not true. If your heart rate goes up too high, this indicates you are no longer exercising aerobically; you are exercising anaerobically, which has no cardiovascular benefits.

When you exercise aerobically, your body is meeting your muscle's increased need for oxygen. "Aerobic" means "requiring air to live." Oxygen serves to release energy from your body's store of fat, glycogen (starchy stored material), and sugars. If you exercise too vigorously and exceed your target heart rate, your body begins exercising anaerobically—not using oxygen. Short bouts of anaerobic exercise are also called isometric exercise. But, while this type of exercise can be useful for building strength, it does not build endurance and can result in muscle fatigue and exhaustion.

To find your target heart range, subtract your age from 220. Multiply that figure by 0.6 and 0.80. That figure will give you your heart rate if you are working at 60 to 80 percent, which is considered a good level for cardiac conditioning. For example, if you're 40 years old, your maximum heart rate is about 180 beats per minute. Your 60 to 80 percent target range is 108 to 144. Often, in aerobics classes, the instructor will have you take a 10-second measurement, feeling your pulse at wrist or neck. Dividing by six, this means your target heart rate should fall between 18 and 24 for a 10-second count. If it's higher than that, don't stop abruptly, but slow down. In an exercise class, an easy way to do this is march in place. If your pulse rate is too low, put a little more intensity into your activities.

❤ Peg's Tip: If you've been tested for your exercise capacity and you were given a target heart rate, use it instead of the above calculations, since the rate is specific to *your* body.

There's another easy way to test the intensity of your activity, especially if you and a friend are walking or using a treadmill or stationary bike. This is called the "talk test." If you can talk to your partner easily, your level of activity is probably appropriate.

❤ Peg's Tip: Individuals vary. Regardless of your heart rate, if the exercise feels too strenuous, slow down or stop! If you're still winded 10 minutes after you stop exercising, or still tired after an hour, you're overdoing it. Contact your doctor if exercising brings on difficulty breathing, faintness, dizziness, nausea, confusion, chest pain, extreme fatigue, or leg pain.

Here are some tips for two of the most popular types of exercise.

Walking

Studies find that a brisk walk three times a week can afford the type of cardiovascular benefits once associated with more strenuous activities like running and jogging. Walking is a great exercise, and all you really need is a pair of well-fitting walking shoes. You can get earphones and enjoy tape-recorded music while you walk; you can walk with a friend, or you can walk alone. If you live in climate where it is sometimes too cold or rainy, consider walking in a shopping mall. Many have organized walking clubs.

❤ **Peg's Tip:** Browsing doesn't count! If you pick a mall for walking, but also love to shop, go before the stores open. *Briefly* window-shop and then take your walk. Afterwards, you can return.

Eventually, you might want to increase your walking speed to an easy jog, or even run. Be sure to increase gradually. To go from walking to running, you might start out by alternating between them. For example, if you walk on a track, try running past the bleachers, and then resume your walking pace. If you are walking in a city or town, alternate a block by walking with a block of running. Increase very gradually, and before you know it, you may be out jogging or running instead of walking.

If you're a beginning runner, here are couple of tips:

Beware of hard surfaces. Running on grass can be easier on your ankles and legs and help you avoid injury. Once you're accustomed to running, try doing it on an uneven surface. This forces you to lift your legs higher, helps your balance and strengthens your ankles.

Put your money where your feet are. Once upon a time, sneakers were the only "athletic shoes" available. But the sneaker has grown up, and proper running shoes can help you exercise better and prevent injuries. Shop for them at the end of the day, since your feet swell during the day. Wear the type of socks you'll run in and be sure to try on both the left and right shoes, suggests *Consumer Reports* magazine. The magazine is filled with such tips, and ranks exercise equipment as well; it's a great guide for those who are money-savvy, or want to be.

Swimming and Water Exercises

Swimming and water exercises are a refreshing way to condition yourself if you've been sedentary, or if you're elderly, disabled, or have previously injured yourself. Working out in the water provides overall fitness and conditioning and can also strengthen your body. If you swim, doing laps is a terrific way to get into good condition. But even if you don't swim, check with health clubs or community pools to find out the availability of water aerobics classes. Sometimes these classes are surprisingly intense, so be certain to find one that is at the right level for you.

One of Peg's favorite pool exercises is water walking. It's harder to do than you think. Stand in waist-deep to chest-deep water and try to walk as you would on land, swinging your arms you go. Belts available in mail-order catalogs can help maintain buoyancy.

As with other exercise, warming up and cooling down are important. Lap swimmers always start off with some stretching. Do a slow lap at the end, or some slow exercises, to "cool down" before you leave the water.

❤ Peg's Tip: Take care, particularly if you have joint problems, not to overdo your water exercise. The extra activity is tempting because using your limbs in the water feels so good.

Exercising at Home

Some people enjoy exercising alone at home. That's great. Others prefer to exercise in a group. Consider getting a few friends together to form your own class, with the help of a videotape. The advent of cable television and VCRs have made it easier to exercise at home than ever before. There is a wide variety of exercise videos designed for women of all ages, exercise ability, and musical tastes. You can order them at video stores or through mail-order catalogs. Some tapes, such as Richard Simmons's more recent videos, are particularly good because they incorporate not only aerobics but some simple strength-building exercises as well.

❤ Moneysaving Tip: Your library or local video store probably has many different exercise tapes available to borrow or rent. Try them out and find the one that's right for you.

Choosing a Health Club

A health club can be a terrific place to exercise, or an expensive rip-off. Too often people sign up for an expensive health club contract, go a lot during the first few weeks, and then stop, because they're bored, they've overdone it, or their needs are not being met. Before joining a club, ask yourself these questions:

- How convenient is the facility to you?
- Do the exercise times fit in your schedule?
- What is the facility like?
- Are exercise classes too crowded?
- Is there a long wait to use equipment?
- Does the facility offer a variety of equipment?

The answers to these questions can indicate you'll use the club for years, or whether it will be just a passing fancy.

A main reason that many people join health clubs is to take advantage of the schedule of exercise classes offered, but the class is only as good as its leader. Ask to meet the staff and participate in a trial workout. You should be able to tell if the exercise leaders seem sincerely interested. Here are some clues to look for. Is the leader absorbed in his or her personal exercise? The answer should be no. The leader should exercise along with you, but be concentrated on your needs.

If an instructor is a certified exercise fitness instructor, so much the better. But skill and enthusiasm are very important; some instructors may not have credentials, but still lead excellent exercise groups. Also, while the fitness instructor does not necessarily have to look like Jane Fonda or Arnold Schwazenegger, she or he should appear to be in good shape. It's easier to be inspired by someone who lives by what they teach. But watch out for the instructor who looks "too" good, and is just there on an extended ego trip.

The right music can make exercise seem effortless; the wrong music can be torturous. If you enjoy working out to Motown, make sure the leader doesn't favor heavy metal. If it's a dance-oriented class, check out the routines. You may be unfamiliar with the steps at first, but it should be easy to catch on. If you always feel lost, you won't be getting the kind of workout you need.

Most of us like to feel that we fit in. Peek into the class ahead of time, or ask the instructor what clothes people usually wear. If a great-looking leotard makes you feel more like exercising, "buy" all means. If you don't look great in a leotard (and many of us don't), opt for a colorful, oversized T-shirt. Some women won't step into an exercise class without full makeup, while others wouldn't give it a second thought. Do what's comfortable for you.

❤ Peg's Tip: Don't feel embarrassed to leave a class if you don't feel well, if it is too intense, or if you don't like it. You're there for you.

♥ Moneysaving Tip: Joining a health club can be a substantial monetary investment. Be sure to read any contract very carefully before you join. In many cases, there is a three-day "cooling off" period in which you can cancel a contract without penalty. Also, some health clubs will be on firm financial footing, but they have been known to go out of business. Check with your local Better Business Bureau and state consumer protection division to find out whether any complaints have been filed against the club you are considering or what monetary protections you might have.

♥ Moneysaving Tip: Often, colleges and hotels have excellent physical fitness facilities that they may allow the public to use; the fee may be less than a health club membership. If you live near your alma mater, your alumni status may enable you to use its facilities free or at a reduced rate.

Ten Principles of Becoming Active

Some of our principles may sound a little unconventional to you. Probably no one had ever suggested that you "underdo" an exercise "plan," or that you lower your standards. But especially if you are unaccustomed to exercising, we believe these are the keys to becoming more active. If you go easy on yourself, you'll find that exercise can be fun. Eventually, you'll be surprised at how much you're actually doing, and you'll be having fun, too!

1. **No matter how little activity you do, it's better than doing no activity at all.** For example, a brisk 20-minute walk three times a week is a good form of exercise, but if you are very sedentary, this may be too ambitious. Even a 10-minute walk is far better than no walk at all!

2. **Safety first!** For women, it is especially important to keep safety in mind. If you are going to walk, bicycle, jog, or do other outdoor activities, make sure you pick an open, well-lit park or other place that is safe. Go with a friend and steer clear of high-crime areas. If you are choosing a health club, particularly if you are going to use it at night, make certain the parking lot is well lit and that it is located in an area where you feel safe. If you ride a bike, you *must* wear an approved helmet.

3. **Underdo, don't overdo.** By far the biggest mistake people make when they begin exercising is that they overdo it. You sign up for a bunch

of exercise classes, or you decide to swim five days a week, or walk everywhere instead of taking the car. What happens? You exhaust yourself, become waterlogged, or get drenched in the rain. Before you know it, you're back on the couch again. So, if you're busy, instead of trying to squeeze in an exercise class three times a week, find one that meets twice a week. You'll be more apt to stick with it, and that's what counts in the long run.

4. **Choose the activities you enjoy.** You're an individual; why should you tailor yourself to someone else's idea of exercise? There are many ways you can build activity into your day, so why should you waste your time doing something you hate?

5. **Build in variety.** Pursue different activities; drop the ones you don't like, keep the ones you do, and always be ready to try a new one. Besides staving off boredom, different types of activities use different parts of your body. For instance, alternate running with bicycle riding.

6. **Always have a backup plan.** You should be able to switch to another activity if the need arises—if your exercise class has a break, your walking companion gets sick, or you mildly twist your ankle. In each of these cases, if you've planned ahead, you can switch to swimming, or some other activity, without skipping a beat.

7. **Lower your standards.** Often, people new to athletic activities tend to compare themselves to the pros and become discouraged. We could compare ourselves only to ourselves, but we usually have unrealistic expectations of ourselves as well. So relax your standards! If your prowess at tennis consists mainly of running around the court chasing balls, but you enjoy it, that's fine. On the other hand, if feeling perennially klutzy is making you uncomfortable, consider finding an activity to which you are better suited, or take a few lessons—but you don't have to be perfect!

8. **Increase your activity level gradually.** If you're doing a mile on a treadmill, don't add another mile; start with doing a quarter of a mile for, say a week, then continue for a few weeks at one and a quarter miles, then add another quarter of a mile, and so on. The same holds for other activities.

9. **If you stop exercising, when you resume, cut back significantly on your activities.** It is sad, but true, that it does not take long at all for your body to begin getting out of condition again. So, if you have to stop for awhile because you're ill, or even after a vacation, you'll have to start out slow again.

10. Give yourself permission to quit (occasionally). Far too often, we decide we are going to exercise for a given time. Then, we go on vacation, get sick, or just bored, and miss a time or two. "That's it," we say to ourselves. "It's no use!" You can't stay on the couch forever. At some point, pick yourself up and go back to the health club or try another type of activity. The most difficult part of going back to a health club is returning for the first time, but almost everyone has been through a similar experience. Before you know it, you'll be happily exercising again!

Glossary

ACE Inhibitor—Type of drug that blocks a specific enzyme (angiotensin converting enzyme); used to treat high blood pressure and heart failure.

Acute coronary syndrome—Blockage of a coronary artery caused by the formation of a blood clot. If temporary, it is referred to as "unstable angina." If the blockage is prolonged, it results in a heart attack resulting in an injury to the heart muscle. Doctors call this a myocardial infarction.

Aerobic activity—Exercise in which the body is able to meet the muscle's increased demand for oxygen continuously during increased activity. Aerobic exercise conditions the cardiovascular system.

Anaerobic activity—Strenuous activity in which oxygen is used faster than the blood circulation can supply it.

Aneurysm—A ballooning-out of the wall of a blood vessel or the heart muscle, resulting from a weakening caused by disease, injury, or an abnormality present at birth.

Angina pectoris—Discomfort or pressure, usually in the chest, caused by a temporarily inadequate blood supply to the heart muscle that is due to coronary heart disease. Discomfort may also be felt in the neck, jaw, or arms.

Aorta—Large artery that leaves the left ventricle and branches into other arteries to carry oxygen-rich blood to the body.

Aortic stenosis—Malformation of the aortic valve, or a stiffening of the aortic valve that comes with age, preventing it from opening normally.

Aortic valve—The heart valve between the left ventricle and the aorta.

Arrhythmia—An irregular heart rhythm.

Arteriography—A testing procedure in which dye is injected into the bloodstream and x-ray pictures are taken in order to study the condition of the arteries.

Artery—A blood vessel that carries blood away from the heart to various parts of the body.

Artificial heart—A mechanical version of the heart generally used as a temporary measure to keep a patient alive until a heart transplant can be performed.

Atherectomy—Procedure designed to dilate (widen) a blood vessel, similar to angioplasty, but uses an instrument other than a balloon.

Atherosclerosis—A buildup of fatty material in the artery wall, causing it to become thick and irregular. This buildup is sometimes called plaque. The condition it causes is known as coronary heart disease or coronary artery disease.

Atrial fibrillation—An arrhythmia caused by to impulses from the atria that are disorganized, irregular, and rapid. Many, but not all, of these impulses reach the ventricles.

Atrial septal defect (ASD)—A congenital defect that consists of a so-called "hole" dividing the upper chambers of the heart.

Atrium (plural, atria)—An upper chamber of the heart.

Bacterial endocarditis—See *Endocarditis*.

Balloon angioplasty—Procedure used to dilate (widen) narrowed arteries, this procedure calls for a catheter with a deflated balloon on its tip to be passed into the narrowed segment of artery, the balloon is then inflated and the artery dilated. Also known as percutaneous transluminal coronary angioplasty (PTCA).

Balloon valvuloplasty—A procedure in which a balloon is inserted in the opening of a narrowed heart valve. The inflating of the balloon dilates, or widens, the valve.

Beta-blocker—Type of drug that reduces adrenaline-mediated stimulation of the heart; slows heart rate, lowers blood pressure, and reduces angina.

Biological valve—Artificial valve made from animal tissue, usually from a pig, used to replace a malfunctioning heart valve.

Blood clot—Blood tissue transformed by clotting factors in the blood from a liquid to a solid form. Blood clots can form inside an artery whose lining is damaged by atherosclerosis, causing a heart attack or stroke.

Blood pressure—The force or pressure exerted in the arteries by blood as it is pumped around the body by the heart.

Bradycardia—A slow heart rate of less than 60 beats per minute (*Brady* ["slow"] and *cardia* ["heart"]).

Calcium channel blocker—Type of drug that blocks spasm of the blood vessels, lowers blood pressure, and reduces angina.

Capillaries—Tiny blood vessels that allow oxygen-carrying red cells to pass through and nourish the tissue cells.

Cardiac—Pertaining to the heart.

Cardiac arrest—The stopping of the heartbeat, usually because of interference with the heart's electrical system.

Cardiac catheterization—Procedure in which a catheter (inserted into an artery in your arm or leg) is guided to the heart, contrast dye is injected, and x-ray movies of the coronary arteries, heart chambers, and valves are taken.

Cardiac rehabilitation—A program of exercise and psychological and social support designed to return people to normalcy or better after a heart attack or other cardiac crisis.

Cardiac spasm—A potentially dangerous constriction of the heart's blood vessels.

Cardiology—The study of the heart and its functions.

Cardiomyopathy—A serious disease involving deterioration of the heart muscle that results in decreased cardiac function.

Cardiopulmonary resuscitation (CPR)—Emergency life support effort where the rescuer provides breaths and chest compressions to help circulated oxygenated blood to the victim until emergency help is available.

Cardiovascular—Pertaining to the heart and blood vessels. "Cardiovascular system" refers to the circulatory system of the heart and the blood vessels.

Cardiovascular drugs—Medications that control blood pressure, reduce cholesterol, and ease the symptoms of heart disease.

Cerebral embolism—A blood clot formed in one part of the body and then carried by the bloodstream to an artery of the brain, where it may cause a stroke.

Cerebral hemorrhage—Bleeding within the brain, usually resulting from a ruptured aneurysm or a head injury.

Cerebral thrombosis—Formation of a blood clot in an artery that supplies blood to part of the brain.

Chest pain unit—A specialized area of the Emergency Department where rapid evaluation and treatment of acute coronary syndromes is performed.

Cholesterol—A pearly, fat-like substance that is an essential component of the body's cells. Also found in some foods.

Circulatory system—Pertaining to the heart, blood vessels, and circulation of the blood.

Coarctation of the aorta—Congenital defect in which the aorta is pinched or constricted.

Congenital heart defect—Malformation of the heart or of its major blood vessels at birth. Also known as congenital heart disease.

Congestive heart failure—The condition created when the heart is not able to circulate adequate amounts of blood; the accumulation of fluids in the lungs, hands, ankles, or other parts of the body that results from inadequate circulation.

Coronary arteries—The heart's major arteries arising from the aorta. They arc down over the top of the heart and branch from the aorta to provide blood to the working heart muscle.

Coronary bypass surgery—Procedure in which a graft (a "conduit") is sewn in such a way as to shunt blood around an area of blockage in a coronary artery. Referred to also as coronary artery bypass grafting (CABG).

Coronary care unit—A specialized hospital area designed specifically to treat heart patients.

Coronary thrombosis—Formation of a clot in one of the coronary arteries that carries blood to the heart muscle.

Costochondritis—Inflammation of the rib joints that may cause chest pain that can be misinterpreted as chest pain from heart disease.

Cyanosis—Blueness of the skin caused by insufficient oxygen in the blood.

Descending aorta—Large blood vessel that channels oxygenated blood from the heart out to the rest of the body.

Diabetes—A disease in which the body doesn't produce or properly use insulin, the substance that converts sugar and starch into energy. There are three forms: Type 1, which is inherited and occurs before age 40; Type 2, which occurs in adults after that age; and gestational diabetes, which occurs during pregnancy and disappears afterwards.

Diastolic blood pressure—Pressure in the arteries when the heart is relaxed between heartbeats. In a blood pressure reading, reported as the lower of the two numbers.

Diuretic—Type of drug that enables the kidneys to rid the body of excess salt and water. May be referred to as a "water pill."

Dyspnea—Medical term for shortness of breath.

Ebstein's anomaly—Congenital defect in which the tricuspid valve of the heart is malformed.

Electrocardiogram (ECG or EKG)—A diagnostic test resulting in a representation on graph paper of the electrical impulses traveling through the heart muscle. The graph is drawn by a computer from information supplied by electrodes attached to the chest.

Echocardiography—A diagnostic method used to detect structural and some functional abnormalities of the heart, utilizing ultrasound, in which pulses of high-frequency sounds are transmitted into the body and the echoes returning to the surfaces of the heart and other structures are electronically recorded. See also *Transesophageal Echocardiogram*.

Edema—Bodily swelling caused by an excess accumulation of fluid.

Eisenmenger's syndrome—Irreversible condition in which the small blood vessels of the lungs are damaged by prolonged high blood pressure within the heart and the lungs.

Electrophysiological study (EP or EPS)—Diagnostic test in which wires are threaded into the heart and stimulated in hopes of simulating an irregular heartbeat.

Endocarditis—A serious bacterial infection of the heart lining or valves. People with abnormal or replaced heart valves or congenital heart defects are among those at risk for developing this disease.

Esophageal dysfunction—Malfunction of the esophagus that can manifest symptoms that can be misinterpreted by the body as chest pain coming from heart disease. Also known as esophageal spasms or esophagitis reflux.

Esophagus—Muscular tube that carries food from the back of the mouth to the stomach.

Estrogen—A group of hormones essential for normal female sexual development and the healthy functioning of the reproductive system.

Estrogen replacement therapy (ERT)— Estrogen prescribed for women to counteract the decline of their natural estrogen in conjunction with menopause or surgical removal of the ovaries.

Exercise stress test—Diagnostic test in which an activity, such as walking on a treadmill or riding a stationary bicycle, is used to evaluate the effect of physical exertion on the heart.

Exercise echocardiogram—Diagnostic test that combines an exercise stress test with an echocardiogram.

Fainting—Temporary loss of consciousness caused by insufficient oxygen reaching the brain.

Fibrillation—Rapid, uncoordinated contraction of individual heart muscle fibers that results in the heart's inability to efficiently pump blood.

Fingers prick test—A simple blood test that involves only a finger prick and that is used to obtain a total cholesterol level.

Genes—Units of inherited material contained in our body's cells.

Genetics—The study of how traits are passed down from one generation to another through genes.

Heart—The four-chambered, muscular organ is responsible for pumping blood through your body.

Heart attack—Permanent damage to the heart muscle caused by a lack of blood supply to the heart for an extended period; known also as a myocardial infarction (MI).

Heart block—Disorder of the heartbeat caused by an interruption in the passage of impulses through the heart's electrical network, causing the heart to beat irregularly and usually more slowly.

Heart murmur—Clinical finding that refers to abnormal sound made by the heart. Heart murmurs that do not signify a heart problem are known as "innocent" murmurs.

Heart-lung machine—A machine that temporarily takes over the function of the heart and lungs and makes possible certain types of operations, including open-heart surgery.

Heart transplant—Replacement of a damaged or diseased heart with a healthy heart taken from a donor.

High blood pressure—An unstable or persistent elevation of blood pressure above the normal range.

High-density lipoprotein (HDL)—a substance believed to relieve the accumulation of low-density lipoproteins (LDL) and very-low-density lipoproteins (VLDL) by transferring them away from the artery; the so-called "good" cholesterol.

Holter monitor—A small, portable recorder, connected by electrodes to the chest, that records the heartbeat over a 24-hour period.

Hormone replacement therapy (HRT)—The use of synthetic or natural hormones to treat a hormone deficiency. In the context of this book, the combined use of estrogen and progestin, the synthetic form of progesterone, to counteract the symptoms and effects of menopause.

Hormones—A group of chemicals each of which is released into the bloodstream by a particular gland or tissue to specifically affect tissues elsewhere in the body.

Hypertension—The medical term for high blood pressure. There are two types. Essential hypertension, the most common, occurs for no apparent reason. Secondary hypertension is caused by an underlying disorder, such as with the kidneys, the adrenal glands, or a congenital disorder.

Hypertensive cardiovascular disease—Type of heart disease caused by untreated high blood pressure.

Hysterectomy—The surgical removal of the uterus. Sometimes, the ovaries are removed as well.

Implantable cardioverter defibrillator (ICD)—A device implanted under the skin that can deliver an electric shock to restart the heart.

Ischemia—Condition in which there is not enough oxygen-rich blood supply to the heart muscle to meet the heart's needs. "Silent ischemia" refers to an inadequate supply of oxygen-rich blood to the heart muscle without symptoms.

Kawasaki disease—An acute illness of children, characterized by fever, rash, swelling, and inflammation of various parts of the body. In 20 percent of cases, the coronary arteries or other parts of the heart are affected.

Keloid—The outgrowth of a scar. Another type of scarring abnormality is known as a "hypertrophic" scar.

Lipid—A fatty substance insoluble in blood.

Lipid profile—A blood test that measures the different amounts of lipids in the blood.

Lipoprotein—The combination of lipid surrounded by a protein; the protein makes it soluble in blood.

Low-density lipoprotein (LDL)—The main carrier of harmful cholesterol in the blood; the so-called "bad" cholesterol.

Magnetic resonance imaging (MRI)—Diagnostic test that uses superconductive magnets and radio waves to obtain high-quality, detailed images of the body's internal organs.

Mammary artery—Also called internal thoracic artery; located in the chest wall, it can be used as a bypass graft for coronary artery bypass surgery.

Marfan's syndrome—Rare inherited congenital disorder of the connective tissues, affecting especially the heart, eyes, and musculoskeletal system.

Mechanical valve—Artificial valve made from materials such as titanium and ceramic, used to replace a malfunctioning heart valve.

Menopause—The term commonly used to describe the stage in a woman's life in which physiological and psychological changes occur as a result of reduced production of estrogen hormones by the ovaries.

Microvascular angina—A type of chest pain not caused by coronary artery disease or spasm. Known also as Syndrome X.

Mitral stenosis—Stiffening and thickening, due to calcification, of the heart's mitral valve.

Mitral valve—The heart valve between the left atrium and the left ventricle.

Mitral valve prolapse—An anomaly in which the leaflets of the mitral valve move out of normal position during the heart cycles. Most of the time this is not serious, but in rare cases it can cause serious mitral valve leakages.

Mitral regurgitation—See *Regurgitation*.

Mitral stenosis—See *Stenosis*.

Multiple gated acquisition (MUGA)—Diagnostic test that evaluates the strength of the heart.

Nitroglycerin—A drug that causes dilation (widening) of blood vessels and is often used in treating angina pectoris, the chest pain from coronary heart disease. Known also as "nitrates."

Obesity—A body weight 20 percent or more above the accepted standard for a person's age, sex, and body type.

Open-heart surgery—Surgery performed on the heart while the blood is diverted through a heart-lung machine.

Osteoarthritis—Degenerative type of arthritis that occurs in various joints of the body. When occurring in the neck, the body may misinterpret the pain signals as coming from heart disease.

Osteoporosis—A disease of aging that chiefly afflicts women and results in a loss of bone density that causes brittleness, fractures, and posture distortion.

Ovary—An almond-shaped gland situated on either side of the uterus that produces the so-called "sex" hormones of estrogen and progesterone.

Pacemaker—The heart's "natural pacemaker" is the sinoatrial node, a small cluster of specialized cells in the top of the heart's right atrium that produces the electrical signals that causes the heart to contract, or "beat." The term "artificial pacemaker" refers to an electrical device that can be substituted for a defective natural pacemaker. The artificial pacemaker controls the beating of the heart by emitting a series of rhythmic electrical discharges.

Palpitation—Heart rhythm disturbance, also described as a "pounding" or "flopping" heartbeat.

Patent ductus arteriosus—Congenital defect in which the passageway between the heart's two major blood vessels fails to close shortly after birth.

Pericarditis—Inflammation of the outer membranous sac that surrounds the heart.

Pericardium—The translucent outer sac that surrounds both the heart and the roots of the major blood vessels emerging from it.

Peripartum cardiomyopathy—Type of heart failure that may occur late in pregnancy or shortly after delivery.

Peripheral vascular disease—Narrowing of the blood vessels carrying blood to the legs and brain. A condition often found in people with heart disease.

Plaque—Hard, fatty matter embedded in the artery wall that develops with atherosclerosis.

Positron emission tomography (PET)—Diagnostic test that uses a radioactive isotope to create metabolic images of the heart.

Postural hypotension—Type of fainting caused by sudden changes in body position.

Pregnancy-induced hypertension (PIH)—General term referring to high blood pressure disorders occurring during pregnancy.

Premature ventricular contractions (PVCs)—An irregular heartbeat in which the lower chambers of the heart (the ventricles) beat before they are supposed to.

Pulmonary artery—The large artery that receives blood pumped from the right ventricle and channels it to the lungs.

Pulmonary hypertension—Type of high blood pressure that develops within the blood vessels of the lungs.

Pulmonary stenosis—Malformation of the pulmonary valve that prevents it from opening normally. Also called valvular pulmonary stenosis.

Pulmonary valve—The heart valve between the right ventricle and the pulmonary artery.

Radio frequency ablation—The use of low-frequency radio waves to destroy heart tissue transmitting an abnormal heartbeat.

Regurgitation—The abnormal backward flowing of blood through a valve in the heart. When this occurs with the mitral valve, it is known as "mitral regurgitation."

Restenosis—The recurrent narrowing of a blood vessel following angioplasty or a similar procedure.

Rheumatic heart disease—Damage done to the heart, particularly the heart valves, by rheumatic fever.

Risk factor—Behavior or traits that have been proven to contribute independently to the development and progression of heart disease.

Sedentary lifestyle—A way of life characterized by lack of exercise.

Septum—Muscular wall that divides the heart into the right and left sides.

Shingles—Known also as herpes zoster, this is an infection of the nerves that causes symptoms that the body may misinterpret as chest pain from heart disease.

Silent heart attack—Heart attack that occurs but is not recognized, owing to the body's misinterpretation of pain signals.

Stenosis—The narrowing or constriction of an opening, such as can occur with a heart valve.

Sternum—The breast bone.

Stress—Any interference that disturbs a person's mental health and physical well-being.

Stroke—A sudden and often severe attack caused by a loss of oxygen to part of the brain. Known also as a cerebral vascular accident (CVA).

Sudden death—Death that occurs unexpectedly and instantaneously, usually from a cardiac cause. If a person is successfully revived after such an event, this is known as having undergone an episode of sudden death.

Syncope—Medical term for fainting.

Syndrome X—See *Microvascular angina.*

Systolic blood pressure—The pressure in the arteries during the heart's contraction. In a blood pressure reading, reported as the higher of the two numbers.

Tachycardia—A fast heartbeat; technically, a rate of above 100 beats per minute.

Telemetry—A term referring to electronic monitoring devices for the heart.

Tetralogy of Fallot—Quartet of four separate heart defects occurring together.

Thallium stress testing—Diagnostic test that combines an exercise stress test with a special nuclear study to create images of the heart.

Tilt study—Diagnostic test in which the body is tilted at certain angles; useful in diagnosing causes of fainting. Also called a tilt table test.

Thrombolytic therapy—The administration of drugs called "clot-busters" used to minimize damage to the heart from a heart attack.

Transient ischemic attack—A temporary stroke-like event caused by a blocked blood vessel. Also called a TIA.

Transesophageal echocardiogram—Type of echocardiogram used to obtain images of harder-to-visualize structures of the heart, in which the sound probe is swallowed and positioned behind the heart.

Tricuspid valve—The heart valve between the right atrium and the right ventricle.

Triglycerides—Fatty compounds implicated in causing atherosclerosis.

Ultra-fast CT—Diagnostic test that uses X rays to rapidly create three-dimensional images of the heart.

Valve—A structure controlling blood flow between two chambers of the heart or between a chamber of the heart and a blood vessel.

Vasospastic angina—Discomfort or pressure usually in the chest resulting from a blockage of blood flow to the heart caused by a spasm of the coronary artery.

Vasovagal syncope—Type of fainting caused by overstimulation of the vagus nerve, the major nerve running from the brain to the upper gastrointestinal tract.

Veins—Blood vessels that take the blood back to the heart.

Vena cava—Either of two large veins that return oxygen-depleted blood to the heart.

Ventricles—One of the two main chambers of the heart.

Ventricular septal defect (VSD)—Congenital defect in which there is a so-called "hole" between the heart's lower chambers.

White coat hypertension—Form of high blood pressure caused by anxiety, such as a visit to the doctor.

Wolff Parkinson White syndrome—Cardiac syndrome caused by abnormal conduction of electrical signals to the heart, resulting in episodes of rapid heartbeats, from 120 to 200 per minute.

Resources

BOOKS

Compulsive Eating

Orbach, Susie. *Fat Is a Feminist Issue: The Anti-Diet Guide to Permanent Weight Loss* (Berkley Publishing Group, 1994).

Bruno, Barbara Altman. *Worth Your Weight: What You Can Do About a Weight Problem* (Rutledge Books, Inc., 1996).

Diet & Nutrition

Brody, Jane. *Jane Brody's Nutrition Book: A Lifetime Guide to Good Eating for Better Health and Weight Control* (Bantam Doubleday Dell, 1989).

Kwiterovich, Peter O., Jr. *Beyond Cholesterol: The Johns Hopkins Complete Guide for Avoiding Heart Disease* (Johns Hopkins University Press, 1989).

Nelson, Miriam E., PhD, with Sarah Wernick, PhD. *Strong Women Stay Slim* (Bantam Doubleday Dell, 1999).

Piscatella, Joseph. *Controlling Your Fat Tooth* (Workman Publishing, Co., 1991).

Piscatella, Joseph. *Don't Eat Your Heart Out Cookbook* (Workman Publishing Co., 1994).

Cookbooks

American Heart Association Quick & Easy Cookbook (Times Books, 1995).

Jenkins, Nancy Harmon. *The Mediterranean Diet Cookbook: A Delicious Alternative for Lifelong Health* (Bantam Doubleday Dell, 1994).

Robertson, Robin. *The Soy Gourmet* (Plume Books, 1998).

Exercise

Price, Joan, M. A. *Joan Price Says, Yes, You Can Get in Shape! Make Exercise a Treat, Not a Treatment* (Pacifica Press, 1996).

Nelson, Miriam E., PhD, with Sarah Wernick, PhD. *Strong Women Stay Young* (Bantam Doubleday Dell, 1997).

General Medicine

Berkow, Robert; Beers, Mark; Fletcher, Andrew, eds. *The Merck Manual of Medical Information: Home Edition* (Pocket Books, 1999).

Genetics and Genealogy (Tracing Your Family Medical History)

Milunsky, Aubrey, MD. *Heredity and Your Family's Health* (Johns Hopkins University Press, 1992).

Krause, Carol. *How Healthy Is Your Family Tree?: A Complete Guide to Tracing Your Family's Medical and Behavioral History (Gale Group, 1995).

Where to Write for Vital Records (free pamphlet), Superintendent of Documents, U.S. Government Printing Office, Washington, DC, 20402.

Health Care Issues

Inlander, Charles B., and Ed Weiner. *Take This Book to the Hospital with You: A Consumer Guide to Surviving Your Hospital Stay* (St. Martin's Press, 1997).

Barron, Bruce A. *Outsmarting Managed Care* (Times Books, 1999).

Heart Disease

Budnick, Herbert N., PhD, with Scott Robert Hays. *Heart to Heart: A Guide to the Psychological Aspects of Heart Disease* (HealthPress, 1997).

Kowalski, Robert E. *8 Steps to a Healthy Heart: The Complete Guide to Heart Disease Prevention and Recovery from Heart Attack and Bypass Surgery* (Warner Books, 1992).

Levin, Rhoda F. *Heartmates: A Guide for the Spouse and Family of the Heart Patient* (Minerva Press, 1994).

Topol, Eric J., MD, ed. *The Cleveland Clinic Heart Book* (Hyperion, 2000).

Internet Guides

Price, Joan, MA. *The Complete Idiot's Guide to Online Health and Fitness* (Que, 1999).

Menopause & Hormone Replacement Therapy

Love, Susan M., MD, with Karen Lindsey. *Dr. Susan Love's Hormone Book* (Random House, 1998).

Nachtigall, Lila, MD, and Joan Rattner Heilman. *Estrogen: The Facts Can Change Your Life* (HarperPerennial Library, 1995).

Notelovitz, Morris, MD, and Diana Tonnessen, *Menopause & Midlife Health* (St. Martin's Press, 1994).

Stress Reduction

Davis, Martha; Elizabeth Eshelmans Robbins; Matthew McKay. *The Relaxation & Stress Reduction Workbook, 4th Edition* (New Harbinger Publications, 1988).

Women's Health

Boston Women's Health Book Collective. *Our Bodies, Ourselves for the New Century* (Touchstone Books, 1998).

Healy, Bernadine, MD. *A New Prescription for Women's Health: Getting the Best Medical Care in a Man's World* (Penguin, 1996).

Hoffman, Eileen, MD. *Our Health, Our Lives: A Revolutionary Approach to Total Health Care for Women* (Pocket Books, 1996).

Laurence, Leslie and Beth Weinhouse, *Outrageous Practices: How Gender Bias Threatens Women's Health* (Rutgers University Press, 1997).

Libov, Charlotte, *Beat Your Risk Factors: A Woman's Guide to Reducing Her Risk for Cancer, Heart Disease, Stroke, Diabetes, and Osteoporosis* (Plume Books, 1999).

INTERNET WEB SITES

Mediterranean Diet
http://www.oldwayspt.org/html/p_med.htm

NEWSLETTERS

Harvard Women's Health Watch
P.O. Box 420234
Palm Coast, FL 32142-0234

Heart Advisor
P.O. Box 420235
Palm Coast, FL 32142-0235
800-829-2506

Women's Health Hot Line
Free Internet newsletter offering health news for women, founded
    and edited by Charlotte Libov
http://www.libov.com
char@libov.com

OTHER MATERIALS

For a free catalog listing of government publications that are free or very
inexpensive and include health topics, write:

Consumer Education Center
P.O. Box 100
Pueblo, CO 81002

The federal government offers useful information on diet, nutrition, and
exercise free or at very low cost. For a free catalog, write:

Consumer Information Catalog
Pueblo, CO 81109

ORGANIZATIONS AND SUPPORT GROUPS

American Diabetes Association
1600 Duke Street
Alexandria, VA 11324
800-232-3472
http://www.diabetes.org

National Diabetes Information Clearinghouse
One Information Way
Bethesda, MD 20892-3560
301-654-3327

Lupus Foundation of America
1300 Piccard Drive, Suite 200
Rockville, MD
301-670-9292
LupusInfo@aol.com

President's Council on Physical Fitness and Sports
701 Pennsylvania Avenue, Suite 250
Washington, DC 20004
202-272-3421

General Medicine

These organizations have information on a variety of health issues and, in particularly, their Internet sites generally also have worthwhile Internet links.

The American Medical Association
515 North State Street
Chicago, IL 60610
312-464-5000
http://www.ama-assn.org

The Centers for Disease Control and Prevention
1600 Clifton Road NE
Atlanta, GA 30333

404-639-3311
http://www.cdc.gov

National Institutes of Health
9000 Rockville Pike
Bethesda, MD 20892
301-496-4000
http://www.nih.gov

U.S. Department of Health and Human Services
200 Independence Avenue SW
Washinogton, DC 20201
202-619-0257
http://www.os.dhhs.gov

Heart Disease

American Heart Association
731 Greenville Avenue
Dallas, TX 75231
800-227-2345; 214-373-6300
www.amhrt.org

National Heart, Lung and Blood Institute (NHLBI)
  Information Center
P.O. Box 30105
Bethesda, MD 20824-0105
800-575-WELL; 301-251-1222
The NHLBI offers recorded messages and free information about
  controlling blood presure, cholesterol levels, and other risk fac-
  tors for heart disease.

Minority Health Issues

American Indian Health Care Association
245 E. 6th Street, Suite 499
St. Paul, MN 55101
612-294-0233

Asian American Health Forum
116 New Montgomery Street, Suite 531

San Francisco, CA 94105
415-541-0866

National Black Women's Health Project
1237 Ralph D. Abernathy Boulevard SW
Atlanta, GA 30310
1-800-ASK-BWHP

National Coalition of Hispanic Health and Human Services
    Organizations
1501 16th Street NW
Washington, DC 20036-1401
203-387-5000

Office of Minority Health Resource Center
P.O. Box 37337
Washington, DC 20013-7337

Nutrition

American Dietetic Association
216 West Jackson Boulevard
Chicago, IL 60606-6995
312-899-0040
312-899-1979 (fax)
www.eatright.org

Stroke

American Heart Association. See above listing.

National Institute of Neurological Disorders and Stroke
9000 Rockville Pike, Building 31, Room 8A-06
Bethesda, MD 20992
1-800-852-9424

National Stroke Association
300 East Hampden Avenue, Suite 240
Englewood, CO 80110-2622
1-800-STROKS
http://www.stroke.org

Women's Health Issues

National Women's Health Network
514 10th Street, NW, Suite 400
Washington, DC 20004
202-628-7814

The Older Women's League (OWL)
666 Eleventh Street, NW, Suite 700
Washington, DC 20001
202-783-6686
A Washington, DC–based organization that promotes older
women's issues and publishes several free reports on women's
health issues, including heart disease and osteoporosis.

SMOKING—HOW TO QUIT (SPECIAL SECTION)

Books

Fisher, Edwin B., Jr., PhD, with Toni L. Goldfarb. *7 Steps to a Smoke-Free Life* (John Wiley & Sons, Inc., 1998).

Klesges, Robert C., PhD, and Margaret Debon, MS, *How Women Can Finally Stop Smoking* (Hunter House Publishers, 1994).

Pamphlets and other materials

There are many free publications on the hazards of smoking and how to
quit available for free from following organizations:

Office on Smoking and Health
Mail Stop K-50
4770 Buford Highway, NE
Atlanta, GA 30341-3724
404-488-5705

Environmental Protection Agency
Indoor Air Quality Information Clearinghouse
P.O. Box 37133
Washington, DC 20013-7133

National Cancer Institute
Building 31, Room 10A24

9000 Rockville Pike
Bethesda, MD 20892
1-800-4-CANCER

Center for Substance Abuse Prevention
National Clearinghouse for Alcohol and Drug Information
P.O. Box 2345
Rockville, MD 20852
(301) 468-2600
1-800-Say-No-To

National Heart, Lung, and Blood Institute
P.O. Box 30105
Bethesda, MD 20824-0105
301-951-3260

Organizations

Action on Smoking and Health
2013 H Street, NW
Washington, DC 20006
202-659-4310

The Advocacy Institute
Suite 600
1730 Rhode Island Avenue, NW
Washington, DC 20036-4505
202-659-8475

American Cancer Society
1599 Clifton Road, NE
Atlanta, GA 30329-4251
http://www.cancer.org

American Heart Association (AHA)
See listing under *"Heart Disease."*
Promotes smoking intervention programs at schools, workplaces,
and health care sites. Refer to your phone book for the AHA
chapter in your area or contact the national office above for
further information.

American Lung Association (ALA)
1740 Broadway
New York, NY 10019
1-800-586-4872
http://www.lungusa.org

Americans for Nonsmokers' Rights
Suite J
2530 San Pablo Avenue
Berkeley, CA 94702
510-841-3032

Selected Bibliography

BOOKS AND REPORTS

"Cardiovascular Disease in Women: A Statement for Healthcare Professionals by the American Heart Association" (1997).

"Cardiovascular Health for Women: A Clinical Practitioner's Guide." The Cleveland Clinic Educational Foundation, 1999.

"Health Concerns Across a Woman's Lifespan: 1998 Survey of Women's Health" (The Commonwealth Fund, 1998).

"Health Care Access and Coverage for Women: Changing Times, Changing Issues?" Policy Report of the Commonwealth Fund Commission on Women's Health (1999).

"1999 Heart and Stroke Statistical Update" (American Heart Association, 1999).

"The Face of Medicare Is a Woman You Know," OWL Mother's Day Report (1999).

"Postmenopausal Hormone-Replacement Therapy," Harvard Health Publications Special Report (Harvard Women's Health Watch, 1996).

Vogel, Steven. *Vital Circuits: On Pumps, Pipes and the Workings of the Circulatory Systems* (Oxford University Press, 1992).

Weiner, Gabrielle, MS, and Charlotte Libov. "Women and Heart Disease: A Special Report from the Editors of Women's Health Advisor." (The Center for Women's Healthcare, Weill Medical College of Cornell University, Torstar Publications, 1999).

JOURNALS AND ARTICLES

Al-Hani, AJ. "Women Take Heart: A Pioneering Study of Women's Health," presented at the American Heart Association's 22nd Science Writers Forum, Santa Barbara, Calif., 1995.

Anderson, JW, Smith, BM "Fantastic Fiber," *Women's Health Digest*, 1995; 1(1):27.

Anderson, JW, Johnstone, BM, Cook-Newell, ME. "Meta-analysis of the effects of soy protein on serum lipids," *The New England Journal of Medicine*, 1995; 333(5): 276–281.

Arnold, AZ, Moodie, DS. "Coronary artery disease in young women: risk factor analysis and long-term follow-up," *Cleveland Clinic Journal of Medicine*, 1993; 60(5): 393–398.

Arnold, AZ, Underwood, DA. "Coronary artery disease in women: a risk-factor analysis," *Cleveland Clinic Journal of Medicine*, 1993; 60(5): 387–392.

Aufderheide, S, Lax, D, Goldberg, S. "Gender differences in dehydration-induced mitral valve prolapse," *Journal of the American Heart Association*, 1995; (129): 83–86.

Blumenthal, RS, Post, WS. "Woman and heart disease: current concepts and controversies," *Mediguide to Heart Disease*, 1999; 2(2): 1–8.

Budoff, MJ, Georgio, D, Brody, A, et al. "Ultrafast computed tomography as a diagnostic modality in the detection of coronary artery disease," *Circulation*, 1996; 93 (5): 898–904.

Caralis DG, Deligonul, U, Kern, MJ, et al. "Smoking is a risk factor for coronary spasm in young women," *Circulation* 1992; 85(3): 905–909.

Castelli WP, Garrison RJ, Wilson PW, et al. "Incidence of coronary heart disease and lipoprotein cholesterol levels," The Framingham Study. *Journal of the American Medical Association*, 1986; 256(20): 2835–2838.

Chandra, NC, Zieglelstein, RC, Rogers, WJ, et al. "Observations of the treatment of women in the United States with myocardial infarction," *Archives of Internal Medicine*, 1998; 158(9): 981–988.

Cohn, LH, Adams, DH, Couper, GS, et al. "Minimally invasive Cardiac Valve Surgery," *ACC Educational Highlights*, 1999; 14(2): 1–6.

Edwards, FH, Carey, JS, Grover, et al. "Impact of gender on coronary bypass mortality," *Annals of Thoracic Surgery*, 1998; 66(1): 125–131.

Ernster, VL, Grady, D, Miike R, et al. "Facial wrinkling in men and women, by smoking status," *American Journal of Public Health* 1995; 85(1): 78–82.

Fletcher, GF, Blair, SN, Blumenthal, J, et al. "Statement on exercise: benefits and recommendations for physical activity for all Americans," *Circulation*, 1992; 86(1): 340–343.

Frasure-Smith, N, Lesperance, F, Juneau, M, et al. "Gender, depression and one-year prognosis after myocarial infarction," *Psychosomatic Medicine*, 1999, 61(1): 26–37.

Freed, L A, Levy, D, Levine, RA, "Prevalence and clinical outcome of mitral-valve prolapse," *The New England Journal of Medicine*, 1999, 341(1): 1–7.

Fuchs, CS, Stampher, MJ, Colditz, G A, et al. "Alcohol consumption and mortality among women," *The New England Journal of Medicine*, 1995; 332(19): 1246–1250.

Greenlund, KJ, Giles, WH, Keenan, NL, Croft, JB, et al. "Prevalence of multiple cardiovascular disease risk factors among women in the United States, 1992 and 1995: the Behavioral Risk Factor Surveillance System," *Journal of Women's Health*, 1998; 7(9):1125–1133.

Healy, B. "PEPI in perspective: good answers spawn pressing questions," *Journal of the American Medical Association*, 1995; 273(3): 240–241.

———. "Homocysteine—the next treatable risk factor?," Harvard Heart Letter, 1996; 6(11): 1–2.

Hennekens, CH, Judelson, DR, Wenger, NK, "Coronary disease: the leading killer," *Patient Care*, August 15, 1996; 116–141.

Hu, FB, Stampfer, MJ, Manson, J E, et al. "Dietary fat intake and the risk of coronary heart disease in women," *The New England Journal of Medicine*, 1997; 337 (21):1491–1499.

Hurt, RD, Dale, LC, Fredrickson, P A, et al. "Nicotine patch therapy for smoking cessation combined with physician advice and nurse follow-up," *Journal of the American Medical Association*, 1994; 271(8): 595–600.

Jacobs, AK, Kelsey, SF, Brooks, MM, et al. "Better outcome for women compared with men undergoing coronary revascularization: A report from the Bypass Angioplasty Revascularization Investigation (BARI)," Circulation: *Journal of the American Heart Association*, 1998; 98 (September): 1279–1285.

Jacobs, AK, Kelsey, SF, Yeh, W, et al. "Documentation of a decline in morbidity in women undergoing coronary angioplasty: A report from the 1993–94 NHLBI Percutaneous Transluminal Coronary Angioplasty Registry," *American Journal of Cardiology*, 1997; 80(8): 979–984.

Jensen, P, Coambs, RB, "Health and behavioral predictors of success in an intensive smoking cessation program for women," *Women & Health*, 1994; 21(1): 57–72.

Kawachi, I, Colditz, GA, Stampfer, MJ, et al. "Smoking cessation and time course of decreased risks of coronary heart disease in middle-aged women," *Archives of Internal Medicine*, 1994; 154(2): 169–1750.

Kawachi, I, Colditz, GA, Stampfer, MJ et al. "Prospective Study of Shift Work and Risk of Coronary Heart Disease in Women," *Circulation*, 1995; 92(11): 3178–3182.

Kawachi I, Trois, RJ, Rotnitsky, AG, Coakley, EH, et al. "Can physical activity minimize weight gain in women after smoking cessation?" *American Journal of Public Health*, 1996; 86(7): 999–1004.

Keller, C, Fleury, J, Bergstrom, DL, "Risk factors for coronary heart disease in African-American women," *Cardiovascular Nursing*, 1995; 31(2): 9–15.

Kenford, SL., Fiore, MC, Jorenby, DE, et al. "Predicting smoking cessation: who will quit with and without the nicotine patch," *Journal of the American Medical Association*, 1994; 271(8): 589–594.

Kenyon, LW, Ketterer, MW, Gheorghiade, M, et al. "Psychological factors related to prehospital delay during acute myocardial infarction," *Circulation*, 1991; 84(5): 1969–1976.

King, AC, Haskell, WL, Young, DR, et al. "Long term effects of varying intensities and formats of physical activity on participation rates, fitness and lipoproteins in men and women aged 50 to 65 years," *Circulation*, 1995; 19(10): 2596–2604.

Knox, SS, Siegmund, KD, Weidner, G., et al. "Hostility, social support and coronary heart disease in the National Heart, Lung and Blood Institute Family Heart Study," *American Journal of Cardiology*, 1998; 82(10): 1192–1196.

Kokkinos, PF, Holland, JC, Andreas, PE, Pittaras, et al. "Cardiorespiratory fitness and coronary heart disease risk factor association in women," *Journal of the American College of Cardiology*, 1995; 26(2): 358–364.

Kuller, LH. "A time of change: early signs of atherosclerosis in perimenopausal women." Presentation, American Heart Association's 22nd Science Writers Forum, 1995.

Kushi, LH, Folsom, AR, Prineas, RJ, "Dietary antioxidant vitamins and death from coronary heart disease in postmenopausal women," *The New England Journal of Medicine*, 1996; 334(19): 1156–1162.

Lauer, MD, Pashkow, FJ, Snader, CE, et al. "Gender and referral for coronary angiography after treadmill thallium testing," *American Journal of Cardiology*, 1996; 78(3): 278–283.

Lauer, MD, Pashkow, FJ, Snader, CE, et al. "Sex and diagnostic evaluation of possible coronary artery disease after exercise treadmill testing at one academic teaching center," *American Heart Journal*, 1997; 134 (5 Pt. 1); 807–813.

Marenberg, ME, Risch, N, Berkman, LF, et al. "Genetic susceptibility to death from coronary heart disease in a study of twins," *The New England Journal of Medicine*, 1994; 330(15): 1041–1046.

Matthews, KA, Owens, JF, Kuller, Lewis H., et al. "Are hostility and anxiety associated with carotid atherosclerosis in health postmenopausal women?" Psychosomatic Medicine, 1998; (Sept.–Oct.), 633–638.

Mehta, Jawahar, "Inflammation, infection and Coronary Artery Disease," *ACC Educational Highlights,* 1999; 14(2): 11–14.

Miller, M, Byinton, R, Hunninghake, D, et al., "Sex Bias and Underutilization of Lipid-Lowering Therapy in Patients with Coronary Artery Disease at Academic Medical Centers in the United States and Canada," *Archives of Internal Medicine*, 2000; (160)3: 343–347.

Ness, RB, Harris, T, Cobb, J, et al. "Number of pregnancies and the subsequent risk of cardiovascular disease," *The New England Journal of Medicine*, 1993; 328(21): 1529–1533.

Nishimura, RA, McGoon, M. "Perspectives on mitral valve prolapse," *The New England Journal of Medicine*, 1999; (341) 1: 48–50.

Pashkow, FJ, "The Mona Lisa Smiles: Impact of Risk Factors for Coronary Artery Disease in Women," *Cleveland Clinic Journal of Medicine*, 1993; 60(5).

Pirie, PL, McBride, CM, Hellersteadt, W, et al. "Smoking cessation in women concerned about weight." *American Journal of Public Health* 1992; 82(9): 1238–1243.

Pirie, PL, Murray, DM, Luepker, RV. "Gender differences in cigarette smoking and quitting in a cohort of young adults." *American Journal of Public Health* 1991; 81(3): 324–327.

Pollock, M, Brechue, WR, "Exercise guidelines for the older woman." *Women's Health Digest*, 1995; 1(1): 31–33.

Roger, VL, Jacobsen, SJ, Pellikka, PA, "Gender differences in use of stress testing and coronary heart disease mortality: a population-based study in Olmsted County, Minnesota,"*Journal of the American College of Cardiology*, 32(2): 345–352.

Ross, RK, Paganini-Hill, A, Pike, M. "Effect of Hormone Replacement Therapy on Breast Cancer Risk: Estrogen Versus Estrogen Plus Progestin," *Journal of the National Cancer Institute*, 2000; (92)4: 328–332.

Salonen, JT, Nyyssönen, K, Korpela, H, et al. "High stored iron levels are associated with excess risk of myocardinal infarction in Eastern Finnish men," *Circulation*, 1992; 86(3): 803–811.

Scharier, C, Lubin, J, PhD, Troisi, R, et al. "Menopausal Estrogen and Estrogen-Progestin Replacement Therapy and Breast Cancer Risk," *Journal of the American Medical Association*, 2000; (283)4: 485–491.

Schulman, KA, Berlin, JA, Harless, W, et al. "The effect of race and sex on physicians' recommendations for cardiac catheterization." *The New England Journal of Medicine*, 1999; 340(8): 618–626.

Schwartz, LM, Fischer, ES, Tosteson, NA. "Treatment and health outcomes of women and men in a cohort with coronary artery disease," *Archives of Internal Medicine*, 1997; 157, (July 28), 1545–1551.

Sesso, HD, Kawachi, I, Vokonas, PS, Sparrow, D. "Depression and the risk of coronary heart disease in the Normative Aging Study." *American Journal of Cardiology*, 1998; 82(7): 851–856.

Sempos, CT, Looker, AC, Gillum, RF, Makuc, DM. "Body iron stores and the risk of coronary heart disease [see comments]." *The New England Journal of Medicine* 1994; 330(16): 1119–1124.

Stampher, MJ, Hennekens, CH, Manson, J E, et al. "Vitamin E consumption and the risk of coronary artery disease in women," *The New England Journal of Medicine*, 1993; 328(20): 1444–1449.

Steinberg, D. "Antioxidant vitamins and coronary heart disease," *New England Journal of Medicine*, 1993; 328(20): 1487–1488.

The Writing Group for the PEPI Trial. "Effects of estrogen or estrogen/progestin regimens on heart disease risk factors in postmenopausal women." *Journal of the American Medical Association,* 1995; 273(3): 199–208.

Thun, MJ, Day-Lally, CA, Calle, EE, et al. "Excess mortality among cigarette smokers: changes in a 20-year interval," *American Journal of Public Health,* 1995; 85(9): 1223–1230.

———. "Unraveling the carbohydrate puzzle," Harvard Heart Letter, 1997; 8(4): 1–3.

Vaccarino, V, Parsons, L, Every, N R. "Sex-based differences in early mortality after myocardinal infarction," *The New England Journal of Medicine*, 1999; 341(4): 217–225.

Waldron, I, Weiss, CC, "Interacting effects of multiple roles on women's health," *Journal of Health and Social Behavior,* 1998; 39 (September), 216–236.

Wenger, NK, "Exclusion of the elderly and women from coronary trials: is their quality of care compromised?" *Journal of the American Medical Association,* 1992; 268 (11), 125–131.

Willet, WC, Green, A, Stampfer, MJ, et al. "Relative and absolute excess risks of coronary heart disease among women who smoke cigarettes," *The New England Journal of Medicine,* 1987; 317(21): 1303–1309.

Williams, JK, Adams, MR, Herrington, DM, Clarkson, T B. "Short-term administration of estrogen and vascular responses of atherosclerotic coronary arteries," *Journal of the American College of Cardiology,*" 1992; 20(2): 452–457.

———. "Women losing health insurance coverage," *The Commonwealth Fund Quarterly,* 1999; 5(2): 1–5.

Woodfield, SL, Lundergran, CF, Reiner, JS, et al. "Gender and acute myocardinal Infarction: is there a different response to thrombolysis?," *Journal of the American College of Cardiology,* 1997; 298(1): 35–42.

Index